BISCUITS, THE DOLE, AND NODDING DONKEYS

FOCUS ON AMERICAN HISTORY SERIES
The Dolph Briscoe Center for American History
University of Texas at Austin
Don Carleton, Editor

Biscuits, the Dole, and Nodding Donkeys

Texas Politics, 1929–1932

NORMAN D. BROWN
EDITED AND WITH AN
INTRODUCTION BY RACHEL OZANNE

University of Texas Press
AUSTIN

Publication of this book was made possible in part by support from the Jess and Betty Jo Hay Endowment.

Requests for permission to reproduce material from this work should be sent to:
Permissions
University of Texas Press
P.O. Box 7819
Austin, TX 78713–7819
utpress.utexas.edu/rp-form

♾ The paper used in this book meets the minimum requirements of ANSI/NISO Z39.48–1992 (R1997) (Permanence of Paper).

LIBRARY OF CONGRESS CATALOGING-IN-PUBLICATION DATA

Names: Brown, Norman D., author. | Ozanne, Rachel, editor, writer of
      supplementary textual content.
Title: Biscuits, the dole, and nodding donkeys : Texas politics, 1929–1932 /
      Norman D. Brown ; edited and with an introduction by Rachel Ozanne.
Other titles: Focus on American history series.
Description: First edition. | Austin : University of Texas Press, 2019. | Series:
      Focus on American history series | Includes bibliographical references
      and index.
Identifiers: LCCN 2019011617 | ISBN 978-1-4773-1945-1 (cloth : alk. paper) |
      ISBN 978-1-4773-1946-8 (library e-book) | ISBN 978-1-4773-1947-5
      (nonlibrary e-book)
Subjects: LCSH: Texas—Politics and government—1865–1950.
Classification: LCC F391 .B8466 2019 | DDC 976.4/06—dc23
LC record available at https://lccn.loc.gov/2019011617

doi:10.7560/319451

Contents

Foreword

Dr. Norman D. Brown: An Appreciation

Norman D. Brown will be remembered as a distinguished scholar, beloved teacher, generous colleague, loyal University of Texas Longhorn, and devoted husband and father. Over the course of his lifetime (1935–2015), he wrote and edited a number of books on U.S. southern and Civil War history, but he is best known for his 1984 monograph *Hood, Bonnet, and Little Brown Jug: Texas Politics, 1921–1928*. At UT, where he taught from 1962 until his retirement in 2010, he stood out for his mastery of twentieth-century Texas politics, and he stood out among his colleagues and students in Garrison Hall—literally.

His children, David and Tracy Brown, are proud that their father, in their words, "inspired many students over his forty-eight years of teaching with his love of history," a sentiment they often heard from those who had studied with him. David notes that his father was fortunate to be able to make a career out of his passion for history: "I have fond memories of his dedication, working away at home day and night on his typewriter on his latest book project."

Norman was also masterful in amassing and collating information and quirky details about the state's politicians—their machinations and personal ambitions, their feuds with one another, and their quests for power, ill-gained or not. He spent many hours in the Eugene C. Barker Texas History Center (now The Dolph Briscoe Center for American History) poring over its archival collections. When classes were in session, he would come to campus early in the morning and proceed to the conference room on the first floor of Garrison Hall, where he spread out his rumpled, dog-eared notes for the day's lectures. Many mornings his colleagues in the history department also saw him hunched over the department copying machine, feeding it stacks of newspaper articles and obituaries. Later that day they would find in their department mailboxes photocopies relevant to their own interests, provided by the department's "one-man clipping service." Norman was ever on the lookout for newspaper stories his colleagues would find enlightening or entertaining.

To have a word with him in his office on the building's main floor (near what is today the conference room), colleagues, undergrads, and graduate students would enter and wend their way through the maze of bookshelves and towering stacks of books and papers—and piles of those ubiquitous photocopied clippings—that ended at his desk. Norman was appreciated as an inspiring, knowledgeable, and caring teacher, for he possessed an uncanny ability to bring the past to life—to make it accessible to undergraduates and graduate students alike.

He was a giant in the field, but also a giant in real life—a large man, well over six feet tall, who commanded the attention of his colleagues and his students even as he impressed them with his gentle demeanor and wry sense of humor. Though reticent, he was an accomplished punster, with gems worthy of Austin's annual O'Henry Pun-Off World Championships. He rarely spoke in department meetings, but when he did, colleagues listened. He was unfailingly kind to junior faculty and graduate students in a time when rigid academic hierarchies based on tenure status could smother otherwise ordinary personal courtesies. Even during the last months of his life, he was eager to help students with their research, a reflection of his deep, abiding interest in Texas politics, past and present.

Norman Donald Brown was born in 1935 in Pittsburgh, Pennsylvania. His family moved to Kokomo, Indiana, where he completed high school. He went on to graduate summa cum laude from Indiana University and to earn his MA and PhD in history from the University of North Carolina at Chapel Hill. As an advanced graduate student, he began teaching history at the University of Texas at Austin in 1962, holding that lectureship until he was promoted to assistant professor three years later. He married Betty Jane Aldrich the following year. In 1969 he received tenure and the rank of associate professor. In 1983 he was promoted to full professor, and a year later was named Barbara White Stuart Centennial Professor in Texas History, an endowed chair he held until he retired twenty-nine years later. (A grateful former student provided the eponymous endowment for his chair.) He taught undergraduate courses on the Old South, the South since 1865, writers of the modern South, and the image of the South in nineteenth-century American literature, as well as the U.S. survey course. At the graduate level his courses included reading and research seminars in southern history and Texas in the 1920s. Unlike many conventional southern historians, early in his career Norman offered courses on slavery and spoke to wider audiences about lynching and the struggle for civil rights in Texas.

Norman was an excellent classroom teacher—low-key, well organized, and plainspoken. Appreciative of his carefully structured lectures, his undergraduates marveled, "He makes it so easy to take notes!" His exam essay questions and writing assignments forced them to keep up with the required readings, attend class regularly, and make a logical argument based on the facts at hand—all valuable skills they would draw upon for the rest of their lives.

His graduate students learned the fundamentals of historical research. Norman encouraged them to burrow into the archives to discover the facts behind Texas historical trends and events that had been rendered previously as myths or hearsay. For example, in the seminar "Texas in the 1920s and 1930s" students mined (as deeply as they could in the allotted time) the raw primary documents that illuminated the Red River Bridge War between Texas and Oklahoma in 1931 or the gubernatorial administrations of Miriam A. "Ma" Ferguson and Dan Moody. He impressed on his students his conviction that the correspondence between relevant actors furnishes insights into their motivation. He also reminded them that political history encompasses much more than campaign speeches and vote tabulations, and he required that his students have an understanding of larger social, cultural, and economic contexts. Each graduate seminar culminated in student presentations, and Norman's insightful comments on each one represented a collegial effort that his students remembered and appreciated long after graduation.

His lengthy *curriculum vitae*, which covers thirteen single-spaced typed pages, is a fascinating historical artifact in itself, listing every book review Norman wrote and the title of every talk he delivered in addition to his publications and courses. Lopsided strips of paper with additions and corrections are stapled onto the pages—by the 1980s there was no need to retype the whole document when only a single line here or there needed updating!

Norman was a good citizen of the UT history department, serving on virtually every committee at least once, and he participated in search committees and prize committees galore. He supplemented his service to the department by serving the university (on the Faculty Advisory Committee for the Lyndon Baines Johnson Library, for example) as well as by engaging with the larger public (as a member of the Texas Constitutional Revision Commission's local citizens' advisory committee in the early 1970s). He served a term (1999–2000) as president of, and was an active member of, the Texas State Historical Association (TSHA), which was founded in 1897 by the first chair of UT's history department, George P. Garrison. Norman was also a longtime member of the editorial advisory board of the association's scholarly journal, *Southwestern Historical Quarterly*. He was named a fellow of the association in 1995.

By the 1970s his books on Daniel Webster of Massachusetts and Edward Stanly of North Carolina had earned him a national reputation as a specialist in the history of late-antebellum politics. Edited volumes of the reminiscences and diaries of two Confederate officers, Capt. Samuel T. Foster and Capt. Elijah P. Petty, followed (in 1980 and 1982). For the latter book, *Journey to Pleasant Hill: The Civil War Letters of Captain Elijah P. Petty, Walker's Texas Division, CSA*, Norman won several awards, including a citation from the San Antonio Conservation Society "for a work of great beauty which conveys, as only letters can, the truth of a monumental moment in history." Other forms of recognition include the Earle R. Davis Award for Contributions to Texas-Confederate History, the United Daughters of the Confederacy's Jefferson Davis Medal, and the George Washington Honor Medal for Excellence.

The publication of *Hood, Bonnet, and Little Brown Jug* by Texas A&M Press in 1984 marked Norman's turn toward twentieth-century Texas, a fertile field for any historian intrigued by idiosyncratic personalities engaged in bare-knuckled politics. Here were great tales to be told about contentious public policies and demagogic appeals to a largely white populace, all set against a national backdrop of partisan political intrigue. Norman shows how James E. "Pa" Ferguson was able to navigate the shoals of factional Democratic in-fighting and rise to power when he was elected governor in 1915. Ferguson was reelected two years later, only to be impeached by the Texas House of Representatives and convicted by a senate committee for misapplication of public funds, among other charges. Not to be denied what he considered his political due, Ferguson sought the Democratic gubernatorial nomination again but lost to William P. Hobby. Pa also aspired to the presidency and the U.S. Senate, ambitions that were thwarted by members of his own party. When Ferguson managed to get his wife Miriam A. "Ma" Ferguson elected governor in 1925, he returned to the governor's office and continued his corrupt ways with gusto. *Hood, Bonnet, and Little Brown Jug* also details the relatively brief but robust hold that the Ku Klux Klan had on state politics in the 1920s, when "others"—defined as immigrants and Catholics as well as blacks and Hispanics—became scapegoats for a depressed agricultural economy. Ma Ferguson's successor, the state's young

attorney general Dan Moody, enacted good-government, progressive principles in an effort to bring efficiency and honesty to state government and to
promote private business interests in the process.

This current volume, the sequel to *Hood, Bonnet, and Little Brown Jug*
picks up that story in 1929. Soon after Norman's retirement in 2010, Josiah
Daniel, a former student of his, generously provided resources to the history
department to ensure that this new book would be published and receive
the broad, appreciative readership it deserved. The first step was to convert
the typescript to an electronic file, a time-consuming process that required
considerable (human) effort to "clean up" and prepare the final version of
text. The department then hired Dr. Rachel Ozanne, a newly minted UT history PhD who had been teaching Texas history, to edit the manuscript. Dr.
Ozanne wrote an introduction to the study and enhanced the footnotes with
sources published since the early 1980s, offering mini-historiographical surveys on relevant topics. Like *Hood, Bonnet, and Little Brown Jug*, this volume fills a gap in the historical literature related to Texas politics.

In keeping with Norman's playfulness in choosing book titles, Dr.
Ozanne calls this study *Biscuits, the Dole, and Nodding Donkeys: Texas Politics, 1929–1932*, making reference to the volume's themes: Pa Ferguson believed that politicians should keep their constituents well fed with political
"biscuits" by giving the voters what they wanted. The "dole" references the
enduring tension between the federal government and the State of Texas, a
tension exacerbated by the Great Depression, when the economic desperation of many residents challenged the state's historic emphasis on personal
self-reliance and its traditional contempt for governmental social welfare
programs. The "nodding donkeys" are the oil rigs that fueled the state's economy but also prompted calls for regulation in the face of a glut in the oil market during the 1930s.

Norman was most definitely a political historian in the traditional—even
old-fashioned—sense of the term. At the same time, readers of his books
and articles will find neither dry recitations of voter registration statistics nor explications of long-forgotten party platforms. Instead, he brings
to life the personal dynamics that inflected Texas politics—the euphemis-
tically labeled "colorful" characters who dominated the political landscape
and wrangled backroom deals to get what they wanted. Moreover, he was
keenly aware of the larger contemporary context for his political studies:
the state's oil-based economy, which brought fabulous, untold riches for a
few; and its cotton economy, which brought backbreaking, unremitting toil
for the many, including almost all Mexican Americans and African Ameri-

cans. Impoverished whites were little better off than their disenfranchised counterparts, but at least they were a valued constituency of the Democrats, and party regulars gave them their due, if only in a rhetorical way and only right before election day.

I arrived at UT in 2008, just a couple of years before Norman retired. With a shared love of southern history, we soon forged a connection that I valued. After he moved to an assisted living home here in Austin in 2013, we continued to keep in touch. Norman never used a computer, so he had no email address. But I would call him on the phone and make a lunch date, and we would enjoy hashing over the week's news headlines. His mind was as sharp as ever, and I considered it a rare privilege to listen to his entertaining stories about the historical roots of any number of current political scandals and debacles. Every morning he still read through a stack of newspapers and journals, and though lacking a copying machine, he still preserved items of interest by cutting them out and filing them away. He would invariably write a letter of thanks after we had met. In his last to me, in the spring of 2014, he offered to talk to one of my students who was writing a research paper on the Texas Klan in the 1920s. Norman Brown was a generous scholar, teacher, and friend to the very end.

Special thanks to those who provided their reminiscences and thoughts on Norman: David Brown, Josiah Daniel, Barbara White Stuart, Michael Stoff, Bill Brands, Neil Kamil, Clarence "Bud" Lasby, Howard Miller, Evan Ross, and George Forgie.

JACQUELINE JONES, Ellen C. Temple Chair in Women's History and Mastin Gentry White Professor of Southern History, University of Texas at Austin

Editor's Introduction

Rachel Ozanne

Norman D. Brown is one of the great master storytellers of twentieth-century Texas politics. This volume is the sequel to his groundbreaking *Hood, Bonnet, and Little Brown Jug*, published in 1984. In that book he explored the major themes shaping the rough-and-tumble world of Texas partisan politics from 1921 to 1928: among them the power of the Ku Klux Klan over local and state officeholders and opinion makers, the role of newly enfranchised white women in the body politic, and the enduring clash between the "Drys" and the "Wets"—those who wanted to ban the distribution, sale, and consumption of alcoholic beverages and those who did not. Brown's work combines a scholar's resourcefulness in seeking out historical sources, both printed and archival, and a dramatist's eye for character development and the illuminating quotation. In the process he reveals the political dynamics of a state struggling between its Old South and New West identities, and his account remains always conscious of what its chief protagonists considered Texas's "exceptionalism."

Hood, Bonnet, and Little Brown Jug concluded with the Democratic Party of Texas deeply divided between business-minded, laissez-faire Hoovercrats, who had bolted from the party to support Republican Herbert Hoover for president, and Al Smith Democrats, who had remained loyal to the party ticket, despite Smith's Catholic faith and antiprohibitionist stance. Brown writes that as the forty-first Texas legislature convened and with the 1930 Democratic primary in sight, "the stage [was] set for a bruising intra-party fight," whose results would "either confirm the Hoovercrat triumph of 1928 or give a verdict of 'Love's Labor's Lost.'"[1] The conflict between supporters of federal initiatives and regulations and those unalterably opposed to them, however, took on heightened significance with the onset of the Great Depression and the hopeless poverty that many Texans experienced during that decade.

That poverty could be traced in the demographic trends of the 1920s. Between 1920 and 1930 Texas's population grew significantly, from 4,663,228 to 5,824,715, adding more than 1.16 million people. Between 1930 and 1940, however, population growth slowed: the 1940 census recorded 6,414,824 people, a growth of 590,109. The population of Texas remained a white majority throughout the 1930s: by the end of the decade, the population of Texas consisted primarily of whites (74.1 percent), blacks (14.4 percent), and people of Mexican or other Latinx descent (11.4 percent). Despite overall trends toward urbanization in the 1920s, in 1930 the majority of Texans still lived in rural areas: over 63 percent of the population lived in towns or regions with a population under five thousand. Among both blacks and whites, 55 percent lived in rural areas. These rural-dwellers would bear the brunt of the hardships of the Great Depression.[2]

When the stock market crashed in 1929, however, most well-to-do Texans initially assumed that its effects would leave the state unscathed. New York City seemed far away, and the stock market was irrelevant, except to its investors. The Texas cotton crop had already been sold that year for a good profit; Texas cities boasted strong economies; and the state's newest oil fields, recently discovered in East Texas, were gushing. These signs of prosperity convinced many that they would weather the economic storm of the crash well. Rural and small-town Texas told a different story; these residents did not at first notice a significant contrast between their lives before and after the crash, because they had always been impoverished. Sharecroppers, subsistence farmers, and oil field roustabouts just barely survived, even in the so-called Roaring Twenties. Still, Texas leaders, both political and economic, persisted in projecting a bright future for the Lone Star State throughout 1929 and 1930. In 1931, however, as overproduction caused prices for cotton and oil to drop to alarmingly low levels, more and more Texans reluctantly began to admit that they were suffering, just like the rest of the country.

The Hoover administration proved unequal to the task of managing a catastrophe of the magnitude of the Great Depression, and most Texans, who had supported Hoover in large numbers in 1928, repudiated his leadership. Hoover's failure caused state Democrats to close ranks, for few of them (and few Americans) wanted to side with Hoover after the Great Depression led to a spike in unemployment and a precipitous drop in consumer purchasing power. Their votes contributed to the landslide victory of Franklin D. Roosevelt in 1932. Between 1929 and 1938, led by Governors Dan Moody (1927–1931), Ross Sterling (1931–1933), Miriam "Ma" Ferguson (1933–1935), and James V. Allred (1935–1939), Texas political leaders grappled with how best to respond to the economic and social challenges presented by the Great Depression and to the challenges and opportunities presented by FDR's New Deal.[3]

These leaders often relied on familiar political tools. As Brown demonstrated in *Hood, Bonnet, and Little Brown Jug*, the progressive impulse remained strong in some Texans in the 1920s despite the end of the Progressive Era. As governors, Pat Neff and Dan Moody both tried to implement certain kinds of reforms in the "business Progressive" model, which emphasized "administrative reorganization, tax reforms, good roads, better schools, and expanded health services," while they refused to try to improve "capital-labor relations" or to institute "broad social programs, such as state protection for women and children in industry and workmen's compensation laws."[4] Notably, this progressive impulse did not extend to efforts to improve the lives of African Americans, Mexican Americans, or other minority groups in Texas.

Indeed, Texas progressivism veered toward economic efficiency and away from "small p" progressivism—social justice. Despite the fact that the unprogressive Ma Ferguson—supported by her husband, former Texas governor Jim "Pa" Ferguson—served a term between Neff and Moody, many Texas voters believed that the state government should be free of corruption and cronyism, though implementing reforms proved problematic in a state with a long tradition of deep suspicion toward government regulations and toward federal intervention in particular. Brown focused his attention on the movers and shakers of state government, noting in passing that most women, most non-Christians, and virtually all black people were shut out of the many robust partisan political discussions that marked this period in Texas history. It was, after all, an era that saw the all-white primary, the mass disfranchisement of African Americans and Mexican Americans, and the violence-backed segregation of public schools and other public institutions and services.

Despite the deepening economic and social crises of the 1930s, in many ways Texas politics at the state level proceeded as business as usual. For example, the challenges faced by the Texas legislature to fund and to create good roads—an ongoing issue for Moody and a topic of heated debate between Sterling (pro) and Ferguson (anti) during the 1930 Democratic primary—pointed both to the need for state intervention and to the growing pains experienced by state governments unused to providing such services.[5] Moral reforms of various kinds proved to be enduring, and enduringly divisive, issues. Moody's second administration grappled with whether to pass a bill to legalize gambling. Prohibitionists and alcohol advocates battled for control of the Democratic Party until the Eighteenth Amendment (Prohibition) was finally repealed in 1933. In the midst of all this, Pa and Ma Ferguson still challenged the ideals of business progressivism in favor of a more rural, tradition-based politics that prized personal relationships over political philosophy or public policy. The Fergusons thus demonstrated that their brand of politics had staying power, despite the expectations of their fellow Democrats and of city-based journalists. While the political machinations of the 1920s had indeed "ended with the Klan virtually extinct in Texas," Texas politicians and politics were, to a degree, predictable and bound by the prejudices and expectations of rural white folk.[6]

The images of the title of this volume—*Biscuits, the Dole, and Nodding Donkeys*—evoke the major issues of Texas politics between 1929 and 1932—emphasizing both continuities in and disruptions to the story of the 1920s.[7] Always an excellent source for a colorful quote, Jim "Pa" Ferguson wrote of the Texan electorate in 1932:

> There now are only two ways in which a man can make himself governor. One is to convince people that he will give them something they want and the other is to convince them that he will relieve them of something they don't want. You might call it giving the people a biscuit. As long as the biscuits last they are for you. But when you cease to deliver the biscuits they will not be for you any longer.[8]

The Fergusons continued to make certain that they provided their constituents with "biscuits," thereby ensuring their continued political influence. Though the elections of Moody and Sterling appeared to be a rejection of Fergusonism, Ma's 1932 reelection revealed voters' discontent with reformists. Ma and Pa still had plenty of populist biscuits to distribute to the ordinary white men and women who had little patience for urban reformers.

The desire of Texans to be "fed" by their leaders spelled disaster for politicians who could not deliver, and in the context of the Great Depression, it was difficult to deliver much of anything of tangible or material value. During Ma's second term the Fergusons found themselves in trouble once again for allegedly diverting federal money to their own supporters. As Brown shows, Ma Ferguson ran for office one last time in 1940 and was defeated soundly by W. Lee "Pappy" O'Daniel. The populist biscuits, however, passed into Pappy O'Daniel's hands: his campaign slogan, "Pass the Biscuits, Pappy!," made him popular with many former Ferguson supporters. Personality politics in Texas endured, albeit in slightly different form, with a new generation.[9]

At the onset of the Great Depression, those Texans resistant to federal "interference" opposed the idea of direct financial relief—"the dole" (a pejorative term that included public-works projects)—assuming that those who worked hard would not starve and that those who were starving ought to work. However, this notion did not last. Brown highlights the shifting attitudes toward the dole and other New Deal programs in Ma Ferguson's 1932 campaign for reelection. She promised to provide direct relief to the unemployed, using federal funds, and she won reelection. At one point more than four hundred thousand Texans were receiving direct relief.[10] Her successor, James V. Allred (1935–1939), often considered the last progressive governor of Texas, promoted direct relief, too, and governed over the state while federally funded and directed organizations such as the Works Progress Administration (WPA) and the Civilian Conservation Corps (CCC) put many Texans to work. Average Texans began to accept and even expect direct governmental support, and they elected Pappy O'Daniel in 1938 in part based on his pledge to create an old-age pension. He never delivered on that promise, suggesting division between the electorate's wishes and its leaders' intentions.[11]

Finally, the term "nodding donkeys" describes the pumpjack (a common oil pumping technology) and reflects the importance of oil to Texas's economy during the 1920s and '30s. As noted above, Texans had hoped that oil would insulate their economy from the Depression, but circumstances determined otherwise. During Sterling's governorship in particular (1931–1933), Texas legislators reasoned that a decline in production would boost prices and save oil companies large and small, but producers in East Texas refused to submit to state mandates. Those producers resisted any and all attempts to cut back on their production, and smaller companies especially feared that larger oil producers would put them out of business. Though some regulation was finally adopted, it was difficult to enforce—and this theme of resisting economic regulation was repeated in other sectors of the Texas economy.[12]

Biscuits, the Dole, and Nodding Donkeys brings into focus the high drama of the aspirations and machinations of leading state political figures in Texas from 1929 to 1932 as they dealt with challenges old and new. This insular group of white male politicians—with only scant influence from women—governed the state without much consideration of the needs of its black, Latinx, impoverished, or female residents. They understood their political world as a closed system with limited players. Their vision of politics was narrow; the electorate, intentionally restricted to white voters whenever possible, they treated mostly as pawns to be manipulated for votes. With elegance and a keen eye for the perfect quotation, Brown homes in on this world marked by petty jealousies, feats of grandeur, and the schemes of its players.

In the decades since Brown completed this work, scholars have expanded their definition of politics to include political actors outside of the closed system of Texas partisan wrangling. When Brown wrote this manuscript, relatively few studies existed that examined the history of Texas in the twentieth century, let alone the politics of nonwhite men. However, many new works now incorporate this broader view of politics, emphasizing trends toward conservatism, providing insights into the history of racial ideologies, and noting important milestones in the history of civil rights. These works provide a critical context for the high politics that Brown emphasizes.[13]

Historians have shown that openness to state planning and intervention during the Great Depression facilitated modernization in certain aspects of Texas society, especially as the New Deal meant even greater involvement of government bureaucracy in most aspects of society.[14] State agencies—often with federal support—encouraged the adoption of improved cotton growing techniques, regulation of the oil industry, and development of waterways, among other initiatives.[15] The state government even promoted the Texas Centennial as a way to draw attention to the potential of the Texas economy.[16] These state interventions achieved popularity among many Texans.

Despite this popularity, some Texas political leaders began to move in a more conservative direction—a trend that scholars have recently begun to investigate in depth. They have traced how Texas was transformed from a solidly Democratic state, which had supported Lyndon Baines Johnson Jr. in the 1960s, to a Republican-controlled state that boasts several leading figures of the twenty-first century's political far right.[17] Some historians identify the 1930s as the decade in which the seeds for the eventual rise to power of far-right politicians were planted. Many Texas conservatives voted for Herbert Hoover, but they were still a long way from switching parties. Nevertheless, a group of businessmen banded together to oppose the liberal policies of FDR, forming a political core that would push back against more egalitarian policies (such as civil rights legislation) of the federal government. During this era Protestant evangelicals began to hold sway over not only Texas's religious life but also its political dynamics. These disparate groups would eventually band together under the aegis of the Republican Party, which would become home to the conservative coalition brought together by Barry Goldwater and Ronald Reagan.[18]

Scholars of Texas have examined these macro trends in political history, but they have also researched the lives of everyday Texans, especially peoples of color and poor Texans, to see how members of these groups responded to the economic, social, and political challenges posed by the Great Depression. These marginalized groups have had to contend with discriminatory public policies for many generations. Studies of Texas cotton farming, in particular, have revealed how race was constructed uniquely in Texas given its large population of Mexican migrants, Mexican Americans, and African Americans. Whiteness, for Anglo Americans and other European immigrants, was defined by social segregation and state-sanctioned discrimination and was cemented by violent attacks on both black Texans and Texans of Mexican descent.[19] Investigations of the modernization and regulation of cotton production further demonstrate that African Americans, who often worked as sharecroppers, were disproportionately affected by 1930s policies that drastically reduced the number of sharecroppers and tenant farmers in favor of larger-scale commercial production.[20] As agricultural employment opportunities decreased, both African Americans and Mexican Americans migrated to urban areas, carving out opportunities for themselves as best they could—some working within the New Deal to make the best of its unfair policies.[21]

Historians have also discovered that Jim Crow Texas, a bastion of white supremacy and its practices of segregation and disfranchisement, nevertheless provided a home for some of the most significant early civil rights battles of the twentieth century. African Americans, working with the NAACP, fought against the white primary, one of the main tools white Texans used to prevent black Texans from voting. In 1923 the Texas legislature passed a statute that explicitly banned African Americans from participating in Democratic primary elections. In 1924 Dr. Lawrence Nixon, a physician living in El Paso, unsuccessfully attempted to vote in the Democratic primary. With the support of the NAACP, Nixon challenged the legality of this statute. The case, *Nixon v. Herndon*, was dismissed by the U.S. District Court in West Texas, but that ruling was later overturned by the U.S. Supreme Court, which determined that the Texas statute was unconstitutional. In 1927 the Texas legislature struck the 1924 statute but immediately passed another that upheld the right of political parties to determine their own membership. The Democratic Party then created a rule explicitly banning black voters' participation in primaries. Nixon brought forward a second suit to challenge the 1927 law (*Nixon v. Condon* [1932]), but the white primary was not overturned for good until the Supreme Court case *Smith v. Allwright* (1944).[22] Nevertheless, 1930s Texas was an important site in the history of black civil rights.

Historians have also shown how Mexican Americans living in Texas began organizing to fight for their civil rights in the 1930s. Middle-class Mexican Americans worked under the banner of several fraternal organizations in Texas to create the League of United Latin American Citizens (LULAC), officially founded in Corpus Christi in 1929.[23] Mexican Americans in Texas were often discriminated against in hiring, education, and housing and were subjected to both legal and informal segregation. Because there were not many laws explicitly mandating segregation and other forms of discrimination against Mexicans and Mexican Americans, LULAC did not use the court system to fight their battles as often as did African Americans in the 1930s.[24] Instead, they used their connections to white civic leaders to advocate for educational opportunities for Mexican American children in Texas, insisting that they be educated with white children. They also conducted poll-tax drives to encourage Mexican Americans to pay poll taxes and to vote.[25]

New Deal policies intentionally excluded agricultural laborers from the protections afforded to organized labor in the manufacturing setting. In Texas, as in other parts of the U.S. South, a significant portion of the labor force worked on farms, so New Deal protections largely did not apply to them. Because African Americans and Mexican Americans comprised the bulk of the agricultural labor force, they were essentially excluded from the New Deal.[26] Organized labor resistance remained weak throughout the state, especially when viewed in the larger national context of robust union building among automobile and steel workers; still, signs of union activity were not entirely absent from Texas.

Mexican American laborers in particular led the way in organizing and striking for better pay during the Great Depression. In 1938, for example, Emma Tenayuca, a well-known labor organizer, took charge of a spontaneous decision to strike by the women who worked at the Southern Pecan Shelling Company in San Antonio when bosses threatened to cut the workers' already low wages. They succeeded in getting the company to agree to pay the minimum wage guaranteed by the Fair Labor Standards Act—although the company chose to mechanize their operation a few years later, enabling them to let go ten thousand of their twelve thousand employees. Such were the contradictions of the New Deal: many of its worker-welfare measures did not apply to the most vulnerable Texas workers, and when those workers struck for higher wages they were in danger of being replaced by machines.[27]

Ultimately, the histories of civil rights organizing of African Americans and Mexican Americans in Texas revealed that conservatism was not the only political movement born in reaction to the New Deal. A liberal, interracial coalition, formed from the activist groups of the 1930s and '40s, made substantial contributions to the cause of civil rights in the 1960s. Indeed, reactions to this interracial coalition and the changes it brought to the Texas Democratic Party help to explain the rise of the Republican Party that Brown alludes to in his epilogue.[28]

These stories—whether about the long-term changes to Texas's political orientation or about the working conditions of African Americans, Mexican Americans, or poor whites—remain in the background of Brown's narrative. Still, his work intersects with these groups in interesting ways. He shows how racial prejudice motivated white Democrats to prevent black Texans from voting in primaries throughout the 1930s. After the 1928 election Democrats who had remained loyal to the party and voted for Al Smith (no matter how distasteful they might have found the New Yorker's political pedigree) discussed various options to prevent bolters (those who voted Republican) from being allowed to vote in primary elections in 1930. The executive committee of the Democratic Party of Texas passed a rule preventing any bolters from running for office in the 1930 primaries. They did, however, adopt a resolution allowing "all qualified voters" who were willing to take a loyalty pledge to vote in the primary. Leading Democratic Party member and Hoovercrat Tom Love pointed out that this might have the inadvertent effect of enabling black Texans to vote in Democratic primaries again—something to be avoided at all costs in the opinion of white Democrats.[29] The issue of race was raised again when white Texans learned that Lou Henry Hoover, wife of President Hoover, had hosted Jessie Stanton DePriest, the wife of Oscar DePriest, an African American congressman from Chicago, at a tea for congressional spouses at the White House.[30] Indeed, Brown's narrative shows that it is difficult if not impossible to write about Texas politics without attending to racial ideologies in some form or another.

Overall, Mexican Americans, laborers, and women (aside from Ma Ferguson) play a limited role in *Biscuits, the Dole, and Nodding Donkeys*, a neglect that underscores the biases of the insular political system that Brown investigates. He presents Mexican Americans as an easily manipulated voting bloc in the minds of white Democrats, who at various points in the narrative worry about whether Mexican migrants are masquerading as U.S. citizens and therefore as legal voters.[31] Though labor organizing was an important project among Mexican Americans living in Texas, in this work labor disputes emerge primarily in the context of Texas politicians' opposition to the New Deal's sympathy toward organized labor. In addition, unlike *Hood, Bonnet, and Little Brown Jug*, which describes the political leadership and activities of the newly enfranchised women of Texas, the main narrative of this volume sidesteps women's political leadership and activity, except when women appear to offer ongoing support for Prohibition or otherwise push for reforms considered by male politicians as "womanly," including those in the realms of education or public health.[32]

Hints of the eventual rise of Texas's far-right establishment recur throughout these chapters, especially in the person of evangelical minister J. Frank Norris, who became famous for his outspoken speeches and his political involvement—a portent of the significance that conservative Christianity would have in Texas politics and culture.[33] Toward the end of the narrative, Brown writes about the unsuccessful congressional bid of Joe Bailey Jr., who went on to become a key member of the Jeffersonian Democrats, a group of conservative Democrats—generally wealthy businessmen—who hoped to undermine the Roosevelt administration's labor-friendly policies and social welfare reforms. Scholars have in recent years identified groups like Texas's Jeffersonian Democrats as central players in the history of the rise of present-day political conservatism. Brown's inclusion of Norris and Bailey supports the general argument that the 1930s were a foundational period for this rightward trend, a trend that would eventually culminate in the Republican Party's dominance of state politics in the late twentieth and early twenty-first centuries.[34]

Overall, this work makes a critical contribution to the study of Texas: in telling the story of its political leaders and in bringing together the histories of politics at both state and national levels, Brown writes an account that has yet to be told in its fullness—and must be told to obtain a clear picture of Texas politics in the late 1920s and 1930s. While other scholars have explored the role of Texas in the national political scene in the 1930s, Brown uncovers how the old guard of politicians who supported Woodrow Wilson helped to secure Texas's support for FDR and to ensure the vice presidency for John Nance Garner. Indeed, Brown's blow-by-blow account of Garner's presidential bid in 1932 (see chapter 6) is a highlight of the book.[35] Brown also sheds light on how bolters were brought back into the Democratic Party fold and how figures like Tom Love failed to regain control of the party. Despite internal debates and disputes, the Democrats maintained a semblance of unity through the 1930s, even though they disagreed among themselves on issues such as Prohibition, Fergusonism, and reform. Understanding how Democrats kept the party together is an important piece of Texas history, instructive not only of the Lone Star State but also of southern history in general. Finally, scholarly biographies of the Texas governors of this era have not yet been written. This volume, along with *Hood, Bonnet, and Little Brown Jug*, remains the best resource for details of their political careers.[36]

Brown concludes this book by outlining the limits of the reform impulse in Texas. He cites the work of George Norris Green, who argues in *Establishment Politics* that 1938—the year in which this epilogue concludes—was the critical year in which the hope for a progressive, reformist political leadership was squashed and the foundation for the conservative cohort that would guide Texas politics moving forward was laid. Brown observes that the 1938 Texas primary not only signaled the rise of Green's new establishment but also marked the defeat of New Dealers in Texas. Average Texans may have liked the New Deal, but their leaders largely did not, harboring suspicions that even popular programs such as Social Security and public jobs projects were a form of creeping socialism. Garner rejected the vice presidency in 1940 and put himself forward for the presidential nomination in an effort to subvert FDR's leadership. FDR secured the nomination for himself, but he failed to eliminate other Texas politicians hostile to the New Deal.[37] The passing of the Populist mantle to Pappy O'Daniel and, eventually, Lyndon B. Johnson's election to Congress indicated that a new generation of Texas political leaders were coming to prominence. Texas politicians would continue to fight old battles even as they introduced new ones—with forces of liberalism and conservatism striving for dominance in the ensuing decades.

In concluding *Hood, Bonnet, and Little Brown Jug*, Brown suggests that "issues seem to reappear in Texas politics, and conflicts in public values are not finally resolved but only advance and recede in prominence."[38] In the mid-1980s Brown wrote about the continued influence of Prohibition in the form of blue laws and dry counties, some of which persist to this day.[39] By the 1920s the Klan had lost its political clout, and efforts of politicians in 1930s Texas to raise the specter of the Klan were mostly ignored. Nevertheless, racism and nativism continued to shape Texas politics throughout the 1930s and beyond. Indeed, at the end of *Hood, Bonnet, and Little Brown Jug*, Brown describes a group of over five hundred Klan members whose 1983 march along the streets of Austin provoked violence.[40] Recent national events in Charlottesville, Virginia, reveal that the influence of the Klan lives on in the various newer white supremacist organizations that have joined its ranks.

In Texas the legislative session of 2017 exposed the nativist sentiment of many lawmakers. Republican governor Greg Abbott championed and signed into law SB4, a bill banning the creation of "sanctuary cities" in Texas. The bill makes local law enforcement officers criminally liable if they do not follow federal requests to enforce immigration laws, and it forbids local law enforcement to create any policies to that end. Law enforcement officials in Austin, San Antonio, Houston, and Dallas argued against this bill, saying it deprived police officers of the ability to exercise discretion in deciding when it is necessary to hold undocumented immigrants on behalf of the federal government. Proponents of the law claim that it will make communities safer, but its opponents point out that SB4 requires law enforcement to target members of the Latinx community for verification of their legal status, potentially leading victims to avoid reporting crimes because of fear of potential deportation.[41] In addition, it is difficult to see the desire by some politicians, including the forty-fifth president, Donald Trump, to build a border wall through Texas and other parts of the Southwest in any other light but a nativist one—especially given the hostile language employed by the president and his appointees to describe undocumented immigrants.[42] Finally, the state's decision to cut Medicaid funding to Planned Parenthood, though ostensibly done in the name of preventing abortions, will limit access to medical care for thousands of women, especially low-income women. These issues pit more liberal, Democratic cities of the state against the rural Republicans who dominate the state legislature.[43]

At the same time, Texas Republicans themselves are split between business progressives and rural evangelicals—a split that Brown's work has located as early as the 1920s. This division was nowhere more evident than in the opposition of business interests to SB6, also known as the "Bathroom Bill." This bill was designed to require people to use restrooms (and other places where a person "might be in a state of undress") based on their "biological sex" as assigned on their birth certificates—and was understood by most to target transgender individuals. The business community perceived that this law might inhibit its profits—and some even speculated that Texas might have lost its bid to bring Amazon to the state because of the specter of the Bathroom Bill's possible reemergence in the next legislative session. Conflict over this bill caused a rift between Texas Senate and House Republicans—and the bill was not passed in the 2017 legislative session.[44]

The final chapters of *Biscuits, the Dole, and Nodding Donkeys* foreshadow the rise of a statewide Republican Party that essentially replaced the Democratic Party in terms of its political and cultural dominance. Even so, a countermovement has arisen—one that Brown did not foresee—that consists of people of color, immigrants, and women.[45] An inconstant ally of these groups is the federal judiciary. In 2017 a panel of three federal judges in San Antonio ruled that Texas must redraw some of its most flagrantly gerrymandered districts—those that give disproportionate power to rural interests over the growing, more diverse cities. The U.S. Supreme Court put a temporary hold on the order to redraw the districts, but in June 2018 it ruled that all but one of the voting maps currently in use did not need to be redrawn. Prior to this ruling, progressive political forces hoped that, if all nine districts were redrawn, minority voters—often Democratic supporters and members of this progressive movement—would have been able to exercise their voting power more effectively.[46] After all, the demographic face of Texas continues to change. According to journalist Lawrence Wright, "Texas leads the nation in Latino population growth," and some observers project that "if Latinos voted at the same rate in Texas as they do in California, the state would already be blue."[47] Whether Wright's prediction is correct remains only to be seen.

In *Hood, Bonnet, and Little Brown Jug* and *Biscuits, the Dole, and Nodding Donkeys*, Norman Brown gives us a clear picture of Texas politics in the 1920s and 1930s—not only of the feuding politicians who cast a suspicious eye on the federal government but also of the issues that proved enduring across the decades. Indeed, politicians today are still debating the efficacy of economic regulations—those affecting the oil industry no less than those affecting controlled substances such as alcohol and drugs—in addition to questioning cultural issues and the meaning of a diverse society. As we make our way toward the uncertain and unknown future of Texas politics, Norman Brown remains a steady guide to inform and instruct us in the history of the state's political maneuverings.

BISCUITS, THE DOLE, AND NODDING DONKEYS

CHAPTER 1

Tom Cat Lands on His Feet

A ccording to newspaper reports, the morning after the 1928 presidential election students found Thomas Jefferson's statue on the University of Virginia campus draped in black crepe—mourning, no doubt, the fact that Virginia had for the first time voted for a Republican candidate. Other reports stated that a resolution would be introduced into the Mississippi legislature asking that Jefferson's remains be removed from the Republican soil of Virginia to the good Democratic soil of Mississippi. In Texas R. B. Creager, leading member of the state's Republican Party, said the results marked the beginning of a new era in the politics of Texas and the South.[1] "For years I have advocated the two-party system for my home State and I am overjoyed at the prospects of its realization," he declared. "I am grateful beyond words to express to Republicans and Hoover Democrats alike. It is my hope that we may continue united in future battles for good government in the State and Nation." Creager's pronouncement hardly signaled the end of conflict between pro- and anti–Al Smith forces within Democratic Party or the rise of a truly viable Republican Party in Texas, as leading politicians fought amongst themselves to control the state's destiny in the aftermath of the 1928 election's surprising results.

On the day after the election, Tom Love, a Democratic Texas state senator and leading so-called Hoovercrat, wired Hoover his congratulations. "It was my glorious privilege to aid in smashing the brass collar in Texas and to serve the Democratic Party by helping to give you her electoral vote. On yesterday Texas and the American people met the acid test." The leaders of the Anti–Al Smith Democrats of Texas, the Texas Republican organization, and the Associated Hoover Clubs of Texas invited the president-elect to visit the state on his return trip to Washington from California. Hoover was unable to come, but Creager wrote Lawrence Richey of the Republican

National Committee that he was "exceedingly anxious" to have Hoover visit Texas for a day or two before he took office. Nothing else could be done that would be more helpful to southern Republicans in gaining a permanent advantage from the recent breaking of the Solid South.[2]

The Anti–Al Smith Democrats of Texas had no thought of becoming Republicans; they intended to take possession of the "House of Our Fathers." "I think we have rendered a tremendous service to the Democratic Party in carrying Texas for Hoover," Love wrote William Gibbs McAdoo. "It will break Tammany from sucking eggs as nothing else could have done. In every speech I made, I said I was fighting as a Democrat to make Herbert Hoover's election as overwhelming as possible in the interest of the Democratic Party." At a victory dinner in Dallas on November 9, it was resolved "that the fight for good government in Texas shall be continued inside the Democratic Party, and, to that end, the campaign organization known as the Anti–Al Smith Democrats of Texas shall be continued as a permanent organization under the name of 'The Anti-Tammany Democrats of Texas,' its present officers to continue in office until changed by vote of its Executive Committee." The organization's purpose was to prevent the domination, in both Texas and the nation, of New York's political machine, Tammany Hall, and its allies and methods; to preserve, strengthen, and enforce the immigration laws; to support and uphold the U.S. Constitution, including the Eighteenth Amendment; and to promote the fair and honest enforcement of all state and national laws. All qualified voters in Texas who approved of and adhered to these purposes could become members regardless of past political views or affiliations.[3]

In sending a copy of this resolution to Love, Alvin Moody, who had been chairman of the Anti–Al Smith Democrats, spoke of maintaining "the skeleton of an organization." Love immediately took him to task.

> It certainly was not my idea and is not of anybody's I can hear from that the anti-Tammany Democrats should maintain the "skeleton of an organization." On the contrary, it is imperative that we should maintain a real, virile organization, which should be perfected in every county in this state. There will be no difficulty whatever in preventing Tammany's domination, not only in Texas politics but national politics and the Democratic Party in Texas and in the nation if we do this thing.

Love stated that the headquarters in Dallas should be kept open and in touch with the organization's key men in every county. "The association against the Prohibition Amendment is not going to shut up shop or maintain any 'skeleton of an organization' nor is Tammany Hall," he admonished Moody. "Nothing has been worse needed in Texas in her whole history than a permanent organization of the moral forces in the Democratic Party. We have such an organization built up as a result of this great campaign and we must maintain and strengthen it." Love had some anti-Tammany Democratic contribution notes printed and persuaded Carr Collins of Dallas to serve as treasurer. Love pledged ten dollars per month for twelve months, sent out a considerable number of letters to friends over the state, and vowed to push the matter until the organization had an income of $1,000 per month.[4]

Immediately after the election, a number of Love's admirers urged him to run for governor in 1930. He was receptive if coy. "We are going to elect the next Governor of Texas," he advised Joseph Hyers. "If necessary to that end, which I hope it won't be, I will run myself." To an Eagle Pass man who wrote that the Democratic Party "will badly need a big man to succeed Little Dan" and Love must run, he replied: "I heartily agree with you that it is imperative that the good Democrats of Texas should control the next election and nominate a governor who stands for all we stand for and has the courage of his convictions. I am willing to make any sacrifice to accomplish that result."[5]

Looking beyond Texas, Love hoped that anti-Tammany Democratic organizations could be spread throughout the South, especially Mississippi, Arkansas, Louisiana, and South Carolina, before being taken nationwide. In a letter to George Fort Hilton of the *Chattanooga News*, he blamed the leadership of Joe Robinson and Pat Harrison for the debacle; they had helped Tammany to dominate the last three Democratic national conventions. The two-thirds rule had nominated Smith by driving everyone who might have beaten him out of the contest. "It has been proven this year that this rule cannot prevent the nomination of a wet Tammany candidate for president, and everyone knows that it does enable the powers of evil, by governing a compact minority of one-third, to beat the brains and heart out of the Democratic Party and ensue [*sic*] its defeat. The two-thirds rule must go."[6]

Love did not care who controlled the Democratic National Committee because its only real power was to select the national convention city, and that did not make much difference. He was content to allow John J. Raskob, whom Smith had nominated to head the committee, to have it and pay off the deficit.[7] As he explained to H. D. Lightfoot of Missouri:

My ideal of an organization would be like the Silver Democrats put on throughout the Nation in 1895, which resulted in their controlling the Democratic National Convention in 1896 and nominating [William Jennings] Bryan. They didn't seek to force out of office the existing National Committeeman but to capture the Party by capturing the next National Convention, which I think is the plan we should follow. My judgment is that such a plan cannot fail to be successful.[8]

Love hoped to regain control of the party for Drys from within.

Bolters Back into the Fold

Captain J. F. Lucey, the vice president of the Associated Hoover Clubs of Texas, had lunch with Love, former governor O. B. Colquitt, and Orville Bullington in December 1928 to discuss ways in which Republicans and anti-Tammany Democrats could cooperate in the future. Love and Colquitt recommended that a cabinet officer for the South, preferably for Texas, be appointed to work for a strong enforcement of Prohibition and for the stabilization of cotton prices; such an officer would also prevent prominent recognition of "the Negro." Love spoke to Lucey about the anti-Tammany headquarters, which were still open. Writing about this matter to George Akerson, Lucey asked, "To what extent, if any, do we wish to contribute to the support of that headquarters?" He continued:

If, for example, we were to defray one-half of the cost, or $12,000.00 for two years, and we could obtain the same kind of co-operation two years hence that we obtained in the recent campaign, we would drive a permanent wedge into the Democratic majority of this State. Incidentally, the Hoover Democrats will endeavor to take charge of the Democratic State organization two years from now, and it is the opinion here that they will not be able to succeed in taking over the organization. If they fail, this is again our opportunity. Furthermore, these Hoover Democrats are just as anxious for Mr. Hoover to make good as we are, and if we keep in close touch with them and not antagonize them in any way, will we not be in a position to ask for their co-operation four years hence[?][9]

A statewide conference of Republican and anti-Tammany leaders was convened in Houston on January 10, 1929, to discuss methods of continued cooperation. Creager was unanimously endorsed for a cabinet post, and a committee was named to call on the president-elect to make this and some other recommendations pertaining to Texas's welfare.[10]

Peering into the political crystal ball to see what the future in Texas politics held for them, anti-Tammany leaders met on February 2, 1929, at the state headquarters in Dallas. Among those in attendance were Alvin Moody, Mrs. J. T. Bloodworth, Judge B. D. Sartin, Cato Sells, J. V. Hardy, Dr. C. M. Rosser, H. Bascom Thomas, O. B. Colquitt, Dr. J. B. Cranfill, and V. A. Collins. Moody told reporters that their discussions had covered mere organization matters and that no definite decisions as to actions were reached. A second conference would be held to decide such questions as the need for a permanent organization and headquarters, depending on the financial feasibility to care for these things. The assertions of defiance heard in the aftermath of their victory against the regular Democratic organization were muted. Indicative was Moody's statement that "we intend to stay in the Democratic Party if we are allowed to. If not, we will do the best we can. If we remain within the party, we shall remain as a faction bound together by our continual opposition to Tammany Hall and its desire to control Texas politics."[11]

Uncertainty surrounded the legislature's disposition of two pending antibolter bills. The Al Smith Democrats wanted to keep control of the Democratic Party and to castigate the Hoovercrats by amending the election code. Representative Luke Mankin of Williamson County introduced a bill to bar bolters from the primary tickets of their parties in the succeeding election. On February 8, 1929, the senate killed Love's "freedom of conscience" bill (which would have allowed party bolting) by voting 20 to 6 to refuse to print it on a minority report. The measure had received only two favorable votes in the Committee on Privileges and Elections: those of Love, who had been added to the committee at his request, and W. R. Cousins of Beaumont. The Dallas senator made an "ardent plea" for its consideration, warning that unless his bill was enacted, the Hoover Democrats would not be able to challenge an exclusion by the state Democratic Executive Committee at a time when the state supreme court was in session. "The Legislature should fish or cut bait on this question," Love challenged. "They should say that we may vote or that we may not. The ranks of the Hoover Democrats have grown enormously since the November election and we can take care of ourselves but the State and the party needs this protection."[12]

Three days later the house defeated the Mankin bill on engrossment by a vote of 61–58. Before killing the bill, however, the house adopted an amendment, 79 to 22, that delayed implementation until after December 31, 1930, thus allowing Hoover Democrats to file for places on the 1930 primary ballot. One killing amendment offered by George Purl would have barred from the ballot anyone who had failed to support the party nominees in general elections from the time they had been qualified voters. It was voted down 70 to 42. Another failed amendment would have barred bolters from the ticket going back ten years. The debate assumed a review of the history of party bolting in Texas, shining a bright light on George Peddy's 1922 senate race against Earle Mayfield and Dr. George C. Butte's 1924 gubernatorial campaign against Mrs. Miriam A. Ferguson. Even the Populist days of the 1890s were mentioned, and members were reminded that the present chief justice of the Texas Supreme Court, C. M. Cureton, had supported the Populist ticket![13]

When Mankin's measure, which Love derisively characterized as the "sackcloth and ashes" bill, was defeated in the house, a similar bill by Senator Will Martin that the senate was preparing to take up was also lost, since legislative rules prohibited the house and senate from considering bills that had been killed by the other body. Love's point of order removed Martin's bill from further consideration. However, on February 12 Senator Alvin Wirtz of Seguin introduced a bill, signed by fifteen other senators, to amend article 3107 of chapter 13 of the revised civil statutes to read as follows: "Every political party in the State, through its State executive committee, shall have the power to prescribe the qualifications of its own members and shall in its own way determine who shall be qualified to vote or otherwise participate in such political party and the qualifications of those entitled to have their names placed on the official ballot at any primary election of such party."[14] On February 26, after two days of constant debate, the Wirtz bill was engrossed 17 to 8 with two pairs (indicating that two representatives had planned to vote yes and another two had planned to vote no, but none of them actually voted that day). Thirty minutes later the bill passed 16 to 8, after Love had a last say that was mostly devoted to answering the attacks that had been leveled against him.[15]

It passed to a third reading in the house on March 4 by a vote of 73 to 47, indicating that the final bill would pass without difficulty. George Purl, leading the fight against the bill, predicted: "You'll never get Gov. Dan Moody to sign this measure." His amendment requiring the state committee to go back only ten years, if party bolters should be barred at all, was tabled 72 to 47. The house also voted down an amendment by Rev. B. J. Forbes that would have made the proposed law effective after the general election of 1930. "This law will keep the bellwethers and bell mares like Tom Love from being Democratic candidates," W. K. Hopkins of Gonzales stated. "Tom Love, O. B. Colquitt, Larry Mills and Cato Sells knifed the Democratic Party and now they want to come back. We don't propose to bar bolters but leaders like them." The bill was passed on the night of March 7.[16]

Proponents and opponents of the Wirtz bill now turned their guns on Governor Moody, the former seeking his approval and the latter wanting a veto. Moody was confronted with another dilemma, similar in the forces behind it to the one that he faced in the Beaumont convention.[17] One horn of the dilemma was adorned with the anti-Tammany or Hoover Democrats, the other with the regulars that had stayed with the ticket all down the line and wanted the bolters punished. That a great majority of the bolting Hoover Democrats had also supported Moody for reelection made his choice even more perplexing. If he vetoed the bill he would go against some of his staunchest Wet supporters in the 1928 intraparty struggle with Love, and if he approved it, he would antagonize the Hoover Democrats who had voted for him.[18]

Alvin S. Moody warned that the Wirtz bill would divide the Texas Democratic Party into two distinct factions, each of which would be a party in itself and, disregarding the Republican element, would make Texas a two-party state. If the bill became law, the Hoover Democrats would be called into mass convention and would nominate a complete ticket in the 1930 state elections. They would designate themselves either as Independent, Progressive, or Constitutional Democrats. If two Democratic parties were formed, Moody believed the "progressive element" would lead the regular Democrats by about 150,000 votes.[19]

On April 2 Moody ended the speculation by vetoing the Wirtz bill.

I have nothing to say about parties controlling their own destinies as voluntary organizations. Under ordinary circumstances, a Bill of this kind would excite little interest and it would have my approval. However, the Bill comes at this time as one of the indirect results of the division which occurred in the Democratic Party in the campaign preceding the recent General Election. It appears evident to me that if the Bill becomes law it will prolong the bitterness which that campaign aroused and will continue and widen the breach in the Democratic party. I am of the opinion that the welfare of the party and the welfare of the State are to be advanced by promoting harmony among those whose views are in accord with the principles of the Democratic Party.[20]

Privately Moody wrote that "it looked to me like the so-called 'Bolter's Bill' could only serve to fan the ashes of old fires and possibly lead to a division in the Democratic Party." He noted that "if it had become a law one of the issues for the next campaign would have been should the law be retained or repealed, and certainly, we have bigger issues than this that need public discussion."[21]

Love wired the governor his hearty congratulations for the great service he had rendered to the Democratic Party cause and to the cause of good government by vetoing the "Wirtz-Tammany force bill": "You have defeated the most audacious and discreditable enterprise in wet machine politics in American history. Whatever may have happened or may happen, your veto of this measure marks you as a great governor of Texas."[22]

"Poor Dan drew a speedy punishment for his veto of the Wirtz anti-bolter bill," sneered the *Houston Gargoyle*. "He was immediately congratulated by Tom Love." The *Gargoyle* saw no reason to heal the split in the Democratic Party. "The wider and longer, the better," it editorialized.

> The elements that left the Democracy in Texas last fall are the elements of reaction. They are a liability, rather than an asset to any party that is seeking to become progressive and liberal. It is their retention instead of their expulsion which will be calculated to continue the strife and friction. For only by its thorough liberalization can the Democratic party hope to stage a come-back ... and liberalization is what the bolters will fight to the last ditch as long as they are permitted to invade the party's councils. Here again, though, as with Mexico, it is the mutinous generals, not the misled foot soldiers, who should feel the stern hand of discipline.[23]

The *Ferguson Forum* chimed in: "The Ku Klux are holding war dances in honor of their pet politician Dan Moody because he vetoed the Wirtz bill that sought to protect the Democratic party from political bolters and rascals."[24]

The Hoover Democrats were embarrassed when an outcry arose in the South over Mrs. Hoover's tea-party invitation to the wife of Oscar DePriest, a black congressman from Chicago. The *Houston Gargoyle* chortled that the invitation had "served to let the Hoovercrat bolters down with a terrific thud." Colquitt warned Rev. J. Frank Norris: "The DePriest matter is being used to arouse a prejudice in the south as one way of discrediting Hoover's law enforcement programme especially as it relates to prohibition. Think you preachers ought to burn them up on it."[25] Norris vowed to "go after Raskob strong in this part of the country," as he was the issue. "The Raskob Tammanyites missed it in trying to make political capital out of the DePriest affair in Texas," the Fort Worth minister assured Mrs. Hoover. "The administration is stronger in Texas today than ever before."[26]

Nevertheless, Hoovercrats used their influence at the national level to bar access to higher offices to certain vocal anti-Hoover Democrats. One early casualty of the political fallout from 1928 was former governor Pat M. Neff of Texas. President Coolidge had appointed him as a member of the U.S. Board of Mediation to fill an unexpired term ending December 31, 1928, at which time he named Neff to a full five-year term. His name went before the Senate Interstate Commerce Committee for consideration. Senator Mayfield, a "lame duck" member of the committee, had approved Neff's original appointment and in return had expected his support in 1928. He did not receive it. Furthermore, the railway unions had been angry at Neff since 1922, when he proclaimed martial law and ordered Texas Rangers and national guardsmen into railroad strike centers. Declaring him to be their enemy, they urged Mayfield to defeat his confirmation.[27]

On December 17 U.S. senator-elect Tom Connally wired Neff: "Have letter from Texas stating that newspapers carry report that the Brotherhood of Railway Engineers and Mayfield were in conference regarding your nomination. This indicates that your attitude in some wage dispute or perhaps your course in strike may be used as pretext. Some think Mayfield wants job himself. Shall remain on lookout." Wounded and disappointed over his own defeat, Mayfield mustered his senatorial friends and made a bitter fight. When Neff sought a meeting to discuss his confirmation, the senator replied tersely: "I think it only frank to advise you that I have reached a definite conclusion to oppose the same and a conference would result in no change of my attitude in the matter."[28]

Neff appealed to his friends back home to write or wire Mayfield on his behalf and enlisted the aid of Senators Morris Sheppard and Connally. He wrote to Senate minority leader Joe Robinson and to the members of the Interstate Commerce Commission, and he asked clerical friends in Alabama to intercede with Senator Hugo Black on his behalf.[29]

Meanwhile, Mayfield enlisted the help of Texas Republicans and Hoover Democrats to block Neff's confirmation. He wrote Love on January 3, 1929:

"Will call upon the President this morning to request him to recall Governor Neff's nomination as member of Board of Mediation. Have Creager wire President immediately urging request be granted and suggest you wire Senator Borah and ask him to cooperate with me in having nomination recalled. Messages should be sent immediately. Send affidavit from Captain Lucey concerning Neff's statement concerning support of Hoover."[30] J. Frank Norris also entered the lists against Neff. "I supported him for Governor, and organized labor never had a worse enemy in the governor's chair," he informed a railroad union lobbyist in Washington. "He did everything on earth he could to carry Texas for Al Smith," he explained. Norris told Hoover's personal secretary that the Hoover headquarters in Dallas had used every effort to persuade Neff to introduce Senator William E. Borah when he spoke in Dallas, but he had refused and had also declined to sit on the platform.[31] "There are plenty of Hoover Democrats that fought to the last ditch in this state, overturning a four or five hundred thousand majority and giving the state to President Hoover, without bestowing favors on our worst enemies," he argued.[32]

The Interstate Commerce Committee reported favorably on Neff 8 to 6, but Mayfield evoked the senatorial courtesy rule—the tacit agreement among senators that an appointee should not be approved against the objections of senators from his or her home state—and the nomination died on the Senate calendar. Neff hoped that Hoover would resubmit his name, but Creager and the Hoover Democrats persuaded the president to appoint O. B. Colquitt to Neff's position.[33]

There was some opposition from regular Democrats to Colquitt's appointment. Nineteen Texas state senators telegraphed Sheppard and Connally protesting that he represented "no political group in Texas" and had so altered his political opinions as to be "obnoxious to the great mass of citizens of the State." Colquitt claimed that the opposition to him in Texas was led by "Jim Ferguson and Lynch Davidson." Senator Robinson, in a letter to Senator James Couzens of Michigan, the chairman of the Interstate Commerce Commission, opposed Colquitt. At Colquitt's request, Governor Moody asked D. W. Wilcox to wire Robinson to withdraw his opposition in view of the committee's favorable report. Opposition to Colquitt was based in part upon the belief that his nomination was for a Democratic vacancy; but when it was learned that this was not the case, some of the Texas opposition was withdrawn. The Senate confirmed him on May 10, 1929; neither Sheppard nor Connally objected and no fight was made. "Heartiest congratulations on your splendid vindication by the committee," Love wired.

"Your enemies have kicked you up stairs."[34] For the time being, Democratic Party regulars and bolters had been able to call a truce, if an uneasy one.

To the Victors Go the Spoils

Patronage soon became a point of contest between Creager's regular Republican organization and "our allies in the campaign," as he termed the Hoover Democrats. At the beginning of the Hoover administration, Creager, who had been the referee in passing out federal jobs since the Harding presidency, announced that no change was contemplated in the Texas patronage set-up. Republicans who had carried the party banner in Texas, in and out of season, were not to be disturbed. But the Hoover Democrats wanted a substantial share of the federal patronage to go to them, since they claimed to have "put it over in Texas." Of the 375,000 or more Texas votes cast for Hoover, the strictly Republican end of the avalanche was said not to have exceeded 100,000, if that many.[35]

After Hoover's inauguration Creager recommended W. H. Holmes of Amarillo as governor of Alaska; O. B. Colquitt of Dallas as a member of the Board of Mediation; B. D. Sartin of Wichita Falls as an assistant attorney general; Robert Van Wyck Maverick of San Antonio to a position in the diplomatic service; John W. Philp of Dallas as an assistant postmaster general; and George C. Butte of Austin, who was serving as an assistant in the solicitor general's office in the Department of Justice, as solicitor general or for appointment to the Supreme Court of the District of Columbia. "Each person named has the unanimous support of the Republican State organization of Texas," Creager wrote Hoover. "The Associated Hoover Clubs of Texas ... and the Anti-Smith pro-Hoover Democrats of Texas, through their responsible leaders, fully concur in these endorsements." However, Philp, who was named fourth assistant postmaster general, and Colquitt were the only ones initially appointed from this list, and Colquitt had other endorsements. Senator George Moses of New Hampshire, through whom the Texas Hoover Democrats maintained their chief White House contact following the inauguration, supported Colquitt for the Board of Mediation; Hoover received a favorable word in the former governor's case from Senator Smith Brookhart of Iowa, who was feuding with Creager. However, in December 1930 Hoover nominated George C. Butte to the post of vice governor and secretary of public instruction of the Philippines.[36]

One of the choice places sought by the Hoover Democrats was collector of internal revenue for the Northern District of Texas, headquartered in Dallas, a position held by George C. Hopkins. The aspirants were Bascom Thomas of Dallas and Cato Sells of Fort Worth, who had been former commissioner of Indian affairs in the Wilson administration.[37] Alvin Moody and Tom Love urged Sells's selection, and Creager was said to approve, providing Hopkins could be transferred to Washington, but the appointment did not go through. Commissioner Blair "did not see his way clear" to transfer Hopkins, although he appeared anxious to appoint Sells, realizing it would strengthen the Republican Party in Texas.[38] Hoover Democrats continued for months to press the president to "do something" for Sells, and the White House appeared sympathetic, but no concrete offer materialized.[39]

Texas would get a large number of census jobs in 1930, and Hoover Democrats maintained an attitude of watchful waiting with assurances from Republican leaders that the places would be divided. They complained that as the situation was shaping up, they were dependent on the generosity of Creager and his lieutenants, whereas they were entitled to at least half the places as a matter of right. At Alvin Moody's request, Colquitt sought a meeting with one of Hoover's secretaries, Walter H. Newton, "to discuss the matter of selecting census enumerators and assistants and other matters of interest to our people." J. F. Lucey supported Colquitt's request for an interview, but Newton, after talking with Creager, replied that "the question of census supervisorship recommendations is one that is left to the Republican National Committeeman. It is, therefore, being handled by Colonel Creager." Newton suggested that the best way to handle the matter would be for Lucey and the others who had assisted Hoover in the campaign to take the matter up directly with Creager: "I am sure you will appreciate the delicacy of the situation and the advisability of handling it somewhat along those lines," the secretary concluded soothingly.[40]

On March 26, 1929, Hoover warned southern Republicans that to be recognized in party and patronage matters they must recognize and select respectable committeemen. The nation's welfare called for breaking down sectional lines, creating two-party representation, and building on political organizations in the South by the people themselves. He explained: "I highly approve and welcome the movement of the leaders of Texas, Alabama, Florida and other States to broaden the basis of party organization by the establishment of advisory committees of the highest type of citizenship to deal with administrative questions and who will also cooperate with independent Democrats." The president's pronouncement plainly contemplated consideration of the Hoover Democrats. However, by July 1929 only Florida had erected an executive committee to do this work, and if Creager had moved in the direction of Hoover's declaration, the Texas Hoover Democrats had not been advised. To do so would make them an integral part of the recommending authority in the state. They made no secret of their belief that Creager wanted to retain control as he had in the past.[41]

When Alvin Moody joined with the Hoover Democrats of North Texas in urging W. L. Carwile's appointment as postmaster at Dallas, Creager opposed the appointment, giving his reasons in a letter to Walter H. Newton:

> We will undoubtedly have to appoint a Republican at Dallas. Mr. Carwile is a Democrat and, while he supported our ticket last November, he, like Moody, Love and others, are going back into the Democratic primaries this coming year in an effort to capture the Democratic machinery in Texas. It would be folly for us to foster a declared Democrat for an important office like that at Dallas. I believe you will agree with me as to this policy.
>
> Of course, if these people could be persuaded to come over and join us permanently, as Republicans, there is nothing I would not do for them. The situation in this State has some interesting possibilities for next year. If Love is defeated in his race for the nomination for the governorship in the Democratic primaries and particularly they select a candidate of "wet" leanings, such as the present Lieutenant Governor, it may easily result in another coalition with the same elements with which we combined last year, and, in such an event, there is a possibility of our electing a State ticket.
>
> Please keep always in mind the fact I advisedly use the word "possibility."[42]

Creager saw no reason to entrust valuable political positions to allies whom he deemed temporary at best.

By October 1929 Alvin Moody had concluded that no Democrat or anyone else in Texas could receive a federal appointment without Creager's personal endorsement, and he was firmly convinced that the national committeeman would not recommend any Democrat for any position that could be filled by a Republican. "I continue to make my recommendations to him, not that I think it will have any effect whatsoever on him, but merely that I must do whatever I can for our people when they request it," he grumbled to Love. The following April the Hoover Democrats were still complaining that they had not been recognized in a single instance. "They do not regard the appointment of Governor Colquitt, who replaced Governor Neff, as a recognition of their faction," Captain Lucey reported to Secretary of the Interior Ray Lyman Wilbur. In March 1931 Alvin Moody complained to Walter Newton that "almost every day I receive letters from the leaders of the groups of Democrats in Texas which I had the honor of leading in 1928 protesting against the lack of recognition that has been accorded them and us by Mr. Hoover's administration." Many events had been played up by the press in the South as slaps at Hoovercrats by the administration. "While this has not affected me any in my belief and my attitude, yet it has afforded Mr. Hoover's Democratic friends in Texas opportunities to protest, and you may be assured that they have done so vigorously many times."[43]

These were also difficult years for R. B. Creager, who found his patronage practices receiving adverse national publicity. Senator Smith Wildman Brookhart, a maverick progressive Republican from Iowa, was named to chair a subcommittee of the Senate Committee on Post Offices and Post Roads to investigate the dispensing of federal patronage in the South. Brookhart was one of that group of insurgent senators dubbed the "sons of the wild jackass."[44] After a conference with president-elect Hoover on February 23, 1929, Brookhart predicted a revision in the method of handling federal patronage. "I am convinced," he said, "that the Daugherty and Fall scheme of patronage is over forever. I am convinced that the Hoover Administration will be honest in this respect, as it will be in all others." Fortified by his exchange of views with Hoover, Brookhart declared that the situation in Mississippi, Georgia, and South Carolina would require a shake-up, which he was confident would take place; his own investigation would be carried into other states, including Texas, from which complaints regarding patronage had been received.[45]

In 1929 hearings in Washington, DC, and San Antonio, the Iowa senator, abetted by Congressman Harry Wurzbach, subjected the Creager organization to intense scrutiny and bitter criticism, referring to it as "the autocratic machine in Texas," and in a letter to Hoover speaking of "the corrupting influence of Mr. Creager's political machine." There were sharp exchanges between the senator and Creager at the hearings:

Senator Brookhart: Every leader like you, Mr. Creager, fought me in Iowa.

Mr. Creager: Well, I probably would fight you, too, if I were in your State. If I was a resident of your State, I think very probably I would cross lance with you.

Senator Brookhart: I think I would clean you out. I do not think you could be elected for anything in Texas or any place else, taking the view you do of politics.

Mr. Creager: I would like to cross lance with you before the public in my State or your State with a decent opportunity to get myself before them.[46]

Wurzbach told the committee that Creager was protecting hotels in the state from raids by Prohibition agents. Creager responded by openly admitting his hostility to the congressman: "Because of underhanded and deliberate efforts on his part to undermine and destroy the influence of myself and friends in Texas and for many other amply sufficient reasons, I did not support or assist him in his last two campaigns, but openly stated I regarded him as unfit and hoped some good Republican might be elected from his district."[47] Creager charged that Wurzbach had violated the federal election laws by accepting campaign funds in the 1926 election from federal employees, the truth of the charge being affirmed by twenty-four affidavits from Texas citizens at the hearings. Wurzbach claimed the charges were an attempt on Creager's part to discredit him with Hoover and that these same tactics had been used against him during the Coolidge administration. He based his defense on the fact that the contributions had been made prior to the primary election rather than the general election, and hence did not fall under the federal law.

An indictment was returned against Wurzbach in Waco on March 4, 1929, formally charging him with receiving and being concerned in receiving contributions from three federal employees for election purposes in the 1926 Republican primary. After a change of venue, San Antonio federal judge DuVal West quashed the indictment on the grounds that the Federal Corrupt Practices Act of 1925 did not extend to primary elections. After the case was taken to the U.S. Supreme Court, that body stated the law extended to primaries and remanded the case to the lower court. However, Wurzbach died before the case was brought to trial.[48]

In its final report the Brookhart committee found that the Republican organization in Texas "based its support upon the solicitation of notes, in a large majority of cases, from prospective office seekers at the time the organization started under R. B. Creager. Later on the majority of the notes secured were from Federal employees or, those anticipating appointment to Federal office through R. B. Creager and his Texas organization." It further alleged that "Creager's only interest in building up a two-party system in the

State of Texas is to perpetuate himself in office as national committeeman of that State." He had done everything he possibly could to defeat Wurzbach for the sole purpose of giving himself absolute control of all federal patronage in the state, the better to retain his hold as leader of the state organization. Senator Kenneth McKellar, D-Tennessee, the only active member of the committee apart from Brookhart, added his brief comment to the unanimous report: "It is but fair to say that Mr. Creager created rather a favorable impression upon me. I agree with Senator Brookhart entirely that Mr. Creager's system of collecting money for party purposes in Texas was beyond the pale, and while not illegal, might well be prohibited by law, but Mr. Creager has adopted and used the plan openly and above board."[49]

As far as Texas Republicans and most of the Democratic newspapers in the state were concerned, Creager came through Brookhart's investigation very well. "The rank injustice and the malice of the man are almost beyond belief," Creager said of the Iowa senator. "I really believe he has done me good instead of harm as the impression seems to be universal that he was a persecutor and a prosecutor instead of an investigator." When the *Houston Post Dispatch* published an editorial calling the Brookhart committee's report "rather a weak effort to discredit the G.O.P. organization in the Lone Star State," Creager sent copies of the editorial to Hoover and his three personal secretaries. "I will appreciate your personally reading the enclosed editorial," he wrote the president. "The *Houston Post Dispatch* is, as you know, one of the leading Democratic dailies of the South. Its editor, Hon. W. P. Hobby, has twice been Governor of Texas."[50]

Creager's efforts to maintain his standing with Hoover were unavailing. Walter Newton, formerly a congressional colleague of Wurzbach, convinced Hoover that Creager's actions could only result in the permanent loss of Wurzbach's seat to the Democrats. At the time of the Brookhart committee hearings in Washington, Creager requested an appointment to see the president for a few minutes. He was put off—a notation on his telegram reads: "Hold for few days." In the face of an increasingly chilly reception at the White House, Creager had to rely on the influence of Captain Lucey, an independent oilman from Dallas who had worked closely with Hoover in war relief programs. "The regular Republican organization is more or less dissatisfied, and Creager's leadership at the moment is at a low ebb," Lucey wrote a member of the cabinet in April 1930. According to historian Roger Olien, "Creager found Lucey's help essential to obtain a hearing at the White House and to continue his control of Texas patronage."[51]

Creager suffered his first major patronage setback when he was unable to secure a vacancy on the U.S. Fifth Circuit Court for Orville Bullington, a member of the state executive committee who had sided with the national committeeman against Wurzbach. Wurzbach, temporarily out of office, opposed the Wichita Falls man's nomination on the grounds that he carried a stigma as a result of his business association with railroads. Bullington and Creager, Wurzbach charged, were simply two railroad lawyers who were trying to pull off a private deal involving the federal courts. Senator Tom Connally warned the president that any other nominee other than his choice, federal district judge Joseph C. Hutchinson, a Democrat, would find it difficult to secure confirmation from the Senate Judiciary Committee. It was learned that Bullington favored repeal of the Fourteenth and Fifteenth Amendments. Senators smarting under the African American opposition to Judge Parker of North Carolina, who was defeated by two votes for confirmation to the Supreme Court, did not want to face another fight. Creager explained matters to Bullington, breaking the news that a prize plum was going to a Democrat.[52]

Meanwhile, Creager had become embroiled in a controversy with *Collier's* magazine that further injured his standing with the administration. In its June 15, 1929, issue, *Collier's* offered "the unique correspondence course (positions guaranteed) which Congressional investigators are studying in an effort to locate and punish the job merchants." Patronage brokers John W. Martin of Georgia and Perry Howard of Mississippi were the principal villains of "Getting a Job for Jack" by William P. Shepherd, but "Ralph [*sic*] Creager" was attacked for running a fundraising system that was allegedly providing about $60,000 every two years for the Republican organization in Texas. Senator Brookhart supplied much of Shepherd's information. Creager was included in the ranks of the job sellers, most of whom, the writer claimed, had already been cut off from White House influence because of the Brookhart committee's revelations. He suggested that Creager ought to suffer the same fate.[53]

In the following issue of *Collier's* on June 22, 1929, Owen P. White directed his article "High-Handed and Hell-Bent" against the regime of Sheriff A. Y. Baker of Hidalgo County, "The Free State of Hidalgo," on the lower Rio Grande. It described how Baker, a former Texas Ranger, and his handpicked bunch of county officials had managed to get away with millions of dollars of the "American" taxpayers' money. White intimated that Creager joined with the old-line Democrats to perpetuate the Baker regime "through a system of handling the Mexican voters that is as old as American domination along the Rio Grande."[54]

In 1928 the Hidalgo County taxpayers united behind a Republican reform ticket to oppose "The Ring." They held an enthusiastic convention and nominated a full ticket for county offices. During the convention, five delegates, two of whom were said to have voted that same day in the Democratic primary, bolted and held a rump convention. Wrote White: "The bug under this chip appeared when Hon. R. B. Creager, Republican National Committeeman, who, for reasons best known to himself, has always encouraged the DEFEAT of his own party in Hidalgo County, recognizing the five bolters, who made no nominations, as the real Republican organization, and thus deprived the taxpayers of their right to have the names of their candidates printed on the ballot." In the general election Hidalgo County was the last county in the United States to send in its returns. Of the nine thousand votes cast, more than five thousand bore the written-in names of the Republican candidates, and yet by taking a little time to count the ballots, the Democratic county commissioners certified the returns as "a sweeping Democratic victory." White's article concluded by quoting Marshal McIlheney, the chairman of the Hidalgo County Democratic organization: "*Regardless of party lines, R. B. Creager and the Democratic organization of Hidalgo County ran the show down in their own corner of Texas.*"[55]

In his autobiography Owen White related that before writing his story, he sought a meeting with Dan Moody. The governor refused to talk about Hidalgo County at his office or the Executive Mansion, but agreed to see White in his hotel room the next day. The reporter told him about the thievery that was going on in Hidalgo County right under his nose. It was true. Moody admitted it and even said that the handsomest and most costly office building in Austin, which he facetiously called the "Hidalgo Building," had been paid for with cash from Hidalgo County, and yet he pleaded with White for at least an hour not to write a word of it for *Collier's*: "It would be bad publicity. It would give Texas a bad name; you're a Texan, aren't you, and—" White interrupted, "Yes, I am a Texan. A damn sight better Texan than you are because instead of covering these thieves up I'm going to expose them."[56]

In August 1929 Creager filed two suits in the federal district court at Brownsville against Crowell Publishing Company, publisher of *Collier's*, asking one million dollars in libel damages in connection with the two articles, which he contended maligned him. "The case has every prospect of becoming a *cause célèbre*, seemingly destined to attract as much national attention as did the monkey trial in Tennessee," commented the *Houston Gargoyle*. According to the magazine, "The ultimate question at stake is a fundamental issue ... the method of distributing federal patronage in those states unrepresented in Congress by neither congressmen or senators belonging to the party in power."[57]

Creager managed to have his case against Crowell and White tried in his hometown of Brownsville, but Charles E. Kelley, the attorney for the publishing company, secured the appointment of a special trial judge in place of the regular judge, DuVal West, who was a friend of Creager's. He then had this special judge order that the jury be drawn from counties in Texas as far as two hundred miles from Brownsville. Kelley argued that Creager would enjoy influence over local jurors because he had promised to donate any damage award to Brownsville for a public park and recreational system. Witnesses testified for *Collier's* that it was "generally known" that the Republican leader, Creager, and the Hidalgo County Democratic chieftain, A. Y. Baker, had an understanding. Creager denied the charges from the stand. After hearing the testimony, the jury found in favor of Crowell and White on May 15, 1930. On his way to the jury box to congratulate the jurors, White paused for a look at Creager: "I never before had seen a man of his color. Two kindly sympathizers were helping him to his feet, and from a ruddy red he had faded off to a pale, sickly gray!"[58]

The news of the trial's outcome was carried in the *New York Times* and *Washington Post*. Creager dropped his second suit against *Collier's* for the Shepherd article. Following the introduction of affidavits in the *Collier's* suit that the Baker ring had tampered with the returns in a federal election, a federal grand jury indicted the sheriff and his retainers. Four or five of the outfit were sent to the penitentiary, but Baker died suddenly of a heart attack only a few days before his case was to come to trial. Unsubstantiated rumors had him alive and well and living in Mexico.[59] The political patronage battle left some of its combatants battered and bruised beyond repair.

Love and War

The Great Depression, which was ushered in by the stock market crash of October 1929, was making itself keenly felt in Texas by 1930 and was perhaps responsible in part for the large number of candidates for public office. "Any year marked by economic discontent is a good year for the candidate who holds no office," wrote historian Ralph Steen, "and is a particularly good year for those individuals who have mastered the arts of demagoguery." A crowded field was anticipated for the gubernatorial campaign if the number of early and rumored entries was any indication. Frank C. Davis talked with former lieutenant governor T. W. Davidson and gathered that he expected to get in the race. President S. P. Brooks of Baylor University was boomed. John Henry Kirby was mentioned, but he indicated to Governor Moody that he had no intention of ever becoming a candidate for any public office. Alvin Moody said privately he would like to run for governor, but yielded to Tom Love's superior claim on the affections of Hoover Democrats. On March 9, 1929, one hundred voters in Precinct 88, Dallas County, banded together as the first Tom Love for Governor club and petitioned the senator to announce immediately. It was in this precinct that the first Hoover-Democratic club was instigated in 1928 by J. V. Hardy, who was now chairman of the anti-Tammany Democrats in the county. The *Ferguson Forum* reported "a whisper" that Love, Mayfield, and Alvin Moody had met in an Austin hotel in mid-May to discuss the governor's race and that Mayfield would not run if Love did. In its July 14, 1929, issue the *Houston Gargoyle* listed Love, Barry Miller, T. N. Mauritz, Katie Daffan, E. G. Senter, Earle Mayfield, Pat Neff, Robert Lee Bobbitt, Walter C. Woodward, Ross S. Sterling, Oscar Holcombe, and Miriam A. Ferguson as possible candidates, "according to an Austin rumor factory."[60] As the various candidates announced their intentions to run, public opinion, in the form of newspapers and leading figures, lined up to support or oppose them in turn.

On July 3, 1929, Love formally announced his candidacy. "With malice toward none and charity for all, I shall be a candidate for Governor as an anti-Tammany Democrat before the Democratic primaries next year," the senator stated. "During the last two months literally thousands of men and women in all sections of Texas have expressed their desire that I become a candidate and I feel that the time has now come when my friends, and my enemies as well, are entitled to know that I choose to run." He framed the significance of his campaign in national terms in a speech given in Cleburne: "It is not going far afield to predict that as the Democracy of Texas goes in 1930, whether Tammany or anti-Tammany, so the Democracy of the Nation will go in 1932." Love immediately began to gather information about Tammany-backed civil rights legislation and black legislators for use as campaign ammunition.[61]

The liberal *Houston Gargoyle* greeted his announcement with delight. "Nothing, really, could be sweeter," it declared. "Because, you see, Tom is our idea of about the worst possible champion that could have been chosen by the elements he is so anxious to represent. Time was, undoubtedly, when Tom's gleaming expanse of bald head possessed a hypnotic potency, when he ruled the state's Democracy with the iron fist of a Mussolini. But those days are happily past, let us hope forever. Tom has become one of the most disliked politicians in Texas."[62]

Serving his third term as lieutenant governor, Barry Miller, a party regular, a Wet, and a political foe of Love, announced his candidacy on July 17. J. Frank Norris, the evangelical minister, was dead-set against Miller and offered to come to Austin and in his presence present proof of his drinking. The minister tried to get congressman John Box to run against Miller, offering to arrange "a monster meeting" before Congress met, but Box declined to make the race.[63]

Pat Neff received some encouragement from admirers. However, he was warned that since he had been governor for two terms, a third term, even if nonconsecutive, would militate against him. The public would also feel that his entry was simply a personal grudge against Mayfield, who had opposed his confirmation to a full term on the Federal Board of Mediation. "Frankly I believe that race is between Barry Miller and Mr. Love," a Mexia woman wrote Neff, "and the Miller element will welcome as many other candidates like you, Dr. Brooks or Cullen Thomas in the race to split the vote of the pros, which would give him a chance to slip in." In any event, Moody removed Neff from consideration by appointing him, in October 1929, to a vacancy on the Texas Railroad Commission caused by the death of C. E. Gilmore.[64] Neff had managed to find a position in Texas despite being slighted by the Hoover administration for national consideration.

In mid-August 1929 Love was informed that Mayfield would run for governor and that Carl Phinney was in the Rio Grande Valley working for him on salary and would continue working for him in the field to the close of the campaign. Mayfield would declare for an elective highway commission "and some rather spectacular changes in that connection." A Hillsboro man wrote Governor Moody to say that his father had received a letter from Mayfield that stated he would definitely be a candidate. Moody was "somewhat surprised," since he had been unaware that a Mayfield candidacy was anything but a rumor. "It seems to me that it is mighty early for prospective candidates in next July's primaries to be laying the groundwork for a campaign," he grumbled. "There is such a thing as a candidate wearing out his campaign before the election time comes."[65]

Potential candidates were interested in knowing whether Moody himself contemplated running for a third term. Congressman James Young of Kaufman sounded out the governor through a mutual friend, saying that he would not think of running against him since they were very good friends and both saw the needs of Texas from very much the same angle. Moody's only reply to this feeler was a noncommittal: "I am interested in what you say about Mr. Young." Reporter Mark L. Goodwin reported from Austin on July 11 that Moody would not challenge Senator Morris Sheppard in the 1930 senatorial election and would retire to practice law at the end of his term. He was said to have expressed having had enough of the strife of legislatures, budgets, and hot-weather campaigning. Still, other news reports indicated the possibility of a third term. Dr. J. B. Cranfill informed the governor, "You have legions of friends throughout the State, and, while there will be a large number of candidates in the field, that would be no bar to your entrance into the fight if you desired to do so."[66]

O. B. Colquitt advised the Hoover Democrats to stay out of the Texas Democratic primaries in 1930. Instead, he urged them to hold their own convention, nominating a full slate of officers from governor down. Only in this way, he contended, could the party determine whether Raskobism and Tammanyism would continue to sit in the saddle of the Democratic Party in Texas or whether control would revert to the "real majority" of the state's Democrats. He also predicted that the Hoovercrats would refuse to align themselves with the old-line Republican forces in Texas headed by Creager. "I foresee no coalition with the Creager Republicans," Colquitt said, "since fully 50 per cent of the old Republican party of Texas voted for Tammany and Smith in the 1928 national election."[67]

Reflecting the views of Love and other anti-Tammany leaders, party chair Alvin Moody rejected Colquitt's suggestion, warning that any attempt to rule the bolters out of the Democratic Party would be resisted, and even if such an attempt succeeded, it would result in another independent movement. On a visit to Washington, DC, in early September, Moody told reporters that his organization's purpose was to control the Texas Democratic Party in 1932 on a platform of maintaining Prohibition and freeing the party from "Tammany control." "We want to see a Texas delegation to the national convention that will stand against these things," he asserted. "The New York idea of control is still rampant in that State. They may not try to nominate Governor Smith again, but probably would take a Protestant and a wet who would make Governor Smith's pronouncement on the liquor question."[68]

Meanwhile, Love was trying to raise money from the old McAdoo crowd for the 1930 primaries. He talked with Daniel Roper in Washington, but the response was not encouraging.[69] "I have conferred further with persons from Texas and elsewhere who are your friends," Roper wrote him after his return home. "They say there is no great enthusiasm in the Anti-Tammany group in Texas and they doubt the possibility of connecting it with National conditions. They say that while your winning next year would help yet your failure will not necessarily greatly weaken their national chances in 1932." They were unlikely to divert funds to Texas because they viewed the outcome of the state gubernatorial election—positive or negative—as negligible to national victory in the next presidential election.[70]

On September 21 B. D. Sartin, Hoover's campaign manager in Texas and a candidate for Congress, started a movement in Wichita Falls for a state mass meeting of anti-Tammany Democrats to demand that the state Democratic Executive Committee either ratify or denounce a recent statement by party chairman D. W. Wilcox that in his opinion a person who took the Democratic Party pledge in 1928 and then voted Republican should not be allowed to run for office on the Democratic ticket in the next election. Wilcox made the statement in a letter to Edgar Scurry, chairman of the Wichita Falls Democratic Committee. Sartin warned that if the committee sustained Wilcox's view, then the anti-Tammany faction would enter a full list of candidates in 1930 to oppose the Democrats.[71]

Alvin Moody called an "informal and private conference" of anti-Tammany leaders in his room at the Worth Hotel in Fort Worth for Friday afternoon and night, September 27, and asked them to be prepared to stay over Saturday if necessary. When news of the closed meeting became public, Moody explained that it had been called only to discuss Wilcox's statement and added that there had been no discussion of fielding an anti-Tammany ticket in the 1930 Democratic primaries. When the Democratic Executive Committee had made its plans public, the anti-Tammany group would then announce its program to combat any bar being raised. However, in a later statement, Moody admitted that "definite plans were formulated for promoting the purposes of the conference."[72]

On October 2 Moody sent a letter to Wilcox drafted by himself, Love, and Cato Sells requesting a meeting of the executive committee to determine officially its attitude "toward those Democrats who had refused to support Governor Smith last year." The letter stated: "If it decides in any way to attempt the curtailment of what we believe to be our moral and legal right, let us urge your cooperation in the utmost good faith to bring about the prompt and full and fair determination of the courts, including the Supreme Court, of the legality of the action of your committee." Moody sent copies to the committee members and released the letter to the press on October 7. Most of the replies were from those who were bitterly antagonistic. "State Senators Wirtz, Holbrook and Martin, of course, were pleased at the opportunity of gouging some skin off all those who differ from them," Moody reported to Love. "The Executive Committeeman from Richmond, Texas, says we should not be permitted to be candidates. Steve Pinckney of Houston was glad of an opportunity to vent his spleen and to assure us that should he have his way we should not be permitted to become either candidates or voters."[73]

The statewide Democratic Executive Committee took no action on Alvin Moody's request, and the defeat of the pro-Hoover Democrats headed by Bishop James Cannon Jr. in the 1929 Virginia gubernatorial election was a discouraging blow. "The result of the Virginia election has disappointed our crowd down here," admitted the editor of the anti-Tammany organ the *Southern Advance*, "though most of them will stick to the last ditch against Brother Raskob and all his works." Senator Morris Sheppard called the strayed sheep of Democracy back to the fold: "Let all who believe in equality of right and justice be made to feel that they are not only welcome, but needed in the Democratic party," read his statement. The *Dallas Morning News* approved this graceful, gentle overture, even if it was essentially unnecessary. It predicted the bolters in Texas would come back because there was nowhere else to go. "The Republican party in this State is not conducted on the hypothesis of local victory," it commented. "The Republican party of Texas, if we are to be painfully frank about it, is an organization concerned with appointed offices and delegates to conventions. When a Republican is elected to anything in Texas he is almost a museum specimen. Even the Republicans would begin to suspect his party purity. Judge Wurzbach can testify to that."[74]

Despite these apparent setbacks to Hoover Democrats, Love believed that there was "little doubt" of his nomination for governor. As he explained to Roper:

> There are fourteen candidates announced and suggested for Governor of Texas before the next Democratic primary, including myself. Of these, thirteen voted for Al Smith last year and I am the only one who voted for Hoover. It is obvious that a large number of those who voted for Smith, certainly a hundred thousand, will vote for me, and substantially all of those who voted for Hoover will also vote for me. Everyone agrees that I will be one of the two high men in the first primary, and that I will beat my opponent in the second primary, unless some new man develops who has strength enough to get into the second primary with me, and there is no such animal, certainly no one in sight.[75]

Love admitted that he would be better off if his name was kept off the ballot, but he did not think the executive committee would pursue that course. "If they do I can certainly compel them to put my name on the ballot through the courts; and even if I should fail in that I would win overwhelmingly as an independent Democratic candidate," he told Roper. "In any event, the fight is one that I can't evade. The only way I can lose, regardless of results, is to run away from the fight and abandon my duty, and that—I am determined not to do." Alvin Moody urged Love at the end of December 1929 to go forward with his plans to bring a test case before the Texas Supreme Court. "We want to know at the very earliest possible moment whether the Hoover Democrats [sic] are going to be able to run as democratics in the democratic primaries next year."[76]

On January 6, 1930, Love became the first gubernatorial candidate to ask for a place on the Democratic ticket in the July primary election as he forwarded his application by registered mail to Wilcox. He stated that since becoming a voter he had supported every Democratic nominee for every office at every election except when he supported George Butte in 1924 and voted for the Hoover electors in 1928. Breaking a silence that he had maintained for months as to how the party organization would deal with the bolters, Wilcox replied in an open letter to Love on January 7 that in his opinion the state Democratic Executive Committee under Article 3107, revised statutes of 1925 as amended in 1927, had the authority to determine the qualifications of those seeking places on the Democratic primary ticket. "Personally, I think the committee has the authority to leave your name off the ticket, but I do not intend at this time to engage in a discussion of this question through the press or otherwise," Wilcox stated. He promised to call an executive committee meeting sometime in the latter part of January or early February to pass on the question of whether Love's name and those of others in like position would be placed on the primary ticket.[77]

The Texas Senate voted 15 to 12 on January 20 to table Love's resolution asking the attorney general to decide whether Democrats who voted for Hoover electors could get their names on the Democratic ticket as candidates or participate as voters in the primary election. After the vote was taken, Love heatedly announced that the Federal Relations Committee would meet immediately after adjournment. Love was chairman, and with four of the seven members present, the committee voted 3 to 1 to request the opinion. Love personally delivered the request to Attorney General R. L. Bobbitt, who stated that he would not be rushed into "a hurried answer." An opinion written by Assistant Attorney General L. C. Sutton, released on

January 30, held that "no executive committee of a political party has the power to bar any person from participating in a party primary either as a candidate for office or as a voter, because such person has voted against the nominee of such party at an election heretofore held, after participating in the primary conventions and primary elections of such party." However, the opinion specifically refused to say what the committee could do as to future exactions. The bolters claimed the opinion sustained their position, but others said the door was left open for the committee to impose qualifications, pledges, or other stipulations, as to the future.[78]

Pleas for harmony, for "healing the wounds," for "presenting a common front to the common and traditional enemy" were now raised loudly on all sides by such "regulars" as Dan Moody, Lynch Davidson, and others whose sympathies were with the Drys, although they had cast their ballots for Smith to keep their records clear. The *Dallas Morning News* editorialized that the state executive committee should accept the attorney general's ruling. "It provides a pleasant outlet from a situation no less embarrassing to the committee than to the candidates who faced exclusion."[79] But the pleas fell on deaf ears. The young liberals on the committee believed that to permit the bolter element to return unchastened would mean, in effect, to turn the party back over to them. As Allen V. Peden recalled:

> They saw, furthermore, that they had the opportunity of a lifetime to make the natural cleavage of the two irreconcilable wings of the party permanent, and forever end the bitter strife which had rendered the organization so impotent for far too long. They made up their minds to re-establish a unified party, even at the cost, if need be, of losing a few state elections to the Republicans. They felt sure that all intelligent Democrats, who really comprehended and espoused the fundamental Jeffersonian principles, would support them in their stand. They were prepared, in other words, to tell all Hoovercrats not ready to acknowledge their error and promise to behave, to take themselves bag and baggage out of the Democratic party and into the Republican, or any other party which could stomach them as a regular diet, and good riddance of bad rubbish![80]

On February 1, 1930, the executive committee agreed by a vote of 21 to 9 that any person who voted in the Democratic primaries or conventions in 1928 and took the party pledge and then broke his pledge and bolted the ticket in the general election had forfeited his right to have his name placed on the Democratic primary ballot in 1930. Vitalization of the policy was effected by the adoption, viva voce, of a bolting test proposed by Steve Pinckney. In addition to the qualifications prescribed by law for Democratic candidates for state offices, any such candidate "in the last preceding general election must not have voted against any nominee or presidential elector of the Democratic party, if he participated either in the primary elections or conventions of the Democratic party in 1928, and took a pledge to support the nominees of the Democratic party"; that he "must in good faith without any reservations pledge himself in writing filed with the chairman of the executive committee ... to support all nominees of the Democratic party during the year 1930"; and that he must declare that he "does not now advocate a voter's entering a party primary or convention and taking the prescribed pledge with reservations mental or otherwise." Connie C. Renfro, on the committee as a proxy holder, was the author of a resolution inviting the Hoover bolters to return to the primary, but only as voters and with the proviso that they take the statutory party pledge. The Renfro resolution as adopted read: "Be it resolved, that this committee hereby extends an invitation to all qualified voters, regardless of previous political views or affiliations, to enter and participate as voters in its nominating primaries and conventions who are willing and do take the statutory party pledge."[81]

Love was present during the committee session but made no effort to speak, and motions to permit him or any outsiders to address the committee were voted down. It also was decided not to read any telegrams or letters bearing on the issues. Throughout the course of the rapid-fire proceedings, Love guffawed frequently and loudly, but when the committee adjourned the strain of "acting the merry part" proved too great for him. To a group of reporters he exploded in angry condemnation of the committee and its action. His face grew red with emotion; he jerked his watch chain from his pocket and whirled the dangling fob nervously around his thumb. After the reporters left, Love encountered Pinckney in the hallway. When the Houston man asked him what the anti-Tammany "party" was going to do now, Love almost shouted. "All right. All right. I'm as good a Democrat as you and these other men that have been in there MISREPRESENTING their party, and you know it. We're the BEST part of the party." Pinckney replied discreetly, "Oh, I see."[82]

Love embarrassed the committee the following day when he charged that the Renfro resolution had deliberately invited every qualified black voter in Texas to participate in the Democratic primary under the 1927 statute passed solely for the purpose of enabling the state committee to bar African Americans.[83] Noting that a group of Al Smith African Americans from San Antonio had attended the meeting to urge this action but had not been heard, Love claimed that "nevertheless, they took home the bacon without being heard." He added: "Gooseneck Bill McDonald knew what he was doing when he was making speeches over the radio in 1928 urging the negroes of Texas to vote for Al Smith." D. W. Wilcox admitted that the resolution was "on its face" subject to Love's construction but insisted that was not its intent. The committee would consider the question at its regular June meeting, he said, and he claimed that "there is no doubt about the fact that, as in the past, negroes will not be allowed to vote in our primaries."[84]

Anticipating that the executive committee would bar him from the ballot, Love had already prepared Senate Bill No. 16, signed by twenty-five senators, giving the Texas Supreme Court and the Courts of Civil Appeals original jurisdiction on appeals of candidates from actions taken by state executive committees in primary elections. The purpose of the bill was to assure that a final court decision was handed down before the executive committee met on June 9 to certify candidates for the July primary ballot. On February 11 Love pushed his measure to final passage in the senate; only A. J. Wirtz, senator from Seguin, was recorded against it. (For three days the Seguin Democrat had waged a one-man fight against the bill's passage.) An identical measure introduced by Representative Jack Keller and endorsed by sixty-four other members passed the house, and Governor Moody signed it on February 14.

Love announced that he would immediately appeal his exclusion from the primary ticket to the Texas Supreme Court. The suit, filed on February 24, was signed by three lawyer-members of the legislature: Senators Walter Woodward and W. R. Cousins and Representative Charles H. Jenkins. In an answer to Love's mandamus petition filed in the state supreme court on April 15, Wilcox and other committee members contended that they were justified in refusing to certify his name as a candidate for nomination by a party that "he has heretofore betrayed and at all times asserts his right to betray at his pleasure." It was claimed that the supreme court did not have original jurisdiction in the case because it was a purely political matter, and the court was asked to dismiss Love's petition.[85]

The state Republican Executive Committee, meeting in Dallas on February 15, took steps to strengthen its own party in Texas by feeding on the dissension now rife in the ranks of the Texas Democrats. It unanimously adopted Creager's resolution inviting all Democrats and other progressive and forward-looking citizens to affiliate with the party. Decrying the actions of the Democratic Executive Committee against the Hoover Democrats, Creager declared that "no man will remain in a party where he is relegated to a position of inferiority. Those who voted for President Hoover will not stand for this." Dr. J. B. Cranfill made a brief address to the committee in which he expressed a desire to work out some means of bringing the dissenting Democrats and the Republicans together for political activity. He wanted them "branded together for progress."[86]

Of course, the Republicans had no intention of turning their organization over to the Hoovercrats, who, if they marched in sufficient numbers on the Republican primary, could take possession of the state party by sunset. They had no hope of getting enough bolter recruits to guarantee victory and thus felt confident of not being swamped by newcomers. "A great scare thrown into Texas Democracy, however, would be a victory of the kind that Texas Republicans relish," observed the *Dallas Morning News*, "for it would find its echo in consideration at Washington and, perhaps, in more fat appointments for the faithful."[87]

Love was by no means the choice of all the Hoover Democrats to lead a campaign within the Democratic Party; some of them wanted an independent movement. "One even hears talk of such radical dissatisfaction among the Hoovercrats over the way Tom Love has seized the limelight and set himself up as virtual dictator as may result in their selecting some one else as their champion," gloated the *Houston Gargoyle*. "Should anything of the sort be done and Tom refuse to stand aside the ensuing scrap would be highly entertaining."[88] Dr. J. B. Cranfill complained, "We are still in the hands of Tammany Hall, the worst part of it being that our own crowd are in Tammany Hall and don't know it." He thought that if Love had not been a candidate, he would have led the Hoover Democrats in a more wholesome direction. "As the matter now stands, there will be a revolt among the Hoover Democrats, but we will split to pieces," the doctor complained to George W. Armstrong, president of the Texas Steel Company in Fort Worth:

> We would have disintegrated anyway, but we will disintegrate more rapidly now.... For my part, I think we will have to give up a number of our friends who are going to stay with Tammany, no matter what Tammany does. That is to say, they will stay in the primaries and then

kick out of the primaries like they did in 1928. That is mighty poor politics and frankly and confidentially, I think there is an element of positive dishonesty in it. I will not be a party to it.[89]

The Hoover Democrats held a meeting in Fort Worth at the end of February and consented to bide their time while Love fought his battle for "liberty of conscience" before the supreme court. George Armstrong argued all day for his and Cranfill's plan of holding county conventions to select delegates to a statewide convention for the purpose of organizing an independent movement or a coalition with the Republican Party. "There isn't any doubt but that the majority of those present desired to take this course and would have done so except for Mr. Love," Armstrong informed Cranfill, who had left the meeting early. "Judge Lightfoot made a speech arguing that while he believed this plan should have been adopted it now would be a slap in the face of Mr. Love, would discredit him in the senate and elsewhere,—and of course Senator Love agreed with this view,—with the result that the meeting, in my estimation, was futile and accomplished nothing."[90]

Armstrong approached Alvin Moody about taking control of the *Southern Advance* and making it an independent paper, with the understanding that it would oppose the Democratic Party and ticket regardless of whether Love's name was on it or not: "My own position is that if I am forced to choose between following Mr. Love back into the democratic party or going to the republican camp I will choose the latter, for I am more of a Hoover-republican than a Smith-democrat." Cranfill talked with Creager and Orville Bullington and arranged to temporarily subsidize the *Advance* with a weekly $100 check until it could be moved to Dallas and Cranfill installed as editor. Love, meanwhile, downplayed any dissension within the Hoovercrat ranks. "There is a little jealously existing on behalf of our mutual friend at Houston [Alvin Moody] and his close friends, which happily cannot do any harm and I do not think will become acute," he advised Daniel Roper.[91]

Love was optimistic about the outcome of his election suit, and much to the surprise of his opponents and to some of his friends, his optimism was justified. On May 17 the Texas Supreme Court, speaking through Associate Justice Thomas B. Greenwood, decided that the executive committee had exceeded its powers and granted Love a mandamus requiring that body to certify his name as a candidate for governor. Article 3107 of the statutes, Greenwood pointed out, forbade the committee to exclude a person from the primaries "because of former political views or affiliations." In adopting the statutory pledge found in Article 3110—that a candidate is a member of a party and agrees to support its nominees—the legislature had explicitly rejected one more exacting in character. The committee could not add to or subtract from the test thus prescribed by law. Since no penalty existed for violation of the pledge, it involved a purely moral obligation and was binding no longer than it could be conscientiously performed.[92]

Love hailed the high court's decision as "a great victory for freedom of conscience and rule of the people" and "a smashing blow at machine politics in Texas." He wrote McAdoo, "It was altogether the greatest legal victory of my life, and about the greatest of anybody's life. The general feeling on all sides is that I have the race won. There are about 18 candidates who voted for Al Smith in 1928 and they are going after each other. I am the only candidate representing the majority of the people who voted for Hoover. I really think there is little doubt of my success."[93]

Jim Ferguson professed to be pleased with Tom Cat Love's victory. "You can't any more raise the wail of a misfit martyr and moan about your conscience," he lectured Love in the *Ferguson Forum*. "You have got to walk up to the lick log and take your medicine. What we boys will do to you will be a plenty. You will get licked more ways than a country boy can work on a Tom Cat and you will look like one when the people get through with you."[94]

According to Harry Benge Crozier of the *Dallas Morning News*, Love "willed that no other Hoover Democrat should be a candidate for state office"; he wavered once and consented to a running mate for lieutenant governor, but his first thought prevailed and he stood alone as the one Hoover Democrat seeking office. Love immediately wired the *News* that this statement was "without the slightest semblance of foundation." He stated, "On the contrary, I urged other anti–Al Smith Democrats to become candidates for State offices." Alvin Moody was certainly contemplating a race for lieutenant governor, for he asked Love, "What do you think I should say if I should announce for Lt. Gov.?" But whether because of Love's disapproval or for some other reason, Moody did not run.[95]

"Indefatigability and perspicacity are munitions in Love's political war kit," noted Crozier in one of his series of word portraits on the gubernatorial candidates. In politics he was something of a paradox. He was not the back-slapping kind of politician, binding men to him after the fashion of a Jim Hogg, a Joe Bailey, or an Al Smith. He always appeared to know exactly what position he wanted to achieve and the shortest and most direct way to it. As a member of the forty-first legislature, he kept up the battle for "freedom of conscience" and lost round after round only to rise and fight again. He stormed at newspapermen for not giving him a square deal; he enticed his colleagues in the senate to give him battle on any subject that would permit him to denounce Tammany Hall and its minions. Day after day his name was in the newspapers. In his thirty years in politics he had created political hatreds that were magnificent in their intensity. Noting that Love's enemies regarded him as a "mere trickster," the *Dallas Morning News* conceded that he had a conscience, even if he did speak of it overmuch. "He is in earnest.... He bristles up on short notice. He is forever challenging, forever moving to amend, forever rising to personal privilege. If his epitaph doesn't do him justice, Tom Love will come up out of his grave to right the matter." The paper saw this "eternal contentiousness" as his "final and fatal enemy":

> The foes he makes in his Armageddons are strength to his arm. But the multiplicity of his Armageddons and the inconsequentiality of some of them keep down the sum of his constructive achievement. If he were to attain the Governor's chair they might easily absorb all his energy and a large part of the attention of the rest of the State Government as well. It is unfortunate that so able, so well-informed, so well-intentioned a man should handicap his own career.[96]

As the man Jim Ferguson called "Tom Cat" headed toward his next back-fence fight it remained to be seen if the state's voters shared the *News*'s view that his contentiousness disbarred him from the governor's office. He had, for the time being, kept himself in the running despite the conflict over the 1928 election, and Democratic Party in-fighting, the mainstay of Texas politics of the previous decade, would continue unabated.

CHAPTER 2

Daniel in the Legislative Lions' Den

Amidst the political machinations and personal ambitions of 1929–1930, the business of running the state fell to Dan Moody. In contrast to his first inauguration, there was little interest in his second, and the ceremony on January 15, 1929, lasted only twenty minutes. "Governor Moody worked even harder for governmental reforms during his second term than during his first," noted Ralph Steen. He made a strong plea for the reforms he had asked for two years earlier. In his first message to the regular session of the forty-first legislature on January 9, 1929, and in subsequent messages to five special sessions, he proposed the reorganization and consolidation of state departments, the adoption of the merit system for civil service employees, the introduction of the short ballot, highway legislation, the elimination of unnecessary duplication in the state colleges, the centralization and industrialization of the prison system, a complete reorganization of the tax system, and state regulation of public utility companies, "to stand between the consuming masses and the company or companies furnishing public utility service to the public."[1] Moody's second term as governor would mark the only term of the 1930s in which the economic hardships of the Great Depression could be ignored.

The *Houston Gargoyle*, which had taken its fair share of editorial cracks at Moody, promptly praised "his courageously conceived and forcefully phrased message to the legislature." The paper stated that it was a progressive program, which if adopted even partially would carry the state a number of healthy leaps forward. The *Gargoyle*, having regarded the governor, by his previous exhibitions of naiveté, as "still moist behind his political ears," was rather surprised at the unusual quality of superior leadership he was now displaying. "We wish him luck with his measures, almost without exception, and we hope that he will have so far profited by past bitter experience as to avoid such errors of strategy as were responsible for the torpedo-ing of the major administration proposals during his first term."[2]

However, the "unusual apathy" and "general absence of interest in the session" that William M. Thornton of the *Dallas Morning News* detected among the lawmakers just before the regular session opened did not bode well for Moody's ambitious program. In fact, some observers saw this lan-guor as portending the proverbial calm before the storm that would come when important and far-reaching measures were introduced. "It is generally conceded that these bills ... will provoke heated legislative battles," Thorn-ton predicted.[3]

W. S. Barron of Bryan and W. R. Montgomery of Edinburg both claimed a majority in the contest for house speaker. A third candidate, H. Grady Woodruff of Wise County, withdrew and announced he would support Montgomery. He charged that special interests and lobbyists were inter-fering in the process and that Jim Ferguson was attempting to dictate a choice. Ferguson was in evidence in hotel corridors, talking with members and hangers-on; the Montgomery people pointed out that he had not been to their headquarters. Jim had issued no statement indicating any prefer-ence in the contest. Barron was elected 87 to 59, a wider margin than had been expected.[4]

Senator Walter C. Woodward of Coleman was a candidate for president pro tem of the senate, and Governor Moody's name was mentioned among those favoring him. The previous November, Woodward had warned Tom Love that Archer Parr, state senator from Duval County, and T. J. Holbrook, state senator from Galveston, were trying to create a following for Gus Rus-sek of Schulenburg for the post: "And in confidence I am saying to you that it was nothing more or less than an effort to control the Senate with anti-administration forces and possibly pro-[Al] Smith forces." Parr told Wood-ward that he had never heard of his candidacy at the time he started the movement for Russek, and that he was going to get Russek out of the way. "Whether I believed this statement or not is immaterial to you," Woodward stated. Although Russek was understood to be making a "strong bid" for the place, Woodward was chosen as president pro tem by a vote of 16 to 14.[5] With leadership in place, legislators returned to long-standing issues in Texas politics of major concern to business progressives like Moody: reforms in the civil service, prison system, and taxes.

Escaping the Ruts Which Time Has Worn

Moody had carried his fight for governmental reorganization to the 1928 state Democratic convention, which recommended the consolidation of administrative agencies and the establishment of a "modern uniform system of accounting" among the agencies. "We believe," the platform said, "that the legislature can, without impairing the public service, consolidate existing departments, bureaus and commissions and thereby reduce the number of departments and employees necessary to conduct the public affairs."[6] Emphasizing again the necessity for action, Moody observed in his message to the forty-first legislature:

> Improvements and economies are being practiced in everyday business life, where the standard of value is efficiency, but there is too much of a disposition to run governmental business in the ruts which time has worn.... There is no reason why the government should not take advantage of new methods that will make for more efficient and more economical administration of public affairs. Reorganization of State government with a view to reducing expenses, increasing efficiency and fixing responsibility, has been undertaken and accomplished in other states, but in Texas there has been no such progress even attempted.[7]

Noting that the state governmental structure had hardly been changed for fifty years (except that the legislature had created additional boards, bureaus, and commissions from time to time), Moody complained that the governor, under the present apportionment of governmental responsibility, "hardly has the opportunity to form a policy, and is without power to enforce departmental efficiency."

Moody believed that the governor should be made an officer of greater responsibility; that he should be given the opportunity to fix policies and the power to carry them out; and that, to this end, he should have power to appoint and remove the administrative department heads. He wanted to see the legislature go "thoughtfully" into the reorganization of the state departments, commissions, and bureaus, coordinate the efforts of the various departments, and fix additional responsibilities on the chief executive so that he could have a policy and some power to execute it. When this was done, bureaus and boards could be abolished or consolidated, and instead of having a hundred, the number could be reduced to fifteen or twenty. "This is in line with the best thoughts of the time on administration of state governments," he argued, "and is the system employed in those states which at the present are showing the greatest progress in administrative efficiency. The Legislature could hardly address itself to a greater project than the modernization of our state government."

Refusing to heed Moody's plea, the legislature took no definite steps toward governmental reorganization at the regular session but during the first special session created the office of State Auditor and Efficiency Expert, to be appointed by the governor. It was this official's duty to promote efficiency, to audit the books of the state departments, and to prevent, insofar as possible, the duplication of functions. An amendment requiring that the auditor be a certified public accountant was defeated as being undemocratic. Moore Lynn of Dallas was appointed to the position, and his first report made charges of misapplication of state funds against Comptroller Sam Houston Terrell. The house launched an investigation, but Terrell resigned and impeachment proceedings were dropped. By 1933 the auditor's special report and two biennial reports had provided "a wealth of material on state administration," according to a student of reorganization.[8]

Moody renewed his plea for the enactment of a civil service law that would apply to all but the highest state officials, saying, "Merit, qualification and integrity should be the test required of the public employees as it is required in the ordinary business affairs of life." A bill providing for a classified civil service system was introduced at the regular session by Representative W. T. Williams of Austin, but it failed, 60 to 46, to pass third reading in the house and never reached the senate. Robert Holliday warned Moody that he could not secure any kind of legislation that "would be worth a damn on your Civil Service program." He claimed, "The House has made up its mind, and any further effort on your part to force this on the Legislature is only, in my judgment, going to further antagonize them, and thus decrease your influence to carry out your further Legislative program." Moody ignored this advice and again submitted civil service to the first special session, only to see the house turn down the bill 71 to 48. Texas did not get a merit system for her state social security agencies until 1940–1941 and then only in response to federal pressure.[9]

No reform claimed so much of Moody's attention as the perennial problem of the Texas prison system.[10] The governor reported to the legislature in 1929 that some progress had been made under the prison board's management. The system had shown a small profit for 1927, but due to an increase in the number of convicts (from 3,000 to 4,500), poor crops, and price fluctuations, it had operated at a loss in 1928. Moody said the system was twenty-five years behind the times and overcrowding made prisons a spreading point for diseases; moreover, the system had no reform or segregation facilities. During his second term Moody frequently pointed out that the penitentiary at Huntsville was a "firetrap." The governor declared that the development of a proper prison system required the concentration of the prison plants and activities. In his opinion such concentration would promote both efficiency and economy, would permit the keeping of practically all prisoners within the walls, and would provide suitable employment at industrial pursuits while still allowing enough farmworkers to produce the food the system needed.[11]

Senator T. J. Holbrook of Galveston sponsored a bill that provided for centralization and a new prison plant, authorized relocation, and gave a locating board final authority for the purchase and sale of land. The house rejected this plan—which Moody and the organized women of the state favored—70 to 59, and voted to concentrate the system on the Darrington farm in Brazoria County. Senator W. R. Cousins offered the same bill in the upper house. "Nobody seems to love Dan any more," commented the *Houston Gargoyle*. "The Hoovercrats can't forget he was so half-hearted. Neither can the Smithsonians. So everybody takes a kick at the convicts."[12]

For nearly four hours one day, senators directed a scathing attack at the Moody-Holbrook bill. Senator A. J. Wirtz of Seguin ("Smith lieutenant and 'bum looser,'" according to Mrs. Moody) declared that "but for the bullheadedness of those sponsoring this bill, we would have prison legislation." Everybody craned his or her neck to see how Moody, who was sitting in the chamber, would take this thrust. He sat quietly, his expression unchanged. "The men who are pushing this bill," Wirtz pursued, "are saying 'we will have this or no other.'" "Isn't it true," interrupted Tom Love, "that the legislature refused to follow the governor two years ago?" Wirtz claimed the opposite: "No, the governor refused to follow the legislature." He added, "You can get your prison system, if you will take it in any of three lower counties."[13]

Even politics and Senator Joe Bailey were drawn into the debate, when Love demanded of Holbrook if "most of the prisoners aren't down there because they followed the principles advocated by the senate's distinguished visitor yesterday?" Love's clash with Bailey over the wet-dry issue and old-time democracy had furnished the showiest display of verbal fireworks of the session.[14]

Although the senate approved the Holbrook bill, the house refused to recede from its opposition, and all the prison bills died when the regular session ended. As a compromise the special session created the Texas Prison Centralization Commission, consisting of the nine members of the prison board, four senators, and five representatives: W. A. Paddock of Houston served as chairman, A. H. King of Throckmorton County as vice president, and Bob Barker of Fort Worth as executive secretary. The commission made a careful investigation of the Texas prison system and visited a score of prisons in other states. The members were unable to reach an agreement on recommendations, and the commission submitted majority and minority reports to Moody, who submitted both to the legislature. The majority report called for the centralization of the system within twenty-five miles of Austin and for the use of convict labor in prison-operated industries. The minority report favored keeping the present system, which combined farms and industry, and patching it up a bit. The minority members listed several reasons why the system should not be removed to Austin; among them was its great need to be "freed from the blight of every changing political fortune," which was why, they claimed, it "should be removed as far as possible from the influence of partisan politics."[15]

Moody called a special session to meet in January 20, 1930, to consider the commission's reports. When it took no action, he summoned a fifth special session to follow immediately on February 19. Some public interest was aroused, and many hoped that some constructive legislation might be forthcoming. "It would be more than unfortunate if the subject of Texas prison reform should be made a political football," said the *Dallas Morning News*: "The State is fully aware that its prison system is no source of pride. Texas has been informed by a national survey that the system is among the poorest in the country. It has been told by its own prison board and by the prison location commission of the many flaws in present administration. Confronted by a disgraceful condition, it is the task to initiate immediate improvement."[16]

Moody's reversal of the Ferguson liberal pardon policy coupled with prison conditions that the governor himself said were "not fit for a dog" contributed to a sharp increase in prisoner unrest and escapes. The *Dallas Morning News* card index of prison-system stories printed in 1929–1930 contains such entries as

- January 6, 1929 — Sixty-five convicts escape from prison farms in one month;

- June 21—Forty-three convicts kidnap guard; eighteen caught; others penned in bottoms of Brazos River by prison forces;
- June 22—Twenty-six convicts caught; four shot; one dead;
- September 29—Eighteen convicts dig their way out of prison farm;
- October 1—Three more convicts flee prison farm;
- October 26—Three buildings on Wynne State Penal Farm burn;
- January 18, 1930—Convicts go on hunger strike;
- January 19—Wynne convicts abandon hunger strike; try to burn chapel; guards put out fire;
- February 25—Swamps of Trinity River block flight of seven convicts after prison break.[17]

"It is not denied now that the penitentiary system is in the worst condition in its history," Jim Ferguson charged in January 1929. "As a result of Moody's policy not to issue any pardons, there is no work being done, the morale of the system is broken down, diseased and unsanitary conditions are on every hand, mutiny and escapes are an every day occurrence." He asserted (without citing proof), "There were not two dozen escapes during the whole time my wife was governor." He pointed out that according to testimony in a legislative hearing there were 763 escapes in 1928, and Ferguson assured his readers "there were nearly as many in 1927."[18]

Convinced that the only way to induce the legislature to do something with the prison system was "by taking the issue to the people," Moody made several public speeches before the legislature convened, and once it was in session he spoke over the radio in favor of the majority report. If the legislature failed to end the disgraceful, wasteful, and dangerous conditions then overwhelming the system, he would make arrangements with the Highway Commission to use the convicts in the construction of state highways. Hoping for popular support, he invited interested citizens to inspect the penitentiary and demand necessary reforms from their legislators. "Our prison system has proved a dismal failure from many standpoints," he said in an address to a joint session on January 21:

The prison at Huntsville is a dilapidated, run-down and worn-out makeshift. It makes one shudder to think what might be the result of any large fire within the walls of the State penitentiary. The facilities for caring for the men are of the most archaic type. The physical properties fit my idea of a Siberian prison. The enforcement of sanitary and health regulations is almost impossible. Nothing worth mentioning is done, or can be done, in the present surroundings for the moral reformation of the prisoner, or toward restoring him to useful citizenship.[19]

However, Moody's commitment prison reform was not limited to making impassioned speeches. On January 26, 1930, he took one hundred members of the legislature and others to inspect the main prison at Huntsville.

Because of overcrowding in the system, the Texas Prison Board issued an order on March 3 that no more convicts be admitted into Huntsville or any of the prison farms "until the normal capacity of the system is reached." The order aroused a storm of indignation in the legislature, where opponents of centralization considered it a form of pressure to pass the desired pending prison bill. Senator McFarlane assailed the order as "another glaring example of incompetency and inefficiency." A few lawmakers demanded that the board membership be cut from nine to three. Others advocated the passage of a resolution requesting the entire board's resignation. The Tarrant County district attorney threated to charge the manager of the prison system with contempt of court if he refused to accept convicts from his county. Dr. A. C. Scott, the vice chairman of the prison board, defended its action: "Concerning charges of the Board's incompetence, if I thought the prison board had shown as little ability to manage the system as has been shown in the unstatesmanlike manner with which some members of the Legislature have dealt with the same problem, I should advocate the board resign in a body." Moody supported the board's action, terming it both wise and necessary.[20]

The senate mustered a majority in favor of the Beck bill, which favored the establishment of two plants: one in a central location and the other located on property already owned by the prison system. The house majority, on the other hand, was content to patch the existing system and incorporated its wishes in the Graves bill. Debate in both houses was heated. Some of the sponsors of the proposed relocation insisted that East Texas was "too unhealthy for convicts." East Texas asked, "Unfit for convicts but fit for Sam Houston and the rest of us?"—noting that Houston had his home at Huntsville. Lee Satterwhite suggested that the idea of changing the location of the prison system was born when a committee of the thirty-sixth legislature had inspected the prison properties when rain had made the ground soggy. He said: "They came back to Austin, a bunch of city legislators for the most part, used to smooth city streets, concrete sidewalks, and steamheated offices; and one of them suggested that the penitentiary should be moved near Austin where the Legislature could get to it. That was the start of this agitation to change prison location."[21]

The Beck and Graves bills were sent to a conference committee, to which Lt. Gov. Barry Miller (who did not support relocation) appointed four senators who were opposed to any change in the prison system—an act that flew in the face of the senate that had voted consistently by a small majority for reorganization. On March 15 Moody issued a scorching statement that said in part: "In appointing the free conference committee on the prison bill, the Lieutenant Governor betrayed the majority vote in the Senate on this bill and he probably ended the hope of substantial prison reform for the present." Mrs. Moody wrote in her diary: "Lt. Gov. Barry Miller, in political peeve (and maybe fear of the third term [he's running for Governor]) stacked the cards in the Penitentiary muddle by giving a four-to-one committee for Graves project; thus he hopes to pass the buck to Dan through a veto almost assured. Dan stated publicly that he (Lt. Gov.) 'betrayed the Senate.' The Senate held out against sinking more money in antiquated system, and wanted reorganization."[22]

From the conference committee came a bill authored by Senator Clint Small of Wellington that provided some improvements in the prison system but stopped far short of the proposed concentration. It provided for the improvement of the Huntsville plant by the installation of a better sanitary system, the provision of adequate hospital facilities within the walls, and the installation of equipment for additional industries. A sufficient number of prison farm units were to be erected to relieve the existing congestion, and the prison board was authorized to dispose of the Shaw farm in Bowie County if this should appear desirable. The bill carried an appropriation of $575,000. It passed the house 80 to 21, and the senate approved it 29 to zero. Moody was displeased with the bill but felt that nothing better could be obtained, and he permitted it to become law without his signature. "I have tried it now with two Legislatures; and I have advocated it in my campaign speeches," he wrote privately of his efforts to improve prison conditions. "There seems little to justify hope of substantial improvement at this time, but if the papers will continue in the campaign I believe public sentiment will be aroused that will result in worthwhile accomplishments in the field of prison reform."[23]

The legislators were not particularly proud of the compromise measure. Small termed it a temporary solution of the prison problem, and Senator Woodward, a supporter of the Moody plan, declared it to be "a bill of apology to the Forty-First Legislature on Prison Reformation." On the other hand,

William B. Teagarden of San Antonio, a Fergusonite, wrote representative Harry Graves: "The gallant fight you made against Moody's plan to sell out the penitentiary farms and convert the system ultimately into a manufacturers business has saved the people not less than ten million of dollars."[24]

The dissatisfaction did not extend to the choice of a new general manager to succeed W. H. Meade, as almost everyone was pleased when Lee Simmons, a Sherman businessman and member of the prison board, agreed to serve after having refused the post the previous year. On April 12, 1930, Simmons met at Huntsville with the board. As soon as he had administered the oath, Chairman Paddock turned to Simmons and said: "Here it is; it's yours. Do the best you can with it." Simmons held the post for several years and was generally considered to be a very capable manager.[25]

In 1929 the legislature, at Moody's suggestion, created the Board of Pardons to replace the Board of Pardon Advisers. The lawmakers added a third member to the board and provided for overlapping terms of six years. The new board was to maintain offices in the Capitol and hold its hearings in that building. It was directed to fulfill such duties as the governor instructed. However, he retained the constitutional responsibility for granting pardons.[26]

Herman L. Crow, a historian of the Texas prison system, wrote that Moody's conception of penal reform "exerted a powerful influence upon the policies of the Texas prison system, although the changes, impressive as they were, fell far short of the complete realization of his ideal." Lee Simmons asserted, "Governor Dan Moody deserves much of the credit for the creation of a responsible prison authority in Texas.... From the Legislature and other bodies he got the co-operation he demanded. I thought him a great man then. I still do."[27]

Tax reform continued as part of the Moody program in his second term. He still believed that the ad valorem tax should be eliminated for state support. A tax survey committee made a report to the forty-first legislature, but it occasioned little comment. Income and sulfur tax bills and other measures affecting gross receipts and severance were killed in the House Committee on Revenues and Taxation during seven days in May. This inspired Senator Edgar E. Witt of Waco, an apostle of tax reform, to challenge the people to furnish a "'peoples' lobby' big enough in personnel and in wisdom to match blades with the spokesmen of the business and corporate interests of the State." He said of the lobbyists: "These men will not deny that the real estate and other real properties of Texas are carrying an undue share of the cost of government. The tax system we are using is makeshift, fashioned nearly a century ago when gainful employment in Texas was represented only by pastoral and agricultural pursuits."[28]

In an address to the second called session, Moody suggested that the state adopt an income tax on individual and corporate income based on the general outlines of the federal income tax law, but levying only that proportion of the federal rate that would yield an income equal to, or approximately equal to, the state ad valorem tax. His proposal garnered sensational headlines in the Texas press, and there was some misunderstanding, perhaps deliberately fostered by opponents of the idea, of his position. "I did not advocate an income tax in addition to other taxes which are now paid, but I advocated the partial *substitution* of an income tax for the present state ad valorem tax," he explained to one irate citizen, who had read a *Fort Worth Star-Telegram* editorial to the effect that he wanted a state income tax equal to the federal tax. "I said that the farms, the ranches, and the homes of this State ought to be relieved of the present unjust burdens imposed upon them by the present ad valorem method. I believe this is a correct and sound principle."[29]

The second special session took no action on Moody's income tax proposal, and he mentioned it again only in his final message to the forty-second legislature before leaving office. Opposition to an income tax was formidable; critics charged that it would retard industrial development. "A Texas shunned by expanding industries and being rapidly denuded of those it now has is a by no means improbable result of its adoption of such a tax measure," warned the *Houston Gargoyle*. "We suggest to Dan Moody, Senator Witt, et al. that they re-read the fable of the goose that laid the golden eggs." Moody's friend Peter Molyneaux editorialized in *Texas Monthly*, saying, "Keep It Out of Texas": "In plain language we think that the adoption of a State income tax in Texas would be so obviously inimical to the best interests of the State that the people would have to become completely blind to the present situation in Texas to countenance any such move."[30]

The taxation of sulfur began in 1923 with a rate of 2 percent of the market value of production. In the fourth special session of 1930, the house approved a sulfur tax of one dollar per long ton of production, while the senate stood fast for a 50-cent tax and refused to compromise on 75 cents. A rate of 55 cents was finally agreed on. Representative Phil Sanders of Nacogdoches, the sponsor of the original dollar-a-ton proposal, raged against the sulfur industry in a mimeographed broadside:

The sulphur industry marched into Austin the most powerful and unscrupulous lobby seen here in a generation. They first attempted to horn-swoggle the House of Representatives into passing a 50¢ tax which would have kept in the pockets of the sulphur companies ONE MILLION DOLLARS A YEAR to which the people of Texas are just entitled. Six times the House of Representatives rejected this attempt to have them barter away the birthright of the people. *But the lobby which failed in the House was successful in the Senate.* In the face of the astounding facts a majority of the Senate voted steadily for the sulphur companies' tax of only 50¢ per ton. The House of Representatives, at the closing hour of the legislature, was crowded to the wall and was forced to accept the pitiful sum of 55¢ per ton in order to get anything at all for the sadly neglected school children of the State.

Sanders urged the people to elect no one to the legislature unless he represented them and not the special interests and was irrevocably committed to a sulfur tax of not less than one dollar per ton. "These interests will attempt to elect men to office who are friendly to their cause," he warned. "We predict that at the coming election this State will be secretly flooded with campaign funds reeking with sulphur fumes. It is up to every patriotic citizen to rise up and fight this situation." Sanders himself served one more term in the legislature, but the sulfur tax was raised only to 75 cents in 1931, and not until 1936 was it set at $1.03. The taxation of natural gas, cement distribution, and cigarettes began in 1931.[31]

State regulation of public utilities was another Moody cause that got nowhere. By 1920 the use of natural gas as a fuel for domestic and industrial purposes was important enough to cause the thirty-fifth legislature to pass a law declaring the gas industry to be a public utility and placing it under the control of the Railroad Commission, effective September 16, 1920. The commission's original jurisdiction extended to all gas utilities outside of cities and towns of less than two thousand inhabitants, and its appellate jurisdiction applied to the rates and services of all gas utilities within cities of two thousand or more.[32] On October 1, 1920, an engineer was appointed at a salary of $4,000 to take charge of the Gas Utilities Division, and all the work was handled by him until 1921, when an assistant engineer (who was supposed to be a "practical gas man"), an accountant, and a stenographer were added.

The commission had the authority to fix the price for the sale of gas at the wells, to fix the rates for the sale of gas in cities and towns of fewer than two thousand inhabitants, and to fix the rates to be charged by gas pipeline companies at the city gates. However, it took no effective steps to exercise this authority. Jack Johnson, a PhD candidate at the University of Texas, was writing his dissertation on state regulation of public utilities in Texas. When he asked one of the commissioners why the commission had not exercised its authority to fix gas rates in cities and towns of fewer than two thousand inhabitants, he seemed surprised at the question and stated that it had no authority to fix such rates. After reading the appropriate section of the 1920 gas utilities law, he remarked, "That does seem like we have such authority, doesn't it?" Commented Johnson: "This would indicate that the Commissioner had not had much time to familiarize himself with the law which he is charged with the duty of administering. This occurred in 1931, eleven years after the passage of the Gas Utilities Law."

The question of the reasonableness of city gas rates came up in case after case heard by the commission on appeal, most notably in the Wichita Falls and Fort Worth cases. Since the commission (for lack of funds) had no authoritative information on the value of the transmission systems used in supplying gas at the city gates, it was forced to pass over the main contentions of these cities and decide the cases on minor issues, some of which the cities were not even contesting. Between 1921 and 1929 the commission heard and determined ten cases on appeal: nine of them involved the question of rates and fair return on the value of the property used in supplying natural gas and natural gas service; the other concerned inadequate service. Only one petition for a rate increase (in the Fort Worth case) was denied, and a federal district court later overruled the decision.[33]

At length, public opinion became thoroughly aroused and mass-meetings were held in numerous Texas cities to protest unreasonable gas rates. In his first message to the forty-first legislature, Moody had urged state control of public utility companies. Bills to create a public utilities commission with power to fix rates for natural gas companies and other utilities were introduced and defeated three times in 1929, once each in the regular and first and second special sessions. "The lobby on the Utility Bill is going to be sufficient to defeat it at this Call Session," Moody was warned during the first special session. "In fact both hotels are full of fellows in opposition to the enactment of that bill and several who were elected on the platform or by friends of the administration are the ones who are fighting you the hardest and you do not have to go very far from Greenville, Hillsboro, Waco, Weatherford or Sherman to find them."[34]

Moody planned to convene a fourth special session in January 1930 to consider public utility regulation and prison reform, and he spoke across the state before then in support of a utilities commission. Moody fired the first gun of his campaign in a speech at the Old Settlers' Reunion at Round Rock on July 9, 1929. He ripped the utilities and did not mince words in pleading for a law to regulate them and to protect the public against what he termed exorbitant charges. He said the utilities had maintained a powerful lobby in Austin during the sessions of the legislature to defeat utility regulation and likened it to the brewery and liquor lobbies of fifteen years earlier.[35]

"Now Dan you should go after these birds without gloves," representative Adrian Pool advised. "You may loose [*sic*] if you put up a real fight you will strengthen yourself with the public win or loose." Pool offered to come to Austin two weeks before the fourth special session met to start an organization that would put a utilities commission bill through the house. "Fight d—n it fight," he exhorted. Harry Graves told Moody that the bill could be forced out of committee on a minority report, at least, and that would "put it square up to the Senate, and let the burden for its not passing rest upon the Senate alone." At Graves's request, Moody sent him a copy of the bill proposed by J. D. Hall at the last session.[36]

However, the legislature continued to ignore his recommendations on public utilities. In his farewell message to the forty-second legislature, he again urged the establishment of a state commission to regulate public utilities. He also called attention to "what appears to be a partial monopoly in facilities for transporting petroleum and what is almost an absolute monopoly in the facilities for refining and marketing products of petroleum," with a suggestion that this subject would bear legislative scrutiny.[37]

Wanted: Sterling Roads for Texas

No state in the Union needed a statewide highway authority more than Texas did, along with financial allocations for construction and maintenance. There were 180,000 miles of roads of all kinds in the state at the beginning of 1929, only 4,000 miles of which were hard surfaced; there were only 20,000 miles in the entire state system. Yet the Highway Commission had been in existence for a decade. Indiana, a much smaller state with much less roadway mileage, had 50,000 miles of improved roads, while Ohio had 42,000 miles. Texas roads (or most of them) were too narrow and too temporary and were unable to accommodate growing traffic. There were many gaps in major highways, and under the present system, whereby counties had to originate a project, it was seldom that a state road was completed. Highway No. 1, also known as the Bankhead, which ran between Texarkana and El Paso, was incomplete after ten years of effort, although a contract had been let recently that would close the last unsurfaced stretch in Mitchell County. The principal north-south road was also incomplete, with a gap in Bell County. Remedying these deficiencies would be a costly investment.[38]

Texas counties continued to build odd, unconnected bits of what they called highways. The usual specimen was a twelve-foot-wide strip of tar poured atop a little gravel. The stack of county and district road bonds was growing thicker than the pavement. It was customary for delegations to call on the Highway Commission every month to request designation, maintenance, and funds. Sometimes as many as two hundred "delegates" crowded into the small commission room, and when their county was called, a dozen or more lined up in front of the counter and talked to the three officials, all at the same time, as well as to the chief highway engineer. A million-dollar project had been known to go through in ten minutes. On the other hand, at almost every session some county presented an aid proposal that the commission had previously approved and since totally forgotten. Almost invariably those seeking aid were asked whether the county had voted bonds. If it had not, it was out of luck. As one highway expert explained:

Maybe the county is in such condition that it can not put up more bonds; maybe there is such opposition that a bond issue would not carry, in which event no State and Federal aid is forthcoming and the highway is neglected, although use of that highway is needed by the people of the State. There are no gaps in a railroad line. Why permit them in a highway, which in the good year 1929 has become a right-of-way and artery of commerce for the private car, buses and trucks, all of which apparently fit in with public needs and demands?[39]

The highway commissioners addressed themselves to this problem. Veteran reporter Raymond Brooks recalled an afternoon in the big workroom of the highway department in the old land office building when he was present with Austin publisher Charles E. Marsh and Cone Johnson: "Texas has got to build roads," Marsh opened. "We can move only when Texas owns its highways," Johnson replied, adding, "Maybe it could buy what there is now." "You mean buy that pile of road bonds?" Marsh asked. "Well," Johnson mused, "at least there's some right-of-way—a place to put some paving." Johnson took an old-fashioned pen and somewhat shakily wrote half a page, something to this effect: "Be it enacted: The State shall acquire and own all rights-of-way in its designated system of highways and shall construct, maintain and own all structures and paving thereon. It shall compensate counties and road districts by assuming all bonds and indebtedness outstanding on roads taken into the designated system." According to Brooks, writing in 1965, "That document became the charter of the Texas highway system, the core of a program in which the state has spent more than two billion dollars, the key of much legislation since then." Brooks does not say when this conversation took place, except that it was a holiday.[40]

In an address to the South Texas Chamber of Commerce on May 3, 1928, Ross S. Sterling, then chairman of the Highway Commission, proposed a state bond issue of $350 million (later reduced to $300 million) to build a connected system of state highways, to relieve the counties of their road-bond indebtedness, and to allow them to improve their lateral roads. He proposed to set aside a portion of the gasoline tax to pay off the bonds. By means of such a plan, Texas could complete ten or eleven thousand miles of paved roads during a ten-year period, or in less time, which, added to the five or six thousand miles already hard surfaced, would constitute a network including every important highway.[41]

On January 20, 1929, Moody submitted to the legislature for its study both the majority and minority reports of the Citizens' Advisory Committee on Highway Matters, the so-called Committee of 31, which he had appointed the previous year. D. K. Martin of San Antonio, a former member of the Highway Commission, served as its chairman. The majority report favored a constitutional amendment giving the legislature authority to vote bonds in the sum of $225 million, with not more than this amount to be outstanding at any one time. The minority report opposed the bond issue. Moody told the legislature that in order to complete a connected system of state highways, the highway department must have a guarantee of certain and continuous funding.[42]

Beside the Committee of 31 reports, four other plans were submitted: one by the Highway Commission itself, the so-called Sterling plan, which called for a $300 million statewide bond issue; one by a committee of county judges and commissioners; one by representative A. H. King requiring counties to give aid or reimbursement to the state for highways; and one by Leonard Tillotson, a representative from Sealy. Tillotson wanted the state to build and maintain highways and pay for them with funds derived from the gasoline, license, and weight taxes, as well as a higher tax on commercial vehicles. He would leave to the counties all income and constitutional sources of credit for the building and upkeep of the lateral roads.

West Texas endorsed the Committee of 31 majority plan, while East Texas favored the Tillotson pay-as-you-go plan. Most of the county judges and commissioners endorsed the Sterling plan. Sterling thought that a three-cent gasoline tax would provide enough funds for all highway improvements, but some individuals disagreed with him. Tillotson wanted a four-cent tax, as did Clarence Ousley, representing the East Texas Chamber of Commerce. A. M. Bourland, president of the West Texas Chamber, as well as W. B. Hamilton of Wichita Falls (chairman of its oil and gas bureau), wanted the tax no higher than three cents. Since September 1, 1928, the state had been collecting two cents a gallon.

A resolution submitting an amendment to the Texas constitution must receive approval of two-thirds of the membership of the house and senate. A bond issue resolution, embodying a proposed amendment authorizing the issuance of a total of $175 million in bonds for highway purposes, passed the senate by the required vote and received 97 votes in the house on passage to engrossment. Jim Ferguson was in the background "swinging his war club" at the bond issue amendment. When it was brought up for final passage, there were present one hundred members regarded as bond issue supporters, and the resolution needed that many votes to win. On the roll call, however, it was found that five of the members present had paired with five absent members. Three of those present and paired members were announced supporters of the resolution. By pairing they eliminated their votes from the official count, and thus the resolution fell three votes short of the total necessary for submission.

It was known before the regular session adjourned that the bond issue advocates would "carry on," and Sterling made an announcement to this effect shortly after the session ended. However, because of a constitutional prohibition, the bond issue could not come up again until the forty-second legislature met in January 1931. Thus proponents had two years in which to lobby statewide for their plan, and it was expected to figure largely in races for state offices in 1930. By choosing legislators based on their advocacy of or stance against the bond issue, voters were expected to decide whether the pay-as-you-go plan under which the state would operate for the next two years was to be abandoned for a state bond issue.[43]

Contrary to the view of the casual observer, the truly new idea brought forward in the highway discussion was not that of a state bond issue but that of having the whole cost of roads borne by users of motor vehicles. The legislature increased the gasoline tax from three to four cents a gallon, while greatly reducing license fees, and a larger portion of the fees was allotted to the counties. Trucks operating on the highways were placed under additional regulations. The state, not the counties, was to have the initiative in improving major roads. Critics of the highway department established an investigating committee, but after holding hearings, the committee found no irregularities and expressed "utmost confidence, in the honesty, integrity and ability" of the commissioners. "The 'probe' of the Highway Commission has turned out to be as much of a fizzling farce as was prophesied at its inception," jeered the *Houston Gargoyle*.[44]

The highway department was authorized to employ fifty license and weight inspectors who would function as a state highway patrol. They were empowered to enforce motor vehicle laws and regulations on the public highways. Far too small to handle its assignment, the patrol was expanded to 120 men, including supervisors, through a 1931 law that also created a law enforcement division within the highway department.[45]

Ross Sterling, Cone Johnson, and W. R. Ely—the three men appointed by Dan Moody to the board of the Texas Highway Commission—worked out an ambitious highway program, first with the assistance of R. A. Thompson, who served as chief engineer during 1927, and then with that of Gibb Gilchrist, who succeeded him on January 1, 1928. The department's "working machine" was "organized like an army, with the chairman of the Commission as Generalissimo, and the three commissioners together forming the headquarters command." The eighteen division engineers, who had general supervision of both construction and maintenance within their districts, had periodic meetings in Austin, at which problems were threshed out with their superiors. "These meetings have served to knit up the whole organization into a working unit covering the whole State, and to develop an esprit de corps which permeates down to the humblest maintenance worker," reported P. J. R. MacIntosh in the December 1929 issue of *Texas Monthly*. "So far as possible, a merit system is maintained throughout the organization, and it is kept free from politics." In 1966 the *Dallas Morning News* noted, "This cleanup in the highway department laid the foundation for its remarkable record of rectitude in the almost half a century that has followed. Moody's demand that it operate above the slightest suspicion of financial irregularities and the selection of Gibb Gilchrist as state highway engineer assure Moody a place as one of those most responsible for the subsequent performance of this biggest of state agencies."[46]

The forty-first legislature also saw another round in the continuing fight between "Baptists and Bangtails." During the regular session the Rev. J. Frank Norris of Fort Worth led a successful fight to defeat a camouflaged racetrack gambling bill supported by W. T. Waggoner of Dallas. Waggoner wanted to build a racing operation on land he owned between Dallas and Fort Worth. It repealed the twenty-year-old racetrack law and substituted "The Fair Commission of the State of Texas," appointed by the commissioner of agriculture, which would put pari-mutuel betting in its place. "If I can get the dead, broken down Baptist leadership to respond I will stir them up also," Norris wrote the editor of the *Texas Christian Advocate* before the session opened, "but I would rather try the graveyard. I am going to bombard the thing in my paper and over the radio." The minister claimed to have proof that the Waggoner interests had sent agents throughout Texas the previous summer before the primary offering to pay the campaign expenses of legislative candidates who would support the return of racetrack gambling in Texas. "In a nutshell it means to move Tia Juana [*sic*] to the Waggoner estate at Arlington, and make this beautiful residence section a cesspool of iniquity," Norris warned.[47]

W. S. Barron told Norris that the bill's supporters in the house claimed fifty-two votes and predicted, "Without doubt it will pass the House." To fight it the minister arranged for a big mass meeting in Austin and asked clergymen, laymen, and "especially good women" to wire their representatives to stand up against the gamblers. This turned the tide. The vote to kill the bill by striking out the enacting clause was 74 to 55. Some of the bill's proponents were game enough to congratulate Norris on his victory. Others, however, were "mighty mad" and promised to be back before the legislature in two years. In turn, Norris announced that he would just stay on the job until then. He boasted:

> I have the roll of all who voted against the bill and am going to circularize their districts and see that every one of them is defeated. It will become an issue in every gathering and we will settle the question as to whether old man Waggoner's millions can buy the legislature of Texas—in fact, I have kinda had it in for that crowd all these years, and am glad of the opportunity of seeing the day of judgment come.[48]

The challenge of building roads, whether for driving across the state or racing on tracks, would continue.

The Veto Governor Strikes Again

The use of the special session in Texas hit its peak during the Depression years, with four governors calling nineteen sessions between 1929 and 1937. Moody set a record with five during his second term, and they embroiled him in acrimonious controversy with the legislature. His legislative tactics were probably too abrasive. He admitted privately that he enjoyed "scrapping" with the lawmakers. Both friends and opponents testified that his frequent vetoes and special sessions caused irritation and friction, and the results in important legislation were disappointing. "About all a bill seems to need, in the current Legislature, to be promptly sidetracked or killed, is the endorsement or even faint approval of Governor Dan," noted the *Houston Gargoyle*. "Let him merely give it the chautauqua salute, and it shall not pass."[49]

The forty-first legislature met in its first called session on April 22, 1929. Moody submitted civil service, prison concentration and relocation, and educational measures. He withheld the appropriation bills in any form until his pet measures were acted on. On April 29 he submitted taxation and public utilities measures, recommending the establishment of a utility commission. "Then the legislature got angry with the governor," recalled the wife of Senator Tom Pollard. "Most of them wanted to go home where they could look after business and law practice." Eighty-five-year-old Judge Walter Acker, a representative from Harris County, was the oldest member of the legislature and the only Confederate veteran. Serving his fourth term, Acker described the special session as the most discordant in his memory. "To my mind this session is most peculiar," he told a reporter. "Administration supporters seemingly are unable to agree on anything and anti-administration forces are exhibiting an extraordinary stubbornness."[50]

The first called session ended on May 21. "All the time the Legislature was in session, a crazy 'wild' group, and Dan sweating so hard to put over constructive measures," Mrs. Moody noted in her diary. "Reactions were deadly, to the recent Smith-Hoover fight, with Dan the 'goat,' both sides." Her husband had spent "night and day at the Capitol and was so fair with unfair legislators (Jim Ferguson still working his hate there too)."[51]

Jim continued to "grill" Moody in the *Ferguson Forum*. After the regular session quit, the former governor said Moody reminded him of an Irishman he saw in a gambling house in Leadville, Colorado: "He made thirteen bets at the roulette wheel and did not win a bet. With the face of a stone, he turned around and said 'Faith it will be well for me to quit such a dam seesaw game.' And out he walked." During the first called session, Ferguson declared that through no fault of its own the legislature had become the "Big Joke" and Moody the "Big Disgust." With embarrassment and chagrin his friends expressed their keen disappointment in his failure to measure up to even mediocrity as an executive. Moreover, his "frivolity" was causing universal discussion. Jim specified: "They say Moody plays dominoes with the members of the legislature and drinks soda water at the stand in the Capitol with the flapper employees and they say he is quite the thing when it comes to dominoes and the jelly bean stunt with the Capitol clerks."[52]

The second special session convened on June 3. Moody was absent but had his message read. He submitted eight subjects: taxation and revenue, appropriations, education, highways, blue sky laws, public utilities, water rights, and judicial reform. Another thirty days passed for the tired and frayed legislators. On July 3 the third called session met to reconsider major appropriations after Moody vetoed the whole $50 million program. "A devotee of the balanced budget, Moody steadfastly refused to sign appropriation bills enlarging the state's deficits," wrote Fred Gantt Jr., a student of the chief executive's office in Texas, "and so adamant was he that he openly threatened to go on vetoing bills until the lawmakers found a solution." Legislators present were at the explosion point. Although there was no quorum, the legislature succeeded in tearing off enough to reduce the appropriations to about $48 million and handed the bills back to the governor. It was now July 20, and members had been in session most of the time since January 1. Five dollars a day did not begin to pay their living expenses while in Austin. Noted Mrs. Pollard: "The men were worn out, under-paid and disgusted, so the houses adopted adjournment motions and departed for home." There had been a perpetual strain between a rather financially liberal senate and a very conservative house, and Moody added the strength of his office to the latter.[53]

Moody vetoed a little over $3 million out of the appropriation bills. "Of course, I got a general raking over the coals about this," he wrote Carl Estes. "I don't think that the tax payers generally were offended by these reductions, but some of the folks who spend the money were very much offended and some of them were a little bitter in their criticisms. I think I left enough to adequately support all of the activities of the government and its institutions. Certainly I hope that I did not impair the efficiency of any department or institution."[54]

The fourth special session convened on January 20, 1930, and adjourned on February 18. Moody was pressing for the passage of his penitentiary bill and the sulfur tax law. The fifth special session followed immediately. The senate's conservative handling of revenue bills that the house had rushed headlong to pass was evident. It had pared the sulfur tax from one dollar per ton to half that amount (eventually forcing the house to accept fifty-five cents) and had failed to pass any of the three other house revenue bills. Common ground was difficult to locate. The governor and the legislature had drifted farther apart, and the only penitentiary faction that had achieved anything in that long struggle was the one dedicated to the status quo. In a March 15 editorial entitled "The Muddled Session," the *Dallas Morning News* took the legislature to task for its lack of performance: "The fact remains that the fourth and fifth called sessions have accomplished practically nothing, and that they are unsatisfactory to the Governor, to the legislators themselves, and to the people of Texas. There is no majority opinion. The Governor has no working control in the House, and his slight majority in the Senate on prison reform is not certain to stand behind him on the tax measures."[55]

Moody's uncompromising attitude on supplemental appropriation bills—refusing to submit them until revenue was provided—was assailed by senators equally uncompromising in demanding submission in advance. The explosion against the governor over this issue came in the senate on March 13. "When did the Governor become a Czar whose actions cannot be questioned? Is our chief executive a king who can do no wrong?" asked an angry A. J. Wirtz. Saying that some members apparently believed the "legislature should cringe and bow and scrape to a Governor who can not be questioned," he declared that condition had ceased to exist when the Magna Carta was signed and now existed only in Italy with Mussolini: "And thank God we haven't set up a Mussolini here, although there are some ambitions in that line." The senator challenged Moody's good faith. If he was willing to meet the legislature halfway, he could submit appropriations, and if the lawmakers failed to pass revenue measures, he could veto appropriations again as he had done before. Wirtz asserted that Moody's policies had been an "attempt to browbeat and coerce the Legislature by gubernatorial dictation." Executive domination of legislatures was the peril of governments from Washington to Austin, he warned.[56]

For Moody, who usually calmly accepted political attacks, Wirtz's speech was the last straw. He said before senate secretary Bob Barker and his wife that "only a coward took advantage of the Senate floor to make a personal attack." He added bitterly: "I just hope he (Wirtz) runs for reelection. I will have some fun making speeches in *his district*; I've got the goods on him and I will make him squeal." His wife questioned him afterwards. "Wasn't that a lot for you to say?" Moody answered: "I did it deliberately to Bob, for I wanted and expected for it to get back to Wirtz."[57]

The forty-first legislature adjourned on March 20, 1930, bringing its stormy career to an end. The differences between Moody and the legislators amounted to a repudiation of his leadership in the lower house and gave a new aspect to the coming campaign for governor. Many of Moody's friends believed he would be a candidate for an unprecedented third term, and the Wirtz incident almost persuaded Mrs. Moody to say that she wanted him to run again. "Last session of the Legislature this winter was a miserable aftermath of dirty politics, selfishness, corrupt lobbies, and legislators run wild," Mrs. Moody wrote in her diary. "Dan [bore] the brunt of it all."[58]

Moody also set a record for vetoes. During the eight legislative sessions held over his four years in office, he vetoed fifteen bills and used the post adjournment veto 102 times, "a record which should readily earn him the title of 'Veto Governor of Texas,'" according to Fred Gantt.[59] His veto was overridden only once, in connection with Senator Clint Small's riverbed validation bill (SB 150). This issue became important following the discovery of oil in West Texas. In Texas the legal definition of a navigable stream was any stream thirty feet wide, regardless of the amount of water flowing. Many West Texas streams that were technically navigable had water in them only when it rained, and others were not navigable by any kind of water transportation vehicle at any time. The surveyors failed to recognize some of these streams as navigable, and titles had been issued to surveys that extended across or partly across them. The possibility of oil profits led outsiders to claim these dry creeks as navigable rivers and to file on them as public land. The Small bill validated titles in all cases in which the patent had been outstanding for a period of ten years.

A large group of West Texans crowded the gallery when the senate debated the Small bill, and when the measure passed with only six opposing votes, they waved hats and whooped, a la West Texas. The senate, seeking to participate in the celebration, recessed for a half hour, and there followed unusual floor scenes—embraces, songs, and handshakes. Tom Love had opposed the bill, and after it carried a young man who did not like his speech called his hand. Love, always belligerent, did not hesitate, and the altercation ended in a telephone booth. Only twenty votes were cast against it in the house.[60]

The Small bill was submitted to Attorney General Claude Pollard, who declared it unconstitutional. Independent authorities who examined it agreed, and Moody concurred with their opinion and vetoed the bill—suggesting that a constitutional amendment with similar provisions be submitted. "My veto of the Small bill did not please everybody," he wrote Senator W. H. Bledsoe of Lubbock. "Naturally I regret very much that I should have thereby offended some, but these things just can't be avoided." On March 5, 1929, despite Moody's veto, the bill was passed in the senate 24 to 6, and in the house the following day 112 to 18. Always happy to fish in troubled (non-navigable) waters, Jim Ferguson editorialized against the veto, proclaiming "Dan and Claude in Disgrace." The Texas Supreme Court sustained the constitutionality of the act on June 1, 1932, in the case of *State vs. Bradford.*[61]

An interesting sidelight marked the passage of the Small bill in the house. Cecil Storey was expected to handle the measure there, but a district judge had set a trial date for a case in which he was chief counsel and would brook no delay. Storey pleaded, and Small (an old friend of the judge's) pleaded, but in vain. Temple Harris McGregor overheard Small's phone conversation with the judge and suggested a remedy. "Clint," he said, "they've got a law in Missouri that takes care of a situation like this. I'll get it from the library for you." McGregor found the law, which allowed the continuance of civil and criminal cases when the parties or their attorneys were actively engaged in legislative duties until ten days after the end of the session. "Talk about speeding up justice?" Attorney General James V. Allred declared during his campaign for governor in 1934: "In the face of such a statute it never can be done. The law says in effect, 'Go hire a member of the Legislature or a state senator and you can put your case off as long as you want to.' I am for the repeal of this law. It is strange what good lawyers some people get to be just as soon as they are elected to the Legislature or to the State Senate."[62]

The forty-first legislature submitted seven proposed amendments to Texas voters. If ratified, they would increase the standard length of a regular session from 60 to 120 days; increase compensation for lawmakers to ten dollars per day for the first 120 days of a session and five dollars per day thereafter; permit the taxation of university lands for county purposes; authorize the investment of a part of the university permanent fund in university bonds; provide for a continuous term of the supreme court; increase the governor's salary to $10,000; and enlarge the supreme court from three to nine members.

Jim Ferguson, hoping to repeat his success of two years before when he had raised the slogan, "Agin 'Em All," proclaimed, "Agin 'Em Both," referring to the amendments increasing the governor's salary and enlarging the supreme court.[63] He warned that Moody would have the power to appoint six new judges at once:

And when he gets the list made out the Small bill will have no more show to stand up than a snow ball will have in the lower regions. He and his side partner Claude Pollard, the "West Texas Navigation twins" will begin to paddle their political boats around like puddle ducks in a rain quacking "We told you so." "See what the Supreme says." "And soon." Also, there were too many corporation lawyers and oil company lobbyists for the judiciary amendment to be much in it for the people. The Moody-appointed judges would hold the gasoline tax unconstitutional.

"Yes, the cat is out of the bag," Jim proclaimed, after the Gulf Oil Corporation urged its workers to vote for the judiciary amendment. "'You tickle me and I will tickle you,' so sayeth the governor's salary $10,000.00 crowd to the corporations who want six brand new judges appointed by the governor."[64]

Ferguson again drew blood. The voters turned down the governor's salary and judiciary amendments while approving the others. "We had a big scrap with the big dailies over the amendments and they were the worst fooled idiots that I ever saw," Ferguson crowed to fellow-editor Pitchfork Smith. "We are going to have warm politics in Texas and the pot is already simmering."[65] Ferguson's prediction was correct, as usual, but Austin was not the only hotbed of political controversy that Moody had to muck.

King Mob Runs Amok

During his second term, Moody found it necessary on two occasions to place areas under martial law. In March 1926 oil was discovered in Borger, a small town in the Panhandle. Almost overnight, 45,000 oilmen, roughnecks, panhandlers, fortune seekers, gamblers, bootleggers, prostitutes, and dope peddlers descended on Borger, turning it into the most corrupt and violent town Texas had ever seen. "Anything goes in Borger," became the slogan of those fleeing from the law. In a few months the boomtown was firmly in the hands of an organized crime syndicate. One resident, departing for safer climes, cursed Borger with a poem that began

> Let's sing a song of Borger,
> Famed for its graft and rot,
> It's just a wide place in the wood,
> This town that God forgot,
> For this village large boasts deeper sin,
> Than Sodom ever knew;
> Come lend an ear, kind stranger,
> And I'll whisper them to you.

Early in 1927 the respectable residents of Borger petitioned Moody to declare martial law and send in the National Guard. Instead he sent Ranger Frank Hamer to investigate. "The worst crime ring I have seen in my twenty-three years as an officer exists there in Borger," Hamer reported. His investigation revealed that nearly all the city officials, including law officers, were deeply involved with, if not actually directing, the criminal activities in Borger and Hutchinson County. Moody ordered Hamer and Ranger Tom Hickman, with detachments from their companies, to move to Borger. The mayor was told to put all police officials under Hamer's control, and the cleanup began with the arrest and resignation of almost all of them. The exodus of crooks and parasites began. "They were strung out along the highways in droves, some in cars and trucks, others afoot," one ranger recalled. "Outbound trains, both passenger and freight, also did a land office business in transporting these undesirables." When a new prosecuting attorney, John A. Holmes, began trying cases, Hamer returned to Austin, leaving in charge Captain William W. Sterling, who had been summoned from Laredo and arrived on Easter Sunday. After three months, Sterling was sent back to South Texas.

By early fall most of the ousted city and county officials had either regained their positions or had been replaced by others just as crooked. On September 13, 1927, Holmes was murdered by an unknown assassin. After visiting Borger, Hamer conferred in private with Moody on a train between Dallas and Terrell. The governor sent word to Gen. Jacob Wolters of the National Guard to meet him in Austin, while Hamer, after testifying in a trial

The largest illegal still ever found, Borger, Texas, circa 1927–1929. Roy Wilkison Aldrich Papers, Briscoe Center for American History, University of Texas at Austin, DI 06299.

at Brownsville, returned to Borger. He placed Mayor Glenn A. Pace under arrest for forcing a witness in a forthcoming murder trial to leave town.

Moody declared martial law in Borger and sent in the National Guard from Fort Worth under Wolters. "There exists an organized and entrenched criminal ring in the city of Borger and in Hutchinson County," his proclamation declared. Nearly all city and county officials were suspended from office, and most of them were jailed. The jail became crowded, and Rangers had to set up a chain "trotline" along the main street and handcuff their prisoners to it to await filing of charges. Peace officers from all over the Southwest came in to search for wanted men from their territories. Before the end of the year, Moody ended martial law. "There was a clean-up all around," one paper noted approvingly. "There is a new Borger. There is a happy Borger. There is a law-abiding Borger. Borger has been tamed."[66]

While the rowdiness of an oil boomtown had prompted Moody's first

George Hughes handcuffed and chained by a white lawman before lynching by a mob, Sherman, Texas, 1930. Roy Wilkison Aldrich Papers, Briscoe Center for American History, University of Texas at Austin, E RWA 138.

use of federal troops, lynching, all too common in this era of Texas history, prompted Moody's second declaration of martial law. Sherman, the county seat of Grayson County, was proud of its two colleges, fine school system, twenty-seven churches, and twelve city parks that gave it the title of "the Athens of Texas." But for fourteen hours on May 9–10, 1930, "King Mob" ran amok in its streets. George Hughes, "a Negro transient and underworld character," was accused of raping a white woman on a farm five miles southeast of the city. Trial was set for May 9. A mob began to gather, described in a report to the NAACP as "composed largely of the ignorant and illiterate tenant-farmer class—the hoodlums and scum of the rural districts—the riff-raff and underworld characters of the city—besides Oklahoma and the neighboring towns contributed their quota of the worst element." On May 7 Sheriff Arthur Vaughan asked Moody for help. The governor called Frank Hamer, who rushed to Sherman with three men.

On the morning of May 9, an angry, sullen crowd of more than a thousand persons gathered around the courthouse. At noon the sheriff and Rangers had to draw their guns to keep the mob from forcing its way into the building. After the jury was sworn in, Hughes pleaded guilty, but the trial proceeded to fix the degree of punishment. When the crowd began to clamor for Hughes, the jury was sent out of the room. According to some accounts, Moody wired the Rangers to "protect the Negro, but do not shoot any one," but he later said this report was erroneous. In any event, the Rangers three times drove the crowd back with tear gas. Meanwhile, Hughes had been locked in the district clerk's vault.

About 2:30 p.m. two boys dashed five gallons of gasoline through the broken window of the tax collector's office on the east side of the courthouse. In a minute the lower floors of the building were burning. Hamer could not find anyone with the combination to the vault. The Rangers and the town's firemen dragged out the fire hoses, but members of the mob cut them. The courthouse was left in smoking ruins; Hughes suffocated and roasted in the vault.

Several hours later a detachment of seventy National Guardsmen arrived, sent from Dallas by Moody at Sheriff Vaughan's request. That night a "hooting, howling mob" drove them off the square and through the streets. Three guardsmen were injured by bottles and other missiles; two men in the mob were wounded. Shortly before midnight, the mob cut through the steel door of the vault and pulled Hughes's body out. It was tied behind a truck and dragged through the streets, with two thousand yelling men and boys following. When East Mulberry Street (the heart of the black district) was reached, the mob hung the body from the lower limb of a tree outside an old brick building housing a drug store and other black businesses. The body was burned, and the drugstore, which was regarded as a bootlegging joint, was also set ablaze. The entire black business section on East Mulberry was destroyed. According to the report made to the NAACP, more than 350 African Americans fled the city the next day, going to Denison, Independence Springs, Van Alstyne, and McKinney. A few went to Dallas, and a number to California. It was rumored that 700 more would leave as soon as the soldiers departed and things quieted down.

On May 10 Moody declared martial law, which lasted for two weeks. On May 12 a military court was established to conduct an investigation. Over the next week sixty-nine men and women were arrested and questioned. Twenty-nine were jailed to await grand jury action; they were later indicted on evidence furnished by the military tribunal. The Texas attorney general went to Sherman and offered his office's services to the local authorities. However, only two sentences of two years each—for rioting and arson— were secured.[67]

The Sherman Riot attracted national and even international attention and condemnation. "King Mob Runs Amuck in Texas," headlined the *Literary Digest.* "The dark conclusion is inevitable that this was, more clearly than any other in many months, a preventable lynching," declared the *Virginia-Pilot.* "It was preventable because sufficient precautions could have been taken in advance, as has been done in many instances in other States where troops have guarded court-houses during trials." The *Houston Post-Dispatch* supplied a Texas view of the horror: "Texans will share the astonishment of the outside world at this exhibition of lawlessness. It defies apology—almost defies explanation. Most of us would have said a few days ago that such a thing could not happen in the Texas of to-day." Some Texans agreed: "In reality thousands of Texans share with me the most powerful humiliation that such an awful thing has happened," wrote Mrs. Percy V. Pennybacker to a friend in the North. "Of course the reports are exaggerated, as usual. I never was more indignant than at the entirely unfounded statements in the article in that terrible London paper. It pictures Governor Moody as an illiterate, whereas he is a University man, with splendid constructive ideas and the courage to carry them out."[68]

The year 1930 saw another lynching in Texas: at Honey Grove a black man accused of murder was killed by a deputized posse while resisting arrest. A mob of a thousand persons was standing by; they seized the body, dragged it facedown for miles, and then burned it in front of a black church. The Southern Commission on the Study of Lynching said that the facts "probably justify its classification as a lynching."[69]

Moody's Legacy

To properly judge the Moody administration, it is necessary to remember the circumstances of his entry into the governor's office.[70] He campaigned on the issue of destroying "Fergusonism" and all its works, and his support was bound together largely by that one issue. His mandate was in that sense a negative one. As Alonzo Wasson wrote in the *Dallas Morning News* near the end of Moody's tenure as governor: "His candidacy for Governor was not a response to the call for great legislative enterprise needing a leader. He did improvise a program of legislative projects. But they were the surplusage of his appeal, which brought him but few of the votes he got. His candidacy was primarily, and almost exclusively, a pledge to rescue public services from the grievous state into which they had been brought by maladministration." Moody carried out this narrow mandate to the end, but when the highway department had been made efficient and graft free, when the state textbook situation had been corrected, and when the Ferguson's liberal pardon policy was reversed, he found, especially in his second term, that his constructive program largely met with defeat. "Governor Moody's record as the State's chief executive is much more noteworthy for its administration than for its legislative endeavors," Wasson concluded. "A severe scoring of his legislative endeavors probably would show that his failures outnumbered his successes. Certainly they outweigh them." A few decades later Ralph Steen conceded, "Moody was not successful in his fight for complete governmental reorganization, but perhaps his work paved the way for such a reorganization at some future date. Moody was really the leader of one of the most progressive administrations of this century."[71]

Moody came to believe, based on his own experience, that men should be trained for the work of state administration and should not be discarded after a temporary period of service. In what may have been an implicit apology for his own shortcomings as Texas's chief executive, he told a reporter for the *Austin American*: "The business of running a state is no different from any other business. It is wrong to train a man for this business and then discard him in favor of an inexperienced person. It is equally wrong to put an inexperienced man in politics and expect an outstanding success." Moody's own rise had been meteoric: from district attorney in 1925 to governor two years later.[72]

As governor Moody became known for his courage and uncompromising honesty, and admirers gave him the nickname "Honest Dan." He left office as he entered it, a poor man financially. He was blind to the trading power of patronage or vetoes and would not "swap votes" with the legislature. A story is told of a legislator who offered to vote for an important administration measure if Moody would promise to sign one of his bills. He refused the trade, and the administration measure lost by a single vote. Then the legislator's bill came to Moody's desk. He signed it, as he had planned to do all along. He would not threaten to discipline those who opposed his measures. "It is a question of ethics whether a Governor ought to be willing to sandbag a Senator or Representative into line," noted the *Dallas Morning News*. "Mr. Moody answers that question in the negative." Still, critics charged that he was unable to see the viewpoints of others.[73]

A frequent criticism of Moody was that he procrastinated and found it difficult to make up his mind. One man said to Representative Ray Holder that "if Moody would now snap into it, and make the appointments that he has delayed from month to month, and make some snappy and quick decisions, even though one half of them are wrong, he would become the most popular Governor Texas has ever had, and would go out in a blaze of glory!" In passing the man's comment along to the governor, Holder declared, "We are inclined to believe that he is right about it."[74]

Moody felt keenly the frustrations of an office that the framers of the post-Reconstruction Texas constitution had kept deliberately weak by scattering powers and responsibilities.[75] His favorite expletive, when ladies were present, was "Dad burn it." One day, when things were going badly, he blew up and shouted at his secretaries: "Dad burn it, when I get out of this office I'm going to make some money, and when I get independent of everybody I'm going to get back into politics and maybe I can get something done." When a Memphis, Tennessee, newspaper published a report that, in order to pass his program, Moody would be a candidate for the state legislature when his term as governor expired, he said he did not have any plans along that line, but added wistfully: "I do see a splendid opportunity to put in a little energy and a little thought upon public questions in the forum mentioned. I have frequently wished, when the Legislature was in session, that I could join in the debate and discuss the merits—and sometimes demerits—of the pending propositions."[76] In a very true sense, Texas has legislative government, but nevertheless the governor's leadership determines to a great degree the course of legislative events and the popular instinct is not far wrong in attributing to him credit or blame for them.

Unfortunately for Moody, the Texas legislature probably reached the nadir of its effectiveness during the 1920s. An organization built on Reconstruction conditions broke down under modern demands. It was so constituted that it had little statewide responsibility, its members being accountable to purely local constituencies. And it was lobby-ridden. "No man who has sat in the gallery of either the Senate or the House has failed to go away with a sense of confusion and general loose-ended-ness of public business as there transacted," complained the *Dallas Morning News*. "The wonder then becomes not that the legislation is sometimes foolish, but that it is ever anything else." The constitutional amendment that increased its pay and altered the conditions of its sessions came too late to save the Moody legislative program, but the very failure of that program made more manifest the necessity of "a better Legislature better able to do its best."[77]

The animosity of political rivals like Jim Ferguson and Barry Miller, who hoped to succeed Moody, also contributed to the governor's difficulties with the legislature. "I saw how Tom Love and Barry Miller acted with the rest of them just like a bunch of Monkeys," one senate visitor wrote Moody afterwards. "Old man Jim Fergerson [*sic*] was sitting in the back tickled to death because the Senate would not do anything."[78] Senator Margie E. Neal told the governor that the people of Texas did not know what an obstacle Ferguson had been in his path:

> Never in the life of any Governor of Texas, while in service, has he had to contend with what you have had to contend with. The out-going Governor has always left Austin and has retired to the shades of private life or to more peaceful political and professional pursuits. It has been quite the contrary with Jim Ferguson. He has remained in Austin, right under the Governor's nose and under the dome of the capitol, to vex and annoy, browbeat and try to defeat, the Governor in what he tries to do for the state.[79]

Mrs. Moody recalled in a 1968 interview that "Jim Ferguson still had a great many people in the state government who had been there, you know, had put people in office by appointment. And everything Dan tried to do was fought by the Ferguson forces." Moody himself offered two reasons for his troubles. First, he believed that during his second term he was regarded as a lame duck because of the two-term tradition. Second, he declared that Ferguson "does not like me personally, and is ready to do anything which he can to defeat my purposes."[80]

Some legislators of the Moody era disagreed on this point. Alfred Petsch, a Moody leader in the house, told Josiah Daniel in 1975 that the Ferguson clique was able "to block Moody without visible demonstration." But W. S. Barron, the speaker in the forty-first legislature, informed Daniel that while there was a substantial Ferguson crowd in the house, it did not greatly influence the outcome of events. From these comments Daniel concluded: "It is safe to say that between the natural recalcitrance of the legislators and Ferguson's machinations, the Moody program had rough sailing."[81]

In a 1975 interview, this author asked former state senator and lieutenant governor Walter F. Woodul why Moody's legislative program was not more successful. He replied that "the legislature didn't have as good sense as he did," and added that "Ferguson had lots of friends in the legislature," while Moody "picked up enemies along the way."[82]

Barry Miller presided over the senate for six years, and he performed his duties so well that he became almost an institution. A colleague once said to Senator T. J. Holbrook, "You might as well attempt to play Hamlet without the ghost as to conduct the sessions of a wild Senate without Barry Miller as its president." "And," Holbrook added, "so it seemed." Born on Christmas Day 1864, near Barnwell, South Carolina (the first state to secede after Abraham Lincoln's election), Miller "early imbibed the political ideas and ideals of the Old South. Having sprung from such surroundings he believed in the Democracy which had always been nurtured in these Southern States, and embraced it as though it were a religion." Holbrook continued, "In all that pertains to the welfare of the State he was, indeed, one of the old guards whose lives are fast breaking but whose spirit will never die." With this background and philosophy, it is not surprising that Miller, in Woodul's words, "was not interested in Moody's program."[83]

Moody's failure to successfully mediate the bitter fight between Texas Democrats who supported Al Smith's 1928 presidential bid and those who opposed him left both factions dissatisfied with his leadership and embittered his relations with the forty-first legislature. According to his wife's later recollection:

> He made a great many enemies among the big Democrats [in] the state who were for Al Smith. And that soured the whole second term he had because those people fought him. They felt that he didn't really support Al Smith in his heart. And when Texas went for Hoover, they blamed Dan Moody a lot for it. And so, all through those last two years, anything that he tried to put over in the Legislature, he ran into foes, Al Smith foes, who were fighting him.[84]

On March 16, 1930, Mrs. Moody summed up her feelings about her husband's difficulties with the legislature in the following angry words:

> The legislature, meeting in one extra session after another has consistently failed to do anything (its only consistency). All Dan's fine plans for accomplishment for the state have come to naught. The Boy has worked and slaved so hard and yet held his head and hand too high to stoop to conquer ("political trading"). He has been too fair and honest and above-board, and old-line politicians, stopping at nothing, took malicious advantage. Enemies have taken every dirty trick possible. Old Jim Ferguson, out of bitter spite, has worked unceasingly. Socalled friends have betrayed him shamelessly. A succession of unfortunate events in his term have helped the statement: the "Al Smith fiasco," the "rule-or-ruin Amon Carter," a legislature unusually lobby-ridden—all

these things have contributed to the mess. I am really so mad I am in the mood to run to *hit back*.[85]

Yet this very personal view of developments as seen from the Executive Mansion, while correct in the main, does not explain why, during Moody's first six months in office, when his popularity was still high and the only organized opposition to him was a small Ferguson clique in the senate, his legislative program was still rejected. According to the *Houston Chronicle*, it "was a bit too advanced for the legislators, especially on the subject of civil service.... Some of his friends opposed some of his measures and supported others."[86]

Part of the explanation then must be sought in the mental attitudes of Texas lawmakers and of the voters who sent them to Austin. While Texas had undergone marked changes in its economy and in population distribution, to a very great degree it was unchanged psychologically—its characteristic habit of thought was rural. Peter Molyneaux, editor of *Texas Monthly*, gave the following description of this mental set: "In general it is a habit of thought to which almost anything which transcends a purely agricultural form of society is in some degree alien. In its most narrow form the rural habit of thought is a neighborhood habit of thought, prescribed in its outlook by the interests and horizons of a rural countryside." Because of this circumstance, Molyneaux noted, successful candidates for state office in Texas, either sincerely or for political purposes, were habitually rural in their thought. In fact, not a few of them had been animated by "a point of view absolutely untouched by economic changes going on all around them— a point of view not unlike that held by the average office-holder in Texas thirty years ago."[87]

It is not surprising then that when rural voters participated directly in the legislative process through referenda on constitutional amendments, those who bothered to vote turned down proposals for the general welfare, costing each taxpayer the equivalent of a few cents a year, if no apparent local benefit would result. The classic instance of this parochialism was an amendment that would have permitted Galveston County citizens to do certain things to provide storm protection. "It did not affect anybody outside of Galveston County a particle, and yet it was defeated by the rural vote," Molyneaux noted. "It is the precise truth to say that it was defeated for the very reason that it did not concern anybody outside of Galveston County."[88]

This same rural habit of thought put legislative roadblocks in the path of the business progressive reforms advocated by Neff and Moody. In addition, the inevitable crowd of lobbyists representing the state's oil and gas, sulfur, and lumber companies throttled severance or income tax proposals that would have lifted the burden from the backs of property holders while providing added revenues for education and other worthwhile projects. The powerful utilities lobby blocked bills advocated by Moody in the forty-first legislature to create a utilities commission with the power to fix rates. "These lobbyists are master psychologists," Attorney General James V. Allred declared in 1934. "They work on a member of the Legislature or the Senate from the standpoint of his weakness. They study him, try to find out what his weak points are. Whatever weak point there is in his moral make-up, they play up to that weakness.... They will furnish whatever it takes to the members of the Legislature if they will take it. Whatever they like, that is what they get. They will furnish them anything they will take." No wonder, then, that when Dr. John C. Granbery wrote Moody commending his 1929 message to the legislature, the latter replied pessimistically: "Some parts of it, as you would imagine, have not met with any great amount of enthusiasm at the hands of the legislature and likely will not be enacted into law. I believe the time will come when some of these matters will be enacted into law. I have sometimes felt that our attitude in Texas is a little too reactionary and that we were not ready to accept progressive measures which worked successfully in other states."[89]

The farewell address of a retiring governor is mostly retrospective, a recounting of things done and attempted. Such addresses have dealt lightly, when at all, with present and future needs lest they trespass on their successor's prerogative. Moody took cognizance of the custom but put himself under none of its restraints. He concerned himself much more with what he thought the forty-second legislature should do than with what the two previous legislatures had done. Outlining what he saw as Texas's paramount needs, he raised the question of prison reform, a red flag to many lawmakers; advocated a highway bond issue to continue the present program of highway building; urged taxation of natural resources and a state commission to regulate public utilities; offered the income tax as a solution of taxation problems; expressed the hope that the short ballot would be adopted some day; suggested that the governor should have more authority over the expenditure of state funds; and advocated the reorganization of the state government to reduce expenses. He urged adoption of the cabinet plan, used by many states, with elections only of the governor, lieutenant governor, and attorney general. Administrative offices, such as the comptroller, treasurer, land commissioner, state superintendent of public instruction, and commissioner of agriculture he wanted placed under executive supervision. "With such authority, the governor could and would be held responsible by the people for the administration of state government," he argued.[90]

It was a bold, far-ranging reform program but had value only as an expression of his views, and like other reformers who had failed to realize their dreams, he could only hope that it would win acceptance in the future. "Some of the reforms included in this program are progressive and did not have the benefit of [a] previous campaign waged for their adoption," he declared in his brief farewell address at the inauguration ceremonies. "Reforms come slowly and the way must be prepared for them. If I could not always hope for the present adoption of reform measures of my program, I could, and did, avail myself of the opportunity to help prepare the way, and I find pleasure in the hope and belief that many of them will ultimately be placed in the Constitution and upon the statute books of Texas."[91]

In an era of rapid industrial and urban growth—and if "progressive" reforms are defined as improving the prison system, improving health care delivery systems, developing mass transportation, and implementing better regulation of utilities, a more equitable educational system for Texas children, tax reform, enforcement of air pollution standards, and a new constitution to replace the 150-year-old document—Moody's criticism of the Texas mind, expressed in his letter to Granbery, remains essentially valid. Although Texas has a sizable, vocal liberal movement, the dominant forces are conservative. Rural and small-town conservatives join with corporate interests in the wealthy Republican suburbs of Texas's burgeoning cities to carry statewide elections. Except for Ann Richards (1991–1995), no governor since James V. Allred, Texas's "New Deal Governor," has been politically liberal; and, in such areas as public utility regulation and tax reform, no governor has been as progressive as Neff and Moody. In 1949 V. O. Key Jr. wrote in his classic *Southern Politics in State and Nation* that Texas was a "Politics of Economics": "The Lone Star State is concerned about money and how to make it, about oil and sulphur and gas, about cattle and dust storms and irrigation, about cotton and banking and Mexicans." Seventy years later, Texas politics is "Still the Politics of Economics," according to two more recent students of southern politics.[92]

CHAPTER 3

A Sterling Victory

A t the close of Miriam A. "Ma" Ferguson's first administration (1925–1927), the Fergusons and their daughter Dorrace moved into the Driskill Hotel in Austin. After a few months at the hotel they rented a residence at the corner of Eighth and Lavaca Streets while they built a Spanish Colonial home at 1500 Windsor Road. It had a large garden where Miriam could putter with her flowers. The 1928 elections marked the first time since 1914 that a Ferguson was not a candidate for office in Texas. Jim Ferguson supported Louis Wardlaw against Dan Moody in the governor's race and Col. Alvin Owsley in the first primary and state senator Earle B. Mayfield in the second for the U.S. Senate. Ouida Ferguson Nalle believed that if the family's political enemies had left matters as they were, "we Fergusons would have been content to retire then." However, Mrs. Ferguson's defeat in the 1926 gubernatorial election, together with the repeal of the Ferguson amnesty bill in 1927, "spurred them both on to try again."[1] The Fergusons would highlight time-honored issues that appealed to their base—opposition to the Ku Klux Klan, protection for rural interests, and the like—but would find strong opposition during the race as business progressive interests rallied around a new standard bearer, Ross S. Sterling.

The Fergusons Were "Willing"

In the *Forum* of September 6, 1928, Ferguson announced that he was suspending publication. "If the *Forum* appears again it will be at the request of its friends and subscribers," he stated. "For nearly eleven years the *Forum* has been on the firing line. It has had its ups and downs, its victories and its defeats." The suspension was short-lived; on January 24, 1929, the paper resumed publication. "I realize the shortcomings of the *Forum* in the past and promise to do better in the future," Jim wrote. "I realize that I was not out-spoken enough in former discussions of public issues. I realize that I have been too mild in talking about public men and candidates in the past." The *Forum* had been started again, he claimed, to help restore the Democratic Party in Texas, to make certain the integrity of the party pledge. This from a man who had bolted the Democratic Party in 1920 and 1922! As Don H. Biggers noted sardonically: "If the Democratic pledge had forever prevented the return of prodigals and deserters Jim wouldn't have had any luck get-ting back into 'the house of the fathers' in 1922 after the American Party 'had performed its great mission in 1920 and been disbanded.' And where would Jim have landed in 1924, after his bolting stunt in 1922?"[2]

On his fifty-eighth birthday, August 31, 1929, Mrs. Ferguson presented her husband with a red-bound book and suggested that he begin keeping a personal diary. On September 9, he made the following entry:

> I find, as I am growing older, a growing fascination for Livestock farm-ing. I find my thoughts unconsciously drifting more and more to cattle and politics, I have many times resolved to quit taking any part in cam-paigns but there is an irresistible influence that continually draws me into political campaigns. One reason is, that I realize the necessity more and more that everybody take more interest in governmental af-fairs or the government will fall. To be effective in this service one must take an active interest in politics.
>
> I have recovered much of my strength and vigor that I had lost in the last few months my wife was in the governor's office in 1926 and I feel a rising desire to again enter a political campaign. At this writing I do not know what role I will play in next year's 1930 campaign but I am sure I will be on the firing line somewhere.... We talk about it in the family circle very often.... Time will prove whether we are again on the way to another campaign.[3]

Jim, like Barkis, was "willing" if the people demanded him.[4] "Do you want me?" he asked coyly in the October 24, 1929, issue of the *Forum*. "Then write me, wire me. I am willing, if the people want me. I am not hankering but I am willing, if the people want me." His platform would have ten cardinal planks: "We will reform more convicts, we will do more religion, we will ex-tend more forgiveness, we will do more like the Savior did, we will do more for the State than has been done since Texas made the mistake of sending a boy [Moody] to mill." In the next issue, Ferguson reported that he had already received about three hundred personal letters and stated, "There is every evidence that the 'Old Guard' is still in line and full of pep." In his diary on November 5, he noted, "Am receiving many letters asking me to run for Governor." Beginning with the November 7 issue of the *Forum*, Ferguson discussed each week one of the planks in his "contingent platform," concluding on January 16, 1930: "This ends the discussion of my platform. I will soon make up my mind what I am going to do. The doings of the legislature will tell the tale. 200 new letters this week."[5]

On February 19 Ferguson formally announced his candidacy for governor, responding, he said, to "the petition and suggestion of a very large number of Texas voters." His announcement, addressed "to the people of Texas," said in part:

> In this campaign I will be seeking an office which I have already had. I will not be seeking an honor, for me and my family have had that, too. I will not be seeking vindication because that has been given me. When I am elected, as I am sure I will be, I will feel that the people of Texas have called me to render a public service which they have not received for the last three and one-half years and for which my experience with State affairs has especially qualified me to perform.

He would not enter into a "frantic mental or physical struggle for election" but would "conserve his strength" for the performance of the governor's duties; nor would he "murmur or protest" against personal abuse and vicious criticism of himself or his record. "I have long since made my peace with God and I shall not now permit the heat of politics to engage me in personal hatred." The Ferguson platform called for:

> (1) A business administration and the veto of any liquor legislation by pro or anti—something to eat and something to wear without a row over something to drink; (2) The reduction of public offices, notably the combination of the office of the Assessor and Collector, and the limitation of fees to $6,000 a year; (3) Preventing any bank from loaning over ten percent of its capital and deposits outside of Texas; (4) The right of the borrower to redeem any home or other real estate within two years after foreclosure; (5) The abolishment of the landlord's lien, so that a tenant could mortgage his crop to his merchant for yearly supplies; (6) An elective five member highway commission, one at large and one from North, South, East, and West Texas; (7) Opposition

to the issue of any state road bonds and for a 3¢ gasoline tax and the building and grading of less expensive roads which would give more roads to the farm and mill; (8) Against the road hog and the banishment of the present truck and bus vehicles which used the public highways for profit to the exclusion of the traveling public; (9) A luxury tax on factory made cigars and cigarettes; (10) Putting the state convict farms in the hands of farmers and liberal issuance of pardons to meritorious prisoners.[6]

Ferguson's platform contained no surprises.

While in Dallas in early April on political business, Ferguson declared that prisons and highways would be the major issues in the forthcoming campaign. Prohibition would not be an issue because "the question is not what to drink but what to eat." He continued: "The disinterested, discriminating public has looked over the State's condition and finds it serious. There is no money and no credit. Foreclosures take place all over, and Texas delinquencies, occur more than ever before in the State's history. The public is convinced that the best men available should be Governor. They can see that all candidates have their faults, but they know that Jim Ferguson is the best qualified."[7]

Despite his peace-pact with God, Jim was soon tearing into his enemies in his good, old-fashioned way. He decried Moody's "promiscuous special sessions and this wicked waste of money" and tried to exploit the racist anxieties of white Texans by reminding them of Mrs. Hoover's invitation to the wife of Oscar DePriest and Tom Love's vote in the Texas senate against a resolution denouncing the action. "The crookedest Tammany politician that was ever born in New York is a saint by the side of any political deserter in Texas who says that any negro woman is the social equal of any white woman," Ferguson demagogued. "If Tom wants to eat with the negroes let him do it, if the negroes will let him, but by the eternal love of our Confederate dead I object to him being allowed to eat with the white folks. This is the real difference between Loveism and Fergusonism."[8] Despite these strong appeals to his base, Ferguson's efforts were soon thwarted, leading his wife to enter a primary race with many strong competitors.

Portrait of Governor James Ferguson as a younger man, undated. Prints and Photographs Collection, Briscoe Center for American History, University of Texas at Austin, DI 02430.

A Crowded Primary

As he had in 1924, Ferguson tried to secure a place on the Democratic primary ballot, contending that the amnesty act passed in 1925 had removed the disqualification placed on him in 1917 and arguing that the repeal of this act in 1927 had no effect. Attorneys for the state Democratic Executive Committee denied this contention, and thus the main issue was joined. A special supreme court consisting of two special and one regular justice ruled on May 23, 1930, that the amnesty act had been unconstitutional and that the legislature could not remove the penalty the state senate had imposed as a court of impeachment. According to the opinion, only a constitutional amendment could forgive the offense of impeachment and restore the right to hold office.[9]

Ferguson was in the courtroom when the decision was read. He commented that should the court refuse to grant a rehearing and reverse its position on his eligibility, his wife would again be a candidate for governor. The court denied his motion on May 26. Anticipating the adverse ruling, Miriam Ferguson announced her candidacy on May 24, but she differed from her husband's platform on the Prohibition issue. She declared herself solidly in favor of the Eighteenth Amendment, saying, "We who have been prohibitionists all these years have suffered much discouragement recently, and I want to see one honest effort made to outlaw the liquor traffic, before we give up the struggle." Jim had announced that he would veto all liquor legislation, but his wife favored the passage of a law or laws providing

> that no one shall be allowed to hold an office, legislative, judicial or executive, that in any way drinks or uses intoxicating liquors unlawfully obtained, and that no person shall take any office to which he or she may have been elected until an affidavit of said person is filed with the Clerk of County stating that said person has not during the six months preceding the making of said affidavit drank any (bootleg) intoxicating liquor unlawfully bought or obtained. If said affidavit is proven to be false, it shall forfeit said office and be subject to prosecution for perjury.

Mrs. Ferguson also favored a law stipulating that no trial for a liquor law violation should proceed until the judge, prosecuting attorney, sheriff, clerk, and deputies of said court filed the same affidavit. Failure to file the document "shall at once, without further procedure, at once vacate any or all of said offices." This was a neat slap at the so-called Drinking Drys, those officeholders who were politically Dry but personally Wet. "So boys, just come and get busy," Jim said of his wife's announcement. "Ma will be waiting for you with a good supper and you can throw your feet under the table and again do business at the same old stand. Bring all our friends with you and tell them that they will be welcome, too, and no questions asked, only to sit right down and make yourself at home." In a short set speech in Waco on June 20, Mrs. Ferguson asserted she would make the best governor because she would have "the best Governor Texas ever had" to help her. "If you want two Governors for the price of one, just give me your vote and Jim will get busy," she promised.[10]

Lt. Gov. Barry Miller became an active candidate for governor on March 17, 1930, the day he retired as grand master of the Odd Fellows of Texas. He had withheld his formal announcement until he retired from the lodge office, refusing to mix lodge work and politics. Asked by newspapermen if Dan Moody was going to run, Miller replied: "I don't know. I hope not. I like that boy, and if he runs he'll get the worst defeat of his life." Something of Warren G. Harding's blandness—as well as his loyalty to friends—characterized Miller, although he was credited with better judgment in choosing friends than Harding had shown.[11] It was said of him that he "will fight harder for an other than he will for himself." Older Democrats remembered him as the chief speaker for the ailing Senator Charles Allen Culberson in his 1912 and 1922 races. It was in keeping with the man that he began his campaign without a platform other than his record in both branches of the legislature, as a district judge, and as lieutenant governor. But circumstances forced him to speak his mind on the issues. In asking that he be "promoted" to the governorship, he claimed that he could always "get along" with the legislature and that such a trait would ensure far better results than having controversies between the lawmakers and the governor. "I know the psychology of the Legislature for I have been connected with it for sixteen years and always worked in harmony with it," he said in a Beaumont speech. If elected governor, he promised to call no special sessions unless there was an emergency. He opposed any tax increase and also opposed the prison relocation plan as extravagant and unnecessary. A longtime Wet, if he was asked about Prohibition, he would say that it was the law and he was for law enforcement; but to every Dry, Miller was at least "moist." To Atticus Webb, he was "wet inside and out—dripping wet." His political strength was difficult to estimate, although he was known to be strong in Dallas and North Texas. Some of the machine leaders in San Antonio were "warm in his support" and considered him to be one of the leading candidates. The *Dallas Morning News* thought he had an outside chance to be in the primary runoff with Ferguson or Mayfield or Love and suggested that against one of them Miller would have better than an outside chance. "But, win or lose, Barry Miller will be Barry Miller still, suave, debonair and undismayed."[12]

On April 5 a Hunt County audience heard E. G. Senter, a candidate for governor, say he would retire from the race if Lynch Davidson became a candidate. When Senter finished, a resolution was adopted and a message sent to Davidson demanding that he be drafted. In reply, Davidson, who had made unsuccessful races in 1924 and 1926, made it clear that he would not be a candidate unless he believed there was a widespread call for him to run. At the same time, he noted a general belief that the presently announced candidates were not qualified either by training or temperament to conduct the state's business. "The problems of the Governor's office are practically the problems of the executive of any great corporation, calling for much training in business management, finance and economics," he stated. "It is my fervent hope that some man capable of meeting that need will offer."[13]

Representative A. P. Johnson of Carrizo Springs told Governor Moody that Davidson hoped to get into the governor's race, provided Tom Love dropped out or did not earn a spot on the ticket, and that Davidson was doing as much pre-announcement campaign work as possible. "I sensed exactly what you tell me in your letter about the Houston party," Moody replied. "The letter he had in the paper a day or two ago led me to believe that he was awaiting the results of the law suit. I don't think he would do much, even if he did get in."[14]

Confronted with the impossibility of summarily forcing Love and his followers out of the Democratic Party as they had hoped, the young Wets carried their fight for party integrity into the July primary by supporting sixty-three-year-old James Young for governor. A resident of Kaufman, a small East Texas community, Young had served creditably in the U.S. Congress from 1911 to 1921, when he voluntarily retired. He was a quiet, conservative country farmer, lawyer, and banker and was reputedly so Dry that he refused to defend citizens accused of liquor law violations. He had left his dying brother's bedside to return to Washington to vote in favor of the Eighteenth Amendment, and he now asserted that the amendment and its supporting laws "will not and never should be changed." He was thus not an ideal candidate from the Liberal viewpoint. But despite his Baptist beliefs and residence in a hotbed of Hoovercrats, he had accepted chairmanship of the Smith campaign in Texas and denounced the political preachers of his own and other Protestant denominations for their religious bigotry. This made him suspect among the ardent Drys. "Jim Young of Kaufman voted with us all along while in Congress," Atticus Webb stated privately. "I think he is personally dry, but seems to me to be the tool of the wets."[15]

Young was undertaking a very difficult thing, trying to stage a comeback in politics after almost ten years in obscurity. Jim Ferguson paid him the compliment of announcing in the *Forum* that he was the best-qualified man yet to appear in the race but added that he "didn't have a chance." For once Ferguson and Dan Moody agreed about something. "I know Mr. Young personally and I like him," Moody wrote. "It strikes me that he is in the unfortunate position of having some folks that have been very busy in politics for a long time crowding him back in this campaign. His chances are somewhat hampered by the presence of Earle Mayfield, Senator Love, Old Jim, and Lieutenant Governor Miller, who have been busy for a long time and getting one group or another in the habit of voting for one or the other of them."[16]

However, Young could count on the support of the Al Smith leaders—with the exception of Barry Miller and his intimates. Among his supporters were John Boyle, Paul Page Jr., Gen. M. M. Crane, Steve Pinckney, Connie Renfro, Claude Hudspeth, Jed Adams, Mike Hogg, Rice Maxey, B. K. Goree, and Mrs. Cecil Smith. Albert Sidney Burleson, who had been U.S. postmaster general during the Wilson administration, endorsed Young and scored those who "delivered this State to the enemy two years ago." He pointed to the recent North Carolina election where bolting Senator Furnifold Simmons had been defeated and urged Texans likewise to "blot the stigma from this State" by electing the Kaufman man. Some of the most ardent Baileyites were for Young for no other reason that he was the late senator's friend. He could count on comparatively little newspaper aid, although the *Houston Gargoyle*, edited by Allen V. Peden, lent support. "The first preliminary … to liberalizing the state government is to reestablish party principle and discipline in the Texas Democracy," Peden declared in endorsing Young. "But to do so no sane man would want to throw himself or the party into the hands of Earle Mayfield or Jim Ferguson, any more than to leave it in the hands of Dan Moody, who has become little more than a Satrap for the witchburners, besides being woefully indecisive and ineffective."[17]

Practically speaking, Young's one claim to the governorship was that Tom Love ought to be punished for bolting and that he, Young, was the man to do it. According to the *Dallas Morning News*, the Kaufman man was "living over the national election of 1928 as vividly as Tom Love," adding that "the dream of his nights and the vision of his days" was his hope of "trying strength with Sir Bolter of the Hoovercrats." The *News* concluded that "so tipped against the Shining Conscience [Love] is the lance of Young that it loses point against all others."[18]

The candidate's appearance was not particularly prepossessing. A slight, spare man, his thin face—with its tightly drawn skin and heavy lines, surmounted by a shock of bushy hair—was not one to warm on first acquaintance. He was not outstanding in language or delivery. Young's friends made a mighty effort to remedy the ravages of time and prick the people's recollection of Young's past services, but the attempt was only partially successful. "Jim Young looks like a seventh place horse," was Ted Dealey's opinion. "His campaign started out with much fanfare and trumpets but it is dwindling rapidly, according to all political prophets. The real trouble with Mr. Young's candidacy ... is that he apparently is out of step with the times. His present campaign speech might as well have been delivered fifteen years ago as today."[19]

Senator Clint Small's entry into major state politics was more or less the result of chance; or perhaps it would be more fitting to call it a "break." The independent oilman was a resident of Wellington in the Panhandle, and he was, his friends said, the sort of fellow who "carried the baton of a field marshal in his knapsack." Never given to bluster or assertiveness, his manner was quiet, almost reticent, but he had the knack of plowing ahead to achievement.

His break came when as a freshman senator in the state legislature he championed the cause of West Texas ranchers by sponsoring a law to validate their titles to property that had been classified as navigable streambeds (and accordingly surveyed as state property, which was available to oil speculators). The property owners (and Small) contended that the land in question was situated in the beds of dry creeks that never ran except during floods. Small pushed his bill through the legislature only to have Moody veto it. He did not pause, but quickly rallied his forces and passed the measure over the veto.[20] Whereupon his ranchmen friends importuned him to become a candidate for governor. In and out of season, the northwestern Texans talked "Small for Governor." Newspapers took him up, and in April 1930, he announced as a candidate on a "let's adjourn politics" platform. "In my race for Governor I shall present a short business program," he stated. "The State needs careful business management a great deal more than it needs new legislation. In fact, I think everybody would enjoy a legislative truce. Texas should be ready for a political armistice."[21]

Small was the only candidate for governor from West Texas, a section that was becoming politically self-conscious, and he was expected to run strongly there, but the hint of segmented support injured him with voters elsewhere, who were trying to decide who was the most likely man to beat Mrs. Ferguson in the runoff. Furthermore, Small entered the race late. He had angered Hoover Democrats by voting for the Wirtz bill to expel them from the party. The candidate explained that his reason for supporting the measure was to "prevent the chaotic conditions that now exist in the Governor's race." Small had the support of almost every state senator, constituting a sort of unofficial campaign committee. He was the favorite of the independent oil operators. Amon Carter and his *Star-Telegram*, which had the largest and most widely distributed circulation of any newspaper in the state, were behind him. His candidacy syphoned votes from Tom Love and James Young; Lynch Davidson, who at one time had urged voters to center on Young and Small and put them in the runoff, came out for Small, but Small and all other contenders were soon dwarfed by the entrance of a Houston-area mogul into the field.[22]

Sterling Outmaneuvers Moody

It was said of Ross Shaw Sterling that he was "a Horatio Alger hero come to life." The bespectacled Texan towered over six feet tall and weighed about two hundred and fifty pounds. He was ruddy-faced and square-jawed, and he covered his full head of iron-gray hair with a size seven and three-eighths hat. Sterling was born on a farm near Anahuac, a town east of Houston, on February 11, 1875, one of twelve children. His father, Benjamin Franklin Sterling, was a native of Mississippi who had been a captain in the Confederate army; his maternal forebears had come with Stephen F. Austin's colonists and fought at the battle of San Jacinto. Ross attended public schools and farmed until about 1896; a little later he and his father and brothers operated a schooner on Galveston Bay, carrying vegetables to supplement the farm earnings. In 1898 he married Maude Abbie Gage, who had $65 saved up; he had nothing. They spent the money to furnish the modest home they rented in Anahuac. He told his wife that he had worked out his philosophy of life while hoeing on the family farm. It was to "take three or four licks while the other men took two."

Sterling opened a general store at Double Bayou near Anahuac; he went on the road to buy and sell produce for his brother, John Sterling of Galveston; he opened a store and bank at the little town of Humble in Harris County; and he operated a fruit, vegetable, and feed store at Sour Lake that had branches in Saratoga and Batson. In 1910 he bought two producing oil wells in the Humble field, and a year later organized the Humble Oil Company with $150,000 capital. The company failed to get the customary level of production from a Sour Lake district well, and some of his partners got cold feet. "Drill it deeper," Sterling ordered, and at two hundred feet further down they struck a gusher. In 1917 Sterling and other South Texans organized the Humble Oil and Refinery Company around this well and other holdings, with a capitalization of $4 million. Sterling became the president and later chairman of the board. In 1925 he sold his holdings in Humble to Standard Oil and started developing real estate near Houston. A member of the Houston Port Commission since its inception and its chairman since 1922, he was one of the guiding spirits in building the Houston Ship Channel to bring the Gulf of Mexico fifty miles inland to Houston's door. He bought two weak Houston newspapers, the old *Post* and the new *Dispatch*, employed practical newspapermen to operate them, and in August 1924 launched the successful *Post-Dispatch*, which later became the *Houston Post*. In 1927 Governor Moody named the fifty-two-year-old millionaire chairman of the Highway Commission.[23]

Gen. Jacob Wolters intimated that he was the "original Sterling man" for governor, writing that "on several occasions I had casually mentioned to him the possibility of his candidacy. He lent no encouragement." In February 1929 Wolters met Sterling on the front steps of the state capitol. Some legislators had charged that the highway chairman was using his department to build a political machine to elect himself governor. Sterling told Wolters that he was going up to the pressroom to tell the newspapermen that he would not be governor "if he were hog-tied, gagged and dragged into the office." A seasoned political bellwether, Wolters urged him not to be hasty; Texas might need him, and his first duty was to the state. Sterling finally promised he would not give out any such statement. "From then on I began systematically to investigate what the chances were of his winning," Wolters recalled. "I didn't get any encouragement from any of the politicians with whom I talked.... [They] told me frankly that we couldn't elect a millionaire governor of Texas. I kept driving away."[24]

William P. Hobby, Sterling's associate on the *Houston Post-Dispatch*, also promoted a Sterling candidacy, although Wolters stated, "He was not so confident about success." Late in 1928, when Hobby and Sterling were both honored guests for the opening of the South Texas State Fair at Beaumont, the ex-governor (Hobby held the office from August 1917 through January 1921) remarked in the course of a brief speech that the audience might not realize it was beholding, in himself and the highway commission chairman, "one governor in retrospect and another in prospect." In October 1929 Hobby spoke at the dedication of a new highway from Corpus Christi to the Rio Grande Valley. Again he hinted that Sterling, who was on the platform, might well be the next governor of Texas.[25]

Jesse H. Jones and W. O. Huggins, the publisher and editor, respectively, of the *Houston Chronicle*, came out publicly for Sterling's nomination. But according to Ed Kilman, Sterling's wife, his son Walter, and W. M. Cleaves (his attorney) did not want him to run. Cleaves warned Sterling that financial clouds were growing darker on the horizon, and the millionaire's private affairs urgently needed his closest attention to weather the storm. Tom Love tried to convince Sterling that he (Love) would do better for the state and that Sterling should continue promoting his "good roads" program until it was further advanced and then run for governor. "I think I'm entitled to run now," said Love. "It's free for all," was Sterling's laconic answer.

In early 1930 Sterling was still turning aside all suggestions that he run with a noncommittal, "Why bring that up?" He went a little further—but still left the question of his intentions unanswered—when Al Prince, editor of the *Mercedes News Tribune*, told him there was a strong local sentiment for him to run. "That's very nice," Sterling smiled. "I'm afraid I can't be a candidate; but don't say I won't in your paper until you hear it from me." Concluded Kilman: "Thus evidently, as late as early April 1930, he was disinclined to make the race—but not definitely decided."[26]

In mid-May some of Sterling's South Texas friends began contacting leaders in other sections of the state to find out how the Houston man would do if he should announce right away. The response from President S. P. Brooks of Baylor University was not encouraging:

> I have no doubt that his business success shows that he would give a business administration as governor, and in all probability would make a capital governor. I doubt, however, if he goes out on the hustings whether he could be elected. He has not enough of the bullragging and rough oratorical stuff that takes with the rabble. I have an idea that other candidates with infinitely less ability would embarrass him. There are some candidates who do not know enough to be embarrassed.[27]

According to Steve Pinckney, Sterling "had a hard time making up his mind to get in" because "Moody would not get off the nest." Some of the current governor's friends wanted him to run for a third term. The large number of candidates seeking the office was to Moody's "very great advantage," and in the runoff he could be elected against anyone now in the field. They argued that well-informed people recognized that Moody had been right in most of his controversies with the legislature and that a statewide campaign would convince the people at large that his recent recommendations had merit. "Make you a platform advocating penitentiary reform, . . . advocating the abolition from A to Z of the fee system, and the creation of a public utility commission, and tax reform," urged the director of the Baylor University School of Business. "Nerve yourself to fight it out with all opposition, before the people, from border to border, and you can win—and what is more you will go back to Austin with a Legislature ready to co-operate with you in rendering great service to our great State." Another well-wisher advised, "You can do for Texas what R. M. LaFollette did for Wisconsin if you will stand firm."[28]

To these suggestions Moody replied with a form letter noting that the writer was paying him a "distinct compliment," which he sincerely appreciated, but, it concluded, "I am sure I would want to think a good bit about this step before taking it." These thoughts tended more and more in the direction of a third term. "Until today or the last few days, I could not believe that Fate would play us the trick of making possible or probable another two years," Mildred Moody noted in her diary on March 16, 1930:

> I can't think of it now; perhaps I cross bridges. And Dan, who keeps his own council even from his wife, has talked to me of marvelous "offers" of positions when he should be *free*. He has planned on the time it would take to get out of debt and breathe once more. I could not conceive of his running once more, still events of the last few days are ominous. I do believe he wanted out; but he is so hurt over various treacheries; he hates to see certain dreams go glimmering, who knows perhaps he fears to feel no more the "zest of power, the price [pride?] of place." Joe said to me the other day, when we met briefly at the hotel, "But Dan has a positive genius for politics" and I wondered if having been bitten by the bug he would never be quite happy outside![29]

In the latter part of March, Moody solicited his friends' views on the governor's race. The replies were not very encouraging. T. W. Carlock of Pecan

Gap reported that everyone he talked to thought it would be a mistake for Moody to run. "As a reformer and humanitarian, they say you are all right; but as a business executive you fall down," he stated bluntly. "They feel that you take up half-baked and untried measures and try to put them over in the form of legislative enactments and constitutional amendments, when the sober second thought of the legislature and the people condemn them as unsound.... As Lynch Davidson says: —you are 'a petulant boy' blaming the legislature for breaking your play things." A hotel owner in Sulphur Springs told the governor that he had found only one man among his guests that would vote for him and only one letter in the *Dallas News* and the *Fort Worth Star-Telegram* supporting him—and "that letter was written by a lady." Moody admitted that he had been "pretty badly 'winged'" in West Texas because of his veto of the Small riverbed bill.[30]

At Moody's request, newspaperman Frank Gibler investigated the political situation in Harris County; he reported that Moody would run first in the primary there and win the runoff against either Mayfield or Ferguson but that his support would not be as enthusiastic as it was in 1926. "Many people express themselves as being disappointed in you and say that you have not shown the strength of personality that your widely publicized 'red hair' led them to believe." One of the disappointed ones was Will Hogg, who wired Moody from Cannes, France: "As Texas appears politically quite demoralized a third term candidacy probably will give a certain old hungry thieving privy rat [Ferguson] a better chance to succeed you or to name your successor. Obligation to your administration would seem direct. You unflinchingly support an available candidate perhaps Jim Young. Another fragrant frankness I hope worth the soul of a Mexican frijole. Thanks."[31]

On April 14 Moody announced that he was preparing three statements relating to the fortieth and forty-first legislatures and the state government's work during his tenure of office. The first would show what the two legislatures had done and what the state government had accomplished under Moody; the second would enumerate his recommendations to the legislatures and note "what those sessions failed to do in response to executive urging"; and the third would cover "a program of what should be done in Texas during the next two years in the matter of legislation and improvement in the government."

Most of the state's political leaders accepted this announcement as preliminary to a third-term candidacy, at least under certain circumstances. Some analysts said it depended on the supreme court's action in the Love case (discussed in chapter 1); the governor would run if the court sustained the executive committee but would not enter the contest if Love were admitted to the ballot. Others disagreed, saying Moody could better capitalize on a third-term candidacy with Love on the ballot because it would open such a bitter feud between the regulars and the Hoover Democrats that the governor would win in the second primary against a candidate of either faction. A third opinion held that Moody would not be influenced by Love's fate but would like to delay his own announcement until the court had acted so he would not alienate any of Love's most ardent supporters who might be expected to look kindly on the candidacy of a governor who had vetoed the antibolter Wirtz bill. "It is no secret now that Governor Moody would like to succeed himself," reported William Thornton of the *Dallas Morning News*, "and that he wants more than anything the enactment of a law putting the prison system within short distance of Austin or in Central Texas, the introduction of industry into the system as an occupation for the convicts and a gradual abandoning of farming as the major effort."[32]

Mike Hogg greeted Moody's April 14 announcement with what his brother Will called "a red hot statement" criticizing the governor's performance in office. "Hope MH burns him up for the Legislators who *tried* to work with and for him." Puzzled by Hogg's attack, Moody blamed the Houston man's "intemperate statement" and "bitter personal feeling" on his 1927 reappointment of a lady to the University of Texas Board of Regents, which had so offended Will Hogg that he declined to serve on the board. The Hogg brothers' critique of Moody was motivated by their displeasure with his attitude at the 1928 national convention on Smith's stand on Prohibition and Jesse Jones's presidential candidacy; furthermore, Mike Hogg supported James Young for governor. "The principal trouble with him is that he and a little group have anointed one to be Governor of Texas and he was afraid that I might get into the race, and in some small way embarrass their plans," Moody confided to D. K. Martin of San Antonio. He added: "I can only trust that the people of Texas who read the statement will recognize it as intemperate and know that he did not substantiate his statement by reference to the record of facts, — because he could not."[33]

In May veteran Dallas Democrat Pat O'Keefe talked in Port Arthur with Hobby, Pat Neff, Roy Miller, William Pool, Judge Helms, Joe Moore, Tom Henderson, William Stone, and other prominent Democrats. "All were of the opinion that you ought not to run," he reported to Moody. "You know most of these were your friends. Bill Hobby and Roy Miller asked me what chance Mr. Sterling would have so it looks like they want him to run. I told [them] I did not think the farmers would vote for a millionaire. The reason they gave was what have you to gain. You can weigh this as you see fit." Mrs. Moody noted in her diary on May 15: "Dan away for most of two weeks here and there over the state (beginning of a campaign, not official, but might as well be)."[34]

On May 20 Moody talked with Hobby, Sterling, and Rep. Alfred P. C. Petsch of Fredericksburg, the administration's floor leader, and they advised him against seeking a third term. The following day the governor saw Highway Commissioner Cone Johnson, a staunch supporter, at breakfast and later they talked with Sterling. After that Tom Love called at the executive office and conferred briefly with Moody. "I did not mention to Governor Moody the question of his reported candidacy for a third term," Love told reporters, "but I did tell him that I am a party regularity man and that of the twenty candidates in the race for Governor, the Supreme Court gave me a clean bill of health as the most regular." He denied that the two men had discussed the question of one or the other making the race or had made any agreement about support. Moody told friends that a definite announcement regarding his political intentions would be made soon. According to Steve Pinckney, "Dan Moody would not commit himself, but continued his course of throwing sop to RS [Ross Sterling], encouraging him to run in one breath and discouraging him in the next breath."[35]

On May 21 William Thornton reported that a conference was contemplated at Houston in a day or two at which the decision would be made as to whether Moody would seek a third term. If the answer was no, the conference would decide who would be recognized as the administration candidate. "Should Moody not run it is said that R. S. Sterling, millionaire Houston publisher and business man, might make the race. It is known that like Governor Moody, Mr. Sterling has the affirmative idea as to entering the contest. Since he is part of the administration he would represent it effectively." Should both Moody and Sterling remain out of the contest, the talk in Austin was that the administration group would probably support Love. Moody had said several times he would support Love in preference to several others in the race, and a statement from Petsch echoing Moody's support was considered significant.[36]

Moody remained in Austin on Thursday, May 22, and did not attend the informal Houston conference. The significance of his absence was amplified by a statement made several times during the day that he had made no elimination agreement with anyone and had not abandoned his inclination to get into the race. He would not be quoted directly for publication, except to say that his formal decision still was in abeyance. However, it was made unmistakably clear that he would not support Love as long as there was a chance for a third term. Governor Moody wrote Alvin Moody that while Love would get a great many votes from anti-Smith Democrats, he would be in a predicament if he got in the runoff with someone other than Mrs. Ferguson. Argued the governor:

> It's my candid judgment, that Senator Love misses his guess badly when he thinks that all people who voted against Smith will vote for him for Governor. Among my personal acquaintances here in Austin, and even in Dallas, I can name man after man who refused to vote for Smith who are supporting some other candidate than Senator Love in this campaign.
>
> My concern in the present election is to see someone elected Governor of Texas who will carry forward progressive measures, and I am deeply concerned that this State government shall not fall into the hands of a Ferguson or Earle Mayfield. No man can foretell the outcome of any election, but I have thought the thing over from every angle, and made inquiries from every quarter of the State, and I have just about concluded to enter the campaign.[37]

Love attended the Houston conference but refused to be eliminated, whereupon, according to Steve Pinckney:

> Governor Hobby, at the instance of Sterling, called up Dan Moody and told Dan that RS had decided not to run, whereupon Dan said, "My goodness, tell him not to do that—that won't do—I would rather get out and make speeches for him than to run myself. Tell Mr. Sterling for goodness sake not to decide, but wait until next Sunday at least." (Sunday being next to the last day for filing). In the meantime friends of Sterling continued to urge him to run, whereupon two or three days later Hobby called Dan up over long distance and told him that RS was having so much pressure brought to bear on him that he was reconsidering the matter and would like to know if anything had happened since his last call to Moody that would change the situation so far as Moody was concerned. Of course, there was nothing to do but say "no," but he suggested that Sterling withhold final judgment for a day or two longer. Hobby was too wise for that and got Sterling to announce immediately.[38]

On Thursday, May 29, Sterling announced in Houston that he would be a candidate for governor, and this caused a "real political flurry in Austin." His entrance upset Moody's plans and severely hampered the draft movement on behalf of his fellow Houstonian, Lynch Davidson. The next day the governor, who was on a speaking tour, sent a long telegram to the capitol pressroom saying he had intended to announce in Sunday's newspapers, but he indicated that "Mr. Sterling has been a staunch political friend of mine and I would not like to run against him." He did not say, however, that he would not run. When called over the telephone, the governor refused to amplify his statement. When told that many were construing it to mean that he would not be a candidate, Moody said he was "not encouraging any one to put any construction on it." William Thornton asserted, "Governor Moody has a reputation as a procrastinator, particularly in matters of politics, and that disposition may have cost him his opportunity to seek a third term." Thornton's opinion was that "had he made his announcement when he first determined to run it might have kept Mr. Sterling out of the race, his friends say." Privately Moody explained that he had not wanted to announce until the last minute because he preferred short campaigns. Moreover, he thought that something might happen that would clarify a chaotic situation. Furthermore, he had accepted a number of speaking engagements, which he felt obligated to fulfill before making an announcement. "I had been invited to make these speeches as Governor and I felt that I ought to appear as Governor and not in the character of a candidate."[39]

A move to draft Moody was started on Saturday, May 31, when twenty-five East Texas citizens from Upshur, Smith, Cherokee, Wood, Henderson, and Gregg Counties signed a petition requesting that the state Democratic Executive Committee put his name on the ballot as a candidate for governor. The petition was started on its rounds by Carl L. Estes, publisher of the *Tyler Telegram* and the governor's close friend. Included with the petition was Estes's check for the $100 filing fee. Moody knew of the action, since he had a telephone conversation with Estes on Friday night, but his only comment when told the petition had been filed was "I have nothing to say."[40]

In a telegram to the *Dallas Morning News*, Estes stated that Moody had not wanted his friends in East Texas to draft him but they had done so anyway. Moody went to Victoria on Monday, June 2, to attend the funeral of a friend, and when he returned to Austin in the afternoon he again refused to make any statement regarding his political plans. "So quiet is the Governor as to his future plans that not even his closest political friends have fathomed his intentions," noted one observer. "He apparently is waiting for something to happen, and it may be forthcoming soon. It is no secret that he hankers to enter the contest and that he has particularly vitriolic shafts to shoot at two or possibly three of the candidates."[41]

James Young asked Moody to join in a request for Sterling's resignation from the Highway Commission, now that he had become a candidate, "in order that this important function of our Government may be kept free from political controversies and entanglements." All Moody would say was "I have read Mr. Young's letter." Representative Petsch conferred with Moody on Wednesday night, June 4, and then went to Houston where he conferred with Sterling and others. Claiming to be a harmonizer between Moody and the Houstonian ("not that it was necessary, but merely as a matter of convenience"), the legislator said he thought Sterling would win with the governor's support. "I am very much encouraged over Mr. Sterling's candidacy," he declared. Asked whether he thought Moody would withdraw his name from the ticket, he replied emphatically, "Oh, certainly I do," adding: "It is my guess that he will make a statement to the State Democratic executive committee when it meets at Austin Monday." By June 7 Moody's decision was made. That day he wrote Frank Gibler: "Mr. Sterling concluded to become a candidate, and I do not want to run against him. He has always been a loyal supporter of me in all of my campaigns and throughout my administration. I do not want to have even the appearance of selfishness or ingratitude towards my friends. There are some men who have been such loyal and consistent supporters of me that I would not want to contest with them for any office, and Mr. Sterling happens to be one of them."[42]

Moody and Jim Ferguson had a bitter exchange at the executive committee meeting on June 9 after the governor requested that his name be left off the primary ballot. He indicated that he did not want to confuse the situation by running or possibly cause the election of Ferguson, "who is running behind his wife's petticoats," or Earle Mayfield, "neither of whom should hold public office." Ferguson jumped to his feet, his face white with rage, and shaking a finger at Moody, only a few feet away, shouted: "I dare you to get into the race: You are afraid to get into it, and you know you are." Moody, his face blood red, his voice angry, and his finger pointed at Ferguson, retorted: "I met you on the stump as a candidate and I defeated you. I am not afraid of you. Jim Ferguson is a man who stands against good government and I stand for it. I met you before and I beat you." Ferguson, interrupting, said in a loud voice, "Get in again. You won't do it: You are afraid!" Moody again pointed his finger at the ex-governor and with more deliberation said: "I am not afraid of you, I beat you ignominiously before and I could do it again, even by more thousands of votes, but I am not going to lend my name to anything that will further muddle the waters and make it possible for a return to Fergusonism in this State."

The melee ended when the committee voted to grant the governor's request to remove his name from the primary ballot. Moody told the members he would have more to say about Ferguson, and this was interpreted to mean that he would go on the stump to fight the Fergusons, and Mayfield as well, to a finish. Earlier in the day, in a stormy session and over Connie Renfro's bitter protests, the committee had put Love's name on the ballot. On June 4 the Texas Supreme Court had denied the committee's motion for a rehearing in the Love case, and thus the bolter was eligible to run.[43]

The January 4, 1931, entry in Mildred Moody's personal diary throws an interesting sidelight on her husband's decision not to run. She wrote:

New Year's Eve we led the grand march at the big ball, and in the evening I thought long over things Charles Marsh said to me, as we danced: "You and I are always one to take the long chance. I wanted Dan Moody to do that. I had already talked to Franklin Roosevelt and it was as good as settled, a Governor of Texas breaking a third term precedent was unbeatable, and a young popular man.

It was a cinch that he would have been vice-president, and then President. (He mentioned Roosevelt's health:) In other words Dan had a ten to one shot had he just held firm to his decision, maybe Dan's fatal weakness. He let his friends trick him out. "Now as a mere Ex in private life, well F.D.R. now has nothing to say. Dan now has only a chance in a hundred or a thousand. But you and I will always take the long chance and gamble." And I thought to myself, "King-maker," "God???"[44]

On June 9, 1930, Moody telegraphed Marsh, who was in Chicago on his way back from the East, that he had conferred with friends of good judgment from various parts of the state and it was their unanimous opinion that it was time for him to get out or get in.[45] "I believe they are correct," Moody stated, "Houston party [Sterling] seems convinced of a hands down winning and will run it out. Other party from Houston [Lynch Davidson] thinks he can win and seems bent and determined upon running. Friends of both Houstonians believe that both of them will be in race. It is my judgment our analysis of the other evening needs revising and that I should act today."[46] This telegram confirms that Moody and the Austin publisher had discussed a third term and that the governor's decision not to run contradicted the two men's understanding. Of course, Roosevelt or his managers undoubtedly dangled the vice presidency before many men as he pursued his campaign for the nomination; still, it should be remembered that the office did fall to another Texan—John Nance Garner.

Provoked at Sterling's sudden announcement, Moody said privately that he would vote for him, but at first expressed a lack of confidence in his ability to make the runoff. "He [Moody] wasn't a pleasant friend to talk with during those days," Wolters stated. "He could emit more pessimism than any natural optimist I ever heard talk. He was 'young man gloom' every time I made contact with him." There were suggestions that Moody make some speeches for Sterling, but the candidate's managers agreed they did not want him to make any open declaration in the first primary campaign. As Moody explained: "I believe the prevailing thought among his friends is that he has considerable strength in certain counties that have gone against me in my campaigns for Governor and that there would be danger of alienating some of his votes in these counties." As a courtesy Sterling asked for Moody's advice, particularly on the subject of highways, and he sent the governor a tentative draft of his opening address at Huntsville, promising to call him long-distance to get his reaction and any criticisms. In mid-July, Moody described the governor's race as "a very, very muddled situation" but now conceded that "Mr. Sterling has been making some rapid gains."[47]

The Field Narrows

In addition to Moody, several others who had been expected to run had withdrawn or failed to file for a place on the ballot. State Treasurer W. Gregory Hatcher, E. G. Senter, and Katy Daffan dropped out, as did Lynch Davidson, who had been placed on the ballot by thirty-five Hunt County citizens. Davidson's fifteen-hundred-word statement, sent to the newspapers on June 19, gave no sign that he would support Sterling's candidacy. One section in fact was accepted among political observers as indicating opposition to Sterling. "With every ounce of energy" that he possessed, Davidson said, he would "work to save the State" from a state highway bond issue. Still, his withdrawal probably helped Sterling more than anyone else. "Certainly it hurts Tom, Maw and Earle, which is what Davidson hoped," commented the *Houston Gargoyle*.[48]

The other Davidson, T. Whitfield, tested the waters for his candidacy but announced on June 1 that he would not run because every additional entry from those in the center only made more certain a runoff between the two extremes, Ferguson and Love, and such a result would mean a Republican victory in Texas. Crosby County friends of state senator Pink L. Parrish of Lubbock filed his name as a candidate while he was absent from the state. He was a huge man, weighing 310 pounds, who enjoyed wide prowess as a trencherman and kept a senate page busy bringing him sandwiches, fruit, milk, and other dainties. "Senator Parrish handles a sandwich as the ordinary man handles an aspirin tablet," commented William Strauss. "Just puts it on his tongue and swallows." Popular at home but not widely known over the state, Parrish declined to make the race and announced that he would support Clint Small. Both came from the plains section, and they had almost adjoining desks in the senate. Senator T. N. Mauritz of Ganado, called by Seth McKay "one of the ablest and most progressive of the state senators," was expected to run but did not. Mayor Oscar Holcombe of Houston was boomed but made his peace with Sterling, with whom he had been feuding, and said he would back him. The *Houston Gargoyle* guessed that "Oscar might be thinking of making another mayoral race, and that he would not like to have The *Post-Dispatch* oppose him, as it did the last time."[49]

The four "minor" candidates simply added numbers to the race as their polling numbers would scarcely make a dent in the total number cast. Paul Loven of New Braunfels, known as a "big butter and egg man," announced as a Wet, but an opponent claimed that "he did not say how wet or what he would do about it if elected." Clement C. "Soapy" Moody, a delivery man for a Fort Worth laundry, said he wanted to "redeem the family name," but he did not elaborate on that statement. His candidacy was considered a joke, and an unsuccessful effort was made to keep his name off the ballot. His platform, issued from his headquarters in Charley Holder's barbershop, was such a masterpiece of spoofing that Roscoe E. Wright, a reporter for the *Houston Gargoyle* saw "the fine Spencerian hand of Silliman Evans, former political writer, maker of Dan Moody and now his foe." Dr. C. E. Walker of Grapevine was a physician, a Dry, and a political unknown. Frank Putnam of Houston was a newspaper and public relations man running on a "dripping wet" platform. He said he would reduce drinking by 50 percent by making it legal, respectable, and unromantic.[50]

Ferguson greeted Sterling's entry into the race with the prediction that he would not take one hundred votes from Mrs. Ferguson but would upset most of the other candidates. "While he has no chance to be elected yet any man with two or three million dollars and the nerve to spend it can always stir up a brass band campaign that looks dangerous until the ballot box is reached when the blow-up comes," he asserted. In addition to labeling Sterling "the big rich candidate," Ferguson also questioned his mental competence and lack of formal education:

> Let a man have money and there are many substitutes for having brains. Sterling can take many people down to that million dollar residence on the bay on that public highway built since he became highway commissioner and show them that fine furniture and all of them books that have pictures in them that he looks at and knows by sight and he will just make a lot of people think he is a big man.
>
> They say that somebody was reading out of one of his books to him and read something about the Mason and Dixon line and Sterling said he didn't know where that railroad was located.[51]

In July Ferguson concentrated his efforts against Sterling's proposed road bond issue and his opposition to an elective highway commission. "I notice in Mr. Sterling's speech Friday he wants the people to have a chance to vote on $350,000 road bonds, but that he is opposed to the people electing the officials to spend it," he said in a Waxahachie speech. "If they've got a right to vote on one, why haven't they a right to vote on the other? That's one reason my wife is opposed to issuing State bonds." He told a Houston audience that for Harris County to recover the $7 million in voter-approved road bonds out of Sterling's $350 million in bonds, the county would have to assume its per capita portion in the amount of $22 million. In the case of Tarrant County, the bond plan would take away $5,739,000. He sprinkled his Fort Worth speech with striking metaphors to describe what had happened when the bond proposal came before the legislature in 1929:

> I got as busy as a one-eyed man at a three ring circus and Ross Sterling and Tom Love had little Dan as busy as a cat on a hot rock. There was every kind of political skullduggery. With wine, women and song. I don't know whether any of the Legislature were bought, but they kept over half of them drunk for a long time. The battle ebbed and flowed, but finally we got a vote and we licked 'em. Now the, hydra-headed monster has bobbed up again, when everybody's broke and thousands are walking the streets out of work.[52]

Sterling was attacked for having named William Strauss, "who is Jesse Jones' high finance henchman for approach to the big money in New York," to manage his campaign; and for being a "Tom Love bolter" because he had strongly supported Felix Robertson in 1924, had voted for George Butte, and had allegedly voted for Hoover in 1928. He was also exposed for having been a Klansman at one time. He was charged as a member with sponsoring a proposition "to sell a $3 robe and sheet for $18 and now is offering a road bond issue that is a bigger holdup than that."[53]

The boiling flow of brimstone and vitriol did not end there. Sterling and his associates were accused of draining oil and gas underlying the Imperial state prison farm through fifty-seven producing wells on land within a stone's throw of the prison property. If Sterling was a good businessman, why was it that the Reciprocal Insurance Company and the Lumberman's Reciprocal Company had gone broke paying commissions to Will Hobby, and Sterling was one of the directors? "If you think he's a business man," Ferguson challenged his audiences, "go to Houston and look in the records and you'll find that he's the biggest ignoramus in business or the crookedest fellow in business."[54]

It was generally assumed that Mrs. Ferguson, because of the Ferguson "vest-pocket" vote, would be in the runoff, and her supporters expected the campaign to develop into an assault by several of the leading candidates on what they denominated "Fergusonism." William B. Teagarden recommended that the Fergusons accept the challenge and make the issue Fergusonism against Moodyism and Loveism. "Our position, it seems to me, is that Moodyism is bad enough, but Moodyism and Loveism combined—and that will be the real issue when Moody takes the stump—is infinitely worse," he wrote Jim.[55]

Ferguson had no editorial support among the big city dailies, with the exception of the *Houston Press*. Except for the *Fort Worth Star-Telegram*, which had a special aversion to Moody, they refused to publish any criticism of the governor or his administration because he was not a candidate. When Teagarden asked Ferguson for a list of favorable city and county papers that would publish his series of letters contrasting Fergusonism with Moodyism, he was provided with the following (in addition to the *Houston Press*): *Cutover Land Farmer* (Newton), *Record* (LaGrange), *Fletcher's Farming* (Hondo), *Wolfe City Sun*, *Review* (Athens), *Camp Wood Crony Courier Gazette* (McKinney), *Sun* (Alvin), *Wood County Record* (Mineola), and *News* (Canyon City).[56]

Tom Love began his campaign while his case was still before the Texas

Supreme Court, attacking Tammanyism and Fergusonism, John J. Raskob, and the state Democratic Executive Committee, which was characterized as a "blown in the bottle Tammany utility of the first order." James Young was singled out for attack as the chairman of the "Tammany campaign committee for Texas in 1928." He was running as a Dry candidate with the enthusiastic support of John Boyle, Steve Pinckney, and a number of the leading Wet politicians and corporations and public utility lawyers and magnates in Texas. His campaign had been opened at a sort of Belshazzar's feast held in the Adolphus Hotel in Dallas. "My friend, Jim Young, is not the only Tammany candidate for Governor of Texas," Love declared. "There are others. There will be other Belshazzar's feasts. Tammany is just trying out the boys at this state of the campaign."[57]

"The booze issue is the fundamental issue of this campaign," Love told a Navarro County audience on May 3. "The issue is whether the financial greed of the bootlegger and the alcoholic thirst of the booze-fighter shall control the Government and the Democratic party in Texas and in the Nation." His political scenario had the well-financed Association Against the Prohibition Amendment, a large, nationwide action group dedicated to overturning the Eighteenth Amendment, planning to take over the Democratic Party and make it the tool of the outlawed liquor traffic. "They are planning to make the Democratic party the wet party of the Nation and to renominate Alfred E. Smith for President in 1932," he warned. "They are hoping to elect a satisfactory Governor of Texas this year, and it would suit their purposes better to elect a dry Democrat who will advocate harmony with booze, than to elect an avowed wet." (This was an obvious reference to Jim Young.) When Governor Moody issued a harmony statement, Love insisted that "there must be no harmony with booze, or with Tammany Hall, which stands for booze and graft and political corruption and Wall Street domination of the Democratic party and the Government."[58]

Love had a progressive platform where state affairs were concerned. He advocated abolition of the ad valorem tax and the substitution of a state income tax; a "complete, comprehensive, economical and humane reformation of the prison system" along the lines of the Beck bill; state aid for cattle, sheep, and goat raisers and state cooperation to help them obtain aid from the federal farm marketing act; and improved living conditions for farm families. The farmer should be able to obtain reasonable educational opportunities for his children, to live on good roads, and to have electric lights and power and other such conveniences. The tenant farmer should be given a reasonable opportunity on fair terms to become a farm owner. Love favored labor legislation, since "good wages for the workers is not alone indispensable to their welfare, but to the general welfare." He advocated the enforcement of child labor laws; protection for the rapidly growing group of women workers; and state regulation of motor busses, trucks, and public utilities. Love argued that although the courts should determine rates and service, not a rate-regulating tribunal, a state fact-finding agency should be created. He praised Governor Moody's legislative program, saying: "I have never heard sounder or more statesmanly recommendations to the Legislature of Texas than those contained in his messages." Love favored a road bond plan, but realizing that it was known as Sterling's idea, gave it little emphasis. "My advice to you is not to push the state bond issue," V. A. Collins wrote Love in early June. "It may be all right to say you have no objections to submitting to the people, but as an issue it will lose two to one in Texas."[59]

In six weeks Love traveled eight thousand miles, going from El Paso to Texarkana and from the lower Rio Grande to Amarillo, touching eighty-one counties and making sixty speeches, the last at Fair Park, Dallas, on July 25. Love spent no money from Anti-Tammany Democrats of Texas funds in promoting his candidacy; he paid his own expenses, and J. V. Hardy of Dallas, the anti-Tammany finance chairman, furnished him a car, gasoline and oil, and drove him around the state. Love borrowed $500 from McAdoo for one year to pay his expenses until he could devote his attention to private business. All told, he spent less than $5,000 in the race. Still, he professed optimism about the outcome of the first primary. In a San Antonio radio talk on July 9, he predicted that he would lead the ticket with a plurality of not less than seventy-five thousand votes, noting: "All of my opponents voted for the Smith electors and thus the opposition is divided into ten equal parts."[60]

In his speeches former senator Earle B. Mayfield opposed Sterling's road bond plan and argued that he was the only candidate in the race with statewide support and a comprehensive understanding of the state's needs. Imitating Governor Huey Long of Louisiana, he made war on the chain stores and criticized the ad valorem tax as unjust and out of date. Early in July his denunciation of the chain stores tapered off, as he realized the issue was not catching fire with Texans. "Political Analyst" in the *Austin American* pointed out that Mayfield was strong with women voters and that several women's organizations had endorsed him. His friends made an effort to line up former Klansmen behind his candidacy. "Earle Mayfield may be no statesman in the highest sense of the word," commented the *Dallas Morning News*, "but none can say he does not look the part; while thousands hail him as bearing a brain to match Wilson's and a tongue tipped with Bryan's fire."

During July Mayfield concentrated his attack on Sterling's millions, insisting that the highway commissioner had brought Standard Oil back into Texas by selling his Humble Oil stock to the Standard Oil Company of New Jersey after Senate Bill 180 was enacted into law. Now the oil company was "opening its bags of gold to put one of its henchmen in the Governor's chair." One of Mayfield's rivals, Frank Putnam of Houston, suggested that Mayfield was "dry in principle but not in practice" and that he "uses the radio a lot lately—must have struck oil."[61]

The First Primary

When Sterling announced he would be a candidate for governor, there were just eight weeks until the primary on July 26. The politicians were not enthused about a millionaire candidate. Sterling's campaign manager, William Strauss, knew nothing about state politics but took hold of the job and began to organize. The first week saw the headquarters staff more or less groping in the dark for a starting point. The beginning of the second week saw more progress in the naming of county leaders in South and East Texas. "We were feeling carefully but surely into doubtful territories before attempting to establish any definite contact for organization," Strauss recalled. "Some political sage has commented, and with truth, that most fatal blunders are made during the first days of any political campaign. This mistake was successfully avoided." Sterling clubs were soon organized in many parts of the state, and again the greatest activity was clustered in the south and east. At the organization of the Sterling club in Houston, J. W. Evans predicted that the candidate would poll more than thirty thousand of the forty-five thousand votes expected to be cast in Harris County. At the same meeting, Jesse Jones certified Sterling's clean personal life and said the best way to elect him was to tell the story of his career to 1930.[62]

The first month saw South Texas formed gradually into almost a solid front for Sterling. William H. Scott, one of his managers, predicted that sixty-five South Texas counties would give 80 to 90 percent of their votes to Sterling, and in a June meeting of the Houston real estate board, 100 of the 103 members present preferred Sterling. Alvin Moody was one of the three dissenters. "Mr. Sterling's candidacy seems to be going over strong in South Texas, all the way from Beaumont to Brownsville," Moody reported to Love. "It is somewhat discouraging to some of your supporters in Houston, but when the campaign develops, the sentiment may change." But the outlook from the areas in which Sterling must gain his winning strength were not encouraging. Hobby, Strauss, Paul Wakefield, Jesse Jones, and Wolters went to Dallas but accomplished little; a second trip and the opening of headquarters held out some hope for the still doubtful territory. Murphy Townsend, a lawyer with no political experience, was named manager for North Texas; a grocery merchant, Ernest Alexander, handled Tarrant County and West Texas; and Hilton Howell, a Waco lawyer but also no politician, was handed McLennan and a tier of adjoining counties. Wolters was skeptical at the beginning about managing a campaign with key men who were not in the least politically minded, but he was won over by their good performance.[63]

San Antonio presented probably the most complex situation in the state because internal political strife made it dangerous for the outsider to transgress on what was generally conceded to be machine-controlled territory. Hobby went to the city and started things for Sterling. Wolters received promises from machine leaders that while they intended to vote for Barry Miller, they would keep hands off. Then Sterling, Hobby, and Strauss visited the city. Strauss prevailed on Albert Steves Jr. and Reagan Houston, two businessmen with no political experience, to chair Sterling's campaign committee in Bexar County. Col. Chas Tobin, brother of the late mayor, joined the organization as campaign manager. Some machine support was won over. "The committee is composed of administration and anti-administration men who are working in perfect harmony," a Sterling man informed Jesse Jones in early July. "I believe we will get the entire influence of the 'city machine' and I also believe Frank Huntress will soon announce for Sterling. Mr. Grant of the Express said to-day that he thought it possible for us to carry this county over the combined opposition, in other words get a majority for Sterling. The Sterling sentiment is growing daily."[64]

Sterling's platform included a demand for a $350,000 state bond issue to improve the highway system and to relieve the counties of payments on highway bonds. Almost all of his opponents attacked this proposal, warning that if adopted it would increase taxes and saddle the state with gigantic debts when the future of the economy was highly uncertain. "It is a wise man, and a wise state, in these days who treads carefully, cautiously," warned the *Houston Gargoyle*. "Far better to wait awhile." Rather gleeful that the Houston man was irrevocably "tied to" the issue, Sterling's opponents anticipated, in James Young's words, that he would soon "abandon his own child," or slur over the issue in the campaign. Instead, Sterling himself raised the issue in his opening speech at Huntsville on June 20, declaring that the

*Ross S. Sterling stands on a stage with microphones during his run for governor,
Walker, Texas, 1930. Ross Shaw Sterling Papers, Briscoe Center for American
History, University of Texas at Austin, DI 05549.*

people should be given the chance to decide at the ballot box whether the
bond program should be adopted. He denied that the bond issue would raise
taxes; in fact, it would lower them. The farmer, the rancher, and the small
property owners would obtain relief rather than an additional load. The cost
of the highways would be borne by the users as the bonds would be secured
by a gasoline tax.[65]

At the suggestion of William Clay Grobe, a reporter for the *Houston
Chronicle*, Sterling began to call his highway bond plan the "unbending
plan," noting that he wanted to return to the counties the $75 to $100 million
they had already contributed to state highways. He remarked that thirty-
three states had adopted the state bond plan and were finding it worked.
At the same time, he did not claim that his plan was the only answer; if the
legislature could devise a better plan, one that would take the road tax burden from farmers and home owners, he would be glad to approve it.[66]

Sterling was no orator and realized the fact, modestly telling his audiences that they need not expect any flowery speeches from him. He started

out on his first speaking tour through East Texas with a written speech, but reading interfered with his delivery. "It isn't going over so well," an observer told Ed Kilman of the *Houston Post-Dispatch*. "Reading the speech takes the punch out of it." Kilman agreed: "He'd do much better without a speech." At the next town, Sterling's script was "mysteriously missing" and he had to talk freehand. "It upset him for a while, but before long he quit trying to remember his lines and cut loose, saying what was in his heart, rather than what was on the written page," Kilman recalled. "Then the crowds began to sit up and take notice." They interrupted more frequently with applause, and the Texas political war-cry rang out: "Pour it on!" On June 25 Sterling first made the request that was to bring smiles to audiences all over Texas: "If you ladies will pardon me I'll shuck this coat."

Massive, gray, and a little grim, perspiring in shirtsleeves, he would earnestly plead the cause of business in government. To appear more "folksy," he began to refer to himself as "the old fat boy" and even essayed some humor. Speaking on the courthouse lawn in Victoria, he was remarking, "I don't recall exactly how many candidates are in this race," when the courthouse clock began striking the hour of eleven. He paused, counted the strokes as they sounded. "That's it—there are eleven of them," he said, adding: "In two hours that clock will strike one, and after a month from today there will be just one candidate in this race. That will be Ross Sterling." Of the Ferguson promise, "Two Governors for the Price of One," he remarked in a speech at Scotland: "It's darned hard to make an omelette, out of two rotten eggs, or a good Governor out of two that have been tried and found wanting."[67]

While campaigning in northeast Texas on July 18, Sterling for the first time took cognizance of the charge that he was spending more money than the law permitted. He emphatically declared that he would not violate any law to become governor and asserted that he was not spending as much money as some of the other candidates. "If my friends like me well enough to spend money to have me elected Governor, it is a compliment and a testimonial that they think me worthy and that I have more local friends than the other candidates," he argued. He said he had not answered this "untruthful charge" before because he "did not want to get down into the mud and wallow with those who were slinging mud."[68]

Because the large number of candidates seeking the gubernatorial nomination made it difficult for many voters to make up their minds, Texas newspapers played a more decisive part in the primaries, especially the first, than in any similar contest veteran political observers could recall. In retrospect, the race was really between four candidates: the two with the greatest per-

sonal followings, Mrs. Ferguson and Love, and the two with regional newspaper support on which to build, Sterling and Small. In that sense it was
a contest between the newspapers and the factions, on the one hand, and
between Sterling and Small for a preponderance of newspaper support on
the other.

It was both Small's strength and his handicap that he was regarded as a
regional candidate—the favorite son of West Texas and the Panhandle. As
the campaign got underway, he obtained the increasing support of that region's newspapers, headed by the *Fort Worth Star-Telegram*, the *Amarillo
News*, and the *El Paso Times* and *El Paso Herald*. "There can be no question
about the importance of newspaper support to Senator Small," noted Peter
Molyneaux. "It was the newspapers of the region from Fort Worth to El Paso
and up into the Panhandle to Amarillo that aroused the people of that territory to a pitch of enthusiasm for Senator Small seldom if ever equaled in
the political history of the state." However, outside that territory Small obtained very little press backing, and as the final outcome showed, the great
bulk of his vote came from the region in which he had almost unanimous
newspaper support.[69]

Before he announced, Sterling was already assured of a nucleus of newspaper support, with Jesse Jones's *Houston Chronicle*, Hobby's *Beaumont
Enterprise*, and his own *Post-Dispatch* strongly behind him. During the two
or three weeks following his entrance, newspaper after newspaper in southeast Texas announced for him, and in due course he had as much general
support among the newspapers in that section as Small had in his home territory. It then became a question of which of the two could obtain the greater
amount of newspaper support outside his home territory.

Sterling made steady progress among the smaller dailies and weeklies
in East, Central, and North Texas. A few newspapers switched to him from
other candidates, and he gained a few press adherents even in West Texas
and the Panhandle, notably the *Abilene Reporter News*. Sterling's publicity
department, headed by Paul Wakefield, carried the story of the candidate's
successful business career to the people through more than five hundred
weekly and ninety daily newspapers. In a Fort Worth speech, Jim Young
charged that the Sterling forces were offering advertising in exchange for
editorial support. "Ross Sterling is attempting to buy editorial support in
Texas country newspapers and this causes the newspapers to betray what is
generally regarded as a public trust."

The San Antonio and Dallas newspapers remained neutral during the
early part of the campaign, contenting themselves with reporting its prog-

ress in the news columns. Sterling's popularity with the reporters who followed him over the state was reflected in their writing. Meanwhile the road bond proposal became the most discussed issue of the campaign and had some impact on the course of newspaper support. "Newspapers which are not supporting Sterling, though favorable to the bonding plan, are beginning to speak out in its favor," Molyneaux wrote at the end of June. "Recent expressions of this kind having appeared in such publications as the Dallas *News* and the Dallas *Times-Herald*." On June 29 the Marsh-Fentress chain of newspapers, which included the *Austin American, Austin Statesman, Waco News-Tribune, Waco Times-Herald*, and nine smaller daily newspapers, came out in favor of the bonding plan and against the "would be Bryans and big stick politicians" who were opposing it on the stump. Sterling's candidacy was not mentioned, but the net effect of this advocacy of the bond plan was to help him at the expense of all the other candidates except Love.[70]

By early July Sterling had more newspaper support outside of West Texas and the Panhandle than all of the other candidates put together. It was now generally conceded that Mrs. Ferguson would make it to the runoff, but there was no agreement as to who would be her opponent. "As I see the race now, there is a very large percentage of the voters as yet undecided as to how they will cast their ballot," John E. King, the managing editor of the *Dallas Morning News* reported to owner George Bannerman Dealey. "These voters want to cast their ballots where they will mean something—in other words, they want to vote against Ferguson and Love, and they want to vote for a man they believe can beat these two. This puts Sterling in a strategic position, and if he can show sufficient strength to win a large part of this as yet undecided vote, he may get in the run off with either Love or Ferguson." King added that "if such was the case, his nomination in the second primary would be assured."[71]

On Tuesday, July 14, the *News* printed on its front page an analysis of the primary outlook by E. M. (Ted) Dealey, a member of the editorial staff. Dealey summarized his views after an extended trip over the state, and he gave it as his opinion that the people were centering on Sterling.

> The crucial point lies in the answer to the question: Is there any chance of the voters centering on one of the candidates, Sterling, Small, Young, or Miller? The answer seems to be yes. There are straws in the wind which indicate very clearly that this crystallization of sentiment is taking place. And the trend which apparently has set in seems to be

favorable to the candidacy of Mr. Sterling.... Ross Sterling ... was only a few weeks ago almost out of the running. Now he is most decidedly in it.[72]

That afternoon the *Dallas Dispatch*, which was not friendly to Sterling and had attacked his bond proposal, began to publish the results of a poll of about two hundred and fifty newspapers covering the entire state, as to how the candidates would run in the different counties. Sterling took the lead at the post and kept it until the last results were published several days later. On Wednesday, July 16, just ten days before the election, the *Dallas Morning News* formally endorsed Sterling. "In the opinion of The News," said this announcement, "the outstanding candidate, who has no past to conceal, but does have a constructive policy and a clear vision of the needs of Texas, is Ross Sterling. It is the intention of The News to favor his candidacy as the one best suited by experience and character to carry on with efficiency and economy the important duties that devolve on the executive of the State."

The support of the *News*, probably the most influential paper in Texas, was pivotal in the campaign. "It was indeed the climax," conceded Molyneaux, "and as a result the last ten days of the campaign was a march to victory for Mr. Sterling. It put new vigor into the Sterling campaign workers, and it solidified into a solid conquering phalanx, the great number of newspapers which had rallied under the Sterling banner." The endorsement even made a dent in the Tom Love and Barry Miller fronts in their home sector. On the eve of the primary election, the *News* published the results of its poll of the state's newspapers, which placed Sterling in the runoff behind Mrs. Ferguson with Small in third place, just as they stood when the votes were counted after the primary.[73]

As election day approached every major candidate was touted for a place in the runoff by his friends and his organization. "East Texas and North Texas, the Rio Grande Valley, and South and central Texas are going to give me my fair share of votes Saturday," Clint Small declared, "and if West Texas sticks by me instead of following after some old, spavined politicians, then I am in the second primary as sure as the sun rises." He forecast that he, Ferguson, and Sterling would be the first three. According to Dan Moody, a "large majority" of those people around the capitol placed Sterling first, Ferguson second, and Small third. Mayfield, Young, and Love contended for fourth place, and Miller last. In her brief closing address at Temple, her old home, Mrs. Ferguson thanked the other candidates for not saying anything mean about her or her husband, and she admonished that all differences will and should be forgotten as "life's shadows lengthen toward the great beyond." In the *Forum* Jim exulted, "WE FINISH, WE WIN." He continued to predict until the day of the election that Sterling's vote would disappoint his friends and that either Love or Mayfield would be pitted against his wife in the second primary. Making his last appeal to the voters in Palestine, Sterling concluded his address by lapsing into poetry. "In the words of the poet I want to say this as a final message to the people of Texas":

> I live for those who love me,
> For those who know me true,
> For the heavens that shine above me
> And for the good that I can do.[74]

The early election returns indicated that the two leaders would be Mrs. Ferguson and Sterling. With 242,959 votes, Mrs. Ferguson carried a bloc of Central Texas counties, won some counties from the northeast, and carried seven German counties, for a total of ninety-eight. She ran strongly in counties where she had received a large vote for reelection in 1926. Sterling, with 170,754 votes, took the southern part of the state and won occasional counties in deep East and far West Texas giving him pluralities and the lead in fifty-eight counties. Third-runner Clint Small, with 138,934 votes, carried the Panhandle and the northern half of West Texas with perhaps a greater unanimity than a candidate for office ever carried any section of the state. In most of Small's eighty-nine counties, he polled majorities over the aggregate totals of the other ten candidates, and in some of them he had two-thirds majorities.[75]

An interesting feature of the contest was the small vote totals polled by Love (87,068), Young (73,385), Miller (54,652), and Mayfield (54,459). Young led in five counties, including his home county of Kaufman, its neighbor Gregg, and three sheep and goat counties, Bandera, Edwards, and Sutton. Miller led in his home county of Dallas, in Comal (a German county), in Archie Parr's Duval, and in Kenedy, a ranch county along the Gulf Coast between the lower Rio Grande Valley and Corpus Christi, for a total of four. Love carried Hays County. Mayfield did not have a plurality in any county in the state. The minor candidates received an insignificant number of votes.[76]

"I was defeated by the overwhelming use of money in support of two candidacies; that of Small in West Texas who got 100,000 of my votes in that section; and that of Sterling in South Texas who got 100,000 of my votes there," Love wrote McAdoo. "If either of these candidates had not gotten in the race ... I would have been nominated. As it was, I beat three strong men and was beaten by three."[77]

Pro-Smith Democrats rejoiced to note that Love ran fourth. On the other hand, James Young, who led the fight for Smith, could do no better than fifth. "Well, our horse didn't run very fast, did he?" admitted the *Houston Gargoyle*. "In the gubernatorial derby, that is. Too bad, but that gallop is definitely over. He was game.... If the run of Democrats can't see the crying need for restoring the integrity of their once great party, it's no fault of Jim Young."[78]

But the important thing was not the defeat of these men, for Texas Hoovercrats were obviously back in the fold and the Democratic revolt was over. Rather it was the large vote for Ma. Jim had always given strong showings in the hinterlands; and hard times, and now drought, were powerful Ferguson allies. "The surprising Ferguson vote, in my opinion, is due to the disgruntle [*sic*] frame of mind of the people as a whole," the organizational director of the Texas Cotton Cooperative Association told Dan Moody. "Almost everyone has suffered some financial loss, and many people are really in a serious predicament. They are extremely resentful, and they are likely, by reason of a certain perversity that is common to nearly all of us, to vent their spleen upon anyone who is obviously more fortunate than they." William G. McAdoo wrote Jesse Jones: "It seems inconceivable to me that the people of Texas would deliberately take another dose of Fergusonism. However, Democracy has strange ways."[79]

The attorney general's contest attracted almost as much attention as the gubernatorial race. The three chief candidates were the incumbent, Robert Lee Bobbitt of Laredo, James V. Allred of Wichita Falls, and Cecil Storey of Vernon. Also in the field was Ernest Becker, an obscure attorney for the Dallas Development Corporation. This was Allred's second try for the office; he had been narrowly defeated by Claude Pollard in 1926. In October 1928 Allred alerted his immediate staff to begin "lining up" for a race in 1930. "I will sure be in the race for Attorney General next year," he advised Representative Elwin Gerron, who had warned him that a petition asking Cecil Storey to run was circulating in the legislature. "In fact, I am already running, and ... you can tell them all I said I was going to run regardless of who runs." Allred unofficially announced his candidacy in a speech at the Old Settlers' Reunion in Granbury, Texas, in August 1929.

When Pollard suddenly resigned on September 15, 1929, Allred considered asking Moody to be appointed for the unexpired term, but his brother Ben warned that "you haven't a chance in a million with Moody," and Allred

was unwilling to be embarrassed in the 1930 campaign as a rejected applicant. Moody first offered the job to Wright Morrow of Houston, and when
he declined, the governor named the forty-year-old Bobbitt, a lawyer and
former speaker of the Texas House of Representatives. Bobbitt had been
mentioned as a candidate for governor in 1928 before Moody announced
for reelection.

Allred was not afraid to take on Bobbitt, who was uncertain whether to
run for a full term as attorney general or to shoot for the governor's office.
"I talked to Bobbitt for a few minutes about his plans and he does not know
what he wants to run for," Allred wrote his brother Oran. "He suggested that
I come down to Austin later and we would talk things over, etc.... No one is
overly pleased with the appointment."[80]

Allred found an issue in advance of the campaign by opposing chain
stores. One of the most colorful opponents of the chains was W. K. "Old
Man" Henderson of Shreveport, Louisiana, whose radio station, KWKH,
"Hello World" Broadcasting Company, specialized in antimonopoly propaganda. Allred enlisted with Henderson's "Merchants Minute Men" in January 1930; for four months he crisscrossed Texas speaking by invitation only
at rallies of independent merchants, publicizing his name and reinforcing
his reputation as the "little man's" champion. "Two months ago everybody
thought you could beat 'anybody except Bobbitt,'" Ben Allred wrote Jimmy
on February 22; "Now the general opinion here [Pampa] is that you can beat
him—'if he runs.'"[81]

On March 5, 1930, Bobbitt announced as a candidate for attorney general. Described by the *Houston Gargoyle* as a "highly provincial Prohibitionist," Bobbitt had the ringing endorsement of the two Moodys (Dan and
Alvin), Tom Love, and most of the Hoover Democrats. "Love and Bobbitt,
in fact, form the crux of their ticket," stated the *Gargoyle*. Love's longtime
political ally, Marshall Hicks, was one of Bobbitt's law partners.[82]

Cecil Storey, the floor leader of the Fergusonites in the house of representatives, spent much of his time attacking the Moody-Bobbitt legislative
program and Bobbitt's conduct of the attorney general's office. He accused
him of official neglect in permitting the University of Texas regents to hire
a firm of San Antonio lawyers to recover certain oil leases. Storey switched
much of his attack to Allred after it became apparent that he was being well
received by the voters. In a speech at Belton, Storey said: "Jimmie is a good
looking boy but when he boasts that he is running on his record as a lawyer,
I believe he is a bit optimistic since his legal record is largely before him. I
think he has been in the Civil Appeals Court once."[83]

Dan Moody defended himself in the press by denouncing Storey for mouthing the Ferguson line while concealing his partiality for the discredited former governor. "I want Mr. Storey to understand that whenever I see a man trying to conceal his Fergusonism and to slip in to public office when the folks are not aware of his attitude, it is my purpose to expose him." Ferguson retorted that he was not concerned in anybody's race except his wife's. "My wife's race is a great success and the only trouble with Little Dan is that he sees his appointee Sterling slipping and his appointee Bobbitt not doing any better," Jim sneered. "He's afraid he's going to lose 'em both and he's just fretting."[84]

At times Allred seemed almost lost in the crowd. "Moody has given Storey more publicity than he could have ever gotten by himself but I don't know whether it will make a dent or not," Oran Allred fretted. "I really believe he did it with malice aforethought to switch the Ferguson vote to Storey so that Bobbit [sic] might lead in the first primary." Yet while his opponents bickered, Allred worked the state vigorously, methodically, and effectively. "He is said ... to be an extremely personable chap, and a whiz of a campaigner," commented the Houston Gargoyle. "He blows unannounced into a town in his rattling Ford, hires a truck, backs it up to the courthouse square, mounts its rear end and begins haranguing. In a very few minutes he has gathered a crowd that grows rapidly and listens gleefully to his denunciation of his opponents."[85]

Allred believed that he had lost in 1926 by coming out for Moody, and this time he was determined to stay out of the governor's race. In his speeches he emphasized his antitrust position, while assuring businessmen that "legitimate" enterprise had nothing to fear. He insisted that he was uncompromisingly "anti-chain, anti-merger, anti-monopoly, anti-Wall-Street." He constantly reminded voters that he had lost by a mere four thousand votes in the 1926 runoff and appealed for a "square deal." To emphasize his role as an underdog, he recalled for his audiences his experiences as a boot-black in Bowie, working the streets and shops for nickels and dimes. Oran Allred saw the value of the rags-to-riches Horatio Alger tale: "I figure this shine boy story will go big," he commented, "and put you in the lead again."

In the July primary Allred led the field with 286,906 votes. Bobbitt was second with 257,821; Storey was in third place with 125,239; and Becker placed last with 75,593 votes. These results set Allred and Bobbitt against one another in the runoff.[86]

In contrast to the interest shown in the gubernatorial and attorney general races, the contest for the open U.S. Senate seat attracted little attention. Senator Morris Sheppard, the "father of national prohibition," sought a fourth term and was opposed by former congressman Robert L. Henry of Houston and C. A. Mitchner of Sherwood. Mitchner was a political unknown and made no campaign. Henry was one of those politicians who give opportunism a bad name. He had run for the senate in 1922 as a Klan candidate (but without the order's backing) and finished last in the July primary. In 1928 he had vocally supported Al Smith for the Democratic presidential nomination. Henry was regarded as politically dead, and his candidacy on a Wet platform was not taken seriously. "Of all men of any prominence in Texas he is about the easiest one to beat for any office," a Waco friend advised Senator Sheppard. "Bob was a 'wet,' then he turned 'dry' for the benefit of the Ku Klux, bidding for their support but failed to get it, and now he is 'wet' to complete satisfaction.... Bob won't get enough votes to 'wad a shot gun.'" Sheppard had sorely disappointed some of his Prohibition friends and made them nervous when he championed Al Smith in 1928, but when Henry threw his hat into the senatorial ring, they hurried back to the senator's standard. Wrote a Decatur lawyer: "I believe my friends, the Hoovercrats, will join me in almost solid phalanx and forever efface little Bob, from the political horizon."[87]

Henry tried to improve his dismal chances by repeatedly challenging Sheppard to debate the merits and demerits of prohibition on the stump, but the senator remained in Washington, explaining that his "official duties" as Democratic whip would not allow him to return home to campaign.[88] Between them, the three candidates spent less than $2,000, and almost one hundred thousand fewer votes were cast for senator than in the heated governor's race. Sheppard won by a large majority, polling 526,193 votes to Henry's 174,260 and Mitchner's 40,130. Although Sheppard carried eight of the ten German counties, Henry's opposition to Prohibition secured him forty percent of the vote in those counties and he carried Comal and Kendall. "The antipathy to the Ku Klux Klan seemingly cost Henry few votes," wrote Seth McKay, "and that question must have been regarded as a dead issue." Despite the size of Sheppard's majority, the 214,000 votes polled by two weak opponents—and the large number of voters who registered no choice—indicated considerable opposition to Sheppard's strong Prohibition views. The Wet *Houston Gargoyle*, which in January had called in vain for "some (comparatively) young man" from the "liberal" camp "to tweak Morris Sheppard's Dry nose," thought a stronger candidate with a thoroughly organized campaign might have unseated him. "The Henry showing at least indicates what can be done in the future."[89]

The race for lieutenant governor attracted numerous candidates: state senator Edgar E. Witt of Waco, ex-senator H. L. Darwin of Paris, former Klansman Sterling P. Strong of Dallas, J. D. Parnell of Wichita Falls, Virgil E. Arnold and James F. Rogers of Houston, and J. F. Hair of San Antonio. State senator William H. Bledsoe of Lubbock announced his candidacy in November 1929 but withdrew on June 6, 1930. This race also caused some excitement. Strong led in the first primary with 175,777 votes, closely followed by Witt with 173,874. Parnell trailed in third place with 121,865 votes, followed by Rogers (85,254), Darwin (75,721), Hair (43,317), and Arnold (42,459).

Former governor Pat M. Neff spoke at many points on his candidacy for a full term as railroad commissioner. He was opposed by state senator Nat Patton of Crockett, W. Gregory Hatcher of Dallas, and H. O. Johnson of Houston. Despite the opposition of the four railroad brotherhoods, who had never forgiven his intervention with Rangers and state militia at Denison and other Texas cities during the 1922 strike, Neff led in the first primary by a wide margin, polling 362,067 votes to Hatcher's 175,229, Johnson's 109,334, and Patton's 93,067. Neff was just 15,564 votes short of a majority and had to face Hatcher in the second primary—in which the gubernatorial race again took center stage.[90]

The Runoff

"The real issue before the voters during the next four weeks is to put Fergusonism permanently out of State politics," editorialized the *Dallas Morning News* after the first primary. "Texas has a job of housecleaning on hand and will probably complete the task satisfactorily at the second primary by eliminating the Fergusons from political life. The Ferguson vote in the primary was large, but presumably the best that Jim and Ma can do." Still there was no overlooking the fact that Sterling was starting 70,000 votes behind the Fergusons. He had to make up that number and get a majority of the remaining ballots as well.

Plenty of warnings sounded that the road bond issue would beat Sterling. Five of the seven candidates who opposed the proposition had polled about 70 percent of the votes in the first primary. "Men are saying on this street this morning—men who never did vote for Ferguson, they will vote for Ferguson rather than Sterling because he will bond the State for roads," a Stamford man informed Dan Moody. Secretary of State Jane Y. McCallum hoped that Sterling would stress honesty in government from now on more than road bonds because "everything points to a real honest-to-goodness bear fight." His critics conceded that Ferguson was a master of political strategy and platform appeal; none was more sure of his touch as he played on the mass reflexes of his crowds, many of whose "faces were work-worn and weary," showing "the sharp pinch of poverty." They were a collection of "downhearted tenant farmers, dispossessed mortgagors, jobless day laborers — simple and unpretending, perhaps, but all desperately in earnest and utterly engaged in the toils of the wizardry of his words."[91]

In the first Democratic primary, Clint Small had polled 138,943 votes, mostly from the Panhandle and West Texas, which at once became the battleground in the second primary. Both the Ferguson campaign and the Sterling group recognized the importance of securing as large a part of the Small vote as possible. Although senators Walter C. Woodward and Pink Parrish and many other Small leaders in West Texas promptly announced for Sterling, the defeated candidate refused, saying that "he would not attempt to dictate to his supporters." Small told Alonzo Wasson he would be neutral, even to the degree of not letting anybody know how he was going to vote. According to Wasson:

> He thinks the showing and impression he made in this contest will put the Governorship easily within his reach two years hence, so that his ambition to occupy that office has been heated rather than cooled by his defeat. Also he thinks, for several obvious reasons, that the Fergusons would be a weaker opponent than Sterling, who, if nominated, would be fortified behind the second term tradition. So he hopes for the election of the Fergusons, though not out loud, since in speaking for them he would incur the political liability of having aided and abetted in electing them. Hence the silence, hence the neutrality, hence the secresy [sic].[92]

Sterling's managers tried to convince Small to make a speech for their man, but the senator pleaded legal business as an excuse for refusing. However, after Sterling talked with Amon Carter, the *Fort Worth Star-Telegram* endorsed him. Small then agreed to make a speech at Waco on August 20, which was broadcast over San Antonio, Waco, Amarillo, Houston, and Fort Worth radio stations. Urging Texas to rid itself of "that shop-worn politician, Jim Ferguson," Small predicted that Sterling would "inaugurate a new era of Texas politics." The road bond issue was no longer before the people, and in all other matters he approved Sterling's platform. Small also spoke in San Antonio and Fort Worth. A furious Jim Ferguson waded into Small at Terrell. "I want to tell you people something about this man Small," he sneered. "Small, too small, I say." He quoted Small as telling him over the phone, "I would not be caught with the Sterling crowd," and asserted that at a meeting in Fort Worth the following day, Small "suddenly broke out and abused Ross Sterling," saying that the Houston crowd had mistreated him and showed him no respect. Ferguson claimed that Small had indicated his intention to support Mrs. Ferguson, a statement that Small called "ridiculous and absurd." However, Small did not say what had caused him to change his mind about remaining silent in the campaign.[93]

Tom Love issued a statement saying, "I have fought the best fight I could and I have kept the faith and have lost and I have no regrets." He pledged to "continue to fight against restoring Fergusonism to power in the State Capitol at Austin by heartily supporting Ross Sterling." The Woman's Christian Temperance Union (WCTU) also lined up for the Houston man. "The runoff primary will be a furious fight with all of Jim Ferguson's ancient enemies, including the preachers, the Governor and his cabinet and Tom Love and his bolters, behind Sterling," predicted a Ferguson man in San Antonio. James Young endorsed Sterling in the second primary, as did Jed C. Adams, Gen. Martin McNulty Crane, and Mike Hogg, who had managed the Kaufman man's campaign in South Texas. "It looks like—The plain people of Texas are about to let maudlin sentiment run them off again with the Fergusons," Hogg declared. "I consider this the greatest mistake they can possibly make. There is no use in rehashing the past Ferguson record—everybody knows it." A. M. Ferguson of Sherman, president of the Ferguson Seed Farms, Inc., denied he was backing his brother. "The real Jim Ferguson that I have known from childhood has no more interest in the 'common people' than a hog has in a rockpile or a 'bee course.' His whole life has been centered in 'me and my wife, Ma' and those who can be induced to kick in."[94]

Barry Miller and Earle B. Mayfield advocated Mrs. Ferguson's election, prompting Sterling to remind the voters that in 1928 Mayfield and Ferguson had entered into an "un-holy alliance" to deliver the latter's vest pocket vote. "Evidently they have now entered into alliance of the same sort," the candidate stated. Mark McGee, a former state commander of the American Legion, who had managed Mayfield's campaign, announced that he would support Sterling in the runoff. Col. Alvin Owsley, on the other hand, switched from Sterling to Ferguson. "He is a double-barreled warrior who shoots in either direction with equal facility," was the *Fort Worth Star-Telegram*'s acid comment on Owsley. "He is a vocal ambidexter of an orator, with permanently meshed forward and reverse gears, capable of either pushing or pulling on short notice, or no notice at all. He is a fore-and-aft statesman with reversible and interchangeable parts."[95]

On July 29 a few of Sterling's friends met with him in his Houston office, among them Governor Moody, Hobby, Wolters, Cone Johnson, W. R. Ely, Thomas H. Ball, Walter Woodward, Judge J. M. Wagstaff, Ernest Alexander, and William Strauss. It was decided that while there would be no surrender of the candidate's views on state road bonds, the issue to be stressed in the runoff campaign was "Honesty and Responsible Government Versus Dishonest and Proxy Government." The attendees also decided that a statewide rally of Sterling forces would be held at the Adolphus Hotel in Dallas on August 4.

In the meantime Sterling issued a long campaign opening statement, which devoted considerable attention to past Ferguson misdeeds. "It is going to be a real hard scrap from now on," the candidate wrote a banker friend, "though I am sure that the [*sic*] most of the good people of Texas will rally to the standard of good government and bury the Fergusons for all time to come." Ferguson responded, "I understand that Mr. Sterling's friends in order to save him from espousing the State Bond issue have persuaded him to repudiate the only issue he had in the campaign." He continued, "They are so desperate they now are about to deny their maker, not for thirty pieces of silver but for $350,000,000." Veteran Fergusonites knew what was coming. "Moody, Sterling and Love declare that the issue *now is* '*honest government*,'" William Teagarden wrote Jim. "From this it is evident that they will try to reorganize the Old Anti-Ferguson crowd and conduct a campaign of vituperation, as they did in 1926."[96]

Sterling's managers had kept Dan Moody off the stump in the first primary, but the governor's friends were now urging him to get into the fight against Fergusonism. "Now Dan the time has come when you can 'Cut your wolf loose,'" wrote a Gonzales lawyer. At the Dallas rally, Walter Woodward presided and Moody and Thomas H. Ball were among the speakers, both making pleas for good government. "When he [Moody] delivered that short speech," Wolters recalled, "not only the crowd present, but from all over Texas our friends realized that the strategy was to let the candidate and Walter Woodward carry the battle into West Texas, and let Dan make speeches throughout North, East, Central, and South Texas." Moody was invited to make his first speech for Sterling at Waco on August 7, the day before the candidate opened his runoff campaign at Hillsboro. Leaving Austin for his speaking tour, Moody carried a large folder. He explained to reporters: "I am carrying the official records showing the true situation as to the administrations of James E. Ferguson and Mrs. Miriam A. Ferguson, that the people of Texas may know that the extravagant claims of deeds and accomplishments are entirely without merit."[97]

Six thousand people turned out to hear Moody at Waco and cheered repeatedly as he delivered, amidst considerable heckling from Ferguson partisans, a powerful philippic against "Fergusonism, the only issue in this race." He declared that in "a contest between honesty and Jim Ferguson, you'll find Dan Moody fighting early and in all places he can get to." The governor followed this address with a swing through North and East Texas. "It is really amazing how the East Texas voters especially the women are flocking to Sterling," reported a Sterling worker who was backtracking Moody to check up on his effectiveness. "Urge Dan to keep up the good work and hit hard where ever he goes. He is making thousands of votes for Sterling each day." On August 19 Moody spoke in Dallas before a crowd that Tom Love called the largest he had ever seen in Dallas County. "This meeting convinced me that Sterling will be nominated by a 100,000" votes, he wrote the governor.[98]

When Jim Ferguson charged that Moody was "afraid to come to West Texas" and offered to give him fifty dollars a day to make four speeches there, Moody replied to the offer by saying that he had accepted a Ferguson wager in 1926 and it had not been made good. Still, he scheduled two speeches in West Texas at Brownwood and San Angelo, telling his audiences: "Old Jim now owes me $100 for this day's work. He can keep his money, though. I don't want it. I would be afraid it was tainted." Moody ended his campaign for Sterling with a three-hour speech before twenty thousand citizens in the bowled slopes of Austin's Wooldridge Park. His theme was "Sam Houston at the beginning of the first 100 years; shall it be Ferguson now? . . . Time and again the vast audience cried No! No!"[99]

Speaking at Hillsboro on August 8, Sterling declared there was only one major issue in the runoff and that was "honesty and responsibility in government." He attacked "Fergusonism," particularly in the matter of Mrs. Ferguson's pardon record, and finessed the unpopular road bond plan by saying that it was for the people to decide whether it was desirable. He would favor "any sound plan that can be worked out to speed highway improvement and equalize the tax burden for highway and other purposes." Following this speech, Sterling toured West Texas with Walter Woodward, who usually spoke first for about forty-five minutes to an hour, followed by the candidate. In one week the two men spoke to perhaps fifty or sixty thousand people. Occasionally Senator William H. Bledsoe of Lubbock and other friends traveled with Sterling. A Ferguson speaker trailed the candidate throughout most of the western tour.[100]

After leaving West Texas, Sterling, now joined by Albert Sidney Johnson of Dallas, carried his campaign from the Oklahoma line through the heart of Texas to Galveston on the Gulf of Mexico. In five days, August 18–22, he spoke in Denton, Gainesville, Paris, Kaufman, Ennis, Marlin, Cameron, Georgetown, San Marcos, San Antonio, Columbus, and Galveston, not to mention the side trips and speeches. "I do not believe there has ever been a campaign just like that," marveled Jacob Wolters. A *New York World* reporter heard Sterling make a speech. "It was stilted and cold, but full of hard facts and good business sense, and he outlined a fine program he would carry out if he were elected." A newspaper poll published in the *Austin American-Statesman* on August 17 showed Sterling as the probable winner with 56 percent of the vote, and it showed that he was leading in every section of the state that had been polled. A few days later another estimate gave his probable majority as sixty thousand votes, showing that he was the leader in all five sections of the state polled. In an election eve statement, Sterling predicted a majority of not less than one hundred thousand votes; his last word to the voters was "to march forth to the polls ... and clinch the victory for which they have battled and bury Fergusonism forever."[101]

Opening her runoff campaign at Cooper on August 7, before an almost record-breaking throng from all parts of East Texas, Mrs. Ferguson defined the issue as "whether you want an elected Governor or a bought Governor." She clarified: "Yea, whether you want a Democratic Governor or a plutocrat Governor." Invoking the name of "the immortal Jim Hogg," who had fought corporate power in his day, she warned that "this same hydraheaded monster has raised its head in Texas and I call to arms the same faithful people of Texas to do for our posterity what our fathers have done for us." Jim spoke after his wife and turned loose what Ted Dealey of the *Dallas Morning News* called "the most vitriolic attack on Sterling" he had ever heard. "It was awful," he wrote his father: "He makes Sterling out a thief and a crook and a liar and a man who was saved from the penitentiary only through his, Ferguson's, aid. He mentions the failure also of the Lumberman's Reciprocal Insurance Co. and includes Hobby as another crook. Jesse Jones he referred to as an ex saloon keeper. In general he gave them all up and down the country." According to Dealey the crowd "ate this part of his speech up"; it had had a tremendous effect, and "Ferguson undoubted will use this stuff all over the State." If allowed to go unchallenged, Dealey believed he would beat Sterling with it, but that presented a problem. Sterling could not very well answer Ferguson publicly unless his charges were published, and "they are libelous in the extreme."[102]

In a speech at Dallas the following evening, Ferguson repeated what Ted Dealey referred to vaguely in print as "the serious personal charges against Ross Sterling and his associates" that he had first made at Cooper, and he criticized the newspapermen on the platform for not reporting a portion of his Cooper speech. At the same time he put Texas newspapers on notice that if they libeled him in the campaign, he would sue for damages. "These big newspapers wanted to get a license to lie on me again," he shouted. "But they can't do it. I'll pop it to them every time they do."[103]

Ferguson's most damaging charge against Sterling was that when he (Ferguson) became governor in 1915, he had appointed a banking commissioner named John S. Patterson, who examined the condition of Sterling's banks. Finding them in bad condition, he informed Sterling that matters must be straightened out at once or the banking department would take prompt action. This Sterling could not do on short notice; he was using too much of the banks' money to carry out his oil exploration operations. As Ferguson told the story, the Houston man came to him in great distress and asked for time in which to complete drilling one, and possibly more, wells. He got down on his knees, wept, and pleaded for time. Ferguson then urged Patterson to be lenient and give Sterling time to complete his drilling operations, pointing out that if the well or wells came in, Sterling could save himself, the banks, and the depositors. Patterson finally agreed to take no action; Sterling struck oil and made good on his debts.[104]

Moody defended Sterling against this charge in a speech at Cooper on August 9: "I understand Jim Ferguson charged when he spoke here at Cooper, that Mr. Sterling got in financial difficulties and came to him [Ferguson], got down on his knees and cried," he stated. "I asked Mr. Sterling about this, what I could say about it, and he replied 'It's not true. It didn't happen.' I suggested to Mr. Sterling he denounce it as a lie." However, Ferguson got affidavits from some banking department employees who substantiated the main elements of his charges. They had been present when Ferguson and Sterling had called on the banking commissioner.

On August 12 Sterling released all newspapers and news services in Texas from any danger of libel suits and challenged Ferguson to do his worst. At the same time, he challenged him to follow this example and release the newspapers from any libel suits that might be filed as a result of Sterling's criticisms of the former governor. "If James E. Ferguson refuses to do this, then it is an open admission on his part that he is afraid for the people of this

State to know the truth," commented the *Dallas Morning News*. But Jim did refuse to let the papers off the hook.[105]

To refresh the people's minds about the evils of "Fergusonism," the well-financed Sterling forces flooded the state with pamphlets and broadsides. Tom Love's *Fergusonism Down to Date: A Story in Sixty Chapters Compiled from the Records*, which had first appeared in O. B. Colquitt's *Free Lance* during the 1926 campaign, was reedited and brought up-to-date. Copies of the articles of impeachment filed against Jim Ferguson in 1917 were distributed, along with a statement from Secretary of State Jane Y. McCallum, which certified that according to records on file in her office: "During Miriam Ferguson's last twenty-nine days in office she granted full, unconditional pardons to 33 RAPISTS, 133 murderers, 124 robbers and 127 liquor law violators. During her last three days in office, from January 15, 1927, through January 17, 1927, she granted clemency in 160 cases, including full pardons to 35 violators of liquor laws, 40 robbers, 22 murderers, and 10 RAPISTS."[106]

The Langhorn case provided exhibit A in the indictment of the Ferguson pardon record. On February 4, 1925, twenty-five-year-old William H. Langhorn Jr., of Fayette County, confessed to the rape of one girl and the murder of her sister, who was fighting to protect her. He was tried for murder and given the death penalty on March 21, 1925, but his sentencing was deferred pending an appeal to the Court of Criminal Appeals, which confirmed his sentence in December 1926. In January 1927, just before leaving office, Mrs. Ferguson commuted Langhorn's sentence to life imprisonment. The commutation was presented to the District Court of Fayette County by Temple Harris McGregor, Jim Ferguson's law partner, on May 20, 1927, before the death sentence could be pronounced. On May 10, 1927, a mortgage on 2,556 acres of land and two other farms in Washington County was given by Langhorn's parents to F. L. Denison, as trustee, for the benefit of James E. Ferguson and T. H. McGregor, to secure and enforce the payment to the two attorneys of six promissory notes bearing 6 percent annual interest.

Sterling's state headquarters distributed a pamphlet entitled *Womanhood Murder and Rape. Commutation of Sentences Under Fergusonism. The Langhorn Case, Wherein Jim Ferguson Extracted Blood Money by Selling Executive Clemency*. The document reproduced Langhorn's confession (which offered explicit details of the rape and murder) and the subsequent legal proceedings and deed of trust from his parents. Ferguson defended himself by noting that Sterling's "political key note friend" Jacob Wolters, Senator Gus Russek, several priests, and some former county officials and

prominent citizens had urged clemency because the young man was of unsound mind. The deed of trust was a fee for defending Langhorn against a
civil damage suit for $20,000 brought by the victims' parents. The suit was
settled for an agreed judgment of $5,000. "I had no connection with the
Langhorne [*sic*] boy's second case until my wife had been out of office for
nearly five months," Ferguson insisted in the *Forum*. "I have never collected
my fee or received any land from the Langhorne's or anybody else yet, and
I have a slow note secured by a deed of trust and if anybody wants it they
can have it, for thirty cents on the dollar." In a second pamphlet the Sterling
forces urged voters to "figure it out for yoursel[ves]." According to *Fergusonism and the Record of a Crime. A Sequel to the Langhorn Story*, voters must
"consider whether you want 2,000 more felons loosed upon society at one
fell blow."[107]

The Fergusonites were outgunned in the pamphlet war, but they reminded voters that Sterling had been a member of the Ku Klux Klan, re-
printing an open letter from the *Houston Chronicle* of January 14, 1923, to
twenty Houston Klansmen, including Sterling, asking their help in finding
the men who had recently flogged a woman and her male visitor at Goose
Creek. Don H. Biggers and four others called the attention of "sincere prohibitionists" to *Sterling's Wholesale Whiskey Business* at Dayton, Liberty
County, 1910–1913. "We feel the cause of prohibition will suffer by the eastern
newspapers headlining 'EX-WHOLESALE LIQUOR DEALER ELECTED
GOVERNOR OF TEXAS,'" the circular warned. Mrs. Kina Mae Crabb of
Ranger, a widow and mother of a little daughter, sent Sterling a telegram
on August 21, which the Ferguson camp printed, requesting that the $14.41
per week benefit due her from the Security Union Insurance Company for
the death of her husband be paid. "I have just received notice from Wright
Morrow receiver that claim draft must be returned unpaid although there
are approximately three and one half years of the award to run. We are in
dire need of this money in order to live. Mr. Sterling will you please have
your company to pay us the money we are entitled to for the death of our
loved one."[108]

"It is a great show in a dull month," commented the *New York Times*
in an August 19 editorial entitled "Texas Enjoys Herself": "What with 'Old
Jim' and the herd of spouters and amplifiers, Texas must be a continent of
sound. The favorite cry at meetings is: 'Pour it on.' For four days more it will
be poured."[109]

According to Seth McKay, by the last weeks of the campaign the array
of speakers who had volunteered to work for Sterling "rivaled the group of

political leaders who had entered the lists for Senator Culberson against Colquitt in 1916." In addition to Moody, Woodward, and Small, they included Cone Johnson, Cullen Thomas, Jim Young, General Crane, and T. W. Davidson. Senators Morris Sheppard and Tom Connally announced they were supporting Sterling. In a telegram to William Strauss, Tom Love congratulated the candidate on the anti-Ferguson campaign he was running and urged "every friend of mine" to leave nothing undone to swell his assured majority to the largest possible limit. "Responsible government and honest government and the good name of Texas are at stake," he declared. "We want a Governor who believes that the Ten Commandments are not dead and that it is wrong to steal."

Barry Miller and C. C. McDonald of Wichita Falls made speeches for the Fergusons. Speaking in LaGrange, Fayette County, to a mostly German and Czech crowd, Miller attacked the Klan, which he said was "militantly active in this campaign." Forty thousand Klansmen had been recruited in recent weeks and had actively thrown their support behind their preferred candidates for governor and lieutenant governor. While Miller did not explicitly charge that Sterling was a member of the newly reorganized order, he declared that the Houston man's previous membership would influence him in its favor.[110]

Following a rally at Fair Park in Dallas, where his crowd was estimated at twelve thousand, Ferguson swung through West Texas. He gave his usual argument against the road bond issue, saying it would amount to a billion dollars and claiming that the roads would only last for ten years, while "the Sterling bond grabbers will make slaves out of your children for forty years." He defended his own and his wife's pardon record by saying that "if forgiveness is a sin, then Jesus Christ was a hypocrite and the Bible is a lie." He added, "And if my wife is elected, she is going to pardon 2,000 convicts as soon as she gets into office." Moody was sharply criticized for wanting to move the penitentiary to "the cedar brakes of Austin, where nothing but skunks and armadillos can live." Sterling's alleged meeting with him in his office in 1915 was related in intimate detail. "My heart went out to him and I laid my head on the block for Ross Sterling," he declared at Floydada. "When I got into trouble at Austin, Ross Sterling was the first arrival they put in the witness chair against me. I made three major mistakes: when I elected Hobby Governor, when I elected Moody Attorney General and when I kept Sterling out of the pen."[111]

Ferguson jumped from the south plains to Port Arthur on the gulf at the beginning of the last week of the campaign. In his speech he described

Sterling as the only candidate he ever saw who could neither read, write, or think. "At Lubbock he sat on the platform like a Barnum & Bailey rhinoceros and never opened his mouth. He had somebody else make his speech." The former governor then worked his way up East Texas, speaking at Nacogdoches, Terrell, and Fort Worth, before he closed at Marlin. While Ferguson was in Fort Worth, his wife joined Miller and McDonald at a San Antonio rally. "Well boys, we are up to the last round," Jim crowed in the *Forum*. "I am going strong and we have the political liars on the run. In prize ring parlance Moody is groggy and wobbling, Sterling is holding on to the ropes and his backers are in the act of throwing up the sponge in admission of defeat that is sure to come next Saturday."[112]

But it was Ferguson who was knocked out. Sterling defeated Mrs. Ferguson by almost 89,000 votes (473,371 to 384,402) and carried 150 of the 250 counties reporting. While his greatest majorities were in the urban counties, his vote was large in all parts of the state. A dozen of the larger counties accounted for more than two-thirds of his majority. The four largest— Dallas, Harris, Tarrant, and Bexar—combined to give the Houston man a lead of nearly 45,000. In proportionate gains, as compared with the July 26 primary, Sterling ran his best race in the so-called Clint Small territory. In Donley County Sterling polled 30 votes in July and 1,425 in August. In Hale County he received 105 votes in July but led Ferguson two to one in the runoff (2,131 to 1,030). Sterling won Potter County (Amarillo) 4,352 to 1,661, after receiving only 220 votes on July 26, whereas Mrs. Ferguson had received 754. However, she carried Clint Small's home county, Collingsworth, 1,183 to 978, although Sterling's vote increased markedly from 40 in the first primary. Mrs. Ferguson carried all of the ten German counties except Kendall; she won Bell County, the Ferguson's old home; and also carried Williamson, home of Governor Moody. Sterling led in almost all of the Rio Grande Valley counties, but Archie Parr's Duval gave Mrs. Ferguson 1,171 votes to Sterling's 78.[113]

The Texas press made its quadrennial announcement that Fergusonism was dead. Raymond Brooks of the *Austin American* noted that "not a single pro-Ferguson legislator was elected this year on the Ferguson issue." A writer for the *Dallas Morning News* enthused, "'Two Governors for the price of one' did not appeal to the democracy of Texas." The writer continued: "The indications are that Jim Ferguson will never again be a factor in the politics of Texas. He has been weighed in the balance, and found woefully wanting. Texas has redeemed itself from Fergusonism." Out of state, the *New York Times* was pleased that the people of Texas "in a time of economic

discontent and even distress, refused to follow adroit and popular demagogues." Jacob Wolters believed that "this is the end of old Jim," but he added
a prophetic caveat: "Of course this depends upon the success that Mr. Sterling will make of his administration."[114]

Other veterans of the political wars were consigned along with Ferguson
to the scrap heap. The people had wanted a businessman, Raymond Brooks
wrote later, and "unerringly" they had turned to Sterling, "simply because he
ignored the cherished traditions on which the politicians of an outworn day
were still living." He remarked that the Sterling victory had routed not only
the Fergusons but also Mayfield, Young, Miller, and Love, all of them old-
timers, skilled in Texas politics. Jacob Wolters wrote Moody that the results
of the campaign, aside from placing Sterling in the governor's chair, would
be very helpful to Texas, to wit: "The permanent evacuation from the zone
of political activity in Texas of certain well-known battle-scarred veterans,
and the confinement to various political sanitariums of a number of younger
gentlemen who gained some prominence by activity in your campaign in
1926, and came to regard themselves seriously as political leaders. These
latter are not bad fellows. They will recover and probably in time still be of
some worthwhile service to the public."[115] The "younger gentlemen" Wolters
referred to were "liberal" Democrats like Steve Pinckney and Connie Renfro,
who had tried to kick Tom Love out of the Democratic Party and had supported Jim Young for governor.

The state press and many of Sterling's followers gave Dan Moody a large
share of the credit for the defeat of Fergusonism. His was one of the most
spectacular campaigns ever made in Texas to that date; in two weeks of
lightning-like campaigning, he spoke in twenty counties, most of which had
been carried by Mrs. Ferguson in July. Only two of them voted for Ma in the
runoff. "The handiwork of Texas' fighting young Governor, Dan Moody, was
very apparent on the face of the returns," noted the *Dallas Morning News*. "In
many doubtful counties where Moody spoke there was a sudden and great
accession to the Sterling standard that is unintelligible and unexplainable
except upon the theory that the young Governor's slashing attack against
James E. Ferguson and 'Fergusonism' had a tremendous effect." Sterling
wired the governor that "I feel that your efforts contributed materially to the
success of my candidacy." Veteran newspaperman Hugh Nugent Fitzgerald
termed Sterling's victory a public endorsement of Moody's administration
and suggested that Texas should get behind Moody for the presidency in
1932. Moody himself was described as "jubilant." "The people of Texas are to

be felicitated," he said in a telegram to Sterling, "upon the leadership which they have placed in your hands and in your nomination for Governor." Asked if he had a statement for the press, he replied: "I'm going fishing."[116]

Ferguson credited Sterling's "big vote in the cities" for his victory, noting that his wife had been the favorite in the small towns and the country. He called for the repeal of the poll tax, saying: "Every day during the campaign I would speak to hundreds of poor people who were good people who would walk up and tell me that they wished they had paid their poll tax so they could vote for my wife. There are no less than 250,000 of such people in Texas who are deprived of this vote by the poverty of their occupations." Upon further reflection, Jim blamed his wife's defeat on a coalition between the Republicans and the "Ku Klux Sterling crowd." He elaborated: "These windies who are going around here like Moody, Small, Woodward and Parrish bragging about how they elected Sterling are just plain political looneys—Sterling money and Boss Creager's political sagacity is what turned the trick and a close analysis of the facts and figures will prove that I am correct." Creager was looking to 1932 for Hoover and had played his game well. Ferguson predicted that if Sterling were beaten in the 1932 primary, he and most of his friends would yell fraud and go straight body and soul into the Republican Party. As things turned out, this was not bad as predictions go.[117]

In the heated attorney general's race, Robert Lee Bobbitt, surprised to find himself in second place, launched an aggressive campaign to discredit Jimmy Allred, whom he privately acknowledged to be a master campaigner and the best voter-getter in Texas. Disparaging him as too young, "not qualified," and "just sprouting his wings," he claimed that Moody had made the same assessment when considering a replacement for Claude Pollard. He announced that Allred had "scurried to San Antonio," where he closeted himself with Mayor Chambers and promised a "hands-off" policy on local elections, thereby obtaining the support of the most notorious "ring" in Texas. "Allred calls me a 'drowning man,'" Bobbitt stated, "but I would rather drown than … traffic with … [that] political machine." Realizing that his close relationship with Moody had thoroughly alienated the Ferguson crowd, Bobbitt had nothing to lose by attempting to link Allred with "Old Jim" and to ride into office on Sterling's coattails. In a speech at Plano on August 8, he charged that Allred was obligated to Ferguson because the latter had appointed Ben Allred as district attorney of Wichita County and that Allred's picture and campaign ads had appeared in the *Ferguson Forum.*

"Old Jim has young Jim securely tucked away in a little trundle bed," Bobbitt warned. And unless the public acted quickly, he predicted that "Texas ... [would] have another Jim Ferguson on its back for the next 25 years."[118]

Allred replied pointedly but good-naturedly to each charge; he noted that Bobbitt had not only carried San Antonio and Bexar County in the July primary but also had won most of the machine-controlled counties in South Texas as well. He concluded that the incumbent's concern for Bexar County was a sham. It was, he observed tartly, "just as illegal to vote unenfranchised Mexicans on the border ... in San Antonio." Allred denied being obligated to any individual or faction. "I have never received any favors at the hands of Ross Sterling or James Ferguson," he declared, and he promised not to embarrass any other candidate by linking his fortunes with theirs. In any case, the Ferguson vest-pocket vote was his without asking. Cecil Storey endorsed him, and Ferguson blasted Bobbitt in the *Forum* as "the hot tamale statesman of the Rio Grande, appointed by that political misfit, Dan Moody." He noted pointedly: "Bobbitt's opponent is Hon. James V. Allred, an honest and capable lawyer of Wichita County. Nuff said: Here's at it!"[119]

Allred polled 57 percent of the vote, defeating Bobbitt 472,087 to 343,292. In a gracious concession statement, the loser reflected: "I have just got some of Jimmie Allred's dust out of my eyes. He is a most successful campaigner and a great vote mobilizer." Moody wired his congratulations on "a spectacular race." "Jimmy Allred is a figure to reckon with in Texas politics from here out," said the *Houston Gargoyle*. "He is fairly bursting with energy and ambition. Attorney General today. Tomorrow? Governor, senator, perhaps even President—who knows." Allred himself was "tickled with the election," although he admitted: "Out of the first twenty thousand votes, Bobbitt had a lead of about 2,200; and I must confess that I was a sick horse." In two other important statewide races, Edgar Witt was nominated for lieutenant governor over Sterling P. Strong (431,060 to 363,467), and Pat Neff handily won the nomination for railroad commissioner by defeating W. Gregory Hatcher 463,601 to 339,878.[120]

The Democratic state convention met in Galveston. Still game, Tom Love urged that as many anti-Tammany delegates from the different counties attend as could do so conveniently. "I think it is a good idea for us to keep our eye on the gun," he advised Cato Sells. "There will undoubtedly be a carefully planned and well organized movement in Texas to ram Al Smith or some one like him down our throats in 1932." Love speculated: "If Dallas County and Harris County and Tarrant County co-operate wisely and timely we can prevent Texas from siding in this movement, and I am in favor of keeping the matter in mind."[121] On the surface, however, all was tranquil in advance of the gathering as Sterling leaders moved into Galveston in force, led by Jacob Wolters and Walter Woodward, who was to be the temporary chairman and keynoter. George Purl of Dallas, Love's successor in the senate, voiced a plea for harmony; the past should be buried, and nothing more should be said about pro-Klan and anti-Klan parties, or pro-Smith and anti-Smith parties. Jim Ferguson did not attend the convention, and the small number of Ferguson delegates present offered no serious opposition to Sterling's forces. Arriving in Galveston on September 8, Sterling issued a statement that said in part:

> Tuesday's State Democratic convention, while prospectively one of the quietest in years, and therefore one of the most harmonious, will mark the beginning of a new day of progress in Texas, it is my hope and belief. Texas has put away irresponsible proxy government forever, and the bitterness and strife of that and other disruptions of the State Democracy during the last decade are but unpleasant memories. The people wish peace and the advancement of the State's interests, which can only come with peace.[122]

One concrete sign of the desire for harmony and need to bury the dead past was the convention's willingness to accept Carr P. Collins of Dallas as a member of the state executive committee. Collins had been a bolter in 1928, as was his father, V. A. Collins, and both had fought Smith hard. Sterling's candidate for state chairman, Judge W. O. Huggins—the editor of the *Houston Chronicle* and an original Sterling man—was chosen to succeed D. W. Wilcox. Huggins's chief function was to sit on the lid and preserve a nice, quiet peace in the family. The general lack of interest in the convention was clearly shown by the small attendance; there were no more than two or three hundred delegates on the floor and many vacant seats. The *Houston Gargoyle* commented: "After two such rousing shows as those staged in Beaumont in May and in Dallas in September of 1928, each packed full of comedy and tragedy, this one was a very pale pink tea party, which could have pleased only those who like such tea-parties." The apathetic delegates did stand and shout when Moody came forward in his customary white linen suit and black bow tie to address the gathering. It was obvious that he was the most popular man in the convention, which was something of a paradox to practical politicians who had counted the governor's political fortunes at low ebb. Moody said he was glad to have witnessed the burial of "political charlatanism in Texas" and noted that "the time has come to turn our backs on this new-made political grave."

The only serious threat to the harmonious proceedings came when Love persuaded the platform committee, with Sterling's approval, to endorse submitting a constitutional amendment abolishing ad valorem taxes at the end of two years. But Sterling was persuaded to change his mind, and at his request the platform committee reconvened and voted 10 to 6 to remove the plank. Love was first asked to withdraw it but refused. Senator Paul Page, who had been a bitter political enemy of Love's for many years but was on his side on this issue, gave notice of a minority report. Opponents of Love's proposal accused him of wanting a state income tax. In the end the weary delegates voted down the minority report by voice vote and then shouted approval of the majority report. Page asked for a roll call, but the chair ruled the request came too late.

Love was more successful on the Prohibition issue, as the platform declared: "The Democracy of Texas is unalterably opposed to the repeal or emasculation of the Eighteenth Amendment, and stands for the strict and efficient enforcement of our national and State prohibition laws, and for such legislation as will strengthen them and contribute to their enforcement."

Another feature of the platform was the recommendation that highway traffic bear the expense of constructing and maintaining state-designated highways and that the counties be reimbursed for bonds and other expenditures on such state roads. This plank placed the burden entirely on a gasoline tax and answered in the negative speculation as to whether Sterling would insist on a platform expression of his statewide bond issue proposal. The document praised the Moody administration and congratulated the people on the defeat of proxy government. It favored liberal support of all education, flood control, the development of a system of state parks, and simplified court procedure. The incoming administration was urged to work for the improvement and modernization of the prison system and to instigate tax reform, conservation, public utility regulation, and enforcement of the antitrust laws.[123]

The Republicans, having polled more than one hundred thousand votes in the gubernatorial election of 1928, were required by law to hold a primary election to nominate candidates in 1930. This primary was the first held by the party since 1926. Believing that Mrs. Ferguson would be in the runoff, the Republican leaders anticipated a bitter August fight among the Democrats, especially if her opponent was Love or Mayfield. Plans were made to launch a fusion movement of Republicans and independent Democrats immediately after the August primary, in an effort to defeat the Democratic nominee. The Republicans had polled almost three hundred thousand votes for Dr. George C. Butte in 1924 and expected to do even better in 1930 if Mrs. Ferguson was again the nominee. Butte received 5,016 votes of the 9,792 votes polled statewide, giving him a majority over his three opponents: Henry E. Exum, John Pollard Gaines, and John F. Grant.[124]

Sterling's victory in the runoff left the Republicans still hopeful but caused them to change their strategy and fish for the Ferguson vote. "Texas Democrats are so divided they can not lie down together in the same bed," Creager said flatly. At the Republican state convention at San Angelo on September 9, the national committeeman said there were between 150,000 and 200,000 Republican voters in Texas; that the Republicans would receive between 80 to 90 percent of the Ferguson vote; and at least 100,000 of Sterling's votes had come to him because of opposition to Mrs. Ferguson. "With Dr. Butte as our candidate, and a constructive platform, there are bright hopes for Republican victory in November," he announced. The platform adopted "almost bodily" several planks of the Ferguson platform.[125]

In a *Forum* editorial published just after the Republican convention ended, Ferguson hinted at a bolt. "Moody led again his anti Ku Klux friends into the Sterling Ku Klux crowd led by Sterling and by the use of money the democrats of Texas are asked to vote for a millionaire Ku Klux candidate. In other words we have no choice between Big Butte and Little Butte. Yea, between the real Butte and a counterfeit Butte. Yes, ... only a choice between a Republican and a millionaire Ku Klux." Ferguson wondered, "Shall we give this crowd a dose of their own medicine? Or shall we not? Aye, that is the question." He invited the "boys" to drop him "a line on this question and let me know how you feel and how your neighbors feel about the question."[126]

A short time after the state convention, Butte withdrew as the party's gubernatorial candidate, and the state executive committee on September 24 named Col. William E. Talbot of Dallas to replace him. Talbot had served in the Texas Rainbow Division in France. He "is highly popular," Creager and Capt. J. F. Lucey said of Talbot in a telegram to the White House. "Will make vigorous and aggressive campaign and will receive very large support from dissatisfied elements Democratic Party." The press interpreted the change as an effort to please the Fergusons and their partisans, since the 1924 campaign between them and Butte had been a bitter one. It was not clear whether Butte had withdrawn voluntarily or possibly had been withdrawn. The former seems to have been the case, since he had congratulated Sterling on his runoff victory: "It was the spectre of the return of the Fergusons to power—now happily removed—that brought me into the campaign. I breathed a sigh of tremendous relief as the returns of your magnificent victory came in last night."[127]

Republican hopes were dashed when Jim Ferguson advised his followers to "grit [your] teeth, hold [your] nose and walk up to the ballot box in November and vote the democratic ticket straight from top to bottom even if Sterling's name is on it." By taking their bitter medicine now, the Fergusonites would be free to say in 1932 that they were so loyal to the Democratic Party that they "even voted for a Ku Klux bolter." Moreover, a bolt to Talbot would provide an excuse to bar them from voting in the 1932 primary.[128]

Talbot campaigned on the general theme of "Buy It Made in Texas," always wearing a complete wardrobe of clothing made in the state. He never criticized his opponent or the Democratic platform. Sterling did not even bother to campaign. On October 30, at the request of the Legislative Amendment Committee, he issued a statement urging support for the four proposed constitutional amendments on the ballot. Ferguson had appealed to the people to vote "Again' 'em All, Again."

Election Day

On November 3 Sterling broke his silence for a second time to urge Texans to go to the polls.[129] In a light turnout, he polled 252,738 votes to Talbot's 62,224, a ratio of a little more than four to one. The Republican candidate carried three German counties—Gillespie, Guadalupe, and Kendall. The Socialist candidate, L. L. Rhodes, received 829 votes and Communist J. Stedham 231. Senator Sheppard defeated his Republican opponent, Dr. J. Doran Haesly of Dallas, by a ratio of more than seven to one (258,929 to 35,357). In the attorney general's race, James V. Allred polled 268,900 votes; W. A. Sanborn, the Republican nominee, won 37,033 votes; and Socialist George Clifton Edwards polled 895 votes.[130]

There was considerable interest in the race for a U.S. House seat in the fourteenth congressional district. As Texas's sole district with a Republican congressman, its return to the Democratic fold might be a deciding factor in swinging control of the next U.S. House of Representatives. Republican Harry M. Wurzbach was facing Democrat Henry B. Dielmann, a San Antonio attorney and former legislator. Both U.S. senators from Texas were among the "big guns" of the party who campaigned for Dielmann. "The San Antonio *Express* wants Dielmann elected and we hope to get Hearst and the San Antonio *Light* to support him," Representative John Nance Garner wrote Tom Connally. But Wurzbach continued to enjoy some Democratic support. John Boyle, the Texas Al Smith leader in 1928, spoke on his behalf. "Mr. Wurzbach is such a splendid fighter, such a sturdy personality and such a thorn in the side of the Texas Republicans, that the Democrats would almost hate to see him lose," commented the *Dallas Morning News.* "Indeed, there is reason to suspect that Democratic votes have kept him in office when Republican vengeance would have removed him."[131]

Wurzbach won the election, carrying Bexar County by six thousand votes and the entire district by over eight thousand. However, he died in San Antonio on November 6, 1931, before completing his term. Richard M. Kleberg, a Democrat and descendent of the King Ranch dynasty, took both the Texas Republican organization and the "San Antonio crowd" to a thorough drubbing in a special election later that month, stepping into Wurzbach's seat with a majority over all his opponents and making John Nance Garner's chances of becoming speaker of the House stronger than ever. Not until 1950, when Ben Guill won a special election, would another Texas Republican serve in Congress.[132]

Nationwide, the congressional elections of 1930 handed the Hoover administration a stunning rebuke. In the South voters who had favored Republicans in 1928 were returning to the Democratic fold. Outside the South, farmers, disillusioned over Hoover's promises to alleviate their plight, voted Democratic; the party won Republican-held seats in Ohio, Indiana, Illinois, Wisconsin, and Nebraska. Urban districts that Smith had helped to carry in 1928 remained Democratic in 1930, and additional seats were won in such localities as Chicago, northern New Jersey, and southeastern Connecticut. When the new Congress met in the winter of 1931, the Democrats organized the House and elected John Nance Garner speaker. In the Senate, where six new Democrats had been elected, the Republicans had only a one-vote edge.[133]

Equally gratifying to Texas opponents of the Eighteenth Amendment were the Wet gains in Congress and the state house. In Ohio, birthplace of the Anti-Saloon League, Robert J. Bulkley, running on a Wet platform, won his U.S. Senate seat by one hundred thousand votes. Governor Franklin D. Roosevelt was reelected with a plurality of 725,000 votes in New York.

Forward-looking Democrats saw FDR as the most likely candidate for president in 1932. Despite his Wet views, he was a Protestant without connections to Tammany Hall, and he would fare better in Texas than Al Smith had in 1928. "At the moment ... Roosevelt stands at the head of the list of wets, with no dry Democrat in sight around whom the party might rally," editorialized the *Dallas Morning News*. "Much less objectionable than Jim Reed of Missouri or Ritchie of Maryland, he has a personal appeal not far from that of Al Smith, over whom he has the advantage in matters affecting prejudice against creed or against Tammany. Roosevelt is a challenge to dry Democracy to bring forth its champion. There is but short time in which to do it."[134]

Among the first to hop on board the Roosevelt bandwagon in Texas was former lieutenant governor T. W. Davidson, who dictated an early morning telegram to the New York governor. "Your splendid victory gives heart and courage to the hosts of Democracy and promise[s] a return of the party of Jefferson, Jackson and Wilson." He told reporters: "If Franklin D. Roosevelt should become our standard bearer in 1932, I think there is no influence under heaven that can prevent an overwhelming Democratic victory." Albert Sidney Johnson, the secretary of the state Democratic Executive Committee, thought that even though the Texas delegation to the next Democratic national convention might be Dry, the Prohibition question would not disturb Texas Democrats as much in 1932 as in 1928.[135] At any rate, he said, if it did, Dry Democrats would not be able to find dry comfort in a Wet Republican party. Agreeing with the *Dallas Morning News*, Johnson was favorable to Roosevelt's candidacy and saw no danger of his losing Texas in 1932, since Smith had lost it by only 25,000 votes and Roosevelt had the advantage over Smith of having no Tammany ties and being a Protestant. On the other side of the Prohibition question, Tom Love was reported silent in the face of the uncertainties that surrounded the election.[136]

The rupture caused by the bolters' departure from the Democratic Party was healed, and the party was back in one piece. Prohibition and Fergusonism remained central to the election, and while Ferguson raised the specter of the Klan, it failed to rile up Texas voters as it had in the past. Sterling had secured his victory.

CHAPTER 4

The Sterling Years

"Nineteen-thirty-one looks like a Sterling year," predicted the *Dallas Morning News* after the Houston man won the general election in November 1930, and the sun beamed down on his inauguration ceremonies in January. Sterling's address had a Coolidgean smack to it as befitted a plainspoken man. Examples: "If we cease building, we suffer and die"; "One good medicine for tax ills is economic government"; "I believe that good roads are the most potent single factor in the forward march of the State generally." Politics is something of a game, with its rules, its strategy, its habits of thinking, its traditions. By all of these one politician can judge another and measure him. But Sterling was no politician, and for that reason he was a puzzle to official Austin. Practically half of his first message to the legislature was devoted to the 1930 Democratic platform. "The platform is an obligation," said the governor, "second only to the Constitution itself." This was new doctrine in Texas, where party platforms were generally ignored after the election.[1]

Sterling's First Legislative Session

As it turned out, there was no friction between the businessman governor and the legislature. Both did as they pleased and neither complained of the other; the result was peace and harmony but little cooperative action. Sterling felt no compulsion to be forceful or to pressure the lawmakers, and he believed that he should not substitute his judgment for theirs on the constitutionality of laws. He thought that the veto power had been granted only to negate acts contrary to the public interest. Only seven bills were vetoed (three of them appropriation measures)—all after the legislature had adjourned.[2] The governor sent a special message endorsing a bill favored by the Texas League of Municipalities and the City Attorney's Association to create a state utilities commission, but the measure died on the house calendar. Another message strongly urged creation of a state conservation commission to supervise the oil and gas laws, and it too died on the calendar. A constitutional amendment authorizing $212 million in highway bonds, the proposal that caused Sterling such difficulties as a candidate, passed the senate by the necessary two-thirds vote but was killed in the house, where the one hundred votes needed could not be mustered. The Ferguson men, led by Temple Harris McGregor of Austin and Coke Stevenson of Junction, were grimly determined to beat the bond amendment, and they bent every effort to that end. McGregor laconically told reporters: "You can say we're going to beat the goddam bond issue." In the house several members played cat-and-mouse politics with the plan, unable to resist the idea of making a record on both sides for future campaign use. Some would watch the count and cast their votes so the measure fell just below the necessary one hundred. On one roll call, the measure received ninety-nine votes, and the catchword became "Who'll be No. 100?"

Sterling watched the progress of his bond plan through the legislature with grave concern, but he took no direct steps to save it, even at crucial moments. According to Senator Clint Small, he talked with lawmakers about the amendment, but he neither logrolled with them nor subjected any of them to pressure. Indirectly, however, he may have been more active than has been assumed. Among the Sterling papers in the Texas State Archives is a fourteen-page typed list: "Check of those originally against issue made March 23rd, 1931." The list indicated whether the representative was still "hopeless" or open to persuasion and gave the names of men in their districts who might be asked to contact them. On April 15 Sterling called Carl L. Estes of Tyler to discuss the position of the Smith County legislators on the highway bond plan, and later that day Estes wrote the governor: "Beg to advise that we have Representative [H. H.] Hanson and Senator Pollard 'in line' and I have taken the matter up with a number of Mr. [J. S.] McGee's personal friends, who in turn are endeavoring to persuade him to change his view point." Sterling had earlier wired John Henry Kirby in Chicago to ask him to use his influence with Senator John Hornsby of Austin. Hornsby announced he was against the bond but would give his vote to permit citizens a statewide expression on it.

According to Sterling's friend Ed Kilman, the *Houston Post-Dispatch*'s capitol correspondent, some of the Ferguson men in the house offered the governor a deal during the bond fight.

At this point, when the bond proponents were straining day and night on a final desperate still-hunt for the needed votes, Sterling was subjected to about as strong a temptation as a governor ever underwent. A certain person came to his office, gave him a list of eighteen House members' names, all on record against the bond issue, and told him that everyone would vote for the resolution if he would appoint a certain friend of Jim Ferguson's to a certain office. At that moment a hundred House votes for that measure was the thing he wanted most in life. He could have had them for a nod of his head. But instead he shook it. "I'll be damned if I do!" A week later the bond resolution was put to a vote for the last time. It mustered 95 ballots—five short of the necessary 100.

Instead, the lawmakers in a special session in September 1932 set aside one fourth of the revenue from the gasoline tax to reimburse the counties for money spent in building roads that were now part of the state system. On the final roll call, two or three representatives, who had pledged that if present they would vote for submission, just happened to be busy in a domino game in one of the committee rooms.[3]

Sterling's restraint toward the legislature was the subject of unfavorable comment. "Since nomination and inauguration he has shown honesty, sincerity, industry and moderation, it is only fair to say," the *Dallas Morning News* said of Sterling in October 1931. "But it can not be justly said that he has yet found himself in the Governor's chair." The newspaper gave poor ratings of his dealings with the legislature and his understanding of the processes of governing: "Mr. Sterling has had almost as poor success as did Moody while his grasp upon the constitutional outline of State government seems to fall short of his predecessor's." A private assessment of Sterling's performance was much harsher. "There never was a man honored with the office of Governor of Texas, that had so little knowledge of the object and function of Government as our present incumbent," Judge Robert W. Brown of Coryell County complained to Attorney General Allred. "He does not have the slightest idea what government is for, or where it came from nor the objects it is expected to accomplish. I can take any High School Boy that has passed a Civics Examination and give him Sterling's record and he can whip him on any stump in Texas."[4]

Although the forty-second legislature was the first to hold a regular session for the ten-dollar per diem wage (raised from five) through a full 120-day period, it neared the end of that period with little constructive work done. A constitutional amendment approved by the voters in 1930 provided that the first thirty days of the session be devoted to the introduction of bills, the second thirty days to committee work, and the final sixty days to the disposition of bills in the house and senate. The wholesale suspension of the time allocations was followed by the worst bill congestion ever experienced as a record number of measures were introduced. Sterling suggested a short recess in an effort to salvage preliminary work. The senate voted to recess for thirty days, but the house balked, agreeing only to meet for one more day. The governor then notified both houses that they would be recalled within twenty or thirty days. However, the first special (called) session, from July 14 to August 12, 1931, also showed a lack of results, so a second special session met from September 8 to October 3. There were two more special sessions in 1932.[5]

The regular session saw a few important bills passed, including the adoption of a fairly comprehensive child welfare program, a provision to handle adequately (at least) the criminally insane, an effort to ease the burden of state and county taxes on "Old Man Texas" by implementing a semiannual payment plan, and bus and truck regulation measures. The University of Texas (UT) was authorized to use $4 million of its funds to erect permanent buildings, and Texas A&M College was allowed $2 million for the same purpose. A companion bill split the university's royalty income from the permanent university fund after three years, giving UT two-thirds and A&M one-third. In the interim A&M was to receive $2 million each year. The legislature passed a state budget bill, one of the governor's measures, making him in effect the state's chief fiscal manager, and authorized a Joint Legislative Committee on Organization and Economy to make a survey of the state government for reorganization purposes. "We are hoping Texas will benefit from the investigation and recommendations made by our legislative committee," Sterling wrote Gov. William H. Murray of Oklahoma.[6]

Kidnapping was added to the list of crimes for which the death penalty could be assessed, the law prohibiting Sunday movies was repealed, the birthday of Robert E. Lee was made a legal holiday, the Texas Centennial Committee was established to make plans for the centennial celebration in 1936, and it was decided that Texas should have a poet laureate and that a new one should be selected each second year. The legislature also found time, late in the session, to authorize Dan Moody to buy the chair that he used while governor.[7]

Many more important bills failed. Although this was the first session following the decennial census, no redistricting bill was passed; bills to revise

Texas Centennial celebration poster depicting a man holding a Texas flag and a woman holding a bluebonnet, 1936. Ephemera Collection, Briscoe Center for American History, University of Texas at Austin, DI 04411.

the election laws failed to make the grade; a lobbyist registration bill was turned down; efforts to have a constitutional convention were abandoned early in the session; no tax equalization bill was accepted; and no cotton acreage control plan was voted. An effort to materially enlarge the powers of the Railroad Commission to enforce oil proration, supported by the independent producers, was defeated, as were other bills to regulate the oil industry. One bill cherished by the independents that attracted much attention, SB 338, sought to divorce filling station ownership from control of production, refining, and transmission pipelines. House Bill 586 directed the Railroad Commission to limit pipeline companies to earnings of not more than 10 percent on their investment. Another bill proposed to raise taxes on pipelines. The Senate State Affairs Committee killed Pink Parrish's resolution calling for a forty-day investigation of public utilities.

In 1932 legislators, lobbyists, and newsmen made a talismanic charm out of the elongated and white skeleton of a horse's head. Fitted nicely over the mirror of a dresser in the Driskill Hotel, the head was presently covered with scrawled names and sometimes liquor was consumed as signers toasted the "Order of the Horse's Head."[8] Its dry bones perhaps served as a metaphor for the way that Texas's economy was drying up, requiring leadership more effective than Sterling seemed to provide.

Depression and Deficit

The economic downturn of the Great Depression created a most difficult situation for the state government. In preparing the biennial appropriation bills, lawmakers were embarrassed by the triple difficulties of slow tax collection, shrinking revenues, and a mounting deficit. Their stumbling efforts to find new revenues encountered heavy opposition from the swarms of business lobbyists who descended on the capitol. A state income tax bill failed to pass, along with a bill to enlarge the intangible assets tax law to include fifteen thousand corporations not paying the gross receipts tax. The intangible assets tax gave oil company lobbyists a bad scare. "The representatives for the oil companies have rather depended upon the business men of the State to oppose this Bill," Jacob Wolters of the Texas Company wrote W. O. Huggins.

There is a business men's organization represented here. I am afraid their work has been rather noneffective. It has not been aggressive enough. We have been rather active in the last two or three days. But there ought to be a general alarm, and thousands of telegrams poured in here Monday and Tuesday against that bill. A few strong delegations from Houston, Dallas, Fort Worth, Waco and San Antonio would be very effective. Judge, I am scared.[9]

A cigarette tax of three cents on a package of twenty was approved over the opposition of the tobacco lobby, which included the Retail Druggists Association; half of the revenue was to go to the school fund and the other half to the general fund. Sterling called in several lobbyists for major Texas corporations and appealed to them to help pass the tax on cigarettes. They agreed, but rather than approach the legislature directly, they arranged for the lawmakers' constituents throughout the state to bring pressure on their representatives. Representative E. M. Davis charged in the house that the cigarette tax was due to "six sets of lobbyists who want this tax because they believe it will restrain the Legislature from applying other taxes."

Such hopes, however, were short-lived. Sterling called lobby members back to his office and told them that a deficit was still anticipated, which was considered a bald hint that more money was needed. The lobbyists registered "pain." "It is hardly thought they willingly will surrender additional taxes to the State, as they have been fighting tax bills to the last ditch," commented William Thornton of the *Dallas Morning News*. But there was no alternative. Six members of the house signed a letter urging an increase in the sulfur tax from 55¢ to $1 a ton. This prompted a rebuttal letter to the legislature from L. Mims, the vice president of the Freeport Sulphur Company, and Roy Miller, director of public relations for the Texas Gulf Sulphur Company. The two men alleged that the six house members "have been imposed upon by the enemies of the sulphur industry" and that the "honest facts" about its present condition should convince any reasonable and fair-minded person that sulfur in proportion to its earnings was assuming a larger portion of the costs of government in Texas than any other industry, and that its tax burden should not be increased. Despite this appeal the sulfur tax was raised to 75¢ a ton. Also, a tax of 5¢ per four-hundred-pound barrel was levied on cement, and a 2 percent tax on natural gas was approved. The gasoline tax law was revised to capture about fifty million gallons that had escaped being taxed each year when payment was made at the point of first distribution at refineries in Texas or at the wholesaler where the gas was shipped into the state. At 4¢ a gallon, this measure meant an additional $2 million in taxes.[10]

Despite the increased sulfur tax and the other new taxes, appropriations still greatly exceeded the expected revenue, and on June 11 Sterling—trying, as he expressed it, "to cut the garment to fit the cloth"—vetoed almost $3 million in funding, eliminating new buildings for the state's colleges and university and cutting money meant for the summer schools in 1933. These vetoes allowed Sterling to reduce the prospective deficit in 1933 to a little more than $1 million, which would enable him to hold down the state tax rate, possibly to the desired 27¢, and to depend on an upward turn in oil prices to restore much of the state's income.[11]

The Red River Bridge War

A minor but colorful episode of Sterling's administration was the so-called Red River Bridge War of 1931.[12] The ruckus began over a new $225,000 bridge between Denison, Texas, and Durant, Oklahoma, one of three nontoll bridges built jointly by the two states. Parallel to the Denison-Durant bridge was a toll bridge. Its operators obtained a federal injunction prohibiting the use of the new bridge until the Texas Highway Commission fulfilled its contract obligations to compensate the toll company for its lost business. On July 16, 1931, Gov. William "Alfalfa Bill" Murray of Oklahoma grew impatient about opening the new bridge. He sent highway crews to remove the barricades from the three free bridges and to plow up the Oklahoma approach to the toll bridge.

Murray apprised Sterling of his action. "It is absurd for any individual person or corporation to hold up two sovereign states and the project of the nation itself," the Oklahoman declared. "Urge that you give like instruction on your side of the line." Murray claimed that he had the right to cross into Texas because under "old Spanish treaties" Oklahoma held title to both sides of the river—and because each state owned a lengthwise half of the new span. Sterling retaliated swiftly. He ordered Texas Rangers to close down the south end of the Denison-Durant free bridge. Adjutant General W. W. Sterling and Texas Ranger captain Tom R. Hickman of Company B took over the scene with the backup of two of Hickman's Rangers. This time the bridge stayed closed. The Terral-Ringgold bridge was allowed to remain open. The Gainesville bridge remained unused because its southern approach was not finished. "I feel you have extended your jurisdiction beyond all reason," Sterling wired Murray. He maintained that Texas had to obey the federal court injunction to keep the free bridge closed. Citizens of Grayson County, Texas, wanted the new bridge open. Their state senator, J. J. "Jake" Loy of Sherman, said the governor had exceeded his authority in calling on the Rangers.[13]

Alfalfa Bill had his whimsical moments. He suggested that a quilting bee be held between Texas and Oklahoma women. The women, he said, would remove the barricades on the free bridge in order to get together. He further suggested that Ma Ferguson might lead the Texas delegation of quilters, but Jim Ferguson, speaking for his wife, declined the invitation. Sterling called the idea "tom-foolery." He said, in a huff, "Texas believes in law and order, and the womanhood of the state have shown themselves to be the foremost exponents of that principle." He added, "As Governor of Texas, I trust they will not be led astray by such a questionable proposal."[14] At mass meetings in Denison and Sherman, indignant citizens cheered Murray's name, and it was suggested that Grayson County secede from Texas and join Oklahoma. Finally, Murray took the boldest step of all. He declared martial law in the toll bridge area and dispatched thirty-five National Guardsmen from Durant to the scene. Adjutant Generals Charles Barrett of Oklahoma and W. W. Sterling were good friends. "I sent him word that the Texas end of the bridge was being held by four Rangers," General Sterling recalled. "If he was sending a brigade to open it, I would keep all four of them. If only a regiment was to be used, I would let a couple of the boys go home." Captain Hickman of the Rangers and Lt. Col. John McDonald of the Oklahoma Guard met midway on the free bridge for a brief talk. There were no hostilities; all the fighting was done in the newspapers. The Rangers maintained their vigil at the south end of the free bridge, spending a considerable part of their time on the bank of the river in target practice, while the Oklahoma troops were grouped at the north end of the nearby toll bridge to keep it closed.

On the night of July 23, Ross Sterling, seated at a table in the San Jacinto Inn near Houston, signed a bill hurriedly passed by the legislature that got Texas out of its legal snarl and enabled it to open its end of the free bridge. "It's all history now," said Governor Sterling as he signed the bill. The Rangers were called off their posts on July 25. Federal judge Colin Neblett in Muskogee, Oklahoma, declared that the bill passed by the Texas legislature offered the toll bridge company the legal means to settle its contract dispute, and he temporarily rescinded the injunction prohibiting the opening of the free bridge. At the same time, however, Neblett issued a restraining order prohibiting Oklahoma officials from interfering with the operation of the toll bridge. The judge said if Murray interfered with the injunction he would cite him for contempt of court.

Murray took umbrage at the injunction and defied it by personally taking command of the National Guard. On the evening of July 25 he showed up at the toll bridge packing an ancient horse pistol and ate liver and onions with some of the guardsmen. Murray said he would "hold the fort" in keeping the toll bridge closed. But the next day he changed his mind, saying: "If folks are fool enough to pay seventy-five cents to cross here, let 'em do it." The toll bridge could stay open as long as the free bridge was. However, on July 27 he changed his mind again, declared a second martial law zone around the free bridge, and posted sentries on both sides of the river to make sure it stayed open.

That just about wound up the Red River Bridge War. With both bridges open, all the business naturally went to the free bridge. Governor Sterling took no action on the presence of Oklahoma troops on the Texas side of the river. A Sherman lawyer warned him that "to again close the bridge would be met with almost universal indignation, and I doubt if level-headed people would be able to stem the tide."[15] On August 6 a federal district judge in Houston permanently dissolved the injunction against opening the free bridge, and a few days later the Oklahoma troops went home. There was peace along the border again. A later court ruling recognized the south bank of the Red River as Oklahoma's southern boundary.

Murray's use of troops to keep the free bridge open made the cantankerous governor a folk hero on both sides of the Red River. In Durant plans were made for a gigantic barbeque in Murray's honor. By the end of the summer a Murray for president movement had blossomed in Texas and Oklahoma, although his Bread, Butter, Bacon, and Beans campaign never got off the ground. "Stay in there and pitch," a Henderson man told Murray when "Oklahoma's man on horseback" made a triumphant visit to Dallas in August 1931. "I can't play pitch," Alfalfa Bill laughed, "but I'm the best bridge player in the country." On February 18, 1932, a reception was held for him at Collinsville in Grayson County. Murray had been born in the nearby hamlet of Toadsuck. There was a five-mile-long parade, after which a monument bearing Murray's likeness was unveiled.

On the other hand, Ross Sterling won few friends by using Texas Rangers to enforce the unpopular federal injunction. He was accused of favoring corporate interests over the people's. The fact that Sterling, as chairman of the Highway Commission, had signed the disputed contract with the toll bridge company did not help matters. Jim Ferguson made great sport with Sterling in the *Ferguson Forum*. He reprinted an editorial from the *Holland Progress*: "Now, if we had 'Ma' and 'Pa' in the governor's chair of Texas—a governor for the people and not corporations—what a relief we could rightly expect.... People would enjoy travelling on the state and national highways without being 'held up' at these toll bridges."[16]

Martial Law in the East Texas Oil Field

On October 5, 1930, an elderly wildcatter named Columbus Marion "Dad" Joiner discovered the giant East Texas Oil Field, one of the largest petroleum deposits in the world. His Daisy Bradford Number 3 well was near Henderson in Rusk County, forty miles north of Nacogdoches. Although Joiner's gusher precipitated the usual boom, it came nowhere near revealing the vastness of the reservoir that fed it. It first ran 52 barrels in seventeen minutes, but its full daily production only amounted to 226 barrels. Just after Christmas, Ed Bateman's Lou Della Crim Number 1 spouted oil in a little valley nine miles north of the Joiner well. Not quite a month later, on January 26, 1931, the Lathrop Number 1 near Longview blew in at 20,000 barrels a day before a cheering audience of 18,000 farmers and townsfolk. The Lathrop site was twenty-six miles north of the Daisy Bradford Number 3.

Geologists did not believe at first that the wells were drawing from the same pool. Heeding their advice, the major oil companies showed little interest in East Texas and permitted the wildcatters to move in, sinking wells and pumping oil as fast as they could with no regard for the consequences. The oil lay at an average depth of no more than 3,500 feet, and a well could be drilled for approximately $20,000. The majors soon saw their mistake, for subsequent drillings revealed that a single immense pool, the Woodbine formation, underlay Rusk, Gregg, Smith, Upshur, and Cherokee Counties. Forty-five miles long and from five to twelve miles wide, the field encompassed over 140,000 acres. Even after the field was a year old, the major oil companies owned less than 20 percent of the producing wells and proven acreage. Leases were in the hands of four thousand or more individuals and companies.[17]

On March 8, 1931, the *Dallas Morning News* carried a timely cartoon by John Knott. It bore the caption, "In the Wake of the Gold Rush." The sketch depicted a crowd of men headed for the new oil field in East Texas. Close on their heels was a large wolf branded with the word "Lawlessness." In the wake of the boom, tiny, dirt-poor communities were transformed forever. In less than a month Kilgore grew from a sleepy hamlet of seven hundred to a bustling city of ten thousand fortune hunters. Petty thievery, gambling, and prostitution were rampant. Texas Rangers, led by Sgt. M. T. "Lone Wolf" Gonzaullas, were ordered to clean up the town. Within two hours they had rounded up some three hundred suspects. The lawmen herded them down the main street into a Baptist church—Kilgore's jail was unfinished—and booked them from the pulpit. Forty were held for detention; the rest were hustled out of town. For almost a month arrests averaged one hundred a day.[18]

Gas and oil drilling raised problems concerning subsurface property rights, and the courts had come up with a solution. In 1889 the Pennsylvania Supreme Court had devised the "rule of capture." Analogizing gas and oil to a wild animal—a feral nature—that moved from one property to another, the court ruled that what was "captured" by a well belonged to the driller regardless of its effect on the pool under adjacent land. This principle resulted in an absurd amount of over-drilling. Anyone who did not drill a well on his or her own property was surrendering the oil beneath it to the neighbor who did. The more wells a person drilled, the more moving oil might be captured. This principle was responsible for the hasty drilling in the East Texas field; no one wanted someone else to get his oil. Buildings were torn down to make room for drilling rigs. Derricks were built so close together that their legs crossed. It was commonplace to drill two wells on the front and back half of a twenty-five-foot-wide city lot. One downtown block in Kilgore had 44 wells.

Eventually 31,000 wells would be drilled into the black giant. According to one estimate, ten to fifteen times as many wells were developed in the field as were needed to drain the pool. The overdrilling not only destroyed natural pressures; it also led to a glut of oil. Crude oil was dumped into open earthen pits to evaporate while the owner searched desperately for buyers. It ran bank-full in streams and a foot deep through the field in the Gladewater area.

But to the poverty-stricken residents of the area, the flood of oil was providential. The booming oil industry did much to ease the strain on unemployment rolls by creating new jobs for filling station operators, mechanics, oil drillers, truckers, and others. The discovery of oil fields affected directly such places as Kilgore, Midland, and Taylor, while opening new investment and sales territories for Dallas and Houston. "The church people of Kilgore look upon oil as the discovery of God's manna reserved to His children against a time of sore need," commented the *Dallas Morning News*. "Certain it is that much of East Texas would face a lean year indeed had it not been for the fruit of the driller's derrick."[19]

Under Texas law the Railroad Commission was charged with the super-

*East Texas Oil Field, derricks and buildings, undated. Verkin Photo Company
Collection, Briscoe Center for American History, University of Texas at Austin,
DI 02378.*

vision of the state's oil and gas. In 1917 the legislature declared that pipelines
were common carriers and placed them under the regulation of the commission. This act further empowered the commission to make such rules
as might be necessary to prevent the physical waste of oil and gas. In 1919
the legislature passed "An Act to Conserve the Oil and Gas Resources of the
State of Texas," which served as the basis for most of the regulation that followed. An Oil and Gas Division was organized under Dr. George C. Butte;
and on July 8, 1919, thirty-eight conservation rules were issued for the guid-
ance of oil operators. Perhaps the most famous of these was number thirty-
seven, which prohibited the drilling of a well within 300 feet of a completed
well (or of one being drilled) and ruled that wells could not be drilled within
150 feet of a property line.

A few days later the commission issued the first proration order, to be
effective in thirty days, in the Burkburnett oil field. This order, which grew
out of inadequate pipeline facilities in the area, provided that oil going into
pipelines would be distributed equitably among the field's producing wells.

In 1927 operators in the Yates field voluntarily made a prorationing agreement to limit production, which the Railroad Commission approved. Later it assumed the administration of the Yates field. The following year the commission ordered operators in the Hendricks field in Winkler County to limit production to 150,000 barrels daily, prorated to a formula giving equal weight to acreage and well potential. The revised statutes of 1929 added to the definition of waste, which the commission was empowered to prevent. It provided that "neither natural gas nor crude petroleum shall be produced, transported, stored or used in such manner of under such conditions as to constitute waste; provided, however, this shall not be construed to mean economic waste."[20]

The first commission order limiting Texas oil production statewide was issued on August 27, 1930, a little more than a month before Dad Joiner's discovery. It limited production to 750,000 barrels a day—a cut of 50,000 barrels a day from the 1929 average. The Danciger Oil and Refining Company of North Texas promptly challenged the commission's orders in the district court in Austin, filing an injunction suit on August 30. The company argued that the orders were not authorized by law since they had no reasonable relation to preventing physical waste but were concerned primarily with price fixing and with economic waste and were therefore specifically prohibited by the 1929 law. The company lost the suit. In February 1931 the court held that the orders were effective in preventing physical waste and that any effect on price was incidental. The company appealed to the Court of Civil Appeals, but a decision would not be forthcoming for some time.[21]

Some of the major oil companies appeared before the Railroad Commission early in 1931, urging it to extend its 1930 orders to the new East Texas field. R. R. Penn, chairman of the Texas Central Proration Committee, announced in Tyler on January 18 that "nominations" for all Texas oil fields, including East Texas, would be needed at least for a period between January 25 and April 1. "Crude oil will be selling at thirty cents a barrel if unprotected production is allowed to continue," he warned.[22]

On January 2, 1931, the Marion County Chamber of Commerce at Jefferson, well outside the limits of the new East Texas field, denounced proration as high-handed monopolistic interference with private property and warned the major oil companies to keep "hands off" of East Texas "in view of the fact that this section is just entering the possibilities of the largest oil field in the state." One week later Carl Estes, the fiery editor of the *Tyler Morning Telegraph* and the *Tyler Courier-Times*, blamed overseas imports for the glut on the market and called proration nothing more than a nefarious scheme by the majors to manipulate prices at the expense of independents and gasoline consumers.

At the first meeting of independent operators in Tyler, Senator Tom Pollard was appointed chairman. In turn, he appointed a committee representing both sides of the controversy to study the proration question. On January 21 a meeting between independent operators and the committee appointed by Pollard was held in the courthouse at Tyler, where a heated discussion of proration lasted more than five hours. Although a few sentiments were offered in favor of the basic theory of proration, the meeting as a whole was strongly against it. "We have just started in with our field here," thundered Judge Charles Brachfield of Henderson. "When other fields were turning out millions of barrels of oil nobody thought of proration. It certainly ought not to start here until our millions of barrels are developed." Brachfield asserted: "Operators have spent their money to try to develop this field; and, now, before we have shipped the first hundred thousand barrels, they want to stop us with proration!" Toward the end of the meeting, Carl Estes took the floor to offer a resolution requesting postponement of any form of proration in the new field for one year. The proposition was discussed at length. Finally, R. R. Penn promised that if Estes would withdraw his resolution, he would not ask for proration for the new field at the time. The resolution was withdrawn.[23]

Beginning February 3 and continuing for more than a week, oil operators, merchants, and land owners held a series of mass meetings in the East Texas field to discuss proration and to act to prevent it. In Kilgore 250 lease and royalty owners, independents, and merchants passed a strong resolution bitterly protesting any proration in the new field prior to the next proration period in April. They formed a permanent organization to oppose the measure. "We cannot expect any help from the governor of this state, who is the big chief in both the state and the Humble Oil & Refining Company, from whom R. R. Penn receives his instructions!" Dr. A. D. Lloyd bitterly declared. At Overton three hundred operators and lease and royalty owners organized the Lease & Royalty Owners' Association of Overton and passed a resolution requesting the Railroad Commission to refrain from proration in Rusk County until April. On the same day, the district court room at Henderson hosted a similar meeting. Those present organized the Henderson and Joinerville Lease and Royalty Owners' Association and requested that the commission refrain from proration in East Texas until April. Two days later Longview held a meeting with Carl Estes in the chair. He disclosed that his paper's poll so far had revealed a preponderance against any form of proration. On February 6 representatives of the various local operators and royalty and lease owners' organizations met at Longview and formed the East Texas Lease, Royalty & Producers' Association to coordinate the efforts of the local associations in the fight for a square deal for independents in the new field. Another group, the Proration Rules Committee of the Gregg and Rusk Counties Proration Advisory Committee, met in Longview and urged the Railroad Commission to call a hearing "as soon as possible" to prorate East Texas production in relation to market demand. In this group was H. L. Hunt, who with the purchase of Dad Joiner's five thousand acres had become one of the largest leaseholders in the field.[24]

On March 16, 1931, Governor Sterling proposed to the legislature that an appointive state conservation commission be created and that the Oil and Gas Division of the Railroad Commission be transferred to the new body. The governor attributed a break in the oil market on March 5 to the commission's failure to place East Texas under its conservation orders. He believed that because the Railroad Commission was an elective body, a majority of its members were unwilling to make an unpopular decision and were bidding for the favor of East Texas independents. "Find through reliable resources that favorable reaction[s] outweigh by far opposition of message," Paul Wakefield, one of the governor's secretaries, wired Sterling. "It is evident that the message will tend to show your administration just who it can depend on in future. One senses all through the Capitol today that a battle is brewing and the lines are being tightly drawn." Two of the commissioners, Chairman C. V. Terrell and Lon A. Smith, along with gas division supervisor R. D. Parker, had earlier issued a statement criticizing the governor's stand on the conservation of natural resources and inferring that he was influenced by special interests. However, the third commissioner, Pat Neff, commended Sterling for criticizing the commission's failure to conserve natural gas, saying 500 million cubic feet were being wasted daily in Texas.[25]

East Texas members of the legislature prepared to fight Sterling's conservation bill. Representative H. E. Lasseter of Henderson distributed a letter charging the governor with favoring a policy that benefited the large oil companies and hurt the small independent producers. Senators Pollard and Pink Parrish introduced a resolution in the senate calling for a complete investigation of proposed proration in the new field. The East Texas Lease, Royalty & Producers' Association retained Dan Moody, Judge Charles L. Harty, and Judge Edwin Lacy to try to prevent East Texas from being included in the Railroad Commission's next proration program, which was due to start on April 1. At a called meeting, the association expressed a willingness to accept proration if importation of foreign oil was reduced to 16 million barrels annually, a figure proposed in the Capper bill that was pending in Congress. "The great oil combines should not be permitted to crush the small independents—the men who made possible the great East Texas field!" shouted Carl Estes, amid loud approval. Plans were made for a "march on Austin" to protest proration when the subject came up for consideration before the Railroad Commission on March 24. The East Texas delegation traveled to the capital in thirteen Pullman cars.[26]

After a one-day postponement, the hearing before the commission got underway. Moody contended that all operators violated the state's antitrust laws when they prorated output prior to orders issued by the state. The independents argued that the only legal ground on which the state could prorate production was for the prevention of physical waste, and they claimed that the East Texas field was marketing without such waste. "Price has nothing to do with the state's right to prorate," Chairman Terrell declared in response to R. R. Penn's argument that without proration the price structure would collapse. The following day the Texas Central Proration Committee recommended an allowable of 50,000 barrels daily for the East Texas field and 656,058 barrels for the entire state. The allowable for the new pool would be increased by 5,000 barrels daily each month, beginning May 1, and would continue until an allowable of 70,000 barrels should be reached. Carl Estes protested vigorously against this recommendation: "The field probably already is making its fifty thousand barrels allowable on that basis, and new wells are coming every day. The little operators and land owners of East Texas will be heard from—in an emphatic way—if such an order goes into effect, even if you put us in jail and keep us there for forty years!" When three major oil companies operating in Texas announced their agreement to cut their oil imports, the East Texas delegation muttered that it was "a trick to get this recommendation through." The hearing came to a close on Saturday, March 29, when the commission refused to recess until the following Wednesday at the request of the independents.[27]

The following day Moody announced that East Texas would appeal to the courts for an injunction to restrain the application of proration in that section regardless of the amount of the allowable. Asked whether East Texas would accept an allowable of 100,000 barrels daily—double the figure recommended by the Central Proration Committee—he answered: "My clients will not accept that amount and their instructions are to enjoin any proration order made." The Railroad Commission issued an order on April 3 bringing East Texas under proration for the first time and fixing production as of April 10 at 90,000 barrels daily and gradually building up to 130,000 barrels on June 15. Moody and Estes then secured a temporary injunction from district judge J. D. Moore in Austin restraining the Railroad Commission from enforcing its 90,000-barrel proration order in Smith, Rusk, and Gregg Counties.[28]

The relief obtained by the independents through the injunction was short-lived. On April 13 Assistant Attorney General Fred Upchurch ruled that the order obtained by Moody and Estes applied only to a single tract of land embracing seventy-two acres owned by Estes; the Railroad Commission then announced that it would be ready within a few days to start prorating. After much dickering and delay, proration finally started on May 1. The allowable was upped to 160,000 barrels, divided between the three main sections of the East Texas field as follows: Joiner, 65,000; Bateman, 60,000; and Lathrop, 35,000. These figures represented a compromise between the commission and representatives of the independents, and the latter looked upon the proration order as a sort of truce. Wells were allowed to pump from 260 to 570 barrels a day, depending on potential and location.[29]

In the meantime Representative Andrew M. Howsley introduced a bill providing for the further regulation of oil production in East Texas and giving the Railroad Commission greater power to enforce its regulations. Estes sent a "call to arms" to members of the East Texas Lease, Royalty & Producers' Association and all independents in the field to go to Austin to fight against the measure. The Tyler Chamber of Commerce wired its protest. On May 11 a mass meeting in Tyler denounced the measure. The bill was reported favorably out of committee, and a petition drive in East Texas on its behalf almost pushed the measure through the house. Estes, Cone Johnson, Colonel T. N. Jones, and Earle B. Mayfield, who were representing the independents, heard of the petition and sent scores of telegrams warning citizens not to sign it. The Howsley bill died on the last day of the regular session when the house voted to suspend the rules and pass uncontested legislation during the last hours of the session. Even then proponents of the bill had the house clock set back two hours to prevent adjournment at the legal hour of midnight, but to no avail.[30]

The legislature also refused to pass Sterling's state conservation commission bill and adopted instead a proposal calling for the creation of a study commission. The commission held two meetings, one in April and one in May, but it offered no constructive plan. As soon as the regular session ended, there was talk of a special session to deal with the oil situation. The Wichita Falls and Graham chambers of commerce, several Fort Worth bankers, and Amon Carter, publisher of the *Fort Worth Star-Telegram*, asked Sterling to call one. Hugh Roy Cullen of Houston argued against a special session, saying that "the only thing that will control the oil industry is supply and demand." When asked for his opinion, Senator Tom Pollard said: "Oil ills can be best dealt with only by the U.S. Congress limiting imports." A few days later he told the *Dallas Morning News*: "The present state of affairs is due to depressed market conditions of the world and the importation of foreign oil from Mexico, Venezuela and Russia. Neither of these conditions could be remedied by an act of the Texas Legislature." Sterling could best serve the people of Texas by influencing the U.S. treasury secretary to suggest to President Hoover that Congress be called into special session "to place an effective embargo which will close the great flood gates of foreign oil which is pouring into this country."[31]

By this time even those most rabidly against proration realized that some sort of control in the new field was inevitable. The East Texas Chamber of Commerce, meeting in convention at Marlin, adopted a resolution favoring some form of proration, and its action represented a turning point in the attitude of many people toward the idea. A group of independents headed by Charles Roeser and Ed Landreth formed the Texas Oil Emergency Committee to pressure the governor into calling a special session to enact a stronger conservation law. The RoeserLandreth group argued that proration orders focused solely on the prevention of physical waste could not possibly restore the industry to health and called for proration to address market demand. Tom E. Cranfill, the president of the Independent Producers' Association of Texas, proposed a "voluntary" 300-barrel per well and twenty-acre unit production plan for all the state's flush fields. The proposal would allow East Texas about 250,000 barrels daily.

Estes and the East Texas organization agreed to give the plan a fair trial. Sterling issued a plea to operators on behalf of the plan, but many independents suspected the governor of favoring the large companies. The mere fact that he asked them to follow the Cranfill plan alienated many independents. Moreover, the governor indicated publicly that he did not look forward to any degree of success through the plan. "If it works it would be fine and it should be tried out," he said, but he pointed out that there was no restraint on violations of the agreement. He also doubted if all operators would agree to it.

On Saturday morning, June 20, all East Texas wells theoretically choked down to an average of three hundred barrels daily. Many of the freewheeling operators actually obeyed the agreement, but others preferred to follow the

Railroad Commission's proration order. Still others ignored both the Cranfill plan and the Railroad Commission. The chaotic situation showed little improvement. "East Texas looks over a troubled oil sea and is apparently unable to agree on what raft to trust itself," editorialized the *Dallas Morning News*. "Governor Sterling, however, has the right idea. Temporary measures will not be useful. A permanent policy preferably directed by law is a better solution than cure-alls that only promise to cure."

The Cranfill plan had been operating for less than a week when the major oil companies that were still taking East Texas crude posted prices of twenty cents a barrel. There was practically no market at that price. By July the price of oil had dropped to ten cents a barrel (compared to three dollars a barrel in 1919). A speakeasy on the Texas-Louisiana border advertised beer at "10 cents a glass or one barrel of oil." Two members of the Railroad Commission, Terrell and Smith, passed a proration order on July 3 allowing 250,000 barrels daily, to be distributed equally over the East Texas field under the Cranfill twenty-acre-unit plan. Actual production on June 27 was 359,000 barrels daily, according to reports to the commission. The 250,000-barrel flat allowable would remain in force for the months of July, August, and September, "unless sooner modified or changed," but in no event would the 250,000-barrel allowable be changed prior to August 1. "The entire hearing was under the direct supervision of attorneys whose compensation for services rendered was paid by the oil companies sought to be regulated," charged Pat Neff. "Considering the background of this order, the manner of its making, the uncertainty of the meaning, the inequities in its provisions and knowing full well that no effect will be made by the Railroad Commission to enforce it, I do not desire that my name be signed to it." However, at a mass meeting in Tyler on July 7, East Texas operators agreed to give the commission's new proration order a fair trial. They stressed they preferred the Cranfill plan and intended requesting its reinstatement if the commission's order did not work out satisfactorily.[32]

When the price of oil dropped to ten cents a barrel, Sterling called the legislature into special session on July 14 to consider laws adequate to conserve the state's natural resources. Production in the East Texas field averaged 408,786 barrels daily for the week ending July 15—a new record. This brought the total production from East Texas to approximately 30 million barrels. "A grave crisis confronts the State of Texas in the conservation of its natural resources," Sterling stated solemnly in an address to a joint session of the house and senate. "The earth's reservoirs of oil and gas are being drained and virtually thrown away, and an enormous underground waste is resulting from the orgy of disorderly production." He urged that the legislators immediately set to work to devise means of regulating production in the East Texas field to eliminate oil waste. "I don't want pricefixing," the governor told the senate in a special message on July 22. "If the necessary laws are passed to enforce orderly production, prices will come back of themselves, to something like a dollar a barrel."

The administration's oil and gas conservation bills, prepared by Senator Walter Woodward and Representatives R. M. Wagstaff, Alfred Petsch, and A. P. Johnson, created an appointive conservation commission with greatly enlarged enforcement powers; the bills redefined physical waste but omitted any mention of economic waste due to an excess of production over market demand. As planned by Sterling, the commission would consist of three members not less than thirty years old: a petroleum engineer, a lawyer with experience in oil practice, and a practical oilman of at least five years' experience. The salary would be $6,000, and the first appointments would be for two, four, and six years, with all future reappointments for six years.[33]

Jim Ferguson chimed in with a proposal for a graduated tax on oil production. "Tax daily production only one cent a barrel up to 300 barrels and these small owners of small wells will save their small wells and the land and royalty owners upon which they are located will save their investment," he wrote in the *Forum*. "Then tax the next 200 barrels 10 cents a barrel and oil people will begin to look around for a small well to invest in. Then to clinch the thing just tax the next 500 barrels 25 cents a barrel and we won't hear any more about overproduction." If the legislature would pass this tax law and implement a graduated tax on cotton to make the raising of cotton by "land barons and corporation big machinery farming" unprofitable, Ferguson promised to help pass the redistricting bill and the bill establishing Sterling's conservation commission, as well as proposed amendments to the present proration law. With tongue firmly in cheek, Jim also promised "to sign a petition to ask the governor to appoint Dan Moody, Tom Love and Jesse Jones for the commission and will ask my friends in the senate to vote for their confirmation, and after the governor appoints them or anybody else I will begin to support him for re-election and ask all my friends throughout Texas to do likewise."[34]

On July 28 a federal district court decision in the MacMillan case invalidated the Railroad Commission's April order on the grounds that it was directed against the loss of market price and was based on unsound engineering concepts.[35] Despite the fact that he wanted a workable law and despite the fact that he was accused of playing ball with the major oil companies, Sterling announced that he would veto any law that authorized the consideration of market demand, the very thing the majors most wanted, as the federal court had outlawed this device. On August 7 both houses killed the conservation commission. "It's not my funeral," was the governor's only comment. "I can only recommend. It's up to the Legislature to legislate." The vote in the senate was 17 to 11, in the house 79 to 53. In both chambers, but especially in the house, the idea of an appointive commission was thought to be undemocratic. In addition, a deal that Sterling had made with Smith and Terrell for them to support the legislation in exchange for receiving the chairmanships of the new and old commissions blew up when Neff criticized his two colleagues at the legislative hearings and they spent their time on the stand defending themselves—and by implication the Railroad Commission. It appeared to the lawmakers that the three men could not agree among themselves on what legislation was needed.

The house passed a bill that applied a graduated tax on oil: one cent per barrel up to and including five barrels; one and a half cents up to twenty barrels; two cents up to forty barrels; three cents up to one hundred barrels; four cents up to one thousand barrels; and six cents per barrel for all production over that figure. The senate killed the measure by refusing, 12 to 11, to adopt the minority report from the State Affairs Committee. Near the end of the session a conference committee worked out a weak bill, adopted overwhelmingly by both houses, prohibiting all types of physical waste but specifically forbidding the Railroad Commission to limit production to market demand. The commission was required, moreover, to post a ten-days' notice and then to hold public hearings before issuing proration orders. Asked if the bill dispelled any possibility of martial law in East Texas or the convening of another session, Sterling replied that he "would have to wait and see."[36]

Oil was now flowing at a rate of one million barrels a day in East Texas—enough to meet one-third of the nation's crude oil requirements. One day while discussing the Ranger cleanup drive in Kilgore with Adjutant General Sterling, the governor said:

> It looks like I am going to be forced to take a hand in that mess over there. One of my responsibilities is to conserve the natural resources of the state. They must be saved for future generations. I am not going to allow a bunch of reckless operators to waste them. Landowners are being cheated out of their royalties, and are threatening to take the law

into their own hands. If the commission is powerless to put a stop to that kind of abuse, I am going to do it with martial law.[37]

Governor Murray of Oklahoma was also confronted by overproduction and a market decline, and on August 4 he declared martial law for a distance of fifty feet around each well and closed down his state's oil fields with troops. On August 5 he telegraphed Sterling: "I trust you may see your way clear to join me in shutting down all flush wells in Texas, which beyond a doubt would bring the desired results." Sterling replied that Texas was not in a position to follow Oklahoma's lead in shutting down flush oil wells. "Our Legislature is making splendid headway today in passing conservation laws," he declared. "I am sure that our Legislature is going to pass the necessary measures to correct our deplorable condition." This was two days before the house and senate killed the conservation commission bill. On August 10 Sterling, forsaking his hands-off policy, issued a statement saying that many citizens felt that the state's conservation laws were being "trampled under foot," and they were asking him to use the militia to protect them. "I sincerely trust it will not be necessary to do this, but that the Legislature will meet the occasion," he stated bluntly. Conjecture was rife at the capitol as to whether the governor intended to follow Murray's example. Sterling's statement did not say how far he would go in responding to the citizens' requests, and when asked directly, he curtly told newspapermen to "use his statement as he had written it." However, the next day he said that if martial law was declared, it would not be done until after the legislature ended its special session, when he had the opportunity to measure the results. "I want it plainly understood," he added pointedly, "that I will not call the Legislature back if a conservation measure is passed."[38]

"I think that everything should be done in an orderly manner to uphold the law and the orders of the Railroad Commission," Sterling said in a telegram to a mass-meeting of East Texas oilmen in Tyler on August 14. "The men engaged in the oil business are as intelligent as the average business men in the other lines of endeavor and it does appear to me that they should discontinue their grand scramble which is resulting in drowning themselves in oil as well as dissipating and destroying the heritage of the land and royalty owners of East Texas." The meeting petitioned the governor to impose martial law and shut down oil production completely before and during a reasonable period necessary to put proration into effect under the new law. This was a surprising resolution to come out of East Texas. More surprising still, it was signed by the East Texas Lease, Royalty & Producers' Association. It represented the first vital breach in the ranks of East Texas independents. Sterling also received a petition signed by twelve hundred oil producers and royalty owners in East Texas likewise requesting him to issue an order shutting down the production of all oil and gas wells in Smith, Rusk, Upshur, and Gregg Counties and to declare martial law to enforce his order.[39]

Faced with this industry appeal to end the orgy of waste and in answer to a confirming report from special observer Ray Dudley, whom he had dispatched to the scene, Sterling made a hasty decision on the morning of August 15, 1931, to put the East Texas field under martial law to enforce proration. He did not consult the Railroad Commission. Chairman Terrell, for one, did not think the action was legal. Sterling believed the production of oil in excess of the maximum allowed by the commission was wasteful and immoral. In the words of his biographer, Warner E. Mills Jr., "The key to Sterling's use of martial law lies in his confusion of policy and law and morality and law."

On the night of August 15, Sterling summoned Adjutant General William Sterling to his capitol office for a conference. Assistant Adjutant General Horace H. Carmichael was also present. The group worked out the details of martial law. The governor asked what branch of the National Guard should be used and was told the cavalry. Mounted men were best for any kind of semipolice duty, he was told, and patrolling the muddy oil fields could best be done on horseback. One hospital unit and one ambulance unit would also be needed. The adjutant general requested the governor let him command the troops. "I can't do that, Bill," the governor replied. "General Jacob F. Wolters is an authority on martial law and has written two books on the subject. I am going to place him in charge. It would break old Jake's heart to be left out of this campaign. Governor Murray of Oklahoma has put Cicero Murray in charge of the troops up there. Although we are not related, if Bill Sterling was in command during martial law people will think it is a family affair."

The governor's proclamation, released on August 17, cited the state's policy of conservation as found in the Texas constitution and state law. Sterling said that the facts, as presented to him, pointed to the existence in East Texas of "an organized and entrenched group of crude petroleum oil and natural gas producers ... who are in a state of insurrection against the conservation laws of the State ... and are in open rebellion against the efforts of the constituted civil authorities in this State to enforce such laws." He asserted that these conditions had angered citizens in the oil district and provoked threats that they would enforce the conservation laws if the state did not. The situation amounted to a state of insurrection, tumult, riot, and breach of the peace and there was now imminent danger that this condition would be extended.[40]

Shortly after Sterling's proclamation was made public, 1,203 troops of the Texas National Guard's 112th Cavalry Brigade moved into four counties in East Texas and shut down all the wells. "What is the meaning of all these soldiers?" a stranger inquired of a Gregg County resident, who replied: "They mean dollar oil." General Wolters established his headquarters at "Proration Hill" near Kilgore. "Companies shutting down rapidly," he wired Sterling. "Sinclair shutting down. Expressing desire to cooperate." On August 21 Wolters denied a group of unemployed oil field workers permission to hold a protest meeting in Tyler.

"Allow no well to produce any oil until specifically ordered to do so by the Governor of Texas," Sterling wired Wolters on September 1. The governor's action confirmed the suspicions of many East Texans that he was partial to the major oil companies. Wolters was the chief attorney for the Texas Company (also known as Texaco), and Walter Pryon, one of his colonels, was a production official for the Gulf Oil Company. One legislator remarked that "the governor proposes to take East Texas out of the hands of the civil authorities and put in the hands of the Texaco Company." Martial law brought this angry reaction from the *Gladewater Journal*: "Governor Sterling is proving himself even more to be dreaded than E. J. Davis, the carpet bag Governor who locked his legislature up until they passed a law justifying his proclaiming martial law whenever his whims dictated.... Ross Sterling is a greater enemy to Texas than E. J. Davis, his prototype."[41]

Jim Ferguson charged that Sterling's action had been taken at the insistence of the big oil companies. "The East Texas field was the small independents' field," he declared. "This field is looked upon as the poor man's brake [break] that he never had before and to shut him off with the threat of shot and shell from a peaceful occupation is looked upon by not only these small operators and their friends, but by the great overwhelming majority of the people of Texas as poor sportsmanship, and an inexcusable crime against personal liberty and private property."[42]

However, Mayor J. Malcolm Crim of Kilgore, the Kilgore Chamber of Commerce, the Kilgore Lions Club, and Harold G. Anthony, the editor of the *Kilgore Daily News*, commended Sterling on his imposition of martial law and pledged to cooperate in every way possible. According to the governor, out of several thousand telegrams and letters he had received, only seven had disapproved of his action. One of the seven was from Houston banker R. M. Farrar, who wrote: "When I read of your action I recalled the headlines of the story on Hidalgo County in Colliers a year or two ago—'HIGH HANDED AND HELL BENT'—and I am wondering if the large majority of citizens do not, in fact, feel likewise."[43]

"Governor Sterling has taken a popular step," admitted the *Dallas Morning News.* "Its freedom from risk has been pointed out by the more precipitate Governor of Oklahoma." Their concerted shutdown in the oil fields displayed a new tendency to cut through red tape to get results. "In shearing through it, executive sword wielders should exercise care not to injure the contents," the paper warned. "The present precedent is dangerous."[44]

Martial law ostensibly was declared to prevent riots and insurrections from people who objected to having the wells run wide open. In reality it was intended to control the flow of oil from East Texas until the Railroad Commission could act; afterwards it was left in force to carry out proration orders. The East Texas field was reopened on September 5 under an order permitting a flow of 225 barrels daily (supposedly until October 31) from each of the more than 1,800 wells in the field. But on September 18 the allowable on each East Texas well was reduced to 185 barrels, and on October 13 it declined to just 165 barrels. Crude oil prices advanced over the next few months from 24 cents a barrel in the week ending August 21, 1931, to 67 cents a barrel in the week ending March 12, 1932. It had been as low as 5 cents a barrel.

Sterling's resolute action had at least prevented total anarchy, but the price jump that resulted from his shutdown encouraged the production of "hot oil," the name coined for crude produced illegally on the sly. Every kind of subterfuge was employed. A "hot oil" operator might tap into someone else's flow line or put a secret bypass on his own. He might install a "lefthand" valve so that when the troopers turned the pump off and padlocked it, they were actually sealing it open. A Gladewater producer built a concrete blockhouse around his well to confound the soldiers. In one instance a state gauger found that a steel stairway had been cut away from a 55,000 barrel storage tank so that he could not measure its contents. In New London the "Tower of London" arose when Tom C. Patten erected a penthouse over his derrick, registered it as his homestead, and pulled up the portable electric staircase when the authorities appeared. Railroad Commission employees were repeatedly turned away from the small refinery plants in the field with shotguns and threats of violence.[45]

The second special session of the forty-second legislature considered a bill to give the state an income from wells drilled in the beds of navigable streams in proven oil territory, especially the Sabine River, which meandered for nine miles through the East Texas field. Private interests were obtaining this oil by drilling up to the banks of the Sabine. According to Sterling twenty million barrels of oil that belonged to Texas lay beneath the river and should be recovered for the state's benefit. "It looks to me as though it will put the State in the oil business, and that you will put me in the oil business for the State," he remarked, and added, "I don't think I have forgotten how to drill a well." When the streambed bill was killed because of the twenty-four-hour rule at the end of the session (Senator Margie E. Neal having talked it to death), Sterling charged that the oil lobby was largely responsible. Senators Joe M. Moore and T. A. Deberry affirmed that there was an oil lobby in Austin and that a glance at the "sidelines" any day of the session would disclose its personnel.

The irate governor persuaded the lawmakers to postpone final adjournment by threatening to call another special session immediately. At that juncture a free conference committee worked out the minor differences in the streambed bill passed by the two houses. "I think it very important if it can be done that one hundred votes be secured adopting the Free Conference Report on the leasing of the River beds," Sterling wrote Speaker Fred Minor. "You realize that ninety days' delay will be expensive to the State." However, there were only 86 yes votes in the house to 29 nays. The senate voted in favor 20 to 6. Still, it was Sterling's most notable victory of the session. Although no executive order could be issued until January 1, 1932, he asked that negotiations start immediately for the sale or recovery of the oil beneath the Sabine.[46]

Independent oil operators accused the major oil companies of violating Texas's antitrust laws in order to put them out of business. The legislature decided, after holding hearings, that certain monopolistic practices probably existed in the oil industry. Sterling himself was summoned before the house probers to explain a contract he made with the Humble Oil Company in January 1930, when he and two partners received $175,000 from the company as part of the lease contract for oil and $225,000 advance royalties for oil on a fifteen-hundred-acre lease that had one well on it that was subsequently shut in. At the first special session, both houses passed by overwhelming majorities a resolution directing Attorney General James Allred to seek evidence of oil company conspiracies and to bring suit against any violations of the state's antitrust laws. Sterling added his unqualified endorsement. Thirty thousand dollars was appropriated to finance the investigation.[47]

After completing his investigation, Allred filed a quo warranto suit in district court on November 12, 1931, against seventeen major oil companies. He accused them of violating the state's antitrust laws, of systematically monopolizing the distribution of oil, and of conspiring to fix prices on gasoline, oil, and service station equipment. By way of penalties he demanded the forfeiture of eleven Texas oil corporation charters, the cancellation of nonresident permits for four out-of-state holding companies, and the dissolution of the American Petroleum Institute and its regional council, the Texas Petroleum Marketers Association. Fines for each day of violation since 1929—a maximum of $17,850,000—were sought.

Predictably the oil companies and their business supporters were outraged. Humble announced that it would lay off five thousand men in Houston and cancel contemplated plant expansion. Ray Leeman, manager of the South Texas Chamber of Commerce, predicted that the suit would result in the unemployment of twenty-five thousand men and a loss of half a million dollars from the state's tax base. The *Fort Worth Star-Telegram* editorialized that Allred had selected the worst possible time to "rock the economic boat." But the independent operators were pleased with the attorney general's action. On December 16, 1931, the Independent Petroleum Association of Texas met in Dallas and endorsed the state's antitrust laws and Allred's suit against the majors. "I have no doubt but what you will win in this fight," Allred's close friend and former law partner, Bernard Martin, wrote him.

> I was delighted to see in the paper yesterday that some of the independent oil men have come out openly approving your fight against those violating the anti-trust laws. As time goes on, I think it the duty of these real honest-to-God independent oil companies to take a greater stand openly in the press against the major oil companies. Since you have started the fight in their behalf, as well as in behalf of all the people they ought to no longer be afraid to stand up for their own rights and they should gladly seize the opportunity to defend the officers who are seeking to enforce the anti-trust laws.[48]

Privately Allred complained that most of the big papers in the state had taken an "unfair attitude" about the suit by asserting that he had sued the companies on a "technical" violation of the law. "I assure you there is nothing technical about this suit," he wrote the editor of the *Houston Press*, "and

I believe, when the matter comes before the court, that any newspaper of any chamber of commerce will have some difficulty defending the practices of these oil companies." Still, he told his brother Rene in early January 1932 that "we are getting along in pretty good shape. Of course I could expect dilatory tactics to be employed, but I am feeling mighty good about everything." However, the case dragged on. The litigants argued more than seventy points of law, accumulated hundreds of depositions, and amassed the most voluminous court record in Texas history.

When the National Industrial Recovery Act (NIRA)—one of FDR's short-lived attempts to stabilize the economy by suspending antitrust laws and making price- and wage-fixing legal—became law in 1933, the trial judge, J. D. Moore, dismissed Allred's suit on the grounds that the NIRA superseded the Texas antitrust laws. Conceding that the decision had left him "stunned" and "groggy," Allred in December 1933 appealed to the Court of Civil Appeals, which in April 1935 not only upheld Judge Moore's opinion but ruled that the state's antitrust laws were unconstitutional! (Allred was elected governor before this decision was reached.) In June 1937 the Texas Supreme Court sustained the constitutionality of the antitrust laws and the case was sent back to the trial court. Not until 1938 did Attorney General William McCraw reach an out-of-court settlement with the seventeen companies.[49]

Martial Law Comes to an End

Meanwhile, on October 13, 1931, Eugene Constantin, J. D. Wrather, and the Brock-Lee Oil Company brought a suit in the U.S. District Court for the Eastern District of Texas at Tyler for an injunction to halt temporarily the enforcement of proration orders for their wells. In granting the injunction, Judge Randolph Bryant ruled that Sterling had exceeded his authority in declaring martial law initially and that he had been without warrant of law in interfering with and depriving the plaintiffs of their right to operate their properties in a prudent way.

Sterling defied the court's injunction. He declared that the "principle of State rights is involved and the Federal Court will not be permitted to throttle the will of the people. This is the State's affair and Federal Courts should let the State take care of it." When he was asked what he would do were a federal court to order its marshal to open the wells, he replied: "I guess I have more men than they do." The governor ordered Wolters verbally not to permit any well in the military district to produce more than 165 barrels a day and to shut down any well producing over that amount. The same day he sent a written order confirming his verbal command. For legal aid he turned to Dan Moody, Edgar F. Smith, and Paul D. Page Jr. The plaintiffs were represented by Luther Nickels and Joseph W. Bailey Jr., both of Dallas.

On February 18, 1932, a special three-judge federal court at Beaumont ruled in the case of *Constantin v. Smith* that Sterling had exceeded his authority in declaring martial law, and pending the final disposition of the case the governor and the military must be enjoined from interfering with the plaintiff's properties. Sterling angrily instructed Wolters to continue martial law except on the Constantin and Wrather leases. (The Brock-Lee Oil Company quit the suit before it went to trial.) Carl Estes wired the governor to keep soldiers in the field to preserve peace.

Moody and Edgar Smith went to Washington to obtain an order from Supreme Court justice Louis Brandeis staying the injunction until they could carry an appeal to the Supreme Court, but Brandeis refused to grant a stay. On February 29 Moody and Smith filed an appeal on behalf of Sterling and other state officials with the Supreme Court. "I believe that we have the situation in the East Texas field well in hand since the Railroad Commission is co-operating 100% with me," Sterling wrote.

> I have not the least doubt but what the Supreme Court will hold that a chief executive has a perfect and constitutional right to use the military forces to enforce the law and that his findings as to whether it is necessary or not cannot be inquired into by any court during the term of martial law. The Railroad Commission admits that they are powerless to cope with the situation as it now exists on account of their not having sufficient force to handle such a vast area. General Wolters tells me that he and his men are going day and night and they are pretty well worn out.[50]

The end of martial law came rapidly. Other producers began applying for injunctions in Judge Bryant's court. Bryant speedily granted these petitions as well as those already on file. As each was granted, Sterling was required to remove the troops from the properties of those receiving injunction relief. The effect was to transfer jurisdiction of the wells back to the Railroad Commission. In June 1932 Commissioner Pat Neff resigned to become president of Baylor University. Sterling persuaded Ernest O. Thompson, who had made a record battling the utilities as mayor of Amarillo, to take an interim appointment and to announce for election to the office in the upcoming Democratic primary. According to Sterling's recollection, Thompson declared: "Governor, I can eat that job up." He stayed for thirty-two years, until his retirement in 1965.[51]

Texas oil operators now filed suits against the Railroad Commission charging that under the 1931 act it did not have the power to allocate production allowables in relation to market demands. Many operators again went ahead to indulge in an unrestrained production spree, encouraged by the Federal District Court for East Texas, which on October 24, 1932, in its ruling on the Peoples' Petroleum Producers suit, enjoined the Railroad Commission from enforcing its proration orders. Sterling at first resisted calls from oil producers for another special session. "At this time ... I am not at all sure that it would be the right thing to call the Legislature together," he wrote on October 27, "as I have serious doubt as to whether they would pass any corrective legislation within a reasonable time, and besides it is so near the time of the regular session. Of course the majority of the oil people are clamoring for a special session of the legislature. They are so easily excited these days, and sometimes without proper cause for excitement."[52]

However, Sterling shortly changed his mind and called the legislature into session on November 3 to enact a market-demand proration law. "I could not afford not to call another session, knowing as I do what would take place if something is not done to correct the situation," he explained. "If the Legislature does not pass a law to correct the defects in the present law, the responsibility will be theirs, not mine." The harrowing experience of the past year had had a sobering effect. With a minimum of debate the lawmakers passed the Market Demand Act, which authorized the Railroad Commission to consider market demand in prorating oil production. The act defined "waste" as any oil production in excess of what transportation or market facilities could absorb.[53]

In December 1932 the U.S. Supreme Court through Chief Justice Oliver Wendell Holmes affirmed the judgment of the lower federal courts in *Sterling v. Constantin*. The court said that the fiat of the governor could not supersede the U.S. Constitution as the supreme law of the land. "Martial law is a dangerous as well as a costly weapon," declared the *Dallas Morning News* sternly. "Democracies do not trust its coercive force and their orderly institutions. The Supreme Court decision is a merited rebuke of abuse of power conferred by the electorate that applies to other executives than the well-motivated Governor of this State."[54]

The East Texas field was again thrown in turmoil as oil prices skidded. Hundreds of wells were running wide open and crude was being offered at twenty-five cents a barrel. On December 17 the Railroad Commission ordered both production and transportation shut down in the East Texas field until January 1, 1933, ostensibly to permit the gauging of wells to determine accurate bottom-hole pressure. In March the commission again closed the East Texas field for two weeks to take bottom-hole pressures and check the findings against the first shutdowns. The commission's proration order of April 22, 1933, based on a well's potential (to be determined by key wells) was the first order upheld in federal court and gave the commission legal standing at last. Ernest Thompson complained that the commission had been thrown out of court 212 times before it got a valid order and that he himself had been enjoined seven times in one day between the capitol and the Driskill Hotel, where a statewide hearing was scheduled.

The petroleum code of NIRA, which gave the president and the Interstate Commerce Commission the power to regulate the transportation and pricing of petroleum, brought more order to the East Texas field in the fall of 1933.[55] In February 1934 the legislature enacted a refinery control bill, requiring all refineries in the state to report the sources of oil that they processed. East Texas refiners bitterly opposed the measure and staged a demonstration at Austin to influence Gov. Miriam Ferguson (in her second term of office, 1933–1935) against signing it, but in this they failed. By the mid-1930s the Market Demand Act, the Refinery and Tender Act, and other legislation had allowed the Railroad Commission to take control of the once rampaging output. By 1938 more than 80 percent of the field had been brought under the domination of the major companies, and by 1941 only three independents were left in East Texas. In retrospect, Sterling commented: "I have no apology for martial law in East Texas. It saved the state $6,000,000 in taxes, and it saved the people of Texas $40,000,000 in the value of their products." But Warner E. Mills Jr. concludes that while Sterling's declaration of martial law held down East Texas production to a rational figure for six months, it also delayed for that period a court test of the conservation act of 1931 and hence postponed the day when the act had to be changed. "His control of East Texas affairs could be best characterized as wooden, and he himself came close to ruining the price structure of the industry."[56]

A Cotton Holiday, or Washing the Baby

In addition to the troubles brought about by the oil glut, the low price of cotton caused problems for the Sterling administration. Governor Moody had proposed a "buy a bale" campaign in 1930, which asked Texas business-men to buy cotton and hold it until the price rose, but there were entirely too many bales and the campaign was abortive. In 1930, in the fourth called session of the forty-first legislature, lawmakers recommended that cotton acreage be reduced at least 30 percent. Later that year a call went out for a special session to pass a cotton acreage reduction law, but Moody refused to act, saying such a law would be of no benefit unless similar measures were passed by the other cotton-producing states.

Late in the summer of 1931 farmers were receiving 5.5 cents a pound for middling cotton. A farmer who borrowed money in 1928 now needed three times as much cotton to repay his obligation as the loan had represented when it was made. Acting under a resolution adopted by both houses of the legislature on July 28, 1931, Sterling invited the governors of fifteen cotton states to attend a conference in Austin on August 4 to consider possible "national and international co-ordinated action" on the cotton situation. The response was limited: only five other states besides Texas were repre-sented—Oklahoma, Louisiana, Arkansas, Tennessee, and New Mexico. The delegates recognized the dependence of the cotton farmer on European con-ditions and endorsed a proposal to restrict cotton acreage by law and to unite the South in a program of industrial development. The representatives from the other states declared that if Texas would take the lead and enact a cotton acreage control law, their state governments would do likewise.[57]

However, it was Governor Huey Long of Louisiana who took the initia-tive, suggesting that all cotton-growing states should enact legislation for-bidding the planting of cotton in 1932. He sent telegrams to the governors and other officials of seven cotton states, inviting them to meet with him in New Orleans on August 21 to discuss ways to implement the plan. Only the governors of Arkansas and South Carolina accepted the invitation; the other five sent representatives or regrets. Sterling named Commissioner of Agri-culture J. E. McDonald to represent Texas. "You may say to the conference for me that I am willing and ready to do everything I can toward helping the great cotton industry of the South and I wish you much success in your meeting," Sterling wired Long. At Long's urging the delegates approved a resolution recommending the moratorium to their states, provided that the plan was adopted by states producing three-fourths of the total American cotton supply. The proviso was aimed chiefly at Texas, which produced more than a fourth of the crop. Sterling, on being informed of the conference's action, said he would not convene the legislature in special session to consider the cotton question until he was sure the people wanted such action, and he was asking for their opinions on Long's plan. He indicated that Texas had no intention of passing the first moratorium law. "Well, that is Huey's baby," he said. "Let him wash it first."[58]

"We'll be glad to wash the baby first," Long responded. He wired Sterling: "All right old boy we are getting ready to start out to wash the baby and dress it. It will be on your desk and yell 'da da' before the week's out." Summoning the Louisiana legislature into special session—the "wash the baby session"—Huey urged the lawmakers to enact his plan. The bill, with a proviso that the governor was authorized to suspend the law's operation if states producing three-fourths of the cotton crop did not enact similar legislation, won unanimous approval in both chambers. Although it was nearly midnight, the measure was rushed to the executive mansion for Long to sign. He received it in his bedroom, wearing a cotton nightshirt he had bought for the ceremony. Before retiring, he instructed his chief lieutenant, O. K. Allen, to charter a plane and take a copy of the act, bound with blue ribbon, to Sterling. On the yellow cover, Long wrote in green ink:

Dear Governor Sterling and Texas Legislature:
Adopt this baby and it will save Texas and the farmers of the South.
Huey P. Long
Governor—U.S. Senator-elect, Chairman, Cotton States Conference

In Austin, Allen learned that Sterling had gone to Houston for the weekend. With Commissioner of Agriculture McDonald in tow, he went on to Houston and caught Sterling in the airport. Handing the act to the governor, Allen said: "Here is Governor Long's baby, all washed, powdered, and wrapped in a cotton dress." Sterling's only comment was, "That is up to the legislature. I'll have more to say after conferring with legislators."[59]

Sterling was swamped with replies to his request for advice on a special session and Long's plan. On September 1 the *Galveston Daily News* reported that 52,693 persons had declared in favor of a special session—6,799 had signed petitions, 44,256 had voted for a session at mass meetings, and 1,638 had written the governor. Only 514 persons had expressed opposition to a special session. By September 5 between 70,000 and 80,000 people had expressed themselves on the issue. About half favored the Long plan, and the others preferred a partial reduction in cotton acreage, typically one-third to one-half of the 1931 crop. "Your state needs leadership as much as any state I know of and it is going to be up to you to save your people and to help save the people of the balance of the country," Long wired Sterling. "If you do not act at once any action that you take will be of no avail. We have more cotton on hand that we can use for two years and by prohibiting planting next year we can get the farmers fifteen to twenty cents per pound for their cotton if Texas and other states will act."[60]

Long's proposal raised many pertinent questions. If his plan went into operation, what would happen to those who made their living by planting cotton or to those down the line—the ginners, gin machinery manufacturers, repair shops, and the people they employed? What would be the effect on buyers and shippers? Would America's cotton markets be captured by foreign competitors? Some members of the Texas Cotton Association, an organization of buyers and shippers, quietly worked behind the scenes in opposition to a special session to enact a cotton acreage control law. "I feel that even if the Legislature were to pass some acreage control law, which appears doubtful, that it would not have the desired effect and would probably result in no good," Burris C. Jackson of Hillsboro, who was active in the association, wrote to Sterling. "What the cotton trade needs now is less government in business and a free hand to work out its own problems." The *Beaumont Enterprise* thought Long's proposal would do more harm than good. The fate of the cotton industry, it said, rested in the hands of farmers, not with "lawmakers, ballyhoo artists, candidates for public office and politicians." Unable to resist the pressure any longer, Sterling called the legislature into session on September 8. "I have waited and investigated," he said, "until I have become convinced that a majority of the cotton farmers of Texas and their legislative Representatives desire an emergency law, and I am now ready and glad to act in their behalf." While leaving the provisions of legislation to "the wisdom of the lawmakers," the governor noted: "There is much sentiment among our farmers as well as among those engaged in other lines of business in favor of a half reduction of cotton acreage."[61]

Invited by the Texas lawmakers to address them, Long prepared to fly to Austin, but political problems with Lt. Gov. Paul Cyr kept him at home, and he had to be content with a radio address to thousands of farmers gathered in Austin's Wooldridge Park. Sterling received an ovation and some heckling when he spoke after Long and counseled caution and calmness in approaching the acreage reduction question. When the legislature delayed taking action, Long's impatience boiled over and he attacked that body over the radio. He stated that it was well known "that the members of the Texas legislature have been bought like a sack of corn to vote against the cotton prohibition plan." Temple Harris McGregor, a staunch Ferguson man, berated Long's "ignorance, imprudence and ignorance" in a house speech, implying that he was "poor white trash." Members liked the speech so well that McGregor was invited to repeat it in the senate.

The senate passed a resolution 21 to 7, declaring that Long's statement "is a lie made out of the whole cloth, and its author a consummate liar." After softening the resolution by striking out the section that called Long a liar, the house voted 64 to 47 to postpone its consideration indefinitely. A defiant Long refused to apologize. His plan was defeated in the house 92 to 37, and in the senate 19 to 9, after which the legislature passed a law providing that no one could plant cotton in 1932 and 1933 to exceed 30 percent of the area in cultivation during the preceding year. After 1933 cotton could not be planted on the same land two years in a row. The penalty for breaking the law was from $25 to $100 for each acre of cotton planted or cultivated in violation of the act.[62]

Most Texas farmers disregarded the law, which was virtually impossible to enforce, and only Arkansas, Mississippi, and South Carolina enacted similar legislation. A mass meeting of Central Texas landowners in Waco on December 5, 1931, urged Sterling to convene the legislature to repeal the cotton acreage reduction law unless by December 20 he had positively ascertained that the governors of the states producing 75 percent of the 1930 cotton crop would agree to call their legislatures into session prior to January 10, 1932, to pass laws reducing their cotton acreage a minimum of 50 percent. On February 1, 1932, District Judge W. C. Davis in Franklin ruled the law in violation of both the Texas and U.S. constitutions because it deprived citizens of their property without due process of law, impaired the right of contract, and was a retroactive measure. Enforcement of such a law, in the opinion of the court, would have worked "unthinkable hardships upon the tenants" and an injustice on small land-owning farmers. Davis's ruling was upheld by the Tenth Circuit Court of Appeals in Waco on March 5, 1932, and the case was not carried to the Texas Supreme Court. Thus Texas was left without any regulatory laws for cotton planting.[63]

Texas farmers in 1931 planted 1.5 million fewer acres of cotton than in the previous year, and many predicted that the acreage in 1932 would decline another 1.5 million acres. This reduction came about not because of any state or federal law but because cotton was priced so low that it did not pay to grow it except on the very best land. The total value of all Texas crops declined from $585,422,000 in 1929 to $306,872,000 in 1931. Cotton prices continued to drop, reaching a thirty-three-year low on June 1, 1932, of 5.05 cents a pound. Since about half the voters in Texas were tenant farmers whose major crop was cotton, the cotton problem brought even more distress to Texas than did the ruinously low price of crude oil, and the state of the cotton market promised still more political trouble for Sterling in 1932 should he seek the traditional second term.[64]

Maury Maverick and the Diga Colony

The nation's initial reaction to the Great Depression set off by the stock market crash of October 1929 was to beat it through magical incantation and by showing the kind of booster spirit that had made the 1920s hum. Administration officials' optimistic statements about business conditions were echoed in the Texas press. "The country is sound economically, and, so far as anyone can see, will remain so indefinitely," said the *Beaumont Enterprise* on February 12, 1930, summing up the paper's reaction to the economic difficulties. In a September 3, 1930, editorial, the *Dallas Morning News* commented reassuringly: "Hard times can be made a blessing to the people of Texas if they result in retrenchment, greater thrift, a deeper insight into the real needs of the State, and careful plans for putting the State on the high road to prosperity. Texas is too wealthy inherently to live on Poverty Row, when Comfort Avenue is just around the corner."[65]

The optimistic editorial in the *News* brought a prompt rebuttal from the old Populist James H. "Cyclone" Davis. "I am glad that The *News* can see a blessing in hard times," he wrote. "But the millions of jobless, homeless and hungry wage-earners and millions of sunburnt, drought-scorched, sweat-soaked, tax-burdened, debt-ridden farmers and common business men can't enjoy those blessings." But the *News* was not converted to Cyclone's angry pessimism. "What we need to do is to laugh and whistle, and then to look trouble in the face and snap our fingers at it," the paper advised a few weeks later. "There may be need of some retrenchment in the purchase of unnecessary luxuries, but conditions are fundamentally sound and the next few months will show a marked improvement here and there, and a general but slower movement forward all along the line."[66] Instead, the Depression got worse. A year after the crash, six million men were walking the nation's streets looking for work.

Unemployment statistics for Texas during the first years of the Depression are unreliable since no state agency was capable of compiling such figures. However, Governor Sterling estimated in February 1932 that at least 300,000 people were unemployed in the state. By December there were an estimated 348,000 unemployed. Mexicans and blacks, most of whom were unskilled and poorly educated, were especially hard-hit. Since they performed manual labor or worked as domestics, they were the first to be discharged in a depression. Dallas and Houston gave no relief to Mexican or black families.[67]

Once the problem of unemployment was recognized, the first reaction of most of Texas was orthodox: to provide relief for the jobless by reliance on friends, neighbors, relatives, churches, private agencies (including the Red Cross, Salvation Army, and Community Chest), and local or state government. "An emergency need exists in Beaumont," the *Enterprise* stated in November 1930, during the Community Chest campaign. "There is not as much suffering here, or as much unemployment, as there is in other cities, but quite enough to warrant the charitable people of Beaumont in straining a point to make their community chest subscriptions as large as possible." Within a relatively short time, however, the funds of private groups and local communities were exhausted, and the inexperience of local and state officials who were overburdened by the demands made on their limited resources precluded any effective state action.[68]

One of the most obvious indicators of increasing unemployment was the appearance of large numbers of transients on the streets. In cities like Dallas and Fort Worth, located on major railroads, hundreds of the homeless would pass through daily. In one six-month period an estimated 45,000 transients moved through El Paso. Newspapers warned about professional beggars and people who actually did not want to work, preferring instead to live off the relief provided by generous people. The editor of the *Hebbronville News* probably represented the thinking of many Texans when he declared in November 1930: "The time has probably arrived when a judicious use of the old fashioned chain gang on that class who refuses to work and roam from place to place fattening off the sympathizing public may be required." The migrants were often accused of responsibility for the growing crime rate, and local law enforcement officials sought to keep them out of the towns. A stranded family with a car was usually given food for a few meals, milk for the children, and five gallons of gas to get them back on the road. Suggestions for solving the problem included the drafting of transients and federal intervention to remove the relief burden from local communities. The State Bureau of Labor Statistics recommended that each city take care of its own citizens first, discourage outsiders from moving in, and encourage its own people to stay at home.[69]

Despite the general hostility, there were occasional expressions of public support for the transients. In his first term as Bexar County tax collector, Maury Maverick saw the Depression "hit like a cyclone," and by the middle of 1932 he viewed its effects in San Antonio as terrifying. He urged Governor Sterling to provide relief assistance and joined in the establishment of a Central Veterans Committee for aid to indigent veterans and their families. His major venture as a member of the committee was the establishment of the War Veterans Relief Camp on October 18, 1932, at the San Antonio Fair Grounds, where some of the remnants of the Bonus Army that had been driven out of Washington were camping. Maverick was named director and R. R. Rogers was the camp commander.

At first the camp was only a place where transients might get a decent meal and a place to sleep. Food was provided partly through relief funds and partly through contributions from local merchants and farmers. On November 21, 1932, a terse "Colony Order No. 2" informed residents that "effective this date this camp will be known as Diga Colony, Frio City Road and Mr. Maverick will be known as the Colony Director. It is desired that the word 'camp' be dropped from the record and conversation entirely." "Diga" was an anagram of letters taken from "agricultural and industrial democracy." The order signaled the colony's relocation from the fairgrounds to a thirty-five-acre industrial site that Maverick leased from the Humble Company for a dollar a year, and it marked the launch of an experiment in self-help communal living. The site had rail tracks, a water well, and several buildings. Maverick arranged with a railroad company to get free freight cars to be used as houses.

The colony was apparently well managed, and it reached a near self-sustaining basis midway in its approximately yearlong life span. "The Texas veteran experiment at the Diga community, near San Antonio . . . stands out strikingly as an efficient combination of veteran self help sustained by outside co-operation," the *Dallas Morning News* noted approvingly in December 1932. But Maverick's experiment failed because people did not "understand cooperation for the common good." He later declared: "Two economies cannot exist side by side within a given area, especially a money and a non-money one. Such things as 'Epics' and the like are bound to be failures because they represent a patch-work economy." The problems were not new: "Our men began to get work on Army projects," he commented wryly. "One worked thirty hours in a week and got a dollar an hour. He had been the meekest, most respectable and hard-working man in the colony. He drew his thirty dollars. He arrived on the scene tight as a drum, swaggering down the street. He beat his wife, turned capitalist, and left."[70]

After Diga Colony was underway, Governor Sterling, at Maverick's request, appointed him in December 1932 to make a "survey of destitute people in the state, particularly in reference to destitute transient population." Accompanied by two friends, Pat Jefferson and Harry Futrell, Maverick dressed as a hobo and "rode the rods." The men drove through part of Texas to study firsthand the plight of the transient unemployed. Maverick found that a very large proportion of those riding freight trains were tenant farmers, sharecroppers, and agricultural workers and that women or boys and girls comprised about one-fourth of this moving population. In his report to Sterling after the trip, Maverick made an impassioned plea for some action to alleviate a situation in which boys between eleven and nineteen were "living without parents or friends to guide them, and are spending their formative years in flophouses, jails, [hobo] jungles, or any available shelter, begging, panhandling, and, incidentally, starving part of the time, living miserably on a wholly improper diet, with no sanitation, no medical attention, and being chased from place to place by the police in the various cities." Maverick told the governor that there were some fifty to seventy-five thousand "destitute, shelterless, homeless people" who were willing to work but could find no jobs. He urged that these conditions be recognized as a national problem and that the information he had collected be forwarded to the federal government with a view to the development of national policies to meet such problems. Back in San Antonio Maverick organized transient relief stations—one in a big four-story building that had been operated by Montgomery Ward—where people in need could get a very cheap meal of coffee, bread and beans, and sometimes Mulligan stew. He had freight train schedules made up, provided information as to the best travel routes, and listed "the best places to board trains without getting into trouble."[71]

"Of all the depression problems, Sterling least understood unemployment," wrote his biographer, Warner Mills. In many instances he saw the suffering of the unemployed as evidence that they had "not the right idea of using what means they may have" to improve their condition. During the second special session Sterling read in the newspapers that cotton farmers needed pickers. He immediately announced that the urban unemployed should go to the fields, oblivious to the fact that factory workers or retail clerks were ill-suited to the backbreaking work of picking cotton. He intimated that if a man really wanted to help himself, he had the opportunity.

As his friend banker J. W. Hoopes of Dallas put it: "The big trouble is that we are playing too damn much and working too damn little."[72]

In early July 1930 Sterling wrote Senator Elmer Thomas of Oklahoma: "I am in accord with any movement that will improve the unemployment situation although I am of the opinion that this state is doing all the work it can, including the greatest road building program in its history." By October of the following year he admitted that unemployment was still widespread and presented serious problems as winter approached.

> While Texas has not been so hard hit as other sections, conditions in our State are far from satisfactory. There has been very meager seasonal improvement in business and employment conditions, and the trend is quite certain to be toward a more general state of forced idleness among our industrial workers. Unless some definite common plan is worked out and given coordinate operation, chaotic conditions may ensue.

Sterling called a statewide gathering of prominent Texans to meet in the hall of the house of representatives in Austin on October 16, 1931. Here he appointed a group called the Committee of One Hundred to be members of the Governor's Committee for Employment, to act in an advisory capacity to the committee recently created by the legislature. "I have been giving our financial situation quite a lot of thought," he wrote U.S. Representative John Nance Garner. "I have become convinced that something should be done by our Federal Reserve Board to expand credit instead of contracting. I hope you will insist on something being done to relieve the situation." Garner replied that the Federal Reserve Board's policies were "entirely in hands of administration," but promised to make "every possible effort to relieve situation."[73]

In fact Sterling himself was a financial victim of the Depression. As he sat in Austin collecting his yearly salary of $4,000, his business empire crumbled away. Cattle and ranches, office buildings, banks, and other properties were taken. The Joseph F. Meyer interest bought control of the Houston National Bank from the governor. A savage joke purported to quote Jesse Jones sending word to Sterling in Austin: "You run the state up there and I'll take care of Houston." Sterling's financial reverses also cost him the *Houston Post-Dispatch*. It was purchased by Jones in the name of J. E. Josey, chairman of the board of the National Standard Life Insurance Company. The newspaper's earlier name, the *Houston Post*, was resumed in 1932.

Jones, who already owned the highly profitable *Houston Chronicle*, sold the *Post*, including the KPRC radio station, to William P. Hobby on easy terms. Hobby had been virtually in control of the paper while Sterling served as highway commissioner and governor.[74]

By the time of the 1932 presidential election—after Hoover's reliance on local and state government initiative and private charity to provide relief for the jobless had failed—many Texans were ready to demand more aid from Washington, even the hated dole. The *Beaumont Enterprise*, which had earlier opposed federal aid because "it weakens the morale of a people who have always felt heretofore that they could take care of themselves," now admitted: "The 'dole' has few defenders, in principle, but starvation does not permit of hair-splitting distinctions—that is, it does not permit them to be long continued, for men may become desperate under the lash of hunger." Since it had been "demonstrated that every community cannot solve its relief and welfare problems," the federal government must act.[75] In the years to come Texans learned to accept federal intervention, although many continued to grumble about how it would destroy personal initiative, states' rights, and the American way of life. The myth of self-help and rugged individualism continued to hold sway over the minds of Texans. Ross Sterling, however, would not be the man to lead them into the future, Texans concluded—regardless of their opinions about federal intervention in the state.[76]

CHAPTER 5

Texas Again Tangled in Ma's Apron Strings

Early in 1932 Jim Ferguson reached the conclusion that hard times among Texans would make it a good "Ferguson year."[1] Farmers were selling their milk for 10 cents a gallon, and oats and corn were going for 15 cents a bushel. Eight-week weaned pigs sold for 50 cents, cattle for 3.75 cents a pound, and cotton for 4 cents a pound. "Pay your poll tax brother," Jim urged his followers, "and let us kick 'em, cuss 'em, fight 'em until we have turned the rascals out and the people in." At the end of January he revealed that neither he nor his wife would be a candidate for congressman-at-large, as generally had been predicted, but he refused to make any announcement on the gubernatorial race. However, he reportedly told friends in Austin that his wife's candidacy would depend on the number of poll taxes paid. If a large number of Texans qualified to vote, she probably would oppose Sterling.[2] "I think Ma would be a very dangerous opponent for Sterling," privately predicted Senator Clint Small of Amarillo. "She would carry this country against him in spite of all that could be done.... Put this down in your book to remember, 'if Ma runs against Sterling, look out for another Ferguson administration.'"[3] Small's prediction proved prescient, as Sterling ran an ineffective campaign in a year in which it was particularly difficult to win as an incumbent—ultimately leaving the state of Texas once again subject to Fergusonism.

The Candidates Line Up

On February 15 Mrs. Ferguson announced her run for governor, stating: "In addition to my connection with and my experience in the Governor's office, I shall avail myself of the advice and co-operation of competent friends, of the Legislature, and my husband in determining a policy that will

relieve the present perilous condition of our State's affairs." In a *Forum* editorial, "Her Hat Is in the Ring," Jim called attention to Sterling's frequent
trips to Houston on business and commented: "My wife thinks the orphan
office of governor should not be further neglected let alone abandoned and
she is willing to take the child and nurse it back to health again." In Dallas
he told a group of admirers: "The people are demanding lower taxation. I
tell you, it's either lower taxes or revolution." What the people needed was
for the federal government to issue two billion dollars in new money, either
currency or gold or silver "coin of the realm."[4]

Ma's remedies for rescuing Texas from its unhappy predicament included a constitutional amendment exempting from all taxes any homestead valued at less than $3,000; consolidation of as many county offices
as possible into one; popular election of the Highway Commission; a suspension of state bond issues for highway construction; replacing machinery
with people on roadwork where hand labor could possibly be used; support
for more public schools; extension of a two-year equity of redemption on
farm and home foreclosures; levying taxes only against an owner's equity
in real estate, leaving the balance to the holder of the vendor's lien; extend-
ing time for payment of taxes accruing before January 1, 1932, for two years
with the proviso that if they were paid within that period all interest and
penalties would be waived; reduction of all interest charges to 6 percent; a
redistribution of the gasoline tax and motor vehicle license fees, amounting
to $43 million, in such a way as to save taxpayers $12 million in ad valorem
taxes; and applying a liberal pardon policy to meritorious and energetic
prisoners. It was a platform carefully crafted to meet the perceived needs of
a depression economy.[5]

For several weeks Mrs. Ferguson's announcement was given little attention. "The Fergusons are shelf-worn political goods in Texas by now," sniffed
the *Dallas Morning News*. "They belong to a passing phase of politics, but
they insist on bringing out the same old show wagon and in performing
the same old song and dance. Discredited and rejected politically, they still
peddle their nostrums of government. Ma with matronly dignity in the cart
while Pa beguiles the crowd with medicine and ballyhoo. It is hard to believe
that Texas will make further investment in Fergusonism." In April the *News*
reported that the Depression had reduced the number of poll-tax payers in
Texas by almost 6.5 percent as compared with 1930 and by 12.3 percent from
1928; the paper thought this would be "sad news for the Ferguson camp"
since Fergusonism was essentially an appeal to discontent, and the most
discontented were the least able to pay the tax. Ferguson territory had been

Miriam "Ma" Ferguson in a yard of chickens, undated. James Edward Ferguson Collection, Briscoe Center for American History, University of Texas at Austin, DI 02364.

notably hit by poll tax recessions. Jim was understood to be recasting his platform appeal to reach the urban dweller, since his "hip pocket" rural vote was going to be materially reduced this election year.[6]

Until late in the spring the big question was whether Governor Sterling would be a candidate for reelection. Lt. Gov. Edgar Witt, state senators Clint Small and Walter Woodward, and Fort Worth businessman George W. Armstrong were said to be ready to enter the race if Sterling did not announce, and there was some speculation that Attorney General James V. Allred or former governor Dan Moody might enter the contest. Sterling told Small that he would let him know early in January what he intended to do. "He told me he had enough and that if he consulted his own feelings he would not run," Small advised a friend:

> But unfortunately Sterling is not "captain of his own boat" and if he gets his orders to run, he will be in the race with plenty of money for

a campaign, regardless of the fact that he is broke world without end. Big business will be for him. They know they are safe with him. As for the oil companies it would be rank ingratitude for them not to support him. He has always signed on the line fixed for his signature and they would be very foolish to experiment on some one else at this time. I think he will run or rather I think they will run him. These people have nothing against me but they know that I would do as I dam well pleased and this might not please them.[7]

At the end of 1931 Sterling had hinted strongly that he would ask for a second term, telling reporters that he "never had [said] he would not be a candidate for re-election," and adding that he had affairs in such shape that he "can visit the people during 1932."

On January 21, 1932, the *Dallas Morning News* reported that Sterling had told Small in a forty-five-minute conference in his private office that he would be a candidate to succeed himself. But the governor held back on a formal announcement, and his silence fueled rumors that he had either changed his mind or was wavering. "I have assumed that Governor Sterling will seek another term and he has not told me anything to the contrary," Walter Woodward commented after a conference with Sterling, Moody, and others in Austin on April 26. "We discussed political conditions generally, but the Governor did not tell me he would or would not run for a second term." It was generally accepted that Woodward would be the administration candidate if Sterling did not run.[8]

James Allred took himself out of the governor's race in early April by announcing that he would be a candidate for reelection as attorney general. "The talk about my running for Governor was embarrassing me in my work here," he explained to his parents. "I felt that it was the best thing from every angle for me to stay in here another term, if the people will return me." He was opposed by Clem Calhoun of Amarillo and Ernest Becker of Dallas. Calhoun announced his platform by saying: "I am running on Mr. Allred's record in office." He claimed that the attorney general had filed the antitrust suits in order to "deal the death penalty to a major industry." Allred professed not to be alarmed by Calhoun's challenge. "I rather think the big oil companies are going to put up a lot of money and try to make it as miserable as they can for me, but I am not afraid of being beaten," he confided to his parents.[9]

Clint Small was not able to keep the pique entirely out of his conditional announcement on May 1: "If Governor Sterling does not want to claim a second term I will run." He thought the governor was "lessening his chances to beat Mrs. Ferguson every day he fails to make that announcement."[10]

In an address to the State Bankers Convention at Austin on May 9, Sterling spoke optimistically of "the rising sun of a new day," and the press interpreted his speech as forecasting an announcement for a second term. That day Small asked the governor for a declaration of his intentions and advised him that he would announce his own candidacy on May 15 unless given "a more definite statement" before that time. On May 11, while en route by automobile to Sweetwater for the West Texas Chamber of Commerce Convention, Sterling telephoned his secretary in Austin that he would make his announcement for governor "in the next few days, setting forth my platform in detail." On May 14 Small told reporters in Sweetwater about his May 9 ultimatum to the governor. "Up to this time I have no positive statement," he noted. "I expect to make my word good." However, Sterling forestalled the West Texan by formally announcing his own candidacy later that day. In a 1953 interview with Warner E. Mills Jr., Sterling's secretary, Jesse Ziegler Wand, recalled: "Mrs. Sterling begged him not to stand for reelection. The Governor told me one day he was NOT going to run. Then Dan Moody came by the office late in the afternoon and was with him for two hours. When he came out Mr. Sterling had changed his mind and he wrote something for a press release."[11]

M. H. Wolfe, a Dallas cotton executive and Baptist leader, entered the race on a two-word platform: "Do Right." Tom F. Hunter, a wealthy independent oil operator from Wichita Falls who aspired to round out his career by serving as governor, also filed for a place on the ballot. Hunter was short, heavy-set, and stoop-shouldered, but his appearance was offset by a personality that appealed to voters. Roger Q. Evans of San Antonio announced on a platform calling for state loans to servicemen. George Armstrong decided to remain in the race on a "To Hell with Wall Street" platform after Sterling announced. The Fort Worth man bolted the Democratic Party and ran as an Independent when Roosevelt was nominated for president, but he did not withdraw from the race in time to keep his name off the Democratic primary ballot and received a scattering of votes. Three other names appeared on the ballot: C. A. Frakes of Jefferson County, J. Ed Glenn of Bosque County, and Frank Putnam of Harris County. Some of the Young Democrats wanted to draft Wright Morrow of Houston, an assistant attorney general under Dan Moody, and a Bexar County group started a draft movement for state senator W. K. Hopkins of Gonzales. Asked what he thought of the Morrow and Hopkins drafts, Sterling invited all candidates to enter with the statement that the weather was hot and the water fine, and for good measure he added the more the merrier. A conference of Young Democrats announced for Austin on June 9 (to choose between Morrow and Hopkins) failed to materialize; and after thinking the matter over, both men decided not to run.[12]

Wet Texas

Some of Sterling's backers, headed by former governor Hobby and Jacob Wolters, started a movement to have the state Democratic Executive Committee at its Austin meeting vote to hold a referendum on repeal of the Eighteenth Amendment at the July 23 primary, with the thought that it would bring out a large Dry vote and help the governor's candidacy. Senator Woodward wrote Tom Love that "with this question on the ballot, we could expect practically every man and woman in Texas who opposes the 18th Amendment, to go to the polls and it would draw an issue between Ferguson and Sterling that would result unquestionably in the defeat of Ferguson." Representative Walter Beck of Fort Worth, one of Sterling's strongest North Texas supporters, recognized the groundswell for repeal and warned him that opposing the repeal movement would cost him thousands of votes. "Fergusonites would like to harness you up with a camel and let Jim profit by the tremendous swing that had developed for repeal of the Eighteenth Amendment," Beck stated, reminding the governor that his Dry views were well known and suggesting that he state publicly that he had never attempted to dictate to the people as to what their views should be, but was disposed to let them say what they wanted.[13]

On the other hand, Carr P. Collins of Dallas, a devoted "Pro," advised Sterling: "In my judgment, your friends should insist that no such referendum be taken on this prohibition question." Repeal might carry, and such an outcome would do more to destroy the Eighteenth Amendment than any other thing that had been done by any of its enemies. Moreover, it would have a direct bearing on the governor's race. "This prohibition question ought to be kept out of the Governor's race, because there are literally thousands of people who are in favor of repeal but who are honest citizens and believe in honest government. If we try to draw the lines on prohibition by creating some situation that would make you the candidate of the prohibitionists and Ferguson the candidate of the anti-prohibitionists, you would be certain to lose by such a lineup." After discussing Woodward's letter with other Drys, Love reported that it was his and their unanimous opinion that a referendum on the Eighteenth Amendment would not be advisable "and would keep more Dry voters out of the primaries than it would bring in and hurt Sterling more than it would help him." At the same time, he had found staunch Drys determined "to leave no thing undone to aid in Sterling's reelection."[14]

Although some of Sterling's close political advisers inferred publicly that he favored submission, the governor announced on June 8 that he had no intention of asking the executive committee to place the repeal proposition on the primary ballot. "I am running for Governor and intend to do everything to further my own campaign," he stated. "I have friends on both sides of the prohibition question. Prohibition does not have anything to do with the gubernatorial race and I certainly would not have any right to request the committee to submit the question of repeal." He wrote Carr Collins: "Of course, there are various and sundry opinions as to what effect this would have on the Governor's race. I am sorry that the question has been brought up."[15]

The state Democratic Executive Committee voted 16 to 13, with more proxy holders than committeemen voting, to allow Democrats who voted in the first primary to mark "for" or "against" a proposal that the seventy-third U.S. Congress submit the question of retaining or repealing of the Eighteenth Amendment to the people. Carl Estes of Tyler offered the resolution, and it was seconded by I. Friedlander of Houston. Estes asserted that he, as a prohibitionist, would vote against repeal, but he thought the people, "including the soldiers who were in France the other time it was voted on," should have a chance to say whether they wanted to reconsider. The vote came after a floor fight so heated that Chairman W. O. Huggins, himself "a prime mover of the proposed poll," had to invoke a rule that he would hear only committeemen or proxy members.[16]

Drys and Wets were divided in sentiment about the prohibition ballot, which was seen by both sides as a pro-Sterling scheme to get out a big Dry vote. Many felt that the ballot was a mistake and that there was no reason for it. One prominent Wet said that "neither the sincere wets nor the sincere drys desired it." Carr Collins wrote Alvin Moody: "My own opinion was and is that it was the most colossal blunder from Governor Sterling's standpoint that has been committed. Any time you get the question of prohibition injected into a campaign, you take the people's minds off of everything else." Collins predicted, "People will have an opportunity now to forget all about what a crook Jim Ferguson is."[17]

On June 16 it became known that a group of ultra-Drys, who claimed to control anywhere from fifty thousand to one hundred thousand votes, were planning to mass their strength behind M. H. Wolfe. "Rumors about such a movement have come to me," Wolfe said, "but I am not in a position to say anything about this." Spokesmen for the group were understood to believe that Sterling could not defeat Mrs. Ferguson and that the present Wet tendencies of the Democratic Party would keep the Drys out of the July 23 primary unless they were induced to enter it to vote for an outstanding Dry like Wolfe. The Drys also resented the resubmission ballot and charged that it was a Sterling campaign ruse to get out a large vote by reopening a previously closed issue of major concern to his base of popular support.[18]

On July 6 a committee of forty-five Dry Democrats—including chairman Cato Sells, Tom Love, Alvin Moody, Carr P. Collins, V. A. Collins, Atticus Webb, H. Bascom Thomas, and J. D. Sandefer—issued an appeal to the state's Dry Democrats to meet the challenge of the liquor forces by going into the primaries and voting for Dry candidates. They called attention to the Texas Supreme Court's decision in *Love v. Wilcox*, in which the court held that voters who entered the primaries in Texas were not bound to support the party's nominees except as their conscience approved such support. "In view of the determined effort to destroy our prohibition laws, we feel that no dry Democrat can afford to stay out of the Democratic primaries," the statement read. "Our great party—the party of Jefferson and Jackson and Woodrow Wilson—must not be surrendered to the domination of the outlawed liquor traffic." At the same time the committee urged Drys to ignore the liquor referendum, since under the circumstances, "the vote on this referendum can be little more than a straw vote which can not have any real significance, or constitute any reliable index as to the views of the people." Four or five county executive committees refused to place the submission referendum on their ballots, but Dallas was the only large county that did so.[19]

On July 9 a group of Drys led by Tom Love and Alvin Moody met in Dallas and formed the Texas League of Dry Democrats, sworn to militant and unrelenting opposition to any weakening of the Eighteenth Amendment and national prohibition. Despite the passage of several resolutions, including one urging Drys to go to the polls and vote against the liquor referendum, the group revealed a lack of unanimity in thought and action. Love remarked after the meeting: "We're going to do our duty, but I don't think we know just what our duty is going to be." Some in the league said that Drys should vote Republican, although the GOP stood for resubmission; some said Drys ought to vote Democratic, although there were unanimous expressions of opposition to the party's forthright stance on repeal and open disagreement with the repeal attitude of Roosevelt and Garner.

Some league members like George W. Armstrong wanted Drys to desert both parties and act independently. Dr. J. B. Cranfill announced that he would support William D. Upshaw, the Prohibition Party's presidential candidate. Love, who advocated ignoring the liquor referendum, admitted that "the odds are against us in this fight two weeks from today." Although most of those at the meeting had been active in the Hoovercrat movement in Texas in 1928, there was little talk of a bolt from the Democratic Party. It was apparent that the Hoover-Curtis ticket and the Republican platform did not offer as inviting a haven as it had four years earlier.[20]

Because of the legislature's failure to redistrict, Texas voters had to elect three congressmen-at-large. Unofficially the militant Drys favored W. Erskine Williams of Fort Worth or E. G. Senter of Dallas for Place 1; B. D. Sartin of Wichita Falls for Place 2; and Sterling P. Strong of Dallas for Place 3. The Young Democrats, or "liberals," favored Lawrence Westbrook of Waco for Place 1; Joseph Weldon Bailey Jr. of Dallas for Place 2; and Douglas W. McGregor of Houston for Place 3. The battle in Dallas County to control the delegation to the state convention in Lubbock would find Love arrayed against Maury Hughes, one of the younger liberal leaders, who had emerged as that group's ablest general. Love made it clear that Hughes was the man he and his forces were aiming at. "We are opposed to giving State or local governments control over the liquor traffic," he declared. "We oppose turning the Government over to such men as Al Capone in Chicago, Frank Hague in New Jersey, and Maury Hughes in Dallas."[21]

Alvin Moody suggested that the Dry leadership in the various counties undertake to cooperate with the Wolfe and Sterling forces to capture the precinct and county conventions. Delegations would be delivered to the successful candidate in the July primary. "I am more than pleased to hear of your splendid activities in Fort Worth," he wrote Cato Sells. "I am sure you folks can handle the situation there. If the drys in Dallas and Harris County can carry their precinct and county conventions we will, at the state convention, re-write the Democratic party's position on the Eighteenth Amendment. This possibility should prompt us to make an unusual effort to succeed."[22]

However, at the Dallas County convention the regulars, headed by Maury Hughes, selected their complete delegate slate with slight but ineffective opposition from the embattled Dry faction led by Tom Love and Ray Holder, chairman of the Dallas County League of Dry Democrats. After the initial test of strength, when former mayor and county judge W. M. Holland received 204 votes for temporary chairman to Holder's 130 votes, "the regular program swept through on a clear track with all signals green." The

convention roared its approval of the Democratic national ticket and platform. Love was "the most booed and hissed at man at the meeting." His four
minority resolutions were tabled. The delegates named Hughes state committeeman, succeeding Carr P. Collins, who was put on the state Democratic
Executive Committee in 1930 when the Love crowd controlled it. (Collins
had succeeded Hughes, who now returned to the place.) Ray Holder was put
on the Lubbock-bound delegation, but Love, Alex W. Pope, and Roy Eastus
were conspicuously absent.[23]

In Harris County the Wets carried about 75 percent of the precincts—to
the Drys' 25 percent—and were in complete charge of the county convention. Alvin Moody complained that "we were whipped in Harris County in
the precinct conventions by the lack of support the Sterling forces gave to
us. In many boxes we lost the precinct convention by some 1 to 5 votes—63
to 64—83 to 79—54 to 49—many boxes by just one vote. Any help or assistance from the Sterling forces would have made us overwhelmingly victorious." It was generally conceded that the Sterling people would elect Steve
Pinckney or Jim Kilday executive committeeman from the district. "If they
do it will just about destroy whatever enthusiasm the dry people now have
for Sterling's candidacy," Moody warned Love.[24]

Sterling's Early Campaign Missteps

In the meantime the gubernatorial campaign was underway. The Fergusons opened at the Cotton Palace in Waco on May 21. Reading from a prepared text, Jim charged that the Sterling administration was dominated by
Jake Wolters and the "big oil companies." "One year of the present administration," Jim argued, "has cost the people twice as much as the two years
my wife was governor. The people know the Fergusons know how to reduce
taxes and save money." Noting that the Highway Commission had spent
more than $200 million in the last five years, he charged that it was domi-
nated by the cement trust. "Roads have been built around towns, to help
friends, or where they won't do any good." There were thirty thickly populated counties in Texas where bonds had been voted and in which the people
had been denied state aid. Ferguson alluded specifically to one piece of highway from Palacios to Corpus Christi, which he called the "fisherman's road,"
and said that more people in one day traveled the road between San Antonio
and Waco, or between Waco and Dallas–Fort Worth, than passed over the
fisherman's road in one month. Moving from roads to the penitentiary sys-

tem, Ferguson told his audience that "others have tried the no-pardon plan and lost millions for the State out of the prison system. I have lived to see my idea of mercy to the unfortunate adopted by my enemies." Jim contended that interest and taxes were draining the country and vowed: "If I had the power, I'd abolish interest. Since this can't be done, interest should be reduced to 6 per cent." In her short speech, Mrs. Ferguson read her platform, vowed to use the veto power to cut appropriations "if it shall be necessary to suppress extravagance," and asserted that highway commissioners had grown "arrogant, disrespectful, and dictatorial." Their incompetency and extravagance had wasted millions of dollars, and she promised that if elected she would use all the powers of her office to remove them.[25]

Three weeks after the Fergusons opened at Waco, Sterling made his opening speech in the same city on June 11. He took as his general theme the question, "Shall honest government and responsible government, and businesslike government be continued in Texas?" He insisted that a threatened deficit in the state treasury had been headed off and would soon be wiped out and reviewed the split-tax payment program, truck regulation measures, and the rescue of the oil industry (and the state's tax revenues imperiled by its demoralized condition), as among his administration's achievements. He predicted the riverbeds law would bring in millions in revenue. Looking ahead, he emphasized economy in state government, recommended abolishing the fee system in all branches of government, promised no bond issue for any purpose under present conditions, supported the proposed constitutional amendment to exempt homesteads up to $3,000 in value from state taxes, vowed to promote home ownership in Texas, and urged conservation of the state's natural resources. He hoped farmers would find a constitutional way to regulate their production to accommodate consumption demands and thus stabilize their markets, as had been done in other industries, and he promised to support any measure that gave reasonable promise of aiding agriculture.[26]

Sterling's supporters advised him that economic conditions would necessitate long, hard campaigning to obtain victory, but the governor—less attuned to political currents and lulled by his conviction that a second term, barring scandal, was traditional—felt that he needed only wage a short, intense campaign to remind the voters of his qualifications. Except for his opening address at Waco, he did practically nothing during May and June beyond releasing his platform and laying the groundwork for a campaign organization. He devoted a major portion of his time during this period to attending highway celebrations, church conferences, and other nonpolitical functions. When he finally began a speaking tour on June 23, he found that his opponents possessed the initiative and that he had to defend himself at every turn.[27]

The Ferguson platform proposed as a tax relief plan that the $300 million now collected from the gas tax be divided in three equal parts, one-third to the public schools, one-third to the state highway department, and one-third to the state ad valorem general revenue fund. Sterling objected to this approach on the grounds that the monies diverted to the general revenue fund would in all likelihood be squandered by the legislature and that the highway fund would be inadequate to sustain the state's highway maintenance and construction programs. As an alternative, he proposed that the state assume that portion of the bonded indebtedness of the counties, which represented their contribution to the building of the state highway system, and that part of the gasoline tax funds should be used for this purpose. He admitted that his plan was not a general tax relief plan and would help only those counties with heavy road bond indebtedness. However, he argued that where relief was granted it would amount to many times that which the Ferguson plan would achieve. He repudiated the highway bond plan that he had advocated two years before, arguing that the state government was not justified in contracting itself into debt in a period of economic crisis. Moreover, he had vetoed the Brooks bill the preceding October, at the end of the second special session, which would have accomplished what he now espoused. Sterling had justified his veto on the grounds that the bill would disrupt highway department planning, would grant no immediate tax relief, and was in its existing form unconstitutional, since its object could only be achieved through a constitutional amendment.[28]

Speaking at San Angelo on July 6, Sterling hailed the abandonment of the county aid system in state road financing, announced the previous day by the Highway Commission, as a boon to the taxpayer. "For a long time," he said, "I had been urging the commission to cease letting counties share in the building of State roads, as I have advocated for four years the use of money from the gasoline tax fund to take up road bonds already voted by counties for State construction." The commission's action guaranteed early refunding to the counties that already had contributed to highways, and Sterling promised to exert every effort to have it done as soon as possible. He continued:

> It makes me sick at heart to see farmers and their wives working from dawn till dark in the fields, raising cotton which scarcely sells for the

cost of its production, and having to dig up taxes up to $3 on the $100 valuation, and pay the highways of which others enjoy the most benefits. The State must pay them back that money and shift the burden of highway costs from the homes and farms to the traffic. I have advocated that shift for four years, last year through a separate constitutional amendment, which failed of submission. I shall continue to urge it until some constitutional means is found to accomplish it.

Sterling here told for the first time of an offer he said was made to him during the last regular session to deliver eighteen votes in the house for the county refund amendment and a companion amendment providing for a state road bond issue, if he would appoint a certain friend of Jim Ferguson to a certain office. "I'll be damned if I do," he said his answer was, adding, "and every last one of those eighteen members, who were named to me, then voted against the measure."[29]

Having belatedly adopted the view that the tax diversion change might be made by legislative action, Sterling was pressured to call a special session for that purpose. "It would wreck the Ferguson plans completely—and such a course could be used with the most decisive political effect," Senator Gus Russek advised him, adding that "the people are wild for some sort of relief." Sterling stubbornly resisted until the second week in July, when he weakened and announced that he would convene the legislature on August 1 if he won renomination at the first primary.[30]

Right of Way or Rule of Waste?

As an incumbent in hard times, Sterling faced an uphill climb for a second term. A doctor in Thrall informed the governor: "Our people in this little community seem to think that you and Hoover are the cause of the depression, low price of stock, cotton, cattle and everything bad." While driving through Bastrop County during the election, Adjutant General William Sterling picked up a hitchhiking farmer. "Who is going to get your vote for governor?" he asked. "Ferguson," the farmer replied. "Why?" Sterling inquired. "Because," the Fergusonite explained, "Ross Sterling put the three cent postage stamp on us."

The governor usually defended his administration and outlined his plans for further reforms, leaving the Ferguson record to the numerous other surrogate speakers, including Dan Moody, who came to his aid. Heroic efforts were made to keep the "beer belt" of German and South Texas counties from going for Mrs. Ferguson. Senators Gus Russek, W. K. Hopkins, T. J. Holbrook, Walter Woodul, and W. A. Williamson, along with former senator A. J. Wirtz, Henry Paulus, John L. Darrouzet, and John Walker campaigned for Sterling in this overwhelmingly pro-Ferguson section. In a few cases Moody and Sterling teamed up and spoke at the same rallies. In Dallas, when the governor's chair on the platform crumbled under him just as Moody was warming to his arraignment of Fergusonism, the speaker smilingly told the crowd: "I always knew Governor Sterling was a heavyweight and I see he is upholding my opinion of him now." At Cleburne, Moody praised Sterling's administration and spoke at length on the menace of proxy government. He told the crowd that while Mrs. Ferguson was governor her husband had an income of $149,000, "a most phenomenal record for an unemployed man whose wife was governor."[31]

Every large daily newspaper in Texas except the *Houston Press*, which supported no candidate, backed Sterling. The editor, Marcellus E. "Mefo" Foster, personally favored Tom Hunter.[32] As it had in 1930, the Sterling camp circulated thousands of copies in both English and Czech of a pamphlet giving the grisly details in the Langhorn rape-murder case. Ferguson published an editorial in the *Ferguson Forum* that gave his version of the incident, and he printed a one-page broadside, "The Truth about the Langhorn Case." Frank W. Chudej, president and controlling owner of the *Forum*, filed obscenity charges against Adjutant General Sterling and Ross Sterling's Austin manager, A. C. Bull, in a Travis County justice of the peace court. The charges were dismissed on July 12 for want of prosecution. Chudej, who arrived late, said he had been delayed by a flat tire. Some Texans were indignant at the pamphlet's explicit sexual language. "The Langhorn confession left for my sister to read unappreciated," a Fort Worth man wired the governor. "We are your supporters. Don't believe you would want your sister to read such an indecent confession."[33]

Tom Hunter exposed further details on the subject of Jim Ferguson's tax returns, telling his audiences that for one year Ferguson sent in a return of $759, but the federal government had revised it to $61,123. "And the greater part of that was in checks from combines he promised to subdue," Hunter pointed out. He attacked the "capitalistic combines and chain stores" and the alleged oil trust domination of Texas industries; he charged that taxes were too high and that wealth and monopolies and trusts were escaping taxation. If elected governor he promised to abolish, consolidate, and rearrange the 120 bureaus and commissions; to protect the independent businessman against chain stores; and to guard the people generally against exploitation.

While serving as chairman of the Highway Commission, Sterling had insisted that all rights-of-way for roads destined to become parts of the state system be one hundred feet wide. The boundaries of state-owned property were marked with short concrete posts stamped "ROW." Hunter used these markers as a basis for his attack on the Sterling administration, telling his listeners that the letters stood not for "Right of Way" but for "Rule of Waste." "My reception in the different sections of the state has been very gratifying," the candidate informed Ben G. Oneal in mid-May. "I have, in fact, made more headway than I had hoped for the length of time that I have been on the road."[34]

In line with his new policy, Ferguson spoke in the population centers and not in the rural districts, as he had done in previous campaigns. He believed that the country people were for the Fergusons and that he must convert the urban dwellers, who had not supported them in the past. He made few new charges or speeches during the last few days of the campaign. In a speech at Brenham, Ferguson claimed that the state treasury would have a deficit of $6.5 million by August. "They criticize us because we offer Texas two Governors when my wife is elected," he said, "and I say we will make up for the time Texas has not had any Governor."

The Fergusons spoke to a large crowd at Houston, where Jim again accused the Highway Commission of "autocracy, incompetency, and waste." He said that Sterling had two thousand men on highway jobs for political purposes and that they would not have jobs "thirty days after the election." He renewed his charge of a "shortage" of $100 million in the state highway funds for the last five years. A cartoon in the *Ferguson Forum* shows Sterling taking a $100 million highway melon from the Texas highway department's melon patch; its caption reads, "Here's where a 'Texas Steal' Beats a Georgia Sweet!" In his speeches Ferguson spoke of Sterling as a "fat head" and called him the "present vacancy" and "present encumbrance." The state auditor, Moore Lynn, reported on July 20 that the highway funds were in perfect order, but Ferguson repeated the charge in his closing speech at Dallas on July 22.[35]

The Prohibition referendum on the Democratic primary ballot brought out the expected heavy vote. The ballot was unusually long, and the counting and reporting were slower than usual. The results showed Mrs. Ferguson leading in the governor's race by a wide margin: 402,238 to Sterling's 296,383. Hunter was in third place with 220,391 votes, and M. H. Wolfe trailed far behind in fourth place with 32,241. Submission on the repeal of the Eighteenth Amendment won handily, 405,309 to 117,618. "Texas remains overwhelmingly dry," Tom Love announced, despite this outcome, basing his opinion on the fact that "more than 500,000 majority of the Democrats who voted in yesterday's primary election either voted against submission or refused to vote for it."[36]

Mrs. Ferguson swept northeast, East, and Central Texas, carrying 163 counties by a plurality or majority. The usual Ferguson strength in East Texas was accentuated by resentment against the martial law episode. Jim Ferguson poked some fun at Dan Moody in the *Forum*, saying: "Now, just believe it or not, little Dan Moody has quit Ross and gone to speaking for my wife. He made something like twelve speeches in the campaign in twelve different counties and places and every place where he spoke went for my wife by decisive majorities." Sterling carried sixty-one counties, including the tips of the state: seventeen Panhandle counties (the "Small counties" of 1930); all twelve of the Trans-Pecos counties; and thirteen Rio Grande counties. His best showing was in the larger urban counties—notably Dallas, his banner county, which gave him a lead of 4,844 votes over Mrs. Ferguson—and in Tarrant, Harris, Jefferson, Travis, and El Paso Counties. However, notoriously wet Bexar County gave Mrs. Ferguson a plurality of more than ten thousand votes over the governor. She carried every African American box in the Alamo City by a large majority. Hunter tied Mrs. Ferguson in Wichita, his own county, and led in twenty-nine others, including a dozen of Wichita County's neighbors and the remainder from the counties veering southwest from that area.[37]

In another statewide race, Attorney General James V. Allred won renomination without a runoff, polling 600,768 votes to Clem Calhoun's 270,354 and Ernest Becker's 79,056. According to Allred and his friends, he would not have had an opponent had not Love advised his fellow ultra-Drys to concentrate on Parrish, Davis, and Strong for Congress and Sterling for governor in the runoff primary and to concern themselves with other matters later.[38] John Henry Kirby, chairman of the Texas Federation of Antiprohibition Clubs, urged Wets to vote for Terrell, Bailey, and Burkett. The winners in the runoff were Terrell, Bailey, and Strong.[39]

The Ferguson lead of more than a hundred thousand votes discouraged many Sterling supporters, and they were slow in getting organized for the runoff, but the governor himself professed to be optimistic and pointed to the 1930 contest in which Mrs. Ferguson had secured 45 percent of the total vote in the first primary but in the runoff could do no better than 44.8 percent; she lost the runoff by more than 88,000 votes. The governor felt that history would repeat itself. "The Fergusons in this last primary have polled their full strength, and in the run-off will not reach the 400,000 mark," one of his secretaries assured a Mission man. Some of Sterling's friends were not so optimistic. Col. Sam Robertson of San Benito wired Sterling and urged him to withdraw in favor of Tom Hunter. The telegram read: "You are an 'in.' You cannot win in such a time as this. Thomas Jefferson, George Washington or Abe Lincoln, if in office today could not be re-elected. The voters of 1932 are as rational as the mob who crucified Christ."[40]

It was a bad year for the "ins" generally. Eighty-five new members were elected to the Texas House of Representatives, and most of them defeated an incumbent. George C. Moffett, first elected to the house from Hardeman, Foard, Knox, and King Counties in 1930, had two opponents in 1932. In a 1965 interview he recalled:

> It was right in the bottom of the depression, and in some cases I'd hand the voter a card, and he'd look at it, ask if I was in office, and, of course, I said yes. He says that's all I want to know. I'm not for anybody that's in office. So it was largely a case of the "ins" against the "outs." My opponents didn't present any particular constructive platform at all. They just said that what we needed was a change in Austin. And it was a hard race. . . . I'll tell you, in a depression like we had then, people . . . they were stirred up and many of them . . . they didn't care who the man was, if he was in office, they didn't want him back.[41]

However, in Moffett's case, the voters sent him back to Austin.

Sam Rayburn returned home to Bonham from Chicago to again face two opponents in the Democratic primary on July 23.[42] "It was my thought that I would escape opposition this time," he complained to friends. "But it seems that that isn't in the cards for me." One of his opponents was seventy-three-year-old Choice Randall of Sherman, who had run against him two years earlier; the other was Jesse Morris, a young and well-liked reporter and part-owner of a printing company in Greenville. Morris's cry that it was "time for a change" worried Rayburn, who understood the perils of incumbency in hard times. "Why," he countered, "should voters want to change their congressman any more than they would their doctors, lawyers, tenants, school teachers, or bankers?" Morris told his audiences, "You can expect that Rayburn will be boasting of what he has done. But what has Rayburn done?" Rayburn wired Congressman John McDuffie: "Party in this district has written Speaker about my record. If answer is not strong will do no good. If strong enough will do immense good. Conditions bad and political situation serious." Rayburn squeaked through the first primary with 50.7 percent of the vote, a majority of 503 out of 35,287 votes cast. His hairline victory was made possible only by the fact that he had successfully fought a change in his district's boundaries the year before that would have tacked on a Republican piece of Dallas County. The legislature could not agree on a redistricting bill, and the issue was put off until 1933. "It is a mighty tough deal to try to get more votes than two men in one primary but it happened that I could get through," a relieved Rayburn wrote Amon Carter.[43]

Conniving for Votes in the Runoff

The efforts of both the Sterling and Ferguson camps were bent in the runoff toward acquiring the major part of Hunter's 220,391 votes. The Wichita Falls man's strong showing was the surprise of the primary. "I wish to congratulate you on your splendid race," Sterling wired Hunter. "The run off now appears to be with the Fergusons and myself. I will appreciate your support very much." Dan Moody had a long conference with Hunter in Austin on the governor's behalf. But Hunter declined to take sides, writing Sterling: "Until my tired mind may relax I will take no action. Whatever I do if anything will be in behalf of the great plain people.... My supporters were independent thinkers."[44]

The Fergusons waged a sort of "weekend campaign," usually grouping their night rallies from Thursday to Saturday and resting and making plans during the intervening days. They opened the runoff in San Marcos on August 6. Mrs. Ferguson accompanied her husband to perhaps half of his appearances, usually reading her speech before he appeared, since he was always the main attraction. In his speeches Ferguson brought new issues into the fight, such as the recently increased state tax rate, the alleged heavy deficit, as well as the reduction in the school apportionment from $17.50 to $16 a child. He again bore down hard on his charge of a $100 million shortage in the highway fund, dismissing the state auditor's report as not giving any information. He never failed to mention his wife's majority of 105,855 votes over Sterling, and he predicted she would have twice that majority on August 27.[45]

Sterling's friends held "a good government" rally in Fort Worth on August 1 to plan his runoff campaign. A thousand political leaders from all sections of the state attended, including many who had supported Hunter. It was decided that Sterling should concentrate on the Hunter counties, on the East Texas Oil Field district and other Ferguson strongholds, and on the labor districts of the big cities. Mrs. Cone Johnson, Tom Love, Gen. M. M. Crane, and Maury Maverick made radio appeals for Sterling in the last few days of the campaign. Dan Moody again went "on the firing line for good government," opening his speaking tour with a Gainesville talk on August 7, in which he compared Sterling's record with Ferguson's. "Now look at Dan," Jim sneered. "He's like a chicken snake run over by a hay wagon on a dusty road on a hot summer day. He's biting and snapping at everything trying to wiggle in all directions at the same time."[46]

Beginning with a speech in Wichita Falls on July 29, Sterling made a very aggressive and strenuous campaign, speaking from seven to ten times a day and ending each day with a rally in a large city or county seat. In all, he made 160 speeches in three weeks. He was accompanied on most of his campaign tour by former state senator Robert A. Stuart of Fort Worth, who took the role assumed by Senator Woodward in 1930. Stuart usually made the opening speech, summarized the Fergusons as governors, and gave detailed stories of Ferguson's work as a lobbyist in recent legislative sessions. The governor would review his administration's accomplishments, including a claim that he had vetoed $3.6 million in appropriations to keep the state within its revenues. He said he was asking a second term "on my record, and my record only." In East Texas he went into great detail to show that the state and its citizens had profited from his declaration of martial law in the oil field. He said he had been accused of favoring the major oil companies but declared the record showed he had befriended the independent oilmen. "I did not receive one letter, telegram or telephone call from a major oil company requesting martial law," he stated. "The independents petitioned that action by the hundreds. They held a mass meeting and not one dissented from the plan to shut in that field and restore orderly production."[47]

Sterling hit hard at Jim Ferguson's employment as a paid lobbyist for special interests during the forty-second legislature, charging that he had opposed appropriations for an investigation of alleged violations of the anti-trust laws and for a survey to determine the reasonableness of public utility rates; he had been employed by the sulfur interests to work against a higher tax on sulfur and by the cement and natural gas industries to fight taxes on those products; he had sought to defeat the cigarette tax, a source of $2 million annually for the school fund; he had lobbied against bills requiring the big oil companies to dispose of their filling stations and limiting the profits of big pipeline companies to 10 percent; and he had opposed passage of the riverbed bill. Ferguson advocated limiting the production of oil to the market demand, a proposal for an oil monopoly, Sterling noted, "favored by two persons, Jim and his wife, and by two publications, the Forum ... and the *Lamp*, a magazine published by the Standard Oil Company." Yet, Sterling told his audiences, Ferguson "would make you believe that I am the tool of the major oil companies." Echoing the governor, Clint Small charged that the major oil companies were supporting the Fergusons in the runoff. Dan Moody told a Denton crowd that the ox of Ferguson's pocketbook knew its sulfur company master and quoted Ferguson's own words in opposition to the sulfur tax. Again a pause: "And the ass knoweth its master's crib."[48]

After the July 23 primary, there was general interest in the fact that 132 counties, mostly in the Ferguson stronghold of East Texas, had polled a much larger vote than their total voting strength as indicated by the record of poll-tax payments. In these counties there were issued 359,667 poll-tax receipts for 1932, but 397,386 votes had been cast, the latter figure excluded Democratic poll-tax payers who had not voted in the primary, blacks barred from it, and Republicans or other party voters. In Gregg County the primary vote was 73 percent in excess of registration, although the Ferguson camp claimed this could be explained by oil activity transfers from other counties. A great majority of the people and press agreed with the conclusion of the *Dallas Morning News* that "most impartial observers assume from the relative totals that fraudulent voting in the primary was widespread." Of the 132 excess vote counties, Sterling carried 18, Hunter 20, and Mrs. Ferguson 94. She led by 75,090 in the totals for the 132 counties.[49]

A week before the July primary, the Democratic chairman in Shelby County had warned Sterling that "Old Jim's plan is to steal this Election, and they are telling all of his followers to come and vote regardless of whether they have paid their Poll tax or not. A large percentage of the Ferguson following in East Texas especially have not paid their Poll Tax." A Dublin dentist informed the governor after the election: "There were about 1600 less poll tax receipts in this co (Erath) alone & there were more votes cast than ever before." He continued:

> Thousands of people under 60 years of age voted claiming to be exempt on physical defects, such as defective eye sight, rheumatism loss of eye, loss of fingers, maimed joints.... Thousands of ex soldiers who receive pensions from the government under every kind of pretext voted & their wives also voted & did not have a poll tax receipt. At our small

country box near here 15 world vets & their wives voted & did not have a poll tax receipt, & I understand every one voted for Ferguson.[50]

Revelation of the situation led to a great many investigations or promises of investigations by local county and election officials. "Unless there is something ... done, there will be thousands of illegal votes cast all over this part of the State in favor of Mrs. Ferguson," Tyler banker Gus Taylor warned Tom Love. "I especially refer in East Texas to Gregg, Upshur, Husk and Smith county. If the negro and the illegal votes can be kept out of the next primary I have no doubt but what Governor Sterling will win by a reasonable majority." On August 19 W. O. Huggins, the chairman of the state Democratic Executive Committee, announced that the committee would use full efforts to prevent illegal voting in the August primary and to punish election officials who willfully permitted illegal voting. "It may cost $100,000 to prevent illegal voting but it is well worth the money for the State of Texas," Sterling said with emphasis after talking with Huggins, "for when a pure ballot is destroyed then the foundations of free government crumbles." He issued a proclamation offering a $500 reward for uncovering dishonest election officials and $100 reward for revealing the fraudulent voter. "There will be plenty of men willing and anxious to make this easy money," he warned, "and any person caught violating the election laws will be dealt with in severe terms. I do not want a dishonest vote. If I can not be elected by honest votes I do not want office. Those conniving to get dishonest votes had better watch their step or they will find themselves in serious trouble."[51]

Shortly before the second primary, Adjutant General Sterling received reports of a steady influx of transients into East Texas, particularly into Gregg County. Convinced that it was a "nefarious plot" by the Fergusonites to steal the election with a hoard of floater votes, General Sterling, without telling the governor, made plans to send three companies of Rangers into East Texas to frighten these undesirables into flight. "Crooks always get itchy feet at the appearance of the Rangers, and the wicked flee without waiting to be pursued," he told a group of Ranger officers. "I believe that this move will do more to curb illegal voting than any amount of talk." The zero hour was midnight. Sterling was waiting in his quarters at Camp Mabry in Austin, when shortly after 11 p.m. he received a telephone call from the governor, who was spending the night at his home on Galveston Bay. He asked: "Do you have a bunch of Rangers in the East Texas oil fields?" Sterling replied that he did and that "they are going to strike at twelve o'clock." The governor countermanded the order, claiming that "a move like that would cost us the election." The adjutant general was dumbfounded but managed to say: "On the contrary it will win it. The place is flooded with illegal voters, and they are solidly against you." The governor repeated: "I still want to countermand the order."

General Sterling always thought that it was Jacob F. Wolters who was responsible for the governor cancelling his plan, but Ross Sterling later told Ed Kilman that the man who advised him to get the Rangers out was Amon Carter. In the last conversation William W. Sterling ever had with Ross Sterling, the former governor remarked, "Bill, if I had let you go ahead and knock out those illegal votes in Gregg County, we probably would have won."[52]

The August returns showed that Sterling made large gains in most parts of the state. He secured a far greater percentage of the Hunter and Wolfe vote than did Mrs. Ferguson. The governor increased his July primary vote by 177,463; Mrs. Ferguson topped her first primary total by only 75,406, but that was enough to win, 477,644 to 473,846—a margin of just 3,798 votes. Sterling led again in northwest Texas, the Rio Grande Valley, and in the large urban counties except Bexar, which his opponent carried by 3,457 votes. Dallas County gave the governor a majority of over 13,000. It was the closest vote in a governor's contest since 1869, when E. J. Davis was declared the winner over A. J. Hamilton by 809 votes, and was the closest in Texas history for a Democratic primary election.

The returns showed that the total number of votes cast in more than a hundred counties again had exceeded the number of poll tax receipts. After conferring in his office with Tom Love, Dan Moody, Judge W. R. Ely, Robert A. Stuart, Walter Woodward, Walter Woodul, Alfred Petsch, and other friends, Sterling issued a statement claiming that he had received a substantial majority of the votes lawfully cast in the second primary and that he ultimately would be declared the winner. He charged that thousands of illegal votes were cast and that gross errors occurred in the count. Thanking his friends for reelecting him and for their interest in good government, he promised to "leave nothing undone to obtain an honest ballot and an honest count." "I know that I have won this election if all the illegal votes were out of that count," the governor assured a supporter. Nevertheless, the *Dallas Morning News*, an untiring, unsleeping foe of the two Fergusons, admitted: "Those votes, so far as illegal, after all voiced the will of citizens of Texas, tho technically disfranchised by non-payment of poll-tax or some similar reason. It is an indication that many citizens, not listed, yet preferred Mrs. Ferguson to Mr. Sterling, and their opinion is entitled to consideration."[53]

All Things to All People

Texas faced the prospect of again winding itself up, as the *Cincinnati Enquirer* tauntingly expressed it, "in the apronstrings of 'Ma' Ferguson." Writers for national magazines like *The Nation* and *Collier's* sought to explain the Ferguson phenomenon to their readers. "To some extent, the Ferguson victory denotes an awakening class-consciousness, since 'Ma' was commonly regarded as the candidate of the people against the corporations," wrote Harold Preece from Austin in *The Nation*. "I use the term class-consciousness advisedly, but so long as the Ferguson organization serves as a stop-gap, no party with a genuine program of social readjustment is going to make any headway in Texas." Mildred Adams, a correspondent for the *New York Times*, commented: "Why Texans voted for her this particular year is a question that, asked of fifty people, may evoke fifty separate answers." She continued:

Catholics may vote for her because they are still grateful to her for beating the Klan, business men because they think she will reduce the costs of government, or because they expect to get State contracts. Newly converted Fergusonites may say, "I never did take much interest in politics before, but when it touches your pocketbook I tell you it's a different matter." Certain independent oil men are for her because they are furious at Governor Sterling for sending the State troops into East Texas, for political ineptness, for being a dry, for not bringing prosperity. Disappointed idealists will support her because they are still bitter over the administration of young Dan Moody, who succeeded her as Governor. Thousands of people because they are tired of overdue mortgages and low crop prices.

Out of it all, personality emerged as the one great common denominator. Always it comes back to Old Man Jim, Farmer Jim, Jim and Ma. Jim is all things to all people.

A grizzled, unshaven cotton farmer, wearing overalls held up by a safety pin and broken shoes that showed bare feet, described himself as the poorest man in Hays County and told Adams that he had always voted for Ferguson and always would. "I'll tell you how it is," he said after an hour's talk. He summed up the Ferguson appeal thus: "You go up to the mansion there in Austin and Jim treats you just as good as if you was covered over with diamonds. I know, because I've done it. If Old Man Jim can't get us out of the mess we're in, nobody can, and we might as well give the clanged country back to the armadillos and the hoot owls."[54]

The Sterling camp tried to persuade the fourth special session of the forty-second legislature to create an investigating committee to look into the alleged election frauds, but the proposal was killed in the senate on September 6, when members voted 15 to 10, with three pairs, to send the investigation resolution back to the State Affairs Committee. Again the East Texas counties showed many more votes cast than poll taxes paid, and the issue was particularly acute in the counties comprising Tomas Pollard's and Margie E. Neal's districts. Both were against the proposed investigation, and the former served as "chief pallbearer" to the senate resolution. In a telegram read to the senate on September 3, Pollard gave East Texas a clean bill of health on the charges of election irregularities. On September 9 the house tabled a resolution, 62 to 52, for a ballot probe after almost an entire day of debate. "Just what does that mean?" a newly elected legislator from the brush country asked as the vote was taken. "That it is just about to breathe its last," Speaker Fred Minor gravely replied. "Confidentially, the general talk around the Capitol is that Mrs. Ferguson will be certified as the nominee and will be elected without any considerable trouble," James V. Allred wrote his parents. "You may rest assured that I will do my dead level best to keep down the middle of the road and do what is right. Of course, I am wholeheartedly supporting the Democratic ticket from top to bottom."[55]

Perhaps more importantly, the Sterlingites were defeated in the Democratic state convention at Lubbock. Only a comparatively few Sterling delegates attended, despite imploring phone calls from the governor's state headquarters in Dallas, while the Ferguson partisans came in droves from every section of the state and would not be denied. They took up most of the hotel rooms and crowded the public eating places. There were rumors that Sterling would attempt to seat his delegates with the help of Texas Rangers armed with machine guns, and the Ferguson men, some of whom were armed, had "blood in their eyes."

Crowds greeted the Fergusons at the railroad station. From there the couple were conducted to their hotel in a parade led by the Lubbock High School Band. When the one-day convention opened on September 12, the Ferguson managers quickly took charge. Not a breath of opposition manifested itself on the floor, and the convention went off harmoniously. A new state chairman, Maury Hughes of Dallas, and a new state committee were named—all under the Ferguson influence. Only a few anti-Ferguson men won places. The convention certified Mrs. Ferguson as the party's nominee and recommended her platform to the voters and the legislature. Sterling, who had reached Lubbock the night before, did not go to the meeting. He and about a dozen dispirited friends stayed in a hotel room a few blocks away and listened over the radio to the throaty roars of the victory-hungry Ferguson crowd.[56]

Upon his return to Austin, Sterling filed a suit contesting Mrs. Ferguson's nomination in Judge W. F. Robertson's 126th District Court. The judge was a Sterling appointee and Dan Moody's uncle. The suit alleged that more than twenty thousand illegal votes were cast in the second primary for Mrs. Ferguson; furthermore, it argued that she was not qualified to hold office because of her marriage to James E. Ferguson, a licensed attorney, which made her entitled to a share of his earnings under the community property law. During the time she was governor, the suit charged, her community earnings raised her salary more than $20,000 above her state salary, and this was in violation of the constitutional provision prohibiting the governor from practicing any profession or receiving any reward, fee, or compensation.[57]

"The court proceedings will not succeed," Ferguson declared in the *Forum*, "and the promoters of the litigation should now be branded as enemies of the Democrats and all others who act with them." Ferguson leaders in the legislature prepared a countermove if the Sterling suit was pushed. They contemplated a special session of the new pro-Ferguson legislature on November 10 to investigate Sterling's private business transactions and other matters. Under the law enacted after Ferguson's impeachment in 1917, seventy-six or more members could call to convene a special session if the governor refused to do so. "The opposition is becoming frantic," Sterling wrote Charles I. Francis. "[T. H.] McGregor and [W. E.] Pope are doing everything they can among the legislature to prejudice their minds against me, and the administration. As you perhaps know they have even gone so far as to threaten impeachment proceedings. They are simply trying to throw out a smoke screen or trying to intimidate or frighten me. Of course this they cannot do." Publicly he vowed not to be scared off by "smoke screen threats."[58]

On September 28 Judge Robertson granted a temporary injunction keeping Mrs. Ferguson's name off the general election ballot. The next day her attorneys asked the Texas Supreme Court to issue an order compelling Secretary of State Jane Y. McCallum to certify Mrs. Ferguson's name to the various county clerks and to restrain the secretary from making a partial certification of the nominees. The court did not immediately grant the injunction but set a hearing for October 1 and told Mrs. McCallum in the meantime not to take any action as it had taken jurisdiction. On October 2 Mrs. Ferguson filed a sensational countersuit in Judge Robertson's court, charging Sterling with having spent over $500,000 in the campaign, although the corrupt practices act limited expenses to $10,000. A general denial was made that illegal voting would have changed the election's outcome.

On October 6 Robertson ruled that he lacked jurisdiction to try Sterling's suit and dissolved his temporary injunction. Two days later the supreme court ordered Mrs. Ferguson's name placed on the general election ballot, and to ensure there was no slip-up, the justices executed a sweeping mandate guaranteeing that her name would be on the ticket in every county in Texas and decreeing that its judgment was final. No reference was made to Mrs. Ferguson's eligibility. The basis of the decision was that the contest had become moot because Mrs. Ferguson, a holder of the certificate of nomination, could not be deprived of her rights by legal proceedings that would continue beyond the time for the printing of ballots.[59]

Orville Bullington of Wichita Falls, a lawyer and independent oil producer with farm and ranch interests, was the Republican gubernatorial candidate running on a platform calling for vigorous enforcement of the Eighteenth Amendment. Opening his campaign at Waco on September 20 before two thousand people, he appealed to Sterling supporters and Ferguson opponents to place honesty in government above party affiliation by retiring the Fergusons to private life. He quoted in full Jim Ferguson's statement, made in 1920, advising Texans to bolt the Democratic Party and vote as citizens interested in their country's welfare. The candidate remarked that this was the only good advice Ferguson had even given to the people of Texas. Ferguson told Dallas newspapermen that his wife would poll 600,000 votes and her opponent, whom he called a "political ignoramus," would get about 75,000.[60]

As had happened in 1924, some anti-Ferguson Democrats bolted to the Republican nominee. An anti-Ferguson mass meeting was held in Dallas on September 24 in response to a call issued by thirty people, most of them active in the Anti-Tammany Democrats of Texas movement in 1928. They organized the League of Anti-Ferguson Democrats to exist "so long as Fergusonism is an issue in Texas politics." The gathering voted unanimously to support Sterling for election should he win his case against Mrs. Ferguson but to go for Bullington if he lost. The league formed a nine-member campaign committee with Cato Sells as chairman. On the day the Texas Supreme Court decided in Mrs. Ferguson's favor, the executive committee endorsed Bullington. "This is a Democratic campaign," Sells said as he opened headquarters in Dallas. On his coat lapel he wore a Bullington for Governor button under a Roosevelt-Garner medallion. Members of the group included T. S. Henderson, H. W. Naman, Oscar Calloway, Ed Crane, J. L. Lightfoot, Sam McCorkle, Dallas Scarborough, E. L. Kurth, and R. L. Wheellock. Gen. M. M. Crane announced that he would not vote for Mrs. Ferguson but was "intensely interested in electing the national presidential ticket headed by Governor Roosevelt." Sterling was informed by a member of the Jefferson County Democratic Executive Committee that "at least thirty of the fourty [sic] four members will bolt the party and vote for Mr. Bullington. I feel that he will carry Jefferson County by at least one thousand votes."[61]

Tom Love wrote William Gibbs McAdoo that "Ferguson will be beaten a hundred thousand in November." A group of anti-Ferguson Democrats took over publication of a monthly farm paper, the *Texas Farm Democrat*, to counteract the *Forum*'s influence with rural voters, and Love was installed as editor. According to W. R. Ely, he wrote "every word of the first issue," and it was his purpose to try to keep the paper going as a monthly. Jim Ferguson blasted the former supporters of George Butte in 1924 and Herbert Hoover in 1928 who were now organizing to defeat the national and state Democratic tickets in Texas. The following is vintage Ferguson and deserves to be quoted in full:

> They are headed as usual by Tom Cat Love who has started him a newspaper called the Texas *Farm Democrat*. Of all the people that ever lived he is the last man that has any right to use his name. In the first place, he is not a Texan, but a "pussy-footer" from Missouri who hit Texas running for office as the candidate of the saloon men of Dallas. He is in no sense a farmer and, while he owns a farm near Dallas that he bought by selling influence in the Wilson administration during the war and called his place Love Ridge, he knows nor cares no more about farming than a hog does about the Grace of God. While the boys were taking Vimy Ridge "over yonder" Tom was taking Love Ridge over here. And as to Tom being a Democrat, that is so durn ridiculous that everybody greets that claim with a hee haw of a jackass.[62]

The day after he lost his court fight, Sterling said he would not vote for Mrs. Ferguson in the general election. "Knowing Jim Ferguson's record, and having declared it to the people of Texas, I would consider it an act of positive dishonor to cast my vote to put the government of Texas in his hands," the governor declared. Asked if he intended to support Bullington, Sterling

replied: "The statement speaks for itself. I have nothing to say right now."
He wrote a Dallas supporter: "You have probably seen my statement in the
press today. I assure you that I meant every word of it and there is no language strong enough to express my contempt for James E. Ferguson and his
crowd of criminals and law breakers." Sterling vowed, "I shall continue to
fight for honesty and efficiency in the government of this State, regardless
of my political fortune."[63]

In his letters Governor Sterling urged the anti-Ferguson forces to unite
with Bullington, calling him "a native West Texan, son of a Confederate sol-
dier, and a splendid man." George Armstrong was running as an independent, but Sterling felt that he would not get more than a fifth of the anti-
Ferguson vote and hoped he would withdraw from the race. A Bullington
for Governor button was pinned on Sterling's coat when he left the executive
office on October 20 for a fishing trip. In a statement issued in Austin two
days later, the governor came out unreservedly for Bullington and renewed
his attack on Fergusonism, repeating his charge that Mrs. Ferguson had
been nominated through illegally cast votes. He offered his services to do
everything possible to elect the Republican nominee: "Texas Democrats can
not render the Democratic party a better service than by smashing Fergusonism with their votes at the November election, and I predict this is what
they will do by a substantial majority."[64]

Bullington made an elaborate campaign, visiting all parts of the state.
He bitterly denounced Jim Ferguson but did not mention his wife by name.
"We have them scared and on the run," he said at LaGrange. "They have
tried to laugh this campaign off. We're wrecking Jim's gravy train." He said
he was a Texan first and a party man second, arguing that a victory for him
would be a victory for Texas and that bolting was a civic duty. "It's either vote
anxious for me or nothing." To reassure anxious Democratic state employees, he promised not to claim the spoils of office for the Republicans. "I realize Texas normally is a Democratic State, and I can assure my Democratic
friends that they need not fear a shake-up in the State's appointive offices,
nor a replacing of Democrats by Republicans."[65]

The Fergusons announced on October 13 that they would make ten
speeches, most of them in the larger cities, during the two weeks preceding the election. Jim said he was anxious that Texas should poll a million
Democratic votes. The couple urged people to vote the straight ticket, reminded them of their primary pledges, and preached honesty and the
sacredness of an obligation. "Democrats, vote 'er straight" was also the state

Democratic Executive Committee's slogan as it waged a single campaign to elect the party's whole ticket "from President to Public Weigher." Following the strategy of tying the national and state tickets together, the Fergusons always put in a good word for Roosevelt and Garner.[66] Jim had sent a letter to Roosevelt that had enclosed a copy of the *Forum* with the Lubbock convention platform, had given assurances of Democratic success in Texas for the national and state tickets, and had advised the nominee: "By all means conserve your strength for the performance of official duties beginning March 4, 1933." Roosevelt's cordial reply was as follows:

> Though I have just returned from my "look, listen and learn" trip I am snatching a moment to answer your good letter of Sept. 22.
>
> I was much interested in the copy of your paper, which I shall read through carefully just as soon as possible. Naturally I was especially pleased with the platform adopted at the convention at Lubbock.
>
> I am delighted to have your assurance that prospects for the success of the ticket are so good for writing me as you did.[67]

The League of Anti-Ferguson Democrats of Texas distributed a broadside, "Do Not Be Bluffed or Bulldozed," calling Roosevelt's letter "a part of the routine grist for national headquarters." Voters were reminded that in 1920 Ferguson had pleaded with his followers to scratch the Cox-Roosevelt national ticket, telling them not to be "bluffed or bulldozed" into voting what he then termed the "infernal Democratic ticket." Love sought unsuccessfully to have Roosevelt make a declaration in line with his speech in Nebraska that urged voters to regard public welfare above party regularity and to let their conscience be their guide in the November election. He was "absolutely convinced" from his long acquaintance with Roosevelt, he wrote Jim Farley, FDR's campaign manager and chairman of the New York State Democratic Committee, that if the governor was a citizen of Texas he would not vote for Mrs. Ferguson, even if she was the legal party nominee.[68]

At a Houston rally Ferguson said that there were only six doubtful counties in the state and claimed that his wife would get a 15,000-vote majority in Bexar County, which would be enough to offset the Bullington majorities in Dallas, Harris, McLennan, Potter, Tarrant, and Taylor Counties. In closing at Tyler, he predicted his wife would lead her opponent by a majority of 500,000 votes. "I try to kid myself as little as possible," Jim told Dick Vaughan of the *Houston Press*, during a remarkably frank interview:

People say I've got the vest pocket vote, a vote I can pull out of my vest pocket any time I want it. They think of it as a gift from the sky, like the frost that comes down during the night. The only way a man ever gets people to vote for him is by doing something for them. The day is past when a man can speak himself into office. There now are only two ways in which a man can make himself governor. One is to convince people that he will give them something they want and the other is to convince them that he will relieve them of something they don't want. You might call it giving the people a biscuit. As long as the biscuits last they are for you. But when you cease to deliver the biscuits they will not be for you any longer.[69]

The *Dallas Morning News* urged voters to "shed party collars" and vote against Fergusonism: "Fergusonism must be buried under an avalanche of votes before Texas can hold its head up proudly among its sister states." But 1932 was one of the worst possible years for a Republican to be running for governor of Texas, and the old anti-Fergusonism appeals had lost much of their punch. "Ferguson hatred—as preached by you Drys—is not appealing to people who are near starvation," a Burleson man lectured Tom Love. "They listened to you in '28—to their sorrow. Most of them look upon Drys now, as nothing more than 'henchmen' for the Republican Party.... Mr. Bullington's dryness, Anti-Fergusonism, and promise of Good Government, will not deceive enough people, to elect him Governor of Texas. Wait and see!"

In fact, Mrs. Ferguson won the race with a majority of 211,179 over Bullington (528,986 to 317,807). She carried all but twenty-eight counties. Twenty-five of these were in West Texas. Only Dallas and Potter of the "six doubtful counties" were lost to the Fergusons: Harris gave them a majority of 10,335; McLennan, 1,560; Tarrant, 455; and Taylor, 156. Bexar County fell only a few votes short of giving Ma the predicted lead of 15,000 over Bullington. "I feel somewhat disappointed that Bullington did not win over Mrs. Ferguson," Sterling said privately, "though it was almost an impossibility on account of this being a presidential year and a great landslide was bound to take place on behalf of the Democratic party." However, the Democrats in Texas cast almost a quarter of a million more votes for Roosevelt and Garner than for Mrs. Ferguson, indicating widespread voter disapproval of the Ferguson record. The ill fruits of bolting in 1928 tainted the campaign for independent voting four years later. Roosevelt profited by it hugely and the Fergusons to a lesser degree.[70]

On December 3, 1932, the state Democratic Executive Committee adopted a resolution calling on the state and national heads of the party to appoint only loyal Democrats who had supported the ticket from top to bottom for public office. Chairman Maury Hughes told newsmen there were some Texas politicians who were a menace to the party and to the state and who were engaged in a conspiracy to put stumbling blocks in Mrs. Ferguson's path as governor. Referring to one Democrat who, he said, had bolted the party in 1928 and 1932 and who was now reported to be seeking a federal appointment, Hughes remarked, "This man has more gall than brains." He explained, "As far as the Governor is concerned, only those who supported the ticket will receive appointments."[71]

Appointing Party Spoils

The bolting Democrat in question was Cato Sells, the chairman of the anti-Ferguson league of Texas, who was an applicant for the position of collector of internal revenue for the Dallas District. Tom Love started a letter-writing campaign to Senators Sheppard and Connally endorsing Sells for the job. As Love explained to those from whom he sought letters:

> Although he [Sells] was an outspoken supporter of Roosevelt and Garner after the Chicago Convention and of John N. Garner before that Convention, the Fergusonites are urging that he ought not to be appointed, because he was one of the hundreds of thousands of Texas Democrats who opposed James E. Ferguson, running in his wife's name, for Governor. In view of his life-long, self-sacrificing support of the Democratic Party and of the moral side of all public questions I do not feel that he ought to be slaughtered because of his opposition to Fergusonism.

Both Governor Sterling and former governor Moody (who, Love assured Sells, "was for you as strong as horse radish") wrote letters on Sells's behalf, but the two Texas senators agreed that the appointment should go to W. A. Thomas of Dallas, a member of the Ferguson-Hughes group and a onetime brother-in-law of Sam Rayburn.[72]

In May 1933 Congressman Joseph W. Bailey Jr. candidly told O. B. Colquitt, whose term on the U.S. Board of Mediation would expire on January 1, 1934, that in his opinion there was "very little chance of your reappointment; because Mr. [James A.] Farley has said in my presence and to a number of my friends, that no appointments will be recommended of people who bolted the ticket in 1928 in Texas." Love wrote a long letter to President Roosevelt in December 1933 on Colquitt's behalf. He warned the president that "it is neither good policy nor good government to blacklist" Dry Democrats "for having followed their consciences in 1928; and this is precisely what we are told in Texas is to be done and ought to be done." Colquitt waged a vigorous lobbying campaign in Washington, talking with Connally, Sheppard, Garner, Rayburn, and others, but to no avail. He was not reappointed.[73]

The original Roosevelt men in Texas, headed by T. Whitfield Davidson, were afraid that the Garner camp would exclude them when he came to distribute federal patronage. Davidson warned Col. Edward M. House, who had been a close advisor to President Wilson, that by using national committeeman Jed Adams and by keeping facts away from Farley and others, "there is an attempt being made to wholly ignore and discriminate against those who performed this signal service and in favor of those who were bitter against Mr. Roosevelt and are still bitter against many of his friends." Charles I. Francis of Wichita Falls was dispatched to the East to look after the interests of the Davidson group, who were backing Karl Crowley for administrative assistant to the attorney general of the United States, Alvin Owsley for minister to Canada, and Clyde O. Eastus for district attorney for the Northern District of Texas. The Roosevelt group fared better than the Hoovercrats, for all three men received federal appointments, although Owsley had to settle for minister to Romania. In September 1933 Francis was named as a special assistant to the attorney general of the United States, in charge of all oil and gas litigation for the Department of Justice; he was also counsel for the Petroleum Administrative Board. In February 1936 Roosevelt appointed Davidson to succeed Judge Edward R. Meek as U.S. District Judge for the Northern District of Texas. He spent thirty years on the federal bench, retiring in 1965; at eighty-nine he was the oldest federal judge in the nation. Davidson died in 1974 at the age of ninety-eight, having outlived his life insurance company's actuary tables.[74]

Thomas Watt Gregory, who had been attorney general during the Wilson administration, received "almost innumerable letters" asking for help in securing places under the incoming administration, and he endorsed "quite a number of people for different positions." In February 1933 he went to New York City to confer with Roosevelt. He complained of a cold during the meeting and the president-elect advised him to go to bed as soon as he returned to the Hotel Pennsylvania where he was staying. Pneumonia developed, complicated by pleurisy and acute diabetes, and the seventy-one-year-old Gregory never rallied, dying in his hotel room. House had notified his family, and his wife, son, and daughter were at his bedside when the end came.[75]

House, according to his friend and biographer, Arthur D. Howden Smith, assumed that he was to be the new president's closest responsible adviser, consulted on all questions of major policy, national and international. But House was overoptimistic in this assumption. Political gossip had it that neither Louis McHenry Howe—FDR's closest advisor and confidant—nor Jim Farley was partial to sharing influence with the colonel. Not long after the November election, Smith conveyed to House Farley's patronizing reply to a newsman's question. "Oh, no, we're not worried about him. A very nice old gentleman. We'll take care of him, but I don't think we'll need him." House was skeptical of this intelligence. "I daresay certain people don't want the President to listen to me," he said, "but I'm sure I can influence him. He trusts me, and so does his mother. I've known him ever since he was a mere boy."[76]

According to Raymond Moley, Roosevelt believed that House had long outlived his usefulness. Although the president rarely consulted the colonel, the two men remained on friendly terms.[77] Roosevelt sent House an inscribed photograph, which the colonel promised to cherish and hang alongside that of Wilson. "Just between us and the angels, F. R. lacks many of the qualities that we should have in a dictator of the Philip Dru type," House confided to Frank Andrews in August 1933. "I have not attempted to influence affairs of the administration, and have only given advice when it was sought. If I were younger and more vigorous I would have attempted a more active part, for my relations with the President and his family are exceedingly cordial. He has asked me to Washington several times and I may go down in October and spend a few days with him."[78]

Meanwhile, the anti-Fergusonians gave themselves over to gloomy forebodings about the future of state government under Ma and Pa. "I feel that we are in for a siege of lawlessness and one of tearing down and breaking up the splendid state organization that has taken six years to build up, though I cannot believe that the people of Texas will stand for it to go too far," Sterling predicted. "At least, I am hoping for the best." During the campaign Jim Ferguson had complained about the presence of Texas Rangers at several of his rallies, culminating in several being at the Lubbock convention and even in the courtroom during the arguments on the election fraud. Adjutant General Sterling and some of his men were credited with having originated the

Langhorn brochure, which caused considerable excitement and a damage suit against Sterling's campaign manager, Ernest Alexander of Fort Worth. According to the *Dallas Morning News*, "This means that the rangers will be polled as to loyalty, with some sure to walk the plank. The present force has been built up in six years, four under Dan Moody and two under Sterling." On January 18, 1933, every member of the Rangers was discharged, without prior notice. Their combined service was approximately five hundred years.[79]

Robert Holliday of El Paso, whose term on the University of Texas Board of Regents was about to expire, wanted to protect the institution from Ferguson control by having two regents resign before the governorship changed hands and appointing Judge Robert Batts and Ed Crane in their place. "From two to four more years of Batts' and Crane's influence on the Board will put the University in a position where even the Fergusons could not hurt it, permanently," he wrote Thomas Watt Gregory, "but I feel that the situation is rather serious until the building program is completed and our lands and finances are put on a secure basis." Gregory replied: "I do not know what is going to happen to the University under a Ferguson administration and I can only hope for the best."

Regent O'Dell was prevailed upon to resign, and Holliday hoped Sterling would appoint Crane to his unexpired term, but instead the governor named Charles I. Francis. On January 11, 1933, Sterling announced that he was reappointing Batts, Holliday, and Crane for six-year terms; all had been originally appointed by Moody. Ferguson adherents in the senate prepared to fight against confirmation, and later in the day Batts asked that his name be withdrawn. Mrs. Ferguson indicated that her nominees would be H. J. Lutcher Stark, Dr. H. K. Aynsworth, and L. J. Sulak. On January 16 Sterling withdrew his nominations after Attorney General Allred issued an opinion that the appointive power rested with the incoming governor. The senate confirmed Mrs. Ferguson's nominees.[80]

In line with the governor-elect's campaign threat to replace the entire Highway Commission, Jim Ferguson secured a temporary injunction from Judge J. D. Moore of the Ninety-Eighth District Court of Travis County that restrained the commission from taking bids or contracting for the expenditure of any additional highway funds. If contract letting could be frozen until Mrs. Ferguson's inauguration, road fund expenditures would be in the hands of a commission with at least one and perhaps more Ferguson appointees. However, Attorney General Allred and the commissioners opposed Ferguson's action, and he ultimately lost his suit. The injunction was dissolved and the commission on the night of December 8 hurriedly issued $4 million in contracts. Jim found solace for this setback by asking business-men to purchase twelve-inch ads costing $25 each in the January 17, 1933, inauguration issue of the *Forum*; the ads congratulated "the State of Texas and the Fergusons upon their return to the Governor's office." Texans must have felt a sense of déjà vu; it was 1925 all over again.[81]

In the waning days of Sterling's administration, Cone Johnson's term on the Highway Commission was ending and the Fergusons slated Frank Denison of Temple to replace him. Efforts to induce W. R. Ely, who had been appointed by Dan Moody in 1927, and D. K. Martin, also a longtime mem-ber of the Highway Commission, to resign failed after some negotiations.[82] The Fergusons then moved to gain control of the highway body in their own way by having a bill drafted that raised its membership to five, provided for that number of districts, and allowed for the election of a member in each district for a six-year term after the first two years. The incoming governor would appoint the members for the first two years, which would be dur-ing Mrs. Ferguson's incumbency. As drafted, at the outset, the bill required the resignation of commissions whose terms extended into the Ferguson administration.[83]

In his final days in office, Sterling did what he could to hamstring Mrs. Ferguson for the next two years. Under a law passed by the forty-second legislature, he was required to prepare a budget for the next legislature's consideration. Sterling set to work "with gusto" on the project. With the outgoing governor's budget in the hands of lawmakers, the new governor would find it more difficult to justify her own financial proposals. He also attempted quietly to foster the speakership candidacy of A. P. Johnson of Carrizo Springs, but these efforts came to naught when the Ferguson choice, Coke Stevenson of Junction, won the post. In his final message, the longest of any he had sent to the legislature, the governor sought, in the words of his biographer, "to build around the Fergusons a wall of positive, practical suggestions for legislation, which represented his own thoughts about the needs of the state." In early January he tried to make some appointments in the executive branch, which were ordinarily left to the incoming governor. Finally, he disbursed all the funds received from the Reconstruction Finance Corporation for work-relief projects to the cities and counties. These activi-ties came under the heading of what the governor privately called "rolling a rock in the paths of the Texas enemies."[84]

Sterling was so bitter over his defeat that he refused to take any part in the inauguration ceremonies. He explained: "I will say to the people of

Texas that I do not care to take part in the inauguration of one whom I deem wholly incompetent to occupy the office of Governor and whose husband, who will be the Governor in fact, is ineligible and disqualified to hold any office of trust in the State of Texas, according to the Constitution of the State and decisions of the Supreme Court." On the last day of Governor Sterling's term, Adjutant General W. W. Sterling joined the governor in his office. The corridor was crowded with exuberant Ferguson men. One of the governor's friends suggested that he go out the side door, to avoid any possibility of a clash. He brushed the idea aside, saying, "I came in the front door, and I am going out the same way." It was customary for the outgoing governor to mark a passage in the Bible for his successor. W. W. Sterling suggested to the governor that he underscore the Eighth Commandment, but Ross Sterling vetoed the plan. "The Lord will take care of old Jim," he said. The two men entered the governor's private automobile and drove to his home on Galveston Bay.[85] The Sterling years were over, and Texans would have to see just how well the Fergusons' biscuits could stave off of the hunger pangs of the Great Depression.

CHAPTER 6

Garnering Votes
for Cactus Jack

B y the fall of 1930 the American people were becoming increasingly disgruntled over the collapse of Republican prosperity, and Democratic prospects nationally seemed bright.[1] No president could have prevented the Depression or brought the nation back to good times quickly. Much of the criticism of Herbert Hoover was unfair. He was the first president in history to attack economic depression systematically, but as the economy continued downward he grew more rigid and doctrinaire in trying to cope with the crisis. He was also his own worst enemy—too unyielding to get on well with the politicians and too colorless and aloof to win the public's confidence and affection. People needed a scapegoat for their difficulties, and the president received the blame. As a Texas Democratic leader wrote in December 1930, "Hoover seems to have lost the confidence of this section, among them many who voted for him two years ago; I have myself been compelled to revise my rather favorable estimate of the man." Another Texan declared bitterly, "Truly, I have been hit hard, but I deserve no sympathy, I voted for Hoover." The president's name became a trademark for every artifact of the Depression. Shantytowns were sometimes referred to as "Hoover Heights" or "Hoovervilles." Men who slept on park benches dubbed the newspapers with which they covered themselves "Hoover blankets." A pocket turned inside out was a "Hoover flag." Jackrabbits, eaten by many hungry Texans, were known as "Hoover hogs." Harvest hands sang, "Hoover made a soup hound outa me."[2]

Public discontent with the Republican record was reflected in the congressional elections of 1930. When the new Congress met in December 1931, the Democrats were able to organize the House; in the Senate, where six new Democrats were sworn in, the Republicans had a nominal one-vote edge. This trend portended Democratic victory in 1932. The leading contender for the party's presidential nomination bore a famous name in American politics. Franklin D. Roosevelt, a distant cousin of Theodore, had been assistant secretary of the navy in the Wilson administration and his party's vice presidential candidate in 1920. In 1921 an attack of poliomyelitis paralyzed him from the waist down. With the dedicated assistance of his wife Eleanor and his aide and major political adviser Louis McHenry Howe, Roosevelt recovered sufficiently to place Al Smith's name in nomination for the presidency with the "Happy Warrior" speech at the Democratic National Convention in 1924. In 1928, at Smith's urging, he agreed to run for governor of New York. He was elected by 25,000 votes, although Smith failed to carry the state in his second presidential bid. This gubernatorial win in a Republican year greatly enhanced Roosevelt's prestige, and many people thought it marked the beginning of Smith's coolness toward him. In 1930 Roosevelt was re-elected by a plurality of 725,000 votes, more than double Smith's highest margin of 339,000 in 1922. Despite early certainty among some leading Texas Democrats that Roosevelt was their man, in the months leading up to the 1932 primary, a majority of Texas voters rallied behind their favorite son, John Nance "Cactus Jack" Garner, casting Roosevelt's victory into doubt.[3]

The Only Democrat Who Can Carry the West

For Roosevelt the task of winning nationwide support for the presidency meant finding a consensus position on Prohibition and putting some distance between himself and Tammany Hall. Roosevelt was personally Wet and drank moderately—one or two cocktails at a time. His great concern over Prohibition was that it must not again wreck his party's chances as it had in 1928. As governor he handled the question in a gingerly fashion. But on September 9, 1930, he broke his official silence. In a letter to Senator Robert Wagner, he declared that the Eighteenth Amendment should be repealed and replaced with a new amendment, which would restore to the states real control over intoxicants. In states where the people desired it, the sale of liquor through state agencies should be legal; in states where the people were opposed to liquor, they should have the right to bar its sale. Furthermore, this principle of home rule should extend down to the level of cities, villages, and towns.[4]

To put further distance between himself and Tammany, Roosevelt called Mayor Jimmy Walker on the carpet in Albany, appointed Judge Samuel Seabury to investigate the Tammany district attorney, and supported a Republican-controlled state investigation of New York City government.

But he hedged his attack on Tammany corruption by insulting Seabury and prolonging Walker's tenure in office.

Roosevelt was opposed to the Smith-Raskob plan of making Prohibition the dominant issue of the 1932 campaign. The crucial question was whether the damp "states' rights–local option" position would appease the Wets without alienating the Drys irreparably. The positive reaction from across the country immediately confirmed Roosevelt's belief that he had made the right move. In the South the few attacks on him came from the ultra-Drys who had bolted to Hoover in 1928 and who chose to lump Roosevelt with Smith and Raskob as another wringing Wet. "Let us not blink [at] the facts," Tom Love wrote Daniel C. Roper. "Franklin D. Roosevelt is regarded as a Dry who has gone Wet for political purposes, and as an anti-Tammany Democrat who has gone over to Tammany for political purposes." In the West, William G. McAdoo's reaction was bitterly hostile. "Roosevelt has done exactly what I expected him to do," the Californian wrote Love after publication of the New York governor's letter to Wagner. "He has come out for the repeal of the Eighteenth Amendment; he has done his utmost to suppress the investigation of Tammany corruption in New York, and will go to any length to serve Tammany in order to be reelected Governor. He has an overpowering ambition to be nominated for the Presidency in 1932." To McAdoo's mind that would "simply invite another rout similar to that of 1928."[5]

Roosevelt made his decision to begin an aggressive campaign for convention delegates before the 1930 election. James A. Farley, the genial chairman of the New York Democratic Executive Committee, was given the job of marketing Roosevelt among Democratic leaders from coast to coast, while the governor himself denied that he was a candidate, telling reporters: "I am giving no consideration or thought or time to anything except the duties of the Governorship. I repeat that now, and to be clearly understood, you can add that this applies to any candidacy, national or otherwise, in 1932."[6]

For Roosevelt to win two-thirds of the delegates to the Democratic convention, he had to carry the South and West almost solidly and add a substantial showing in the East. Texas, with its forty-six delegates, was a tempting prize. Roosevelt kept in touch with important Texans like Gov. Dan Moody and Jesse Jones, while his wife Eleanor corresponded with Mrs. Percy V. Pennybacker, a prominent Texas clubwoman whose chief interest in what she termed "organized womanhood" was the Chautauqua Woman's Club, a part of the Chautauqua Institute in western New York.[7] Eleanor cultivated Mrs. Pennybacker with a luncheon in her honor at the Executive Mansion in Albany, visits by the Roosevelts to Chautauqua, inscribed photographs, invitations to social functions, and a proposal of nonresident membership in the prestigious Cosmopolitan Club. Mrs. Pennybacker was completely won over to Roosevelt's cause. "Tell Governor Roosevelt every time I look at his photograph, I offer a little prayer: 'Dear God, give us this courageous spirit for a next President of the United States.'"[8]

In early February 1931 about 160 Texas senators and representatives (out of 181) signed a letter prepared by James G. Holloway, a rank-and-file Democrat from East Texas, inviting Roosevelt to visit the state. So many nonmembers were anxious to sign that Holloway began another for state house officials and employees and the general public.[9]

In March and April 1931 Jesse I. Straus, a New York businessman, issued the results of two polls, one of the 1928 convention delegates and one of business and professional men. Roosevelt led everywhere. Fifty-one replies were received from Texas delegates and alternates and Roosevelt was favored by twenty-five. Owen D. Young of New York, the president of the General Electric Company, was second with nine, followed by Senator Joseph Robinson of Arkansas with eight, McAdoo and Newton D. Baker of Ohio with two each, and humorist Will Rogers and Al Smith one each. Three delegates thought it was too early to express a preference. However, of the twenty-five delegates and alternates favoring Roosevelt, only John Boyle of San Antonio and Robert Holliday of El Paso had any statewide influence.[10]

Early in 1931 an organization was formed in Texas for Owen Young. General Jacob F. Wolters was one of the signers of the call. In the list of signers were found the names of light and power officials and, in Hugh Nugent Fitzgerald's words, "a few practical politicians who train in the light and power camp." Young was given a slight boost by his support for the Veterans' Bonus bill; Hal Brennan, state commander of the American Legion, and other lesser lights in the Legion were active for a while and then apparently dropped out. Young had supporters in Houston, Dallas, and Fort Worth. Former Klansman Bill Hanger, who represented the light and power interests in Fort Worth, favored Young but had no objection to Roosevelt. Magazine literature extolling Young made the rounds of the Young camps in Texas, but by August 1931 Fitzgerald believed the movement to be dead for all intents and purposes. Young himself kept insisting throughout the preconvention period that he was not a candidate, but in light of his many addresses on current issues and the activities of his closest friends, the suspicion that he was a candidate could not be downed.[11]

Roosevelt needed the support of the old Wilsonians in the South and West who still wielded influence within the Democratic Party, and one key to that support was Wilson's Warwick, the elderly Col. Edward M. House of Texas, who was now living in a New York City townhouse. House had known Roosevelt since he was a young man (through Mrs. Sara Delano Roosevelt, the governor's mother) and had taken a fatherly interest in his budding political career. In 1925 House indicated warm support for Roosevelt's stillborn proposal that a Democratic conference be held to heal the wounds of the 1924 Madison Square Garden convention and to move the party in the direction of progressive principles. "The Party is thinking of you," the colonel wrote in rather patronizing fashion, "as one of our principal assets." Shortly before the 1928 election, House wrote a friend: "I was with Franklin Roosevelt all day last Sunday at his country place. I believe he will be elected and if he is and Smith is defeated, he is our best bet for 1932." After the election House wired Roosevelt: "Your election brings consolation and a great hope." The New Yorker replied that "I would rather have your approval than that of almost any other man I know." Roosevelt's smashing gubernatorial victory of 1930 brought forth House's prediction of election to the presidency two years later and ushered in the colonel's activities in Roosevelt's cause. House's friendship and support—along with Roosevelt's own service in the Wilson administration—draped around the governor's shoulders, in the words of one reporter, "at least a little of the sacred Democratic mantle that was Woodrow Wilson's."[12]

On December 29, 1930, House conferred with Louis Howe. Howe briefly outlined some of his plans as House listened attentively. Suddenly Howe said, "What about Texas?" The colonel replied confidently, "You can count on Texas." "Why?" Howe wanted to know. "Because," answered House, "I will send word to my friends there that Roosevelt is our best bet." That seemed to satisfy Howe, who abruptly concluded the conference and shuffled off. "He [Howe] reminded me of Alberich," said Robert M. Field, a friend of House's, who was present.[13] "The only difference was that the gold which Louis guarded was the political destiny of Franklin Roosevelt."[14]

House saw in Roosevelt a candidate whom he could perhaps shape and direct, as he thought he had once influenced Wilson. He urged the governor to strike "a high and progressive note" in his 1931 inauguration speech, because he would have the whole country for an audience, "and what you say now will go a long way toward crystalizing opinion of you as a leader and a statesman.... If you will read Wilson's Inaugural Address in 1913 you will better understand what I mean." House evidently did not think Roosevelt capable of arriving at correct policies on his own. He confided to Robert Woolley that he thought Roosevelt could beat Hoover in 1932 "if we can keep [him] from making any mistakes and get him to take the right view of national and foreign affairs." Later House suggested to Daniel Roper: "I think we are all of one mind as to Roosevelt's availability as a candidate and what we must do is to confer as to the best position for him to take not only on the question of Tammany but also on the question of prohibition and the economic issues which are so vital at the moment."[15]

On his part, Roosevelt found it profitable to nurture House's notion that he could resume his Wilsonian role as president maker and confidential adviser, but nothing demonstrated more clearly how little intention he had of giving real power to House than the fact that he sent Howe to court the colonel. Howe, always distrustful of those who managed to come too close to Franklin, would never have shared his position as Roosevelt's key adviser and would have reacted with rage at the very idea. So far was Howe from that emotion that at the conclusion of a March 1931 meeting, he left the colonel puffed up with importance and full of enthusiasm for the Roosevelt cause. House wrote Roosevelt: "It is a joy to cooperate with him for the reason that he is so able and yet so yielding to suggestions. We never have any arguments and have no difficulty in reaching conclusions satisfactory to us both. I congratulate you upon having such a loyal and efficient lieutenant." Howe thought House bombastic and limited in influence, but he could be useful if carefully watched. In June 1931 Roosevelt sent Howe to see House with a list of proposed "key men" to head his state organizations. House was down for Texas.[16]

Emerging from political retirement, House began an extensive private correspondence to promote Roosevelt's fortunes. In letters to the old Wilsonian group, he wrote as an experienced politician, appealing to the politician's instinctive desire to back a winner. "If we nominate Roosevelt I feel sure we can elect him over Hoover, particularly if times do not change between now and November 1932, and provided nothing untoward happens," he wrote Albert Sidney Burleson. "The reason I mention Roosevelt is because he is the only democrat who can carry the West. It would vote for him as solidly as I did for Wilson in '16 and for much the same reason. Newton Baker and Cordell Hull represent my views perhaps more nearly than any men in the Party whose names are mentioned as possible candidates, but there are reasons why neither one would make anything like as strong a candidate as Roosevelt."[17]

The colonel's maiden effort early in 1931 to recruit McAdoo met with a rebuff. "Replying to your questions about 1932 I can't see Roosevelt or any other New Yorker, at the moment," the Californian stated. "Who, of all men on our side now being mentioned, has any popular hold upon the imagination or the interest of the American people? Without meaning to be vain, but speaking merely of the fact, I think I had a very strong hold upon the masses." House backed off with flattery, assuring McAdoo that he had no more ardent admirer and that he would have been a worthy successor to Wilson, "another Jackson" in his popular appeal. If the Democrats were deadlocked again in 1932, "that would be the chance for your friends to spring your name upon the Convention." The two men agreed to challenge jointly the Smith-Raskob dominance of the party machinery, but McAdoo clung stubbornly to his insistence that the party shun another New Yorker as nominee. "Tammany and the bosses" had chosen Cox in 1920, Davis in 1924, and Smith in 1928. "Each time, disastrous defeat resulted."[18]

The Roosevelt camp asked House to feel out the situation in Texas and advise them as to the best method of proceeding. "In fact, Roosevelt's friends have left the matter wholly in my hands," the colonel boasted. He, in turn, relied on his old friends Thomas Watt Gregory, attorney general in Wilson's cabinet, and Houston attorney Frank Andrews to advise him on Texas politics. "I am counting on you both as being willing to support Roosevelt even if not with enthusiasm," he wrote them. After receiving House's letter, Andrews lunched with Gregory and former governor Hobby, and then reported:

> We talked about the matter a good deal. We were all of the opinion that if Roosevelt got out as a distinctly wet candidate Texas would not be for him for the nomination. If that feature were not especially emphasized, he would stand a better chance to carry Texas. His handling of the Tammany situation will also have something to do with it. In other words, if he shows a disposition to go after the corruption hammer and tongs, instead of in a permissive style, it would help him in Texas very greatly.... We all agree that it is too early to make predictions along a definite line—too many things can happen. We also all agreed that no man who is thoroughly committed to the wet side should be a Roosevelt Manager in Texas. He might be a wet, but he should not be prominent because of that issue.... Unless conditions change pretty rapidly, if Roosevelt should be nominated I think he would be elected. There is, of course, no doubt about his carrying Texas.[19]

Gregory's advice followed similar lines. The best policy for the time being was not to attempt to form an organization in Texas and to keep quiet;

Roosevelt's apparent growing strength in the middle and far West, if kept up, would gradually have its effect in Texas and elsewhere, for a large number of Texans liked to be on the winning side. In case no great Roosevelt active strength developed later, Gregory recommended sending an uninstructed delegation to the national convention and getting as many Roosevelt men as possible on it. He closed with a warning that House, dreaming of again manipulating Texas politics from the seclusion of his Manhattan townhouse, would have done well to heed:

> I am not active in politics down here and my health is such that I do not feel disposed to be very active; of course you will bear in mind that the old machine of 1912 no longer exists, that a world of younger men are largely in the saddle and that Roosevelt would not have that gripping pull on a large body of Texans which the name of Woodrow Wilson carried; your Roosevelt organization would have to be built up almost from the ground, and at this time I do not know where the building material would come from, though it might appear in abundance a little later on.[20]

In addition to waging his letter-writing campaign, House sent his young protégé, Robert W. Field, a Rhodes scholar from the University of Texas who was now practicing law in New York City, to look into Roosevelt's prospects in Texas. "With the situation as it is I am anxious for my native State to cast her potential votes for Roosevelt as she did for Wilson in 1912," House wrote Field. "To have an influence she should have it will not be sufficient to send an uninstructed delegation and then swing to Roosevelt at the Convention. She should be one of the first as she was before to step across the line and be to Roosevelt what she was to Wilson during his fight at Baltimore and throughout his two administrations." Before leaving Field lunched with Roosevelt in Albany. In the meantime House had advised Gregory and Andrews that Field was coming and told them to talk to him "as frankly as you would talk to would to me for he has my full political confidence." Although Field offered to pay his own expenses, House and Howe decided that the Roosevelt organization should reimburse him.[21]

Field's ostensible reason for going to Texas was to attend the second annual Texas Roundup in Austin. He boomed Roosevelt there. "Governor Roosevelt has all the strength possessed by Al Smith and none of Smith's weaknesses," he told reporters. "Governor Roosevelt is a wet, a Protestant and a member of the Masonic order. It will take a wet candidate to win the state of New York." Privately, Field assured his listeners that Roosevelt's health was perfect and that he handled himself well, using only a cane. "There is a good deal of talk as to whether or not he is physically able to take the strain of the Presidency," Andrews wrote House. "Judicious advertising of his physical condition will be exceedingly helpful."[22]

Upon his return to New York City, Field prepared a memorandum for Roosevelt. He identified Tom Connally, Ross Sterling, Dan Moody, and Pat Neff as the most influential political leaders in Texas, in that order. "These four men are drys. If any one of them took a favorable position either express or implied, the effect would be most helpful and would probably control the decision of Texas." Connally was not unfriendly, but his chief purpose in life was to be reelected, and he was unlikely to do anything that would make that more difficult. Sterling knew nothing of politics and was ambitious only to be reelected governor. Jesse Jones had started a movement to have the Texas delegation pledged to him, but Field doubted whether Sterling would permit his name to be used in such a game. Moody, although out of office, had a personal following and was a most effective campaigner, but he was in debt and was chiefly concerned with building his law practice. He was decidedly friendly toward Roosevelt and would continue so unless some of the militant Wets rushed into print with statements purporting to represent the Roosevelt position. As for Neff, he was bone dry and unlikely to help in any way. His ambition was to go to the U.S. Senate.

Field recommended that Gregory be named on paper as head of the Roosevelt movement in Texas. Wilson had been deified in the minds of Texans, and since Roosevelt and Gregory had been part of his administration, they would regard Gregory's leadership as altogether natural. Moreover, Gregory was active and alert but so advanced in years that younger and more ambitious men would not regard him as a threat to their own political hopes.

In conclusion, Field reported that the bulk of the Smith people in Texas were cordially for Roosevelt and that most of them recognized that any effort on their part for him would be resented by the anti-Smith crowd and would play into the hands of the fanatical Drys, typified by Tom Love, who were eager for a bitter Wet vs. Dry, Smith vs. anti-Smith fight. In such a conflict, Roosevelt and the moderate Wets and Drys who supported him would be destroyed. "The important thing therefore is to let all of the earlier public activity and statements on behalf of Roosevelt come from the extreme drys if possible and following that from the moderate drys," Field recommended. "The wets can work under cover without publicity and can come out in the open after the drys have committed themselves. All of the wets with whom I talked and all the Smith men except very few, were entirely agreeable to such a plan."[23]

After talking with Roosevelt, House wrote Andrews and Gregory that the governor would not do anything "in an active way" for the present, which conformed with their advice. If they wanted him to come to Texas in the autumn, he would try and arrange it. "It seems to me if he went to the State Fair at Dallas as Wilson did in '12 it might be helpful," House suggested to Gregory. "He makes friends wherever he goes. He is modest, not opiniated [*sic*] and listens to advice, besides he is genuinely fond of people and shows it." The colonel sounded an optimistic note: "I hope you and I may be able to repeat our performance of 1912 and it looks as if we might."[24]

Gregory, however, showed little real enthusiasm for Roosevelt, personally preferring Newton D. Baker or Senator Cordell Hull of Tennessee for the nomination; in mid-May he confessed to House: "I have not yet discovered any special drift toward Roosevelt." While "feeling around a little for Roosevelt strength," he confined his efforts to suggesting that Prohibition should be forgotten in the next fight and that the Texas delegation to the national convention should be composed of "Simon Pure Democrats" who would support the ticket and who, while perhaps uninstructed, would work for the best interests of the party. He even went so far as to suggest that the best policy in Texas might be for Roosevelt's friends to throw their support to Hull who, although a Dry, favored waging the 1932 campaign on economic issues.[25]

House's undercover work for Roosevelt was brought into the open on June 4, 1931, by Ernest K. Lindley, political correspondent of the *New York Herald Tribune*, who telephoned the colonel at his summer home in Manchester, Massachusetts, and received official confirmation of the rumors that he was a member of the Roosevelt camp. The *Herald Tribune* captioned Lindley's article: "Colonel House Back in Politics to Aid Roosevelt's Cause." Lindley quoted House as saying: "It's the first time that I have taken part in a national campaign since 1916. The only reason is because of my admiration for Roosevelt, and, further, because of my belief in a Democratic victory." Asked by reporters if he had discussed the governor's prospects with him directly, House said he preferred not to answer. He had "no notion" what part, if any, he would take in promoting Roosevelt's campaign. "I have not been in good health for several years," he said, "and I don't know what I may do." But House was careful to write Howe to let him know that his announcement had elicited many approving letters from Texas and elsewhere.[26]

To dramatize his reentrance into politics, House gave a luncheon for

Roosevelt at his summer home on June 13, 1931. Among the guests were Massachusetts's two senators, David I. Walsh and Marcus A. Coolidge, both Democrats. Invited, too, were some of the Wilsonian intellectuals of Boston, including Mayor James M. Curley and the editor of the *Atlantic Monthly*, Ellery Sedgwick. House's purpose in feting Roosevelt, as he explained to Robert W. Woolley the following day, "was to discourage Smith and his followers, and to show them how hopeless it was to oppose our man. Massachusetts has been considered Smith's strongest state, and if he cannot count on it his cause is lost. No one not here could realize how successful the luncheon was. There were seventy-five or a hundred newspaper men, photographers and movie men here, and I believe my object was attained." As events were to prove, House had grossly underestimated Smith's influence in one of the two northern states he had carried in 1928.[27]

Lining Up Texans for Roosevelt

"We must get Texas to declare herself early," House wrote Robert Field on July 4, 1931. "It will not only have a great influence on other Southern States but it will give Texas a dominating position which I very much want her to have." Since the ultra-Drys had spearheaded the opposition to Al Smith in 1928, the Roosevelt headquarters concentrated on converting the moderate prohibitionists. When the time came to organize, Frank Andrews wrote Roosevelt, "Your friends in Texas of the prohibition faith should be, at least theoretically, put in charge of the organization. If we are fortunate enough to properly arrange this when the necessity develops, we ought to make the landing." House asked Gregory, as soon as he thought it was advisable, to get Connally and Dan Moody to come out with him and Andrews stating that, in their opinion, Texas was favorable to Roosevelt. The colonel thought it would be "a real coup."[28]

Gregory had no opportunity to contact Connally and Moody before he met with Roosevelt, Howe, and Field in New York City. Gregory told the group that the drift in Texas was toward Roosevelt, that Connally had publicly declared his conviction that he would be the nominee, and that Moody was friendly. However, a state organization should not be formed, he argued, until a large number of prominent Dry Democrats had pledged their active support, and this was the work he was looking after. There was a possibility that Roosevelt's Wet friends in Texas would start a bandwagon movement before Gregory was ready, and through former national committeeman Joseph Guffey of Pennsylvania, who was closely in touch with the Wet element, Howe took every precaution to keep this from happening.[29]

Gregory also visited House in Massachusetts and outlined a course to be pursued in Texas. After returning home, he would go to Dallas and talk with Gen. M. M. Crane and other North Texas leaders; he would also try to line up the *Dallas Morning News* for Roosevelt.[30] "We consider the Dallas *News* the most influential paper in Texas," the colonel explained to Howe. Gregory would then give a statement to the Associated Press endorsing Roosevelt, which House would first edit. House assured Howe that Gregory "is willing to take the bridle off and make his statement strong as it can be made."[31]

Meanwhile, other Texans not part of the House circle were moving ahead with their own plans to organize the Lone Star State for Roosevelt. At the end of July the first Franklin D. Roosevelt for President club, with a membership of over four hundred, was organized in Waco.[32] Former lieutenant governor T. Whitfield Davidson of Dallas, who was destined to become the Roosevelt organization's front man in Texas, appeared on the scene with an invitation to Gregory to join "a number of Franklin D. Roosevelt Democrats" in an informal, dollar-a-plate luncheon at the Baker Hotel in Dallas on July 30. Gregory immediately asked House whether Davidson had been authorized to organize the Roosevelt movement in Texas and if so, by whom. Although he thought very highly of Davidson, "a rather close personal friend of mine," he still believed that it was too early to organize. However, if Davidson had been authorized to proceed and did so, Gregory would be glad to cooperate with him and be of all the help he could.[33]

Gregory was not back in Texas in time to attend the luncheon but promised to see Davidson in Dallas. He asked Davidson to sound out Crane, Cullen F. Thomas, and the *Dallas Morning News* regarding the Roosevelt campaign. In an effort to restrain Davidson's enthusiasm, he cautioned:

> I feel that the stars in their courses are working for Roosevelt and I am rather distinctly of the opinion that if the Roosevelt people wait a while longer to launch his organization, it will be a distinct advantage as the sweep in his direction seems to be becoming more pronounced every day. I should regard it as a very unfortunate thing for any extreme Anti-Prohibition leaders to dominate, or largely take charge of, the Roosevelt movement in this State.[34]

But those attending the luncheon had already decided to go ahead. Davidson, who presided over the meeting, appointed twenty-nine persons, ten of whom were from Dallas County, to meet in two weeks and perfect a permanent organization. A statewide meeting in Waco was planned for later, at which time a delegation would be sent to Roosevelt with an invitation for him to attend the state fair in Dallas. An effort would be made to have a Roosevelt Day set aside and to hold a mammoth rally. "Like you, I feel that the Roosevelt sentiment is overwhelming," Davidson wrote Gregory. "It is much more general than I anticipated. As a result of our small publicity here, I have large stacks of letters and telegrams. General Crane, I am sure, will be with us. Cullen Thomas is hesitating some what on account of Prohibition, but I believe he will be all right later on. The Anti-Saloon League is fighting Roosevelt."[35]

After scrutinizing newspaper reports of the Davidson meeting, Gregory was unimpressed. About a dozen people had been mentioned by name in the *Dallas Morning News* report, "among whom are unquestionably some light weights," he informed House. Only six or eight men and women on the twenty-nine-member committee were known statewide. Tyler banker Gus Taylor, who knew Davidson well, told Gregory that "he is a good fellow, but is a limelighter, and we ought to get some stronger men than were at the Dallas meeting." Frank Andrews thought that "there was not a single recognized State leader in the bunch," which included a fair sprinkling of cranks like Pat O'Keefe.[36] He also believed the movement was premature, and he doubted that Davidson was the man to handle it. Neither Gregory nor Andrews was willing to become part of the Davidson organization. "I fear that the Davidson movement will concentrate a rather general attack on, and perhaps organization against, the Roosevelt movement, and this before the movement had made the headway which Frank and I thought should be waited for," he fretted to House. Pleading ill health, Gregory declined to serve on the organization's permanent committee but promised quiet cooperation.[37]

House advised Gregory that no one had authorized Davidson to form a state organization, noting: "The Texas situation is supposed to be wholly in our hands, that is yours, Frank Andrews' and mine." Still, Davidson's action did not surprise House. As he explained to Howe: "You cannot have a candidate so far in the front as ours and not expect someone to start an unauthorized organization. The desire to be in the band wagon is too strong to be denied, and this we may reckon on in other states as well as Texas." House recommended that Gregory make the best of the situation and work in harmony with Davidson and others.[38]

Gregory now saw a "tremendous drift" toward Roosevelt. During a recent visit to Austin, he informed House, he had found practically no Roosevelt opposition. "The unquestioned sweep toward Roosevelt in all parts of the country is having exactly the effect in Texas which I anticipated and the tide is growing stronger every day," Gregory noted with satisfaction.[39]

On August 29 Roosevelt's supporters held a statewide meeting in Waco and perfected a permanent state organization. Davidson was elected chairman; Newt Williams of Waco, vice chairman; Harold D. Young of Dallas, second vice chairman; Archie C. Price of Waco, secretary-treasurer; and Mrs. Frank Coffey of Fort Worth, assistant secretary. Davidson privately hailed the meeting as "a splendid success," noting that more than twice as many representative men and women had attended as compared with the Woodrow Wilson meeting in Waco twenty years before. But Gregory, who did not attend the meeting because he thought it was "premature and ill-advised," told House that the state's leading newspapers had paid no more than casual attention to it. He noted that of the sixty people present, thirty-eight were from Waco and seven from Dallas, and there were only four he had ever heard of—Davidson, Williams, Harry Lawther of Dallas, and James G. Holloway of Austin. Moreover, a considerable portion of those in attendance were Wets, and several of the speeches had indicated a strong Wet sentiment. Gregory promised to use his influence to try to get prominent Prohibition leaders to take part in a general state Roosevelt conference to be held not earlier than January or February 1932.[40]

In early September 1931, Davidson, Harry Lawther, R. E. L. Saner, and "a gentleman from Oklahoma" called on Roosevelt at Poughkeepsie, New York. The Roosevelt headquarters decided to treat them with great courtesy and give them all the publicity they wanted, but to firmly decline to visit the Texas State Fair in the fall. "We are still running under the delusion that Roosevelt is not an avowed candidate," House explained to Gregory, who had strongly advised against the state fair appearance, in part because he thought Roosevelt's physical infirmity might make an unfavorable impression on Texans, "a full blooded people with great confidence in physical vigor." The Texas delegation was "delighted" with Roosevelt and satisfied with both his physical fitness and his position on Prohibition.[41]

In October the Roosevelt headquarters sent Samuel I. Rosenman to San Antonio to contact local leaders and talk them into "whooping up the Roosevelt-for-President club in that section of the State." Rosenman had been born in San Antonio in 1896 but had pursued a legal career in New York. A member of the Empire State legislature from 1922 to 1926, he served as bill drafting commissioner from 1926 to 1929 and then became legal counsel to Roosevelt and the founder of the famous group of advisers called "The Brains Trust."

Upon his return from Texas, Rosenman prepared a memorandum for Howe. "San Antonio, or Bexar County, is divided into two Democratic factions," he reported. "One is led by the Mayor of the City, Charles M. Chambers, and the other, called 'The Citizens League,' the so-called reform group, is led by Charles Dickson, a lawyer. I visited the leaders of both groups. They all seemed to be for F. D. as the man most likely to win in the election." In view of the factional fight, Rosenman asked both sides who would be the proper person to lead the Roosevelt movement in South Texas. He was told to see Henry C. Carter, a lawyer; he found him "very friendly disposed towards Roosevelt." Still, Rosenman played it close to the vest: "I, of course, made no mention of any active movement being started, but I think he would be the ideal man in South Texas." Rosenman thought the committee in charge should be Carter, Henry Lee Taylor, and Mrs. S. J. King. Since the Roosevelt for President club in North Texas was completely Dry and was actively enrolling only Drys, he recommended that a separate organization along Wet lines should be started in South Texas, as soon as the Dry organization was well underway.[42]

In the meantime the Davidson organization met in Dallas and selected a five-member committee to arrange for the opening of a Texas headquarters with a paid office staff. Davidson, Charles I. Francis of Wichita Falls, and Walter B. Scott of Fort Worth were named to the committee; two places were left open for representatives from Houston and San Antonio.[43] After receiving Rosenman's report, Howe wrote Davidson that his club was "generally recognized as being composed of the dry element," and he thought that the time had come to give the Wets their place. As long as that element seemed to be focused in the southern part of the state, would it not be wise to let them go ahead and organize a "South Texas Roosevelt Club for President?" Howe tactfully noted: "Of course, we do not want anything that looks like a rival of the Roosevelt Club already organized, but it would be difficult to have the same Club composed of part 'wets' and part 'drys.'" Howe asked Davidson to give him an answer at the earliest possible moment, as there was danger that Wets excluded from the Roosevelt organization might go to Governor Albert Ritchie of Maryland, a Wet, or some other party.[44]

Although Gregory approved of Howe's suggestion, Davidson was unenthusiastic. "I do not think it would be wise to separate Texas into a Dry group and a Wet group," he told Howe. "Those things are looked upon with disfavor by thoughtful people in both groups. We have studiously avoided that and have taken the position that the next campaign should not be fought on the question of prohibition but ... upon the Republican record and nothing else." Davidson then went on to disabuse Howe of the notion that the Roosevelt organization was exclusively composed of Drys; in fact, a majority was possibly Wet, including Newt Williams, Harry Lawther, and R. E. L. Saner. Galveston, which had always been Wet, was thoroughly for Roosevelt, and Fred Pabst was a member of the club's finance committee. Having casually dropped this bombshell on Howe (Gregory had known from the beginning that the Davidson organization was not strictly Dry and had informed House), Davidson promised to go to San Antonio in a few days and confer with Henry C. Carter and other local leaders. What he seems to have had in mind was a Bexar County Roosevelt club with a representative on the board of his own organization. As he wrote Carter: "It is our idea that each club conduct its campaign in its own way but by unified or associated efforts we might extend the organization into the other counties that were more backward." This was not exactly what Howe had envisaged.[45]

Carter refused to commit himself definitely to Roosevelt, and, after visiting San Antonio, Davidson recommended that John Boyle should be the organization's titular head, with somebody younger like Woodall Rogers in the front doing the active work. "Sentiment in San Antonio seems to be fine," Davidson advised Gregory. "In fact, it is growing every where. Frank Davis and John Boyle each assured me they were for Roosevelt, but they have each been very active and are conscious of the fact that they shouldn't work in the front. One of them has been on one side of the controversy for a time and the other on the opposite."[46]

Despite Davidson's continued optimism, Gregory put his finger on the basic weaknesses of the Roosevelt campaign in Texas, writing House: "I find the drift still toward Roosevelt but there is no real enthusiasm for him or for anyone else, and I am not at all satisfied with the organization the Davidson people are working on; it does not seem to me to be Statewide and practically none of the influential Democratic leaders of the State have come out for him."[47]

Yet Gregory's own strategy was essentially passive: to allow the enthusiasm for Roosevelt in other states to act on Texans and cause a "drift" to the governor. Furthermore, Gregory was simply not healthy enough to lead actively. As he told House: "I am not at all well and cannot be an active organizer in this matter, though I am doing all I can for the cause under the circumstances." He constantly harked back to the Wilson campaign in 1912 as a model for 1932.

Gregory opposed paying workers for campaign organization and wanted instead to rely on Roosevelt's friends, well-wishers, and "general patriotic citizens" for such help as they were willing to give. "In the Woodrow Wilson organization of 1912 do not think we had a single salaried person except two or three stenographers," he informed Davidson. But eager volunteers did not come forward in large numbers to work for a man who was not even a declared candidate. Most people's conversations were taken up with the Depression, not politics. Gregory was unable to find anyone to put in charge of organizing Harris County for Roosevelt. "I am about at my row's end," he confessed to Frank Andrews. "I have no general acquaintance with the politicians of this county, especially the young and middle aged ones, and so I am not a good man to make a selection." Not surprisingly, he wrote House at the end of November: "There is no such enthusiastic support of Roosevelt in Texas as there was for Wilson in 1912."[48]

Frank Andrews, the third member of the House-Gregory-Andrews triumvirate, was even less active than Gregory. "I have been so terribly busy that I have not been able to talk much politics lately," he wrote House on December 5. "Have not seen Gregory for a month and only sporadically find time to discuss politics with people who know something about it."[49]

Gregory devoted much of his time from November 1931 to January 1932 trying to secure a general letter addressed to Texas Democrats and signed by about a dozen leading Drys in the state, advising them not to raise the Prohibition question in the national platform or in the general election, to forget factional differences, and to pitch the fight against the tariff and on economic issues. He also hoped to insert in the letter a recommendation of Roosevelt's nomination, but General Crane and others in the Dallas area with whom he consulted thought this would be a bad policy. They were afraid that it would detract from what they hoped would be the practically unanimous acceptance by leading Texas Democrats of the policy advocated. Gregory and Crane together drafted the text and asked Tom Connally, Dan Moody, W. A. Keeling, James V. Allred, S. F. Brooks, W. A. Tarver, Tom S. Henderson, Cone Johnson, Cullen Thomas, Rice Maxey, Luther Truett, and C. L. McCartney to sign it. This would make fourteen signers. "You will observe that nothing is said about Roosevelt in the address; that will come later," Gregory advised Howe. Ultimately, Gregory, Crane, Henderson, Maxey, Thomas, Truett, and McCartney signed the address. Allred, Connally, Johnson, and Brooks refused to sign, and Moody, Tarver, and Keeling would not sign unless the address was redrafted to say more about forgoing a fight on Prohibition and less about the shortcomings of the Republican

Party. To dwell at length on the failures of the Hoover administration, they felt, would not be "wise or necessary" if "a strong appeal is to be made to the 'Hoover Democrats' who broke away from the party in 1928." An exasperated Gregory wrote Crane on February 23, 1932: "Almost three months ago we began work on the address we thought of giving out to the Democrats of Texas," he complained. "Up to some two weeks ago I continued to use my best efforts to get Keeling, Moody and others in Austin to send a draft covering their ideas of the address, but I have been put off so much from time to time that I have given up any hope of securing results from that quarter.... It rather seems to me that, considering the situation at large, we might as well abandon our idea of publishing the address." The address was finally published, over the signatures of the seven original signees, on May 23, 1932, a few days before the Democratic state convention and far too late to be of any use to Roosevelt.[50]

John Boyle warned Roosevelt through a third party, Judge Charles Pope Caldwell of New York City, that the "Democrats of Texas generally are not disposed to follow the leadership of Davidson, because he is primarily for Davidson, and whenever a party battle is on usually 'takes to the bush.'" Representative Temple Harris McGregor of Austin commented: "Roosevelt had the best of it here several months ago. I am not prepared to say that he has now." The canny Ferguson stalwart wrote in early October 1931:

> The band wagon riders took charge of his interest and have organized in his behalf. T. W. Davidson is the driver. While I don't think he will fall off of the seat, yet he may strike a stump or run into a rut and turn the wagon over before he finishes the trip. He is backed by the half and half crowd with the ultrawets and the ultradrys on the outside. This being so, I think it is entirely probable that these political pinquins [penguins] will be in the minority when election comes around.[51]

Howe was disturbed when the *New York Times*, which had always been friendly to Roosevelt, carried a story by its Texas correspondent stating that his supporters were not as busy as they ought to be in the state. "As I told you I had an intuition that things were going slowly," he wrote House. "However if Gregory will get his list of powerful people together and if something ever gets going on the South Texas thing, I think it will help." The colonel replied soothingly: "I think we will have to let Gregory have his way since he is on the ground and in touch with all the leaders." He added, "Personally I feel confident that Texas will be for us."[52]

McAdoo for Roosevelt

"The old McAdoo element tried to hold a rally here last night, Mr. McAdoo himself being present," Davidson wrote James A. Farley on December 16, 1931. "His appearance and speech was a 'boomerang'—everybody there was disappointed."[53] McAdoo's visit to Texas was the culmination of a low-key campaign by Tom Love to secure the state's delegation for his beloved "Chief." "Thomas B. Love has been pursuing his mole-like tactics since the beginning of the session," reported Hugh Nugent Fitzgerald in a memorandum forwarded to Roosevelt. "Those who enjoy his confidence say he has been urging his followers to organize for McAdoo for president and Hull for vice president next year. He has made very little headway under the dome of the state capitol."[54]

Love was convinced that Dry Democrats ought to make their fight within the Democratic Party and carry the national convention if possible, avowing all the time that they would not support a Wet if nominated. He thought there was "a good chance" to nominate a Dry progressive Democrat in 1932, and, if nominated, such a candidate was likely to have "a fair chance" to win, while no Democrat who favored repeal of the Eighteenth Amendment could come as near winning as Smith in 1928. In a March 1931 letter to McAdoo, Love recommended "a general program of friendly co-operation" between Dry favorite sons in various states: for instance, Dan Moody in Texas, Vance McCormack in Pennsylvania, Charles M. Hay in Missouri, Cordell Hull in Tennessee, Joseph Robinson in Arkansas, Walter George in Georgia, Alben Barkley in Kentucky, Harry Byrd in Virginia, Edward P. Costigan in Colorado, and Thomas Walsh in Montana. A movement should be projected in California to send a solid, dependable McAdoo delegation to the national convention as a part of this program. "Your friends will certainly control any delegation which goes from Texas unless present conditions are entirely upset," he assured McAdoo. "I think this should be the Dry program for the present, coupled with a policy of watchful waiting. I believe you can be nominated for President by pursuing this course and that if nominated you can be elected. I do not believe you can be nominated by projecting an overt nation-wide candidacy for the nomination unless and until developments justify that course."[55]

McAdoo conferred with some of his "old war horses" in San Francisco and New York about becoming a candidate. The Dry church leaders looked upon him as the Dry Democratic hope, but former allies, like Daniel Roper, Breckinridge Long, and Robert Woolley refused to join in letting the Anti-

Saloon League or other such organizations run the Democratic Party again. Some of McAdoo's closest friends said privately that he could not stand the disappointment of another defeat and that he was too old to try again. In fact, McAdoo did not want to make a long, hard fight for the nomination, and there was the matter of finances. "I think McAdoo will fall into line, though with a heavy heart," Woolley wrote House on June 18, 1931. "Confidentially he wrote to Roper recently asking if he thought it would be possible to arrange here in the east for the financing of his (McAdoo's) candidacy for the nomination. Roper replied in politic but plain language. In so many words, he told McAdoo that there was not the slightest sentiment for him, nor would it avail to try to work up any for him. Is there anything more tragic than a blasted presidential hope?"[56]

McAdoo, who was operated on for hernia in September 1931, accepted an invitation to speak at a World Disarmament Conference in Dallas on Armistice Day, November 11. Advising Love of his acceptance, McAdoo noted that he was getting letters from all parts of the country urging him to run again and wanted to talk the situation over with Love when he saw him. At this time McAdoo was evidently seriously considering running as an Independent. "What do you think of the possibilities of an independent movement?" he asked Love in an October letter. His own reasoning was as follows:

If I were an active candidate for the Democratic nomination, as I am not, it would be hopeless, in my opinion, because the wets and the bosses and the plutocratic elements in both parties which encompassed my defeat in 1924 would be able to tie up more than a third of the convention and create another deadlock, even if I went into the 1932 convention with as much strength as I had in the 1924 convention. The truth is, my dear fellow, that both political parties are under the same plutocratic control, so far as the national conventions are concerned. They dictate the nominations of the candidates of each of the major parties and no matter which win, the people lose.

If the letters he was receiving from all kinds of people, many of whom he did not know, were a fair indication of underlying sentiment, a political revolution might be possible in 1932—the kind of revolution that would allow some man in whom the people had confidence to lead a successful independent movement. "Of course, this would be almost a miracle," he admitted, "but occasionally miracles happen in the life of a nation, like the nomination and election of Woodrow Wilson, for instance. Certainly his nomination was a miracle."

Love was unenthusiastic. The only possibility of an independent movement assuming substantial proportions, he replied, would be after every effort had been exhausted to prevent a Wet Tammany nomination. "Only in such circumstances could a movement go very far in Texas, in my opinion." To this McAdoo responded: "I note what you say about the independent movement. I don't think I have conveyed to you accurately the general idea that is in my mind, but I shall write you about it in the near future."[57]

McAdoo put off his talk in Dallas until December 15 to allow his voice to recover from the effects of the anesthetic used in his operation. Love and his political allies made plans to meet quietly with him. Accompanied by his wife, McAdoo arrived in Dallas on December 14 to find that his arrival had created what the *Dallas Morning News* called "a small cyclone of interest that may easily develop into a boom to him." Sensitive to this fact, he refused to be drawn into any political discussion that might be construed as even a tacit admission that he was a candidate for the Democratic nomination. But he did say that he was greatly pleased to be back in Texas, recalling with almost boyish delight "the bully fight" that the Texas delegation had made with him in New York in 1924. "We had to fight extraordinary and detestable tactics in that convention," he declared, but quickly added, "only don't say detestable. I don't want to get political in talking of even the past." He continued: "Naturally I hope that we can find and raise up some Moses who can lead us out of the wilderness, including the welter of plans and grandiose schemes that have been advanced to restore prosperity." But, like Governor Murray of Oklahoma, who had declared that "this country needs another Lincoln," McAdoo refused to say where such a leader could be found.[58]

After McAdoo returned to California, he asked Love to send him fifty copies of that part of the *Dallas Morning News* carrying his speech and to have Senator Sheppard put it in the *Congressional Record* to ensure wider distribution. "What was the general reaction to the speech in Dallas?" he wanted to know. He was assured that it had made a "real impression" on Dallas and the state, due largely to the utter absence of any indication of political significance. "The Al Smith–Roosevelt crowd were hoping to discover a deep laid plot to use the occasion for political purposes and were disappointed in their utter failure to find any tangible support of such a charge," Love gloated. "I do not know what conditions are beyond the Texas line, but there is no doubt but that a delegation for McAdoo would be chosen now by an overwhelming vote; and that quite regardless of your candidacy or refusal to be a candidate."[59]

McAdoo also visited Washington in December 1931. Daniel Roper gathered together a group of Roosevelt supporters to give him a luncheon, hoping to win him over to the governor's side. House suggested that Roper should "impress him with the fact that we are centering on Roosevelt as the one man who can clean up the Wall Street, Raskob-Smith combine." He added, "Mac knows, and you may drive it in, that under ordinary circumstances we would both prefer him to anyone." McAdoo, however, was not convinced by Roper's arguments, for the question of him leading an independent movement was the subject of several top-level conferences in the Roosevelt camp during the following months. "I hope much that Roper and House and you," Roosevelt wrote Homer Cummings, "can pour oil on the somewhat troubled waters of his mind. Mac is a fine fellow, but I don't think that he has any perspective about the present situation and that it is only his real friends who can persuade him that a last minute insurgence will get him nowhere and will do harm to the progressive ideals with which all of us were associated in the old days."[60]

Cactus Jack: Texas's Favorite Son

In the meantime another name had been added in the Democratic presidential sweepstakes. In December 1931 John Nance Garner was chosen Speaker of the U.S. House of Representatives by the Democratic caucus and thereby became a national figure. After serving two terms in the Texas House of Representatives, where he introduced a bill to divide Texas into five states (in conformity with the 1845 joint resolution of annexation), Garner, as chairman of the committee on redistricting, brought in a bill to provide himself with a congressional district as large in size as Pennsylvania. In 1903 he arrived in Washington accompanied by his self-effacing, hard-working wife Ettie, who served as his secretary through most of his career. They lived a quiet life in residential hotels around Capitol Hill and mingled in Washington society only to the extent that his office required. Garner made few speeches and offered few bills in his early years in the House. He fostered a populist image of himself as a leading advocate of the graduated income tax and the Federal Reserve Act. When Claude Kitchins's opposition to World War I disqualified him as administrative leader, Wilson made Garner his confidential representative in the House. An adroit politician, Garner maintained his equable course through the twenties, trading public jabs and private drinks with his good friend, Nicholas Longworth of Ohio, the Republican speaker prior to Garner's tenure; they were, cracked Edward T. Folliard of the *Washington Post*, "the Damon and Pythias of Capitol Hill." At the end of the day, Garner, Longworth, and their lieutenants liked to gather in an obscure room in the Capitol colloquially known as the Board of Education to discuss legislation and down bourbon and branch water in a ritual Garner named "striking a blow for liberty."[61]

Uvalde, Garner's home, was a small town in South Texas. In addition to his controlling interest in two small banks, Garner owned a block of business buildings and other city property, a large rambling house in which he lived, pecan orchards and beehives, and a ranch that ran cattle, sheep, and Angora goats. "How did he make his million plus?" a reporter for the *St. Louis Post Dispatch* asked one of Garner's old Texas cronies. "Trading," was the reply. "John's the champion trader of west Texas. I guess he has traded in nearly everything. He trades ranches, banks, goats, stock, bees—John don't care so long as it's a bargain." Garner's one hobby was camping. He liked to go out for a few days on hunting and fishing trips. He was proud of his camp cooking. Poker might have been named as his chief vice, but it certainly could not be termed an extravagance, seeing that he won over $15,000 during one session.[62]

Garner regarded himself as an "old fashioned Jeffersonian Democrat." He said in 1931: "The great trouble today is that we have too many laws. I believe that primarily a government has but two functions—to protect the lives, and property rights of citizens." When it goes further than that, "it becomes a burden." In this spirit he had opposed child labor reforms, women's suffrage, and Prohibition because they interfered with states' rights. But he was also Jeffersonian in his hostility toward big finance. He assailed the domination of government by big business and led the fight in 1924 against Secretary of the Treasury Andrew Mellon's regressive tax reduction program. Garner also denounced public utilities and supported Senator George Norris's proposal for government operation of Muscle Shoals and his "lame duck" amendment. An investigation of Senate lobbyists disclosed that the Insull power interests had contributed $1,000 to a campaign to defeat him for reelection in 1928. While Garner voted against the Smoot-Hawley tariff bill in 1930, he saw to it that his district's goat's hair and Bermuda onions received protection. He still believed that Texas should be divided into five states and in 1930 made two statements on the subject. "When men reach our age they naturally think of their children's children etc. and it is such thoughts that prompted me in making the suggestion of a division of Texas," he wrote Thomas Watt Gregory. "The suggestion is not attractive, especially to our female voters, but to those who understand the situation here it must have some appealing weight."[63]

Washington correspondents vastly overdid the job of puffing Garner up to the public after his selection as speaker. They pictured him as a fiery, stalwart, sombrero-wearing son of Texas and gave him such picturesque sobriquets as "Cactus Jack," the "Texas Tiger," "Texas Jack," and "Chaparral Jack." They recalled that Texans hailed him as the "Chaparral Cock of the Frio" but failed to explain that the local meaning of that term was merely "roadrunner." Photographers took pictures of Garner stalking up the marble steps to the House, his sombrero rivaling the Capitol dome. Cartoonists clothed him in the garb of western actor Tom Mix—and the picture of a rip-roaring, snorting politician was complete. The reality was very different. A small man with a hawk-like nose, ruddy face, short-cropped white hair, owlish eyebrows, cold blue eyes, and a tight, small mouth, Garner, in the words of historian Arthur Schlesinger Jr., "presented at once the appearance of an infinitely experienced sage and of a newborn baby."[64]

Bascom Timmons, a newspaper reporter in Washington and later Garner's biographer, was the first to mention him as a possible Democratic nominee in 1932. That mention was made after the 1930 congressional elections in a routine story to newspapers in the Southwest. If Garner saw the column, he never mentioned it to Timmons. When Timmons remarked to Garner that Texas was proud of his position in the Democratic Party and undoubtedly there would be a movement in his behalf for the presidential nomination, he seemed uninterested and commented instead on Roosevelt's sweep in New York. "I think the Democrats have a real political catch in this fellow Roosevelt," he said. "He looks like the man for us in 1932." His own chances he dismissed. "No Democrat from Texas is going to have availability for his party's Presidential nomination except under extraordinary circumstances." When Timmons asked what effect Roosevelt's physical condition might have on his availability, Garner replied, "For the Presidency you run on a record and not on your legs. If he makes a good record with the legislature at Albany this winter his kind of ailment won't hurt him as a candidate. It might help him."[65]

In November 1931 Garner confided to Howe that he thought Texas would probably instruct for Roosevelt, but as speaker he felt it would be unwise for him to come out openly for the governor. He even requested that Howe find out Roosevelt's position on a number of issues to come before the House

Democratic caucus, since he felt that the probable candidate for president should have an important say in policy. "I certainly wish that I could have the pleasure of a few minutes conversation with you," Garner wrote Roosevelt. "It would be very inspiring and helpful. I had the pleasure of something like thirty minutes to an hour with your secretary the other day—concerning which he will tell you when he sees you. I wish you the best of health, luck and everything else. We are all right in Texas."[66] Daniel Roper approached Garner in December, asking whether he would consider supporting Roosevelt. The Texan told Roper what he had earlier told Howe: that since he was about to become speaker, he should maintain a neutral attitude, but he then added that he felt drawn to Roosevelt because of the financial forces against him.[67]

The first inkling that Davidson received of a Garner movement in Texas was when he visited San Antonio in mid-November. "Judge [Henry C.] Carter told me of a matter that I think is of more significance than he thought," he wrote Gregory. "He has had a letter from some party in Washington suggesting a boom for John Garner as a favorite son from Texas." This "favorite son business," Davidson believed, was being worked in every state in the Union, the ultimate object being to tie up the national convention and rush to a dark horse obligated to Raskob or some select group. "I am inclined that something should be given out to the papers against this universal favorite son propaganda," he stated. "I think I shall prepare something along that line and consider the advisability of giving it out without making any specific charges or calling any names." Subsequently, the *Houston Press* carried an interview with Davidson dealing with the evils of a favorite-son campaign, and editor Marcellus Foster also published an editorial on the subject. The *Dallas Morning News* printed an editorial in which it quoted Davidson's views.[68]

Frank Andrews advised House that he had been told "on most reliable authority," that Jouett Shouse, the chairman of the executive committee of the Democratic National Committee and a Smith man, was now engaged in an active effort to block Roosevelt's nomination. "I am told that he has been rather free in the statement that he has lined up more than a third of the states so that the opposition to Roosevelt will be unbreakable. I am also told that the 'Favorite Son' business is playing a large factor in it, and that the advocacy of Garner in Texas had its origin there."[69]

Andrew's information was correct. In September 1931 Smith, Raskob, and Shouse settled on Newton D. Baker as the man to stop Roosevelt. Identified with the Progressive movement in Cleveland, and secretary of war from 1916 to 1921, Baker had crusaded throughout the twenties for American membership in the League of Nations, which shaped his image as heir apparent to the mantle of Wilson. Yet some people believed that Baker had grown conservative since returning to Cleveland in 1921 to head a large law firm with a prolific corporate practice, including J. P. Morgan and utility companies. When he served one term as president of Cleveland's chamber of commerce, Baker favored the open shop. He sponsored a pamphlet urging the shutdown of a municipal electric power company he had backed when he was mayor of Cleveland. Shouse informed Ralph Hayes (Baker's "Louis Howe") that if Baker "would consent to be supported, 'Z' [Smith] will not only eliminate himself but will throw to you every particle of strength he can muster." Mrs. Belle Moskowitz told Hayes candidly that her choice was still Smith, but added that "if she couldn't have her man—and such a choice did not appear to be in the cards—she much preferred ours." Baker, however, refused to actively seek the nomination and would consent to run only if drafted. Shouse came away from a mid-September Washington meeting with Baker and Hayes "greatly heartened" and determined to carry out a strategy conceived at the conference: to encourage an "open convention" made up of uninstructed and favorite-son delegations and bound by the traditional two-thirds rule. Raskob and financier Bernard Baruch were believed to be bankrolling the stop-Roosevelt coalition.[70]

According to reporter Irvin S. Taubkin of the *Dallas Morning News*, it was in the "fertile, far-seeing brain" of Steve Pinckney "that the Garner movement was really started." An ultra-Wet Houston lawyer, Pinckney was one of the leaders of the liberal Young Democrat faction in Texas. Some weeks before Congress convened in December 1931, Pinckney wrote to some of his Texas friends from Washington to begin organizing for Garner in such a way as to have a liberal organization when completed. He is known to have talked with Shouse and Raskob during this trip to the East, and his advocacy of Garner was part of their effort to block Roosevelt's nomination, leaving the way open for Al Smith—or a satisfactory conservative alternative in Newton Baker.[71]

The first John Garner for President club was organized in Houston in the latter half of November 1931. John Thad Scott, a banker, started the organization and proposed to form a statewide chain of similar clubs. On December 7, the same day Garner was elected Speaker of the House, his neighbors in Uvalde celebrated the occasion by organizing a Garner for President club. Three days later an editorial in the *Ferguson Forum* posed the question, "Why not John?" The article urged Texans to "get busy and make him our successful son as he has proved himself worthy to be." According to the *Forum*, "He knows now more about the actual operation of national affairs than any of the other prospective candidates can learn in 5 years after they are elected. Study the Garner idea and will [it] grow on you?"[72]

What did Garner himself think of the occasional mention of his name as a presidential eligible? "I do not know whether Mr. Garner takes very seriously the movement to make him a candidate or not," Sam Rayburn wrote on January 2, 1932. "I do not think it is offensive to him now but what it will be later on I do not know. There seems to be a great movement for favorite sons now. This is in some wise going to embarrass some of the favorite sons, who really want to elect a President and believe that Roosevelt is the easiest man to elect." According to the Washington bureau of the *Dallas Morning News*, the speaker's attitude was that the "echo from the hill" was pleasing, but he was not seriously impressed with the movement.[73]

The first widespread publicity on the Garner candidacy came with a coast-to-coast radio address on January 1, 1932, by publisher William Randolph Hearst, who had served in the House of Representatives with the speaker before World War I. Surveying the current presidential scene, Hearst classed Roosevelt, Baker, Ritchie, Smith, and Young as "all good men in their way, but all internationalists — all, like Mr. Hoover, disciples of Woodrow Wilson, inheriting and fatuously following his visionary policies of intermeddling in European conflicts and complications." But, he continued, Garner was "a loyal American citizen, a plain man of the plain people, a sound and sincere Democrat in fact, another Champ Clark. His heart is with his own people. His interest is in his own country." As he closed his speech, Hearst emphasized that he was not telling his listeners who should be the next president, but he left no doubt in their minds as to who his choice was, saying: "Unless we American citizens are willing to go on laboring indefinitely merely to provide loot for Europe, we should personally see to it that a man is elected to the presidency this year whose guiding motto is 'America First.'" The following day Hearst's address, in the form of an editorial entitled "Who Will Be the Next President?," appeared on the front page of every one of his newspapers.

Before endorsing Garner, Hearst sent George Rothwell Brown, one of his syndicate's political writers, to find out where the speaker stood on such issues as the retrenchment of government expenditures, the League of Nations, and the cancellation or reconsideration of European war debts. After interviewing Garner one evening in his modest suite on the seventh floor of the Washington Hotel, Brown reported to Hearst that while the speaker had taken no public stand on the League of Nations, he felt sure that he was opposed to all foreign entanglements. Garner believed in thrift, prudence, and economy in government, and as a banker, he abhorred extravagance in every form. He was unalterably opposed to the cancellation or modification of the European war debts owed to the United States and was sound on tariff and finance, having been for years an able member of the Ways and Means Committee. Brown told Hearst that "Mr. Garner had a deep sense of obligation first of all to his own country, that he was an old-fashioned, patriotic American and a rugged Democrat of the Andrew Jackson school."[74]

Brown later performed another task for Hearst. He wrote Garner's campaign biography, giving it the eye-catching title *The Speaker of the House: The Romantic Story of John N. Garner*. Before the book was published, Hearst ran daily installments in his newspapers, beginning on February 21, 1932. It was assumed that any presidential candidate who could claim a log-cabin origin was placed firmly in a category with Abraham Lincoln and thereby had a jump on other contenders. "John Nance Garner was born in a mud-chinked log cabin," wrote Brown. There was some question as to whether the speaker had in fact first seen the light of day through mud chinks, and an extensive search was begun for the humble dwelling in Blossom Prairie, Texas. Hearst, however, refused to be bothered. One of his staff artists was told to draw a picture of a log cabin suitable to presidential nativity, which made a very fetching illustration for the campaign biography.[75]

Garner professed not to be impressed with Hearst's boom. "What have you got to say about your Presidential candidacy?" he was asked at his daily press conference. "I haven't got a word to say," he shot back. "I am trying to attend to my business here. Now I'll talk about anything else you want to." The speaker explained to Bascom Timmons why he felt further presidential talk could do him and his party severe harm. "I have been Speaker less than sixty days," he said.

> I have got a tender majority of three. If I can stay close to the gavel I can get along all right. The biggest single bloc of votes in there is controlled by Tammany. It's more than a tenth of all the Democratic votes in the House. They have got a Roosevelt-Smith split among themselves already. Smith has got support among Congressmen from other states. The Maryland fellows are lined up for Ritchie. There are Roosevelt people in nearly all the delegations. I don't want to jeopardize our cohesion and the legislative program by a Presidential candidacy of my own.[76]

On January 5, 1932, Garner denied that he was a candidate. In a letter to a Texas supporter, a copy of which was distributed to the press, he said: "There are no presidential bees buzzing around my office. My duties as speaker have kept me so busy I have given this matter no consideration and I expect to be kept equally busy until the House adjourns." He followed the same tack in his private conversations. A colleague, Representative John McDuffie of Alabama, reported, "He growls like an old bear" if one mentions his candidacy. Another old friend, Homer Cummings of Connecticut, saw Garner early in January and reported to Roosevelt that the speaker had told him he was not a candidate. His only interest, Cummings observed, was to fulfill the duties of his office to the best of his ability, and consequently "he was giving his entire time, thought and attention to it and he did not intend to be diverted from his purpose." However, Garner agreed to Hearst's request that he designate a go-between so that the publisher could keep him abreast of his editorial policy and the general progress of the newspaper boom that he was conducting. The speaker chose John McDuffie as his contact man. This arrangement enabled him to maintain that he was personally doing nothing to further his candidacy while remaining fully informed as to what his supporters were doing for him. Newspaperman Thomas L. Stokes, who was covering the House during this time, noticed numerous private conferences between the speaker and the Hearst representatives.[77]

Hearst's support contributed little or nothing to the favorite-son sentiment for Garner in Texas. The speaker was already well liked there and needed no endorsement, while Hearst himself was not well liked, largely because of his opposition to Woodrow Wilson's ideas and works. The wartime president remained an idol to Texas Democrats, and the publisher's anti-Wilson diatribes were regarded as "unjust almost to the point of slander." Also, Garner's best friends felt that his interests would not be served by thrusting him forward too rapidly.[78]

On January 12, 1932, Sam Rayburn wrote Lewis T. Carpenter of Dallas concerning the general political situation as it related to the forthcoming Democratic national convention in Chicago.

It appears to me at this time that Franklin Roosevelt is far and away in the lead of all possible Democratic nominees. There is quite a movement throughout the Country, however, designated to be a "Stop-Roosevelt" campaign. Roosevelt with his position in New York has appealed to the popular imagination of the American people as no other man does at this particular time. However, within the next few months there will be developments that will show us all, I think, a clear road whether it leads to Roosevelt or another direction.

Little was left to Carpenter's imagination as to the meaning of "another direction." Rayburn went on to discuss Garner's qualifications as the man who occupied "the highest position of any other Democrat in public life in America today" and who was doing his job in "a masterly way." Rayburn claimed, "He is catching the imagination of the Country and it is not far from possible that quite a myth may be built up around him before the next Convention meets." The congressman did not discourage the movement to organize Garner for President clubs, saying:

Just what Mr. Garner's attitude toward his friends organizing Garner Clubs is pretty hard to find out as he has been so busy trying to do well the big job that he has in hand, that he has given little or no attention to it. However, I am of the opinion that at this time the movement in his behalf in Texas is not offensive to him and whether he makes a statement now or later is entirely a matter which he alone will decide.[79]

Writing in the *Baltimore Sun* on January 20, 1932, political columnist Frank R. Kent reported that within the past week "the Garner boom has swollen quite a lot." However, not all of the unsolicited support was inspired by either Hearst publicity or a personal desire to see the speaker nominated. A considerable portion of it came from politicians in the East, many of them friends of Al Smith, who were hostile to Roosevelt's nomination and anxious to find a way to stop it. In the absence of any candidate behind whom they could center—Smith himself was displaying "a rather sullen inactivity"— and in light of Roosevelt's long lead, they had been almost ready to give up. In this situation the Garner boom was "as welcome as the flowers in May"; the speaker's strength would come from the South and West, which were the sections in which Roosevelt had 90 percent of his support. Word had there- fore gone out from Smith's friends in Washington to "talk Garner." Jouett Shouse gave him an eloquent send-off in a Chicago speech. At the same gathering, Democrats in the South and West who dreaded anything tainted with Tammany turned to Garner as an alternative to Roosevelt. One corre- spondent analyzed the Garner boom as follows: "The impulse is rooted in a deeper and stronger feeling within the party. It arises from the desire of the rank and file Democrats to get away from everything the East implies and to find a good, safe politician with an innocuous record who knows the game and how to play it. Unconsciously, what they want is a Democratic Coolidge, and they instinctively feel that Garner is their man. They are not wrong."[80]

McAdoo for Garner

Meanwhile, McAdoo, who still cherished some presidential ambitions and was also contemplating a California campaign for the U.S. Senate, was closely watching developments. At the beginning of 1932, he viewed two of the major Democratic presidential possibilities with active dislike. Smith had been the major factor in McAdoo's defeat at the 1924 convention and McAdoo never forgave him. The Californian also disliked Roosevelt, whom he associated with Tammany Hall, Smith, and repeal of the Eighteenth Amendment. He thought the New York governor was a mental lightweight, full of "cheap platitudes and generalities," who was physically incapable of undertaking presidential duties. "Don't you know," McAdoo asked Daniel Roper, "that he'll Tammanyize the United States?" Roper replied, "No, I don't." To Arthur Mullen, McAdoo solemnly warned, "We don't want a dead man on the ticket, Arthur." Mullen, Roosevelt's Nebraska manager, retorted, "We won't have one."[81] McAdoo's first reaction to Hearst's speech endorsing Garner was negative. "I think it was a marplot speech," he wrote George W. Lynn. "I don't know whether Garner takes it seriously or not." McAdoo thought Hearst was making a mistake in antagonizing Wilson Democrats by implying erroneously that Garner was not in sympathy with Wilson's principles and ideas.[82]

"Is Jack [Garner] going to ask for the Texas delegation?" McAdoo queried Love on January 5. "If so, there will be no use, I think, in having the conference [in Houston] we discussed when I saw you last. If Jack doesn't want the delegation and if you have the conference we talked about, it might lead to the result that you and other good friends there have had in mind." Love replied, "If John Garner should say that he is opposed to the repeal of the Eighteenth Amendment I think it would be the part of wisdom for our friends in Texas to support him." He continued, "If he does not say this, he cannot get the Texas delegation. Things will crystallize in Texas between now and February 1 and I will keep you advised."[83]

On January 11, 1932, McAdoo wrote Love that he would rather have Garner than any of the Wet candidates, adding: "I think we could probably carry the California delegation for him, provided Texas is going to stand by him, but we will have to move soon, otherwise the wet gang out here will get in the saddle." On the same day that he received McAdoo's letter, Love wrote Garner, quoting the above passage from "a very prominent Dry Democrat of California." He told the speaker:

> I want to support you for President of the United States but I cannot and will not support anyone for that position who is not openly opposed to the repeal of the Eighteenth Amendment and in favor of its enforcement. I do not want the prohibition repeal issue in the campaign, and it can't be eliminated except by nominating a known opponent of repeal. . . . Personally, I earnestly hope you will qualify as the man we are looking for. If you do you can, in all probability, be nominated and elected President of the United States. If not, it is my opinion that there is no chance either for your nomination, or election.

Love sent a copy of this letter to McAdoo, promising to let him know what Garner's response was. Replying immediately, the speaker refused to declare himself on Prohibition, giving as his reason the need to preserve Democratic harmony in the House. "You have been associated with me for many years," he stated. "You have had wide experience as a legislator and I know that if you will give this careful consideration you will realize the wisdom of the course I am pursuing." But Love was not to be placated. He complained to Senator Sheppard that Garner was "going to try to ride through without declaring his opposition to the Raskob program." Dissatisfaction with Garner's reply led Love to again privately raise the McAdoo standard. "If McAdoo will allow the use of his name, and no Texas candidate is in the running who opposes the repeal of the Eighteenth Amendment, I am sure that the great majority of the delegates to the State Convention will be instructed for McAdoo," he advised P. H. Callahan, a Kentucky Dry. "In any event we are not going to take the liquor assault upon the Democratic Party, and the American home, lying down."[84]

But McAdoo's thinking was now diverging markedly from Love's. Within a month of Hearst's speech, McAdoo changed his mind about Garner as he came to realize the value of the approval of the Hearst newspapers. To stage a political comeback in California, McAdoo needed press support and control of the Democratic Party machinery in the state. The organization of a Garner ticket would ensure the newspaper backing and the victory of that ticket would overthrow the existing Justus Wardell–Isidore Dockweiler Wet leadership. By the end of January, McAdoo assumed Texas would be for Garner, writing Love: "So far as I am concerned, I think it is all right." As soon as Love and "our friends in Texas reached any conclusion about Garner," McAdoo wanted to be informed, so that something could be done for him in California.

For once Love refused to follow the chief's wishes. In his opinion Garner's letter meant he would not carry Texas. He told McAdoo flatly that he was not going to support any candidate who favored repeal of the Eighteenth Amendment or who declined to state his position on that question. McAdoo pressed Love to change his mind. "I feel very warmly . . . to Jack Garner, and really, of all the men who are mentioned as available for the Democratic nomination, I would rather support him than any of them," he declared. "I assume, of course, that Texas will instruct for him, and I venture to express the hope that you may think this the wise thing to do." As for himself, he did not wish to be considered for the Texas vote, or any other state, for that matter. Still, he left the door ajar a bit for a draft. "That, of course, doesn't mean that I wouldn't accept a nomination if it came unsolicited, but there is, of course, no chance of that."[85]

Presidential Hopefuls Emerge

In mid-February McAdoo came out enthusiastically for Garner. "I hope you liked the 'blast' I gave you the other day," McAdoo wrote the speaker. He explained to Bernard Baruch that he had been under increasing pressure to permit his own name to be used as a candidate, and he felt that the most effective way to eliminate himself was to declare in favor of someone else. But the elimination was a qualified one. "You have, of course, seen my statement about Garner," McAdoo wrote Love. "I hope you approve it. I think that we should all get behind him. It will do no harm, of course, if the personnel of the Texas delegation should have a secondary choice if it should be impossible to nominate Jack."[86]

Despite the Hearst and Texas booms for Garner, by February 1 it appeared Roosevelt might win the nomination by default. Only Gov. Albert Ritchie of Maryland, a Wet, was making any effort toward securing the nomination, and he was making little headway. The picture looked grim in the Newton Baker camp. Walter Lippmann and Ralph Hayes agreed that "the Roosevelt strength has reached perilous proportions and is in danger of turning into a sweep."

Roosevelt formally announced his candidacy on January 23, 1932, but two weeks later, on February 6, Al Smith came into the race with the statement: "If the Democratic national convention, after careful consideration, should decide it wants me to lead I will make the fight, but I will not make a preconvention campaign to secure the support of delegates." This equivocation contributed to Roosevelt's advantage. Although the 1928 Democratic standard bearer pledged "not in advance of the convention either to support or oppose the candidacy of any aspirant for the nomination," party leaders knew he was gunning for Roosevelt. His announcement slowed the momentum of the governor's campaign: the New York delegation would now be divided, and Smith would win delegates that otherwise might go to Roosevelt in the East and Midwest. Smith had Tammany support plus the backing of John J. Raskob and Jouett Shouse. Also in his camp were Boss Frank "I Am the Law" Hague of Jersey City, Mayor Anton "Tony" Cermak of Chicago, and Gov. Joseph Ely and Senator David I. Walsh of Massachusetts.

"It is impossible to believe," Walter Lippmann wrote shortly after Smith's announcement of his candidacy, "that Smith, who is a great realist . . . expects to be nominated. He had no illusions about his election in 1928 and he can hardly have any now about the party's willingness to go again through an ordeal by fire. But that he does not wish to be ignored, that he believes he represents a political force, that he intends to be consulted on the candidate and the platform is now evident." Lippmann concluded that Smith's friends could do no more than deadlock the convention and nominate someone other than Smith or Roosevelt. That candidate, he predicted, would be Newton D. Baker.[87]

Smith's entry also enhanced Garner's position. Several of the nationally read political correspondents in New York and Washington predicted that if Smith and Roosevelt neutralized each other's chances, the Democrats would concentrate their favor on the speaker. McAdoo noted with satisfaction that Smith's candidacy meant that both he and Roosevelt would have delegate tickets in California. "Neither of them is acceptable to a large element of the Democratic party," he wrote Love, "and I think it is very likely that my friends and I will support a Garner ticket. I believe that we can carry the state for Garner if we make the fight." He saw no possibility of either Roosevelt or Smith being nominated, and predicted "another big row" at the Chicago Convention.[88]

Smith's managers were not worried about Garner becoming a threat to their man in the East. "Garner got the kiss of death from Hearst and McAdoo and he cannot live this endorsement down at least in this part of the country," one of the former governor's campaign workers in New York told a Texas supporter. Smith's Texas friends were told in confidence to back

Garner, since it was felt that all favorite-son strength was probably favorable to Smith in the long run, "either for direct switch, or to detract from Roosevelt's strength."[89] According to Hoovercrat Alvin Moody, Garner's candidacy was "merely the blanket under which Pinckney, Renfro and the rest of the Al Smith crowd hope to secure the delegates to the national convention," but he could see no way to stop them.[90]

By early February 1932 Texas Democrats were organizing enthusiastically for Garner. As a means of achieving harmony in the still rather torn Texas Democracy, the Garner boom was ideal. "It is impossible to oppose it without seriously endangering one's political life here," reported the Texas correspondent of the *New York Times*. "People look askance upon one who would dare to advocate the candidacy of an other when all the country, including Mr. Hearst, is crying for Garner." The speaker's camp was a political melting pot, as Texas leaders of factions hitherto at odds united behind him. The state press, almost without exception, emphasized the opportunity Texas had to present a candidate with wide appeal. On February 16 Senators Sheppard and Connally announced that "the Democrats of Texas" would send a delegation to the national convention instructed to vote for Garner's nomination and "would welcome the support of Democrats everywhere to his banner." They touted the speaker as a man "grounded in the fundamentals of Democracy, a rugged and militant champion of the great body of the American people" whose training and service gave him a wide grasp of national affairs and made him eminently qualified to perform the exalted duties of president.[91]

Two other favorite-son movements had made their appearance in Texas before Garner's. One was in behalf of Melvin Alvah "Mel" Traylor, the president of Chicago's First National Bank. A native of Kentucky, Traylor had lived in Texas from 1898 to 1911 and, after practicing law for a time in Hill County, had gotten his start in banking in Malone and Ballinger. Climbing ever higher in banking circles, Traylor served as president of the Illinois Banking Association in 1924 and of the American Bankers Association in 1927. *Time* chose him for its July 30, 1928, cover story.[92]

In March 1931 Traylor spoke to salesmanship clubs in Dallas and Houston, and Jesse Jones said privately that he would make fine presidential timber. When House heard this, he remarked that "Traylor is the fourth man I have heard that Jones is booming for President. I hope for his sake they do not compare notes." The Smith-Raskob forces made some rather ineffectual efforts to promote him in Kentucky, Texas, and Illinois. News stories depicted this wealthy banker as a "homespun candidate" who had been a teenager before he saw his first train. On August 21, 1931, fifteen hundred West Texans gathered in Ballinger to endorse Traylor, "leading financier of America," for the Democratic nomination for president and to lay plans for a Texas Traylor for President club. "Mel is driving for second place on the ticket or for the Treasury," Robert Field informed House. "He is hard headed and evidently feels that if he shows some strength in the Convention that his chances of a Cabinet appointment will be very much better." When the Garner boom was launched in Texas, Traylor's supporters swung behind it but hoped that the Texas delegation would turn to the Chicago banker if Garner could not be nominated. At the national convention Illinois gave Traylor a complimentary vote on three ballots, but beyond that he was not able to attract any appreciable support. The trouble with the candidacy of the homespun multimillionaire was that it had a false ring.[93]

Texas's other favorite-son candidate was colorful Gov. "Alfalfa Bill" Murray of Oklahoma, the rustic, tobacco-chewing darling of political cartoonists. He was introduced as the "Next President" at a homecoming rally in Collinsville, Texas, on February 18, 1932. Despite bad weather thousands of Texans and Oklahomans turned out. But the *Dallas Morning News* sniffed that his "invasion" of Texas was more spectacular than nationally significant, and his celebrity status as a native-born Texan excited no statewide enthusiasm. "He is something of a combination of Jim Hogg, Jim Ferguson and Cyclone Davis, without being true to type in likeness of any of the three," the paper pointed out. "His very versatility in stagecraft leaves Texas cold, save for a few whoops from the exuberant or roars from the disgruntled by way of approval." The Alfalfa Statesman's strenuous but erratic Bread, Butter, Bacon, and Beans campaign netted him just twenty-two delegates from Oklahoma and one, his brother, from North Dakota.[94]

Texas for Garner

When the first boomings for Garner were heard, the Roosevelt people in Texas criticized it as being "another stop Roosevelt" movement and continued to press their work for the New York governor. But as the Garner movement continued to grow, they changed their attitude from one of criticism to one of "friendliness and amity." On January 23 T. Whitfield Davidson admitted to House, "Garner being popular and a Texas man has considerably handicapped our campaign." He assured him, "We had everything solid, and have it yet except for this Garner boost." He went on to ask House's opinion on how the Garner push should be dealt with, and added: "My present inclination is not to give way to the Garner boom on one hand, nor to vigorously oppose it on the other, but to compose the personnel of the delegation with delegates who will not be unfriendly to Gov. Roosevelt."[95]

That same day Thomas Watt Gregory conferred with Frank Andrews about the Roosevelt situation in Texas, and the two men agreed, Gregory wrote House, that Garner could not resist the temptation of being mentioned as a presidential candidate and would do nothing to deter those who wanted the Texas delegation instructed for him. To oppose the Garner movement would require the most desperate efforts, would not be successful in the long run, and would result only in the elimination of all Roosevelt men from the delegation. They believed that the "stars in their courses" were fighting for Roosevelt, and if his strength continued to develop he would ultimately get the Texas vote at Chicago because Texas Democrats wanted a winner in 1932. In sum, "Frank and I think the best policy is not to antagonize the Garner movement in any way and make no fight against giving what would merely be a complimentary vote. We do not believe that this can be prevented, and that that course should be pursued."

House replied that he, James A. Farley, and Homer Cummings had been working on the "Garner case" and had decided to send Cummings to Washington for ten days or two weeks and sound out the speaker. "Between us and the angels, he will suggest that if we organize the Convention Garner will be our candidate for Temporary Chairman provided, of course, he comes out for our man. *This is very confidential* and to go no further than to Frank Andrews." As for Texas, Farley and Cummings agreed on the Gregory-Andrews position and they could work to that end. "The truth of it is, the Texas end is entirely in your hands and what you two do will be accepted here as final."[96]

On February 19 the Davidson organization spent several hours in an executive session in Dallas wrestling with the problem of how to get on board the Garner bandwagon without getting off the Roosevelt wagon. Among those attending the conference were Davidson, Charles I. Francis, Stuart Smith of Beaumont, and Ernest May of Fort Worth. The next day Davidson advised Roosevelt as to his group's position toward the Garner movement:

> As a matter of political strategy the Roosevelt forces in Texas have decided not to contest with John Garner as a Favorite Son.
>
> This is a disappointment to some of us, but it is good tactics. We still expect to see you nominated overwhelmingly, and, by the latter

maneuver, you can be sure that Texas will not be counted among your enemies, unless, per chance, John Garner should be nominated, and, confidentially, I do not think he is going to be.[97]

The Davidson group viewed the Garner forces as an amalgam of the Stop Roosevelt element, composed of "a few rabid Al Smith men and a certain bunch of Hoovercrats, followers of McAdoo," along with a segment of Garner's admirers who supported him because he was a Texan. "This group is not hostile to Gov. Roosevelt, and it is with them that we want to keep on terms of amity and good will," Davidson explained to House. To this end, Davidson assured Sam Rayburn that the Roosevelt forces in Texas would get behind Garner so that "if possible, there will not be a dissenting note." At the same time they, and many within the original Garner group, were interested in knowing that Garner would not permit his name to be used in any Stop Roosevelt movement that might result in a deadlocked convention nominating Al Smith. "If the people of the U.S. want Mr. Garner and will nominate him, all will be well," Davidson stated, "but if they don't want him, then I think you join me in saying that we want the Texas vote in the Chicago Convention to be free to go to Franklin D. Roosevelt."[98]

The Garner organization in Texas was initially headed by Mayor Charles M. Chambers of San Antonio, a boyhood chum of Garner's in Red River County, and it was in the Alamo City that the speaker's supporters met on February 22, Washington's birthday, to formally launch his campaign. Under the seemingly harmonious surface, the rally was a bitter preliminary skirmish to decide who would control Texas politics for the next two years. "The crowds on the streets and in the auditorium didn't smell the brimstone in the air, but the politicians in the lobby did," reported the *Houston Gargoyle*. "As a matter of fact, they smelled little else, though they were careful not to remark upon the fact outside of the privacy of their hotel rooms."

On the Sunday afternoon preceding the rally, a quietly announced informal caucus of one hundred Texas political leaders assembled at the Gunter Hotel with Judge W. O. Huggins, executive committee chairman and editor of the *Houston Chronicle*, presiding. State senator Walter Woodward of Coleman, who was closely allied with the Sterling administration, shortly arose and announced that Senator Walter Woodul of Houston, another Sterling spokesman, would be named national chairman of the Garner campaign, with P. K. Hornby, a friend and ally of Mayor Chambers, as state chairman. A word was also dropped regarding the desirability of naming Tom Love as a vice chairman for Texas. Governor Sterling himself took the floor several times to urge harmony. But the little group of liberals present realized that if the Sterling-Chambers-Huggins combination gained control of the Garner movement from the outset, it would put them in the driver's seat at the state convention, granting them the power to select the delegates to Chicago, to elect the next state executive committee, and to name the next national committeeman.

One after another, three liberals—Alvin Wirtz, W. K. Hopkins, and Henry Schofield—got to their feet and opposed any such hand-picking of the campaign leaders, calling it a discourtesy both to those attending the rally and to Garner himself. They made it clear that if the attempt persisted, there would be a fight to the finish staged on the floor of the rally against the nominations. Several San Antonians opposed to the Chambers machine spoke to the same effect. Taken by surprise, the hand-pickers retired in confusion. Judge Huggins adjourned the meeting hurriedly with an announcement that the organization would be perfected at the rally the next day. Concrete evidence of the prearranged plan was a story appearing Monday morning in the *San Antonio Express*, a pro-Chambers paper, reporting the appointment of Woodul and Hornby to the national and state chairmanships.

Meanwhile, the liberals were busy rallying their forces. They quickly decided on a strategy that would embarrass the opposition terribly, even if it was able to force its nominations through. Sam Rayburn was contacted by telephone, and he agreed to serve as national chairman of the Garner campaign. To oppose his selection would be tantamount to confessing selfish interests by the Sterling-Chambers-Huggins faction. Word that he would be nominated from the floor was passed to them, together with the liberals' intention to recommend that he be given a completely free hand in forming state organizations in Texas and elsewhere and in appointing chairmen and other officials to manage them. The liberals would approve a temporary state committee, to be composed of one member selected from each state senatorial district, but Rayburn would have the right to dismiss or alter the membership if he desired.

The hand-pickers surrendered. They could not risk a fight against Rayburn on the floor, which presented the real possibility of being defeated and the certainty of an open division within the Garner ranks for which they would be held responsible. The liberals in turn agreed to Chambers's selection as permanent chairman of the rally and of Woodward as chairman of the temporary committee. And with all that arranged, the stage was set for the "harmonious," enthusiastic rally for Garner that the state press so colorfully described for their readers. According to the *Houston Gargoyle*, the net

effect of the liberal revolt was to remove the Garner movement safely beyond the reach of any state faction, while placing the liberals themselves in
a strong position going into the state convention. "Sterling wanted to get his
crew in, but after some fight we defeated his plans," liberal Alvin Romansky
of Houston wrote Josef Israels II, his Smith contact in New York City. "The
Young [Democratic] group is going to perfect an organization and we will
be strong for the Governor [Smith], and I hope to get this group in charge
of the young Democrats division of the Garner Campaign."[99]

It was noteworthy that no outstanding leaders of the anti-Smith forces
of 1928 were in evidence at the rally. Tom Love was not there, nor was Alvin
Moody, Cato Sells, or Mrs. Claude de Van Watts, the "big four" of Texas prohibitionists. The suggestion was dropped that Love be made vice president
of the state Garner organization. "We at least want Democrats to head any
organization that may be created," pointedly commented national committeeman Jed Adams. It was generally believed that McAdoo's endorsement
of Garner removed any doubts that Texas Drys would not support him. Jim
Ferguson, who had taken an active, voluntary interest in preparations for
the rally, was an unobtrusive figure. He rode with a state senator in the
parade but was given no part in staging the show. Sterling held open house
in a hotel suite. "Garner is no longer in the favorite son or dark horse class,"
he declared. "He is a national favorite, and a horse that is in the race to
win."[100]

Another significant feature of the mass meeting was the official abandonment of the Roosevelt for President drive in Texas. Stuart R. Smith announced on behalf of T. Whitfield Davidson that the Roosevelt organization
would cast its support behind Garner. The announcement was met with
scarcely more than a ripple of applause; as the *Washington Herald* noted:
"The Roosevelt movement in Texas died when John Garner's name was first
proposed for the Democratic presidential nomination."[101]

But Louis Howe was not yet ready to read the last rites over his candidate's prospects in Texas. On February 27 he telephoned House, who was
vacationing in Charleston, South Carolina, and asked him to call Gregory
and discuss the advisability of trying to carry the state for Roosevelt. House
told him what Gregory's opinion was; he noted that all of Roosevelt's friends
in Texas concurred with it and therefore it was of no use telephoning. In a
follow-up letter, House noted that both Gregory and Davidson thought "we
would likely lose the second choice for Roosevelt by making a fight." He continued, "I am sorry to see Texas throw her influence away in such a manner,
but luck was against us in having Garner come to the front as he has. We

should have carried the State easily otherwise." Howe then phoned Robert Field and asked him to go to Texas to assess the situation. Field declined because of business, but he also thought it would be a waste of time and that he could be of more use by going to Washington and reaching an understanding with Garner regarding Texas. House agreed.[102]

In January 1932, just before embarking on a cruise to Mexico, Newton D. Baker took the precaution of backing away from the League of Nations. "I would not take the United States into the League, if I had the power to do so," he now said, "until there is an informed and convinced majority sentiment in favor of that action ... I am not in favor of a plank in the Democratic national platform urging our joining the League." Baker's reversal left Roosevelt exposed as the most internationalist of the candidates. House tried to persuade Hearst privately that there was no reason for concern about Roosevelt's views on foreign policy, but the publisher demanded a public statement. On February 2, in an Albany speech, Roosevelt accordingly declared that the League was no longer the League conceived by Wilson; it might have been had the United States joined, but "the fact remains that we did not join." In present circumstances, he said, "I do not favor American participation."

The press promptly denounced the speech as a cynical effort to shake off the Hearst attacks. Roosevelt's internationalist friends were deeply disturbed, and Hearst was not mollified. House told Gregory that "practically all our crowd are disgruntled" with Roosevelt, "and one more blow may detach them from the cause." He warned Farley that if Roosevelt did not come out clearly for the World Court and if he should show a pro-Tammany leaning, then the revolt among the Wilson people would be widespread and formidable and would probably cost him the nomination. "Up to a short time ago I felt that his success was practically certain," the colonel lamented. "I am less certain now than I have been for many months."[103]

"Howe and Farley seem to dominate F. R. and of course their outlook is local," House grumbled to Gregory in mid-February. "They are able and loyal to F. R. and determined to have no interference. Of course, they do not speak the same language as the Wilson crowd." To others over the course of 1932 the colonel lamented his diminished access to Roosevelt.[104] Some observers on the governor's campaign staff blamed House for the loss of Texas. Howe, in turn, complained that Roosevelt was increasingly inclined to act on his own. "Was it a ploy designed to shunt aside the aging puppeteer [House]?" asks Elliot A. Rosen, and answers himself: "In part. Certainly the Howe-House collaboration ended, and from the evidence, it seems that most major tactical decisions, beginning in March 1932, were made by Roosevelt alone." That month the governor began to assemble a group of academic experts on the subjects that would need to be discussed in the ensuing campaign for the presidency. Nicknamed "The Brains Trust," the group included Samuel I. Rosenman, Raymond Moley, Rexford G. Tugwell, and Adolf A. Berle Jr. "During the campaign he [House] wrote long letters to Roosevelt, replete with all sorts or advice," Moley recalled. "Roosevelt turned them over to me to read, remarking on one occasion that House was 'right about 50 per cent of the time.' I found his suggestions only mildly interesting."[105]

Love Letters for Garner

Garner's friends in Washington were disappointed that the San Antonio meeting had tried to launch a national organization in behalf of his candidacy. They had understood that the rally was intended to adopt him as the candidate of the Texas delegation to Chicago and that the national Garner movement was to grow elsewhere of its own force. In accepting the leadership of the Garner forces, Rayburn clearly defined the speaker's stand. "My interpretation of this action is that it named me only the national representative of the Texas committee and not a national campaign manager. Mr. Garner is not an active candidate for the nomination for President and, therefore, there is no national campaign manager." When Judge C. H. Howard of Atlanta announced that he would be Garner's proxy in the Georgia Democratic primary, Rayburn tried to stop him. "Texas is presenting Speaker Garner as its choice for the presidential nomination because Texas has confidence of his superior qualifications for the office," he wired the judge. "We are not in any movement to stop any candidate." Nevertheless, Howard filed, backed aggressively by Hearst's Atlanta newspaper. Georgia selected delegates by counties instead of for the state at large, and there seemed to be a good opportunity for Garner to win a few delegates. But Roosevelt's popularity was great in the state, where he was a frequent visitor to Warm Springs; on March 23 he crushed Garner by a popular vote of almost eight to one and won all twenty-eight delegates. He carried Warm Springs 218 to 1.[106]

As speaker, Garner vacillated between cooperation and obstruction in his attitude toward the Hoover administration. Yet whatever he did, he generally carried his well-disciplined followers with him. "This isn't a session of Congress," the progressive Republican from New York City, Fiorello H. La

Guardia, said one day; "This is a kissing bee." In February Garner formed a Democratic Economy Committee, charged with doing everything possible to balance the budget, including even the enactment of a sales tax. But this proposal went too far, and Democrats began to defy their leader. Garner's closest friends believed that the maneuverings against the sales tax were in part an effort by Roosevelt supporters in the House to destroy the speaker's chances at Chicago. "Garner did not go on the floor when the revolt broke," Thomas L. Stokes remembered. "I was in the lobby during the fight and saw him walking up and down with Representative Isaac Bachrach of New Jersey, a Republican friend. Bachrach had his arm about Garner's shoulder and was admonishing him not to take it so hard. It was a terrible defeat for the Speaker of the House."

Reluctantly, Garner threw himself into the fight. He left the speaker's chair, walked to the well of the House, and made a dramatic "camp meeting" appeal for the sales tax. In his climax, he asked every member who would pledge himself to a balanced budget to rise in his seat. Nearly the whole House stood in a moment of revivalist fervor. But the spell could not last. Under La Guardia's fiery leadership, the sales tax was knocked out of the bill. Roosevelt men made no secret of their belief that the Garner boom had been badly damaged, and newsmen who attended the speaker's news conference on March 24 noted that he no longer was the confident leader they had portrayed earlier in the session. According to the *Washington Post*, he "seemed on the defensive." Republican propagandists devoted the major part of their time to criticizing Garner's fumbling leadership. "Look at the House of Representatives under Democratic rule!" became the stock reply of the Republicans to all critics of the Hoover administration.[107]

Meanwhile, back in Texas, Tom Love sounded the war cry of the ultra-Drys. In an address before the Dallas County Women's Democratic Association on March 2, he predicted that the following resolution, or one substantially like it, would be presented at each of the precinct conventions on May 7: "We are opposed to making the liquor traffic lawful; and we favor instructing the Texas delegation to the Democratic National Convention to vote only for candidates for President or Vice President who are known to stand for maintaining and enforcing the Eighteenth Amendment." Thus he served notice that he expected to fight for control of the Dallas County convention with the same precinct machine methods he used in gaining control of the 1928 and 1930 conventions. Love also served notice that he would oppose Garner for the nomination unless he definitely committed himself against repeal of the Eighteenth Amendment. In making this demand of

Garner, Love set himself publicly apart from other ultra-Dry leaders like McAdoo and Sheppard, both of whom had heartily endorsed Garner.[108]

The state Democratic Executive Committee, meeting in Fort Worth on March 9, moved to purge the party ranks of Hoovercrats by unanimously deciding to demand a written pledge of support for the party's presidential and vice presidential nominees from all participants in precinct or county conventions held for the purpose of selecting delegates to the state convention at which national convention delegates were chosen. Charles I. Francis was author of the pledge resolution. The WCTU asked Love to fight the pledge in the courts. He agreed, and Dan Moody joined him in the suit.[109] On April 9 Judge Robert B. Allen of the 116th District Court upheld the executive committee's right to exact a loyalty pledge from participants in its conventions. Denied the writ of mandamus he sought, Love filed notice that he would appeal. "In Texas, party primaries must be free," he declared in a letter to the *Dallas Morning News*. "The Democratic party must be a public utility; not a private association, beyond the law, pledge-bound and machine controlled." But on April 21 Texas Democratic regulars won a sweeping victory when the Texas Supreme Court held in *Love v. Buckner* that the loyalty pledge was "in entire accord with the governing statutes, as well as with party customs," thus rejecting Love's efforts to have the courts rule the test invalid. Love then announced that he would take the written pledge but would not consider himself bound beyond the limits of conscience and good faith. He also indicated his intention to support Garner, "my friend of thirty years standing," and to seek an instructed Garner delegation to Chicago. Love explained his change of heart by saying: "Of the seven or eight candidates for the Democratic nomination who are mentioned he is one of the only two of them in the running who is not avowedly in favor of the repeal of the Eighteenth Amendment; and, while Garner voted against the Eighteenth Amendment, he has uniformly and dependably supported all other appropriations and other measures for strict prohibition enforcement, by all his votes in Congress."[110]

Before making this announcement, Love had pleaded with McAdoo to get Garner to say that he regarded the effort to legalize liquor as unwise and that he was opposed to it. McAdoo waited almost a month before replying and then curtly brushed off his lieutenant's appeal: "I note what you say about Garner. So far as I can learn his record on prohibition is far superior to that of any other man mentioned for the Democratic nomination; and it seemed to me that he was the only man who had a chance to beat Roosevelt, whose nomination I should regard as being most unfortunate.... I presume he will state his position about the matter in due time."[111]

Love's ally Alvin Moody, the titular leader of the Hoovercrats, wanted all those who planned to vote against any Wet candidate nominated at Chicago to stay out of the conventions entirely and let those who believed in "brass collar rule" and were willing to permit New York–Boston–Chicago machine control of the national party to attend and take the "immoral" pledge. But Love insisted that the "wise thing" for Dry Democrats to do was to attend the convention. As he explained to Moody: "I am led to this view by the conviction that Fergusonism is a real menace this year and that we can be more effective in inducing Dry Democrats to go into the July primaries by going into the presidential primaries than by staying out. I am confident that the more of us who go into the presidential primaries the more of us will go into the July primaries."[112]

Harmony, Hell: The House Is On Fire

In the meantime feuding continued within the Garner camp. On March 21 the temporary state Garner for President committee met in San Antonio. Bitter wrangling broke out over the selection of a permanent chairman; the liberal faction, headed by W. K. Hopkins, opposed the Sterling-Chambers faction, headed by the temporary state chairman Walter Woodward. Newspapermen were barred from the session. When the morning session broke up with little accomplished, Sam Rayburn, who was present, said he was "disgusted." However, the meeting ended in "harmony" when Walter Woodul of Houston was selected as the permanent state chairman over editor Fred Horton of Greenville. Woodul received sixteen votes to Horton's fifteen, six proxies making the difference. Silliman Evans, formerly of the *Fort Worth Star-Telegram* and now an official of American Railways and headquartered in New York City, was named state and national publicity director. Frank Killough of Eastland, a well-known attorney, remained as executive secretary and Hopkins as vice chairman. The state headquarters was moved from San Antonio to Dallas in a trade for Woodul's selection. Mayor Chambers took this decision standing—on the nose. A "political cynic" remarked to a fellow scribe after the skirmish was over: "Yes, Thermopylae had its messenger of defeat; the Alamo had none."[113]

In California Garner's campaign was well organized and vigorous. Mc-

Adoo was his state campaign manager. McAdoo's close friend John B. Elliott was placed in charge of the activities in southern California, while former Democratic state chairman Henry H. McPike headed the Garner drive in the north. So much publicity for Garner appeared in the five Hearst papers, two in Los Angeles, two in San Francisco, and one in Oakland, that a Roosevelt backer was led to comment: "Hearst gives almost as much space daily to Garner as he gives to the Lindbergh baby [kidnapping] or the Japan-China War." The speaker appealed particularly to conservative Drys in the Democratic Party. In southern California, where this element was strong, there was a great growth of Garner clubs. The Texas State Society of California, comprised of a hundred thousand Californians of Texan descent, came out strongly for favorite-son Garner. "I must say that I am surprised by the enthusiasm with which Garner's name has been received down here," McAdoo commented at the end of February, "and I think there is no doubt that he will carry this end of the State by a large majority."[114]

In northern California Democrats tended to be liberal and Wet. Despite this handicap the Garner forces made a strenuous effort to carry the area. "The movement for Garner has gained great momentum," McPike advised McAdoo. "Various ones describe it with the old expressions, 'Groundswell,' 'Avalanche,' 'Landslide,' 'Tidal wave.' It is the equal of the past movements we have had here in past years." The most difficult areas for the Garner forces were the cities and towns of the Sacramento and San Joaquin valleys; Roosevelt's state leaders, Justus Wardell and Isidore Dockweiler, had such a firm control over the party machinery, tying up every county committee, that it was almost impossible to organize rallies for Garner. "Sacramento and Fresno were fortresses into which we could not possible [*sic*] get an entering wedge," admitted a Garner leader.[115]

On May 3 some 538,910 Democrats voted in the California primary—61.6 percent of the state's registered Democrats. McAdoo, heading the list of Garner delegates, received 222,385 votes; Wardell, leading the Roosevelt list, received 175,008 votes; while Smith's chief delegate came in a strong third with 141,517 votes. Roosevelt was badly squeezed between Los Angeles Drys and San Francisco Wets. Garner actually won the election in Los Angeles County. In that Dry bastion he overwhelmed Roosevelt by 79,300 votes, while the New York governor had 31,923 more votes than Garner outside Los Angeles. Roosevelt did best in rural districts. Out of fifty-eight counties in the state, he carried thirty-five, including most of the inland farming areas. Garner carried seventeen counties, including eight out of ten in southern California. One county was evenly divided between Garner and

Roosevelt, while five counties, all in the Bay region, voted for Smith. Smith's biggest victory came in San Francisco—a city that he had come within four thousand votes of capturing in 1928—where he received more votes than Garner and Roosevelt combined. He also surprised the experts by running ahead of Roosevelt in Los Angeles.[116]

One immediate result of the election was the ousting of Isidore Dockweiler as national committeeman in favor of John B. Elliott. In June McAdoo himself assumed the position. That same month McAdoo announced that he was a candidate for the U.S. Senate, although he had earlier admitted to Bernard Baruch that "the office of Senator, while one of the greatest in our government, has never made any appeal to me." He wrote cheerfully to a senatorial friend: "Here I am in politics again. I thought I had more sense, but I ... haven't." He made it abundantly clear that his task consisted of preventing Roosevelt's nomination. "I think what is most in McAdoo's mind," newspaper columnist Mark Sullivan wrote after a postprimary interview with the Californian, "is to prevent the nomination from going to New York State. He has a hate against all of New York because of his experience in 1924."[117]

The Texas press interpreted Garner's California triumph as lifting him out of the favorite-son category and putting him squarely in the running for the presidential nomination. His friends could now count ninety Texas and California delegates in his column. The *Dallas Morning News* good-humoredly editorialized that the "seed of Texas sowing in California" through the years "came to harvest" on May 3. It explained: "Expatriate Texans remembered bluebonnets and northers, chuck wagons and cornbread, East Texas ribbon cane molasses and the good old pumphandle shaking of hands—they could not forget the Alamo, they were not unmindful of Goliad. The eyes of Texas were upon them, and they gave Garner such support that it seemed as if the very rocks and roots brought him aid."[118]

Roosevelt's California leaders explained his defeat by blaming Smith. They pointed out that the combined Roosevelt-Smith vote was 92,000 in excess of the Garner vote. "Every Smith vote was a Roosevelt vote, had Smith been out of the field," Wardell wrote Roosevelt. "If Governor Smith had not permitted the use of his name in our primaries," claimed Dockweiler, "we would have won over the Garner ticket by at least [a] 75,000 majority." The Smith camp readily admitted that their candidate's aim had been to defeat Roosevelt. "I look at the situation wholly from the national viewpoint," said Mrs. Grace Montgomery, a Smith leader. "It is, when so regarded, a signal victory for Smith. He has sounded the death knell of the forces of expediency, and as to it, New England and New York will make short work of them."[119]

Garner's victory was a hard blow to Roosevelt's fortunes. Coming only a few days after a disappointment in Pennsylvania, where the governor did not get all the delegates that he had expected, and the fiasco in Massachusetts, where Smith defeated him by a majority of three to one and won the entire delegation, it all but ended his hopes for nomination on the first ballot and raised serious doubts if he would be nominated at all. "It seems a serious and perhaps irreparable blow to the Roosevelt candidacy," McAdoo crowed. Outwardly Roosevelt remained optimistic. From Warm Springs he wrote Lt. Gov. Herbert Lehman: "All goes well here. I am not the least bit disturbed by the California Primary result because Garner will, I am sure, not join any mere 'block movement.' I am getting real sun and lots of sleep." Roosevelt saw Garner's bloc of votes as the key to his nomination. Prophetically he confided to Josephus Daniels that if he could win them over, that "would cinch the matter" of his nomination. Knowing that McAdoo and Hearst would try to control the California delegates if Garner was eliminated, he asked Wardell to "do some quiet scouting to see whether his crowd, if and when released, will come our way or will sell out." Jim Farley urged another California supporter: "The thing for you fellows to do now is to keep in personal contact ... with the Garner delegates and work on them in the hope that after they see Speaker Garner's nomination is not possible, they will swing their support to the Governor." He predicted, "Every effort you put forth in that direction will be helpful to the Governor's cause."[120]

Although the Roosevelt people in Texas had retired to the wings when the Garner movement appeared on the stage, they believed that the elements supporting the speaker were too diverse and conflicting to ensure any real solidarity behind him and had been quietly urging delegates to be instructed to vote Roosevelt as a second choice as it became apparent that Garner could not be nominated. As Herbert Bayard Swope, former editor of the *New York World*, and Al Smith viewed the situation from Smith's suite in the Empire State Building, McAdoo was as anxious to check Roosevelt as they were. Swope placed a telephone call to McAdoo in California inviting him to join the anti-Roosevelt coalition. McAdoo indicated his amenability—subject to one major condition. "If the opposition to Roosevelt were ultimately to necessitate a conference of Democratic leaders in order that some other nominee might be selected," McAdoo asked, "would ... [Smith] accept Mr. McAdoo as one of the conferees?" Smith readily accepted the condition and added: "I'll do more than that. Unless he is included, I'll refuse to be a conferee myself." The telephone conversation ended on that note, with the understanding that Smith and McAdoo would meet in Chicago when the Democratic convention opened. Bernard Baruch, who favored Baker for the nomination, acted as liaison between the Smith and McAdoo groups. He arranged for the two ancient foes to meet at Chicago's Blackstone Hotel.[121]

The first determined effort to instruct the Texas delegation to back Roosevelt as second choice in Chicago appeared on April 22 when District Attorney Sam McCorkle and B. H. Broiles, editor of the *Mexia Daily News*, issued a call for Central Texas Democrats to meet in Mexia on April 29 to plan such a move. T. Whitfield Davidson was the principal speaker. The Garner camp moved quickly to squelch the plan. "We should go to Chicago with only one flag—Garner," Fort Worth publisher Amon Carter phrased it. Rayburn issued a statement cautioning against a second-choice instruction as inimical to Garner's chances of nomination. Governor Sterling, Walter F. Woodul, and W. K. Hopkins also advised against second-choice instructions.[122]

The second-choice movement made its way across the state. In most instances the Democratic precinct conventions voted to send Texas's delegation to Chicago only with instructions to support Garner. In a few scattered instances delegates to the county conventions were instructed to favor Roosevelt as a second choice should Garner withdraw. One Hillsboro precinct instructed for Melvin Traylor and another commended him without instructing. The topic of Prohibition was sedulously avoided in the precinct conventions.[123]

In the county conventions on May 10, most of the counties again named no second choice but asked that the Texas delegates be instructed to vote for Garner as long as his name was before the national convention. Sentiment for Roosevelt as a second choice, however, appeared at a number of county meetings. In El Paso County the Roosevelt forces, led by Robert L. Holliday, swept the convention to the cries of "steamroller" from the Garner men. The Harris County convention was completely controlled by the Wets, led by Steve Pinckney; it adopted a resolution favored by the liberals containing biting criticism of the national prohibition laws. The resolution came to the floor on a minority report after the majority of the resolutions committee had refused either to endorse or attack the country's liquor laws. Walter Woodul, the chairman of the resolutions committee, protested that taking either side might embarrass the Garner candidacy. James E. Kilday, one of Pinckney's lieutenants, answered Woodul. "Harmony, hell," he shouted, "the house is on fire." The instruction to the county's delegation to the state convention favored voting for Garner, although the words "until released by him" were exchanged by the liberals to "as long as there is a reasonable chance of his nomination." The amended instruction was "of course tantamount to an uninstructed delegation, once the Garner boom has faded," Paul Page Jr., who had written the substitute motion, assured Roosevelt. "It is I think the instruction most favorable to your candidacy which can be secured to Texas." But it would also allow those liberals favoring Smith to try to swing the Texas delegation to him at Chicago. As Alvin Romansky explained to Josef Israels:

> Here is what we are trying to do, we want to capture the delegation to the National convention, of course we are for Garner but when the time comes we want to be able to switch and if we go ahead without making any campaign in this state and do not tell the electorate we can place our men on the delegation without any trouble, we are going to put big men, liberal, and those who would not oppose the Governor [Smith] because of religion, who are Garner men but for Smith in the end, but we can not let anyone know this and we are forced to deny any movement for Smith.[124]

An attitude of "no compromise" was evident among the regulars who dominated the Dallas County convention. W. A. Thomas was named temporary chairman. As Al Smith's Texas manager in 1928, he symbolized party regularity. Murrell L. Buckner, another regular, was named permanent chairman. The Dallas delegation, consisting of more than two hundred regulars and chaired by Maury Hughes, was instructed to support Garner for the presidential nomination "first, last and all the time, and without any second choice," while avoiding either Wet or Dry resolutions. The convention voted down an amendment by Tom Love that would have added to the Garner resolution the statement: "We are opposed to the nomination of any candidate for President or Vice President who stands for the repeal of the Eighteenth Amendment." Love and his fellow Drys George Purl, Shelby Cox, Atticus Webb, Dr. C. C. Selecman, and Alex W. Pope, among others, were conspicuously absent from the delegation to the state convention. Privately Love blamed his defeat on the party pledge, claiming that twenty-five thousand Democrats in Dallas County had voted against Al Smith on the liquor issue in 1928 and that he could "count on the fingers of my two hands" all of those twenty-five thousand who voted in the 1932 presidential precinct primary. The result was that "bootlegger lawyers" had easily controlled the county convention.[125]

The ultra-Wet liberals wanted to replace national committeeman Jed Adams, who was seeking a third term and was regarded as representing the Dry element, with former state senator Alvin J. Wirtz, a Wet and "a good Smith man," according to Alvin Romansky. Wirtz derided the Garner "peace and harmony" propaganda as being designed to "do John Garner an injustice by shushing the prohibition question." He declared, "The Democrats must come out plainly on the live issues of the day, and prohibition is one of them." Furthermore, "It will help Mr. Garner in his race for the presidential nomination for Texas Democrats to say that the party has definitely repudiated Thomas B. Love and his crowd."

But Garner's managers realized that if his home delegation went to Chicago with hatchets sharpened for Prohibition's slaughter, his Dry support in the South and West would be ended. The signal to fight against any Prohibition resolutions in the state convention was given on May 19 by W. A. Thomas, who warned that an attempt to introduce a repeal resolution would bring on "revolution." He took exception to Wirtz's statement, pointing out that the campaign had been "John Garner without any other instructions." Garner himself took no public position as to the state convention's course on Prohibition, but Rayburn warned privately: "If we go into controversial questions like prohibition we might just as well chop his [Garner's] head off to begin with."[126]

At a meeting the day before the convention opened in Houston, the Young Democrats converted themselves into the Texas Democratic Association and named W. K. Hopkins as chair. Resolutions were adopted favoring repeal of the Eighteenth Amendment and for submitting to Texas voters the question of modifying or repealing national and state prohibition. Dallas County friends of Jed Adams succeeded in holding back a resolution endorsing Wirtz for national committeeman. The Garner organization won a notable victory when the state executive committee named Rayburn as temporary chairman and keynote speaker over one of its own members, Charles I. Francis, who was favored by the liberals. The vote was sixteen for Rayburn and eleven for Francis (who did not vote himself). Garner's board of strategy worked out a program to keep him from being branded Wet or Dry by the convention's action and to leave him free to speak his own mind later. The Garner group, headed by Walter Woodul, agreed tentatively to a national referendum touting Prohibition as a Democratic principle but decided to vote down any repeal or antirepeal resolutions on the floor.[127]

From the convention floor Francis was put forward by Hopkins as a candidate against Rayburn for temporary chairman. "There is a demand that these hands be taken off of the throats of the delegates, and permit this convention to name its own officers," he shouted amid loud cheers, "and I charge that this has all been concocted in a group that met in room 1360 of the Rice Hotel." Asserting that Rayburn would be the Garner leader, chairman of the convention, and head of the Texas delegation, Hopkins vehemently inquired: "What manner of man is this, Caesar, that has grown so strong?" But when the votes began to roll up for Rayburn, reaching 662 to 234 for Francis when Lamar County was polled, Francis withdrew his name, pledging his support to Garner. Those who expected keynoter Rayburn to point the way on Prohibition for the convention were disappointed, for in his forty-five-minute speech, he spoke only of Garner and the colossal failure of the Republican Party. As he explained afterwards, "I wanted the Convention to stay out of controversial issues which were not really issues and I did so in my speech and I made what I thought was a straightforward Democratic and anti-Republican speech to the convention." The liberals also lost their fight to replace Adams with Wirtz. Adams was leading nearly two to one when Nacogdoches County was polled, and Wirtz stopped the roll, withdrew his name in a magnanimous speech, and made it unanimous.

"Amid the most uproarious scenes enacted at a Democratic gathering in recent years," the convention urged Congress to submit a referendum on the Eighteenth Amendment to the states, instructed its delegates to Chicago "to vote as a unit for John N. Garner as Texas' sole choice for the presidency of the United States and for none other under any circumstances until released by him," endorsed full payment of the soldiers' bonus, and moved to keep African Americans out of Democratic primaries. The referendum resolution was adopted, 853 to 564, over the opposition of the militant Drys led by W. A. Tarver, chairman of the State Insurance Commission and close friend of Dan Moody's. The convention voted down the Wet minority report calling for the repeal of the Eighteenth Amendment and accepted the majority report, which declined to include any declaration on national prohibition in the convention's resolutions.[128]

On the record the Texas delegation was unanimously for Garner, "first, last and all the time," but when it came to a second choice, opinions differed. There was considerable anti-Roosevelt sentiment in the Garner group, consisting of Jed Adams, Maury Hughes, Walter Woodul, and their associates, who had things pretty much their own way in the Houston convention. Hughes expressed a preference for Newton D. Baker in the event Garner could not be nominated. Adams expressed no second choice, but in a letter to the Texas delegation he said that Jouett Shouse should be made the Chicago convention permanent chairman rather than Senator Tom Walsh of Montana, the Roosevelt choice. "It looks now as though there were a movement not to stop Roosevelt, but a movement to stop Garner by giving the partisans of Governor Roosevelt absolute control of the convention," the national committeeman warned. At Garner headquarters in Chicago Woodul severely criticized the Roosevelt camp. These men reasoned that if they were out to nominate Garner, and if Roosevelt was the strongest man to start with, the speaker's chances could best be served by joining with the other candidates to stop him. With Roosevelt out of the way, they would fight it out with those who remained.[129]

Roosevelt's friends sought to get men and women on the delegation who would vote for him when Garner, in Gregory's words, "passed out." Gregory reported to House that among the 184 delegates and 184 alternates (each delegate having one-quarter vote), there were "unquestionably a large number of men favoring Roosevelt and some of them being quite enthusiastic for him." On the whole, he thought "the Roosevelt people did about as well as could be expected and that after a few ballots Roosevelt will get a very large part of the delegation." Ernest May was "quite sure" that more than half of the delegates were friendly to Roosevelt and would never consent to Texas's vote being used to promote "an indefinitely deadlocked convention." To T. Whitfield Davidson, the most reassuring fact was, as he wrote Roosevelt, "that Texas is not entering into any league or combine 'To Stop Roosevelt.'"[130]

Davidson issued a statement in which he argued that there was more Roosevelt sentiment in Texas than there was for any other candidate except Garner and that the success of the Garner movement in the state was largely because the Roosevelt men had come into it without reservation. He claimed that 80 percent of the Texas delegates were for Roosevelt after Garner, a figure hotly disputed by the Garner people. Walter Woodul sputtered that the delegation, was "whole-heartedly for John Garner" and that Davidson's statement had been "untimely and in poor taste." House and Gregory agreed that Davidson had made a mistake in thus antagonizing the Garner people on the delegation.[131]

Roosevelt had reason to be pleased with the overall results of his preconvention campaign in the South. He had every state below the Mason and Dixon line except Maryland, Virginia, and Texas. The indefatigable Howe had built up an elaborate, very candid card file on delegates and state leaders that might be used to probe their weak spots at a crucial moment. On the three-by-five pink cards that summarized Texas, in the words of Howe's biographer, Alfred B. Rollins, "some of the great figures of the day were nailed down like butterflies." Examples include Amon G. Carter: "Powerful—King-maker type—Loud—Breaks with everyone"; Tom Connally: "Politician—no convictions—Friendly, but noncommittal. . . . *Tremendous* influence—Key man—Delegate at Large—Fears N. Y. City Situation"; Jesse Jones: "Money—Houston Chronicle, owner of—For himself first, last and all time—Ambitious—Promises everybody everything—Double crosser"; Tom Love: "Bitter, Violent dry—Hoovercrat—Against F.D.R. Boosting Dan Moody—Trader, unscrupulous—No real following"; Dan Moody: "Key Man. . . . Hopes to V.P.—Friendly—Very dry political & personally. Would resent any Roosevelt leadership from Al Smith crowd"; Ross Sterling: "Honest. . . . Concerned primarily re-election—No political sense—Grateful to Moody. . . . Key man."[132]

On June 16 the North Carolina convention chose a delegation pledged to Roosevelt, and this convinced Garner that even the Dry South was getting damp. Information also reached him that the platform committee of the Democratic convention would bring out a plank calling for repeal of the Eighteenth Amendment. On June 21 he issued a formal statement declaring for the repeal of the "unsound and unworkable" Eighteenth Amendment; promising to take "no flim flam" from debtor nations; denouncing the protective tariff; viewing with alarm "the constantly increasing tendency toward socialism and communism [as] the gravest possible menace" and advocating that "the government use every means within its power to prevent their further spread"; and pointing with pride to the relief measures he had sponsored. In brief, the statement announced his willingness "to serve my country and my party to the limit of my capacity." He would not accept the vice presidential nomination, however. He was quite emphatic about that, although later he added: "I am in the hands of my friends and they can do anything they want to with me except put me in jail."[133]

Reaction from Democratic Drys to Garner's statement was restrained. Sheppard said that although he disagreed with Garner on repeal, he would continue to support him for the presidency. "I regard him as sound on all other vital questions." McAdoo gave his approval of Garner's statement upon his arrival by plane in Cheyenne, Wyoming. "I think it is fine," he said, adding that he believed the people were entitled to vote on the Prohibition question. However, Tom Love immediately issued a bristling statement declaring that Garner's antiprohibition stance marked the end of his boom "by furnishing obvious and conclusive reasons why he ought not to be nominated and can not be."[134]

Before leaving Washington for Chicago, Bascom Timmons talked the situation over with Garner. The newspaperman was enthusiastic because he thought the Roosevelt-Smith split would give the speaker a chance to run past both men after a deadlock. But Garner was still uninterested. "I have no desire to be President," Timmons quoted him as saying. "I am perfectly satisfied right here in the Speaker's office. I worked twenty-six years to get to be Speaker. If we win this election I will have a considerable majority to work with in the House. If we are on the political upswing as it looks, I will have a longer tenure as Speaker than any other man ever had." But Garner felt that the Democrats could forfeit the public confidence and lose the election if they made a spectacle of themselves as in the 1924 Smith-McAdoo deadlock. Then he told Timmons in confidence: "I am not going to deadlock the convention against the leader. Roosevelt is the leader in delegates." Timmons asked what he thought of Newton D. Baker as a compromise choice if Roosevelt did not win on the first few ballots. "Compromise candidates don't win Presidential elections," he replied.[135]

The Democratic preconvention campaign was ending in doubt. Roosevelt, although assured of a majority of the delegates, fell short of the requisite two-thirds, due mainly to Garner's victories in Texas and California. Smith, who had hoped to exercise a veto, had failed to win the minimum one-third. For either to succeed, support would have to be bargained for at the convention among the ranks of the unpledged and/or among those delegates instructed for favorite sons. With ninety votes, Garner was in a key position to determine the outcome. He was ready to wait for a few ballots to see whether Roosevelt was really strong and whether the convention was likely to be deadlocked. Then he would decide on his future course of action.

CHAPTER 7

Roosevelt and Garner

The Democratic National Convention opened in Chicago on Monday, June 27, 1932, in the air-cooled auditorium the Republicans had recently vacated. Most of the managers of the various candidates—and, indeed, many of the candidates themselves—were on the scene a week before, getting their forces lined up for the battle to come. The forty-eight delegates from California arrived on June 25. Forty of the delegates had one vote each; eight had one-half vote each. They were pledged to vote as a unit for Speaker of the House John Nance Garner unless he released them or unless a majority of the delegation voted to change the rules and vote as individuals. William Gibbs McAdoo, the chairman of the delegation, expressed complete public confidence in a Garner triumph. In private, however, he confessed to his friend Judge William Denman: "It was a grand victory we won in California and I hope that Garner may win at Chicago, but who in the hell can tell where anything or anybody is going these days."[1]

Robert Woolley suspected that McAdoo had his own ambitions. As he explained to House: "On the opening day of the Convention we discovered that our friend from California treasured the idea that we didn't have all the votes we claimed and that, a deadlock resulting, a dark horse could walk away with the nomination—he being the dark horse. He confided as much to a United States Circuit Judge from New York (M.B.M.), who promptly imparted the information to me." According to Breckinridge Long, "He [McAdoo] was obdurate." The devoted Roosevelt supporter reported to Senator Key Pittman after the convention's close: "I had two long conversations with him.... But from McAdoo I got the distinct impression he was playing his own game and could not be counted on to help at all—or unless Baker became a real threat. But, in that case, a deadlock would already have developed."[2]

McAdoo created a mild sensation by calling on Al Smith, and the report spread swiftly that the bitter foes of Madison Square Garden were joining together against Roosevelt. Indeed, Smith informed his friend Joseph M. Proskauer that he and McAdoo had agreed that they would join forces to prevent Roosevelt's nomination. If a deadlock ensued, they were to confer again in an endeavor to unite behind a strong candidate. McAdoo later claimed that he offered no firm commitment when Smith proposed an alliance to stop Roosevelt, but Elliot A. Rosen had concluded that "there is ample evidence to suggest that McAdoo willingly joined the coalition on the eve of the convention, perhaps in the hope of emerging as a 'dark horse' candidate." A November 1932 newspaper article by Frank R. Kent of the *Baltimore Sun* contended that once Smith gave McAdoo a state-by-state analysis of those delegations willing to break from Roosevelt if given the chance, the Californian became a participant in the movement. Kent related:

> Finally McAdoo was convinced and asked, "What then?" "If we go to the fifth ballot," said Smith, "we've got him licked. All right. Then my candidacy is out the window. I can't be nominated, but we can sit down around a table and get together on a candidate." To that the McAdoo query was, "When you sit around the table will I be there?" and the Smith reply was, "If you're not there I won't be there either." That ended the conversation.[3]

McAdoo also called at Roosevelt headquarters and rumors cropped up of a possible trade to give Garner second place on the ticket. "William G. McAdoo, looking just as vital and energetic as he had at Madison Square Garden in 1924, darted about like an elongated hummingbird, lighting for a moment, then flitting away," wrote Thomas L. Stokes. "The lank and lithe Californian was all over the place, enjoying his mystery role tremendously. He beamed and shook hands and slapped backs and was hailed everywhere as 'Mac.'"[4]

Sam Rayburn, Garner's national campaign director, had arrived from Washington on June 24 and swung into action with statements claiming the speaker was growing in strength every day and that additional second choice pledges were being received. He declared that Roosevelt did not have the necessary two-thirds vote for nomination and that he would grow weaker as the balloting progressed.[5] It seemed like it could be anyone's game as delegates lined themselves up to compete for their chosen candidates—and Texans and their favorite son, Garner, had a critical role to play in deciding the final victor.

The Cowboy Spirit

The Texas delegation chartered a special train to take it to Chicago. W. T. "Pappy" Waggoner, a wealthy Fort Worth rancher and oilman, paid the expenses of the forty-piece Old Gray Mare Band from Brownwood. Before leaving for Chicago, the delegates were asked by Amon Carter to wear sailor straw hats and light suits. "It is the further hope that none of the delegation will go to Chicago wearing either boots, spurs, chaps or sombreros," Carter admonished. "It is the idea ... to leave off the wild western cowboy spirit.... This ... will be of tremendous value in impressing upon other states the seriousness of Texas in presenting Mr. Garner as the logical candidate for the Democratic nomination." The Texans were met at the station in Chicago by McAdoo and the California delegation. They paraded to the Sherman Hotel, headquarters for the Texas delegation. Humorist Will Rogers, an Oklahoma delegate, joked that the Texans had arrived in Chicago on burros headed by that "fearless old Statesman Amon G. Carter, the genial dirt Farmer of Shady Oaks Post Office, Texas." Rogers explained to his readers that "Amon is national committeeman, deligate [sic], alternate, steering-wheel, banker, receiver and wet nurse for the Texas Deligation."[6]

When the convention opened on Monday, June 27, Texas pulled off the first real thrill of the day; the Old Gray Mare Band came marching into the auditorium headed by a huge banner on which was Garner's picture. "The Eyes of Texas" sounded, and the Texans were on their feet with a rousing cheer that attracted the attention of everyone, including photographers, who rushed to the Texas section. The Californians cheered lustily, and McAdoo came to the Texas delegation and greeted friends. The 184 delegates were seated in the front row just to the right of the chairman, and the alternates were grouped across the aisle.[7]

In his address to the convention, keynoter Senator Alben W. Barkley of Kentucky announced for repeal of the Eighteenth Amendment, his statement setting off a twelve-minute parade that wound around the hall amid shouts, cheers, confusion, and music. Some of the marchers taunted the seated Texans. "Why don't you get in the parade[?] You are hurting your candidate." This goaded some of the Wets into action; they asked Rayburn if he had given orders that the Texas standard must not be touched. "No," the congressman replied. "It is not my fight." Whereupon the Wets made a move to get the standard but were thwarted by Drys who held to the staff and pushed off those who wanted it. Suddenly Charles Guokas Jr. of Houston made a football lunge, reached the staff, tore off the placard reading "Texas," and joined the parade. The Drys were right at his heels, and a free-for-all scramble followed in the aisle. The police arrived and prevented any actual fighting, but the Drys recovered the card, and it did not get into the procession. Just at the close of the parade, when tempers had cooled, the standard was released at Amon Carter's suggestion and started with the marchers but failed to get very far. After its rough handling, it was torn but still usable. Thus history repeated itself; Wets and Drys in the Texas delegation had scuffled over the standard in the 1928 Houston convention. "If this monkey business continues, some are going to accuse the Texas delegation of making itself the laughing stock of the convention," warned William M. Thornton, who was covering the convention for the *Dallas Morning News*.[8]

Roosevelt had to give up his fight to abolish the two-thirds rule for nomination because of serious defections among his delegates in the South and West. But he was triumphant in an important test when Senator Thomas J. Walsh of Montana was elected permanent chairman against Jouett Shouse, Smith's candidate, by a vote of 626 to 528. The Texas delegation opposed abrogation of the two-thirds rule and supported Shouse. Roosevelt was likewise successful in seating Huey Long's Louisiana delegation and a Minnesota delegation favoring the New York governor. Had Roosevelt lost these two delegations, thirty-two votes would have been added to the opposition.[9]

The auditorium was packed on the third day when Chairman Walsh called the night session to order. Everyone was expecting a dramatic battle on the Prohibition plank. At eight o'clock former Senator Gilbert Hitchcock of Nebraska, chairman of the platform and resolutions committee, began reading the platform. The tenseness in the air revealed itself in cheering and handclapping for almost every plank. Finally, Hitchcock reached the Prohibition plank. "We favor the repeal of the eighteenth amendment," he read. A yell went up from all parts of the hall, and the Wet demonstration began. It lasted ten minutes. The reading of the rest of the platform came as an anticlimax.

The Wets on the platform and resolutions committee, led by Senator David I. Walsh of Massachusetts, had insisted on a forthright Prohibition repeal plank. McAdoo, Cordell Hull, and A. Mitchell Palmer, former U.S. attorney general, fought them hard over it, but in the end the full committee sustained Walsh 35 to 17.

Hull submitted the minority report on Prohibition to the convention. It merely called for the submission of a repeal amendment to the states and did not put the Democratic Party on record as being either Wet or Dry. It differed little from the plank the Republicans had adopted. As Hull took his seat, he was roundly booed and hissed.[10]

The Wets on the Texas delegation obtained Rayburn's consent to a caucus off the floor to determine how the Texas vote should be cast. They contended that Texas would make itself ridiculous and repudiate Garner by opposing the majority repeal plank. What one Wet called "the official Garner organization," along with Rayburn and Senator Tom Connally, wanted Texas to vote for the minority plank, contending that the Houston convention's instructions were specific to go for submission only. They insisted that Garner himself, while personally for repeal, had not asked that it be written into the platform. The result of the poll was 67 to 61 for the majority plan; therefore Maury Hughes, who had gone to the platform to speak for the minority report, flipped and spoke for the majority report instead![11]

The final vote was a better than four-to-one victory for the repeal plank—934¾ to 213¾. "The debate had been not so much a wet and dry fight as it was a dispute as to how wet the party should be," noted two observers of the 1932 campaign. "No one defended prohibition; it was a question of how best to get rid of it. The repealists favored butchering and burying it unceremoniously; the moderates wanted it put away with the customary rites accorded the dead."[12]

Congress remained in session during the Chicago convention, and on the Monday night before the convention opened, Senator Harry B. Hawes of Missouri and Senator Key Pittman of Nevada were in the former's Washington office discussing what was likely to occur. They were deeply disturbed over newspaper reports indicating that a bitter deadlock would destroy the party's chances as it had in the past. They decided to do something about it. They called Roosevelt in Albany to ask if he had any objection to Garner as a running mate. According to Hawes, Roosevelt responded: "Senator, that would be fine; the Governor from New York and the Speaker of the House from Texas—clear across the country." He instructed Hawes to get in touch with James A. Farley, chair of the New York Democratic Executive Committee, in Chicago and relate what had taken place. Hawes wired Farley: "Group believe winning ticket would be Roosevelt and Garner. Ninety votes of California and Texas would eliminate dispute. Am advised would be satisfactory to party here [Garner]. See Sam Rayburn Tom Connally and check my own impression. Best wishes."

After a hurried telephone call to Hawes and Pittman, Farley immediately started in search of Rayburn. First he found the congressman's friend,

Silliman Evans, whom he had come to know in the preconvention fight, and Evans promised to bring Rayburn to Farley's rooms at the Congress Hotel. It was after 11 p.m. when Evans and Rayburn appeared; they had managed to slip in unseen. Farley used all the salesmanship at his command to persuade them of the necessity for a combination of the Roosevelt and Garner forces, pointing out that the New York governor would have a substantial majority over all his opponents on the first ballot and by all the rules of the game was entitled to the nomination without delay. He recalled that Roosevelt and Garner were personal friends and had always thought highly of one another. He pointed out that the delegation that first saw the "light of reason" would naturally be in a strategic position if it switched over and assured Roosevelt's nomination. The Texas delegation was big enough to do the job even without California. Finally, Farley promised to do everything in his power to secure the vice presidential nomination for Garner if Texas made the switch. "We have come to Chicago to nominate Speaker Jack Garner for the Presidency if we can," Rayburn replied. "We are not against any other candidate and we are not for any other candidate. Governor Roosevelt is the leading candidate and naturally he must be headed off if we are to win. But we don't intend to make it another Madison Square Garden." He did not even indicate interest in the vice presidency for Garner. The men promised to keep the conference a secret. Farley explored other possibilities, offering the second spot on the ticket to Albert Ritchie of Maryland and Harry Byrd of Virginia if they would give up their own candidacies and switch to Roosevelt.

That same night Pittman and Hawes got busy and sent hundreds of telegrams to Democratic leaders in Chicago and around the country urging them to place the best interests of the party above everything else and to do their best to obtain a Roosevelt-Garner coalition. To Tom Connally they telegraphed: "We have had a talk with interested parties and we can say no more. All agree ultimate nomination of Roosevelt assured. All believe that strongest ticket will be Roosevelt and Garner. Since abandonment of two-thirds rule fight results will be determined on combination of President and Vice-President tonight."

At 7:30 the next morning, Garner, angry at what seemed an unauthorized and premature surrender of his own candidacy, called Hawes out of bed and gave him an old-fashioned tongue lashing for sending out telegrams to the effect that he was willing to withdraw from the race and accept the vice presidency. The speaker made it plain that he had no desire for the office and had authorized no one to entertain such a proposition on his behalf. Later in the morning Hawes called him in his office to discuss the matter again. He pointed out jokingly that there was less work for the presiding officer in the Senate and then seriously urged Garner to accept the vice presidential nomination as a great honor for his state and as a boon for the party.[13]

On Thursday, June 30, Farley met Rayburn and Evans again. He told them Garner could have the second-place nomination. Rayburn asked Farley what he wanted him to do. Farley told him to have Texas cast its vote for Garner on the first ballot and then switch to Roosevelt immediately after the roll call. Rayburn replied that he had more than 180 delegates and the same number of alternates who had come to Chicago to back Garner for the presidency and argued that it would be unfair to them and to the state to agree to any such arrangements. He said the delegation was bound to vote for Garner for two or three ballots at least until it was shown whether he had a chance to be nominated. Rayburn then asked how long Farley could keep the Roosevelt forces intact. Quite frankly, Farley told him, certainly for three ballots, very likely for four, and possibly for five. "Well," replied Rayburn. "We just must let the convention go for a while, even if we are interested in the Vice Presidency, and I'm not saying that we are."[14]

On Friday, June 30, six Roosevelt supporters in the Texas delegation, Paul Page, Charles I. Francis, Alvin W. Owsley, Richard F. Burges, R. E. Huff, and T. Whitfield Davidson, drafted the following telegram to Garner: "Since Governor Roosevelt has a large majority of the delegates to the convention and feeling that to further contest the nomination will result in injury to the party we as members of the Texas delegation suggest that you seriously consider withdrawing from further pressing the contest. It will solidify the ranks and insure success in November." However, on Burges's advice, the wire was not sent.[15]

Courting the Texas Delegates

The task of launching the candidates occupied ten hours of the afternoon and evening sessions on June 30. Governor Joseph Ely's speech for Smith was by far the most effective, while John E. Mack's speech for Roosevelt was probably the worst. Tom Connally nominated Garner as "a Democrat without prefix, suffix or qualifying phrase." The Texas band led a colorful procession. Mrs. Grace Hargreaves, daughter of William Jennings Bryan, carried the California banner, and McAdoo held aloft the big California gold bear flag. Will Rogers and a group of Oklahoma delegates carried the Sooner banner into the parade, although the state was instructed for Murray. A few other state banners joined, more in friendship than in support.[16]

After the nominating speeches were concluded, the Roosevelt managers forced a first ballot at 4:28 a.m. on July 1, hoping to stampede the weary convention. The first ballot gave Roosevelt 666¼ votes, just 103 short of nomination. Smith received 201¾ and Garner 90¼, while seven others tallied 195¾. At the end of the roll call, a beaming Farley confidently waited for some state delegation to switch to Roosevelt and thus set the bandwagon in motion. To his bitter disappointment, no one arose. The second ballot was soon underway. Farley very cleverly held back a few votes in reserve in order to give the impression of Roosevelt gaining strength on each ballot. As he explained: "It is an old axiom in politics that no matter how strong the leading candidate may be, a decline in strength on succeeding ballots is fatal. The arrow must go up and not down." The second count gave Roosevelt 677¾, an increase of 11½ votes; Smith dropped to 194¼ and Garner held firm at 90¼, while the others totaled 186¼. Still, the break failed to come.

Roosevelt's floor manager, Arthur Mullen of Nebraska, moved for adjournment, but the anti-Roosevelt forces, convinced they had the New York governor "on the run," compelled the calling of a third ballot. This time Farley threw every reserve vote he had into the Roosevelt column. Roosevelt painfully gained another 5 votes to reach 682.79, still 87 short of nomination. Smith dropped again to 190¼, Garner went up to 101¼ (a gain of 11), while all others received 177.21. And still the break failed to come. By this time the limits of physical endurance had been reached, and both sides were ready to quit. At 9:15 a.m. the exhausted delegates gratefully accepted McAdoo's motion for adjournment until 8:30 that evening. The stalemate was complete. The Roosevelt ranks had not broken nor had the anti-Roosevelt allies given ground.[17]

Farley had arranged for Daniel C. Roper and Bruce Kremer, national committeeman from Montana, to keep constantly in touch with McAdoo in the hope of winning over California's forty-four delegates. While the second ballot was being taken, Roper and McAdoo retired to a private room in the auditorium. Roper emphasized the great opportunity McAdoo had to promote Wilsonian policies. At one point he asked whether the Californian would consider the cabinet position of Secretary of State. "No," McAdoo answered flatly. "No personal advantage must accrue to me, either from our conferences or from anything that happens in this convention." But he continued: "If I can get a recess of the convention so I can take a poll of our California delegation, I'll endeavor to get them behind Roosevelt, and that will mean Texas also." Roosevelt, however, would have to accept Garner as the vice presidential candidate and agree to consult McAdoo about federal patronage in California and about the appointments of the secretaries of treasury and state. McAdoo warned Roper that a Hearst representative had visited leaders of the Texas delegation and had insisted that they cast at least seven ballots for Garner. "But," Roper protested, "it won't be possible to hold some of the Roosevelt states in line that long. If the California delegation waits until the eighth ballot, it may mean the nomination of someone else, possibly Smith or Newton D. Baker. I am told there are a hundred votes pledged to Baker as a second choice."[18]

During the balloting, Arthur Mullen went down to the Texas delegation and talked with Tom Connally. He asked why they were holding out for Garner when he did not have a chance. When Connally kept quiet, Mullen continued: "If Jim Farley and I agreed to one concession, we could get the vote of the New York delegation to swing over from Al Smith to Governor Roosevelt." Connally asked, "Then why don't you give it? You've probably promised the sun and moon to plenty of others." Mullen asked, "What do you mean?" Connally smiled wryly and said: "There are, I hear, at least a half-dozen men to whom you've promised the vice-presidential nomination." Mullen demurred, "That's not true. But if Garner will take the vice presidency, maybe it could be arranged." Connally told him he did not know whether Garner would settle for second spot on the ticket. "I hear from men in Washington whom I believe, and whom you'd believe, that Garner will take it," Mullen replied, evidently referring to Hawes and Pittman, and asked, "If he does that will Texas come to Roosevelt?" Connally parried: "I don't know. There are some men in the delegation who're pretty strong against Roosevelt. We'll have to know more about how Garner stands and what can be done for him before we can go ahead." Before he hurried away, Mullen said, "Let's talk about it after we adjourn."

Later, over breakfast, Mullen told Connally that if Texas would come to Roosevelt, the governor's forces would do everything humanly possible to carry the vice presidential nomination for Garner if he would take it. "I'll call a man in Washington who's closer to Garner than any one else, and find out," Mullen continued. "I'll let you know." A short time later Mullen brought Farley to see Connally on the convention floor. According to the latter, he told them that Texas would not come over to Roosevelt unless the delegation had absolute assurance that Garner would be the vice presidential nominee. "We'll do that," Farley agreed. "That isn't enough," Connally said. "I don't want any old *political* assurance. I need your *personal* assurance as man to man that if the Texas delegation comes over to Roosevelt, you'll nominate Garner for Vice President." The two men shook hands on the agreement.[19]

After the convention adjourned, Farley and other Roosevelt leaders went to Louis Howe's suite in the Congress Hotel. Howe, who was suffering from asthma, was lying on the floor in his shirtsleeves between two electric fans. Farley asked the others to step back, lay down beside him, and whispered in his ear, "Texas is our only chance." Howe agreed, but with no enthusiasm. Up to this point, he had felt that the Garner forces would remain adamant to the bitter end and that Farley should negotiate with Harry Byrd of Virginia for his twenty-four votes. A meeting between Farley and Rayburn was arranged by Rayburn's longtime friend, Senator Pat Harrison of Mississippi. Farley, arriving first in Harrison's hotel suite, dropped into a chair and fell asleep. When Rayburn entered with Silliman Evans, Farley aroused himself and once again stated the case for an immediate decision. He said that Roosevelt needed Texas to win; that the alternative was a victory-sapping deadlock; and that the vice presidential nomination could be swung to Garner. The conference lasted only a few minutes. Nothing was said by either of the Texans about the vice presidency and neither man made any promise. Rayburn, as he stood to go, merely said, "We'll see what can be done."

That was good enough for Farley. His hopes soared again, and he raced back to Howe's room. "It's in the bag," he said, "Texas is with us." Howe nodded his head and said only, "Jim, that is fine." Farley later recalled: "Roosevelt was far more effusive when I broke the news to him over our private line." In fact, the nomination was not yet "in the bag."[20]

As Farley stumbled off to bed for a couple of hours' rest, Howe continued to monitor the situation. Daniel Roper rushed in to describe his talk with McAdoo. Howe immediately put him through to Albany, and in Roper's recollection, Roosevelt told him to give McAdoo the required assurances.[21]

Meanwhile, pressure was being brought on William Randolph Hearst at his San Simeon mansion. He received phone calls from Joseph P. Kennedy, a Hearst business associate; Damon Runyan, a noted Hearst writer; Col. Joseph Willicombe, the publisher's confidential secretary; and Farley. All pointed out the danger of a swing to dark horse Newton D. Baker, ardent advocate of the League of Nations, if Roosevelt slipped on the next ballot. "Could I get Ritchie?" Hearst asked Kennedy. "No, I don't think so," Kennedy replied. "I think if Roosevelt cracks on the next ballot it'll be Baker." Hearst consulted his attorney and political adviser, John Francis Neyland, and decided the Baker threat must be prevented. Willicombe promptly transmitted Hearst's decision to George Rothwell Brown in Washington. "Mr. Hearst is fearful," the message went, "that when Roosevelt's strength crumbles it will bring about either the election of Smith or Baker. Either would be disastrous." Garner was to be told that Hearst believed "nothing can now save the country from peril but for him to throw his delegates to Governor Roosevelt, who has proved that he commands a majority of the convention, though he cannot obtain a two-thirds majority."

About 11 a.m. on July 1, Brown met Garner in the speaker's private room in the southeast corner of the Capitol. "Mr. Speaker," Brown said, "I have a message for you from Mr. Hearst." Garner seemed to know what was coming. For a moment they looked together in silence across the green lawns around the Capitol. Then Brown repeated Hearst's message. Garner responded: "Say to Mr. Hearst that I fully agree with him. He is right. Tell him I will carry out his suggestions and release my delegates to Roosevelt." Hearst's advice apparently only reinforced a decision already reached by Garner.[22]

Pressure was brought to bear on Garner from another source. Arthur Mullen called Rep. Edgar Howard of Nebraska, a Garner crony, and told him to ask the speaker whether he would accept the vice presidency. "I've talked to the man [Connally] who knows the temper of the Texas delegates. They're out now, and he's with them. Tell Garner he'll have to decide in a hurry and notify them." Howard called back about 11:15. "John says he's received all the honors he's ever had through the Democratic Party," he reported, "and that no man, situated as he is, can decline the honor of the vice-presidential nomination." Mullen informed both Connally and Farley of this development. "That sets us," Connally said.[23]

Many Texans and others now believed that Garner had a real chance to be nominated. Will Rogers thought there was a possibility that Arizona and Arkansas would go to Garner on the fourth ballot. Garner also had second-choice strength in Alabama, and John McDuffie hoped to switch it to him on the fifth or sixth ballot. As Alabama, Arizona, and Arkansas were the three states alphabetically at the start of the roll call, a three-way swing might have started the bandwagon rolling for the speaker. Representative Lindsay Warren of North Carolina, one of Roosevelt's floor managers, was convinced that if the governor did not make it on the fourth ballot, he was through. Warren's second choice was Garner, and he counted eighteen Tar Heel delegates as pledged to him. "An ex-governor of Texas informed me," historian William E. Dodd wrote Illinois Judge Henry Horner, "how many utility men were here and working upon the Texas delegation with mind, namely, the defeat of Roosevelt. One of my students was with the Mississippi delegation and he reported the same thing there. [Senator] J. W. Bailey and Governor Gardner of North Carolina, both utility sympathizers, were working in that state to change the delegation." According to Jim Farley, it was hinted that the anti-Roosevelt forces might join together in Garner's support and that the speaker could expect up to three hundred votes on the fourth or fifth ballot. Boss Frank Hague of New Jersey offered to switch his thirty-six votes to Garner. All day Friday, Smith leaders, including Belle Moskowitz and Joseph M. Proskauer, tried to get through to Garner, but he would not answer the telephone. He explained later that he meant no discourtesy, but the Smith camp was trying to commit him to a last-ditch stand in which he wished no part.[24]

There was also some activity during the day among the Roosevelt men in the Texas delegation. Fourteen signed a petition authored by Charles I. Francis and Karl Crowley of Fort Worth requesting Rayburn to release the delegation from its instructions: "Upon such release, the forty-six votes of the Texas delegation [will] be case [cast] for the nomination of that matchless statesman, executive and friend of the people — Hon. Franklin D. Roosevelt of New York." Between the third and fourth ballots, some fifty telegrams were sent to Garner requesting that he release the Texas delegation, and state senator Archie Parr called him about 3:30 p.m. and advised him to release the delegates.[25]

In Washington, Garner analyzed the three ballots, state by state, and at about 3 p.m. Chicago time called Rayburn. He was terse, as always. "Sam I think it is time to break this thing up," he said. "Roosevelt is the choice of the convention. He has had a majority on three ballots. We don't want to be responsible for wrecking the party's chances. The nomination ought to be made on the next roll call." Rayburn said he would canvass the situation and call back. According to Bascom Timmons, Rayburn "wanted to talk to some people before the Garner delegates were released." He did phone late in the afternoon. "I do not remember exactly what Sam told me," Garner reminisced to Timmons,

> but this is the impression it made on my mind: Conferences had been in progress all day and Smith's bloc was standing firm. Roosevelt could not break into other delegations, and Mississippi and some other states were about ready to desert him. Feelers showed that California would go to Roosevelt if I released the delegates. Texas would not, unless I went on the ticket with the New York governor. They had to sell the Texas delegates on the idea that Roosevelt, as governor of the most

populous state, and I, as head of one branch of the government which the Democrats held, would be a winning ticket. If Texas and California did not go to Roosevelt on the fourth ballot, Rayburn thought the convention was in for a deadlock.

Garner did not like the idea of taking the vice presidential nomination, but he wanted another Madison Square Garden deadlock and defeat in the general election even less. The Democrats had taken another licking in 1928. "So I said to Sam, 'All right, release my delegates and see what you can do. Hell, I'll do anything to see the Democrats win one more national election.'" In a letter to Richard Burges, Garner succinctly stated his reasons for releasing his delegates: "I realized the situation that existed, and I knew that a deadlock might prove disastrous to our party, and party success means more to me than anything else."[26]

Texas and California for Roosevelt

At 4 p.m. Farley met with two of McAdoo's best friends in the California delegation: Thomas M. Storke, a newspaper publisher from Santa Barbara, and Hamilton Cotton, a Los Angeles oil millionaire. He opened the conversation with the admission that he had thrown his full strength into the third ballot and that five states held in the Roosevelt column by the unit rule—Minnesota, Iowa, the two Dakotas, and Mississippi—were ready to break away on the next ballot. This meant a compromise candidate, probably Newton D. Baker, and possible defeat in November. "Boys, Roosevelt is lost unless California comes over to us on the next ballot," he said. According to Storke, Farley became very emotional, pounding on a chair with his closed fist, and with tears literally flooding his eyes. The two men wanted to know who would control patronage in California if McAdoo switched. Farley replied: "Mac, of course, we will recognize him in everything." Finally convinced, Storke and Cotton promised to try to persuade McAdoo and the delegation to switch to Roosevelt at the earliest possible moment.[27]

Arriving at McAdoo's suite, Storke and Cotton warned him that unless California switched to Roosevelt on the next ballot, his cause would collapse and the "money interests" would put Baker across. "But boys, it's too late now," he protested. "It's past six and the convention meets in less than two hours and a half." The two men sensed that McAdoo was not quite ready in his own mind to suggest a switch to Roosevelt and wanted to test the sentiments of the California delegation. (Perhaps he still cherished some dark-horse hopes of his own.) Finally, he agreed to call a caucus. He then told Storke and Cotton that Garner had phoned him about half an hour earlier and that he thought they had been "kidding him along"; McAdoo continued:

> Garner also added, that he was most grateful for the way the Califor-
> nia delegates had stuck by him, but that frankly he had never taken it
> too seriously. The cards were stacked against him, he felt. But whatever
> the California delegation wanted to do would be perfectly agreeable to
> him, and that he was telephoning the same decision to Sam Rayburn
> and his Texas delegation. Garner is making no suggestions as to whom
> we should switch.

A Hearst representative (Willicombe) had informed McAdoo during the afternoon that the publisher had given up Garner as a lost cause and conceded that the "boys in the smoke filled back room" had apparently settled upon Baker as their choice. (He did not mention his earlier negotiations with the coalition.)

At 5 p.m. Roper, McAdoo, Amon Carter, George Creel, and Joseph Willicombe gathered in McAdoo's suite in the Sherman House. Willicombe announced that he had spoken with Hearst, who could envisage a shift by Texas and California to Roosevelt on a later ballot. Roper recalled that it was the eighth ballot; Brice Clagett, McAdoo's son-in-law, thought it was the sixth. Roper insisted that such a decision would ensure the nomination of Smith or Baker.

At 6 o'clock a delegation dispatched by Smith, unable to reach McAdoo on the telephone, tracked him down. Would California stay with Garner until the sixth ballot? "What," McAdoo inquired, "would the anti-Roosevelt coalition do at that point?" They did not know. McAdoo became testy. Suspicious of Smith's motives, he announced unwillingness to remain in the coalition and go up a "blind alley." He could continue to support the coalition only if he knew its choice as nominee. They could not say. A sentence crossed out in a Clagett memorandum of February 1933 reveals that McAdoo then concluded that he was finished with the "combination" and considered himself a free agent.[28]

Word spread that afternoon that the publisher had given up Garner as a lost cause and McAdoo felt that Hearst would not be unhappy if the California delegation switched to Roosevelt. "Let's see what the delegates want," McAdoo said, half pushing Cotton and Storke out the door. "You boys find

Jack [Elliott] and ask him to help you round them up. We will meet at 7:00 o'clock. I'm sure Jack will understand and go along with the idea."[29]

While the members of the Texas delegation were assembling in the Sherman Hotel around 6 p.m., Rayburn left the room to find a telephone to call Garner for an official release. The speaker was expecting Rayburn's call. The ensuing conversation was a model of brevity:

> Do you authorize me to release the Texas and California delegations from voting for you for the Presidential nomination?
> Yes.
> Do you release the Texas and California delegation from voting for you from the Presidential nomination?
> Yes.

Rayburn said good-bye, hung up, and went back to the Texas caucus with the news that Garner had released both delegations. Only 105 of the 184 delegates could be rounded up, but those awaiting Rayburn's arrival were pro-Garner, with strong Newton D. Baker leanings. According to Tom Connally, when seventeen delegates totaling four and a quarter votes asked for permission to vote for Roosevelt on the next ballot, "far more than a majority booed them down." Rayburn knew that a hard-core group led by Amon Carter would prefer to go home rather than vote for Roosevelt. Cheered by the speaker's acquisition of eleven additional votes on the third ballot, they were hopeful that he could next pick up Mississippi and Arkansas and move on to the nomination.

"Well, I've just been talking to John Garner in Washington," Connally quoted Rayburn as saying, letting his lower lip sag. "And John wants you to know that he is out. He told me to tell you that the instructions binding you to him are no longer in force. He released you without any strings attached." For his biographer, Dwight Dorough, Rayburn recalled the reaction to his announcement:

> A good friend of ours then jumped up and said, "I'm gonna make a speech," and he began telling Garner had said this, that and the other. He kept on going around and around, saying we don't want to run out on Mr. Garner, and then some of the women around me began crying, and then I said, "We're not running out on Mr. Garner. He's not a candidate any more." We just argued and argued. I tried to tell them Garner was out of it.[30]

Just to keep the pot boiling, a couple of Illinois delegates managed to slip by the guards at the door and circled around the room promising that Garner would get thirty votes from their delegation on the next ballot. Senators Cordell Hull and Kenneth McKellar of Tennessee appeared and appealed to the Texans to throw their vote to Roosevelt. Arthur Mullen dropped in and said, "We've got to nominate Roosevelt on the next ballot tonight or we'll lose the fight. So we must get your votes tonight." "I was completely in the dark," confessed James E. Kilday, a liberal delegate from Harris County:

I was on my feet protesting against the switch. My argument was that the mere fact that Garner had released us was not such a thing as to justify us in ceasing to vote for him; that, out of courtesy to our candidate, we ought to cast, at least, one more vote for him after he had released us; that, surely, we ought to go on for the reason that Governor Smith had just sent us word that New York would vote for Garner on the next ballot, and we had other assurances of assistance.[31]

During the proceedings the caucus voted to appoint a new steering committee of five members to direct the delegation's activities on the floor of the convention. The committee was to consist of Amon Carter, Tom Connally, Charles I. Francis, Sam Rayburn, and W. A. Tarver. A few minutes later newsmen waiting outside the room learned this plan had been abandoned and that the caucus was again in an uproar.[32]

According to T. Whitfield Davidson's version of these chaotic events, Connally was asked to make a motion that the delegation go to Roosevelt. He refused. (Connally was up for reelection in 1934.) Rayburn then took the gavel and "with tears in his eyes turned it over to Amon Carter and left the caucus without expressing his wish as to how they should vote or for whom." A fierce argument ensued; Amon Carter spearheaded the opposition to Roosevelt. After about two hours, Davidson moved that the delegation switch to the New York governor. A roll call vote was reported as 54 to 51 in favor of the motion, and there was a hasty exit for the stadium. It was then about 9 p.m.[33]

"Finally, though, when they began to row, I had to squeeze down on them and we voted fifty-four to fifty-one to go for Roosevelt," Rayburn told Dorough. Connally recalled that after an hour of the never-say-die Garner rooters howling, "We'll never vote for Roosevelt! Give us Garner!" Rayburn managed to put the question of supporting Roosevelt to a vote. The senator continued: "Shortly after the roll call began, I caught one delegate voting against Roosevelt for an absentee delegate. I quickly denounced him for his illegal vote and watched carefully from then on as each name was called. How important each vote was showed up when the tally was announced. For only by a three-vote-margin—fifty-four to fifty-one—did the delegation make its switch to Roosevelt."[34]

But Connally neglected to mention that neither he nor Rayburn were among the fifty-four delegates who voted to switch to Roosevelt! Since there were 184 voting delegates and only fifty-four voted to abandon Garner, there is some question as to whether Texas actually went to Roosevelt. Many of the most ardent Garner men were out working for him in other state delegations when Rayburn caucused the Texas delegation. Had the die-hards all been there, it might have stayed with Garner.[35]

In any event Rayburn instructed Silliman Evans to find Farley and tell him what had happened. Senator Harrison of Mississippi met Evans on the stairway leading to the convention platform. "Has Texas done anything?" Harrison asked. "Yes," replied Evans, "and so has California. We've voted to go for Roosevelt." The senator exclaimed, "Good Lord! Mississippi has voted to leave him!" and he rushed back to his delegation to reverse its decision to switch to Baker on the next ballot.[36]

Shortly after 7 p.m. the California delegates had assembled behind locked doors at the Sherman Hotel, in a room next to that where the Texas delegation was holding its caucus. Accounts differ as to McAdoo's attitude. In a 1938 letter to Sam Rayburn, McAdoo recalled meeting him about 5 p.m. in the Sherman Hotel and telling him about the California caucus. "In our conversation, I expressed the opinion that it would be impossible to secure Garner's nomination and that I was going to propose to the California delegation that it authorize me to cast the vote of the State on the fourth ballot for Roosevelt, because I felt that he was fairly entitled to the nomination since he had received, on the third ballot, six hundred and eighty-two votes, or only eighty-seven votes less than the required two-thirds." McAdoo claimed that under the California preference system, the delegates did not need permission from Garner to change their votes, and he expressed the hope that Texas would join California in transferring its vote to Roosevelt, which would give him the nomination on the fourth ballot. If the two states acted together, they could secure Garner's nomination for the vice presidency. As McAdoo recalled it, Rayburn agreed that it would be impossible to nominate Garner and stated that he would talk to Garner almost immediately and explain the California situation. Rayburn, who had not seen McAdoo all day, evidently kept the news of his 3 p.m. conversation with Garner to himself. "Within an hour thereafter," according to McAdoo, Rayburn told him that Garner would release the Texas delegation and would be glad to accept the vice presidential nomination if offered.

Rayburn's recollection of events contradicted McAdoo. In a letter to the Californian, he stated that he had met McAdoo in the hall just as he was leaving the Texas caucus to telephone Garner, and he quoted McAdoo as saying: "What are we going to do? We will vote for Jack [Garner] until Hell freezes over if he or you say so." Rayburn told McAdoo, according to his account, "Go on in and release your delegation, as I am going to the telephone right now to ask Mr. Garner to give me the authority to release the Texas delegation." In a subsequent letter McAdoo claimed that Rayburn "was altogether in error" concerning the incident and insisted that he had decided to swing the delegation to Roosevelt: "It was obvious to me there was no chance to nominate Garner since Roosevelt had polled within eighty-seven votes of the required two-thirds." McAdoo said he feared a repetition of the disastrous 1924 Madison Square Garden convention and the subsequent defeat of any Democrat nominated. He believed that California, as the fourth state on the roll call and the first anti-Roosevelt state, occupied a "dominant strategic position" to start a landslide of votes for Roosevelt. McAdoo stated categorically that he did not know of Garner's release of delegates until he encountered Rayburn on the convention floor, just as the evening session was being called to order.[37]

The conflicting accounts make it impossible to know the precise sequence of events. "Judging by available evidence, both men were partially correct," concluded Lionel V. Patenaude. "McAdoo had already made up his mind to switch, and Rayburn did tell McAdoo to release his delegates, but apparently not at that time ... It appears that the news of the release was probably conveyed to McAdoo while both the Texas and California delegations were scurrying back and forth during the caucuses."[38]

McAdoo called the California caucus to order. Without indicating his own preference, he asked for opinions as to what the state should do in the event of a sudden shift or break during voting at the evening session. McAdoo emphasized one point over and over; he absolutely did not want a repetition of the ruinous deadlock that had occurred in New York City eight years earlier. A few Bay Area delegates favored going over to Smith, but more delegates favored Roosevelt. A large number wanted to stay with Garner for another ballot or two. One delegate expressed a choice for Baker. The meeting became a first-class donnybrook as tempers arose along with voices. The delegates sensed that McAdoo wanted them to switch. "We came here to vote for John Nance Garner and no one else!" screamed Grace Bryan Hargreaves. "McAdoo, you are attempting to betray us!" shouted another delegate. McAdoo turned white and clenched his fists but remained silent. It was soon obvious from the arguments that the delegation could not unite immediately behind any candidate.

Finally, to avoid a disastrous deadlock, a majority of the delegates unenthusiastically approved a steering committee of four, consisting of McAdoo as chairman and spokesman, Henry H. McPike, national committeewoman Nellie Donohoe, and John B. Elliott. It was Elliott, who enjoyed the respect and confidence of every member of the California delegation, who proposed this. The group was empowered "to determine when, and to whom, the votes of California should go in the event of a switch from John Nance Garner." The caucus then broke up without any actual vote on candidates, contrary to McAdoo's postconvention statement that the shift had been voted unanimously. Thomas Storke estimated that "more than half would have insisted on staying with Garner for at least one more ballot. Perhaps fifteen might have gone over to Smith. Possibly a majority favored Roosevelt. The only certain judgment of the situation was that unanimity was impossible." Immediately after the caucus broke up, the steering committee huddled together and instructed McAdoo to go Roosevelt on the next ballot. Based on the available evidence, this was after McAdoo learned that Garner had released his delegates but before the Texas delegation followed suit.[39]

The roll call was underway for the fourth ballot when a flushed and out-of-breath McAdoo came rushing down the aisle to his seat. His limousine had traveled about a mile from the hotel when the motor died and the chauffeur announced nonchalantly that they were out of gas. McAdoo in desperation climbed aboard a policeman's motorcycle, but he could not keep his long, gangling legs from scraping the pavement, so after going about a hundred yards or so, he had to dismount. The policeman then hailed a passing taxi, and with sirens screaming, McAdoo reached the auditorium. He met Rayburn, who told him that Texas had voted to switch to Roosevelt. McAdoo offered to yield to Texas, but Rayburn felt that it might cause further ill-feeling in his delegation to have the Lone Star State make the break first. A vigorous last-minute appeal was made to McAdoo by Amon Carter, who intercepted him on his way to his seat. Carter declared that the vote to release the Texas delegation had been very close and that it was a great mistake to "desert" Garner at that stage of the convention. He urged McAdoo not to change California's vote until the sixth ballot at least, saying that Texas would also stay by Garner in that event, and he could eventually be nominated. McAdoo rejected this appeal; California's decision for Roosevelt had been made and was final. In any event, Carter had no authority to make such an offer, although it is doubtful that a poll of the Texas delegation, once fully assembled in the auditorium, would have sustained the caucus vote for Roosevelt.[40]

Reaching his seat, McAdoo asked permission to explain a change in California's vote. "Please recognize me when California is called, Tom. You will not be disappointed. McAdoo," read the slip of paper a runner carried to Chairman Walsh. When California's name was called, McAdoo moved toward the rostrum. Cheers broke out from the Smith delegates and from the Smith rooters in the gallery, who believed McAdoo was going to switch California's votes to Smith. Then an electric silence descended as he began to speak. He said that he had had enough of deadlocks and that "any candidate who has mustered the strength now held by Franklin Delano Roosevelt should be given the nomination."

Bedlam broke loose. The stunned Smith forces, when they recovered their wits, began booing loud enough to rattle the rafters. McAdoo stood patiently as the booing went on minute after minute. Viewing the scene, H. L. Mencken wrote that the sixty-nine-year-old McAdoo was still "slim, erect and graceful" and "looked every inch the barnstorming Iago of the old school." He continued: "Eight years ago at New York he led the hosts of the Invisible Empire against the Pope, the rum demon and all the other Beelzebubs of the Hookworm Belt, and came so close to getting the nomination that the memory of its loss must still shiver him. The man who blocked him was Al Smith, and now he was paying Al back."

Each time McAdoo attempted to resume speaking, the booing increased in volume. The band started to play "California Here I Come," but nobody heard a note. Finally, Walsh got some semblance of order and into this momentary lull, McAdoo's voice sounded again: "I am going to finish this statement, regardless of what the galleries or anyone else have to say about it." Then, quietly and calmly, he went on to explain that California had not lost one whit of its faith in the statesmanship, character, and ability of John Nance Garner, but that he realized the Texan could never be nominated. "Therefore, California believing the majority should rule, casts its entire 44 votes for the unmistakable choice of the majority—Franklin D. Roosevelt!" Roosevelt, listening intently at his radio in Albany, leaned back and grinned broadly: "Good old McAdoo."[41]

McAdoo's dramatic announcement did the trick. State after state jumped on the bandwagon, Texas among them, and when the stampede was over,

Roosevelt had 945 votes, 175 over the necessary two-thirds. Smith salvaged 190½ votes, and 9½ others were scattered among favorite sons. Smith, with a bitterness in his heart that was to stay there until his dying day, refused to release his votes to the winner, and the fourth ballot went into the history books as above recorded. (One Smith follower wired McAdoo that evening: "The advancement in 2,000 years has been marvelous. Judas got only thirty pieces of silver.")[42]

A *New York Times* reporter discovered Garner on the roof of his Washington hotel looking out over the White House grounds. No one else had recognized the speaker in the hot darkness. "You've gone to Roosevelt?" he asked. "That's right, son, and that is all I'm going to say to you." After a moment the speaker relented a little. "I'm a little older than you, son," he said, "and politics is funny." According to Bascom Timmons, Garner did not even listen to the fourth ballot on the radio, and it was not until he saw newspapers the next morning that he knew his released delegates had brought about Roosevelt's nomination.[43]

Roosevelt wired McAdoo at 9:48 p.m.: "I am grateful to you for your generous and patriotic statement to the Convention and I hope to see my old friend tomorrow." Garner reassured his Californian ally: "Telegram received. Thanks for good wishes and kind sentiments. You did the wise and patriotic thing and Democracy owes you debt of gratitude. Mrs. Garner joins me in regards." The next morning McAdoo made a statement to the press in which he said the action of California and Texas had been dictated by the condition of the country, adding: "It would have been tragic to have deadlocked this convention. California and Texas, united as they were, had it in their power to tie up the convention indefinitely. The final result would have been the nomination of a candidate who did not represent the progressive element of the Democratic party. The hope of this country lies in a change of administration."[44] According to Bernard Baruch, "McAdoo ... thought that Smith intended to swing to Newton Baker, whom he opposed. There were, in fact, many reasons to believe this might occur. Determined not to be caught, McAdoo planned to move before Smith did." Smith's supporters claimed perfidy on the Californian's part. "If McAdoo had not broken the pledges he made," Jouett Shouse informed Newton Baker a few days after the convention's close, "Roosevelt would not have been nominated. On the fourth ballot there would have been serious defections from his ranks with the result that some other nominee would have been certain. That nominee would have been you or Ritchie." (Subsequently Shouse changed his mind and became convinced that the Smith delegates would have gone to Garner.)[45]

Basil O'Connor wisecracked to Roosevelt a few days later: "Of the 55,000 Democrats allegedly to have been in Chicago for the recent Convention, unquestionably 62,000 of them arranged the McAdoo shift." And Frank Freidel has concluded: "Certainly a remarkable number of them were working one way or another for the ultimate compromise, and many of them played notable roles in softening up one or another member of the Texas and California delegations. It is not surprising, therefore, that Mullen, Roper, McAdoo, Hearst, ad others, both in print and orally, have claimed credit for the great climax."[46]

Who was the most influential in swinging the Garner votes to Roosevelt? Both Arthur Mullen, through Congressmen Edgar Howard, and William Randolph Hearst, through George Rothwell Brown, stated their case to the speaker. These conversations, plus the fact that Garner and Rayburn had agreed not to tie up the convention, probably had some effect on Garner's decision. Jim Farley thought his influence was pivotal. Tom Connally enlarged his role—more than the evidence warrants. McAdoo tried to give the impression he was the key man in the switch, but he argued for Roosevelt only by inference in the California caucus, and it was John Elliott who proposed the steering committee that made the actual decision to switch. Lionel Patenaude believed that "the key man was Sam Rayburn," because he had Garner's power of attorney, Garner trusted his judgment, and the information he provided to the speaker in their 6 p.m. conversation "was decisive in helping Garner make up his mind."

"Garner, however, merely was putting his stamp of approval on a fait accompli," Patenaude concluded. "Rayburn's decision at the morning conference with Pat Harrison and Jim Farley on July 1, 1932, had made Roosevelt the future president of the United States." Yet T. Whitfield Davidson, in a 1952 letter to Patenaude, called attention to the failure of "Sam Rayburn, Senator Connally, and Chairman Amon Carter to vote for Roosevelt in the caucus, leaving the caucus without a suggestion or any attempt of guiding it to Roosevelt." Had it not been for the sub rosa campaign to place Roosevelt men on the Texas delegation who were nominally for Garner, the delegation might have disregarded the speaker's wishes and continued to vote for him. On July 5, 1932, Clyde O. Eastus of Fort Worth wrote Roosevelt that "myself and about eight others were responsible for the break in the Texas delegation." In an April 1933 letter he asserted: "Many delegates who claim now to be your friends insisted in our caucus that we cast two more ballots for Speaker Garner and a complimentary ballot for Melvin Traylor." He added, "This was voted down." Another Roosevelt delegate wrote the governor that the switch to him had to be done "on the quiet," because "some of them who purported to lead our delegation were determined to deliver the Texas delegation to the Smith forces."[47]

McAdoo, Elliot, McPike, and Donohoe, however, made their decision to switch to Roosevelt *before* Texas voted to switch. Since Roosevelt was only eighty-seven votes shy of victory on the third ballot, California's switch early in the fourth ballot roll call would have started the bandwagon for Roosevelt, even without Texas. "Keep the following records straight," an angry Will Rogers wrote in his column. "It was California that sold out and not Texas. Texas was for sticking even after California had quit 'em."[48]

Be Sure to Put a Stamp on That Letter

After Roosevelt's nomination a number of candidates were urged for the vice presidency, including Senator Clarence C. Dill of Washington, Gov. Henry Dern of Utah, and Senator Burton K. Wheeler of Montana, all of whom had been steadfast Roosevelt supporters since the beginning. Bernard Baruch spoke to Farley on behalf of Gov. Albert Ritchie of Maryland, but was told it was too late. Boss Ed Flynn of the Bronx, who had labored hard for Roosevelt, thought the vice presidential nominee ought to be someone other than Garner, someone less distasteful to the Irish Catholic Democrats of the North. "They felt keenly that Smith had been defeated in 1928 because of his religion," wrote Flynn in his memoirs. "They knew also that Texas, which was normally overwhelmingly Democratic, had gone for President Hoover. I felt, therefore, that if a candidate were named from Texas, Catholics would use this as an excuse for opposing the national ticket." A westerner or midwesterner would be better than "a representative of perhaps, bigotry's banner state," as the *Catholic Mirror* described Garner. Flynn got nowhere, however, in the effort to convince the Roosevelt leaders. Farley refused even to call a conference on the second-place choice and avoided as many inquiries as possible. He felt that Garner was entitled to the nomination if he wanted it. Roosevelt told him to go ahead and do what seemed best. Farley obtained Rayburn's approval and started lining up Roosevelt support for Garner.

Just before balloting got underway, Rayburn called Garner in Washington, told him he was about to be nominated for vice president, told him that Roosevelt was coming to Chicago to address the convention, and suggested that he also talk to the delegates over a voice-amplifying system connected

Vice President John N. Garner and President Franklin D. Roosevelt, circa 1930–1935. John Nance Garner Papers, Briscoe Center for American History, University of Texas at Austin, DI 01408.

with the telephone. Garner had no desire for an office of relatively little importance and preferred to remain in the powerful speakership. "I can still hear Roosevelt guffaw when he was told the Speaker's opinion of the office," wrote Brains Truster Rexford Tugwell. "'It was,' the Texan said, 'not worth a quart of warm spit.'" He gave his reason for accepting the nomination to Josephus Daniels, who had sent him a telegram in the middle of the night urging him to decline: "In reference to the vice presidential nomination, it was the opinion of my Texas and California friends that acceptance would prove helpful to the ticket, and I acted entirely upon their advice. That is the only consideration that prompted me to accept." There was only one other candidate nominated besides Garner—General Mathew A. Tinley of Iowa—and he withdrew before the balloting began and moved to make the Texan's nomination unanimous. The motion was carried without a dissenting voice.[49]

Was Garner's nomination in the nature of a deal by which Roosevelt got the votes of Texas and California? McAdoo said no. "All this talk about deals and trades is simply and only the echoes of a sharp contest and the disappointments that always follow such a battle," he said in a statement on July 5. "California's course was motivated by one purpose only and that was to save the party from another protracted and factional fight in the Convention which would have destroyed all possibility of success in November. We Californians felt that personal ambitions and factional differences must be submerged in a common and patriotic purpose to save the nation." Farley had repeatedly offered the vice presidency to Garner leaders, but they insisted that they had never made it a condition for switching to Roosevelt. Yet Josephus Daniels insisted that there had been a trade. He recalled: "I didn't like it; but, of course, like all Roosevelt supporters acquiesced because we had won the chief goal." The conditions were the nomination of Garner as vice president and McAdoo to be consulted before any secretary of the treasury was named. If McAdoo had not been elected to the senate, he would have expected to be secretary of the treasury. In his memoirs Cordell Hull stated that he and Daniel Roper, "in conjunction with other leaders, prevailed upon McAdoo to cast California's vote for Roosevelt in exchange for an arrangement to nominate Garner for Vice President. I do not know what other persons, save Farley and Howe, undertook to figure in this arrangement." Individual Texas delegates were assured by Roosevelt supporters that he would be offered the vice presidential nomination. Thus, Charles I. Francis wired Roosevelt at 11:35 p.m. on July 1: "As the delegate from Texas who spoke in your behalf and fought to break the deadlock which turned Texas to you in caucus at six thirty tonight I urge that you have as your running mate John Garner of Texas as was assured me would be done by Senators Hull and McKellar. This ticket cannot lose."[50]

The Texas delegates left Chicago with mixed feelings. They were glad to have a native son on the national ticket, but many were disappointed that he had the second place. "It's a kangaroo ticket," grumbled Archie Parr, who had voted for Roosevelt in the caucus. "Stronger in the hind quarters than in front." Whatever his feelings at the time of the caucus, Rayburn wrote Colonel House after returning home: "It was a great convention and I think nominated a great ticket. Texas, as it did in 1912, was a great factor in this Convention." Richard Burges wrote T. Whitfield Davidson: "The more I reflect upon it, the better satisfied I am with the outcome at Chicago." Burges marveled at what he viewed as a narrow escape for the Texas delegation: "I feel that we have reason to congratulate ourselves. Whenever my thought recurs to the narrow margin of our victory in the caucus, I feel what a narrow escape we had from being placed in a ridiculous position, and that not because we did not have a safe majority, but because the specious pleas of some of our members, ostensibly in aid of Garner, misled at least a few of our voters."[51]

Roosevelt flew to Chicago to accept the nomination. His speech—the joint product of Roosevelt himself, Louis Howe, Raymond Moley, and other members of Roosevelt's Brains Trust—contained the now famous words: "I pledge you, I pledge myself, to a new deal for the American people." Garner, who did not speak to the convention from Washington, asked that he be notified of his nomination by mail. This was done and the speaker wrote a letter of acceptance. "Be sure to put a stamp on that letter," he instructed his wife. "It is not official business."[52]

Roosevelt's nomination was apparently satisfactory to all the Democratic factions in Texas. Some of the Hoovercrat leaders refused to say definitely that they would support him; however, they indicated that if he did not stress repeal too hard they would get behind him. McAdoo's support plus Smith's opposition did a lot to bring them into the Roosevelt camp. Tom Love's reaction was taken as typical of most of his bone-dry followers. "I was certainly proud of my old chief, William Gibbs McAdoo, when he was on that platform, being booed by the galleries and cheered by the delegates, last night," said Love. By his swing to Roosevelt, McAdoo had done the Democratic Party an invaluable service by freeing it from the influence of Tammany Hall and Raskobism. However, Love declined to say whether he would support Roosevelt. "I want to see what he does about the platform, which is the rottenest platform that any man was ever asked to stand upon."[53]

The Republican National Convention had met in Chicago on Flag Day, June 14. Because of the state's large vote for Hoover in 1928, Texas's representation was increased from twenty-six to forty-nine delegates over 1928, although Texas took no active part in the proceedings. Since the death of congressman Harry M. Wurzbach, R. B. Creager had ruled unchallenged over the party machinery in Texas, and when the credentials committee made its report, it contained no dispute regarding the Texas delegation. The Texans cast their votes for Hoover, who was overwhelmingly nominated on the first ballot. Only one other name, that of Dr. Joseph Irvin France of Maryland, was placed in nomination, and he received the support of only four delegates. Six men were nominated for vice president, including incumbent Charles Curtis. Creager nominated convention chairman Bertrand Snell, a New York congressman, for the second spot on the ticket, and although Snell asked that his name be withdrawn, the Texas delegation cast its entire forty-nine votes for him. At the conclusion of the first ballot, Creager moved that Curtis's nomination be made unanimous, which was done with a great chorus of "ayes."

The gist of the Republican Prohibition plank was that Congress should promptly submit to state conventions, not to the legislatures, a new amendment on the liquor traffic that would permit state determination as to whether liquor should be manufactured and sold within state borders. The plank was regarded as a meaningless—but necessary—political gesture, written to save the eastern and northern states for Hoover. A minority plank calling for resubmission of the Eighteenth Amendment was voted down, 681 to 472.[54]

Roosevelt for President in Texas

Garner's nomination for vice president, together with the effects of the Depression, Hoover's unpopularity, and the disarray among Texas prohibitionists, decided the contest in Texas from the start. Thomas Watt Gregory assured Colonel House that "the political condition of National politics in Texas is all right and Roosevelt will undoubtedly carry the State by a large majority." In early August Governor Sterling wrote Garner that there was more harmony in Texas behind the national Democratic Party than at any time since the war days of President Wilson. Texas would support Roosevelt and Garner by the largest majority any national candidates had ever received in the state. No intensive campaign for the national ticket was considered necessary, and Texas's two senators and other leading speakers were sent into other states to campaign for the party.[55]

The only question was whether the Hoovercrats of 1928 would vote for Roosevelt and Garner on a platform calling for the repeal of the Eighteenth Amendment. A few Hoovercrat leaders in Texas initially expressed some degree of optimism about Hoover's chances in the state. Rev. J. Frank Norris reported to the president's secretary, Walter Newton, that "the Democrats are troubled and terribly uneasy about Texas. The general feeling is that the tide of prosperity has set in and we should not swap horses in the midst of the stream. But the thing I hear most is 'Roosevelt and Garner are weak' and this is no time for weakness at the head of our Government." Alvin Moody wrote Newton that in his opinion there were at least 250,000 Dry Democrats in Texas who had supported Hoover in 1928 and who would vote for him again provided he said the right thing in his acceptance speech. "He must let them know that he is in sympathy with the Eighteenth Amendment and that he still wants it to succeed," Moody insisted. As it turned out, there were practically no defections of southern Democrats to Hoover. Most Texas Drys ended up voting reluctantly for Roosevelt and Garner. Hoover, in Tom Love's view, lost a great opportunity when he "abandoned" the Eighteenth Amendment. As Love explained to Senator William E. Borah on Election Day: "I am one of several million Democrats who are voting for Roosevelt today, not because of the dripping Wet Plank in the Chicago platform, but in spite of it."[56]

Donald Richberg, the general counsel for the Railway Labor Executives' Association, on his way from Chicago to New York City to see Roosevelt, stopped in Washington and dropped in on Garner. The speaker mentioned that he had not seen his running mate since the nomination, but he would like Richberg to take one message to him. "Tell the governor that he is the boss and we will all follow him to hell if we have to, but if he goes too far with some of these wild-eyed ideas to have the stuffing kicked out of us."[57] But it was the conservative Garner, not Roosevelt, whom the Republicans tried to portray as a wild-eyed radical and a threat to free enterprise. He was ridiculed and belittled from one end of the country to the other.

By the time Congress adjourned in July, Garner had made himself conspicuous as the strong advocate of a $100 million emergency relief fund to be administered at the president's discretion and of a billion-dollar federal public works program. The speaker had been involved in a noisy quarrel with Hoover about the bill to enlarge the scope of the Reconstruction Finance Corporation. He had demanded that private as well as public borrowers have access to public loan funds, charging that the president's insistence on confining the loans to banks, railroads, and other public and semipublic institutions was a special form of succor to financiers. In turn, Hoover and his lieutenants excoriated Garner's plan for loans to small business as an attempt to make the RFC "the most gigantic banking and pawnbroking business in all history."[58]

These ideas made Garner an anathema to the business interests of the East. "I am very much afraid that Garner's so-called 'relief bill' is going to be a serious handicap to the ticket in the East," Frank Andrews fretted to House. "The President has already denounced it as a 'pork barrel bill,' and so far as I understand the situation it is indefensible." John W. Davis wrote: "I agree that Brother Garner is not making votes for his ticket." The Democratic presidential standard bearer of 1924 concluded: "We shall see what we shall see." Houston businessman W. L. Clayton was "afraid the Texas end of the ticket will be a great handicap. He [Garner] has been a deep disappointment to me." The *Reader's Digest* was also disappointed in the speaker. The editors expressed regret in view of his recent leadership that they had published an article "highly complimentary" to him in the June issue. "We believe that you are now discredited among thoughtful people of America, and that you have already alienated countless numbers who otherwise would have supported the Democratic party in November."[59]

When a Dallas crowd turned out to cheer Garner on his return from Washington, he cut loose with a fiery attack on Hoover, so hot that it stirred politicians and editors throughout the country. The speaker recounted the stormy scenes in Congress in the last several weeks, when Hoover twice vetoed bills he (Garner) had advocated. Shouted Garner:

> I trusted the President enough to be willing to leave the distribution of that [relief] money to his judgment, but he called it a "pork-barrel measure." Then because I demanded that the Reconstruction Finance Corporation make public its use of $2,000,000,000 of the people's property, he said in effect, "No that is for the benefit of my select clientele, and the people must not know what is done with it." We passed that measure anyway. I notice by the morning newspapers he says he will study it a few days, and "probably will sign it." He means he wants to have a few days in which to find out what Wall Street and J. P. Morgan think he should do about it.

Leading Republican journals, such as the *Chicago Tribune*, professed to be alarmed at Garner's pork-barrel measures and to be shocked at his "intemperate rantings" on the hustings in Texas. He was called a Klansman and a "Negro-hater." "Mr. Garner seems to be proving a real godsend to the Republican spell-binders," remarked the *Hartford Courant*; and the *Newark Evening News* added that "that sort of rude, rugged talk will certainly insure the cowboy-goat-herder-horse-wrangler vote for the Democratic ticket, but what it will do north of the mescal and pinto line is just horrible." The *Washington Post* took a slightly different tack by suggesting that while the colorless Roosevelt hedged on everything, the dynamic Garner was speaker was running the Democratic show. "It is an odd and embarrassing situation," the *Post* declared, "in which the tail of the kite becomes more important and influential than the head." Secretary of the Navy Charles Francis Adams asked ominously: "Would any President be able to control Garner?" There were renewed whispers about Roosevelt's physical and mental health, with the implication that a vote for the New York governor was really a vote for Garner for president.[60]

A Sherman, Texas, businessman, after returning from a trip in July to New York and some of the New England states, reported to Sam Rayburn that he had found feelings of apprehension with reference to Garner among a number of manufacturers with whom his firm did business. "They all feel that Garner is a capable man, well seasoned and experienced in Governmental affairs but they have a fear that his extremely progressive program is going to cause a great many people to vote the Republican ticket where they might have voted with the Democrats." Rayburn replied that it was a part of the Republican campaign in the North and East to create the impression that Garner was a radical. "How any one who is acquainted with Mr. Garner could say he is a radical or an ultra-progressive, is strange," the congressman declared. Rayburn knew what he was talking about, but as a publicity director at Democratic national headquarters said to a reporter in August: "It's a funny thing: here's a man who has been before the public for thirty years, and yet nobody don't know nothing about him."[61]

The talk about his alleged radicalism and his running the Democratic show was embarrassing to Garner. He had his wife forward the *Washington Post* editorial, along with a clipping from the *New York Times*, to Roosevelt with the assurance that he was not going to take the initiative in any way, but would be governed by Roosevelt's policies throughout the campaign. He asked Roosevelt to look over his acceptance letter to Senator Barkley and make suggestions before it was released. "I hope you will be very free in your criticisms," he prompted. Garner did offer his running mate some advice on campaign strategy. "My idea is to punch the Administration in the nose, especially Hoover and Mills, at every opportunity, because the Treasury Department has been the Administration for the last twelve years. A short sermon on Mellon, Mills, and Meyers would be good for the people in all this western and southern country. I don't know how it would set in the East."[62]

Roosevelt, implying that he expected Garner to campaign continuously throughout the fall, urged the speaker and his wife to come to Albany for a visit, and said not a word about his supposedly radical views. However, he did caution "My dear Teammate":

I agree with you about hitting the Administration, but it is my thought that in some parts of the country, such as the East and the Middle West, Hoover is so thoroughly down that too many personal attacks on him won't be taken very well by the Republicans who now expect to vote for us. In Democratic territory it is all right, but everything you or I say gets into the papers in every section of the country. Frankly, I think it is best to hammer at the Republican leadership—not the Republican Party—and it is all right to talk about Mills, Mellon, Hyde, etc. without too much reference to Hoover himself. He personally is flat and we can safely leave him there.[63]

Garner became increasingly sensitive to the fears expressed by eastern Democrats that he would alienate voters. "I repeat, I don't know anyway but to give the Republicans hell," he protested to Farley, who had succeeded Raskob as national party chairman, "and that does not seem to be agreeable to the eastern section of the country." Roosevelt tried his best to placate his running mate, assuring Mrs. Garner: "I want you and the Speaker not to worry one bit about these fool editorials in some of the eastern papers. They are grasping at straws and, because of lack of other material, are building up false impressions against us both. Our long standing friendship will mean the finest possible team work."[64]

In mid-August Garner went east to confer with Roosevelt and pose for joint photographs. "All you have got to do is stay alive until election day," he advised his running mate at their first meeting. "The people are not going to vote for you. They are going to vote against the depression." Garner told Howe in New York that he felt the less he had to do with the campaign the better it would be. His motto became "Sit down—do nothing—and win the election." What he wanted was for Howe to arrange it somehow that he could stay down in Uvalde and go fishing until Election Day. Although Howe and Farley tried to talk Garner into campaigning, at least in Texas and California, the speaker clung to his "poker" hunch that "the less we say, and especially myself, the better it will be for us in the campaign." As he settled down in Uvalde, Garner confided to Farley: "Now if I can just be cautious enough to keep up with Governor Roosevelt's viewpoints and not appear to controvert them, thereby giving our Republican friends in the East and elsewhere a chance to say that we are crosswise, I will have accomplished something at least." Farley replied reassuringly: "The situation is all right as I see it and the thing for us to do is to sit tight and I am sure everything will come out all right."[65]

The cautious Howe sent Charles Hand, a newspaperman from New York, to Uvalde to ride herd on Garner's infrequent statements to the press. "I'll bet you ten dollars," Garner said as he greeted Hand at the door, his eyebrows beetling like mad, "that this is another one of that little devil Louis Howe's ideas." However, the Texan cooled down and the two men became good friends, even "striking several blows for liberty" together as time went on.

Messages from the national headquarters to Garner requesting him to take an active part in the battle were funneled through Hand but provoked little more than such statements as: "The Captain is going to be elected and doesn't need me on the stump." In early October Garner wrote Roosevelt: "I do not want to make any set speeches." The speaker explained: "I am certain that this would be to the best interest of the party. Any set speeches from me will not get additional votes, and might give the opposition arguing material. I am most positively set in this view; therefore, good comrade, let me have my way in this thing." Garner participated only twice in the campaign: once when he went to Topeka, Kansas, to appear on the platform with Roosevelt and once when he delivered a radio speech in New York City on a nationwide hookup. Written with the help of Hand and speechwriter Charles Michelson, the speech, in Hand's opinion, was "a rattling good one." Garner opened with a moving tribute to his close friend, former speaker Nicholas Longworth, who had recently died, before moving on to discuss taxation and the need for government economy.[66]

A delegation composed of Farley, fund-raiser Frank Walker, Bernard M. Baruch, and Senators Claude Swanson, Key Pittman, and James Brynes, called on Garner at his suite in the Hotel Biltmore and argued with him for three hours that he should make more speeches. Garner stuck to his guns. "Let's go on the principle of Captain Bill McDonald of the Texas Rangers," Garner said. "A riot was threatened in a Texas town and citizens wired to the Governor to send Rangers. Then they went to the station to meet the train. Bill McDonald got off. 'What,' asked the leader of the citizens' group, 'just one Ranger!' 'Well,' Bill McDonald drawled, 'there's just one riot ain't there?'" The speaker had made his point; one speech per campaign was enough.[67]

The Republican campaign to smash Garner was completely baffled. "How can you smash a man who has simply folded up before you have a chance to smite him?" asked the *Dallas Morning News.* "Mr. Garner saw the point to that first and now the Republicans are seeing it."[68]

Roosevelt and Farley depended entirely on the regular Democratic organization in each state to get out the vote. This policy brought complaints from preconvention Roosevelt supporters in states where the organization had opposed his nomination. When Cordell Hull complained to Farley that

Roosevelt's early supporters in Texas were being sidetracked, Farley replied: "To be very frank with you, Senator, I think we will make a terrible mistake if we fail to carry out the campaign through the regular organization in Texas. . . . If we do it otherwise we are going to be in trouble." After the Chicago convention T. Whitfield Davidson tendered the former Roosevelt organization in Texas to national committeeman Jed Adams. "However, we will not wait to be told what to do," Davidson assured Richard Burges, "but will coordinate activities and do everything that we see to be done."[69]

In early August Davidson talked with Joseph Duffey of Pennsylvania, who said that Adams had given him and Farley assurances that he would extend fair recognition to all factions in Texas. But Davidson was not persuaded. "Candidly, I am fearful that Jed is biased and perhaps jealous of every one who took any part in the preconvention Roosevelt Organization, or who was active in turning the Texas Delegation to Roosevelt at Chicago," he confided to Burges. "I hope I am wrong about this." Davidson warned Rayburn that a few men in the Texas delegation had their minds made up to turn the delegation to a candidate other than Roosevelt should Garner withdraw, and "for political effect, these parties probably put me in a different light to you, other than my true attitude." Rayburn brushed him off with a brief form letter reply: "Thank you for your letter. I am of the opinion that the ticket we nominated at Chicago is a very popular one and I am proud of the part that Texas had in it, I trust that every Democrat both with his voice and pocketbook will get out and elect this ticket. I think it is vital to the country that this change be made."[70] After consulting with Rayburn, Adams named Roy Miller of Corpus Christi, the "boy mayor" of that city from 1913 to 1917, state manager for the presidential campaign. An intimate friend of Garner, Miller was reported to have vigorously opposed his "ditching" in the caucus before the fourth ballot at Chicago. Some Texans protested the appointment: Miller was a lobbyist for the Texas Gulf Sulphur Company in Austin and Washington, and naysayers stated that his appointment would hurt the national ticket. One irate San Antonio man wrote Roosevelt: "I am sure you will understand the rank and file voter cannot see why your loyal supporters have been ignored and paid lobbyists have been given honors in this campaign." But such protests were dismissed. "These things always come along," Rayburn assured Miller.[71]

On Election Day, November 8, Roosevelt wired Garner: "Best of luck to my good old teammate. Everything points to a victory for us. We will vote here at Hyde Park and go to headquarters in New York this morning. Will telephone you from there." The results of the election almost exactly reversed 1928. Roosevelt obtained 22,815,539 popular votes and carried forty-two states with 472 electoral votes to Hoover's 15,759,930 popular votes and six states with 59 electoral votes. Smith, with eight states to his credit, had 87 electoral votes in 1928 to Hoover's 444. Garner had amused himself offering wagers that no one could pick any combination of five states that the president would carry. No one had the right combination, and the speaker won all his bets. "We are happy in the great Democratic Victory," Davidson wrote House. "Your own foresight and wisdom in selecting the right candidate was the real key that unlocked the door. Texas has redeemed itself from four years ago. We had a bunch of boys that fought our man very viciously and vigorously up until he was nominated but they climbed upon the band wagon very nicely."

In September Garner had predicted that Texas would go Democratic by 300,000 to 500,000 votes; as it turned out, these figures were too conservative. Roosevelt got 767,581 votes in Texas while Hoover received only 97,852. The Republican candidate failed to carry a single Texas county. Garner's congressional district elected him to the House for the sixteenth straight time.[72] His nomination for vice president had come after congressional nominations had closed. Consequently, he could have been defeated for vice president and still have been House speaker. Humorist Will Rogers joked after the election:

I advised 'em [the candidates] to go fishing. Let the people alone and make up their own minds. Jack Garner was the only one listened to me. He went fishing, made no enemies, had a good time, caught three big channel cats, a seat in the House of Representatives, and the Vice-Presidency.

That's about a record for one catch. He wanted to throw back the smallest of the "catfish" and the Vice-Presidency, and just keep the seat in the House and the other two fish. Garner will be the only man that ever went from "speaker" in the House to "listener" in the Senate.[73]

CHAPTER 8

The Politics of Relief and Repeal

As Roosevelt and Garner prepared to assume their presidential and vice presidential offices, Mrs. Miriam A. Ferguson returned to the governor's office on January 17, 1933, while four bands played military airs, a squadron of army airplanes circled the capitol dome, and cannons boomed a seventeen-gun salute. A throng of Ferguson partisans overflowed the house of representatives for the first indoor inauguration since 1925, blocked capitol rotundas and departmental offices, and cheered their acclaim. For the second time in seven years, she placed her left hand on a Bible mellowed with age through its long use in that capacity and swore to "faithfully and impartially discharge and perform all the duties incumbent" upon her. Jim was by her side, the only ex-governor who took part in the inaugural. It had been customary for former governors to lend their presence to an inauguration, if possible; but O. B. Colquitt, William Hobby, Pat Neff, Dan Moody, and Ross Sterling did not put in an appearance. Representative Temple Harris McGregor, long a Ferguson partisan, introduced the woman governor as "the people's choice."

Mrs. Ferguson's inaugural address was brief. "On every hand there is want, and need, and hunger that has already led to despair and desperation," she warned. "Hope is nearly gone. The burdens of government are falling heavily on the masses. Reduction of taxes must come and come quickly or the government will fall and fall quickly." She craved "the opportunity to cooperate with you, the members of this legislature, in solving the troubles that now afflict the people who have sent us here to bring relief." She told the forty-third legislature: "Any cause or condition that would lead to unkindliness or unfriendliness must ultimately lead to confusion. So you and I are going to be friendly because we both want to be right." She quoted what she termed an "old valentine verse" that was used by her husband in

Ma Ferguson seated at a desk, circa 1933. Prints and Photographs Collection, Briscoe Center for American History, University of Texas at Austin, E BTE 49.

his first inaugural address in 1915: "If you love me as I love you, / Nothing can cut our love in two." A report in the *Dallas Morning News* noted: "Eighteen years, almost to the day, have intervened between the two addresses, yet the same calculated slips as to grammar are practiced, the same deliberate careless style is employed, the same ingratiating good will is expressed. It is indeed the old familiar tune. We are back in 1915. The voice is that of Miriam, but the pen is that of James."[1] It remained to be seen whether Fergusonism was equal to the challenges facing the state of Texas caused by the Great Depression.

Debt, Taxes, and the Ferguson Machine

A team of lawmakers known as the "Four Horsemen" took charge in the house of representatives and ran things for two years. T. H. McGregor of Austin, Judge John M. Mathis Sr. of Houston, Preston L. Anderson of

San Antonio, and the "intractable, irascible, brilliant" (as Raymond Brooks called him) Walter "Uncle Elmer" Pope, a one-time newspaper publisher, of Corpus Christi.[2]

State revenues had been reduced several million dollars annually by the constitutional amendment, now in effect, exempting from state taxation homesteads to the value of $3,000. Mrs. Ferguson's solution to the deficit and the need for more revenue was a 3 percent sales tax, which she estimated would raise $45 million annually, and a cut of $15 million in the budget for the next biennium. The governor said that such a sum would pay the state's debts, support the state government, and provide a per capita school apportionment of $17.50.

The sales-tax proposal raised many voices to full cry, some for and some against. Peter Molyneaux, editor of the *Texas Weekly*, called it "plain common sense," and a *Texas Weekly* poll of 144 Texas newspapers found that "a definite majority," including the *Houston Post* and *Houston Chronicle*, favored such a tax. An editorial in the *Jayton Chronicle*, however, declared: "The proposed 3 per cent sales tax as advocated by the Governor, would tax everything from diaper pins to pine coffins, if enacted into law, and would cause more hell-raising in Texas than we care to be mixed up in." The *Sterling City News-Record* likewise indicated its disapproval: "The sales tax as proposed by Jim Ferguson would be a mighty fine thing for the big property owner, but it would be hell on the man of small means." However, Ferguson assured his *Forum* readers that the tax would not hurt them. "This sales tax," he explained, "is simply a tax on sales, whether made by the manufacturer, the jobber, the wholesaler or retailer, and if you don't buy, you don't pay."[3]

A press survey showed that house members preferred an income tax; the senate seemed disposed to give the governor what she wanted. Early in March the House Committee on Revenues and Taxation reported favorably on a bill that combined a sales tax and an income tax, although the income tax features predominated. By a vote of 9 to 0 the Senate Finance Committee killed the proposed act late in the session. The governor then asked the state comptroller and the state auditor to prepare a statement about the treasury's condition; this statement she sent to the legislature, calling on the lawmakers to raise revenue "in any way you see fit" in order to end the deficit of $18,207,304 that was forecast for August 31, 1933. If no change was made in the ad valorem tax rate and no new revenue provided, "the total deficit of August 31, 1935," was estimated at almost $32 million. Still the legislators took no action. A few days later Mrs. Ferguson, in a thirty-nine-

word message, proposed an income tax on the gross earnings of corporations, suggesting that such a tax would bring in some $25 million a year. She
said she would extend the intangible tax levy on earnings to all corporations
not then paying a gross receipts tax and declared that such a measure would
"go a long way toward balancing our budget." The legislature did not care for
the proposal; the only revenue-raising measure it passed was one increasing the oil tax to two cents a barrel. The existing law levied a tax of 2 percent
of the value of the oil, which in 1933 averaged a half-cent a barrel. It was estimated that the amended measure would bring in an additional $8 million
a year. The legislature also cut $13 million from the biennial appropriation.
Jim Ferguson exasperatedly gave an account of the governor's stewardship
at the end of the regular session: "My wife and I tried to pass the Sales Tax,
we tried to pass the Income Tax, we tried to pass the Tax on Corporations
on Intangible Values, we tried to pass a graduated Oil Tax but our appeals
seem to have fallen on deaf ears and it is hard to tell what the result will be.
My wife and I have been on the job for five long months."[4]

It was the forty-third legislature that received the Graves-Woodruff Reorganization Bill, perhaps better known as the Griffinhagen Report. The
previous legislature had created a five-member Legislative Joint Committee
on Organization and Economy to investigate all state departments, institutions of higher education, and the judiciary. On the committee were Senators Grady Woodruff and Carl Hardin and Representatives Harry N. Graves,
Phil L. Sanders, and J. T. Terrell. They employed a private firm, Griffinhagen
and Associates, to make surveys and act as consultants. The committee
worked for twenty months and spent $70,000 checking into every facet and
phase of the state government and its administration and prepared a comprehensive report totaling forty thousand words. This report recommended
the reorganization and consolidation of 129 existing state bureaus and commissions into twenty new ones at an annual savings of $1.5 million and pro-
posed a reorganization of state colleges, which would save $2–4 million per
year. "We feel sure that if the contents of this 40,000-word report could become generally understood and appreciated among the people, there would
be no doubt about its major recommendations being put into effect," the
Texas Weekly stated. "However, it is doubtful that even a majority of
the Legislature will digest its contents." According to the *New York Times*,
the report contained "no radical suggestions, no seemingly impossible proposals, nothing that does not appear wholly practical. . . . The plan is designed to save at least $6,000,000 annually but it is thought the proposals,
will be generally discarded."[5]

Shortly after the legislature convened, the Griffinhagen Report was made available to members. Almost immediately a bill was introduced in the house for reorganization of higher educational facilities. The measure created a wave of protest. In brief, it provided for the consolidation of North Texas State Teachers College and the College of Industrial Arts, both in Denton; the abandonment of Southwest Texas State Teachers College at San Marcos, owing to its proximity to the University of Texas at Austin; and abandoning or turning into junior colleges the teachers' colleges at Nacogdoches, Alpine, Canyon, and Commerce. The bill was sent to the Committee on Education and was reported out favorably but got no further.[6]

Two bills were introduced to reorganize the state's executive departments. The Woodruff bill passed the senate and was sent to the house, but it was loaded with amendments that defeated its purpose. The Graves bill was introduced in the house for the same general purposes and passed by a vote of 105 to 22; it then went to the senate, which added minor amendments. However, when it came up for final passage late in the session, it was recommitted to the State Affairs Committee by a vote of 17 to 9, and in that manner was killed. In effect, then, the proposals contained in the Griffinhagen Report were "generally discarded," just as the *New York Times* had predicted. The *Texas Weekly* noted that the chief reaction to the publicity given to the report in newspapers "has been movements in opposition to some of its recommendations by persons who feared they would result in injury to some state institutions located in this or that town or region." No real public support met the report, not even among those who had been most vocal in demanding a reduction in government spending or in opposing proposals to adopt new means of raising revenue.[7]

In 1933 the legislature revived an issue that had lain dormant since 1908 by approving an appropriations bill that carried a rider that legalized racetrack betting in Texas. The rider was written by T. H. McGregor, who knew that it could not be passed as a separate bill. The fact that the state constitution prohibited more than one subject in a bill did not matter, and appropriations and betting on horse races were hardly the same subject. Lush "downs" were opened at Arlington, San Antonio, and Houston. Ministers denounced the law, and many editors and businessmen attacked it, but not until 1937, when Gov. James V. Allred forced its consideration by calling the legislature into special session for that purpose, was it repealed.[8]

Mrs. Ferguson again pursued a liberal pardoning policy, and again she was bitterly criticized for it. Ferguson enemies referred to the Executive

Mansion as "the House of a Thousand Pardons." But Ouida Ferguson defended her mother's pardon record:

> The Governor granted clemency to many whom she thought deserving. To those short-term men, with good prison records, who had been liquor law violators, she opened wide the gates. These pardons the enemy newspapers played up in scareheads accusing the Fergusons of exposing the citizens of Texas to a loosed rabble of murderers and thieves. For carrying out humanely the letter and spirit of the parole and pardon provisions of the law, the Governor was called almost everything short of gangster. Nothing could have been further from the truth. Every pardon granted was the result of careful study of the case. In no instance did Miriam A. Ferguson grant clemency to a convict without the approval of the Board of Pardons.[9]

When the Fergusons moved back into the Governor's Mansion, Jim sought to once more use his wife's patronage powers to become master of Texas's political destinies. In May 1933 he threw his power behind the selection of Charles C. McDonald, a lawyer from Wichita Falls, as national committeeman from Texas to succeed Jed C. Adams, who had been appointed to the Federal Board of Tax Appeals.[10] "I'm for McDonald from start to finish; he is a real Democrat," Jim announced. "He will probably succeed in putting this over," Alfred Petsch advised Sen. Morris Sheppard. "If he does, it will mean that the entire machinery of the Democratic party of Texas is in complete control of a bunch of political bandits, whose leaders have absolutely no regard for the principles of honest public service."

State party chairman Maury Hughes, who had been a loud shouter in the Ferguson camp in 1932, opposed McDonald and favored Vice President John Nance Garner for the post. Garner's selection would have been favorably received in official Washington, but strong opposition developed in Texas against his selection. However, it became unnecessary to present Garner's name when Adams withdrew his resignation at the request of Jim Farley and agreed to serve out his term. In a brief meeting in Dallas on May 15, the state Democratic Executive Committee—driven by Jim Ferguson personally, with B. Y. Cummings of Wichita Falls acting as "right-of-way man"—censured Adams for holding two posts at the same time and endorsed McDonald for national committeeman when and if the post became vacant. "It was amusing how Dallas papers played up the Maury Hughes-

Ferguson fight over the National Committeeman," Tom Love's law partner wrote him in Washington.

> Ferguson certainly did set Maury down, and had a meeting of the State Executive Committee without paying any attention in any manner to its Chairman. Maury was the victory [*sic*] according to Walter Hornaday. I suppose you noticed that B. Y. Cummings accused you, Silliman Evans and Amon Carter of hatching the conspiracy to make Vice-President Garner National Committeeman. Talk is going around here that Maury is being urged by himself to run for Governor, I believe, however, that Allred has taken the leading post in opposition to the Fergusons. His stand on the Ferguson Oil Commission undoubtedly killed that Bill and his public attacks on the lobby at Austin have focused attention to him.

According to Mark L. Goodwin, Washington correspondent for the *Dallas Morning News*, Garner's selection as national committeeman was understood "to have been the wish of the President, and members of the administration in Washington expected the program to go through in Texas." Some of them were said to feel that the state Democratic Executive Committee in Texas had turned its back on the national administration.

During the first one hundred days of the Roosevelt administration, Garner was extremely effective in helping to accelerate the passage of the administration's emergency legislation. Before Congress adjourned, Farley notified the heads of departments, bureaus, and commissions in the nation's capital that "in order to be certain that the interest of the Democratic Party is protected at all times," Garner was to approve every appointment made in or from Texas. As the national chairman explained to Federal Emergency Relief Administration director Harry L. Hopkins: "Texas is his State and it is only fitting and proper that he be thoroughly advised on all recommendations and definitely approve all appointments before they are made. In other words, be certain to consult with him at all times. This is in accordance with the wishes of the President."[11]

The following year, when it became clear that there would be no meeting of the National Democratic Committee until after the Texas primaries and the election of a new state committee, Jed Adams again offered his resignation, and this time it was accepted. On March 24, 1934, the state committee, meeting in Houston, named Pa Ferguson national committeeman. John Bickett Jr. of San Antonio, in a flowery speech nominating Jim, described him as "the noblest Roman of them all." The well-oiled Ferguson machine rolled over the recommendations of retiring state chairman Hughes as if he had made none. "The smooth functioning of the Ferguson machine, as installed at Houston ... commands admiration," one Texas paper commented. "The slate selected for the party posts went through without so much as a shiver of the shock absorbers.... As far as the directing forces of the party in Texas are concerned, those at outs with the Governor are very far out indeed." Ouida Ferguson Nalle recalled: "Daddy's election to this office in the party was a considerable blow to some of the old Ferguson enemies." A rather pointed intimation came from Washington that Ferguson would not be seated, and so the matter rested with Jim nominally occupying the office with at least the semblance of a legal claim to it.[12]

A Good Day's Work for Jim

On July 21, 1932, Congress passed a Federal Emergency Relief law that made Reconstruction Finance Corporation (RFC) funds available to the states for relief. The funds were to be deducted from future highway grants. The Hoover administration required detailed reports concerning the distribution of these funds. Since the average Texas county lacked this kind of relief machinery, relief work in the state was originally organized under the three regional chambers of commerce. Beginning on November 1, 1932, funds were allocated on request of Governor Sterling, who turned them over to the East Texas Chamber of Commerce with headquarters at Longview, to the South Texas Chamber of Commerce with headquarters at San Antonio, and to the West Texas Chamber of Commerce with headquarters at San Angelo. These organizations in turn distributed the funds to county emergency relief committees in their respective areas. In February 1933 A. Wayne McMillen, a RFC field representative, recommended to Fred Croxton, assistant to the directors of the RFC, that no more funds be given to Texas until it organized a central administration agency. Croxton, acting on a resolution passed by the RFC board of directors to make available $1,377,955 for March, stated that consideration of relief needs for April would be dependent upon the progress made toward accomplishing this objective. The resolution further stipulated that Texas take some definite steps toward making state funds available for relief.[13]

Governor Ferguson then created the Texas Relief Commission (TRC) and the old plan was abolished. This caused considerable hard feeling on the part of the three chambers of commerce, as the administration of relief funds had placed their organizations in a very favorable light in the state. The RFC also insisted on the appointment of a competent state director of relief. Governor Ferguson mentioned three names to McMillen, and he reported favorably on Col. Lawrence Westbrook of Waco, who was appointed. According to Westbrook there were 1.2 million people on relief at that time. McMillen recommended that a person experienced in the administration of relief be brought into the state and suggested Aubrey Williams, then with the American Public Welfare Association. Williams arrived in Texas in the first part of March. Operating under the new commission composed of six persons, including the managers of the three regional chambers of commerce, Westbrook organized the work as required by the RFC, and Williams acted as consultant. County committees were organized and personnel hired to administer relief. The commission continued in existence until about June 1, 1933.[14]

In April 1933 the legislature established the Texas Rehabilitation and Relief Commission (TRRC), under the provision that this commission should distribute federal relief through a system of county welfare boards. The governor, lieutenant governor, and speaker of the house each appointed two members, and the governor served as ex-officio chairman. Mrs. Ferguson appointed Westbrook as director. The commission was given $50,000 for administrative expenses.[15] On June 2, the day the bill became law, Jim Ferguson, as his wife's representative, chaired the commission's initial session, as he did all subsequent meetings except one occasion when he was out of Austin. His first act was to give the governor and Westbrook the power to appoint county welfare boards. Ferguson also decided to eliminate the managers of the chambers of commerce from the organization. "This was a good day's work for Jim," historian Lionel Patenaude noted wryly, "especially since he had no legal basis to act as chairman of the new organization." Ferguson and Westbrook then began expanding the relief machine by making selections to the five-member county welfare boards. In smaller counties they relied on "at least five or six of our friends" to recommend names. This caused friction with anti-Ferguson men at the county commissioner level. (The law required that the boards be approved by the county commissioners' court.) Hard-fought disputes over these positions raged in fifteen or twenty counties. As the county boards began to fill with Fergusonites, their power increased in direct proportion to the increases in the relief rolls.[16]

An El Paso man called Senator Connally's attention to the activities of

W. J. Moran, "a very strong Ferguson partisan" in the city. According to this informant, Moran "practically controls the employees of the Federal Employment Bureau and the local R.F.C. employment bureau in El Paso, and these are being used by him to work up a strong political machine in favor of those whose candidacy the Governor may support during the next election." I. L. Martin, a Uvalde lawyer, asked Connally to "use all your vigilance" to prevent Jim Ferguson from gaining control through his appointees of vast federal relief funds. He quoted Judge C. P. Spangler of Uvalde as warning Vice President Garner: "The complete set-up of the Governor is not in operation yet, however it is my personal knowledge that there are a number of men travelling over the State putting the machinery in place. There is no doubt but that these men are being paid out of the relief fund." Martin warned Connally that his own reelection prospects could be injured by Ferguson's relief machine:

> You know that it is rumored that the husband of the Governor is likely to be a candidate for United States Senator, and whether he will be a candidate against you [or] wait to "tackle" our other Senator, we do not know, but its [sic] very likely that he will enter his name at the first vacancy, or chance for the election to some office, and just imagine what he will do politically with a machine behind him, such as he could build up with all that patronage in his hands. I sincerely hope that the powers that be, in Washington will "put on the brakes," and stop his ambition in giving him the power that he could have, if he should succeed in his efforts.

The question posed by a Meridian lawyer to Connally was on the minds of many Texans: "I wonder if the Federal Government is going to allow old Jim to feather his political nest with his political appointments [of] his partisans out of Federal Money."[17]

After the passage of the act establishing the TRRC, Harry L. Hopkins, the Federal Emergency Relief administrator in Washington, took the position that his agency was looking to Lawrence Westbrook to administer relief in Texas, and "very definitely advised" the commission that they were expected to confine their activities to large policy decisions, leaving the actual administration of relief work in Westbrook's hands. Mrs. Ferguson was informed of this fact and it was generally accepted. Aubrey Williams, now a regional field representative for FERA, was pleased with the attitude of Texas leaders. He reported: "The leadership in Texas including, Governor Miriam

Ferguson and her husband, Ex-Governor James Ferguson, Col. Westbrook, the State Director, and the leadership in the State Commission and a large part of the counties, have accepted the desirability of trained social workers as the proper persons to administer these funds, and have also accepted the general position that social work is a public responsibility and should be handled by legally constituted public agencies."[18] Williams had the reputation of being a difficult man to please, but Jim Ferguson managed it. According to another FERA observer, "Ferguson has never crossed Williams on a single proposal. He has agreed to plans whereby he lost some of his power. Westbrook is a fine person, well though off [*sic*] throughout Texas. There is nothing we need to do but stand back of Westbrook. There is not a man in the State who will cross Westbrook; everyone has in him the greatest confidence." Hopkins was told that politically, Texas had "two big factions with many small brackets." One faction was more or less led by Garner and the other by Ferguson. Garner, however, was not a political power in Texas. Ferguson was a politician, but he was clever enough not to play politics in the wrong direction.[19]

In July 1933 Garner intervened in the Texas relief situation with the charge that the chairman of the Uvalde County welfare board was being paid a salary of $500 a month and each member of the board $250 a month. He sent Roosevelt a telegram requesting an investigation. Director Hopkins sent Professor N. B. Bond to investigate the general situation in Texas. In an interview with Garner in Uvalde, Bond learned that the vice president thought that perhaps he had made a mistake in sending the telegram, and he requested that Bond assure Hopkins and through him the president "that he desires to give his full cooperation to the Administration's relief and recovery program."

Bond reported that the San Antonio situation was "not entirely satisfactory" but found the charges made in a letter from Stella Boone, the secretary of the Bexar County Protective League, "to have little if any political basis." The Bexar County Relief Board was in the process of reorganization under provisions of the new law creating the TRRC, and the complaining parties agreed that the new board should be given time to work out its present difficulties. Bond concurred. In the case of Uvalde County, Bond's investigation showed that the FERA was paying the chairman $40 a month and two women $12 a month, for a total of $64 a month, to administer relief in the county. Although Aubrey Williams told Hopkins he was disappointed in Bond's failure to give "something in the way of factual material" in his report, he thought "he got at the crooks of the situations that were brought to his attention by you." As Williams saw it, "The big thing that has been accomplished ... is the silencing of Garner and the showing to the White House the groundlessness of a whole lot of that kind of stuff. It would seem to me that in some way or other this report could be gotten to the President, which would serve a good purpose in the future when similar charges are made."[20]

Governor Ferguson persuaded the lawmakers to pass and send to the voters a constitutional amendment providing for the issuance of bonds not to exceed $20 million for unemployment relief. Jim went to Washington during the first week in July 1933, accompanied by Charles McDonald and Westbrook, to seek help in putting the bond amendment across. "I fell in love with Hopkins," he gushed in the *Forum*. "The President, yes, I saw him. He is as kind as George Washington. He is as bold as Andrew Jackson. He is as plain as Abraham Lincoln. He hailed me with, 'Hello, Jim. I am awful glad you came to see me. How did you leave the Governor?'" Roosevelt bade him tell the people of Texas that he was "deeply grateful for their loyalty and support and that they could rest assured that they would receive every consideration at his hands."[21]

At Ferguson's request, Hopkins, accompanied by Aubrey Williams, flew to Austin to speak three days before the bond election. Hopkins made it clear that if the amendment did not pass, Texas would have trouble obtaining federal funds. In a radio broadcast from a banquet at the Driskill Hotel, where 150 guests had gathered, Hopkins stated that "the Federal Government has no intention of continuing to pay 95 percent of the Texas relief bill after the bond election on Saturday, but it stands ready to go over halfway in a partnership with the State." Mrs. Ferguson introduced Hopkins at the banquet; Jim was speaking in Tyler that evening. Westbrook had set up a nonpartisan, statewide committed headed by Ferguson and William Strauss, Ross Sterling's former campaign manager, to lobby for passage of the amendment.

The director later admitted to a Texas senate investigating committee: "I didn't work at it or make any speeches but for me to tell you gentlemen, who are practical politicians, that I didn't do what I could to get this bond issue passed would be an absurdity. I did everything I could and pulled every wire I knew how and I instructed our force to furnish the steering committee ... with anything they desired, to do everything possible for them." Local county relief administrators exerted pressure on "reliefers" to vote. Tex Alsbury, relief administrator for Bexar County, recalled: "We put the bond issue across by talking to the social workers. We told them if they wanted any more money to give out that they had better vote with us, and we got them to get the precinct vote. The people in the county were out of work and money. They were hungry and they lined up to vote." Federal funds were used to finance part of the campaign. Several big city mayors also used their influence. Governor Ferguson, urging the people to vote for the relief bonds, proclaimed Election Day as "Food and Hunger Day."[22]

Following the passage of the bond issue on August 26, 1933—by a vote of more than two to one—Mrs. Ferguson called a special session of the legislature to meet on September 14 to implement the program. By this time unsavory rumors concerning the activities of some county welfare boards had become so widespread that both houses passed resolutions calling for an investigation. "From the looks of things the boys want to have some fun with Gov. Jim and this is their hour," Aubrey Williams wrote Hopkins. "I suppose it would be cruel not to let them have it. Only afterwards they should be told what they really in their serious moments must do." A senate committee started hearings on September 21. Senator George C. Purl, the committee chairman, announced that "rumors are afloat throughout the length and breadth of Texas concerning the expenditure of funds and charges and counter charges have been made of rank favoritism of one kind or another." However, Williams regarded the investigation as simply a political vendetta against the Fergusons and Westbrook:

> It was openly stated that their purpose was to secure the dismissal of Westbrook and to discredit the relief work in Texas. There can be no doubt whatever that there were two influences behind the investigation; one, the political opponents of Ferguson, who sought to wrest from the Governor any part of the administration of relief; and to capitalize upon a public issue of this character for their own political advantage; and, second, the three state chambers of commerce, who still nursed their resentment over having been forced to relinquish the greatly desired task of distributing the millions of dollars granted the State of Texas for relief purposes.[23]

Regardless of the facts of the matter, the investigation proceeded.

On the day before the hearings opened, Williams appeared before a joint session of the legislature and stated "unequivocally" that the "administration of funds under the Rehabilitation and Relief Commission and the directorship of Mr. Lawrence Westbrook has been and is immensely satisfactory to the Federal Emergency Relief Administration." He later warned Hopkins: "I look ... for considerable backfire on what I have said. This will come largely from the metropolitan press, who are all very bitterly opposed to Ferguson and are ready to condemn anyone who approves anything which they have anything to do with." According to the *San Antonio Express*, Williams had told the legislature in effect to leave Ferguson and Westbrook in charge. In "other words he menaced the State that Ferguson must control those millions or Washington would abandon Texas."[24]

In his testimony before the senate investigating committee, Westbrook admitted that "since I have been familiar with it, I have known of some extremely culpable acts committed by people charged with the responsibility of distributing these funds." Still, he refused to accept responsibility for the existence of the situation and later indicated that even Hopkins knew something was wrong. In the course of the hearings, two revelations in particular made Jim Ferguson look bad. First, the business of bonding employees of the TRRC had been given to one of his cronies, Eugene Smith, an agent for an insurance company. "How came you to select Mr. Eugene Smith?" Westbrook was asked. "Because he was a friend of the governor and I wanted to give him this business," the director replied bluntly. Second, Frank Chudej, an ex-employee of the former governor who had fallen out with him, testified that he had deposited in the American National Bank of Austin $22,100, in denominations from $50 to $1,000, which was given him by Ferguson from January 4 to August 17, 1933. He stated that he did not know where the money came from or what was in a "little black book" in Ferguson's safe in which he kept a record of the money received by him. "Lately, about the last six weeks before the Legislature met it disappeared," he explained, "and I do not know where it is." Senator Clint Small moved that Chudej's testimony be made part of the commission hearings; only three senators objected, one of them Archie Parr.[25]

The hearings revealed that gross violations concerning salaries, administrative expenditures, nepotism, and political favors to influential people were common throughout the state, especially in those areas where Ferguson people occupied the administrative positions. Senator T. J. Holbrook introduced a letter that said that "Mr. Ed Hussion of Houston told Galveston friends he had the naming of county committees and county administrators in 35 separate counties—with Jim Ferguson's authority."

Perhaps the most flagrant example of mismanagement involving relief funds was found in Bexar County. Ruth Kolling, a social worker from Wisconsin, who was put on the Bexar County payroll by Westbrook over the opposition of Tex Alsbury, testified that the county organization was honeycombed with politics and that all sorts of political pressure was brought to bear to give relief benefits to persons who were not entitled to them. Moreover, Alsbury had "dumped" a hundred people from the administrative payroll into the relief department when he heard that his organization was going to be investigated. Alsbury was convinced that the commotion was caused by the old Sterling crowd. He told an interviewer in 1971 that political power was for the asking: "Give a politician at the state level the amount of federal money we had [been] given during the depression like we had and he [could] control any political situation. I could have licked the Chinese government with that kind of money because you've got the power. You've got the food in your hand the people want it." He saw the investigation as a threat to him, as a struggle of Democrats against each other, and "the people out of power against the people in power." Interviewed by a reporter at the time, he cavalierly dismissed his critics, saying, "To hell with 'em, what are they going to do about it?" Angered by this contemptuous attitude, the investigating committee uncovered a powerful combination of city administrators, county judges, and local labor unions in the San Antonio area bound together by relief and politics. In the ensuing shakeup, Alsbury was fired.[26]

Despite the disclosures, the senate confirmed Westbrook as director with only one dissenting vote, and it passed a measure authorizing the sale of $5.5 million in relief bonds. However, the lawmakers set up a new ninemember Texas Relief Commission (TRC), giving the governor the power to appoint only one member and at the same time giving the lieutenant governor and the speaker power to appoint three each; the remaining two were named in the bill. Jim Ferguson was removed from chairing the commission meetings. The legislature also created a bond committee consisting of the attorney general, comptroller, and state treasurer and mandated strict accounting procedures. "This has caused a great difficulty," Aubrey Williams complained, "in that the Attorney General [James Allred] is a candidate for Governor and in spite of protestations to the contrary has not secured speedy action in the issuance of the bonds, and has only responded when pressure was placed by the Federal administration through threatening to stop Federal relief funds." In October 1933 a total of 416,714 Texans were on relief, and of that number, 285,689 were living in cities while 130,485 resided in rural areas. The $5.5 million was soon spent, and early the next year the legislature voted an additional $5 million. This amount, in turn, was quickly exhausted, and in August 1934 the third special session voted more bonds. The last of these so-called bread bonds were issued during the Allred administration.[27]

Following the establishment of the new TRC, Williams met with its members and stated that the governor and Westbrook would be held responsible for the administration of funds allocated to Texas. It was further made clear that federal funds would be provided on a dollar-for-dollar basis, that state matching funds must be administered in accordance with FERA's rules and regulations, and that all state funds must be used for the same purpose for which federal funds were granted. The commission then began a series of attempts to get control of federal relief funds in Texas. Governor Ferguson consistently refused to authorize the body to act for her. The members tried to get the federal government to appoint the commission as its agent in Texas, but Williams balked. As he indignantly reported to Hopkins: "Members of the Commission stated to the field representative that relief in Texas was unnecessary, except in a very few places—some of the large centers; that very few people really need any unemployment relief, and it was one of the worst things that had happened to Texas; that they were opposed to the bond issue and had worked against it."[28]

In November 1933, following the establishment of the Civil Works Administration (CWA), Westbrook was named by the federal administrator as the administrator for the state of Texas, which made him the direct federal agent. He was authorized to appoint CWA administrators and to act in all matters for the head of the agency in Texas. He was told that all appointments to major CWA offices in Texas would be made on his suggestion.[29]

Adam R. Johnson, the city manager of Austin, succeeded Westbrook as director of the TRC. His name was submitted to the relief board by Carl Estes of Tyler as a compromise candidate who "will keep politics out of the thing." Governor Ferguson, who had no vote in the matter, welcomed Johnson to his new job. "I know Mr. Johnson," she said. "He is an honest and efficient man. I can and will work with him." When Johnson assumed control on February 12, 1934, he was determined not to allow relief politics to dominate the commission.

That's the Kind of Thing You Get in Texas

The very success of the Ferguson relief machine resulted in its destruction. During his first months in office, Johnson completely overhauled the organization and established tight accounting procedures and strict reporting of all expenditures. The focus of power shifted from the counties to the state as a reorganized TRC reviewed and approved all county actions. In effect, the county welfare boards were reduced to administering bone fide state relief cases.[30]

Supporters of the old regime complained to Jim Ferguson. As one man said, some county officials were "over-looking their political deal." He contended that the "best political move that I know now, in my part of the country, is to make them get right, and see the old men and women are taken care of." W. H. Kittrell, who until recently had been connected with the TRC as a confidential helper to Westbrook, told H. Bascom Thomas Jr. that the friends of Westbrook's and Jim Ferguson's were trying to get Speaker Coke Stevenson to remove Bob Holliday as a member of the TRC so that a Ferguson man could be appointed in his place. Kittrell also told Thomas that a trade had already been made between Ferguson and Carl Estes whereby Mrs. Ferguson would sign certain oil bills favored by Estes if he would resign from the commission; when that was done, Ferguson and his friends would arrange with Lt. Gov. Edgar Witt to appoint a friend of the Fergusons in his place. This would give the Fergusonites a majority on the board, and as soon as that was accomplished another state director would be selected. Thomas promised to "verify this statement under oath anywhere at any time. Everything said to me indicated that Holliday was to be removed and Adam Johnson removed, not because of any charge brought against them or for any cause except through politics."[31]

The TRC, in a turbulent session on April 9, ousted Adam Johnson by a vote of 5 to 3 on charges preferred by commissioner Jack Reed, whom Johnson had succeeded as director. C. B. Braun, the commission secretary, was authorized to state that Johnson was removed for "inefficiency, lack of sympathy for and understanding of the relief movement, because he had no background, for the good of the service and because it was the choice of the commission." Before the commission discharged him, it gave a vote of confidence to the Travis County relief board after Johnson had demanded the resignation of all the members "for the good of the service." Marie Dresden, a social service consultant with the commission since August 1933, was elected as Johnson's successor.

The majority also recognized Speaker Coke Stevenson's removal of Holliday and voted 4 to 3 to seat Col. Julius Dorenfield Jr. of Amarillo in his place. Holliday was present and attempted to vote, but the majority refused to recognize him. Holliday had been involved in a controversy with El Paso labor organizations that demanded his removal. He challenged all votes by

Dorenfield and that night prepared a court suit contesting Stevenson's right to oust him. His attorneys were Dan Moody and R. L. Batts.

Coke Stevenson insisted that "Ferguson politics had nothing to do with the removal of Bob Holliday from the Texas relief commission." He had petitions from four thousand labor people in El Paso to remove Holliday, and he had given him a whole month to get up rebuttal statements or petitions from his friends: "He ended up with two letters." Furthermore, "Ferguson did not discuss this removal of Holliday with me or suggest it," Stevenson stated. "Dorenfield is supporting Maury Hughes, not the Ferguson candidate." The speaker thought that the real trouble was that "a lot of people have let their prejudices against Ferguson blind them and dominate their actions."[32]

Lorena A. Hickok, Hopkins's chief investigator, confirmed that all was not well with the relief situation in Texas when she stated in her reports of April 11 and 17, 1934, that "Texas is a Godawful mess. As you know, they're having a big political fight in Austin. Adam Johnson, administrator, and one of the members of the state relief commission, both, I am told, anti-Ferguson, and both kicked out Monday, are preparing to fight, according to stories I've seen in the newspapers. And in the meantime—God help the unemployed." Hickok felt that the Ferguson crowd was in the majority, but the other side was "just a strong enough minority to mess things up.... Oh, yes, I met 'Ma' Ferguson—and 'Guv'nor Jim' Ferguson," she added. "Shrewd people!"[33]

By this time Hopkins had had a bellyful of relief politics in Texas. Told by a field representative in a phone conversation that "it is a bad setup all through that region," Hopkins replied: "Yes, I know, but I don't want to open that now. That thing is full of dynamite. I don't want to open up that fight now. I have already got a meeting of minds with those people and I don't want to get those animals stirred up again." He explained: "That's the kind of thing you get in Texas. It is an uncivilized part of America. You've got to recognize that."[34]

The Texas Supreme Court ruled that Holliday's ouster was illegal and confirmed his right to remain on the commission. With Holliday voting, the commission on June 27, 1934, voted 5 to 4 to reinstate him and then voted 5 to 4 to reinstate Adam Johnson as director. The order of April 8 attempting to oust him was held void, and he was voted his salary for the months that he had been idle. However, he was warned that he must work in harmony with the governor and all concerned. Marie Dresden resigned from the TRC in protest of the move, telling the commissioners she considered Johnson "so inefficient" she did not care to serve with him. The commission ordered an investigation of Travis County relief affairs and put it in the hands of the majority group, which had restored Johnson.[35]

The third called session of the forty-third legislature, which met from August 27 to September 25, 1934, enacted legislation giving the State Board of Control full and exclusive authority over the administration of relief in Texas, and the Texas Relief Commission became a division of that body. Section 30 of the law provided that the board would appoint the relief director and assistant director as well as county administrators. Heretofore, these county administrators had been chosen by the local public officials, and the choices had not always been happy ones. The chairman of the State Board of Control was Claude Teer, whose term expired in in 1935; the other members were John F. Wallace, whose term expired in 1937; and H. N. Baker, whose term expired in 1939. Teer and Wallace were reported to belong to the same political faction as governor-elect James V. Allred, and those in a position to know thought that Teer would be reappointed by the new governor. "The Board shows a disposition to cooperate with the FERA and the present Texas Relief Administration in handling the relief work in the State," a FERA regional field representative reported to Aubrey Williams, now assistant FERA administrator in Washington. "Governor Ferguson also expressed her appreciation of the fine treatment that the State of Texas had received at the hands of Mr. Hopkins. She emphasized the fact that she had vetoed a resolution passed at the recent extra session of the Legislature, this resolution being aimed at the relief administration."[36]

Acting on a directive from Hopkins, Johnson, who continued as state director under the new setup, met with county administrators and informed them that the relief rolls had to be purged of those not clearly entitled to help. Also, since many of their former functions had been eliminated, county budgets and staffs were reduced. The Travis County relief situation was regarded as one of the sore spots in the state. Mrs. Val M. Keating, the head of the social service department in the state relief organization, called the county administrator "a very spineless tool in the hands of a Board, which was predominantly vicious. Several members of the Board were men active either in shady politics, or the running of gambling and drinking joints, et cetera." When the administrator failed to clean up the situation, the State Board of Control investigated, went to Johnson, and secured the resignation of the entire local board and the administrator. "We brought in one of the strongest case workers whose special strength lies in intake," Keating reported with satisfaction to M. J. Miller, the FERA regional field representative. "She has been running the entire case load through the intake and to date has cut the load from about 4500 to 2100. Needless to say, many of those cut off were the pets of the previous administration. Many others who were on exorbitant budgets and who are now receiving budgets in line with those we are able to provide for all the clients are now dissatisfied and disgruntled." Those purged from the relief rolls made several visits to the capitol to complain to the Board of Control, the governor, and the legislature. A small group of some thirty-five spent one day in the corridors of the capitol on a hunger strike. "These people unfortunately are being made the victims of vicious leadership," Miller reported to Williams. "A member of the State Board of Control stated to me that he had information that a number of active leaders were ex-convicts. The chief among the leaders is a man that was indicted for deserting his family." Edward J. Webster, after a one-day visit to Austin in late November 1934, reported to Hopkins:

> PUBLIC OPINION is unmistakable with reference to the minimum wage for labor. It has, according to general belief, done much damage.
>
> Feeling is very strong against political interference with the administration of relief. The public does not see why case workers, and others, should be constantly embarrassed by calls from members of the legislature, the majority, and others who know nothing about the problems of administering relief.
>
> The feeling is also very general that the time has come when the future of relief should be seriously considered. "This can't go on forever."[37]

Thus, by the end of 1934, relief, to a degree, had been separated from politics. Relief officials now perceived their problems as coming not from politicians but from those receiving help. The number of Texans on relief had risen considerably, with the peak of 1,110,573 people on the general relief rolls as of December 1934. In 1935 the maximum was reached in January when 1,145,621 were relief recipients. The monthly average number of people receiving relief in Texas from July 1934 to June 1935 was 1,020,554.

Reliefers were changing their attitudes, and some were demanding their rights as welfare clients. The regional FERA staff, while visiting the capitol in October 1934, found the senate gallery packed with six hundred whites, Mexicans, and blacks, former reliefers who had been removed from the Travis County relief rolls.[38] One of their leaders addressed the senate, as did Chairman Teer, whose "most temperate talk" was well received. Johnson complained that the rumors were drifting in from Washington suggesting that Texas relievers would not work. "If that's true, it's a grievous situation and we intend to remedy it," he vowed. "Our relief program was not intended for people who shirk opportunity to earn an honest living." Already there were fears of a self-perpetuating welfare culture. As Edward Webster observed of young children in welfare homes: "Many of them have seen their parents begin to accept relief and treat it as commonplace, although three years ago the acceptance of relief would have carried a stigma to be avoided at all costs. Fifteen or twenty years from now, those children will be voting and, to that extent, making the laws four [*sic*] our children."[39]

Adam Johnson continued to serve as state relief administrator through the governorships of James V. Allred and W. Lee O'Daniel. In 1938 he suggested changes, which ultimately resulted in the establishment of the Department of Public Welfare. Creation of this department meant recognition that the New Deal relief system had become a permanent aspect of the Texas scene—a significant transformation, given Texans' past aversion to most forms of government intervention.

The Good Ship Prohibition Is Already Going Down

Mrs. Ferguson's second administration also saw a revival of the liquor question. Almost before the November 1932 election returns were in, the Baptist General Convention of Texas was busily mapping out a strategy to save Prohibition. At its mid-November meeting, the convention adopted a resolution that ringingly asserted the rightness of Prohibition, called for the continuance and intensification of prayers for the Eighteenth Amendment, and exhorted the Baptist clergy again to "become martyrs for the cause." The convention also called for an interdenominational structure "of all the religious and moral forces of the state [for the purpose of] co-ordinating them into a compact movement that will go on a holy crusade for this cause." A week later a planning conference assembled in Dallas and issued a formal call went out for an organization meeting of the United Forces for Prohibition. On November 29, 1932, the new United Forces chose Charles C. Selecman as their state president. "The Drys Wake Up!" the *Baptist Standard* declared in a headline.[40]

Tom Love wrote Alvin Moody urging him to become a candidate for Congress on a clean-cut platform against repeal and legalizing beer. He believed Moody could win, but even if he lost he would render a great service to the Prohibition cause. As Love explained to Cato Sells, "I think our tactics should be to consolidate our forces behind candidates for Congress, hereafter, who are against repeal and submission of repeal and against legalizing beer and that the Houston District affords an excellent opportunity to initiate such a program."[41]

When the lame-duck Congress met in January 1933, advocates of repeal joined forces as the United Repeal Council, which included the Association Against the Prohibition Amendment (AAPA), the Women's Organization for National Prohibition Reform, the Voluntary Committee of Lawyers, and the American Hotel Association, had drafted a Twenty-First Amendment to the Constitution, which would in effect repeal the Eighteenth Amendment. The council's hope was to craft the new amendment in such a way as to circumvent the various state legislatures, where, it was feared, Dry lawmakers from rural districts might present a serious barrier to ratification. Repeal leaders had calculated that in existing legislatures, as few as 132 Dry state senators in only thirteen states would have the votes to defeat the amendment. To prevent this, constitutional lawyers proposed—for the first time since the Constitution itself was ratified and for much the same reason—that Congress should call for ratifying conventions in each state. Delegates would be elected for the specific purpose of considering the Twenty-First Amendment. Dry leaders protested loudly against changing the "time-honored method, as old as the Constitution," of amending the document. Tom Love warned Congressman Hatton W. Sumners of Dallas that "the obvious design" was "to enable the liquor traffic to carry Texas and other southern States through the aid of the purchasable negro vote." He pointed out that state representatives and senators were chosen in Democratic primary elections throughout the South, while convention delegates could not be voted on in these primaries. "The primaries are in fact white men's primaries in which the negroes do not vote."[42]

A repeal resolution embodying the convention idea was approved by the leaders of the AAPA and submitted to Congress. The immediate action repealers had hoped for, however, was stopped in the House, where the resolution failed by only six votes. The council's lawyers and AAPA leaders then drew up a general measure, which the various states could, with appropriate local changes, use to call their own ratification conventions. Jouett Shouse, the president of the AAPA, sent the proposed bill to friends in each state so that even while Congress debated, the legislatures then in session might prepare the way for the state repeal conventions. Congress approved the AAPA resolution on February 28. By this time the convention bills in most states were ready for passage. According to Norman H. Clark, "Shouse's timing and administrative skills had beaten the clock of legislative adjournment, and his smooth coordination of national and local efforts may have advanced the actual fact of repeal by as much as two years."[43]

In March the new Congress, after midnight, April 4, 1933, modified the Volstead Act's definition of "intoxicating" to allow the manufacture and sale of beverages with as much as 3.2 percent alcoholic content. In the House ten Texans voted to legalize the sale of beer and ten were opposed; in the Senate, both Sheppard and Connally voted against the bill. Tom Love had earlier warned Senator Sheppard that bringing beer back would bring back brewery politics as well. "If we must have beer, it ought either to be made by the government or if made by private breweries they ought to be required to turn into the government all their excess profits," he advised. "Unless this is done they will have a brewery political pay roll in Texas and in the nation within six months after a beer bill is passed and it will be difficult, if not impossible, to prevent them from dominating politics again as they did when the breweries were running before prohibition."[44]

Meanwhile, back in Texas, the prohibitionist campaign to save "the noble experiment" was in full swing. Charles Selecman was gratified when almost one thousand supporters showed up at the Lubbock First Baptist Church to cheer him on. Large crowds heard Methodist Bishop John M. Moore and Reverend George W. Truett at the Dallas First Methodist Church and Truett and Methodist Bishop Hiram A. Boaz of Houston at the Austin First Methodist Church. Similar meetings were held in other major cities and in scores of towns and hamlets. At a January 13 rally in Austin, about two thousand Drys from forty-four counties heard Truett plead anew for a revitalized Prohibition involvement on the part of Christian ministers. Dan Moody addressed the rally on the theme, "The Value of a United Front." Reverend William R. White, pastor of the Fort Worth Broadway Baptist Church and United Forces for Prohibition executive secretary, outlined plans for campaigns in all Texas counties.[45]

Wets in the forty-third legislature moved to amend the Dean Law so that it would not proscribe the 3.2 percent beer that Congress was acting to legalize. Dry leaders bitterly recalled the emphatic promise of Democratic speakers in the 1932 presidential campaign that repeal of the Eighteenth Amendment would in no way affect statewide prohibition. "They say they want to put the bootlegger out of business, and do not want the open saloon back," Don H. Biggers remarked of the proponents of 3.2 percent beer. "And yet some people claim that Baron Munchaussen [*sic*] was the world's champion liar. And they prate and prattle about the revenue, and a lot of poverty stricken fools parrot like repeat the slush. Well, patriotism isn't the only thing in whose names great crimes are committed." Rev. J. Frank Norris charged that the legislature was being "bought" by the liquor interests. "I dare, I double dog dare [you]," he taunted the lawmakers, "to appoint a committee, pass a resolution, making demand of me for the proof of this serious charge." Norris repeated and elaborated on his allegations during a broadcast over a statewide radio network and later during testimony before the Senate Committee on Civil Jurisprudence.[46]

By the overwhelming margins, the Texas House on April 14 and the senate on April 27 approved a proposed amendment to the state constitution that would end the mandatory statewide prohibition of beer with alcoholic contents up to 3.2 percent and that would permit each local jurisdiction to determine whether such sales were to be legal within its bounds. The proposition was to be submitted to voters in a special election on August 26, 1933. The legislature also decreed that convention delegates empowered to act on the proposed Twenty-First Amendment would be elected at the same time, although separate ballots would be used. Preliminary to the August election, the governor was required to schedule two mass conventions in Austin on June 27, one for voters favoring the Twenty-First Amendment, and one for voters opposing it; no individual could participate in both. Each mass convention was to designate a list of thirty-one candidates and thirty-one alternates, one from each senatorial district. Thus the choice before voters in August would be between opposing, at-large Wet and Dry slates; the election would amount to a statewide referendum on the repeal amendment.[47]

Governor Ferguson appointed Senator Sheppard as temporary chairman of the Dry convention, which assembled in the house chamber on June 27. In his keynote address, Sheppard declared that the "way to handle the liquor traffic is to destroy it. The remedy is not less, but more prohibition." Following the election of former Attorney General Walter A. Keeling as permanent chairman and R. L. ("I'm No Kin to Jim") Ferguson as secretary, the nearly 1,500 antirepealers heard speeches by Dan Moody, Tom Love, William R. White, and J. Frank Norris. Various other Dry warhorses were also present, including Judge D. B. Sartin, Jane Y. McCallum, Atticus Webb, Charles Selecman, and Mrs. Claude de Van Watts. The convention selected antirepeal candidates for the August election. In the evening, they reassembled in Wooldridge Park for additional speeches.

In the meantime some 2,500 pro-repealers met in Gregory Gymnasium on the University of Texas campus. An acrimonious contest developed for permanent convention chairman between Jim Ferguson, who was supported by the state Democratic Executive Committee, and John M. Mathis of Houston, chairman of the newly organized Texas Liberal Legion, who had the support of John Henry Kirby, state Democratic chairman Maury Hughes, and Congressman Joseph Weldon Bailey Jr. Ferguson eventually withdrew his candidacy in favor of his longtime friend and political ally Charles C. McDonald of Wichita Falls, who was elected. To Hugh Nugent Fitzgerald, it was "like a close of a battle of the cats on a backyard fence [until] the dove of peace came along and lit on the rostrum." Following the adoption of a resolution deploring the disqualification from voting of many impoverished citizens who "needed every dime to buy bread for their children" rather than pay the poll tax, and another resolution assuring President Roosevelt that "Texas will go wet on August 26," delegate candidates were selected. After McDonald and the Liberal Legion patched up their differences, plans for a "united" Wet campaign were confidently made.[48]

The Texas vote on repeal was taken at a time when the trend for repeal seemed to be almost unanimous. By now the *Dallas Morning News* was fully convinced that the "good ship Prohibition is already going down with all on board, except those astute statesmen who are leaping on to the wet raft." Twenty states had acted favorably on the Twenty-First Amendment, none had defeated it, and among those recently favoring repeal had been found some of the normally Dry southern states. An editorial in the *Guadalupe Gazette-Bulletin* (Seguin) noted:

> Now that Arkansas and Alabama have voted to repeal the XVIII Amendment the anti-repealers have about given up hope, for they had counted on those states to stem the tide about to engulf the South. It seems that the South, like every other section of the country, is tired of an uncontrolled liquor traffic which has sprung up and enriched a number of unscrupulous racketeers under the prohibition law. They are taking the advice of the President to replace the present poisonous concoctions with a healthful beverage that will bring revenue to the government.[49]

Publicly, United Forces for Prohibition leaders maintained a bold front, professed hope, and held outdoor rallies; the largest, in Dallas, drew an estimated 12,000 people to hear Baylor president Pat M. Neff. But Neff privately agreed with J. Frank Norris that "the success of our cause is not very encouraging." Alvin Moody lamented to Tom Love: "Something must be done about our drys in Texas or we are going to lose our battle on August 26th." Moody complained: "The preachers here in Houston are doing absolutely nothing and I am afraid this is the situation all over Texas. If they can not be aroused to make the fight we are indeed lost!" The father of national prohibition, Senator Morris Sheppard, made a number of speeches in Texas, admonishing people that if they "run down the flag of prohibition and run up the flag of the devil and the saddest transformation that ever marked the struggle of mankind for its own redemption will have been achieved. It will be the first time this nation ever abandoned a principle or deserted a responsibility." On the morning of election day, Love wrote Sheppard to "heartily congratulate you upon the splendid fight you have made.... I have a feeling that we may win today," he confided. "However, I have had too much experience in such matters not to fully realize that the outcome is doubtful. Certainly we have fought under handicaps never known before in Texas governmental affairs."[50]

National Democratic chairman James Farley made a radio appeal from New York City to Texas voters on the evening of August 22 on behalf of repeal. He spoke under the auspices of the Texas Liberal Legion over WBAP, Fort Worth; KPRC, Houston; and WOAI, San Antonio. According to Farley the repeal of the Eighteenth Amendment and the legalization of 3.2 percent beer as quickly as possible was "a cause very dear to the hearts of President Roosevelt, Vice President Garner and every one connected with the administration." An overwhelming vote for repeal in Texas would help "not only in the national recovery drive, but in the determined effort of the administration to stamp out bootlegging, kidnapping and racketeering."[51]

On August 26 about half a million Texas voters (half of those qualified) went to the polls and by a majority of approximately three to two elected the slate of proratification delegates to the November convention; by a slightly greater margin they approved the sale of 3.2 percent beer where local jurisdiction would allow. The larger cities, along with the counties of South and Central Texas, gave such decisive majorities for repeal that the Dry strongholds of East, North, and West Texas were left behind. Fort Worth, Dallas, and Austin delivered two-to-one margins for the Wets; Houston provided them with a four-to-one majority; and El Paso went Wet by a one-sided majority of five to one. Even Texarkana, Sheppard's hometown, favored repeal. In the ten German counties repeal carried by a vote of almost twelve to one, registering 20,142 for repeal and 1,703 against. Comal County voted 2,310 for repeal, 38 against. But Duval County was not to be outdone, voting 1,531 for repeal and just 7 against. The German counties gave similar majorities on the amendment to legalize beer sales. Commented the *Dallas Morning News*: "Texas has definitely declared itself wet, a conclusion clear enough in advance and driven home by more than 100,000 majority for repeal and an ever larger majority in favor of legalizing '3.2 beer.'" Beer and wine became legal again on September 15, 1933, after fifteen theoretically dry years.[52]

The Wet victory was not total, however, as numerous Drys were quick to point out. A majority of the 188 counties that held local option elections voted Dry; rural areas remained solidly Dry, except for South Texas. J. Frank Norris explained that the repeal of national prohibition had become inevitable when both major political parties abandoned the cause; in Texas the attitudes of "half a dozen big cities and the Mexican populated counties" made the difference. The real surprise to Norris (or so he proclaimed) was that so many counties remained Dry despite almost irresistible antiprohibition influences, including the impact of the Depression, Wet propaganda, and Roosevelt's great prestige. "I consider we won a tremendous moral victory," he wrote Love, "and the fight has just begun."

Love was undaunted by the Wet wave that had engulfed Texas. He armed himself with figures to show how insignificant the Wet victory actually was. In a letter to H. B. Ballew of Honey Springs, he pointed out that "the wets polled less than 10% last Saturday of the qualified voters of Texas as shown by the last Federal census, and only 35% of the votes cast at the November election last year and only 30% of the total vote cast in the Democratic primaries last year. Nationwide prohibition seems doomed but the brewers will not control Texas politics and government hereafter." Publicly Love predicted that the Drys would be victorious at the polls in 1934. "The wets always have a better chance when they are out; the brewers can win when they are not in Texas. But as soon as they get in they lose. Candidates backed by the brewers are always beaten by candidates who oppose them."[53]

The convention that was to ratify the Twenty-First Amendment met in Austin on November 24. Five out of the thirty-one senatorial districts were not represented by either a delegate or an alternate. Following the election of John Henry Kirby as chairman and Mrs. James M. Loving of Austin, the only women delegate, as secretary, the delegation, without debate, predictably cast a unanimous affirmative vote. State chairman Hughes took the opportunity to pick up the gauntlet Love had thrown down, announcing that "every candidate for state office should be forced to declare himself on the prohibition issue." "Tom Love," he said, "recently declared every candidate should declare himself as to his sentiment about prohibition. For once I join hands with Love." Less than two weeks later, on December 5, Utah sounded the death knell of national prohibition when it became the thirty-sixth state to ratify the repeal amendment.[54]

An organization was created to handle political strategy for the prohibitionists in 1934. William R. White was named chairman of a five-member committee empowered to select a committee of fifteen or more, including themselves, to determine policies and perfect the organization. In a meeting in Dallas in early February, the committee of five increased its membership to twenty-one. "There has perhaps arisen nothing so important and strategic as this movement," White assured Love, who was named to the committee. "The organization is separate and distinct from the existing dry organizations. All the organizations will, I am sure, cooperate with it after it works out the strategy whereby the united front may be presented on the part of the drys." The group decided to set up Texas Recovery League committees in every community in the state to "rehabilitate the forces for civic righteousness and to make ourselves an effective, political force for our cause." Committee members were asked to subscribe five or ten dollars a month toward the effort.[55]

It was an indication of the weakness of the Dry cause in Texas that no major candidate for the 1934 Texas Democratic gubernatorial nomination directly identified himself with the Drys. The victor, James V. Allred, was a professed teetotaler, but he advocated a new referendum on the 1919 Prohibition amendment to the state constitution, a position resoundingly endorsed by the state Democratic convention in September 1934 and by the legislature the following spring when it submitted an amendment giving it the power to regulate the manufacture, sale, transportation, and possession of intoxicating liquors. In a special election on August 24, 1935, Prohibition was once more defeated, this time by a margin of 297,597 to 250,948.

Although Texas had gone almost full circle on the liquor question since 1919, an era of uninhibited trafficking in intoxicants was not at hand. Even as voters rescinded the 1919 state prohibition amendment, they approved a constitutional section that specifically banned open saloons. In November 1935 the legislature in a special session passed a new comprehensive liquor control law to replace the bone-dry Dean Law. Prior to 1919 local jurisdictions had been allowed to choose between only two options, wet or dry. Four distinct choices were now authorized.

James V. Allred delivering a speech, circa 1930. J. R. Parten Papers, Briscoe Center for American History, University of Texas at Austin, E RAP 0458.

1. Comprehensive prohibition (allowing no sale of drinks with alcoholic contents in excess of one-half of one percent);
2. Proscription of alcoholic beverages other than those (like beer) with alcoholic contents of 4 percent or less;
3. Proscription of alcoholic beverages other than those (including wine as well as beer) with alcoholic contents of 14 percent or less;
4. Legalization of all alcoholic beverages, but with the stipulation that beverages with more than 14 percent alcoholic content must be sold only in an unopened package (or full-bottle) basis, with consumption prohibited on the premises where purchased.

Thus, regardless of the wishes of the local jurisdiction, the serving of liquor by the drink remained illegal in public establishments everywhere in Texas and would continue to be so for more than thirty years. Only private clubs could serve mixed drinks. Restaurants and nightclubs could, in wet areas, serve beer and wine and provide ice and mixers.

Jeanne Bozzell McCarty has noted: "After a decade of vigorous and well-funded campaigning, the wets had crushed the reformers' dream of a perpetually dry Utopia; yet, their victory turned out to be drastically circumscribed." Ten years later (1945), after local jurisdictions had an opportunity to react to the liquor control law, 140 out of 254 counties remained completely dry; 141 counties were so committed in 1952; 115 counties in 1965; and 74 counties in January 1980. Many additional counties were dry except maverick wet precincts here and there.[56]

Critics charged that Texas's liquor laws promoted higher consumption of alcohol and argued that the sale of liquor by the drink, under state regulation, would be preferable. But efforts to pass liquor by the drink legislation foundered on the constitutional provision against the open saloon. In 1941 the United Texas Drys and the WCTU sponsored a new movement for statewide prohibition, and Ralph Steen wrote that "the prohibitionists won in 1918, and they believe they can win again." That same year the legislature more carefully regulated the drugstore sale of liquor and restricted the outdoor advertising of alcoholic beverages. It was not until 1968 that a referendum indicated popular support for an amendment to repeal the ban on liquor by the drink. In November 1970 a constitutional amendment that ended the ban and allowed voters in local jurisdictions to legalize the serving of hard liquor and alcoholic cocktails by the drink was approved by a small margin of 979,868 in favor and 914,481 opposed. Heavy urban majorities in favor of the amendment produced the victory. The following year the legislature authorized the serving of alcohol in restaurants, and on May 18, 1971, elections in wet areas restored the public sale of mixed drinks in the state for the first time since 1919.[57]

Should the Ferguson Forces Stay in Power?

Mrs. Ferguson's second administration was generally regarded as up to the average in Texas and met with less criticism than did her first. However, the two-term tradition was so strong in Texas politics that Ma, now fifty-eight and serving her second nonconsecutive term, announced on November 15, 1933, that she would not seek reelection in 1934. For only the second time since 1914, Texas voters were not confronted directly with the issue of Fergusonism, and some political commentators hailed the beginning of a new era in the state's politics. In an article about the Democratic primary of 1934, the *New York Times* described the voters of the Lone Star State as "apathetic" and called the contest "the quietest in more than twenty years." The *Texas Weekly* offered the following explanation for the public's apathy: "It takes a mob-rousing issue like that of Ku Kluxism, prohibition as it used to be, Fergusonism, or something of that kind—as a single issue which divides the people into sheep and goats ... to get the voters excited during the heat of summer. Fortunately, we think, no such issue looms at present."

The three leading Democratic candidates for governor were James V. Allred, Tom F. Hunter, and Charles McDonald. Maury Hughes of Dallas was credited with having first-call on the Young Democrat vote. Edward K. Russell, a Red River County farmer, made an active campaign for several weeks but withdrew from the race a short time before Election Day. He was the only one of the seven candidates to demand the continuation of Prohibition in Texas. "As to the wet and dry issue that is less an issue than for many years," wrote Raymond Brooks in early April. "Allred and Hunter will share the dry side, so far as it is a question decided by liquor sentiment, and the others will share the rest. It balances out as neatly as a wash sale."[58]

Allred announced his candidacy at a dinner given in his honor at Del Rio on December 15, 1933.[59] His platform advocated the creation of a Commission on Public Utilities, a referendum on repeal of the state prohibition amendment, a decrease in taxes and better distribution of tax money, a graduated chain-store tax to curb monopolies (but no sales tax), and the creation of a modern state police system patterned after the Federal Bureau of Investigation. The pardon system and the lobby were the main issues Allred emphasized in his campaign. He proposed a constitutional amendment giving to the Board of Pardons much of the power exercised by the governor. Allred's plan, which was adopted by the voters in 1936, called for the board to be composed of three persons, one appointed by the governor, a second to be chosen by the chief justice of the Texas Supreme Court, and another to be selected by the presiding judge of the Court of Criminal Appeals. Recommendations from the Board of Pardons were to be binding on the governor, except in capital cases where it was sometimes necessary to issue temporary reprieves. In advocating this plan, Allred told a Llano crowd:

> It may be one of your local officers who suffers the same fate at the hands of these fellows that are turned out like cattle on the highways under our present pardon system. It may be your kinsman that has his throat cut from ear to ear by some fellows turned out like a Texas pardoned convict did in New Orleans last year. I am thinking about the safety of your family and my family—common decency demands that something be done. We should have a Board of Pardons appointed by three public officials, and one which will make recommendations on merit and merit alone, and the recommendations of that Board should be binding on the governor of Texas. That is my ticket!

Allred sharply attacked the lobbyists in Austin. "These people who are in the lobby business down there saddle off taxes on your backs," he told his audiences. "They will furnish whatever it takes to the members of the Legislature if they will take it. Whatever they like, that is what they get. They will furnish them anything they will take. I think you are entitled to know the facts." Allred advocated a law that would require lobbyists to report how much money they were spending and what they were spending it on. "I am in favor of keeping them so busy writing out expense accounts that they will not have any time left for monkey business with members of the Legislature or of the State Senate." He warned the crowd: "You are not going to get any relief until you do something about it. You have got to have a real lobby law before you can settle the problem of taxation, court reform or anything else." A legislator could not serve two masters. "He has got no business representing you and drawing ten dollars a day from you, and at the same time drawing down a retainer from some big utility company, oil company, or a sulphur company, or any other great privileged interest, maintaining a lobbyist at Austin."[60]

Tom Hunter, like Allred a native of Wichita Falls, had been a candidate for governor in 1932, securing 220,000 votes and running third in a field of nine candidates. He had refused to take sides in the runoff between Sterling and Mrs. Ferguson. Hunter favored a reduction of taxes on real estate in order to make the "basic wealth of the state" carry more credit value; he backed a "self-sustaining old age pension fund" supported by the employer and supervised by the state; he advocated retaining the $16-per-capita school apportionment; and he favored the liberal support of higher education. He seemed to favor in principle the recommendations of the Griffinhagen Report in that he would reduce the 130 state bureaus to no more than 30 and would create a governor's cabinet of five members to assume the duties of the eliminated bureaus. He was in favor of state regulation of public utilities and the dissolution of oil trusts, and he said a gross sales tax on chain stores was essential to "the preservation of independent business." In his "blended tax plan," Hunter proposed a "net earnings tax" for persons and corporations in the upper income brackets. He charged that many such corporations were paying no more than 2 percent of their earnings, while real estate was paying from 50 to 125 percent of its income in taxes. He also urged an increase in the sulfur tax.[61]

Charles C. McDonald, who had been named Democratic Party chair in 1933, was a candidate in his own right for the first time, although he had wide experience in campaigning for others. He helped O. B. Colquitt in 1910, for which he was appointed secretary of state. In 1914 he campaigned for Jim Ferguson and served as assistant attorney general from 1915 to 1916. Thereafter, he always took the stump for the Fergusons in their many races. It was generally understood that McDonald was the Ferguson candidate in 1934, the "crown prince" or "Ferguson Prince of Wales," and Jim did endorse him in the *Forum*. McDonald promised, if elected, to work for a six-hour workday and a thirty-hour week in order to provide employment for jobless Texans and decrease the need for relief; to defend organized labor's right to bargain collectively; to help every family own its own home; to oppose prohibition in all forms; to abolish all state ad valorem taxes on real estate and personal property; and to cooperate with the Roosevelt administration. He favored increased taxes on utilities and other monopolies, immediate payment of the ex-soldiers' adjusted compensation, equitable taxation, job insurance, and old-age pensions not to exceed fifteen dollars a month.[62]

Allred's campaign resembled Dan Moody's in 1926. Both had been elected attorney general in their early thirties, and both were capable public speakers. As an orator, his friend Herman Jones recalled, Allred had a voice pitched a little higher than normal, and it lacked the deep resonance of some of the other candidates. "It wasn't especially pleasant to hear, but Jimmie could make a crowd yell, 'Pour it on 'em, Jimmie,' more times than you can count." Political writer Harry Benge Crozier said that Allred had talents as an actor and as an evangelist, along with oratorical ability. "The Allred technique in politics is peculiarly individualistic and a little paradoxical," he noted. "His very presence exudes the spirit of friendliness and yet he probably is as reserved in his intimate fellowship with men as was Pat M. Neff.... It has been observed that in the Allred campaign, he has found his way into more offices to call men by their names, assure them of his appreciation of their suffrage and be on his way than any other candidate."[63]

Ferguson made twelve speeches for McDonald at July rallies. He promised that McDonald would "carry out our policies" and centered his attacks on Allred and Hunter. He predicted that McDonald and Allred would be in the runoff. But there were many who said Jim's old fire was lacking, that he failed to arouse familiar cries of "Pour it on 'em, Jim" from his audiences.[64]

During the last two weeks of the canvass, state prohibition gained prominence as a campaign issue. Mississippi had just voted over two to one against repealing her state prohibition laws, and the Texas press urged that the voters reexamine the candidates' stand on the question. Though personally and politically Dry, Allred favored submitting the question of repealing the prohibition amendment in the state constitution to the voters "because this is a Democratic government and the majority must rule." He enjoyed the support of many Dry leaders and of those who hoped for reform on moral questions. However, J. Frank Norris thought the attorney general was "a double crosser" who was "'toting' water on both shoulders." As he wrote Tom Love: "No greater proof of this double position than his opening address in which he absolutely ignores the prohibition issue. I have more respect for an out and out Wet than for a pussyfooter. Among the many reasons that I have for not supporting Allred is his contemptuous treatment of Dr. White when his committee courteously inquired of him concerning his position on vital moral issues." Maury Hughes wanted to repeal both the amendment and the Dean Law; Hunter favored submission of the repeal question; McDonald, Clint Small (once again a candidate for governor), and Edgar Witt favored submission and repeal. Despite his Wet stance, Small received a well-advertised endorsement from Tom Love. According to Love, Small was "the only candidate outspokenly declaring for the repeal of the race-track gambling act, the crookedest bill ever passed by a Texas Legislature; and he is for padlocking the liquor dives and gambling hells and says so." All of the candidates, Love noted, favored submission, and none of them were very strong against repeal.[65]

The results of the first primary showed that Allred had received 298,903 votes; Hunter, 243,254; McDonald, 207,200; Small, 125,234; Witt, 62,376; and Hughes, 58,815. It was to be an Allred-Hunter runoff. "Glory in the highest!" V. A. Collins exulted. "Maury Hughes was the last man and Witt, who seemed to tie his hope of election to his opposition to prohibition, was next to last. And thanks to heaven, Fergusonism seems to be banished from Texas politics."[66]

McDonald asked his supporters to write and inform him whether they preferred Allred or Hunter. He claimed that they held the balance of power and "can elect either man." A week later he announced for Hunter, saying that 1,016 of the 1,052 letters received had so advised him. "The jig's up with Jimmie because it's time for Tom," McDonald declared. Small and Witt also announced for Hunter, as did Jim Ferguson. "To boil it down, Allred is a boy and Hunter is a man," Jim told readers of the *Forum*. On the other hand, former governor Ross Sterling endorsed Allred and his program. Love was now for Allred. "I think to elect Hunter means two years more of Fergusonism in control at Austin," he wrote privately. "Besides, I cannot forget that two years ago Hunter refused to say a word against Ferguson, when by saying only a word for Sterling, he could have saved us the humiliation and financial loss of the last two years."[67]

At the beginning of the runoff race, political writer Raymond Brooks was on his way to Wichita Falls to do a story on Hunter when he stopped for a late breakfast at Waco. A Hunter campaign worker ran into him at the Roosevelt Hotel coffee shop and said: "If you're going to the meeting, I'd like a ride." Brooks had not heard of any Hunter meeting, but he played along and found out that it was being held in Marlin. As he recalled:

> There, I joined eight or 10 people walking into a big ground-floor sample room at the hotel. Everybody took everybody else for granted. I've sat down. The group included the Frank Denison and Sam Roddy "invisible highway" group, Shelby Cox of Dallas, and various of the most conspicuous of the Ferguson administration figures. I served as secretary, and we named district campaign managers, all closely linked with the Fergusons. I made a separate list for myself, eased out of the meeting and got back to Waco in time to get a story in the afternoon paper. It was "Ferguson Leaders Guide Hunter Run-Off."

Hunter himself had gone to Austin to see Ferguson and solicit his support. On his way to the Marlin meeting, he stopped in Waco and saw the afternoon story. He told the editor not to run the story in any more editions. It ran. Allred told friends that he was driving that day from Wichita Falls to Dallas to set up his runoff, wondering on what theme he could pitch the campaign. Flipping on the car radio, he heard an announcer relating Brooks's story that had broken only minutes before in the Waco paper and said to himself, "This is it." That night he challenged: "Shall the Ferguson forces stay in power?" Years later Brooks recalled: "The race was run on that issue." He believed that "Allred's victory is Texas history." Hunter told his own workers that the story changed the whole runoff strategy.[68]

The runoff was personal and bitter. Hunter declared that Allred had no platform and no plan for taxation. He called him the "boy orator," "Jimmy the Giant Killer," and that "little boy over in the Attorney General's department who has the big pair of breeches." He asserted that the suits Allred had filed against the oil trusts for $17 million were for political purposes only, not for any violation of state laws.

Allred was equally sharp-tongued. He ridiculed the Hunter proposal to combine over one hundred state bureaus under the leadership of five men, calling it "Uncle Tom's Cabinet" and declaring that such a plan was dangerous, for if carried out it would lead to a centralization of power and perhaps even a dictatorship. "He wants to be Chancellor in Texas," Allred said of Hunter. "Compared to this man who yearns for power, a radical is a rank conservative. Where do you suppose he got this Huey Long–Hitler idea for a supercabinet in Texas?" Allred charged that Hunter had made a deal to support Jim Ferguson for Democratic national committeeman in return for the latter's support for governor. He said that Hunter was the "missing link" between the big and little oil companies, calling him a leading official among the smaller firms who lobbied for all of the measures favored by the great oil trusts. He produced a statement by Hunter to the House Committee on Revenue and Taxation urging the levy of a sales tax and insisted that Hunter's "blended tax" was the same thing in a different form. There were references to Hunter's shiny Cadillac and his chauffeur and his expensive residence in Wichita Falls (dubbed "Uncle Tom's Cabin"), in contrast to "the little cottage on a dusty street" that was the Allred home in Austin. A picture of the modest frame dwelling on an unpaved street was printed in campaign literature, and it became a symbol of the plain people versus the oil magnates.[69]

Hunter insisted that he was not a wealthy man; he claimed that his total net income for three years, 1931–1933, amounted to $13,664.64. "False reports are being circulated that Tom Hunter is a multimillionaire," he complained. "Allred's statement is easily 400% false, and I now offer that he may, with his hot oil merchants, utilities and pipeline friends, buy my entire holdings, including my personal effects and clothing, on the basis that he is FOUR HUNDRED PER CENT WRONG."[70]

Texas newspapers overwhelmingly favored Allred, especially after Ferguson picked a slate of his favorites and asked readers of the *Forum* to see that they were elected. The group included Hunter for governor, Hal S. Lattimore for the supreme court, and John Pundt for railroad commissioner. The *Dallas Morning News* said editorially: "The Fergusons do not seem to understand that they are politically dead and that there is nothing so dead as a dead politician." The *News* hoped that every voter "will cross from the ballot on Aug. 25 the names of those candidates who have received and welcomed the endorsement of James E. Ferguson." Furious, Hunter referred to the editorial as "an unfair, libellous, mean, below the belt editorial." In a speech at Dallas he stated: "Every daily newspaper in Texas, with one exception has done down the line with the same vicious unfairness that has characterized the Dallas *News*."[71]

On Election Day Allred secured 499,343 votes to Hunter's 459,106. Seth McKay has noted that Hunter was "unable to overcome the endorsement of Ferguson, according to some observers, and perhaps suffered losses also from the lack of clarity in his pronouncements concerning the blended tax and a suspicion that he favored a sales tax for Texas." Hunter did not receive large majorities in the counties known as Ferguson strongholds, while in the counties where sentiment was strongly anti-Ferguson, he made his poorest showing.

A Fire in His Cities

Political experts immediately declared, not for the first time, that the Fergusons, whose candidates had been defeated in both the first primary and the runoff, were finished in Texas politics. "Texas has grown very weary of the Fergusons and their brand of politics," commented the *Dallas Morning News*. "It is not likely that either of them will again hold any important office in the State, nor is it at all probable that any future candidate will seek or welcome an endorsement from Mr. Ferguson." The *New York Times* carried an article that spoke of the "voluntary retirement of one of the most dominant and, at the same time, most turbulent families in Texas political history." But Peter Molyneaux, editor of the *Texas Weekly* and an astute observer of the Texas scene, was more cautious. "Whether this is the final exit of the Fergusons it would require a hardy order of prophecy to say," he wrote, reminding his readers that on four previous occasions the Fergusons had been "eliminated," yet each time had staged a comeback.[72]

The Democratic primary also witnessed a spirited effort by Congressman-at-Large Joseph Weldon Bailey Jr. of Dallas to wrest from Tom Connally the U.S. Senate seat he had won from Earle Mayfield in 1928. The forty-one-year-old Bailey, a World War I veteran, lawyer, and self-professed "State's Rights Democrat," had a good organization and a full campaign chest. Sam Hanna Acheson's 1932 biography of the candidate's father, the late Senator Joe Bailey (who died in 1929), reminded Baileyites that there was a son of Joe Bailey, bearing his name, who they felt should be drafted to carry on the Bailey tradition. At first he turned a deaf ear to his father's friends who pleaded with him to enter politics but finally gave in. He ran and was elected as congressman-at-large in 1932, defeating the old populist James H. "Cyclone" Davis.[73]

Bailey also had a following among the Young Democrats, or liberals. A story in the *New York Times* declared that "the voices of the new deal for Texas are Maury Hughes, chairman of the Democratic State Committee; Representative Joe Bailey Jr., State Senator W. K. Hopkins, Walter Tynan, San Antonio District Attorney, and others of youth and vigor who lead rather than follow and who fearlessly tell the people how they stand on every public question.[74] In late June 1933 Bexar County judge Frost Woodhull, a protégé of John Boyle, announced that Bexar would "boom" Joe Bailey for the Senate. He stated that sentiment was crystalized against Connally's Dry stand and that "the citizenry is disappointed with its fruits of the Democratic victory" in 1932. However, Frank Buschick Jr., a member of the Chambers organization in San Antonio, wrote Connally that this statement reflected Boyle's and Woodhull's disappointment over the failure of their associate in the Citizens League, Walter Tynan, to be appointed U.S. attorney. "Happily the attempt to inspire this opposition to you at this early time shown in this interview does not proceed from the controlling majority in Bexar County, but from a few disgruntled leaders of ephemeral strength and greatly over rated importance." Another Connally partisan assured the senator in January 1934 that he had no cause to worry about the political situation in Texas: "Some of our youngsters in North Texas have let their friendship and admiration for Joe Bailey Jr. get the better of their judgment. Some of our disappointed office-seeking friends in South Texas have let their disappointments get the better of their judgment. The result is we have a youngster in the race against you who is going to be sadly disillusioned when the campaign is over."[75]

When the primary was still six months away, it was already, to quote one of Bailey's managers, "war to the knife and the knife to the hilt." Bailey continually belittled Connally's record, insisting that he claimed credit for many things for which he deserved none, and charged that Connally, Jesse Jones, Silliman Evans, and Amon Carter had organized a clique to control the political future of Texas. He denounced the "vicious" Bankhead Cotton Control Act and criticized Connally for having supported a bill that would promote unneeded and dangerous "regimentation" among farmers. Bailey opposed the Ickes oil bill, which proposed federal control of oil production, claiming that it would allow out-of-state corporations to control the Texas oil industry. A Wet, he scorned Connally's moderate Dry views and his vote against the repeal amendment and the legalization of beer and ridiculed him for saying that prohibition was no longer an issue in national politics.[76]

Guy B. Fisher of San Augustine County, an opponent of the Roosevelt administration who had run unsuccessfully for Congress in 1932, filed for a place on the ticket as a candidate for the Senate but made only a token campaign. "You need not worry about Guy Fisher," one of Connally's supporters wrote him shortly after Fisher announced. "He moves pretty slow."[77]

Connally remained in Washington until Congress adjourned late in June and then made an intense campaign of some four weeks. In his speeches he praised the Roosevelt administration's efforts to ease the burdens of people suffering from the Depression, explained in detail the Bankhead Act, the Farm Credit Act, the Home Owners' Loan Corporation, and the Securities Exchange Commission Act. He said the farmers were getting from ten to twelve cents a pound for cotton instead of the three or four cents it would have brought had the Bankhead Act not been passed. He never mentioned Bailey by name and calmly referred to him only occasionally as "my opponent." He spoke only of "some of my critics" when answering charges made by Bailey or his friends. "Senator Connally slings no mud," commented the editor of the *Cuero Record*. "Others should follow his excellent example." But Connally permitted his partisans to make cracks about Bailey as "somebody else's boy." Bailey, on the other hand, charged the senator with being a "rubber-stamp politician" who was guilty of "pussyfooting" on many issues. In his first campaign for the Senate, Connally had challenged Mayfield to a joint debate. When Mayfield refused, Connally reportedly said: "If a candidate will not debate the issues he is not entitled to hold office." Now Bailey was the one issuing the challenge to a joint debate. When Connally declined, his opponent contended that "according to Connally's own statement, be does not deem himself worthy of election."[78]

President Roosevelt went out of his way to praise Connally at a White House gathering as an "old friend" and "stalwart supporter" while pointedly ignoring Bailey, who was also present. Roosevelt later instructed Secretary of Labor Francis Perkins to see Connally about "helping him a bit in Texas between now and the primaries." Perkins replied that she thought she had already satisfied Connally but would "call him up at once to see if everything is O.K." Both Jim Farley and Secretary of the Interior Harold Ickes assisted Connally by telling him where federal money was about to be spent in Texas; he could then make the announcement first in a political speech. During the last week of the campaign, a letter from Vice President Garner to former attorney general Walter A. Keeling endorsing Connally was made public. Said Garner: "I do not believe there is a man in Texas who could represent the interests of this state as well as he.... In my opinion it would be a great misfortune to fail to return Tom Connally to the Senate."[79]

Connally received 567,139 votes in the first primary to 355,963 for Bailey and 41,421 for Fisher. The Senator led in all but 20 of the 254 counties. Fisher carried only San Augustine County. Bailey won comparatively few counties over the state, aside from what one political writer designated the "beer belt" in South Central Texas. Connally led by 8,095 votes in Harris County and had comfortable majorities even in Dallas County, Bailey's home, and Bexar County, where Wet sentiment was strong. He received his largest majorities in North and Northwest Texas.[80]

After the election Bailey returned to his Dallas law practice. He opposed Roosevelt's reelection in 1936 as a member of the anti–New Deal organization, the Jeffersonian Democrats, and showed his displeasure with the Roosevelt administration's policies by refraining from voting in the general election. Bailey's oratory, somewhat reminiscent of his father's, rolled from Texas platforms in the 1940 campaign for the presidency. As chairman of the Texas for Willkie clubs, Bailey denounced the New Deal and engaged in many debates over the state. Once he declared that Harold Ickes had Communist connections. Ickes called him a liar.[81] After Pearl Harbor, Bailey was commissioned a captain in the Marine Corps. In 1943 he suffered injuries in a collision with an army truck near Gainesville, Texas, as he was driving home from his station at the Norman, Oklahoma, Naval Air Technical Training School. He died without regaining consciousness.[82]

At the Democratic state convention in Galveston in September 1934, the nomination committee accepted Allred's choices for temporary officers. Former attorney general Robert Lee Bobbitt was made temporary chairman and keynoter, and Albert Sidney Johnson was made secretary. Jim Ferguson had J. K. Brim of Sulphur Springs read his resignation as national committeeman contingent on the election of Garner to succeed him. The resignation was accepted, and Garner was elected on the same motion by the retiring state committee—the same committee that had been ready to elect McDonald over Garner several months before. In a letter to Colonel House, Garner explained why he had agreed to serve as national committeeman:

> The situation developed where there would have been a tremendous fight, not only in the Convention at Galveston but probably before the National Committee, and all the bad features of our organization in Texas, including the prohibition question, would have come to the front. A great many of the leading Democrats in Texas, who had no other purpose than party harmony in the State, visited me here [Uvalde] and urged me to bring about the situation as it developed. Without showing bad faith I can hand it back to the Democracy of the State if it, in anyway, interferes with my duties as Vice President.

Senator Connally did not challenge Allred's choice for permanent chairman of the convention. Allred had recommended James E. Kilday of Houston. Some felt Connally would challenge this appointment since Kilday had supported Joe Bailey and had reportedly written a letter to every Catholic Priest in Texas charging that Connally had discharged a Catholic lady employee because of her religion. Elbert Hooper of Fort Worth wrote Allred's platform for the platform committee. All differences were settled in committee, very few changes were made in Allred's program, and it was accepted by the convention. "The result was the most harmonious convention in years, due chiefly to the skillful management of Mr. Allred," the *Texas Weekly* reported.[83]

Allred had practically no opposition in the general election held on November 6, 1934. The Republican Party in Texas had held a primary for the second time in its history, but only 1,554 voters turned out, selecting D. E. Waggoner as their candidate for governor. Neither party campaigned. The results of the election were Allred, 428,734; Waggoner, 13,307; George Clifton Edwards (Socialist), 1,862; and Enoch Hardaway (Communist), 260. In the Senate race Connally received 439,375 votes; U. S. Goen (Republican), 12,895; W. B. Starr (Socialist), 1,828; and L. C. Keel (Communist), 310. Connally carried every county in the state. Even the three counties that voted for the Republican candidate against Connally in 1928 voted for him by a wide margin in 1934.[84]

"My wife's second administration is driving to a close," with the near unanimous approval of people everywhere, Jim Ferguson noted in his diary on November 25, 1934. "I am wondering what I will find to do when my wife goes out of office next January 15, 1935. I am still in debt and don't know whether I will pull out or not. The depression is still on the country. All that can be done is to bide the time with patience and trust in Providence." Seemingly tired—or worried as to the outcome of a foreclosure suit brought in 116th District Court by the Dallas Joint Stock Land Bank against his wife's 626-acre Bell County farm—much of the dynamic force that had more than once carried Ferguson to the political heights in Texas was missing as he told reporters he was through with active participation in politics and would go back to being a farmer, lawyer, and weekly newspaper publisher and editor. "I do not think the depression will be over for a year, and conditions may get worse," he wrote in his diary on January 24, 1935. "I am now past 63, and I realize that my days of physical activity cannot, in the natural order of things, be prolonged to any great extent.... I am philosophical about the situation, and I do not worry much about what comes or goes, because it would do no good."[85]

At the inaugural ceremonies established custom was broken for the second consecutive time when the retiring governor did not introduce the new governor, presumably because Allred did not wish to have Mrs. Ferguson do so. Mrs. Ferguson evened the score, after a fashion, by leaving the Bible on the governor's desk marked at Jeremiah 50:32, which reads, "And the proud shall stumble and fall, and none shall raise him up; and I will kindle a fire in his cities, and it shall devour all around about him."[86]

Epilogue

"Pass the Biscuits, Pappy!"

In retirement the Fergusons remained staunch Roosevelt supporters. In a June 13, 1935, *Forum* editorial, Jim remarked that "I think the people are getting tired of these vicious attacks upon the President just because the NRA law passed by Congress overwhelmingly was declared unconstitutional by the United States Supreme Court. When all is said and done and history is written, President Roosevelt will stand out as the greatest friend to the common people and especially the masses of Texas that ever sat in the White House." He pointedly reminded those who complained about the encroachment of federal authority on state rights that "the President has fed a million people in Texas for the last two years." He added: "I think the rank and file of Texans appreciate the President's efforts on their behalf and if this crowd keeps jumping on him if I were in his place, I would just order Mr. Hopkins to tell these attackers of the President just to take state rights and go on and the Federal Government will take its money and spend it somewhere else where the people appreciate the President." Ferguson sent Roosevelt a copy of this editorial with the comment: "Notwithstanding the howls of these politicians in Texas, the great masses of our people are still with you and we are glad to hold up your hand at this time."[1]

With Mrs. Ferguson's retirement from office in January 1934, Jim had no state patronage with which to support the *Forum*. The commissioner of internal revenue was after the company for back taxes totaling over $20,000. In July 1935 Ferguson announced suspension of the paper because he "needed a vacation." In an October 1935 interview with an Associated Press writer, he remarked: "We have had many honors, more than any other Texan. We are pretty content and we weren't bluffing last year when we said we were getting out." Pushing his big black hat to the back of his head, Ferguson leaned forward in his swivel chair in the *Forum* office and chuckled. "Well, I'll say this, at this time, I don't know any reason why we should ever want to hold public office again." He continued: "But because we are not looking for an office does not mean we are not interested in politics." Ferguson offered the opinion that "one of the meanest persons in the world is one, who has been honored by the people, steps out and then grouches." The biggest state issue, he said, was where to get the money to pay old-age pensions, authorized by a recent constitutional amendment. Two sessions of the legislature had wrestled with the problem. He viewed the amount of taxes as "alarming" and threatening to "overthrow the nation."[2]

The Last of the People's Governors

The most difficult problem the Allred administration faced was, indeed, old-age assistance. The constitutional amendment, while authorizing public assistance to persons over sixty-five, did not specify the amount of the pensions (except for the maximum state contribution of fifteen dollars) or set definite standards for determining eligibility. The pension program was to be "under such limitations and restrictions and regulations as may be deemed by the legislature expedient." Furthermore, the amendment made no provision for raising the money needed to meet the payments.

During Allred's first term, three special legislative sessions wrestled with the subject; it consumed most of the time of the regular session of 1937, and it was the principal reason why Allred called a special session in September of that year. Opinions concerning eligibility, the amounts to be allowed pensioners, and how the pension money was to be raised differed widely. Allred proposed to raise most of the additional revenue by an increase in oil, gas, and sulfur taxes, but the legislature balked. When the law was written lawmakers believed that about 63,000 people would ask for assistance. However, once the payments began in July 1936, approved applications had reached 80,718 before the end of September, and the old-age assistance commission estimated that the number of pensioners would eventually reach almost 150,000. The legislature increased the revenue while at the same time deliberalizing the law sufficiently, it was thought, to cut the rolls to 80,000. Deliberalization was easier said than done, however, and by June 1, 1937, pensioners numbered 125,772. At the time the legislature conducted an investigation of the old-age assistance commission, and it was evident that the subject of pensions was in politics.[3]

Governor Allred cooperated with the New Deal's relief and recovery programs. He helped set up assistance programs for the elderly, the needy blind, and indigent children but could not persuade the legislature to fund them. He successfully taxed the chain stores and opposed a general sales tax as unwise and unfair while favoring a selective sales tax on luxuries. He unsuccessfully attempted to install a state income tax. He earned the enmity of corporate lobbyists after trying to subject them to registration and regulation. No subsequent Texas governor has been as liberal as Allred, with the possible exception of Ann Richards, and veteran liberals in the state regard him as the last of the "people's governors."[4]

Allred sought reelection in 1936. Old-line Ferguson supporters "strongly urged" Mrs. Ferguson to enter the governor's race, but she declined. The Fergusons supported their friend state senator Roy Sanderford of Belton, and Jim spoke in his behalf. Tom Hunter was again a candidate, along with F. W. Fischer and P. Pierce Brooks. Texans had heard a great deal about the late Senator Huey Long's "share our wealth" program; they were well acquainted with Dr. Francis E. Townsend's plan to pay a pension of $200 a month to most persons past sixty; and Father Charles E. Coughlin's National Union for Social Justice was then active. The candidates accordingly leaned toward a more generous pension policy. Allred, who advocated pensions only for the "aged needy" and wanted but a small increase in natural revenue taxes, was more conservative on this issue than his opponents, and the fact that he was nominated in the first primary indicated that Texas voters were still in a conservative mood.

The *Savannah* (Georgia) remarked that the Allred victory involved a rejection of candidates who favored "wild tax schemes" and indicated a "return to sanity." The *Lansing State Journal* pointed out that Allred had favored economy in government and pensions only to the needy and that candidates running on the Townsend plan in twelve congressional districts had all been defeated. "The news from Texas indicates that the era of soft soap is passing." Another surprising feature of the election was the apparent loss of the Ferguson influence in the ten German counties. Sanderford only polled approximately 9 percent of the votes in those counties, running fourth behind Allred, Hunter, and Fischer.[5]

Less Johnson Grass and Politicians

The Fergusons were replaced in the affections of the poorer whites of Texas by the greater showmanship and more lavish promises of Wilbert Lee "Pass the Biscuits, Pappy" O'Daniel, called by political scientist V. O. Key Jr.

W. Lee "Pappy" O'Daniel campaigning for the office of governor of Texas, 1938. Jimmie A. Dodd Photograph Collection, Briscoe Center for American History, University of Texas at Austin, E JD 0100.

"a mountebank alongside whom old Jim looked like a statesman—and was."[6] O'Daniel, the son of a Union veteran, was born in Malta, Ohio, on March 11, 1890. After his father was killed in a construction accident, his mother supported the family by sewing and washing. Wilbert worked on a Kansas farm in his youth, attended Salt City Business College, and then went to work for the Kramer Milling Company of Anthony, Kansas, as a stenographer and bookkeeper. He was soon promoted to the job of sales manager. In 1912 he became the sales manager of the Kingman Mills of Kingman, Kansas, and in 1916 went into business for himself, building the Independent Milling Company of Kingman. It was taken over by a larger firm that went into receivership during the postwar farm deflation, and stockholders lost their investment. O'Daniel joined the Burrus Mill and Elevator Company of Fort Worth in 1925 as sales manager and within three years had become general manager. Later he was made president of the Fort Worth mill and supervised two mills at Dallas and Kingfisher, Oklahoma. He also became master of ceremonies for a daily radio show featuring Bob Wills and the Lightcrust

Doughboys. The show opened with a woman's request to O'Daniel: "Please pass the biscuits, Pappy."

In 1935 O'Daniel organized his own flour company. He had no mill of his own but bought ready-made flour from various mills, had it packed in ready-made bags, and composed the following stanza to be stamped on each bag under a big picture of a billy goat:

Hillbilly music on the air,
Hillbilly flour everywhere;
It tickles your feet—it tickles your tongue.
Wherever you go, its praises are sung.

Beneath this rhyme in glaring black capitals appeared that favorite word among salesmen: "Guaranteed." Printed in red at the bottom of the sack was the slogan: "Please pass the biscuits, Pappy."

O'Daniel's daily radio program advertising Hillbilly Flour became increasingly popular in rural Texas. It featured a new group of musicians, the Hillbilly Boys, and two star performers, Texas Rose and Leon Huff. O'Daniel's on-air personality, the poems and songs he wrote (the popular favorite was "Beautiful Texas"), and the folksy and religious character of the program built a wide following of fans. He began to host programs commemorating the U.S. Constitution, honoring national and Texas heroes, and counseling on personal problems. One of his most successful stunts, many times repeated, was to initiate some crusade favoring a cause that everyone could endorse, regardless of specific political views, and that no sane man would think of opposing. For instance, he organized a statewide safety association for children, sending out badges to all members. The one rule of the organization was that every qualified member should walk on the left-hand side of the street so as to face approaching traffic.[7]

O'Daniel became interested in the governorship, he professed, as a result of letters "every two years" from his radio audience to make the race. On Palm Sunday, 1938, he asked his listeners if he should run. Messages, he said, came from 54,499 people who urged him to run and only four who wrote against it. He announced as a candidate on May 1. One belief was that he went into politics purely to get a bigger audience and hence a bigger market for his flour. O'Daniel campaigned on a platform of the Ten Commandments, adjustment of taxes, opposition to a sales tax, abolition of the poll tax, and pensions of thirty dollars a month for all persons over sixty-five. He said his motto would be the Golden Rule and announced a slogan of "Less Johnson grass and politicians; more smokestacks and business men."[8]

O'Daniel set out rather late in the campaigning season. He left his wife in Fort Worth to receive his mail and manage his headquarters. Taking his three teenage children, Pat, Mike, and Molly, to help Texas Rose and the Hillbilly Boys, he sallied forth on June 7 to tour "Beautiful Texas" in a big white bus with a platform and microphone on top and "O'Daniel for Governor" painted across the side. He composed a new song, "Them Hillbillies Are Politicians Now," to ring down the road as the bus roared along. The old-line politicians openly laughed at the country music O'Daniel peddled on his campaign swings, but his crowds increased. People jammed the highways, sometimes waiting hours to get a firsthand glimpse of the famous radio salesman. They forced him to speak in towns where he was not even scheduled to stop. During five weeks of intense campaigning, he addressed 113 scheduled meetings and 32 that were not scheduled. He also made three radio talks each week. According to Frank Goodwyn,

> The O'Daniel rallies appealed to the same deep human instincts and provided the same emotional outlets which the camp meetings formerly offered. Here again was a chance to enjoy the thrill and glory of a martial movement without risking any physical bloodshed. Christ was still the hero and Satan still the enemy, but both had new mouthpieces now. Christ's good, which had previously radiated from the camp-meeting preacher, was now represented by the flour-salesman. Satan's evil, previously attached to that abhorred aristocracy which had been the pioneer's European superior, was now found to reside in the professional politician. Roles, state plotting, and costumes were changed, but the plot of the drama was the same.

At O'Daniel rallies miniature barrels, marked "Flour; not Pork," for "dimes, quarters, and dollars" were passed among the crowd. When the campaign was over and all expenses were paid, he had $801.30 left to give to the Red Cross.

In his speeches O'Daniel stressed industrialization and tax cuts more than did the other candidates. "Let businessmen have a chance to establish a bigger and better Texas," he cried. "Let the state encourage business—advertise the advantages of Texas—bring new factories here—do something constructive for the Texas businessmen rather than abuse and tax them. All's

Pappy O'Daniel's gubernatorial inauguration, 1939. Prints and Photographs Collection, Briscoe Center for American History, University of Texas at Austin, DI 03132.

going to be well with Texas if we have a business administration instead of a professional political regime."[9]

As O'Daniel's crowds increased and he became more critical of his "professional politician" opponents, the other twelve candidates became more and more alarmed. As the campaign went into its last week, they recognized that he was the man to beat and attempted to pin a "carpetbagger" and city slicker label on him. Bill McCraw of Dallas, a popular attorney general whom the "old pols" believed would win the election, threw in the sponge the night before, telling a newsman: "I'm beat. I got too much flour in my face." O'Daniel's showmanship and his pension promises brought out to the polls thousands who had not voted since 1928, when they joined the moral crusade against Al Smith. Many voting places were swamped and had to stay open until late at night to accommodate the waiting lines. In appealing to the old folks, O'Daniel had a strong advantage in the Texas law that required a $1.75 poll tax as a prerequisite for voting but exempted from the requirement all those past sixty-five. O'Daniel himself was ineligible to vote because he had failed to pay his poll tax.[10]

Pappy was nominated in the first primary, garnering 50.9 percent of the votes and negating the need for a runoff. Historian Seth McKay, after studying the returns, concluded that "the O'Daniel victory of 1938 was due to the power of the radio, or perhaps to the skill of O'Daniel in the use of the radio." O'Daniel himself attributed his success to a higher power. "It is the first time to my knowledge that the Ten Commandments have been used for a political platform," he told the congregation of the Christian (Disciples of Christ) Church in Fort Worth. "I feel that this is a great victory for the clear-thinking Christian people of Texas." (O'Daniel had joined the church twelve days after he announced his candidacy for governor.) "Texas will give the nation its next President," J. Frank Norris wired from Detroit. "You are independent of all politics and combinations and the nation is looking for a Moses to lead it back to such fundamentals as home and God."

In a postprimary interview with a *New York Times* correspondent, O'Daniel asserted that while his band and his songs drew the crowds to his meetings, the real appeal of his campaign was his promise to put the state government on a business basis and eliminate the sinecures of politicians. "There was at first the opinion that my campaign was ballyhoo and entertainment," he went on. "As I explained my idea of a business administration, we made tremendous gains in followers." To aid in keeping his pledge for a businesslike administration, he said, he would appoint an unofficial advisory committee of businessmen, a board of directors as he described it. "I am a business man," he added. "I know nothing about politics and I have the idea that the principles of business can be applied effectively to State affairs." O'Daniel went on to beat his Republican opponent by 473,526 to 10,940. In the runoff, moreover, he threw his support to Coke Stevenson for lieutenant governor, and Stevenson's vote rose from 258,625 to 446,441—a striking example of Pappy's power. Bascom Giles, who received O'Daniel's "nod" for land commissioner, gained more than 200,000 votes over his July total, while his opponent polled some 71,000 fewer. In all, three of O'Daniel's six choices were successful in the August runoff; three were defeated.[11]

One historian sees the 1938 Democratic gubernatorial primary as a turning point in Texas politics. According to George Norris Green, "Conservative, corporate interests took over the state, once and for all, perhaps permanently. They launched the Establishment, a loosely knit plutocracy comprised mostly of Anglo businessmen, oilmen, bankers, and lawyers."[12]

The 1938 primaries in Texas also offered a test of whether the efforts of Vice President Garner and conservative members of the Texas congressional delegation to block further extension of the New Deal reforms met with the approval of the people. Several Texans were on Roosevelt's purge list: Hatton Sumners, Fritz Lanham, Nat Patton, Joseph J. Mansfield, Richard Kleburg, Milton H. West, Clyde L. Garrett, and Martin Dies. Three of these men, Sumners, Lanham, and Mansfield, headed permanent House committees, and Sumners served as chair of the Senate Judiciary Committee and had been instrumental in the defeat of the president's plan to reorganize the federal judiciary. In the Democratic primary Lanham was opposed by a 100 percent New Dealer; Sumners was opposed by Tom Love, who ran as a Roosevelt man; and Maury Maverick and W. D. McFarlane, the only true New Deal liberals in the Texas delegation, were opposed by conservatives. Both Maverick and McFarlane lost, while all of the incumbents marked for a purge won. The results could be interpreted as a direct slap at the administration's reform policies. As a columnist for the *Washington Evening Star* put it: "The Texas primary turned out to be no ball of fire for the Roosevelt New Dealers."[13]

Governor O'Daniel's promise to give a pension to every person over sixty-five made pensions the chief issue of his administration. After the election, however, the campaign promise was pared down to a proposal to give only to needy persons past sixty-five an amount sufficient to raise their income to thirty dollars a month. Likewise, the governor soon abandoned the hope, often expressed to the voters, that new taxes would not be necessary and proposed to the legislature that an enlarged pension program be financed by a transactions tax of 1.6 percent on all business transactions (with certain exemptions). The governor estimated that the transactions tax would bring into the treasury some $45 million a year, a sum ample to meet all social security obligations. The public was unaware that C. A. Jay, head of the Texas Industrial Conference, Dallas's counterpart of the Texas Manufacturers Association, had presented this tax plan to O'Daniel in secret sessions at the Executive Mansion. It was widely and rightly regarded as a multiple sales tax that would fall most heavily on the small wage-earner and small businessman. The reaction of the general public was "decidedly antagonistic," and lawmakers attacked the O'Daniel tax proposal bitterly. The affair widened the breach already existing between the governor and the legislature.

O'Daniel then supported Senate Joint Resolution 12, a constitutional amendment proposing a combined natural resource and 2 percent sales tax;

but after passing the senate 21 to 10 on April 10, 1939, the measure was defeated by the united efforts of fifty-six members ("The Immortal Fifty-Six") of the house of representatives on ten separate roll calls. The legislature liberalized pensions, adding some 75,000 to 80,000 applicants to the list of those eligible in Texas, but it failed to provide additional revenue, and the problem became even more vexing. In spite of vetoes, the deficit in the general fund of items, totaling $5,383,616, continued to increase.[14]

Third-Term Bids

In early 1940 a major struggle began shaping up in Texas between the Garner-for-president element and the Roosevelt third-termers. From 1937 on the vice president constantly caused trouble for the president and became the darling of conservatives. Garner's departure for Uvalde amidst Roosevelt's court reform struggle broke open the long-smoldering conservative revolt in the South against the New Deal's friendship for organized labor. After his return to Washington, Garner was told to make the best settlement possible but instead allowed Senator Burton K. Wheeler, the leader of the opposition, to do as he pleased. Roosevelt felt Garner had sold out to Wheeler and never forgave him. One of the president's intimates summed up the feeling in the inner White House circle with the bitter remark: "Garner was told to compromise, and he did so by surrendering." Relations between the two men were never the same, and the split was now complete. "As he ponders his legislative problems," wrote Thomas L. Stokes, "President Roosevelt often must think of the cost of the block of votes which Jack Garner threw into his pot at Chicago in 1932 to clinch his nomination." Garner had his last private meeting with Roosevelt on December 18, 1938.[15]

In Texas, E. B. Germany, who had been chosen state Democratic chairman by the O'Daniel forces at the Beaumont state convention in 1938, was an active leader for Garner, along with Amon Carter, Roy Miller, Sam Rayburn, Tom Connally, and Morris Sheppard. National polls showed that Garner was the choice of Democrats if FDR chose not to run, and his campaign was assuming major national proportions. On March 9, 1940, he was endorsed by the state Democratic Executive Committee. A week later, however, the Roosevelt men set up a third-term organization in Austin. The leaders were Mayor Tom Miller of Austin, Jim Ferguson, T. H. McGregor, Edward Clark (Texas secretary of state under Allred), and Maury Maverick of San Antonio. Undersecretary of the Interior Alvin Wirtz returned to Texas

From left to right: John Nance Garner, Tom Connally, and Morris Sheppard, undated. Walter Dickson Adams Papers, Briscoe Center for American History, University of Texas at Austin, DI 00837.

to whip up third-term sentiment. Garner people claimed that Congressman Lyndon B. Johnson was also active in the movement. Tom Love, who had failed to unseat Hatton Sumners in 1938, announced the organization of the Franklin D. Roosevelt Democratic League of Texas, with himself as secretary, but the Garnerites, recalling his bolts in 1924 and 1928, questioned whether he was, in fact, a loyal Democrat. By early April the third-termers had a campaign underway in precincts and counties throughout the state. "This is hot a fight between Garner and Roosevelt," Harold H. Young, North Texas chairman for the Roosevelt organization, declared. "It is a battle between the men who are using Garner as a stalking horse, the Roy Millers and Amon Carters on one side, and the 7,000,000 Texas citizens on the other side." In a speech to a Roosevelt rally in Dallas, Wirtz charged that the vice president's campaign was simply a "Trojan horse" with which to capture the Texas delegation. "These ambassadors of Wall Street in Texas want to be able to play poker with the Texas votes at the national convention," he stated. "They want to use the votes in some smoke-filled hotel room where those who hate the new deal will gather with their ill-gotten hoard of favorite son votes."[16]

Wirtz's answer to Germany's activities was to pay for a statewide radio broadcast from Waco by Jim Ferguson, long a Garner detractor. Ferguson put on a good show, telling his audience that he had "known John Garner for thirty years, and I hope he still is my friend," but added that, in the first place, "he won't be elected and hasn't got a ghost of a chance," and in the second place, the "Lord never did enough for him to qualify him to render the great service that has been rendered by Franklin D. Roosevelt."[17]

Despite the heated rhetoric, Garner and Roosevelt leaders in Washington and Austin worked out a fragile peace agreement under which the Texas delegation would be instructed to vote and work for Garner at the Chicago convention but would not use its forty-six votes to join in a movement that might embarrass the president or any effort that might be interpreted as one aimed at stopping Roosevelt. At the state convention in May, Rayburn was chosen to lead the delegation and Lyndon Johnson was named vice chairman. This also carried out the agreed terms of peace.

After Roosevelt captured the nomination, a number of Texas oilmen and financiers turned against the Democratic Party and supported Wendell Willkie, the Republican nominee. Among the better-known leaders of the "Democrats for Willkie" movement in Texas were Joseph W. Bailey Jr., E. B. Germany, Mike Hogg, John H. Kirby, Steve Pinckney, and John Boyle. At the statewide November election Roosevelt garnered 905,156 votes to Willkie's 211,707. Garner exiled himself to Uvalde, "sulking among the goats," as one newspaper put it. Neither he nor O'Daniel endorsed Roosevelt.[18]

O'Daniel sought reelection in 1940 advocating much the same platform as in 1938, since so little of it had been enacted. He asked voters for $60 million in transactions taxes for social security purposes. Jim Ferguson became convinced that only Ma could defeat him. When an emissary from Washington requested that Ferguson help start the ball rolling for a third term for Roosevelt, it fitted in with his own plans to seek a third term for his wife. His strategy was to tie O'Daniel to the Garner camp and make his wife the Roosevelt candidate to battle it out on the third-term issue. "Isn't all this recent ballyhoo in the papers about Mamma's running for governor the most ridiculous thing in the world?" Ouida Ferguson Nalle innocently remarked to her father. "Not so ridiculous as you might think!" Jim retorted.[19]

Mrs. Ferguson, in a formal statement entitled "If Voters Want Me," announced on March 23 that she would be a candidate for governor if enough persons asked her to make the race, and she called on voters to send her a postcard saying they would support her in the primary. Jim said that if his wife ran, he would not make prohibition an issue "but if some one lights the fire, of course, we will be there." Late in March Ouida and her husband left Texas on a business trip to New York. Before starting home on April 2 by way of Virginia and South Carolina, Ouida received a letter from her mother with a note at the end from Jim. "We miss you terribly. Roosevelt and Garner campaign getting hot. I think your Mother may announce next week. Looks like she has a fine chance. Devotedly, 'Daddy.'"[20]

"One of the main purposes of my running for Governor is to help carry out the things Mr. Roosevelt stands for," Mrs. Ferguson said in her announcement of candidacy on April 13, "and with his help I can obtain the cooperation necessary for the success of my administration." She called for old-age pensions, a proposal always distasteful to her husband but one that O'Daniel had popularized. They would be financed by a gross receipts tax of .5 percent, less reasonable exemptions within the constitutional provision that taxation should be equal and uniform. "This is a small tax on the man who sells and not on the man who buys, and it will yield fifty million dollars," she explained. "I would pay everybody eligible under the constitution without other restrictions." Mrs. Ferguson also promised to reduce state appropriations by $25 million a year, or approximately 25 percent, and would use the veto power if necessary to accomplish this reduction. "High taxes [are] now causing high cost of government and must be reduced or trouble will happen," she warned. The Ferguson platform also favored "reasonable demands of organized labor," cooperation of state and nation in aid to tenant farmers by making low interest loans to enable them to purchase homes, and liberal appropriations for the public schools and institutions of higher learning. "If we get our money's worth, let us buy all the education we can pay for," Ma reasoned.[21]

Five other candidates besides Mrs. Ferguson challenged O'Daniel. Among them were two members of the Railroad Commission, Ernest O. Thompson and Jerry Sadler, and the chairman of the Highway Commission, Harry Hines. Thompson, whose slogan was "A Nickel for Grandma," wanted to levy an additional five-cent-a-barrel tax on oil, arguing that such an increase would bring in sufficient money to finance old-age pensions and the other security obligations. Sadler was "unalterably opposed" to a sales tax in any form and advocated financing old-age pensions through higher taxes on natural resources. O'Daniel reiterated his demand for more liberal pensions and a broader social security program. He favored a transactions tax that would raise $60 million but said he would accept any other tax that would raise the revenue that would be needed. Hines wished to increase oil and sulfur taxes and to levy a production tax on natural gas and franchise taxes on larger corporations. "Although they attacked his record and his plan for raising revenue, his opponents did not directly attack his proposal for more liberal pensions," commented historian Rupert Richardson. "Texas had developed a 'share our wealth' movement of its own, and the candidates did not dare to resist it." O'Daniel blamed a recalcitrant legislature for the breakdown of his nebulous program and asked voters to reelect him as a vindication. Slapped by the daily press, he issued for a time his own weekly paper, the *W. Lee O'Daniel News*. Refused free time by the leading Texas radio stations, he resorted to a powerful station located just south of the Rio Grande in Mexico that was free from U.S. regulations affecting misrepresentation and libel.[22]

Mrs. Ferguson asked O'Daniel during the campaign: "How long will it take to to reduce taxes if we depend on the strumming of a bass fiddle in a hillbilly band and the twang of a banjo and violin to the tune of Sugar in the Gourd and Arkansas Traveler or Billy in the Low Ground?" She continued: "I like to hear the old-time songs and tunes. I honor the old-time religion. But when they are preached for profit and played for politics, it is a transaction founded on something besides a tax." In San Antonio she assailed the musical campaigner as a "medicine man governor" who had put the state "under the shameful banner of the flour sack." Jim called O'Daniel "a wandering minstrel." The governor, he said, "is blowed-up, for the people are fed up on banjo-picking, bull fiddling statesmen."

But the Fergusons were no match for Pappy, who was now the hero of the Texas underprivileged. The old fire had died out of the Fergusons' campaign zeal; the old issues were dead; the partisans who had elected the Fergusons originally had turned over political affairs to a younger generation. Ma came in fourth in the primary with 100,578 votes as O'Daniel triumphed with a majority of 102,202 over the total votes given his six opponents. The governor had carried 54.3 percent of the vote. Ernest O. Thompson was a distant second and Harry Hines third.

The Fergusons' supporters blamed the radio for Ma's defeat, for Pa was a stump speaker and could not adjust his free-swinging style of oratory to the new method of vote collecting. "Jim Ferguson," declared his lieutenant, Fisher Alsup, "was a man who had to be seen to be appreciated." Also, the Fergusons could afford only a fraction of the radio time the O'Daniel supporters purchased. Gladys Little, Mrs. Ferguson's campaign manager, often said to Ouida Nalle after the close of the race: "There were several periods during the campaign when I felt we might have turned the tide had we had the money to buy more radio time." Mrs. Ferguson spoke over the radio at seven a.m. two mornings a week. She took one plank from her platform and discussed it thoroughly during each of these sessions. But numerous disciples, now in late middle age, were convinced that O'Daniel was better able to provide them with pensions than a sixty-four-year-old woman whose husband had continually tangled with the legislature. The old folks apparently believed that O'Daniel was a martyr to legislative perfidy.

The Fergusons had run their last race, although an older brother of Jim's, Alex Ferguson of Grayson, made an unsuccessful race for the Democratic nomination for governor in 1944. The name Ferguson was all he had to offer, and the irony was that he and Jim had been personally bitter toward each other in years past.[23]

Communistic Labor Leader Racketeers

On April 9, 1941, Morris Sheppard, the father of the Eighteenth Amendment and a staunch New Dealer, died, leaving a vacancy in the Senate. A special election (with no Democratic primary) was scheduled. Faced with the problem of selecting an interim senator who would not oppose him in the special election on June 28 and whose appointment would meet with popular approval, O'Daniel solved the dilemma by what V. O. Key called "probably the most ingenious appointment in senatorial history." On April 21, the one hundred and fiftieth anniversary of the battle of San Jacinto, he named to the post General Andrew Jackson Houston, the eighty-seven-year-old son of Sam Houston. The general had been the Republican candidate for governor in 1892 against Jim Hogg and the Prohibition nominee in 1910 and 1912. The veteran conservative legislator Claude Gilmer recalled of Houston: "Well, that old man probably couldn't tell you whether the sun was up or had gone down. I mean he was in his dotage." Six weeks after his appointment, Houston managed to make the long trip to Washington in the care of a nurse; took the oath of office ninety-five years after his father did; went three times to the Senate, where he introduced a bill to appropriate $250,000 to complete the San Jacinto Monument; and then fell ill and died in a Baltimore hospital following an operation for a stomach ailment while the campaign to determine his successor was at its height.[24]

The Texas press carried stories predicting that Jim Ferguson would be a candidate, since his impeachment did not bar him from seeking a federal office. Ferguson made a statement to the press on April 29 in which he included several planks in the platform he would advocate if he should decide to run. One of these was opposition to national prohibition, and he said he would be "the only anti in the race." Jim pointed out that a plurality would be required to win the election and said that with twelve candidates already running, "our crowd can put it over." He suggested that the voters advise him on the situation by sending him a postcard or letter. However, on May 10 the former governor announced that he would not enter the contest. He would give no reasons, merely saying that he did not want to run. (His daughter Ouida stated that "he perhaps realized that his increasing deafness had contributed largely to his wife's defeat in her race for governor in 1940, and that it could only prove a greater handicap to him as a candidate.") Ferguson said that he and his wife would vote for O'Daniel if he entered the race, and if he did not run they would consider the field carefully and try to pick out the candidate who would do the "least harm" in Washington.[25]

There were twenty-nine candidates in the field, including Texas's young attorney general Gerald Mann and East Texas congressman Martin Dies, but the race resolved itself into a contest between O'Daniel and Congressman Lyndon Baines Johnson, who ran with Roosevelt's blessing. The president called him "a very old, old friend of mine," which Johnson claimed was equal to an endorsement. O'Daniel, as governor, had denounced "booze debauchery" and lamented that the Liquor Control Board was not enforcing state laws. He grumbled that the legislature would not confirm his "good, clean honest Christian dry citizens" to the board. But the liquor lobby could not be sure that it could hold him off forever. Other business interests, including gamblers and the ever-hopeful racetrack lobby, backed O'Daniel in order to get him out of the state. Late in the campaign, Jim Ferguson suddenly came back into the picture. "It occurred to me one day," he told a reporter, "that if we could get O'Daniel in the U.S. Senate, Coke Stevenson, as lieutenant governor, would automatically become governor. Well, O'Daniel wasn't doing any good. Polls showed it and so did somep'n else. I called up Coke and said, 'How come you ain't out there helpin' O'Daniel get elected to the Senate so you can be governor?" Coke opined he "hadn't thought about it." "Well, you better get busy," Ferguson said he told Stevenson. "Better take the stump and let all your friends know that a vote for O'Daniel is a vote for Stevenson." Ferguson got busy too. "I rustled around among my hog herd and raised about seven hundred dollars," he said. He claimed he spent this money for an ad that ran in five papers and told people to vote for O'Daniel because Stevenson was also "a pension man" like Pappy. If Stevenson's friends added their votes to the votes of O'Daniel, "it is a double barrel cinch that O'Daniel will be our next Senator and Coke Stevenson our next

Governor." Although Ferguson did not say so, Stevenson, like himself, was a Wet and friendly to the liquor interests who were backing O'Daniel to get him out of the state.

O'Daniel led Johnson by just 1,311 votes (175,590 to 174,279), based on "corrected returns" from a dozen or more East Texas counties. As Ouida Ferguson Nalle told a reporter later: "Anytime the Fergusons can't swing 1,300 votes . . ." According to Walter Jenkins, who went to work for Johnson in 1939: "Most of those late-arriving votes for O'Daniel came from parts of Texas where former Governor Ferguson was still active and where a lot of Dies' votes suddenly turned up for O'Daniel. That's what they say happened anyway. That's what won the election for O'Daniel." According to Seth McKay, "A study of the returns shows that the votes 'from the forks of the creek' elected O'Daniel." He concluded: "His strength was greatest in the rural and small town counties." Pollster Joe Belden regarded O'Daniel's sudden jump in the late returns as "somewhat unnatural" and was concerned enough (or was paid) to make a secret postelection survey in two of the Ferguson counties. In one, Angelina, Belden concluded that there was an "amazing change of votes" that "baffles all mathematical laws." O'Daniel ultimately collected 35 percent of the county vote although the postelection poll indicated that only 22 percent had voted for him.[26]

Two years later O'Daniel defeated former governors Dan Moody and James V. Allred for the regular six-year term, after a hard-fought campaign in which it was charged that Pappy had failed to support the president's defense and war policies. During the campaign O'Daniel charged that Moody and Allred were financed by "Communistic labor leader racketeers," a phrase he used as often as sixteen times in one speech. He also charged that there was a conspiracy among Moody, Allred, the professional politicians, the politically controlled newspapers, and, of course, the "Communistic labor leader racketeers"; they joined forces, he said, in the dirtiest campaign of misrepresentation in Texas history. None of these wild allegations was documented. O'Daniel, who had boasted of the greatest majorities in the history of the state, did not get a clear majority in the first primary; in the runoff he barely won over Allred, 451,359 to 433,203.[27]

In the Senate O'Daniel ranked as the most Republican of the southern Democrats, according to V. O. Key's analysis. When 1944 came around, he stumped Texas for the anti-Roosevelt Texas Regulars and attacked the president with the most ferocious vigor. His amazing political career came to at least a temporary end in 1948 when he declined to run for reelection.

Opinion polls indicated that he had lost favor with Texas voters. "All in all, O'Daniel's career presents a puzzling phenomenon," wrote Key.

O'Daniel spent his last years as a Dallas insurance company executive and real estate manager, but politics kept calling him back. A friend said he had "Potomac fever and would never get over it." He ran losing races for governor in 1956 and 1958, stumping the state with another band, a white fire truck, and a campaign bus. The main plank in his platform remained the Ten Commandments and the Golden Rule. A question was raised in 1958 over his right to a place on the Democratic Party's primary ballot because of his nomination by the Constitution Party as a write-in candidate. The state Democratic Executive Committee, however, voted unanimously to certify his name. The aging Pappy charged that incumbent governor Price Daniel was behind the move to keep his name off the ballot, which had "held up for 41 days" the opening of his campaign. He said he was for segregation of Texas schools, opposed a sales tax, and denounced Daniel as a "would-be little dictator." O'Daniel died in Dallas on May 12, 1969, at the age of seventy-nine.[28]

After the 1941 election, Ferguson, partially deaf, troubled by rheumatism, and weighing 230 pounds, was content to end his time and energy on hog raising and his dairy. Miriam was quite satisfied to enjoy her grandchildren and her flowers. In 1942 Jim Ferguson's health began to deteriorate more rapidly, and the family sought medical help from doctors in Temple and the medical center in Galveston. They all gave the same diagnosis; nothing could be done. The next two years were difficult. Ouida took over the complete management of the Fergusons's farm, piggery, and dairy, and Miriam nursed her sick husband. She tried futilely to prepare palatable, nourishing food for him as he wasted away to less than 100 pounds. On February 28, 1944, Ferguson suffered a severe stroke from which he never fully regained consciousness. For seven more months he lingered; then on September 21, 1944, at 2:30 p.m., he died at his spacious home at 1500 Windsor Road in West Austin. He was seventy-three. His wife and two daughters who had accompanied him to the capitol twenty-nine years earlier as a handsome new governor were at his bedside.[29]

Twice governor of Texas, husband of Texas's only woman governor until Ann Richards took office in 1991, James Edward Ferguson was the most significant political figure in Lone Star politics for two decades. The Austin bureau of the *Dallas Morning News* declared he "was matched in his influence on state political history only by Sam Houston." The *News*, which had fought him editorially in many of his and Miriam's races, now stated: "In the one hundred years of statehood, 1845–1945, Texas has had three Governors who stood out above all others for the rugged picturesqueness of their political careers—Sam Houston, James Stephen Hogg and James E. Ferguson. And the same thing may be said of all of them—that they had their faults, made their errors and likewise made their contributions to the welfare of Texas."

Present at the last rites in the family residence were many who had stuck with Ferguson and his wife through twenty years or more of political success and failure. State departments were closed on the afternoon of the funeral in his memory. Flags at the capitol and elsewhere in Austin flew at half-staff. The burial was at the Texas State Cemetery. Friends raised money by popular subscription for a monument, which was dedicated in 1946. A place beside her husband was reserved for Miriam.[30]

In assessing the thirty years since Ferguson first served as governor of Texas, members of the press concluded that his two most significant achievements were his successful push for the law limiting the rent charged to Texas tenant farmers to "a third and fourth" and his advocacy of rural school education. The rent law, although stricken down in the courts, had remained on the statute books long enough to end the regime of "half-and-half," where the farmer contributed only his labor, with the landlord providing the land, house, farm animals, and equipment, and the tenant got only half the cotton and corn he raised. Noted the *Dallas Morning News*: "Not only did he initiate the rural aid, now called stabilization, fund for the poorer school districts but, by his picturesque, though some will say demagogic, advocacy of the rights of the little red school house, he awakened the people to a growing educational injustice."[31]

Miriam lived for seventeen years after her husband's death, free for perhaps the first time in her life to spend as much time in her beloved garden as she wished. She felt that a good gardener should try some new crop every year. One of her most successful experiments was with ornamental gourds of all shapes. Her favorites were "the ugly ones, the squatty variety."[32]

During Jim Ferguson's final illness, Lyndon Johnson called at the Ferguson home every time he came to Austin. Ouida recalled: "When leaving, he would put his arm around Mamma and ask her if there was anything in the world he could do for her. Lyndon Johnson was too big a man to hold it against Daddy that he had not supported him in his Senate race. 'Governor Jim' was critically ill, and Lyndon showed his concern in many ways." So it was, in the 1948 senate runoff between Johnson and former governor Coke

Stevenson, that Ouida went to the capitol pressroom one day with a statement from her mother endorsing Lyndon. The statement said in part:

> Like all other human beings, the Fergusons made some errors. One I admit we made was in not supporting Lyndon in 1941 when he lost the senate race, to the same crowd by 1,311 votes. Lyndon was too big a man to let that stand between us. It speaks volumes for his character that although we did not support him in 1941, he was as helpful and courteous to us as to every other constituent. In my husband's last illness a son could not have been finer and more attentive. I believe that if my husband were here to help me today, we would work to correct that 1941 error in judgment.[33]

"The old Ferguson counties as a whole did not vote peculiarly, but elements of the rusting Ferguson machine did crank up for their last hurrah, especially in several east Texas counties," notes George Norris Green. "Of the twenty counties that switched from Stevenson to Johnson in the grandest way, half of them were Ferguson's best counties." Johnson bested Stevenson by 87 votes in a hotly disputed contest, thanks to some late returns from Parr-dominated Jim Wells County in South Texas.[34]

As Miriam aged, the people of Texas seemed anxious to find ways to pay tribute to her. In 1953 the Texas Senate passed a resolution honoring her as "an example of noble and gentle womanhood, an ideal wife, and a devoted mother." In several interviews with Ralph Steen in May of that year, she talked freely of politics and politicians and of her great love for the game after she ran for governor in 1924. She declined to say which governor she had known ranked as "best" because she did not wish to apply that term to any of them. She rated Hobby and Sterling as the poorest governors she had known; Allred and Stevenson were labeled "nothings"; and Moody she described as "a nice man but too narrow between the eyes." She did not rank Pat Neff but thought he was "a real gentleman." O'Daniel was a monkey who should never have been governor. She said her husband was the best speaker she had ever heard.

On her eightieth birthday, June 13, 1955, about three hundred persons attended a dinner in her honor sponsored by the Austin Jaycees. Governor Allan Shivers served as Master of Ceremonies, and Mrs. Ferguson was escorted to the speakers' table to the strains of her 1924 campaign song, "Put on Your Old Gray Bonnet." Among those in attendance were James V. Allred and Senate Majority Leader Lyndon B. Johnson. This was Miriam's last formal public appearance. Her remaining years passed peacefully. She told a reporter that she felt no bitterness toward former enemies of Ferguson-ism, adding, "Most of them have seen the error of their ways, anyhow." On November 30, 1960, Miriam suffered a heart attack from which she seem-ingly recovered. But a little less than two weeks after her eighty-sixth birth-day, she suffered a second attack and died on June 25, 1961. A simple funeral service was held at her home, and she was buried beside her Jim, while the flag fluttered at half-staff over the Capitol. On the Fergusons' joint tomb-stone is carved the inscription:

> Life's race well run
> Life's work well done
> Life's victory won
> Now cometh rest.

On Mrs. Ferguson's side there is carved "Thy word is a lamp unto my feet and a light unto my path."[35]

"The political love affair with women which began with Ma Ferguson has continued," notes historian Joe B. Frantz. "The state came close to electing a woman liberal, Frances "Sissy" Fahrenthold [*sic*], as governor in 1972, ad-miring her courage as she went around the state blithely committing politi-cal suicide almost everywhere she turned up." During the campaign, the ghost of Texas's first lady governor returned to haunt Mrs. Farenthold, a former state representative and den mother of the "Dirty Thirty" liberals in the House, at least in the pages of William F. Buckley's *National Review*. The periodical reported with an altogether straight face that "in last week's Democratic Primary for the gubernatorial nomination, predicted winner [Ben] Barnes trailed in third behind rancher Dolph Briscoe and reform can-didate, Mrs. Miriam A. Ferguson." Mrs. Farenthold reportedly reacted with a laugh at the *Review's* anachronism, saying: "You know, I know (Buckley's) family and I'm going to do something about this. That's out-dated me."[36]

Dolph Briscoe's wife Janey was so active in the first Briscoe-Farenthold skirmish that bumper stickers cropped up proclaiming: "If We're Going to Have a Woman Governor, We Should at Least Elect Her." In a January 27, 1975, article, "Texas: Boss Lady," *Newsweek* reported:

> Janey Briscoe, people say, is really the governor of Texas—her hus-band, Dolph, just happens to have his name on the door. People say

that because Janey has been known to stay in the governor's office all day and go over his mail in bed at night. She sits in on political confabs and interviews with reporters, and on her rare absences from hubby's side, she spends hours monitoring sessions of the legislature. "Every time I look up, she'll be sitting in the gallery," says one Republican state senator, "knitting and keeping score like Madame Defarge."

"Dolph is a humble person," Mrs. Briscoe told *Newsweek*'s Peter S. Greenberg. "He has no powerful ambitions." As for herself, she conceded: "I don't like the traditional role of the political wife. I do, however, like the possibilities of what can be done from within that role." Senator Oscar Mauzy recalled: "Last session, we were having trouble finding support money for our committee on the aging. It was Janey who unplugged the bottlenecks. She's a very astute political woman." Not all her actions, however, sat well with Texas politicos, noted *Newsweek*. "After Briscoe's first inauguration, legislators arrived for the traditional party at the Executive Mansion and found that the usual bourbon, branch, and back slapping had been replaced by family entertainment, including a merry-go-round, dancing clowns, and fruit punch. Baptist Janey has kept liquor out of the governor's mansion ever since." Ma Ferguson would have approved.[37]

Notes

Note: Because of the author's death, sources may be incomplete in a few cases.

Editor's Introduction

1. Norman D. Brown, *Hood, Bonnet, and Little Brown Jug: Texas Politics, 1921–1928* (College Station: Texas A&M University Press, 1984), 10, 422 (hereafter cited throughout the notes as Brown, *Hood, Bonnet*).

2. The U.S. Census Bureau did not track Hispanic origins in the 1940 census, but 736,433 of the white population identified Spanish as their first language. According to that measurement 4,751,112 white Texans did not have Hispanic origins. The remaining 0.1 percent of the population identified as American Indians, Eskimos, and Aleuts (1,103 people) and as Asians and Pacific Islanders (1,785 people). U.S. census data does not specify the number of people of Hispanic origins living in rural areas in 1930. U.S. Census Bureau, *1930 Census of Population and Housing*, vol. 1, 1055, 1092–1094; U.S. Census Bureau, *Sixteenth Census of the United States—1940—Population*, vol. 2: *Characteristics of the Population*, part 6, 763; Campbell Gibson and Kay Jung, *Historical Census Statistics on Population Totals by Race, 1790 to 1990, and by Hispanic Origin, 1970 to 1990, for the United States, Regions, Divisions, and States*, Population Division, Working Paper No. 56 (Washington, DC: U.S. Census Bureau, 2002).

3. Several books address the South and Texas during the Great Depression: Roger Biles, *The South and the New Deal* (Lexington: University of Kentucky Press, 1994); Walter L. Buenger, *The Path to a Modern South: Northeast Texas between Reconstruction and the Great Depression* (Austin: University of Texas Press, 2001); James Smallwood, *The Great Recovery: The New Deal in Texas* (Boston: American Press, 1983); Donald W. Whisenhunt, *The Depression in Texas: The Hoover Years* (New York: Garland , 1983). For general overviews of Texas during the Great Depression, see Randolph B. Campbell, *Gone to Texas: A History of the Lone Star State* (New York: Oxford University Press, 2003), 377ff; Ben H. Procter, "Great Depression," *Handbook of Texas Online*, accessed August 08, 2017, http://www.tshaonline.org /handbook/online/articles/npg01 (hereafter cited as *HTO*).

4. Brown, *Hood, Bonnet*, 7. Brown relies on the work of George Brown Tindall for his definition of business progressivism; see Tindall, "Business Progressivism: Southern Politics in the Twenties," *South Atlantic Quarterly* 62 (Winter 1963): 92–106; and Tindall, *The Emergence of the New South, 1913–1945* (Baton Rouge: Louisiana State Press, 1967). Here I use the

term "progressive" to refer to the progressive movement of the early twentieth century, which would not have been progressive concerning issues of race or ethnicity. Brown, however, did not follow this practice in *Hood, Bonnet* so I have elected to leave his usage in the body of the text below. It must be emphasized, however, that most white Texans called "progressive" in the 1930s did not have in mind a progressive agenda in keeping with twenty-first-century notions of social justice.

5. Brown discusses the situation of Texas roads in chapter 2 and the 1930 primary race in chapter 3. My note 38 in chapter 2 discusses the history of Texas road construction in brief.

6. Brown, *Hood, Bonnet*, 10.

7. Brown left behind this manuscript without a title, so I had to decide which images best reflect the themes of this sequel. Given the persistence of the Fergusons and Prohibition into the 1930s, I considered using "bonnet" and "little brown jug" again, but I decided to use new, if related, images because I wanted this volume to stand on its own.

8. Dick Vaughan, "Jim Ferguson's Reminiscences," no. 12, *Houston Press*, October 17, 1932.

9. Brown discusses this transfer from the Fergusons to O'Daniel in the epilogue to this book.

10. Miriam Ferguson was successful in getting a bill passed in the Texas legislature to allow for the provision of direct relief. Evidence of corruption—using federal monies to fund the campaign for the bill—killed the program before it could be enacted. See chapter 8 in this book.

11. Brown notes that Allred was the last progressive governor in Texas (see chapter 8). For more on Allred, see Floyd F. Ewing, "Allred, James Burr V," *HTO*, accessed August 19, 2017, http://www.tshaonline.org/handbook/online/articles/fal42. On O'Daniel and old-age pensions, see the epilogue to this book.

12. See chapter 4 in this volume.

13. Walter L. Buenger argues that approaches to Texas history currently fall into three major streams or "truths": updated traditionalists, persistent revisionists, and cultural constructionists. The cultural constructionist approach, which implements insights historians gain from exploring cultural contexts, developed in Texas studies beginning the 1990s. Prior to that trend, histories of Texas tended to emphasize its nineteenth-century past, in particular the heroic actions of white men. When Brown wrote *Hood, Bonnet* and drafted this manuscript, writing about almost any twentieth-century Texas historical topic constituted a unique contribution. See Walter L. Buenger, "Three Truths in Texas," in *Beyond Texas through Time: Breaking Away from Past Interpretations*, eds. Walter L. Buenger and Arnoldo De Leon (College Station: Texas A&M University Press, 2011), 1–49. I have found confirmation of his generalizations in Gregg Cantrell and Elizabeth Hayes Turner, eds., *Lone Star Pasts: Memory and History in Texas* (College Station: Texas A&M University Press, 2007); Light Townsend Cummins and Mary L. Scheer, eds. *Texan Identities: Moving Beyond Myth, Memory, and Fallacy in Texas History* (Denton: University of North Texas Press, 2016); and John W. Storey and Mary L. Kelley, eds., *Twentieth-Century Texas: A Social and Cultural History* (Denton: University of North Texas Press, 2008). For a work with a useful bibliographic overview of recent Texas historiography, see Bruce A. Glasrud, Light Townsend Cummins, and Cary D. Wintz, eds., *Discovering Texas History* (Norman: University of Oklahoma Press, 2014).

14. The following works all show in some way the importance of either state or federal intervention to the modernizing development of Texas: John A. Adams Jr., *Damming the*

Colorado: The Rise of the Lower Colorado River Authority, 1933–1939 (College Station: Texas A&M University Press, 1990); Cynthia A. Brandimarte, *Texas State Parks and the CCC: The Legacy of the Civilian Conservation Corps* (College Station: Texas A&M University Press, 2013); William R. Childs, *The Texas Railroad Commission: Understanding Regulation in America to the Mid-Twentieth Century* (College Station: Texas A&M University Press, 2005); Debra Ann Reid, *Reaping a Greater Harvest: African Americans, the Extension Service, and Rural Reform in Jim Crow Texas* (College Station: Texas A&M University Press, 2007); Richard Schroeder, *Texas Signs On: The Early Days of Radio and Television* (College Station: Texas A&M University Press, 1998); James Wright Steely, *Parks for Texas: Enduring Landscapes of the New Deal* (Austin: University of Texas Press, 1999); Keith Joseph Volanto, *Texas, Cotton, and the New Deal* (College Station: Texas A&M University Press, 2005); Carol A. Weisenberger, *Dollars and Dreams: The National Youth Administration in Texas* (New York: P. Lang, 1994).

15. Nancy Beck Young explores the topic of modernization in Texas in "Beyond Parochialism: Modernization and Texas Historiography" in Buenger and De Leon, *Beyond Texas through Time*, 221–270. Works that explore various facets of modernization in Texas include Patrick L. Cox, *The First Texas News Barons* (Austin: University of Texas Press, 2005); Diana Davids Olien and Roger M. Olien, *Oil in Texas: The Gusher Age, 1895–1945* (Austin: University of Texas Press, 2002); Schroeder, *Texas Signs On*; George Ernest Webb, *Science in the American Southwest: A Topical History* (Tucson: University of Arizona Press, 2002).

16. Kenneth B. Ragsdale, *The Year America Discovered Texas: Centennial '36* (College Station: Texas A&M University Press, 1987).

17. During the 1930s the Democratic Party's hold over the South, if anything, strengthened. Scholars of southern political history have traced this phenomenon since the 1940s, beginning with V. O. Key's *Southern Politics in State and Nation* (New York: Random House, 1949). Key claims that race, the Civil War and its aftermath, and the failed Populist revolt of the 1890s were the major defining issues of southern politics, and he contended that southerners used the Democratic Party to maintain white control over governments (5–6, 8–9). In the late 1980s, as Democratic control clearly began to slip, scholars attempted to understand the decline of "one-party rule" in the South, and they connected this trend to the collapse of the New Deal political coalition and the political turmoil of the 1960s. See Kari Frederickson, *The Dixiecrat Revolt and the End of the Solid South, 1932–1968* (Chapel Hill: University of North Carolina Press, 2001); Dewey W. Grantham, *The Life and Death of the Solid South: A Political History* (Lexington: University of Kentucky Press, 1988); Alexander P. Lamis, *The Two-Party South*, expanded ed. (New York: Oxford University Press, 1988). For journalistic overviews of this transformation, see Nate Cohn, "Demise of the Southern Democrat Is Now Nearly Complete," *New York Times*, March 4, 2014; Lawrence Wright, "America's Future Is Texas," *New Yorker*, July 10, 17, 2017.

18. I don't mean to suggest that the move to the Republican Party by the majority of white Texans and its embrace of far-right conservatism are necessarily the same process, although they are certainly interrelated. The evolution of the Republican Party into its current ultra-conservative form is a distinct story—though one in which Texas plays a central role. On the Republican Party's move to the right more generally, see, for instance, Robert Horwitz, *America's Right: Anti-Establishment Conservatism from Goldwater to the Tea Party* (Malden, MA: Polity, 2013). On the history of far-right conservatism in Texas, see David O'Donald Cullen and Kyle G. Wilkison, eds., *The Texas Right: The Radical Roots of Lone Star Conservatism* (College Station: Texas A&M University Press, 2014); Sean P. Cunningham,

Cowboy Conservatism: Texas and the Rise of the Modern Right (Lexington: University Press of Kentucky, 2010); Ricky F. Dobbs, *Yellow Dogs and Republicans: Allan Shivers and Texas Two-Party Politics* (College Station: Texas A&M University Press, 2005); George N. Green, *The Establishment in Texas Politics: The Primitive Years, 1938–1957* (Norman: University of Oklahoma Press, 1979); Paul Pressler, *The Texas Regulars: The Beginning of the Move to the Republican Party in Texas* (Garland, TX: Hannibal Books, 2001); Donald W. Whisenhunt, ed., *The Depression in the Southwest* (Port Washington, NY: Kennikat Press, 1980). On the history of conservative evangelicalism in Texas, see Cullen and Wilkison, *The Texas Right*; Alan J. Watt, *Farm Workers and the Churches: The Movement in California and Texas* (College Station: Texas A&M University Press, 2010); Robert Wuthnow, *Rough Country: How Texas Became America's Most Powerful Bible-Belt State* (Princeton, NJ: Princeton University Press, 2014).

19. Neil Foley's work examines the racial dynamics of cotton farming in Central Texas that led to a specific construction of whiteness. See *The White Scourge: Mexicans, Blacks, and Poor Whites in Texas Cotton Culture* (Berkeley: University of California Press, 1997). Other works that consider the construction of race include Jason McDonald, *Racial Dynamics in Early Twentieth-Century Austin, Texas* (Lanham, MD: Lexington Books, 2012); Martha Menchaca, *Naturalizing Mexican Immigrants: A Texas History* (Austin: University of Texas Press, 2011); Cynthia Skove Nevels, *Lynching to Belonging: Claiming Whiteness through Racial Violence* (College Station: Texas A&M University Press, 2007).

20. According to Martin Crawford, in the 1930s the overall number of farmers declined by 8.1 percent, as compared to African American farmers, who declined by 22.4 percent. See "The Legal System and Sharecropping: An Opposing View," in *Race and Class in the American South since 1890*, eds. Melvyn Stokes and Rick Halpern (Oxford: Berg, 1994), 104. Crawford calculates these figures based on data collected in Gilbert S. Fite, *Cotton Fields No More: Southern Agriculture, 1865–1980* (Lexington: University Press of Kentucky, 1984), 238. On farming and sharecropping and the massive alterations in agricultural practices and rural society in the South and in Texas between 1900 and 1960, see Roger Biles, *The South and the New Deal* (Lexington: University of Kentucky Press, 1994); Pete Daniel, *Breaking the Land: The Transformation of Cotton, Tobacco, and Rice Cultures since 1880* (Urbana: University of Illinois Press, 1985); Pete Daniel, "The Legal Basis of Agrarian Capitalism: The South Since 1933," in *Race and Class in the American South*, eds. Stokes and Halpern, 79–102; Foley, *White Scourge*; Jack Kirby, *Rural Worlds Lost: The American South, 1920–1960* (Baton Rouge: Louisiana State University Press, 1987); Bernadette Pruitt, *The Other Great Migration: The Movement of Rural African Americans to Houston, 1900–1941* (College Station: Texas A&M University Press, 2013); David Montejano, *Anglos and Mexicans in the Making of Texas, 1836–1986* (Austin: University of Texas Press, 1987); Reid, *Reaping a Greater Harvest*; Zaragosa Vargas, *Labor Rights Are Civil Rights: Mexican American Workers in Twentieth-Century America* (Princeton, NJ: Princeton University Press, 2005); Watt, *Farm Workers and the Churches*; Volanto, *Texas, Cotton, and the New Deal*; Emilio Zamora, *The World of the Mexican Worker in Texas* (College Station: Texas A&M University Press, 1993).

21. Julia Kirk Blackwelder, *Women of the Depression: Caste and Culture in San Antonio, 1929–1939* (College Station: Texas A&M University Press, 1999); Pruitt, *Other Great Migration*; Reid, *Reaping a Greater Harvest*.

22. Charles L. Zelden, *The Battle for the Black Ballot: Smith v. Allwright and the Defeat of the Texas All-White Primary* (Lawrence: University Press of Kansas, 2004); Will Guzman, *Civil Rights in the Texas Borderlands: Dr. Lawrence A. Nixon and Black Activism* (Urbana:

University of Illinois Press, 2015); Darlene Clark Hine, *Black Victory: The Rise and Fall of the White Primary in Texas*, rev. ed. (Columbia: University of Missouri Press, 2003).

23. LULAC has had a bad reputation among scholars of the Chicano movement because its middle-class leadership emphasized its white identity—in order to distinguish Mexican Americans from African Americans—and often held classist views of poorer Mexicans and Mexican Americans. Scholars Cynthia E. Orozco and Craig A. Kaplowitz have argued, however, that LULAC was nevertheless an important organization for the advancement of Mexican American rights, and its poor reputation, while not totally unjustified, has been overstated. See Craig A. Kaplowitz, *LULAC, Mexican Americans, and National Policy* (College Station: Texas A&M University Press, 2005); Cynthia E. Orozco, *No Mexicans, Women, or Dogs Allowed: The Rise of the Mexican American Civil Rights Movement* (Austin: University of Texas Press, 2009). Other works that discuss the significance of LULAC include Carlos K. Blanton, *George I. Sanchez: The Long Fight for Mexican American Integration* (New Haven, CT: Yale University Press, 2015); Mario T. Garcia, *Mexican Americans: Leadership, Ideology, and Identity, 1930–1960* (New Haven, CT: Yale University Press, 1989); Benjamin Heber Johnson, *Revolution in Texas: How a Forgotten Rebellion and Its Bloody Suppression Turned Mexicans into Americans* (New Haven, CT: Yale University Press, 2003); Benjamin Marquez, *LULAC: The Evolution of a Mexican American Political Organization* (Austin: University of Texas Press, 1993); Judith N. McArthur and Harold L. Smith, *Texas through Women's Eyes: The Twentieth-Century Experience* (Austin: University of Texas Press, 2010); Emilio Zamora, *Claiming Rights and Righting Wrongs in Texas: Mexican Workers and Job Politics During World War II* (College Station: Texas A&M University Press, 2009). Some references cited here were found thanks to Cynthia E. Orozco, "League of United Latin American Citizens," *HTO*, accessed August 7, 2017, http://www.tshaonline.org/handbook/online/articles/wel01.

24. There was one critical court case for Mexican Americans in 1930s Texas. In *Independent School District v. Salvatierra*, Mexican American citizens of Del Rio, Texas, led by Jesus Salvatierra and LULAC-sponsored attorneys, argued that the school district's attempt to build new school buildings would perpetuate the segregation of Mexican-heritage children beyond the third grade—and that this decision was based on race. The local trial judge agreed with Salvatierra, but "the Texas court of appeals overturned the decision." Kaplowitz, *LULAC*, 33.

25. Eventually members of LULAC would oppose poll taxes, too, but earlier on their primary goal was to foster Mexican American political participation. See Orozco, "League of United Latin American Citizens," *HTO*.

26. The history of the exclusion of agricultural and domestic workers—and the racist implications of this decision—is now widely known among scholars. For overviews of the legal history of this issue, see Marc Linder, "Farm Workers and the Fair Labor Standards Act: Racial Discrimination in the New Deal," *Texas Law Review* 65 (1987): 1335–1393; Juan F. Perea, "The Echoes of Slavery: Recognizing the Racist Origins of the Agricultural and Domestic Worker Exclusion from the National Labor Relations Act," *Ohio State Law Journal* 72, no. 1 (2011): 95–138. Works on labor history in Texas more generally include Bruce A. Glasrud and James C. Maroney, eds., *Texas Labor History* (College Station: Texas A&M University Press, 2013); Blackwelder, *Women of the Depression*; Foley, *White Scourge*; Sonia Hernandez, "Women's Labor and Activism in the Greater Mexican Borderlands, 1910–1930," in *War along the Border: The Mexican Revolution and Tejano Communities*, eds. Arnoldo De Leon, Sonia Hernandez, and Thomas H. Kreneck (College Station: Texas A&M University

Press, 2011), 176–204; Montejano, *Anglos and Mexicans*; Reid, *Reaping a Greater Harvest*; Rebecca Sharpless, *Fertile Ground, Narrow Choices: Women on Texas Cotton Farms, 1900–1940* (Chapel Hill: University of North Carolina Press, 1999); Thad Sitton and James H. Conrad, *Nameless Towns: Texas Sawmill Communities, 1880–1942* (Austin: University of Texas Press, 1998); Vargas, *Labor Rights Are Civil Rights*; Watt, *Farm Workers and the Churches*; Zamora, *World of the Mexican Worker*.

27. On the importance of labor organizing to Mexican American civil rights, see Vargas, *Labor Rights Are Civil Rights*. On Emma Tenayuca and the pecan-shellers' strike, see Joseph Abel, "Tejana Radical: Emma Tenayuca and the San Antonio Labor Movement during the Great Depression," in *Texas Labor History*, eds. Bruce A. Glasrud and James C. Maroney (College Station: Texas A&M University Press, 2013), 219–243; Richard Croxdale, "Pecan-Shellers' Strike," *HTO*, accessed August 7, 2017, http://www.tshaonline.org/handbook/on line/articles/oep01; R. Matt Abigail and Jazmin León, "Tenayuca, Emma Beatrice," *HTO*, accessed August 7, 2017, http://www.tshaonline.org/handbook/online/articles/fte41; Gabriela González, "Carolina Munguia and Emma Tenayuca: The Politics of Benevolence and Radical Reform, 1930s," *Frontiers: A Journal of Women's Studies* 24 (2003): 200–229; Zaragosa Vargas, "Tejana Radical: Emma Tenayuca and the San Antonio Labor Movement during the Great Depression," *Pacific Historical Review* 66 (November 1997): 553–580; Vargas, *Labor Rights Are Civil Rights*, 134 ff. On the lives of Mexican American workers more broadly, see Zamora, *World of the Mexican Worker*.

28. See Max Krochmal, *Blue Texas: The Making of a Multiracial Democratic Coalition in the Civil Rights Era* (Chapel Hill: University of North Carolina Press, 2016).

29. *Dallas Morning News*, February 2, 1930 (hereafter cited as *DMN*). See Brown's discussion of this event in chapter 1 of this volume.

30. See chapter 1 in this volume. See also Nancy Beck Young, *Lou Henry Hoover: Activist First Lady* (Lawrence: University of Kansas Press, 2004), 65–71. Young notes that Jessie DePriest's visit to the White House was one of the first instances of African American visitors to the White House since 1901, when Theodore Roosevelt had hosted Booker T. Washington. This combined with the fact that white women were present when Jessie DePriest visited made some northern and most southern whites very angry that the racial hierarchy of Jim Crow was being undermined by the president's wife.

31. See especially chapters 7 and 8 and the epilogue in this volume.

32. The consensus among historians is that on the national level women's political activism was hampered by a fracturing of the leadership after the passage of the Nineteenth Amendment. This is not to say that women stopped organizing politically but simply that there was no cohesion among national leadership. Women in Texas, as Brown showed in *Hood, Bonnet*, were very active politically in the 1920s, pushing a reform agenda. Members of the Joint Legislative Council, also known as the Petticoat Lobby, did not continue to work together in the 1930s, as they began to disagree about the best legislative agenda to pursue. The onset of the Great Depression also may have slowed women's political efforts, as many women needed first to provide for themselves and their families during challenging economic times. Blackwelder, *Women of the Depression*; Sherilyn Brandenstein, "Joint Legislative Council," *HTO*, accessed August 8, 2017, http://www.tshaonline.org/handbook/online /articles/wejfg; McArthur and Smith, *Texas through Women's Eyes*, 61–99; Merline Pitre and Bruce A. Glasrud, eds., *Black Women in Texas History* (College Station: Texas A&M University Press, 2008), 129–158.

33. For more on Norris, see chapter 1 of this work, and especially my footnote 25. Vari-

ous recent works discuss the importance of evangelicalism to the political culture of Texas. See, for example, Samuel K. Tullock, "'He, Being Dead, Yet Speaketh': J. Frank Norris and the Texas Religious Right at Midcentury," in Cullen and Wilkison, *Texas Right*, 51–67; Watt, *Farm Workers and the Churches*; Wuthnow, *Rough Country*.

34. Keith Volanto, "The Far Right in Texas Politics During the Roosevelt Era," in Cullen and Wilkison, *Texas Right*, 68–86.

35. Some works that discuss Texas's importance nationally include Anthony Champagne, Douglas B. Harris, and James W. Riddlesperger, *The Austin-Boston Connection: Five Decades of House Democratic Leadership, 1937–1989* (College Station: Texas A&M University Press, 2009); Lionel V. Patenaude, *Texans, Politics, and the New Deal* (New York: Garland, 1983); Donald W. Whisenhunt, ed., *The Depression in the Southwest* (Port Washington, NY: Kennikat Press, 1980); Nancy Beck Young, *Wright Patman: Populism, Liberalism, and the American Dream* (Dallas: Southern Methodist University Press, 2000).

36. I detail works written about the various governors, Moody, Sterling, Ferguson, and Allred, below, as their gubernatorial terms are discussed in succeeding chapters. Check the footnotes to those chapters for more information.

37. I discuss Green and scholarship related to his work in footnote 12 of the epilogue of this book.

38. Brown, *Hood, Bonnet*, 437.

39. Brown, *Hood, Bonnet*, 435–436. According to the Texas Alcoholic Beverage Commission, as of November 2016 there were seven totally dry counties remaining in Texas. The other fifty-three counties are wet, but wet ranges anywhere from allowing the sale of beer only to the sale of beer, wine, and liquor. For more information, see the Texas Alcoholic Beverage Commission website, "Wet and Dry Counties," accessed September 2, 2017, http://www.tabc.state.tx.us/local_option_elections/wet_and_dry_counties.asp. Texas still has blue laws that restrict the sale of beer before a certain time on Sundays and prevent the sale of wine and liquor on Sunday entirely. See chapter 105 of the Texas Alcoholic Beverage Code, accessed September 2, 2017, http://www.statutes.legis.state.tx.us/?link=AL.

40. Brown, *Hood, Bonnet*, 435.

41. Manny Fernandez, "Federal Judge Blocks Texas' Ban on 'Sanctuary Cities,'" *New York Times*, August 30, 2017. At time of writing, the Fifth Circuit Court of Appeals ruled that the State of Texas "can require local police to honor requests from federal immigration officers to hold suspects in jail." Zach Despart, "Fifth Circuit Rules Texas Police Must Start Honoring Immigrant Detainer Requests," *Houston Press*, September 26, 2017, http://www.houstonpress.com/news/federal-court-approves-parts-of-texas-sb-4-immigration-law-9823333.

42. Texans in the border region largely oppose this wall, as recent protests by local politicians and naturalists demonstrate. Fernando Alfonso III, "Plans for Donald Trump's Border Wall on Texas Wildlife Refuge in the Works," *Houston Chronicle*, July 31, 2017, http://www.chron.com/news/houston-texas/article/Plans-for-Donald-Trump-s-border-wall-on-Texas-11720076.php; Michael Hardy, "In South Texas, Threat of Border Wall Unites Naturalists and Politicians," *New York Times*, August 13, 2017, https://www.nytimes.com/2017/08/13/us/in-south-texas-threat-of-border-wall-unites-naturalists-and-politicians.html?mcubz=3.

43. Ashley Lopez, "Advocates: Poor Women Will Be Most Affected by Texas' Medicaid Cuts to Planned Parenthood," KUT, accessed September 2, 2017, http://kut.org/post/advocates-poor-women-will-be-most-affected-texas-medicaid-cuts-planned-parenthood.

44. Alexa Ura and Ryan Murphy, "Here's What the Texas Bathroom Bill Means in Plain

English," *Texas Tribune*, June 9, 2017, https://apps.texastribune.org/texas-bathroom-bill -annotated; Lauren McGaughy, "The Texas Bathroom Bill Is Dead — For Now," *DMN*, August 15, 2017, https://www.dallasnews.com/news/texas-legislature/2017/08/15/transgender-tex ans-cautiously-optimistic-bathroom-bill-declared-dead-now; Anna M. Tinsley, "Will Bathroom Politics Push Texas aside in Amazon's Search for Second Home?," *Star-Telegram*, accessed October 13, 2017, http://www.star-telegram.com/news/politics-government/state -politics/article173521216.html.

45. Max Krochmal argues, however, that this group of political allies is not unprecedented in Texas history. Rather, important examples of interracial cooperation, especially among African Americans, Mexican Americans, organized labor of all races, and white liberals came together in fits and starts in response to the New Deal. This coalition played a critical role in the election of John F. Kennedy and, to a lesser extent, in garnering support for Lyndon B. Johnson's liberal agenda in 1960s Texas. Krochmal, *Blue Texas*.

46. Nate Cohn, "How a Ruling on Texas Districts Could Help Reshape Congress," *New York Times*, July 27, 2017, https://www.nytimes.com/2017/07/27/upshot/how-a-ruling-on -texas-districts-could-help-reshape-congress.html?mcubz=3; Alexa Ura, "U.S. Supreme Court Temporarily Blocks Ruling against Texas House Map," *Texas Tribune*, August 31, 2017, https://www.texastribune.org/2017/08/31/us-supreme-court-temporarily-blocks-rul ing-against-texas-house-map; Adam Liptak, "Supreme Court Upholds Texas Voting Maps That Were Called Discriminatory," *New York Times*, June 25, 2018, https://www.nytimes .com/2018/06/25/us/politics/supreme-court-texas-gerrymandering.html.

47. Lawrence Wright, "America's Future Is Texas," *New Yorker*, July 10 and 17, 2017, http://www.newyorker.com/magazine/2017/07/10/americas-future-is-texas. Wright has also updated this argument in a recently published book, *God Save Texas: A Journey into the Soul of the Lone Star State* (New York: Knopf, 2018). Other journalists have also written — with varying degrees of optimism or pessimism — about the importance of Texas to understanding the future of the United States. See, for example, Gail Collins, *As Goes Texas: How the Lone Star State Hijacked the American Agenda* (New York: Norton, 2012); and Erica Grieder, *Big, Hot, Cheap, and Right: What America Can Learn from the Strange Genius of Texas* (New York: Public Affairs, 2013).

Chapter 1: Tom Cat Lands on His Feet

1. Editor's note: Creager was singled out by President Harding to be his leading "referee" in Texas in 1921. See Brown, *Hood, Bonnet*, 121 ff.

2. *Dallas Morning News*, November 8, 1928 (hereafter *DMN*); Love to Herbert Hoover, November 7, 1928, Thomas Bell Love, Campaign and Transition Papers, 1928–1929, Herbert Hoover Presidential Library, West Branch, Iowa (hereafter cited as Hoover PL); Alvin Moody to Hoover, Hoover PL; Creager to Lawrence Richey, November 22, 1928, Pre-Presidential Correspondence, R. B. Creager, Hoover PL.

3. Love to William Gibbs McAdoo, November 16, 1928; Alvin Moody Circular Letter to anti-Tammany Democrats, Thomas B. Love Collection, Dallas Historical Society (hereafter cited as Love Collection, DHS).

4. Alvin Moody to Love, November 16, 1928, Love Collection, DHS; Love to Moody, November 17, 1928, in ibid. [Editor's note: Alvin Moody was not related to Governor Dan Moody. For more about Alvin Moody, see Brown, *Hood, Bonnet*, 402–403.]

5. John Lee Smith to Love, November 9, 1928; J. W. Sullivan to Love, same date; Love to Joseph F. Meyers, November 17, 1928; E. E. Townsend to Love, November 8, 1928; Love to Townsend, November 16, 1928, all in Love Collection, DHS.

6. Love to George Fort Milton, November 9, 1929; J. W. Sullivan to Love, same date; Love to Joseph F. Meyers, November 17, 1928; E. E. Townsend to Love, November 8, 1928; Love to Townsend, November 16, 1928, all in Love Collection, DHS.

7. Editor's note: On Raskob's nomination, see Brown, *Hood, Bonnet*, 401.

8. Love to Daniel C. Roper, December 12, 1928; Love to M. D. Lightfoot, December 21, 1928, Love Collection, DHS.

9. J. F. Lucey to George Akerson, January 14, 1929; Lawrence Richey to Lucey, February 7, 1929, Pre-Presidential, General Correspondence, J. F. Lucey, Hoover PL.

10. Editor's note: I was not able to confirm Brown's source for this paragraph.

11. *DMN*, February 3, 1929.

12. *DMN*, January 19, February 9, 1929. Voting with Love were Cousins, Holbrook, McFarlane, Parrish, and Pollard.

13. *DMN*, February 12, 1929.

14. *DMN*, February 13, 1929. The bill was signed by Wirtz, Russek, Martin, Stevenson, Berkleu, Beck, Parr, Miller, Hornsby, Gainer, Small, Cunningham, Patton, Holbrook, Thomason, and Williamson.

15. *DMN*, February 27, 1929. Voting to engross the bill were Beck, Berkley, Cunningham, DeBerry, Gainer, Holbrook, Hornsby, Martin, Miller, Moore, Patton, Russek, Stevenson, Thomason, Williamson, and Wirtz; the nays were Greer, Hyer, Love, McFarlane, Pollard, Westbrook, and Woodward. Parrish and Cousins, who would have voted no, were paired with Small and Parr, who would have voted yes. Moore left the chamber and did not vote on third reading. [Editor's note: According to the Texas legislature's website, pairing is "a procedure for voting whereby, under a formal agreement between two members, a member who will be present for a vote agrees with a member who will be absent for a vote that the member who is present will not vote but will be 'present, not voting.'" The website explains that "when two members are paired, the journal reflects how each member would have voted. Two members may be paired only if one would have voted 'aye' and one would have voted 'nay' on a particular measure or motion." Texas House of Representatives, "Legislative Glossary," accessed January 3, 2019, https://house.texas.gov/about-us/legislative-glossary/.]

16. *DMN*, March 6, 1929.

17. Editor's note: For Moody and the Beaumont Convention, see Brown, *Hood, Bonnet*, 390ff.

18. *DMN*, March 9, 1929.

19. *DMN*, March 24, 1929.

20. *DMN*, April 3, 1929; Fred Gantt, *The Chief Executive in Texas: A Study in Gubernatorial Leadership* (Austin: University of Texas Press, 1964), 303–304; Records of Dan Moody, Texas Office of the Governor, Archives and Information Services Division, Texas State Library and Archives Commission (hereafter cited as Moody Papers, TSL).

21. Moody to Peter Molyneaux, April 8, 1929, Moody Papers, TSL.

22. *DMN*, April 3, 1929.

23. *Houston Gargoyle*, April 7, 1929.

24. *Ferguson Forum*, April 11, 1929.

25. *Houston Gargoyle*, June 23, 1929; O. B. Colquitt to J. Frank Norris, June 25, 1929, J. Frank Norris Papers, Southern Baptist Historical Library and Archives, Nashville, Tennes-

see (hereafter cited as Norris Papers). [Editor's note: Rev. J. Frank Norris played a central role in "loosening" the commitment of many Texans to the Democratic Party and encouraging its members' embrace of fundamentalist Protestantism. He supported Hoover in the 1928 election and warned fundamentalist Baptists that Democratic nominee Al Smith, a Catholic, would undermine family values because of his personal lack of support for Prohibition. Throughout his lifetime Norris flip-flopped between parties in his endorsement for presidential candidates—tending to prefer to support winning candidates rather than aligning with a particular party. See Samuel K. Tullock, "'He, Being Dead, Yet Speaketh': J. Frank Norris and the Texas Religious Right at Midcentury," in *The Texas Right: The Radical Roots of Lone Star Conservatism*, eds. David O'Donald Cullen and Kyle G. Wilkison (College Station: Texas A&M University Press, 2014), 51–67; and Robert Wuthnow, *Rough Country: How Texas Became America's Most Powerful Bible-Belt State* (Princeton, NJ: Princeton University Press, 2014).]

26. Norris to James Vance, June 20, 1929; Norris to Mrs. Herbert Hoover, July 12, 1929, Reels 5, 8, 12, Norris Papers. [Editor's note: Presumably Raskob was the "issue," because, as chairman of the Democratic National Convention and a strong supporter of Al Smith, he would have been behind efforts to discredit the Hoover administration in the South.]

27. E. P. Curtis to Neff, January 4, 1929; Thomas D. Barton to Neff, January 16, 1929; Joe T. Robinson to H. C. Couch, February 5, 1929; Neff to G. Wallace Hanger, February 7, 1929, all in the Pat M. Neff Collection, Texas Collection, Baylor University (hereafter cited as Neff Collection).

28. Tom Connally to Neff, December 17, 1928; Earle Mayfield to Neff, December 26, 1928, Neff Collection.

29. Neff to R. B. Walthall, January 3, 1929; Walthall to Neff; Neff to Joe Robinson, December 26, 1928; Neff to Burton K. Wheeler, December 27, 1928; Neff to James E. Watson, February 5, 1929, Box 125, all in the Neff Collection. (There are more than a dozen letters from Neff to Alabamians in Box 125 of the Neff Collection.)

30. Mayfield to Love, January 3, 1929, Love Collection, DHS.

31. Editor's note: Norris is referring to Senator Borah's speech in favor of Herbert Hoover given in Dallas on October 22, 1928. See Brown, *Hood, Bonnet*, 415.

32. Norris to W. H. Doak, January 10, 1929; Norris to George Akerson, January 18, 1929, Reels 7, 12, Norris Papers.

33. Neff to Herbert Hoover, March 15, 1929; R. B. Walthall to Hoover, March 21, 1929; Tom Connally to R. B. Walthall, March 25, 1929, Neff Collection. Memo on telephone call from R. B. Creager, March 5, 1929, Presidential Papers, Individual, R. B. Creager, Hoover PL.

34. *DMN*, April 27, May 1, 11, 1929; Colquitt to Dan Moody, May 8, 1929; Moody to Colquitt, May 9, 1929, Moody Papers, TSL; O. B. Colquitt to J. T. Bowman, May 13, 1929; Love to Colquitt, May 9, 1929, Oscar Branch Colquitt Papers, 1873–1941, Dolph Briscoe Center for American History, University of Texas at Austin (hereafter cited as Colquitt Papers, BCAH).

35. Editor's note: In the manuscript draft, Brown had repeated the citation in note 34 on this note. I was not able to verify the original sources for note 35.

36. R. B. Creager to Herbert Hoover, March 6, 1929, Presidential Papers—Subject—Republican National Committee Texas, Hoover PL; *DMN*, July 15, 1929.

37. Editor's note: Cato Sells had been a central figure in the Wilson administration, and he played a key role in helping to garner Texas's votes for William Gibbs McAdoo in the Democratic primaries of 1920 and 1924. See Brown, *Hood, Bonnet*, 8 ff.

38. Alvin Moody to R. B. Kreager [*sic*], March 30, 1929; Moody to Charles Curtis, same

date; Moody to Walter H. Newton, April 26, 1929; J. F. Lucey to Lawrence Richey, May 1, 1929; Memorandum, W.H.N., May 7, 1929; Love to Newton, September 5, 1929; Newton to Love, September 14, 1929, all in Presidential Papers—State File—Texas, Hoover PL.

39. J. F. Lucey to Ray Lyman Wilbur, April 12, 1930; Alvin Moody to Walter H. Newton, April 14, 1930; Newton to Moody, April 18, 1930, Presidential Papers—State File—Texas, Hoover PL. In a telegram to Hoover, H. E. Exum, the Republican chairman in the 18th Congressional District of Texas, strongly opposed replacing George Hopkins with Sells, warning: "It will cause more dissension in our good organization in the state of Texas than any possible political move that could be made." Exum to Hoover, March 22, 1930, in ibid.

40. O. B. Colquitt to Walter H. Newton, July 22, 1929; J. F. Lucey to Newton, October 30, 1929; Newton to Lucey, November 5, 1929, Presidential Papers—State File—Texas, Hoover PL. The following year Colquitt incurred Lucey's displeasure by backing Democrat Ross Sterling for governor against the Republican nominee, William Talbot. "There was [*sic*] no more vicious attacks made upon the President while a candidate than were in Mr. Sterling's paper," he lectured the former governor, "and I do not see how you can consider you are supporting Hoover by assisting Sterling." Lucey to Colquitt, September 29, 1930, Colquitt Papers, BCAH.

41. *New York Times*, March 27, 1929; *DMN*, July 16, 1929.

42. Alvin Moody to Walter Newton, September 11, 1929; R. B. Creager to Newton, October 1929, Presidential Papers—State File—Texas, Hoover PL.

43. Alvin Moody to Thomas B. Love, October 1, 1929; Lucey to Ray Lyman Wilbur, April 12, 1930; Alvin Moody to Walter H. Newton, March 26, 1931, Presidential Papers—State File—Texas, Hoover PL.

44. Editor's note: Republican Senator George Moses called members of the progressive faction of the party "sons of the wild jackass" in response to his frustration over their disagreement over the Smoot-Harley Tariff. "Sons of the Wild Jackass," U.S. Senate History, accessed July 10, 2017, https://www.senate.gov/artandhistory/history/minute/Sons_of_the_Wild_Jackass.htm.

45. *New York Times*, February 24, 1929. [Editor's note: Harry M. Daugherty and Albert B. Falls were members of the Harding cabinet who later became embroiled in scandal. See Rosemary Stevens, *A Time of Scandal: Charles R. Forbes, Warren G. Harding, and the Making of the Veterans Bureau* (Baltimore: Johns Hopkins University Press, 2016), 187 ff.]

46. U.S. Congress, Senate Committee on Post Offices and Post Roads, Subcommittee on S. Res. 193, *Influencing Appointment to Postmasterships*, part 2, 70th Cong., 2nd sess., 1929, pp. 527, 545–547.

47. Smith W. Brookhart to Herbert Hoover, April 12, 1929, Presidential Papers—Subject—Republican National Committee—Texas, Hoover PL.

48. William Reynolds Sanford, "History of the Republican Party in the State of Texas" (master's thesis, University of Texas at Austin, 1954), 125–126.

49. *Influencing Appointment to Postmasterships*, part 2, 71st Cong., 1st and 2nd sess., 1930, pp. 1,509–1,533.

50. Creager to J. Frank Norris, July 14, 6, 1929, Reel 6, Norris Papers; Creager to Herbert Hoover, June 1, 14, December 23, 1929, Presidential Papers—Subject—Republican National Committee, Texas; Creager to Lawrence Richey, same date, Presidential Papers—Sec'y Files—Creager, Hoover PL. See also Creager to Newton, March 17, 1930, enclosing a clipping from the *Corpus Christi Caller* on Creager's efforts to make Texas a two-party state. Presidential Papers—Subject—Republican National Committee—Texas, in ibid. Creager also pub-

lished a two-part article in the *Houston Gargoyle* answering its recent editorial against his patronage system. R. B. Creager, "Mr. Creager's Case," *Houston Gargoyle*, May 11 and May 18, 1930.

51. Creager to Hoover, February 24, 1929; E. C. Toothman (Creager's secretary) to Hoover, February 26, 1929, Pre-Presidential Correspondence, R. B. Creager, J. F. Lucey to Ray Lyman Wilbur, April 12, 1930, Presidential Papers—State File—Texas, Hoover PL; Roger Olien, *From Token to Triumph: The Texas Republicans since 1920* (Dallas: Southern Methodist University Press, 1982), 56. In March 1930 Creager complained to Walter Newton that the president's delay in sending in the names of four Texas appointments would seriously affect not only Creager's prestige but that of the Republican organization in Texas. Creager to Newton, March 13, 1930, Presidential Papers—State File—Texas, Hoover PL.

52. Presidential Papers—Secretary's File—Orville Bullington, Hoover PL; *DMN*, December 10, 1930; Roger M. Olien, "The Republican Party of Texas, 1920–1961" (master's thesis, Brown University, Providence, RI, 1973), 83–84. [Editor's note: The Fourteenth and Fifteen Amendments were passed during the Reconstruction era and were then, and are now, considered crucial amendments for protecting the civil rights of African Americans and other minority groups in the United States. Orville Bullington's stated position that they ought to be repealed would have met staunch opposition from African Americans.]

53. William G. Shepherd, "Getting a Job for Jack," *Collier's* 83 (June 15, 1929): 8–9.

54. Owen P. White, "High-Handed and Hell-Bent," *Collier's* 83 (June 22, 1929): 8–9.

55. White, "High-Handed," 47–48. For a description of the 1929 election in Hidalgo County, see Dellos Urban Buckner, "Study of the Lower Rio Grande Valley as a Cultural Area" (master's thesis, University of Texas at Austin, 1929), 114–115. See also Myrtle B. Brown to Love, August 1, 1928, Love Collection, DHS.

56. Owen P. White, *Autobiography of a Durable Sinner* (New York: Putnams Sons, 1942), 221. In another book published three years later, White wrote: "It was a spectacular piece of graft; nothing that Jim Ferguson had ever done could even compare with it; yet, because it would be 'bad publicity for Texas' a correspondent of an Eastern magazine was urged by the highest authorities in Austin not to write an exposure article about it." *Texas: An Informal Biography* (New York: Putnams Sons, 1945), 225. [Editor's note: On White's life see Garna L. Christian, *El Paso's Muckraker: The Life of Owen P. White* (Albuquerque: University of New Mexico Press, 2015).]

57. *DMN*, August 4, 1929; *New York Times*, August 4, 1929; *Houston Gargoyle*, December 8, 1929.

58. White, *Autobiography*, 222–223, 239–243.

59. *DMN*, May 16, 1930; *New York Times*, May 16, 1930.

60. Ralph W. Steen, "A Political History of Texas, 1900–1930," in *Texas Democracy: A Centennial History of Politics and Personalities of the Texas Democratic Party, 1836–1936*, vol. 1, ed. Frank Carter Adams (Austin: Democratic Historical Assoc., 1937), 460; *DMN*, July 9, 1929; Frank C. Davis to Thomas B. Love, January 11, 1929; J. V. Hardy to Love, [March] 10, 1929; Love to Hardy, April 1, 1929, Love Collection, DHS; John Henry Kirby to Dan Moody, March 29, 1929, Moody Papers, TSL; *Ferguson Forum* 12, May 23, 1929; *Houston Gargoyle*, July 14, 1929.

61. *DMN*, July 4, 24, 1929; Love to Dr. O. R. Miller, July 5, 1929; Love to Ira Champion, August 1, 1929, Love Collection, DHS.

62. *Houston Gargoyle*, July 7, 1929.

63. *DMN*, July 18, 1929; J. Frank Norris to V. C. Gilbert, June 22, 1929, Reel 9; Norris to

John Box, June 28, 1929; Box to Norris, July 1, 1929, both Reel 3, Norris Papers. Vic Gilbert, a representative from Cisco, wrote Norris: "I have never seen Governor Miller the least bit intemperate in his habits in this regard. Under the circumstances I mentioned, had he been the least bit inclined, or had he indulged to any appreciable extent, I would have known it." Gilbert to Norris, June 21, 1929, Reel 9, Norris Papers.

64. Cecil Horne to Pat M. Neff, July 12, 1929; Mrs. T. A. Kindred to Neff, July 13, 1929; A. B. Reagan to Neff, July 20, 1929; H. S. Lattimore to Neff, same date; T. W. Davidson to Neff, July 23, 1929, all in the Neff Collection.

65. Charles E. Baughman to Thomas B. Love, August 13, 1929, Love Collection, DHS; Burris C. Jackson to Dan Moody, August 17, 1929; Moody to Jackson, August 19, 1929, Moody Papers, TSL.

66. H. W. Hoffer to Dan Moody, July 16, 1929; Moody to Hoffer, July 18, 1929; J. B. Cranfill to Moody, July 23, 1929, Moody Papers, TSL; *DMN*, July 12, 1929.

67. *DMN*, August 14, 1929. [Editor's note: In 1924, 73 percent of Texans who voted in the presidential election voted for Democratic candidate John W. Davis, whereas only 19.9 percent voted for Republican candidate Calvin Coolidge. In 1928, 51.7 percent of voters supported Hoover and 48.2 percent voted for Al Smith. It is impossible to discern from these numbers which voters might previously have voted Republican but chose to vote Democrat in 1928 or vice versa. Nevertheless, the dramatic increase in Republican votes is striking. Data collected from the American Presidency Project of the University of California at Santa Barbara, accessed September 21, 2017, http://www.presidency.ucsb.edu/index.php.]

68. *DMN*, September 4, 1929.

69. Editor's note: Daniel C. Roper, who had served in the Wilson administration, worked in Washington, DC, as a lawyer. He had been one of the central organizers behind William Gibbs McAdoo's failed bid for the presidential nomination for the 1920 election. Brown, *Hood, Bonnet*, 170 ff.

70. Roper to Love, September 4, 1929, Love Collection, DHS.

71. *DMN*, September 22, 1929.

72. Alvin Moody to Love, September 19, 1929, Love Collection, DHS; *DMN*, September 28, 1929.

73. *DMN*, October 7, 10, 1929; Alvin Moody to Love, October 2, 16, 1929, Love Collection, DHS. "Let the Tom Loves and the Alvin Moodys, the Frank Norrises and the John Stratons go their way with withever force they can muster," editorialized the *Houston Gargoyle*, "and good riddance to a party that calls Thomas Jefferson its father!" *Houston Gargoyle*, October 20, 1929.

74. Norton McGriffin to George Fort Milton, November 12, 1929, George Fort Milton Papers, 1828–1985, Manuscript Division, Library of Congress; *DMN*, November 26, 1929.

75. Love to Roper, December 16, 1929, Love Collection, DHS.

76. Love to Roper, December 19, 1929; Alvin Moody to Love, December 28, 1929, Love Collection, DHS.

77. *DMN*, January 7, 8, 9, 1930.

78. *DMN*, January 21, 22, 31, 1930.

79. *DMN*, February 1, 1930.

80. Allen V. Peden, "Texas Free-For-All," *Outlook and Independent* 155 (July 9, 1930): 381.

81. *DMN*, February 2, 1930.

82. Allen V. Peden, "Tom Love's Ejection," *Houston Gargoyle*, February 9, 1930.

83. Editor's note: After the ruling in *Nixon v. Herndon*, discussed above in the introduction, the Texas legislature passed a new law that enabled the Democratic Party to determine who its members could be. It was to this 1927 statute and party rule that Love referred—implying that the Renfro resolution was potentially broad enough to undo the other rule. The white primary, along with the poll tax, was one of the main methods employed by white Texans to prevent black citizens in their state from voting. See Will Guzman, *Civil Rights in the Texas Borderlands: Dr. Lawrence A. Nixon and Black Activism* (Urbana: University of Illinois Press, 2015); and Darlene Clark Hine, *Black Victory: The Rise and Fall of the White Primary in Texas*, rev. ed. (Columbia: University of Missouri Press, 2003).

84. *DMN*, February 3, 5, 1930.

85. *DMN*, February 8, 12, 15, 25, March 19, April 2, 16, 1930.

86. *DMN*, February 16, 1930.

87. *DMN*, February 18, March 4, July 5, 1930.

88. *Houston Gargoyle*, February 23, 1930.

89. J. B. Cranfill to George W. Armstrong, March 1, 1930, J. B. Cranfill Papers, 1844–1941, Dolph Briscoe Center for American History, University of Texas at Austin (hereafter cited as Cranfill Papers, BCAH).

90. Armstrong to Cranfill, March 1, 1930, Cranfill Papers, BCAH.

91. Armstrong to Alvin Moody, March 1, 1930; Cranfill to Armstrong, March 5 and 7, 1930, Cranfill Papers, BCAH; Love to Roper, March 25, 1930, Love Collection, DHS.

92. Love to George A. Carden, April 4, 1930, Love Collection, DHS; *DMN*, May 18, 1930; *Love v. Wilcox*, 28 S.W. (2d), 515.

93. *DMN*, May 18, 1930; Love to William G. McAdoo, May 30, 1930, Love Collection, DHS. On April 17 the Alabama Supreme Court had refused to stop the Democratic primary of August 12; the state Democratic Executive Committee had excluded as candidates Senator Thomas Hefflin and others who had bolted to Hoover in 1928. *DMN*, April 18, 1930.

94. *Ferguson Forum* 12, May 22, 1930. Ferguson begged his readers' pardon for mentioning the Tom Cat so much, "but Tom's political virtues bear such striking resemblance to that animal of the feline species that howls, bites and scratches on the back yard fence in the night time that unconsciously I find myself recurring to the resemblance of the two animals."

95. *DMN*, July 5, 7, 1930; Alvin S. Moody to Love, May 21, 1930, Love Collection, DHS.

96. *DMN*, July 5, 7, 1930.

Chapter 2: Daniel in the Legislative Lions' Den

1. *Journal of the House of Representatives of the Regular Session of the Forty-First Legislature Begun and Held at the City of Austin, January 8, 1929* (Austin: Von Boeckmann-Jones Co., 1929), 20–35 (hereafter cited as *House Journal*); Ralph W. Steen, "A Political History of Texas, 1900–1930," in *Texas Democracy: A Centennial History of Politics and Personalities of the Texas Democratic Party, 1836–1936*, vol. 1, ed. Frank Carter Adams (Austin: Democratic Historical Assoc., 1937), 456; *Dallas Morning News*, January 10, 16, 1929 (hereafter cited as *DMN*).

2. *Houston Gargoyle*, January 15, 1929.

3. *DMN*, January 7 (quotation), 9, 1929.

4. *House Journal*, 41st Leg., Reg. Sess., 5–6.

5. Woodward to Love, November 21, 1928, Thomas B. Love Collection, Dallas Historical

Society (hereafter cited as Love Collection, DHS); *Journal of the Senate of Texas Being the Regular Session of the Forty-First Legislature Begun and Held at the City of Austin, January 8, 1929* (Austin: A. C. Baldwin & Sons, 1929), 3 (hereafter cited as *Senate Journal*); *DMN*, January 8, 9 (second quotation), 1929.

6. J. Alton Burdine, "Shall Texas Reorganize?," *Southwest Review* 18 (Summer 1933): 409.

7. Moody's comments in this excerpt and the paragraphs following are found in *House Journal*, 41st Leg., Reg. Sess., 22–23.

8. Burdine, "Shall Texas Reorganize?," 410; Steen, "Political History of Texas," 456, 459.

9. Holliday to Moody, May 6, 1929, Records of Dan Moody, Texas Office of the Governor, Archives and Information Services Division, Texas State Library and Archives Commission (hereafter cited as Moody Papers, TSL); *House Journal*, 41st Leg., Reg. Sess., 31; *House Journal*, 41st Leg., 1st Called Sess., 92; J. M. Claunch, "The Fight for Civil Service in Texas," *Southwestern Social Science Quarterly* 24, no. 1 (1943): 51–57.

10. Editor's note: In recent years scholars have investigated the history of the prison system in Texas, as Texas in the twenty-first century leads the way—for better or for worse—in the prison industrial complex. Studies of the 1930s show, however, that in the mid-twentieth century, Texas was on the cutting edge of humane prison reform, especially in practices related to juvenile detention. See William S. Bush, *Who Gets a Childhood: Race and Juvenile Justice in Twentieth-Century Texas* (Athens: University of Georgia Press, 2010), 42–70. Paul M. Lucko has argued, however, that despite prison reform efforts during Dan Moody's administration, Texas failed to adopt prison reform in its entirety, thereby leaving the state open to "the most protracted prisoners' lawsuit in the nation's history." Lucko, "A Missed Opportunity: Texas Prison Reform During the Moody Administration," *Southwestern Historical Quarterly* 96, no. 1 (July 1992): 27–52. Other works examine the development of capital punishment and prison culture. See James W. Marquart, Sheldon Eckland-Olson, and Jonathan R. Sorenson, *The Rope, the Chair, and the Needle: Capital Punishment in Texas, 1923–1990* (Austin: University of Texas Press, 1994); Mitchel Roth, *Convict Cowboys: The Untold History of the Texas Prison Rodeo* (Denton: University of North Texas Press, 2016).

11. *House Journal*, 41st Leg., Reg. Sess., 41; Ralph Wright Steen, *Twentieth-Century Texas* (Austin, TX: Steck-Vaughn, 1942), 201; Seth S. W. McKay, *Texas Politics, 1906–1944* (Lubbock: Texas Tech University Press, 1952), 185.

12. *Houston Gargoyle*, February 15, 1929; *DMN*, February 20, 1929. "We DO feel that much of the educational work has been done," wrote the chairman of the Texas League of Women Voter's Social Hygiene division. "Because of the numerous slurs as to its being pushed by women mostly, we thought it best (I know I did) to keep our personalities in the background, and let it go as the Holbrook Administration Bill, merely stating that the organized women of the State endorsed the bill." Mrs. H. F. Ring to Mrs. Kempner, April 5, 1929, Mrs. Henry F. (Elizabeth L.) Ring Papers, 1913–1931, Dolph Briscoe Center for American History, University of Texas at Austin (hereafter cited as BCAH).

13. "Senators Attack Moody for Stand on Pen Location," unidentified newspaper clipping in Dan Moody Scrapbook, 1927–1964, Texas Scrapbooks [ca. 1841–1883, 1898–1941], BCAH (hereafter cited as Dan Moody Scrapbook, BCAH); Mildred P. Moody, "Personal Diary," March 16, 1930, p. 60, Oral History Collection, University of North Texas, Denton (hereafter cited as Mildred Moody Diary); *DMN*, February 23, 1929.

14. On the Love-Bailey clash, see *DMN*, February 20, 1929. "The Senate has passed Senator Holbrook's bill for prison concentration by a dedicated majority," wrote Moody. "It will

be finally passed in the Senate today to tomorrow, and then go to the House. The House has passed a conflicting bill, but I am rather of the opinion that there will be enough support of the Holbrook bill in the House to carry it over." Moody to Miss Grace John, February 28, 1929, Moody Papers, TSL. [Editor's note: It is not clear who the "distinguished visitor" was, but that person was clearly a "Wet."]

15. *General and Special Laws*, 41st Leg., 2nd and 3rd Called Sess., 86–88; Texas Prison Centralization Commission, *Report of the Texas Prison Centralization Commission*, 5, 32; *DMN*, June 14, August 11, October 3, 1929; Steen, *Twentieth-Century Texas*, 201. Adrian Pool of El Paso advised Moody, "The way I see it is you should get back of majority report with both feet. Call the Leg together in Nov. And we will put it over. If it is as important as you say it is in your speeches you should not wait till Jan to remedy it." Pool to Moody, October 7, 1929, Moody Papers, TSL.

16. *DMN*, January 6, 1930.

17. The data derived from the *DMN* Card index is quoted in Lee Simmons, *Assignment Huntsville: Memoirs of a Texas Prison Official* (Austin: University of Texas Press, 1957), 57–59.

18. *Ferguson Forum* 12, January 31, 1929. [Editor's note: I could not easily ascertain the veracity of Ferguson's claims.]

19. Moody to Judge W. C. Wear, February 18, 1930, Moody Papers, TSL; *DMN*, February 25, 1930; *House Journal*, 41st Leg., 4th Called Sess., 23.

20. *DMN*, March 4, 5, 6, 8 (quotation), 1930.

21. Byron C. Utecht, *The Legislature and the Texas People* (San Antonio: Naylor Co., 1937), 176; *DMN*, January 31, 1930.

22. *DMN*, March 16, 1930; Mildred Moody Diary, March 16, 1930, p. 60.

23. Moody to A. W. Grant, March 13, 1930, Moody Papers, TSL; *DMN*, March 28, 1930; Steen, *Twentieth-Century Texas*, 202–203.

24. Steen, *Twentieth-Century Texas*, 203; Teagarden to Graves, March 13, 1930, William B. Teagarden Papers, 1888–1942, BCAH.

25. Simmons, *Assignment Huntsville*, 61.

26. *General and Special Laws*, 41st Leg., 1st Called Sess., 99–104.

27. Herman Lee Crow, "A Political History of the Texas Penal System, 1829–1951" (PhD diss., University of Texas at Austin, 1964), 268; Simmons, *Assignment Huntsville*, 60, 73.

28. *DMN*, May 12, 1929.

29. Moody to E. W. Bone, June 8, 1929; Bone to Moody, June 7, 1929, Moody Papers, TSL; *Fort Worth Star-Telegram*, June 6, 1929.

30. *Houston Gargoyle*, August 4, 1929; See also Peter Molyneaux, "Why a State Income Tax?," *Texas Monthly* 3 (June 1929): 728–746; R. H. James "The Lure of Indirect Taxation," in *Handbook of Texas*, vol. 2, ed. Walter Prescott Webb (Austin: Texas State Historical Association, 1952), 711. [Editor's note: Some historians have argued that Progressive Era reform efforts were responsible for the creation of a permanent federal income tax, especially after the Sixteenth Amendment was passed under Woodrow Wilson's administration. Many U.S. states followed suit, but as of January 2019, Texas still does not have a state income tax. Its specter has been raised at various points in the state's history, but it is generally considered a nonstarter politically. On federal income tax history, see, for example, John D. Buenker, *The Income Tax and the Progressive Era* (New York: Routledge, 2019), and John F. Witte, *The Politics and Development of the Federal Income Tax* (Madison: University of Wisconsin Press, 1985). On Texans' attitudes toward state income tax, see Randolph B. Campbell, *Gone*

to Texas: A History of the Lone Star State (New York: Oxford University Press, 2003), 467. Rick Perry even argued for the possibility of abolishing the federal income tax during his tenure as governor of Texas. Rick Perry, *Fed Up! Our Fight to Save American from Washington* (New York: Little, Brown, 2010), 183.]

31. *DMN*, March 16, 18, 20, 21, 1930; "Representative Phil L. Sanders on the Sulphur Tax," one-page mimeographed sheet, dated March 22, 1930, in Benjamin Grady Oneal Papers, 1905–1961, BCAH; "Taxation," in *Handbook of Texas*, 2:711.

32. Editor's note: For an examination of the history of the Texas Railroad Commission and its importance to the modernization of Texas state regulatory practices, see William R. Childs, *The Texas Railroad Commission: Understanding Regulation in America to the Mid-Twentieth Century* (College Station: Texas A&M University Press, 2005).

33. This account of the operation of the Gas Utilities Law of 1920 is taken from Jack Johnson, "State Regulation of Public Utilities in Texas" (PhD diss., University of Texas at Austin, 1932). See also Nelms Young Henry, "Problems in Municipal Regulation of Public Utilities in Texas" (master's thesis, University of Texas at Austin, 1933); and Dan Rutledge Vining, "Regulation of the Natural Gas Industry of Texas under the Cox Bill of 1920" (master's thesis, University of Texas at Austin, 1935).

34. J. V. Hardy to Moody, June 6, 1929, Moody Papers, TSL.

35. *DMN*, July 11, 1929.

36. Pool to Moody, August 10, 1929; Graves to Moody, August 12, 1929; Hugh (?) to Graves, August 14, 1929, Moody Papers, TSL.

37. *DMN*, May 5, 1930; *Austin American*, January 16, 1931, clipping in Dan Moody Scrapbook, BCAH.

38. Editor's note: Texas was the last state in the union to create a state highway department, and as Brown's work shows, it struggled to manage competing interests to construct a good state roads system. Federal intervention was ultimately necessary to motivate Texans to build good roads. See John David Huddleston, "Good Roads for Texas: A History of the Texas Highway Department, 1917–1947" (PhD diss., Texas A&M University, College Station, 1981); and Karl Edward Wallace III, "Texas and the Good Roads Movement: 1895 to 1948" (master's thesis, University of Texas at Arlington, 2008). The struggle of local and private interests to develop roads for public use and the common good ran parallel to similar challenges facing Texans during this era. Historian John A. Adams Jr., for instance, has shown that private efforts to dam the Colorado River in Texas were unsuccessful, and it was only through joint state and federal efforts that the river could be developed. See *Damming the Colorado: The Rise of the Lower Colorado River Authority, 1933–1939* (College Station: Texas A&M University Press, 1990).

39. The description of the commission office and the quote in the extract are from Byron C. Utecht, "Facing the Highway Problem," *Texas Monthly* 3 (January 1929): 9–11.

40. *Austin American-Statesman*, August 8, 1965, clipping in Raymond Brooks Biographical File, BCAH; *Austin American-Statesman*, October 1, 1954, clipping in Cone Johnson Biographical File, BCAH.

41. Ross S. Sterling, *Good Roads for Texas: Address of R. S. Sterling, Chairman, State Highway Commission, before the Annual Meeting of County Judges and Commissioners, Dallas, October 12, 1928* (Houston: Distributed by the Gulf Coast Good Roads Association, 1928).

42. *House Journal*, 41st Leg., Reg. Sess., 35–53.

43. Utecht, "Facing the Highway Problem," 14–21; Leonard Tillotson, "Our Highway

Problem," *Bunker's Monthly: The Magazine of Texas* 2 (October 1928): 504–518; Edmund Travis, "Solving the Highway Problem," *Texas Monthly* 3 (April 1929): 433–434. The description of Ferguson is in the *Houston Gargoyle*, February 5, 1929.

44. Steen, "Political History of Texas," 458; *Houston Gargoyle*, February 17, 1929.

45. James W. Robinson, *The DPS Story: History of the Department of Public Safety in Texas* (Austin: Texas Department of Public Safety in Texas, 1974), 6.

46. [Editor's note: Brown, *Hood, Bonnet*, 358.] P. J. R. MacIntosh, "The Biggest Highway Job in History," *Texas Monthly* 4 (December 1929): 603–604; *DMN*, May 24, 1966, clipping in Dan Moody Biographical File, BCAH.

47. Norris to Dr. W. D. Bradfield, December 21, 1928 (first quotation); Norris to Ray Holder, February 9, 1929 (second quotation); Norris to Frank Baldwin, February 16, 1929, J. Frank Norris Papers, Southern Baptist Historical Library and Archives, Nashville, Tennessee (hereafter cited as Norris Papers). See also Norris to W. S. Barrow [*sic*], February 2, 1929, in ibid.

48. Norris to Dr. F. S. Groner, February 16, 1929; Norris to Jane Hartwell, February 19, 1929 (Barron quotation), Norris Papers. See also Norris to Holder, February 16, 1929, in ibid.; Kent Demaret, *Baptists and Bangtails* (Houston: Cordovan Press, 1973).

49. *Houston Gargoyle*, February 24, 1929; Fred Gantt Jr., *The Chief Executive in Texas: A Study in Gubernatorial Leadership* (Austin: University of Texas Press, 1964), 224–225; Moody is quoted in Josiah M. Daniel III, "Governor Dan Moody and Business Progressivism" (Paper presented at the 80th Annual Meeting of the Texas State Historical Association, Galveston, March 5, 1976), 12–13. Daniel reached this conclusion about Moody's tactics based on interviews with Alfred Petsch, Walter Woodul, and William S. Barron.

50. *House Journal*, 41st Leg., Reg. Sess., 2, 35; Edna M. Pollard, *Man from Edom* (Ft. Worth: Branch Smith, 1972), 70–71; *DMN*, May 8, 1929.

51. Mildred Moody Diary, May 25, 1929, p. 55.

52. *Ferguson Forum* 12, March 14, May 16, 1929. [Editor's note: I have not been able to determine what the "jelly bean stunt" was. Brown did not write about it in *Hood, Bonnet*.]

53. *House Journal*, 41st Leg., 2nd Called Sess., 2; *House Journal*, 41st Leg., 3rd Called Sess., 2–3; Gantt, *Chief Executive in Texas*, 224–225; Pollard, *Man from Edom*, 71–72. "We have [been] having considerable difficulty with the Legislature to leave us in running condition," wrote R. B. Cousins, then president of South Texas State College. "The spirit of the Senate is very fine; the spirit of the Appropriations Committee in the House cannot be characterized properly in this statement sent through the United States mail." R. B. Cousins to "My dear Marvin," June 8, 1929, Robert Bartow Cousins Sr. Papers, 1861, 1894–1933, BCAH (hereafter cited as Cousins Papers, BCAH).

54. Moody to Carl Estes, August 20, 1929, Moody Papers, TSL. "I think the Governor is a thoroughly honest and honorable man, but it is just a little bit surprising that a young man who is a native of the State and a product of its institutions, and who has been elevated very early in his young manhood to a place of great power in the State, should find it to be wise to build for himself a purely negative reputation." R. B. Cousins to Ralph R. Cousins, July 27, 1929, Cousins Papers, BCAH.

55. *DMN*, March 15, 1930.

56. *DMN*, March 14, 1930.

57. Mildred Moody Diary, March 16, 1930, p. 60.

58. Mildred Moody Diary, May 15, 1930, p. 67; *DMN*, March 22, 1930.

59. Gantt, *Chief Executive in Texas*, 189.

60. *Senate Journal*, 41st Leg., Reg. Sess., 348–351; Byron C. Utecht, *The Legislature*

and the Texas People (San Antonio: Naylor Co., 1937): 175-176; Steen, "Political History of Texas," 458.

61. Moody to Bledsoe, March 7, 1929, Moody Papers, TSL; *Senate Journal*, 40th Leg., Reg. Sess., 1096-1105, 1161; *House Journal*, 40th Leg., Reg. Sess., 1370-1373; *General and Special Laws*, 40th Leg., Reg. Sess., 298-300; *Ferguson Forum* 12, March 7, 1929.

62. *Senate Journal*, 40th Leg., Reg. Sess., 348; *House Journal*, 40th Leg., Reg. Sess., 482-483; *General and Special Laws*, 40th Leg., Reg. Sess., 482-483; typescript, Harry Benge Crozier Papers, Capitol Legislative Reference Library, Austin; "Address of James V. Allred, Attorney General of Texas, in Behalf of His Candidacy for Governor, Delivered at Llano, Texas, on Friday Night, June 15, 1934," 19, mimeographed speech in Selected Names—James V. Allred, 1934-1948, Box 10, Lyndon Baines Johnson Presidential Library, Austin.

63. Editor's note: Ferguson had used the slogan "Agin 'Em All" in summer 1927 to express his opposition to four proposed amendments to the Texas Constitution, which included increasing salaries for the governor and legislators and raising the number of Supreme Court justices—the two that Ferguson opposed again in 1929. See Brown, *Hood, Bonnet*, 369-370.

64. *Ferguson Forum* 12, June 6, 13, 20, July 11, August 1, 1929.

65. Ferguson to Pitchfork Smith, September 19, 1929, Wilford Bascom "Pitchfork" Smith Papers, 1905-1940, BCAH. Ferguson enclosed the current issue of *My Religious Weekly* and good-humoredly asked Smith "to hurry and send that dam nasty rag of yours without any further foolishness or lying."

66. This account of conditions in Borger and the imposition of martial law is based on H. Gordon Frost and John H. Jenkins, *I'm Frank Hamer: The Life of a Texas Peace Officer* (Austin: Pemberton Press, 1968), 143-150; and William Warren Sterling, *Trails and Trials of a Texas Ranger* (Norman: University of Oklahoma Press, 1959), 97-114.

67. This account of the Sherman riot is based on the following: "The Sherman Case," 13-page mimeographed copy in NAACP Records, Manuscript Division, Library of Congress; W. J. Durham to A. Maceo Smith, January 17, 1940, in ibid.; *DMN*, May 10, 1930; James H. Chadbourn, *Lynching and the Law* (Chapel Hill: University of North Carolina Press, 1933), 82, 88; Frost and Jenkins, *I'm Frank Hamer*, 164-168; "King Mob Runs Amuck in Texas," *Literary Digest* 105 (May 24, 1930): 11.

68. "King Mob Runs Amuck in Texas," 11; Pennybacker to D. G. W. Gerwig, June 11, 1930, Mrs. Percy V. Pennybacker Papers, 1878-1938, BCAH. [Editor's note: I was not able to determine the publication dates for the *Virginia Pilot* and *Houston Post-Dispatch* articles. A recent account of George Hughes's lynching can be found in Edward Hake Phillips, "The Sherman Courthouse Riot of 1930," in *Anti-Black Violence in Twentieth-century Texas*, ed. Bruce A. Glasrud (College Station: Texas A&M University Press, 2015), 108-115. Phillips's narration accords mostly with the one related here by Brown, but it draws on a larger body of primary sources and indicates some ambiguity about the sequence of events that led to Hughes's death.]

69. Chadbourn, *Lynching and the Law*, 37-38.

70. Editor's note: No definitive scholarly biography of the political career of Dan Moody exists. In recent years two books have been written about his efforts to weaken the power of the Ku Klux Klan while serving as a district attorney, and they detail how his successes in that arena led ultimately to his rise to the governorship as an enemy of corruption. See Ken Anderson, *Dan Moody: Crusader for Justice* (Georgetown, TX: Georgetown Press, 2008); and Patricia Bernstein, *Ten Dollars to Hate: The Texas Man Who Fought the Klan* (College Station: Texas A&M University Press, 2017). Anderson does discuss Moody's two terms as governor, but he relies heavily on Brown's *Hood, Bonnet* for his analysis. Bernstein's volume

addresses only Moody's work as district attorney. Neither book critically examines Moody's views of race.

71. *DMN*, January 6, 1930; Steen, "Political History of Texas," 460. Said the *Texas Weekly* in a January 10, 1931, editorial titled "Four Years of Moody": "All things considered, Dan Moody had made an uncommonly good Governor, and the standard of public service which he set and maintained during his four years in office has been of an unusually high order." Clipping in Dan Moody Biographical File, BCAH. Pat Neff wrote Moody, "You have kept the Governor's Office during your administration on a high and lofty plane, and around it no questionable shadows have fallen." Neff to Moody, January 20, 1931, Pat M. Neff Collection, Texas Collection, Baylor University.

72. *Austin American*, November 5, 1930, clipping in Dan Moody Scrapbook, BCAH.

73. *DMN*, April 23, 1930; Paul Bolton, *Governors of Texas* (Corpus Christi: Corpus Christi Caller-Times, 1947), n.p.

74. Holder to Moody, August 26, 1930, Moody Papers. TSL.

75. Editor's note: The popular view that the Texas governorship is notoriously weak continues into the twenty-first century, in tandem with the idea that individual gubernatorial personalities and leadership styles, therefore, are significant to a governor's effectiveness. See, for instance, Brian McCall, *The Power of the Texas Governor: Connally to Bush* (Austin: University of Texas Press, 2009).

76. *Dallas Dispatch*, March 18, 1929; Murrell L. Buckner to Moody, n.d.; Moody to R. M. Kelly, March 18, 1929, Moody Papers, TSL; Bolton, *Governors of Texas*, n.p.

77. *DMN*, October 11 (first quotation), January 14, 1931 (second quotation).

78. Dr. A. C. Biard to Moody, February 24, 1930, Moody Papers, TSL.

79. Neal to Moody, July 23, 1930, Moody Papers, TSL.

80. Fred Gantt interview with Mrs. Dan Moody Sr., August 16, 1968, Austin, Texas, in North Texas State University Oral History Collection, No. 25, p. 20; Moody to T. A. Buckner, May 24, 1930; Moody to Earl E. Arnold, March 7, 1930, Moody Papers, TSL.

81. Daniel, "Dan Moody and Business Progressivism," 13.

82. Author's interview with Walter F. Woodul, Austin, Texas, July 11, 1975. Additional research on this question is needed. Roll-call analysis of key votes in the fortieth and forty-first legislatures would identify which lawmakers generally supported or opposed Moody's program.

83. T. J. Holbrook, *Address of Senator T. J. Holbrook at the Memorial Service Commemorating the Life and Public Career of the Honorable Barry Miller (1864–1933) Senate Chamber, Austin, Texas, October 10, 1933* (n.p., 1933), eight-page pamphlet in Barry Miller Biographical File, BCAH.

84. Gantt interview with Mrs. Moody, 19–20.

85. Mildred Moody Diary, March 16, 1930, pp. 59–60.

86. *Houston Chronicle*, July 1927, clipping in Dan Moody Scrapbook, in possession of Mrs. Dan Moody Sr., Austin, Texas.

87. Peter Molyneaux, "Texas at the Crossroads," *Texas Monthly* 4 (September 1929): 154–157, 161–163. Molyneaux's article was prompted by the recent defeat by rural voters of the constitutional amendments that would have increased the governor's salary from $4,000 to $10,000 a year and increased the number of Supreme Court judges from three to nine. [Editor's note: Brown makes a similar point in the conclusion of *Hood, Bonnet*, 429.]

88. Molyneaux, "Texas at the Crossroads," 163.

89. Granbery to Moody, January 16, 1929; Moody to Granbery, January 18, 1929, Moody Papers, TSL. [Editor's Note: Brown, *Hood, Bonnet*, 432.]

90. *Austin American*, January 16, 1931, clipping in Dan Moody Scrapbook, BCAH.

91. *DMN*, January 21, 1931.

92. V. O. Key, *Southern Politics in State and Nation* (New York: Vintage Books, 1949), 254; Jack Bass and Walter De Vries, *The Transformation of Southern Politics: Social Change and Political Consequences since 1945* (New York: Basic Books, 1976), 305–338. [Editor's note: Later works, however, emphasized that race remains a central component of Texas politics. See Chandler Davidson, *Race and Class in Texas Politics* (Princeton, NJ: Princeton University Press, 1990). Davison directly contradicts Key's prediction that class and economic considerations would be the primary dividing factor in Texas politics. Still other studies have examined the ways that race and class must be considered together to understand southern history and politics. See, for example, Melvyn Stokes and Rick Halpern, eds., *Race and Class in the American South since 1890* (Oxford, UK: Berg, 1994).]

Chapter 3: A Sterling Victory

1. Ouida Wallace Ferguson Nalle, *Fergusons of Texas: Or "Two Governors for the Price of One"* (San Antonio: Naylor Co., 1946), 206. [Editor's note: On the Ferguson amnesty bill and its repeal, see Brown, *Hood, Bonnet*, 266–269, 345–346.]

2. *Ferguson Forum* 13, September 6, 1928, January 24, 1929; Don Hampton Biggers, *Our Sacred Monkeys: Or Twenty Years of Jim and Other Jams (Mostly Jim), the Outstanding Goat Specialist of Texas Politics* (Brownwood, TX: Jones Printing, 1933), 80–81.

3. Nalle, *Fergusons of Texas*, 211–212.

4. Editor's note: Mr. Barkis, a character in Dickens's *David Copperfield*, is known for his repeated use of the phrase, "Barkis is willing."

5. *Ferguson Forum* 13, October 24, 31, November 7, 14, 21, 28, December 5, 12, 1929, January 9, 16, 1930; Nalle, *Fergusons of Texas*, 213. On the night of January 18, 1930, Ferguson had a dream and fell out of his bed at home, fracturing a collarbone. He later described the dream that troubled him. "I dreamed that I was attempting to swim the Mississippi River on a high rise. As strange as it may seem, I saw a small house, come floating down toward me with none other than my esteemed friend Judge W. C. Morrow on the front gallery. I thought I heard him call to me to lookout, and in an attempt to make an overhand lunge to surmount the waves I lunged out of bed, landing on my neck and chest. When I awoke the wave had vanished and my friend was gone. But I was left with a strained neck and a broken collar bone." *Ferguson Forum* 13, January 23, 1930; *Dallas Morning News*, January 25, 1930 (hereafter cited as *DMN*).

6. *DMN*, February 20, 1930; *Ferguson Forum* 13, February 20, 1930.

7. *DMN*, April 5, 1930.

8. *Ferguson Forum* 13, February 27, April 10, 1930.

9. *DMN*, April 24, May 9, May 24, 1930.

10. *DMN*, May 25, 27, June 21, 1930; *Ferguson Forum* 13, May 29, 1930.

11. Editor's note: The Harding administration, as noted above, became well known for its abuses of the political patronage system and for other scandals, such as the Teapot Dome Scandal. See, for example, Rosemary Stevens, *A Time of Scandal: Charles R. Forbes, Warren G. Harding, and the Making of the Veteran's Bureau* (Baltimore, MD: Johns Hopkins University Press, 2016).

12. *DMN*, March 18, June 15, 22, July 5, 1930; *DMN*, July 16, 1930, clipping in Barry Miller Biographical File, Dolph Briscoe Center for American History, University of Texas at

Austin (hereafter cited as BCAH); Atticus Webb to Rev. F. Ingram, April 17, 1930, Thomas B. Love Collection, Dallas Historical Society (hereafter cited as Love Collection, DHS); H. P. Drought to Dan Moody, May 6, 1930, Records of Dan Moody, Texas Office of the Governor, Archives and Information Services Division, Texas State Library and Archives Commission (hereafter cited as Moody Papers, TSL); Seth W. McKay, *Texas Politics, 1906–1944* (Lubbock: Texas Tech University Press, 1952), 194.

13. "My general impression is that the public is not at all satisfied with the candidates who have already been announced for Governor," Davidson had written Senator W. H. Bledsoe the previous November, "and are really looking for [a] more desirable candidate." Davidson to Bledsoe, November 21, 1929, Bledsoe Papers, Southwest Collection, Special Collections Library, Texas Tech University, Lubbock (hereafter cited as Bledsoe Papers, TTU).

14. *DMN*, April 11, 1930; A. P. Johnson to Dan Moody, April 11, 1930; Moody to Johnson, April 12, 1930, Moody Papers, TSL.

15. Atticus Webb to Rev. F. H. Ingram, April 17, 1930, Love Collection, DHS.

16. [Editor's note: I was not able to identify the date of the quote from the *Ferguson Forum*.] Dan Moody to W. A. Brooks Jr., April 18, 1930, Moody Papers, TSL.

17. [Editor's note: I was not able to identify the source of Brown's quotation of Albert Sidney Burleson.] Allen V. Peden, "We Support a Dry," *Houston Gargoyle*, July 6, 1930; Pat O'Keefe to Dan Moody, March 21, 1930; C. M. Smithdeal to Dan Moody, May 9, 1930, Moody Papers, TSL; *DMN*, June 22, 1930.

18. *DMN*, July 12, 19, 1930.

19. Ted Dealey, "Sterling Seen as Big Leader in Southeast," *DMN*, July 19, 1930.

20. Editor's note: This incident is described in chapter 2.

21. *DMN*, April 25, July 6, 1930.

22. *DMN*, April 13, July 8, 19, 1930; Clint Small to Judge Joe W. Crudgington, June 18, 30, 1930; Crudgington to Small, July 1 [June 27], 1930, J. W. Crudgington Miscellaneous Papers, Folder 2, Earl Vandale Papers, 1897, 1908–1967, BCAH; George B. Terrell to Martin McNulty Crane, June 30, 1930, Edward Crane Papers, 1883–1963, BCAH; McKay, *Texas Politics*; Seth Shepard McKay and Odie B. Faulk, *Texas after Spindletop, 1901–1965* (Austin, TX: Steck-Vaughn, 1965), 121.

23. On Sterling, see Harry Benge Crozier's profile in the *DMN*, July 11, 1930; *Handbook of Texas*, vol. 2, ed. Walter Prescott Webb (Austin: Texas State Historical Association, 1952), 668–669; Hugh Nugent Fitzgerald, *Governors I Have Known* (Austin: Austin American-Statesman, c. 1927), 62–64; James T. DeShields, *They Sat in High Place: The Presidents and Governors of Texas* (San Antonio: Naylor Co., 1940), 445–447; Walter B. Moore, *Governors of Texas* (Dallas: Dallas Morning News, 1963), 30; William Warren Sterling, *Trails and Trials of a Texas Ranger* (Norman: University of Oklahoma Press, 1959), 287–304. The physical description of Ross Sterling is from Paul Louis Wakefield, *Campaigning Texas* (Houston: Interstate Print Co., 1932), 35. [Editor's note: To date, no scholarly biography of Ross Sterling exists, although Sterling did write a memoir, which has been edited and updated. See Ross S. Sterling et al., *Ross Sterling, Texan: A Memoir by the Founder of Humble Oil and Refining Company* (Austin: University of Texas Press, 2007).]

24. Jacob F. Wolters, "An Epoch in Texas Politics," in Wakefield, *Campaigning Texas*, 52 ff.

25. James A. Clark with Weldon Hart, *The Tactful Texan: A Biography of Governor Will Hobby* (New York: Random House, 1958), 165–166.

26. Ed Kilman, "Sterling—Texan: The Life Story of Ross Sterling," typed manuscript, 154, Ed Kilman Collection, Houston Metropolitan Research Center, Houston Public Library.

[Editor's note: Brown worked from Kilman's unpublished manuscript, which had converted Sterling's words into third person. On the history of this manuscript and its subsequent publication in Sterling's own voice, see Don Carleton's introduction to Sterling et al., *Ross Sterling, Texan*, 1–4.]

27. A. E. Kerr to S. P. Brooks, May 12, 1930; Brooks to Kerr, May 20, 1930, Samuel Palmer Brooks Papers, Accession #91, Texas Collection, Baylor University. [Editor's note: Brown did not name the archive that houses these letters, and Baylor archivists could not definitively confirm that the collection cited above holds them.]

28. Stephen L. Pinckney to Will C. Hogg, June 5, 1930, William Clifford Hogg Papers, 1897–1932, BCAH (hereafter cited as the W. C. Hogg Papers, BCAH); George W. Harris to Dan Moody, February 14, 1930; L. Brann to Moody, March 7, 1929, Moody Papers, TSL.

29. Form letter reply to letters urging Moody to run for a third term, February 1930, Moody Papers, TSL; Mildred P. Moody, "Personal Diary," March 16, 1930, p. 58, Oral History Collection, University of North Texas, Denton (hereafter cited as Mildred Moody Diary). Mildred Moody had bitterly opposed a third term because of "this fiendish financial strain." She wrote: "(I hate living on borrowed money) the physical drain on Dan; the hacking 'expectations of place,' denying us all right of private living and companionship, the death of all illusions and dreams." See also R. B. Cousins Jr. to R. B. Cousins Sr., March 19, 1930, Robert Bartow Cousins Sr. Papers, 1861, 1894–1933, BCAH (hereafter cited as Cousins Papers, BCAH); McKay, *Texas Politics*, 186.

30. T. W. Carlock to Dan Moody, March 24, 1930; J. C. Winder to Moody, March 31, 1930; Moody to J. O. Guleke, March 29, 1930, Moody Papers, TSL.

31. Frank Gibler to Dan Moody, April 9, 1930; Will Hogg to Moody, March 20, 1930, Moody Papers, TSL.

32. *DMN*, April 15, 27, 1930.

33. Will Hogg endorsement on a clipping from the *Houston Post-Dispatch*, April 15, 1930, W. C. Hogg Papers, BCAH; Dan Moody to E. A. Calvin, April 23, 1920; Moody to Dr. Charles S. Field, April 28, 1930; Moody to D. K. Martin, May 8, 1930, Moody Papers, TSL.

34. Pat O'Keefe to Dan Moody, May 13, 1930, Moody Papers, TSL; Mildred Moody Diary, May 15, 1930, p. 62.

35. *DMN*, May 22, 1930; Dan Moody to W. P. Hobby, May 17, 1930, Moody Papers, TSL; Stephen L. Pinckney to Will C. Hogg, June 5, 1930, W. C. Hogg Papers, BCAH.

36. *DMN*, May 22, 1930. Alvin Moody wrote the governor urging him to stay out of the contest. Alvin Moody to Dan Moody, May 23, 1930, Moody Papers, TSL.

37. *DMN*, May 23, 1930; Dan Moody to Alvin Moody, May 24, 1930, Moody Papers, TSL. See also Moody to J. E. Josey, May 24, 1930; Moody to T. F. Temple, May 24, 1930, Moody Papers, TSL.

38. Stephen L. Pinckney to Will C. Hogg, June 5, 1930, W. C. Hogg Papers, BCAH.

39. *DMN*, May 30, 31, 1930; Dan Moody to Frank Gibler, June 7, 1930, Moody Papers, TSL.

40. *DMN*, June 1, 1930.

41. *DMN*, June 2, 3, 5, 1930.

42. *DMN*, June 2, 3, 6, 1930; Dan Moody to Frank Gibler, June 7, 1930, Moody Papers, TSL. See also the following letters dated June 7: Moody to L. B. Gibson, Moody to Jas. W. Wayman, Moody to P. S. Lake, Moody to C. C. Belcher, all in Moody Papers, TSL.

43. *DMN*, June 5, 10, 1930; Roscoe E. Wright, "(Tom) Love Thy Brother," *Houston Gargoyle*, June 15, 1930.

44. Mildred Moody Diary, January 4, 1931, pp. 78–79.

45. Editor's note: Charles Edward Marsh was a well-known newspaper publisher with ties to the Franklin Roosevelt administration through his friendship with Henry A. Wallace, who would become vice president during Roosevelt's third term. Marsh also became a close friend and confidant of Lyndon Johnson. See Brown, *Hood, Bonnet*, 475n83; and "Charles Marsh, Publisher Dead," *New York Times*, December 31, 1964.

46. Dan Moody to C. E. Marsh, June 9, 1930, Moody Papers, TSL.

47. Wolters, "Epoch in Texas Politics," in Wakefield, *Campaigning Texas*, 55; Ed Kilman to Dan Moody, June 16, 1930; Moody to Dr. B. G. Prestridge, July 15, 1930; Moody to Pat O'Keefe, July 15, 1930, Moody Papers, TSL.

48. *DMN*, April 11, May 29, June 20, 1930; *Houston Gargoyle*, June 22, 1930.

49. T. W. Davidson to W. H. Bledsoe, November 16, 1929, Bledsoe Papers, TTU; T. W. Davidson to Pat N. Neff, March 15, 1930, Pat M. Neff Collection, Texas Collection, Baylor University (hereafter cited as Neff Collection); *DMN*, June 2, 21, 1930; *Houston Gargoyle*, September 4, 1930, June 22, 1930; McKay, *Texas Politics*, 190.

50. *Houston Gargoyle*, June 1, 1930; Roscoe Wright, "Voters Crazy-Quilt," *Houston Gargoyle*, June 8, 1930; McKay, *Texas Politics*.

51. *Ferguson Forum* 13, June 5, 1930.

52. *DMN*, June 22, 1930; *Ferguson Forum* 13, July 10, 1930; Bryant to *Houston Chronicle*, July 23, 1930, Jesse Holman Jones Papers, 1880–1965, BCAH (hereafter cited as Jones Papers, BCAH). [Editor's note: Brown cited here the "Jones Papers." I believe he consulted the Jones archival collection at the Briscoe Center for American History at UT.]

53. *Ferguson Forum* 13, June 12, July 10, 1930; *DMN*, July 12, 1930.

54. Bryant to *Houston Chronicle*, July 23, 1930.

55. William B. Teagarden to James E. Ferguson, June 13, 1930, William B. Teagarden Papers, 1888–1942, BCAH (hereafter cited as Teagarden Papers, BCAH).

56. *DMN*, July 11, 1930; T. N. Jones to William Teagarden, June 5, 1930; Teagarden to James E. Ferguson, June 13, 1930; Marcellus E. Foster to Teagarden, June 16, 1930; Ferguson to Teagarden, June 21, 1930; Teagarden to Roy Monk, July 25, 1930, all in the Teagarden Papers, BCAH.

57. *DMN*, April 6, 1930.

58. *DMN*, May 4, 1930.

59. *DMN*, June 15, 1930; V. A. Collins to Thomas B. Love, June 6, 1930, Love Collection, DHS.

60. *DMN*, July 10, 26, 1930; Thomas B. Love to William B. McAdoo, April 19, 1930; McAdoo to Love, April 22, 1930; R. H. Moodie to Oak McKenzie, July 16, 1930; J. V. Hardy to George W. Armstrong, December 19, 1930. [Editor's note: Brown did not indicate from which archival collections these sources came.]

61. *DMN*, July 9, 11, 15, 18, 25, 1930; Carl Estes to Dan Moody, June 14, 1930, Moody Papers, TSL; J. Frank Norris to Dr. I. E. Gates, July 8, 1930, Norris Papers, Reel 10, Southern Baptist Historical Library and Archives, Nashville, Tennessee (hereafter cited as Norris Papers); McKay, *Texas Politics*, 188, 193–194.

62. William Strauss, "The Campaign from State Headquarters," in Wakefield, *Campaigning Texas*, 36; *Houston Post-Dispatch*, June 10, 1930; McKay, *Texas Politics*, 191. See also "Jesse H. Jones Pays Tribute to Ross Sterling in Radio Speech: Stresses Idealism in Government," two-page broadside in Jones Papers, BCAH.

63. Strauss, "Campaign from State Headquarters," in Wakefield, *Campaigning Texas*, 37; Wolters, "Epoch in Texas Politics," in Wakefield, *Campaigning Texas*, 54–55; Alvin S. Moody

to Thomas B. Love, June 5, 1930, Love Collection, DHS; *Houston Post-Dispatch*, June 4, 5, 6, 1930.

64. Strauss, "Campaign from State Headquarters," in Wakefield, *Campaigning Texas*, 37; "San Antonio and Bexar County," in Wakefield, *Campaigning Texas*, 114; Wolters, "Epoch in Texas Politics," in Wakefield, *Campaigning Texas*, 54; C. S. Fowler to Jesse Jones, July 3, 1930, Jones Papers, BCAH.

65. *Houston Gargoyle*, July 6, 1930; *DMN*, June 21, 1930; McKay, *Texas Politics*, 192–193.

66. Paul Wakefield, foreword to *Campaigning Texas*, 7; McKay, *Texas Politics*, 197–199.

67. Kilman, "Sterling—Texan," 172; Ed Kilman, "The First Campaign," in Wakefield, *Campaigning Texas*, 70–71, 83, 85; *DMN*, July 17, 1930.

68. *DMN*, July 19, 1930. According to reports filed by Sterling and Strauss, his expenses in the first primary totaled $6,098.92. Strauss reported expenditures of $5,313.92, and Sterling in his individual report claimed he had spent $785. This total was $1,901.08 under the $8,000 permitted by law. *DMN*, August 5, 1930.

69. Peter Molyneaux, "State Press Wins a Great Victory," in Wakefield, *Campaigning Texas*, 61–63.

70. Molyneaux, "State Press," in Wakefield, *Campaigning Texas*, 64–65; Paul L. Wakefield, "The Candidate and the State Publicity Campaign," in Wakefield, *Campaigning Texas*, 39, 42; *DMN*, July 20, 1930.

71. John E. King to George Bannerman Dealey, July 8, 1930, George Bannerman Dealey Papers, G. B. Dealey Library-Special Collections, Dallas Historical Society (hereafter cited as G. B. Dealey Papers, DHS).

72. *DMN*, July 14, 1930; Sam Hanna Acheson, *35,000 Days in Texas: A History of the Dallas News and Its Forbears* (Westport, CT: Greenwood Press, 1973), 297.

73. *DMN*, July 16, 1930; Molyneaux, "State Press Wins," in Wakefield, *Campaigning Texas*, 65–68.

74. *DMN*, July 26, 27, 1930; *Ferguson Forum* 13, July 24, 1930; Dan Moody to Adrian Pool, July 24, 1930, Moody Papers, TSL. [Editor's note: Sterling loosely quotes a popular nineteenth-century poem by George Linnaeus Banks, "What I Live For," *Peals from the Belfry: Lyrics* (London: Hope & Co., 1853), 29.]

75. Vote totals are taken from Alexander Heard and Donald S. Strong, *Southern Primaries and Elections, 1920–1949* (Tuscaloosa: University of Alabama Press, 1950), 141–145.

76. *DMN*, July 28, 30, 31, 1930; McKay, *Texas Politics*, 200–201. The minor candidates' totals were as follows: C. C. Moody, 4,382; Paul Loven, 2,724; Frank Putnam, 2,365; C. E. Walker, 1,760, from Heard and Strong, *Southern Primaries*, 141–145.

77. Thomas B. Love to William C. McAdoo, August 7, 1930, Love Collection, DHS. "The folks who hunt band wagons and Flesh pots ran to Sterling fast," lamented a Love supporter in Beaumont. "The numbers of the Klan here who went into it originally for the purpose of benefitting society, stuck to you hard and fast. I never knew whether any lodge resolutions were ever passed on the subject, but was close enough to many to know they were sticking with you." W. S. Parker to Love, August 6, 1930, Love Collection, DHS.

78. *Houston Gargoyle*, August 3, 1930.

79. Lawrence Westbrook to Dan Moody, July 31, 1930, Moody Papers, TSL; William G. McAdoo to Jesse Jones, August 11, 1930, Jones Papers, BCAH; "Ma's Come-Back," *Outlook and Independent* 155 (August 13, 1930): 574. [Editor's note: Though cotton farmers would suffer even more as the Great Depression wore on, as Keith J. Volanto explains, the Great Depression "merely accelerated pernicious economic trends that had begun after the end of

the First World War," such as declining prices and a rise in sharecropping. He describes these trends, as well as failed attempts to address them, in Volanto, *Texas, Cotton, and the New Deal* (College Station: Texas A&M University Press, 2005), 12 ff.]

80. James V. Allred to O. H. Allred, December 9, 1929; Ben P. Allred to James V. Allred, February 22, 1930, Gov. James V. Allred Papers, Courtesy of Special Collections, University of Houston Libraries (hereafter cited as Allred Papers). [Editor's note: Brown did not specify which collection of Allred papers he used here, but the University of Houston collection seems most likely based on the dates of the letters and the correspondents involved.]

81. On the chain-store campaign, see James V. Allred to J. M. Gilliam, February 26, 1930; Allred to R. B. Humphrey, March 3, 1929; Allred to Sam Hanna, March 10, 1930; Allred to W. S. Poston, same date, Allred Papers. William Eugene Atkinson, *James V. Allred: A Political Biography, 1899–1935* (n.p., 1978), 121–127. [Editor's note: See also Nancy Beck Young's discussion of Wright Patman's opposition to chain stores in *Wright Patman: Populism, Liberalism, and the American Dream* (Dallas: Southern Methodist University Press, 2000), 73–104. Patman represented "a long tradition of small-business advocacy," and he preferred to support local businesses, banks, and other industries that "originated in and contributed to these communities" (74).]

82. *Houston Gargoyle*, July 20, 1930; *San Antonio Express*, March 6, 1930, clipping in Robert Lee Bobbitt Biographical File, BCAH. "I have no doubt whatever about the integrity, enforcement and permanence of our prohibition laws, state and national," Bobbitt wrote J. Frank Norris. Bobbitt to Norris, April 2, 1930, Reel 3, Norris Papers.

83. *Fort Worth Star-Telegram*, June 28, 1930, clipping in Robert Lee Bobbitt Biographical File, BCAH; *Austin American*, July 20, 1930.

84. *DMN*, July 21, 1930; *Fort Worth Star-Telegram*, July 21, 1930, clipping in Dan Moody Biographical File, BCAH.

85. O. H. Allred to James V. Allred, July 17, 1930, Allred Papers; *Houston Gargoyle*, July 20, 1930; Atkinson, *James V. Allred*, 133–136.

86. James V. Allred to H. M. Gilstrap, March 3, 1930; Allred to Felix M. Bransford, May 13, 1930; Allred to E. M. Brown, September 20, 1930; Oran Allred to James V. Allred, July 3, 1920, Allred Papers; Atkinson, *James V. Allred*, 138–140; George Manning, "Public Services of James V. Allred," (master's thesis, Texas Technological College, 1950), 6.

87. McKay, *Texas Politics*, 211–212; Ralph W. Steen, "A Political History of Texas, 1900–1930," in *Texas Democracy: A Centennial History of Politics and Personalities of the Texas Democratic Party, 1836–1936*, vol. 1, ed. Frank Carter Adams (Austin: Democratic Historical Assoc., 1937), 460; Harry P. Jordan to Morris Sheppard, March 26, 1930; John G. Gose to Morris Shepard [*sic*], April 2, 1930, Morris Sheppard Papers, 1894–1953, BCAH (hereafter cited as Sheppard Papers, BCAH). See also W. L. Estes to Sheppard, March 28, 1930; Robert H. Holliday to Sheppard, May 13, 1930; Cyclone Davis to Sheppard, April 12, 1930; Robert Gibbs Moody to Sheppard, April 2, 1930; V. A. Collins to Sheppard, June 11, 1930, in ibid.

88. R. L. Henry to Morris Sheppard, March 29, 1930; Sheppard to Henry, March 31, 1930; Henry to Sheppard, same date; Henry to Sheppard, April 9, 1930; Sheppard to Henry, April 12, 1930; Henry to Sheppard, April 14, 1930; Sheppard to Henry, April 15, 1930; Henry to Sheppard, July 11, 1930; Sheppard to Henry, same date; Henry to Sheppard, July 22, 1930, all in the Sheppard Papers, BCAH; McKay, *Texas Politics*, 212.

89. McKay, *Texas Politics*, 212–213; *Houston Gargoyle*, January 12, 1930, August 12, 1930.

90. *DMN*, July 6, 1930; Harold J. Marburger, *Texas Elections, 1918–1954* (Austin: Texas

State Library, 1956), 47. On Bledsoe's candidacy, see numerous letters in the Bledsoe Papers, TTU. On the opposition of the railroad brotherhoods to Neff, see H. R. Christian to Pat M. Neff, July 3, 1930; E. M. Wilson to Neff, July 18, 1930, Neff Collection.

91. *DMN*, July 29, 31, August 3, 1930; *Houston Gargoyle*, August 10, 1930; I. H. Terry to Dan Moody, July 28, 1930, Moody Papers, TSL; Jane Y. McCallum to Mrs. O. H. Carlisle, July 31, 1930, Jane Y. and Arthur N. McCallum Family Papers, 1894–1982 (bulk 1910–1956), BCAH. For other warnings that the road bond issue would give Sterling hard sledding, see George A. Harmon to Dan Moody, July 29, 1930; T. W. Carlock to Moody, July 31, 1930; Reagan S. Wyche to Moody, August 1, 1930; W. S. Parker to Moody, August 15, 1930, Moody Papers, TSL; Leffler Corbitt to Mrs. Percy V. Pennybacker, August 15, 1930, Mrs. Percy V. Pennybacker Papers, 1878–1938, BCAH.

92. *Austin American*, August 1, 1930; Alonzo Wasson to George B. Dealey, August 1, 1930, G. B. Dealey Papers, DHS.

93. Wolters, "Epoch in Texas Politics," in Wakefield, *Campaigning Texas*, 56–57; Amon Carter to Ross Sterling, August 24, 1930; *Houston Chronicle*, August 21, 1930, clipping in Jones Papers, BCAH; *DMN*, August 21, 22, 1930. "All the Sterling force are appreciative of what you are doing," W. P. Hobby wired Small. "Your speech last night was masterful and will undoubtedly do great good. Thanks and best wishes." Hobby to Clint Small, August 21, 1930, Jones Papers, BCAH. See also from the same date: Jacob F. Wolters to Small; Paul Wakefield to Small; William Strauss to Small; Jesse H. Jones to Small, in ibid.

94. *DMN*, July 28, August 1, 5, 11, 12, 1930; *Houston Post-Dispatch*, July 31, 1930, clipping in W. C. Hogg Papers, BCAH; William B. Teagarden to John N. Garner, July 29, 1930, Teagarden Papers, BCAH; McKay, *Texas Politics*.

95. *DMN*, August 1, 1930; *Fort Worth Star-Telegram*, August 17, 1930, clipping in G. B. Dealey Papers, DHS; McKay, *Texas Politics*, 202.

96. *DMN*, July 29, 31, August 2, 1930; Walter H. Woodward, "West Texas and the Second Primary," in Wakefield, *Campaigning Texas*, 141; Ross S. Sterling to Guy M. Bryan, August 2, 1930, Ross Shaw Sterling Papers, BCAH; William B. Teagarden to James E. Ferguson, July 31, 1930, Teagarden Papers, BCAH.

97. George W. Key to Dan Moody, July 28, 1930, Moody Papers, TSL; Wolters, "Epoch in Texas Politics," in Wakefield, *Campaigning Texas*, 56; *DMN*, August 8, 1930. According to Alonzo Wasson, Moody was "hopeful" of Sterling's nomination, "but is by no means confident of it, and in this judgment I concur." Wasson to G. B. Dealey, July 28, 1930, G. B. Dealey Papers, DHS.

98. *DMN*, August 9, 15, 16, 1930; Hilton Howell, "Campaigning from Waco," in Wakefield, *Campaigning Texas*, 118; Royal R. Watkins to Murphy W. Townsend, August 19, 1930; Thomas B. Love to Dan Moody, August 20, 1930, Moody Papers, TSL.

99. *DMN*, August 14, 15, 22, 1930; unidentified newspaper clipping in Dan Moody Scrapbooks, 1927–1964, Texas Scrapbooks [ca. 1841–1883, 1898–1941], BCAH.

100. *DMN*, August 9, 1930; Woodward, "West Texas and the Second Primary," in Wakefield, *Campaigning Texas*, 142–147; Wolters, "Epoch in Texas Politics," in Wakefield, *Campaigning Texas*, 56; McKay, *Texas Politics*, 202–205.

101. Wolters, "Epoch in Texas Politics," in Wakefield, *Campaigning Texas*, 56; *New York World*, August 20, 1930, clipping in G. B. Dealey Papers, DHS; *DMN*, August 23, 24, 1930; McKay, *Texas Politics*, 208–209.

102. *DMN*, August 8, 1930; Ted Dealey to George B. Dealey, n.d., 1930, G. B. Dealey Papers, DHS.

103. *DMN*, August 10, 1930.

104. *DMN*, August 11, 1930; Biggers, *Our Sacred Monkeys*, 85.

105. *DMN*, August 13, 1930.

106. Dan Moody to William Strauss, August 5, 1930; Walter C. Woodward to Moody, July 31, 1930; Moody to Woodward, August 1, 1930, Moody Papers, TSL. *Articles of Impeachment of Jas E. Ferguson by the Senate of the State of Texas Sitting as a Court of Impeachment* (n.p., 1930); and *Do Such Acts of Fergusonism Assure Your Home, Your Sister and Your Friend's Safety . . . ?* (n.p., 1930), both in Moody Papers, TSL. The word "rapists" was not capitalized in Mrs. McCallum's original statement. *James E. Ferguson Impeachment* (n.p., 1930) in James E. Ferguson Biographical File, BCAH.

107. *Womanhood Murder and Rape. Commutation of Sentences Under Fergusonism, the Langhorn Case, Wherein Jim Ferguson Extracted Blood Money by Selling Executive Clemency* (n.p., 1930), Moody Papers, TSL; *Ferguson Forum* 13, August 7, 1930; *Fergusonism and the Record of a Crime. A Sequel to the Langhorn Story*, enclosed in Paul Wakefield to Dan Moody, August 8, 1930, Moody Papers, TSL.

108. *Lest We Forget!* (n.p., 1930), one-page broadside; *Sterling's Wholesale Whiskey Business* (n.p., 1930), one-page broadside; Kina Mae Crabb Telegram to Ross Sterling (n.p., 1930), one-page broadside, all in Ross Sterling File, Campaign Materials, Archives Division, Texas State Library.

109. *New York Times*, August 19, 1930, clipping in G. B. Dealey Papers, DHS.

110. McKay, *Texas Politics*, 206–207; *DMN*, August 22, 1930.

111. *DMN*, August 11, 13, 14, 15, 1930.

112. McKay, *Texas Politics*, 207–208; *DMN*, August 19, 23, 1930; *Ferguson Forum* 13, August 21, 1930.

113. McKay, *Texas Politics*, 209–211; *DMN*, August 25, 26, 1930; Heard and Strong, *Southern Primaries*, 143–145.

114. *DMN*, August 1930; the *New York Times* quote is from Steen, "Political History of Texas," 464; Jacob F. Wolters to Dan Moody, August 27, 1930, Moody Papers, TSL.

115. S. Raymond Brooks, "A Business Man Campaigns," in Wakefield, *Campaigning Texas*, 59; Jacob F. Wolters to Dan Moody, August 27, 1930, Moody Papers, TSL.

116. *DMN*, August 24, 25, 1930; *Austin American*, August 24, 1930; Dan Moody to Ross Sterling, August 23, 1930; Sterling to Moody, August 24, 1930, Moody Papers, TSL; McKay, *Texas Politics*, 210. After the election, the governor received many letters crediting him with having elected Sterling, or at least having been a significant factor in the Houston's man's victory. See George B. Dealey to Moody, August 23, 1930; Tom L. Beauchamp to Moody, August 25, 1930; Jacob F. Wolters to Moody, August 27, 1930; C. M. Chambers to Moody, same date; Dr. W. L. Crosthwait to Moody, August 29, 1930; L. W. Kemp to Moody, same date, all in Moody Papers, TSL.

117. *Ferguson Forum* 13, August 28, September 4, October 23, 1930. See also Stark Young, "The Fergusons and Democracy," *New Republic* 64 (September 10, 1930): 93–94.

118. O. H. Allred to James V. Allred, August 1, 1930, Allred Papers; *DMN*, August 7, 9, 1930; *Austin American*, August 9, 1930; Atkinson, *James V. Allred*, 140–143. Ferguson offered Allred a quarter page in a special edition of the *Forum* on May 22, 1930, for $50. Allred bought the space, asked Ferguson to run a brief excerpt from his opening speech at Alvarado as a news item, and expressed his appreciation for "the opportunity to advertise with the Forum." Jas. E. Ferguson to James V. Allred, May 10, 1930; Allred to Ferguson, May 12, 1930, Allred Papers.

119. B. W. King to James V. Allred, July 31, 1930, Allred Papers; *Ferguson Forum* 13,

August 14, 1930; Atkinson, *James V. Allred*, 143–146; *James V. Allred for Attorney General*, broadside in James V. Allred Campaign Materials, Archives Division, Texas State Library.

120. Dan Moody to James V. Allred, August 25, 1930; James V. Allred to Ben P. Allred, September 6, 1930, Allred Papers; *Houston Gargoyle*, August 31, 1930; Marburger, *Texas Elections*, 49. Bobbitt is quoted in Atkinson, *James V. Allred*, 146. "The big corporations and their high powered lawyers are very nervous about the situation," an Allred manager in Harris County reported after the election. "Some of them have already talked to me and I assured them that they could expect a square deal, but nothing more." Sidney Benbow to Renne Allred Jr., August 26, 1930, Allred Papers.

121. Thomas B. Love to Cato Sells, August 27, 1930, Love Collection, DHS.

122. *DMN*, September 8, 9, 1930.

123. *Houston Gargoyle*, September 14, 1930; *DMN*, September 10, 11, 1930; Steen, "Political History of Texas," 464. According to Dan Moody, he and Love were "about the only one[s] in the state" advocating abolition of the ad valorem tax for state purposes, but the governor thought it would be better, under existing conditions, not to mention it in the platform. Moody to M. M. Crane, August 28, 1930, Moody Papers, TSL.

124. Paul D. Casdorph, *A History of the Republican Party in Texas, 1865–1965* (Austin: Pemberton Press, 1965), 138; McKay, *Texas Politics*, 213–214; Marburger, *Texas Elections*, 50.

125. *DMN*, August 27, September 9, 10, 1930.

126. *Ferguson Forum* 13, September 11, 1930.

127. *DMN*, September 25, 1930; R. B. Creager and J. F. Lucey to [?], September 24, 1930, Presidential Papers—Subject—Republican National Committee—Texas, Herbert Hoover Presidential Library, West Branch, Iowa; George C. Butte to Ross S. Sterling, August 24, 1930, Sterling Papers. [Editor's note: Brown did not state the recipient of Creager and Lucey's September 24, 1940, telegram in the note. In the body of the text he said it was directed to the White House but did not name a specific individual. I was not able to identify a recipient.]

128. *Ferguson Forum* 13, October 23, 1930.

129. *DMN*, October 26, November 1, 1930; J. W. Stevenson to Ross S. Sterling, October 25, 1930; Sterling to Stevenson, October 27, 1930; Walter F. Woodul to Dan Moody and Ross Sterling, October 28, 1930; Edgar Witt to Ross Sterling, October 31, 1930, Sterling Papers, BCAH; *Ferguson Forum* 13, September 25, 1930; McKay, *Texas Politics*, 215–216.

130. Heard and Strong, *Southern Primaries*, 143–145; Robert René Martindale, "James V. Allred: The Centennial Governor of Texas" (master's thesis, University of Texas at Austin, 1957), 19; Marburger, *Texas Elections*, 51. [Editor's note: To the best of my knowledge, no scholarly biography of Allred exists to date.]

131. John Nance Garner to Tom Connally, September 30, 1930, Tom Connally Papers, Library of Congress; *DMN*, November 1, 3, 1930, November 7, 26, 1931.

132. Casdorph, *Republican Party in Texas*, 139–140.

133. David Burner, *The Politics of Provincialism: The Democratic Party in Transition, 1918–1932* (Westport, CT: Greenwood Press, 1981), 247–248.

134. *DMN*, November 8, 1930. See also *Houston Gargoyle*, November 9, 1930. [Editor's note: On Bulkley's election, see Leslie J. Stegh, "A Paradox of Prohibition: Election of Robert J. Bulkley as Senator from Ohio, 1930," *Ohio History* 83 (Summer 1974): 57–72.]

135. Editor's note: Albert Sidney Johnson seems to be have been a common name in Texas during this time—one given in honor of Confederate general Albert Sidney Johnston. I was not able to determine readily which Albert Sidney Johnson was indicated here. Brown

names a Representative A. S. Johnson of Ellis County in *Hood, Bonnet* (23), so it is possible that this is the person he mentions here.

136. *DMN*, November 6, 14, 1930.

Chapter 4: The Sterling Years

1. *Dallas Morning News*, November 6, 1930, January 21, 24, 1931 (hereafter cited as *DMN*.)

2. Fred Gantt, *The Chief Executive in Texas: A Study in Gubernatorial Leadership* (Austin: University of Texas Press, 1964), 191; Warner Everett Mills Jr., *Public Career of a Texas Conservative: A Biography of Ross Shaw Sterling* (n.p., 1957), 137; *DMN*, February 14, 1931.

3. *DMN*, April 9, May 21, 1930, September 20, 21, 1932; Byron C. Utecht, *The Legislature and the Texas People* (San Antonio: Naylor Co., 1937), 178–179; Carl L. Estes to Ross S. Sterling, April 15, 1931, Sterling Papers, Texas State Library and Archives Commission, Austin (hereafter cited as Sterling Papers, TSL); Ed Kilman, "Sterling—Texan: The Life Story of Ross Sterling," 241, 249, Typed Manuscript, Ed Kilman Collection, Houston Metropolitan Research Center, Houston Public Library; Mills, *Public Career*, 140, 141; Raymond Brooks, "Transition in Playback: V—Ross Sterling," *Austin American*, November 2, 1966, clipping in Ross Sterling Biographical File, Dolph Briscoe Center for American History, University of Texas at Austin (hereafter cited as BCAH); S. W. McKay, *Texas Politics, 1906-1944* (Lubbock: Texas Tech University Press, 1952).

4. *DMN*, October 1, 1931; Robert W. Brown to James V. Allred, November 13, 1931, Gov. James V. Allred Papers, Special Collections, University of Houston Libraries (hereafter cited as Allred Papers).

5. *DMN*, March 23, May 22, 23, 1931; Paul L. Wakefield to Jesse H. Jones, May 1, 1931, Sterling Papers. [Editor's note: Brown did not always specify in his notes from which Sterling archival collection he took his sources: both the Dolph Briscoe Center for American History and the Texas State Library and Archives Commission contain correspondence from Sterling's years as governor. Thus, I cannot state definitively from which collection some references in this chapter derive. In those instances, I have left the references in as Brown wrote them: "Sterling Papers."]

6. *DMN*, March 3, May 24, 25, 1931; J. Alton Burdine, "Shall Texas Reorganize," *Southwest Review* 18 (Summer 1933), 410–411; Ross S. Sterling to William H. Murray, July 30, 1931, Sterling Papers, BCAH. [Editor's note: The permanent university fund was mandated by the Texas constitution of 1876 and today consists of over two million acres of land, which provide a constant source of income for both the University of Texas and the Texas A&M University systems, primarily based upon leasing the land for oil and gas drilling or grazing. On its current operations and management, see University of Texas Investment Management Company (UTIMCO), "Permanent University Fund," accessed January 22, 2019, https://www.utimco.org/scripts/internet/fundsdetail.asp?fnd=2.]

7. Editor's note: The Texas Centennial has received a fair amount of scholarly attention. For one example, see Kenneth B. Ragsdale, *The Year America Discovered Texas: Centennial '36* (College Station: Texas A&M University Press, 1987).

8. *DMN*, March 6, 14, April 14, May 24, 25, 1931; Wesley Sisson Chumela, "The Politics of Legislative Apportionment in Texas—1921-1957 (PhD diss., University of Texas at Austin,

1959), 86–89; "Horse's Head," typescript in Harry Benge Crozier Papers, Capitol Legislative Reference Library, Austin.

9. Jacob Wolters to W. O. Huggins, April 24, 1931, Jesse Holman Jones Papers, 1880–1965, BCAH (hereafter cited as Jones Papers, BCAH). See also J. M. North Jr. to Paul Wakefield, April 28, 1931, Sterling Papers, TSL.

10. *DMN*, April 14, 21, 30, 1931; Mills, *Public Career*, 143; Kilman, "Sterling—Texan," 244–245; N. Graves, Alfred Petsch, E. M. Davis, Ray Holder, C. H. Akin, and J. O. Johnson to "Dear Sir," n.d.; L. Mims and Roy Miller to the Members of the Legislature, May 2, 1931, both in Jones Papers, BCAH. See also Roy Miller to William Strauss, August 3, 1930, in ibid. On the opposition of Texas druggists to the cigarette tax, see Walter Adams to R. L. Reader, April 14, 1931; Reader to Adams, April 15, 1931; Adams to Reader, April 21, 1931; Henry F. Hein to Harold Kayton, April 30, 1931, all in Walter B. Adams Papers, BCAH.

11. *DMN*, June 2, 12, 1931; Jesse Ziegler to Estella G. Hefley, June 17, 1931, Sterling Papers, BCAH.

12. On the bridge war, see William Warren Sterling, *Trails and Trials of a Texas Ranger* (Norman: University of Oklahoma Press, 1959), 221–224; Robert E. Baskin, "Texas, Oklahoma Feuded along Red River in 1931," *DMN*, March 22, 1953, clipping in Ross Sterling Scrapbook, 1930–1964, BCAH; Keith L. Bryant Jr., *Alfalfa Bill Murray* (Norman: University of Oklahoma Press, 1968), 200–201, 214–236; W. Richard Fossey, "The Red River Bridge Conflict: A Minor Skirmish in the War against Depression," *Red River Valley Historical Review* 1 (Autumn 1974): 233–247; *Ferguson Forum* 14, August 6, 1931; *DMN*, August 16, 1931. The account given here is based on these sources.

13. William H. Murray to Ross S. Sterling, July 16, 1931; Sterling to Murray, July 17, 1931, Sterling Papers, TSL.

14. Red River Bridge Statement, July 21, 1931, Sterling Papers, TSL.

15. G. P. Webb to R. S. Sterling, July 27, 1931, in Sterling Papers, TSL.

16. [Editor's note: I cannot identify the particular issue of the *Ferguson Forum* from which this quote comes.] One Otto H. Shott published a small eight-page pamphlet, *Bill at the Bridge: Otto's Second Epistle to the Oklahomans*, in thirteen verses. Verse one read:

And it came to pass that the Bill, Tzar of Oklahoma, King of Bolivia and sage of Tishomingo, spake unto Barrett the warrior saying: "General, as commander-in-chief of the army and navy, I command thee to select two colonels, ten majors, twenty captains and a coupla privates and proceed at once to the banks of the Red River. There thou wilst engage the crap shooting rangers from the land of Texas."

There is a copy of *Bill at the Bridge* in the Sterling Papers, TSL.

17. James A. Clark and Michael T. Halbouty, *The Last Boom* (New York: Random House, 1972), 76–107; Carl Coke Rister, *Oil! Titan of the Southwest* (Norman: University of Oklahoma Press, 1949); Robert D. Boyle, "Chaos in the East Texas Oil Field, 1930–1935," *Southwestern Historical Quarterly* 69 (January 1966): 340–352; Ruel McDaniel, *Some Ran Hot* (Dallas: Regional Press, 1939), 71; J. R. Parten, *The Texas Oil Case* (Austin: Independent Petroleum Association of Texas, 1933), 3.

18. Harry Harter, *East Texas Oil Parade* (San Antonio: Naylor Company, 1934), 76–92; W. Sterling, *Trails and Trials*, 227–229; Green Peyton, *For God and Texas: The Life of P. B. Hill* (New York: McGraw-Hill, 1947), 1–5; Clark and Halbouty, *Last Boom*, 123–140. [Editor's note: For a more recent interpretation of the impact of the oil industry on Texas, see

Diana Davids Olien and Roger M. Olien, *Oil in Texas: The Gusher Age, 1895–1945* (Austin: University of Texas Press, 2002). The authors argue that oil was an essential component of the modernization process in Texas, which relied on capital from oil. It wasn't until World War II, they suggest, that the oil market was large enough to support Texas's supply, but Texans nevertheless found ways to bring capital to their state prior to the war, by drawing investors to the developing oil industry.]

19. *DMN*, March 28, 1931; *National Observer*, May 12, 1969.

20. "Regulation of Oil Industry," in *Handbook of Texas*, vol. 2, ed. Walter Prescott Webb (Austin: Texas State Historical Association, 1952), 307; Gerald D. Nash, *United States Oil Policy, 1890–1964: Business and Government in Twentieth-Century America* (Pittsburg: University of Pittsburgh Press, 1968), 113–114; Clark and Halbouty, *Last Boom*, 145–146, 149–150.

21. Warner E. Mills Jr., *Martial Law in East Texas* (Tuscaloosa: University of Alabama Press, 1960), 9–10.

22. McDaniel, *Some Ran Hot*, 78–79.

23. McDaniel, *Some Ran Hot*, 75–81.

24. McDaniel, *Some Ran Hot*, 83–84; Clark and Halbouty, *Last Boom*, 158–159.

25. Paul Wakefield to Ross S. Sterling, March 16, 1931, Sterling Papers, BCAH; *DMN*, March 16, 17, 1931.

26. *DMN*, March 18, 19, 1931; McDaniel, *Some Ran Hot*, 89–92.

27. McDaniel, *Some Ran Hot*, 93–94.

28. *DMN*, March 31, April 4, 8, 1931.

29. McDaniel, *Some Ran Hot*, 95–97.

30. McDaniel, *Some Ran Hot*, 99–100; Edna M. Pollard, *The Man from Edom* (Ft. Worth: Branch Smith, 1972), 81.

31. Amon G. Carter to Ross S. Sterling, May 25, 1931, Jones Papers, BCAH; Pollard, *Man from Edom*, 82; Mills, *Martial Law*, 15. See also W. B. Hamilton to Ross S. Sterling, May 23, 1931, Sterling Papers, BCAH.

32. *DMN*, July 9, 17, 21, 1931; McDaniel, *Some Ran Hot*, 119.

33. *DMN*, June 15, 19, 20, 25, July 4, 6, 1931, Jones Papers, BCAH; Pollard, *Man from Edom*, 82; Mills, *Martial Law*, 15. See also W. B. Hamilton to Ross S. Sterling, May 23, 1931, Sterling Papers, BCAH.

34. *Ferguson Forum* 14, July 23, 1931.

35. Editor's note: The U.S. District Court in West Texas found in *Alfred MacMillan et al. v. Railroad Commission of Texas* that "the commission had not proved its case that limitation of production was necessary to prevent physical waste of petroleum." Olien and Olien, *Oil in Texas*, 184.

36. *DMN*, August 8, 12, 1931; Mills, *Martial Law*, 17–22.

37. W. Sterling, *Trails and Trials*, 230.

38. *DMN*, August 5, 11, 12, 1931.

39. Ross Sterling to Gus Taylor, August 14, 1931, Sterling Papers, BCAH; *DMN*, August 13, 1931; McDaniel, *Some Ran Hot*, 122–123; East Texas Chamber of Commerce (Longview), *Martial Law in East Texas* (Fort Worth: Texas Oil and Gas Conservation Association, 1932), 11–14.

40. *DMN*, August 4, 16, 17, 1931; Mills, *Martial Law*, 24–27; Mills, *Public Career*, 167; W. Sterling, *Trails and Trials*, 230–235; C. V. Terrell, *The Terrells: Eighty-Five Years of Texas from Indians to the Atomic Bomb* (Dallas: Wilkison Printing, 1948), 289.

41. *DMN*, August 18, 19, 22, September 2, 1931; *Ferguson Forum* 14, August 12, 1931; *Gladewater Journal*, August 17, 1931, clipping in Ross Sterling Scrapbook, 1930–1964,

BCAH; Jacob F. Wolters to Ross S. Sterling, August 17, 1930, Sterling Papers, TSL; James A. Clark, *Three Stars for the Colonel* (New York: Random House, 1954), 66; W. Sterling, *Trails and Trials*, 235. See also Roscoe Wright, "Gen. Jake on the Job: Texas' Own Riot Router," *Houston Gargoyle*, August 30, 1931. Wolters's book, *Martial Law and Its Administration*, was published by Gammel's Book Store in Austin in 1930. Wolters left the firm of Wolters, Blanchard and Woodul and joined the Texas Company's legal department on August 1, 1931. Notification card in Sterling Papers, BCAH. [Editor's note: The Texas Company was founded in 1902. While it did not officially change its name to Texaco until the 1950s, "Texaco" was the shortened name used in telegraphs, and some of its products carried that name. See L. W. Kemp and Cherie Voris, "Texaco," *Handbook of Texas Online*, accessed January 27, 2019, https://tshaonline.org/handbook/online/articles/doto1. E. J. Davis was a Reconstruction-era governor of Texas (1870–1874), whom many white Texans viewed as an agent of the federal government because of his support for Republican-led reforms under the Constitution of 1869.]

42. *Ferguson Forum* 14, August 27, 1931.

43. J. Malcom Crim and others to Ross S. Sterling, August 20, 1931; R. M. Farrar to Sterling, August 19, 1921; Sterling to Farrar, August 24, 1931, Sterling Papers, TSL. [Editor's note: Farrar is referring to a story by journalist Owen P. White, who wrote about the actions of R. B. Creager and Yancy Baker in Hidalgo County. Brown narrates these events in chapter 1 of this work.]

44. *DMN*, August 18, 1931.

45. *DMN*, September 3, 5, 1931; Howard Peacock, "East Texas: Where Oil Became an Industry," *Exxon USA* (First Quarter, 1980), 4–5; Rister, *Oil!*, 321–322; W. Sterling, *Trails and Trials*, 235; Harter, *East Texas Oil Parade*, 115–124; Clark and Halbouty, *Last Boom*, 173–180.

46. *DMN*, September 30, October 2, 3, 4, 7, 1931; Ross Sterling to Fred Minor, October 2, 1931, Sterling Papers, BCAH.

47. *DMN*, July 30, 1931; William Eugene Atkinson, *James V. Allred: A Political Biography, 1899–1935* (n.p., 1978), 194.

48. Bernard Martin to James V. Allred, December 17, 1931, Allred Papers; Atkinson, *James V. Allred*, 201.

49. James V. Allred to Marcellus E. Foster, December 15, 1931; Allred to R. Allred, January 7, 1932, Allred Papers; Atkinson, *James V. Allred*, 202–208; Robert René Martindale, "James V. Allred: The Centennial Governor of Texas" (master's thesis, University of Texas at Austin, 1957), 29–30.

50. Ross S. Sterling to Walter Beck, February 27, 1932, Sterling Papers, TSL; *DMN*, October 15, 1931, January 4, 5, 6, 7, February 27, March 1, 2, 1932; Mills, *Martial Laws*, 34–39; E. F. Smith, *A Saga of Texas Law* (San Antonio: Naylor Co., 1940), 357–364.

51. Kilman, "Sterling—Texan," 255. On Thompson, see Clark, *Three Stars*, and Douglas Carter, "The General and the Umbrella," *Reporter* 16 (March 21, 1957): 11–15.

52. *DMN*, November 3, 11, 13, 1932; Ross S. Sterling to N. H. Phillips, November 4, 1932, Sterling Papers, TSL. For calls for the special session from East Texas, see Carl L. Estes to Sterling, October 24, 1932; Gus F. Taylor to Sterling, October 25, 1932; J. K. Adair to Sterling, same date; J. W. Barton to Sterling, same date; George A. Dementroad to Sterling, same date; C. D. Bynum to Sterling, October 29, 1932, all in ibid.

53. *DMN*, November 3, 11, 13, 1932; Ross S. Sterling to N. H. Phillips, November 4, 1932, Sterling Papers, TSL. Railroad Commissioner Ernest O. Thompson wired the governor on October 28: "Believe it highly desirable that you call special session now so that our conservation law can be made to stand up. It should allow us to consider economic waste

and market demand. The best people are now ready for it and the occasion demands it. Best regards." Thompson to Sterling, October 28, 1932. See also Thompson to Sterling, October 31, 1932, both in ibid.

54. *DMN*, December 13, 14, 1932. See also Charles Fairman, "Martial Rule in the Light of Sterling v. Constantin," *Cornell Law Quarterly* 19 (1933–1934): 20–34. "The learned gentlemen did not believe that there existed any imminence of riot or bloodshed," Adjutant General Sterling wrote of the Supreme Court's decision. "They chose to disregard the oft-proven fact that men will shoot to kill in defense of their property. I made a personal survey of the situation, and will always believe that Governor Sterling was right in declaring martial law." W. Sterling, *Trails and Trials*, 236.

55. Seventy-third Congress, *National Industrial Recovery Act of 1933*, Section 9, 48 Stat 195.

56. *DMN*, December 16, 18, 1932; Mills, *Martial Law*, 41; Rister, *Oil!*, 323; Frank Goodwyn, *Lone-Star Land: Twentieth-Century Texas in Perspective* (New York: Knopf, 1955), 201; Clark, *Three Stars*, 101; Mills, *Public Career*, 171–172.

57. Ralph W. Steen, "A Political History of Texas, 1900–1930," in *Texas Democracy: A Centennial History of Politics and Personalities of the Texas Democratic Party, 1836–1936*, vol. 1, ed. Frank Carter Adams (Austin: Democratic Historical Assoc., 1937), 56–57; *DMN*, July 29, 1931. See the "Buy-a-Bale" Campaign editorial in the *DMN*, August 29, 1930. [Editor's note: Robert E. Snyder covers the events of the cotton crisis of 1931 in an in-depth study of the various attempts to try to address rapidly dropping prices and of Huey Long's call for a "cotton holiday," a proposed agreement among southerners to plant no cotton in 1932. While Texans initially showed interest in Long's plan, Texas legislators came into conflict with Long and the state ultimately repudiated his plan, instead attempting to get other southern states to pass acreage reduction laws similar to the one described here. See Snyder, *Cotton Crisis* (Chapel Hill: University of North Carolina Press, 1984).]

58. Huey P. Long to Ross S. Sterling, August 16, 1931; Sterling to Long, August 21, 1931, Sterling Papers, TSL; Sterling to Long, August 17, 1931, Sterling Papers, BCAH; *DMN*, August 23, 25, 1931.

59. Huey P. Long to Ross S. Sterling, August 24, 1931, Sterling Papers, TSL; T. Harry Williams, *Huey Long* (New York: Knopf, 1969), 530–533.

60. Huey Long to Ross S. Sterling, September 1, 1931, Sterling Papers, TSL; *Galveston Daily News*, September 1, 5, 1931. For the public response, see letters and telegrams in Sterling Papers, TSL.

61. Theodore Saloutos, *Farmers' Movements in the South, 1865–1933* (Lincoln: University of Nebraska Press, 1964), 280; Burris C. Jackson to Ross S. Sterling, September 3, 1931, Texas Cotton Association Papers, University Archives, Texas A&M University Library, College Station. See also Jackson to J. W. Garrow, September 3, 1931; Jackson to L. T. Murray, September 5, 7, 1931; Lamar Fleming to Murray, September 5, 1931; Garrow to Sterling, same date; Murray to Jackson, September 8, 1931, in ibid. [Editor's note: Robert Snyder explains that large cotton planters also had deep concerns about "labor unrest" that motivated their opposition to a cotton holiday. In 1931 cotton planters struggled to find enough seasonal pickers to work in the fields to harvest an usually large crop. Wages were very low, and many migrant laborers refused to work for such low wages. Local communities resorted to using vagrancy laws to force transient laborers, especially African Americans, to work in the cotton fields or in other industries in which enough voluntary low-wage laborers could not be obtained. Overall planters feared that a cotton holiday would cause their already-diminished workforce to flee the South for opportunity elsewhere. They also feared that such a measure

could lead to a labor revolt among tenant farmers and laborers who remained behind and would have no work at all during the proposed holiday of 1932 (Snyder, *Cotton Crisis*, 73–91). On the longer history of the ways in which southern states used vagrancy laws and other misdemeanor crimes to force African Americans to labor in southern industries, see Douglas A. Blackmon, *Slavery by Another Name: The Re-Enslavement of Black Americans from the Civil War to World War II* (New York: Anchor Books, 2009).]

62. *DMN*, September 10, 16, 17, 18, 23, 1931. [Editor's note: In his account of these events in Texas, Snyder notes that in its haste to strike back at Huey Long's "personality and politics," the Texas legislature "had neglected to incorporate an escape clause" in this law that would allow them to back out if other southern states did not join them in acreage reduction (*Cotton Crisis*, 115).]

63. Editor's note: Snyder explains that in the months after the acreage reduction law was passed, government officials in Texas, led by Commissioner of Agriculture J. E. McDonald, endeavored to obtain the cooperation of other southern states to pass similar laws and perhaps to promote a plan of regional inter-cooperation. When these efforts failed, the court decision mentioned here by Brown saved Texas from its mistake of having left out an escape clause in the law. Snyder, *Cotton Crisis*, 115–127.

64. *New York Times*, June 2, 1932; *Texas News* 6, November 15, 1932; Seth Shepard McKay and Odie B. Faulk, *Texas after Spindletop, 1901–1965* (Austin, TX: Steck-Vaughn, 1965), 128. On the cotton acreage control question see Peter Molyneaux, "Texas Cotton and Moratorium," *Review of Reviews* 85 (March 1932): 51–52; Gilbert C. Fite, "Voluntary Attempts to Reduce Cotton Acreage in the South, 1914–1933," *Journal of Southern History* 14 (November 1948): 481–499; Karl E. Ashburn, "The Texas Cotton Acreage Control Law of 1931–1932," *Southwestern Historical Quarterly* 61 (July 1957): 116–124; Donald W. Whisenhunt, "Huey Long and the Texas Cotton Acreage Control Law of 1931," *Louisiana Studies* 13 (Summer 1974): 142–153.

65. Paul E. Issac, "Laissez-Faire to National Planning: The Editorial Policy of the *Beaumont Enterprise* from the Great Crash through the Hundred Days" (East Texas Historical Association, 1965), 130; *DMN*, September 3, 1930.

66. *DMN*, September 6, 18, 1930.

67. Editor's note: Scholarship written in recent decades addresses in greater depth the effects of the Great Depression on the lives of Mexican Americans, African Americans, and poor whites living in Texas. In general these groups bore the brunt of the Great Depression's negative effects, but they also found ways to thrive by adopting creative economic solutions, migrating, and organizing. See Julia Kirk Blackwelder, *Women of the Depression: Caste and Culture in San Antonio, 1929–1939* (College Station: Texas A&M University Press, 1999); Neil Foley, *The White Scourge: Mexicans, Blacks, and Poor Whites in Texas Cotton Culture* (Berkeley: University of California Press, 1997); David Montejano, *Anglos and Mexicans in the Making of Texas, 1836–1986* (Austin: University of Texas Press, 1987); Bernadette Pruitt, *The Other Great Migration: The Movement of Rural African Americans to Houston, 1900–1941* (College Station: Texas A&M University Press, 2013); Debra Ann Reid, *Reaping a Greater Harvest: African Americans, the Extension Service, and Rural Reform in Jim Crow Texas* (College Station: Texas A&M University Press, 2007); and Zaragosa Vargas, *Labor Rights Are Civil Rights: Mexican American Workers in Twentieth-Century America* (Princeton: Princeton University Press, 2005). Vargas and Reid in particular show how the New Deal, despite its prejudicial implementation, provided opportunities for Mexican Americans and African Americans in Texas, who worked the system to their best advantage.

68. Donald W. Whisenhunt, "The Texas Attitude Toward Relief, 1929–1933," *Panhandle-*

Plains Historical Review 46 (1973): 96–98. For a full discussion, see Donald W. Whisenhunt, "Texas in the Depression, 1929–1933: A Study in Public Reaction" (PhD diss., Texas Technological College, 1966). [Editor's note: This dissertation has since been published. See Whisenhunt, *The Depression in Texas: The Hoover Years* (New York: Garland, 1983).]

69. Whisenhunt, "Texas Attitude," 98; Donald W. Whisenhunt, "The Transient in the Depression," *Red River Valley Historical Review* 1 (Spring 1971): 7–20.

70. Richard Henderson, *Maury Maverick: A Political Biography* (Austin: University of Texas Press, 1970), 52–56; Maury Maverick, *A Maverick American* (New York: Covici-Friede-Publisher, 1937), 167–176; *DMN*, December 23, 1932. See also Donald W. Whisenhunt, "Maury Maverick and the Diga Relief Colony, 1932–1933," *Texana* 9 (Summer 1971): 249–259. [Editor's note: Robert Snyder notes that Maury Maverick had begun investigating the plight of transient Texans in the context of the of crisis in 1931. Maverick posed as a transient laborer to learn more about their lives, and he claimed that most of them were average tenant farmers or seasonal pickers who were economically overwhelmed due to the volatility of the agricultural labor market at the time. These observations would later inspire his work at the Diga community. Snyder, *Cotton Crisis*, 87–89.]

71. Henderson, *Maury Maverick*, 56–57; Maverick, *Maverick American*, 150–166.

72. Ross S. Sterling to D. G. Burke, January 14, 1931, quoted in Mills, *Public Career*, 162; *Houston Post-Dispatch*, August 4, September 25, 1931.

73. Editor's note: Brown did not cite these sources in his manuscript. I assume they are from letters held in one of the Sterling archival collections.

74. Raymond Brooks, "Transition in Playback: V—Ross Sterling," *Austin American*, November 2, 1966, clipping in Ross Sterling Biographical File, BCAH; Bascom N. Timmons, *Jesse E. Jones: The Man and the Statesman* (New York: Holt, 1956), 159–161; James A. Clark with Weldon Hart, *The Tactful Texan: A Biography of Governor Will Hobby* (New York: Random House, 1958), 170–171; Allen Peden, "The P. D. Purchase: A Glimpse of the High Bidder," *Houston Gargoyle*, December 6, 1931.

75. Isaac, "Laissez-Faire," 132–133.

76. Editor's note: Brown's interpretation of the effect of the Great Depression on Texans holds true today. Historians agree that average Texans became receptive to federal intervention as it became increasingly clear that local measures were not going to be sufficient. Nevertheless, many Texans, as a general rule, continued to be suspicious of the federal government—a mind-set that exists to this day. See Walter L. Buenger, *The Path to a Modern South: Northeast Texas between Reconstruction and the Great Depression* (Austin: University of Texas Press, 2001); Donald W. Whisenhunt, ed., *The Depression in the Southwest* (Port Washington, NY: Kennikat Press, 1980); and Whisenhunt, *Depression in Texas*. On the Great Depression in the South more generally, scholars have shown that it was a crucial turning point in the history of the region. Federal and state policies ultimately undermined an agricultural system reliant on tenant farming and sharecropping, and, despite cultural biases against government intervention, it became more common. See Roger Biles, *The South and the New Deal* (Lexington: University of Kentucky Press, 1994); and Buenger, *Path to a Modern South*.

Chapter 5: Texas Again Tangled in Ma's Apron Strings

1. Editor's note: Since Brown wrote this manuscript, only two monograph-length treatments of Miriam Ferguson's political career have been written: Carl McQueary and May

Nelson Paulissen, *Miriam: The Southern Belle Who Became the First Woman Governor of Texas* (Austin, TX: Eakin Press, 1995); and Carol O'Keefe Wilson, *In the Governor's Shadow: The True Story of Ma and Pa Ferguson* (Denton: University of North Texas Press, 2014). McQueary and Paulissen's work is not written from a historical-critical perspective but nevertheless hopes to challenge the view presented by many scholars, including Brown, that Miriam Ferguson "was governor in name only." Brown, *Hood, Bonnet*, 269 quoted in McQueary and Paulissen, *Miriam*, 310. Wilson, however, takes a critical approach to the Ferguson administrations, attempting to show in detail how they defrauded the people of Texas. A recent volume examines critically the governorship of Jim Ferguson, including the events surrounding his impeachment, his conflicts with the University of Texas and women's suffrage advocates, and his hot-and-cold relationship with the press, among other issues. Jessica Brannon-Wranosky and Bruce A. Glasrud, eds., *Impeached: The Removal of Texas Governor James E. Ferguson* (College Station: Texas A&M University Press, 2017).

2. *Ferguson Forum* 14, December 31, 1931; *Dallas Morning News*, January 31, 1932 (hereafter cited as *DMN*); Alfred Steinberg, *Sam Rayburn: A Biography* (New York: Hawthorn Books, 1975), 102.

3. Clint Small to "Dear Bill," December 29, 1931. This letter was reprinted on the reverse side of a single-page broadside, "400,000 Democrats Can't be Wrong," published by the Harris County Ferguson Campaign Committee during the runoff primary. There is a copy in the Thomas B. Love Collection, Dallas Historical Society (hereafter cited as Love Collection, DHS).

4. *DMN*, February 16, 18, 1932; *Ferguson Forum* 14, February 18, 1932.

5. *Ferguson Forum* 14, March 17, 1932; *DMN*, March 17, 1932.

6. *DMN*, February 17, April 3, 5, 1932.

7. *DMN*, October 18, 1931; Allen Peden, "Who for Governor? Has Ross Had Enough?" *Houston Gargoyle*, November 1, 1931; Clint Small to "Dear Bill," December 29, 1931, Love Collection, DHS.

8. *DMN*, December 31, 1931, January 22, April 1, 27, 1932.

9. James V. Allred to Mr. and Mrs. Allred, April 9, 22, 1932, Gov. James V. Allred Papers, Courtesy of Special Collections, University of Houston Libraries (hereafter cited as Allred Papers); *Austin Statesman*, July 12, 1932; Robert René Martindale, "James V. Allred: The Centennial Governor of Texas" (master's thesis, University of Texas at Austin, 1957), 20. "It has been impossible for even his closest friends to get the Governor to say what he is going to do," Houston businessman J. E. Josey complained to Allred in early April. Josey to Allred, April 8, 1932, Allred Papers.

10. *DMN*, May 2, 1932.

11. *DMN*, May 10, 15, 1932; Ed Kilman, "Sterling–Texan: The Life Story of Ross Sterling," Typed Manuscript, 154, Ed Kilman Collection, Houston Metropolitan Research Center, Houston Public Library, 306; Wand with Warner E. Mills Jr., May 18, 1953, cited in Mills, *Public Career of a Texas Conservative: A Biography of Ross Shaw Sterling* (n.p., 1957), 188.

12. *DMN*, June 4, 5, 6, 9, 10, 12, 15, 1932; "Armstrong for Governor," one-page broadside, Steve M. King to Ross Sterling, June 8, 1932. Sterling to King, June 11, 1932, Sterling Papers, Dolph Briscoe Center for American History, University of Texas at Austin (hereafter cited as Sterling Papers, BCAH); S. W. McKay, *Texas Politics, 1906–1944* (Lubbock: Texas Tech University Press, 1952), 224–224; William Warren Sterling, *Trails and Trials of a Texas Ranger* (Norman: University of Oklahoma Press, 1959), 257.

13. Walter C. Woodward to Thomas B. Love, May 27, 1932, Love Collection, DHS. Beck is quoted in Kilman, "Sterling–Texan," 310.

14. Carr P. Collins to Ross S. Sterling, June 7, 1932; Thomas B. Love to Walter C. Woodward, same date, Love Collection, DHS.

15. *DMN*, June 9, 1932; Ross S. Sterling to Carr P. Collins, June 9, 1932, Sterling Papers, BCAH.

16. Kilman, "Sterling—Texan," 310.

17. *DMN*, June 16, 1932; Carr P. Collins to Alvin Moody, June 15, 1932, Love Collection, DHS.

18. *DMN*, June 18, 1932.

19. *DMN*, July 7, 8, 1932.

20. *DMN*, July 10, 1932.

21. *DMN*, July 11, 17, 23, 1932; Thomas B. Love to John H. Eaton, July 18, 1932, Love Collection, DHS; "J. W. Bailey Enters Contest for Congressman," *DMN*, May 24, 1932, clipping in Joseph W. Bailey Jr. Biographical File, BCAH.

22. Alvin Moody to Thomas B. Love, July 12, 1932; Moody to Cato Sells, same date, Love Collection, DHS.

23. *DMN*, July 23, 26, 30, 31, August 2, 1932.

24. Alvin Moody to Thomas B. Love, July 29, 1932, Love Collection, DHS.

25. *DMN*, May 22, 1932.

26. *DMN*, June 12, 1932.

27. Mills, *Public Career*, 189–191.

28. Mills, *Public Career*, 192–193.

29. *DMN*, July 7, 1932.

30. Gus Russek to Ross S. Sterling, June 7, 1932; Sterling to Russek, June 9, 1932, Sterling Papers, Texas State Archives; Mills, *Public Career*, 194.

31. *DMN*, July 12, 13, 1932; S. B. Kirkpatrick to Ross S. Sterling, July 4, 1932, Sterling Papers, BCAH; W. Sterling, *Trails and Trials*, 253.

32. *A Sterling Record, Written by Public Opinion in the Editorial Columns of the Leading Newspapers of the State—the People's Responsive Representatives for Good Government. Including ... Governor Sterling's Platform* (n.p., 1932), Sterling Papers, BCAH.

33. *Ferguson Forum* 15, July 14, 1932; "The Truth about the 'Langhorn Case,'" one-page broadside in Fred Acree Papers, BCAH; *DMN*, July 13, 1932; Thomas W. Fite to Ross S. Sterling, July 6, 1932, Sterling Papers, BCAH.

34. *DMN*, March 27, 1932; Tom F. Hunter to Ben G. Oneal, May 14, 1932, Benjamin Grady Oneal Papers, 1905–1961, BCAH; W. Sterling, *Trails and Trials*, 257.

35. *DMN*, July 15, 16, 22, 23, 1932; *Ferguson Forum* 15, July 21, 1932.

36. *DMN*, July 25, August 9, 1932; Alexander Heard and Donald S. Strong, *Southern Primaries and Elections, 1920–1949* (Tuscaloosa: University of Alabama Press, 1950), 146–148. Other totals: Roger Q. Evans, 3,974; Frank Putnam, 2,962; C. A. Frakes, 2,338; J. Ed Glenn, 2,089.

37. *DMN*, July 29, August 28, 1932; McKay, *Texas Politics*, 233–234. The black votes for Mrs. Ferguson in San Antonio are mentioned in Hirschie Johnson to Pat H. Dougherty, August 1, 1932, Sterling Papers, BCAH. For press comment, see "Can 'Ma' Ferguson Finish Her Comeback?" *Literary Digest* 114 (August 6, 1932): 34.

38. Harold J. Marburger, *Texas Elections, 1918–1954* (Austin: Texas State Library, 1956), 56–58; Bruce W. Bryant to Tom Garrard, July 7, 1932, Allred Papers; *Austin American*, July 15, 26, 1932; Martindale, "James V. Allred," 20–25; William Eugene Atkinson, *James V. Allred: A Political Biography, 1899–1935* (n.p., 1978), 259–273. See also Harry and Tom King

to James V. Allred, March 1, 1932; Allred to Mr. and Mrs. James V. Allred, March 1, 1932; Allred to Mr. and Mrs. R. Allred, April 22, June 1, 22, 1932; Walter David to Allred, June 24, 1932; W. J. Johnson to Allred, June 25, 1932; W. F. Daniel to Allred, July 1, 1932; Hollis M. Kinard to Allred, July 5, 1932; Tom B. Bartlett to Allred, July 7, 1932; Bruce W. Bryant to J. S. Edwards, July 21, 1932; Thomas B. Love to Allred, July 23, 1932; W. S. Poston to Allred, July 25, 1932; Jas. H. Aynesworth to Allred, same date, all in the Allred Papers; "James V. Allred Attorney General of Texas—The Case of the People of Texas and Attorney General James V. Allred Versus the Oil Companies and Their Candidate Opposing Mr. Allred," four-page broadside in "Who Are Backers of Opposition to James V. Allred," *Austin Labor Journal*, July 15, 1932, clipping in James V. Allred Scrapbook, July 9, 1932–June 16, 1968, BCAH.

39. Marburger, *Texas Elections*, 56–59; J. H. "Cyclone" Davis to Thomas B. Love, July 27, 1932; Love to Bishop H. A. Boaz, August 13, 1932, Love Collection, DHS; *DMN*, August 1, 23, 1932.

40. *DMN*, July 26, 1932; Secretary to Samuel M. Duffie, July 30, 1932, Sterling Papers, BCAH. Robertson is quoted in W. Sterling, *Trails and Trials*, 262.

41. Editor's note: The interview with George C. Moffett, 1965–1966, is part of the University of North Texas Oral History Program, accessed February 6, 2019, https://digital.library .unt.edu/ark:/67531/metapth223568/?q=George%20C.%20Moffett.

42. Editor's note: Samuel T. Rayburn was a Texas representative to the U.S. Congress for nearly fifty years between 1913 and 1961. He would eventually be chosen Speaker of the House and majority leader for Democrats. No scholarly biography has been written about Rayburn since the late 1980s, but many works cover his life and career, including Anthony Champagne, *Sam Rayburn: A Bio-Bibliography* (New York: Greenwood Press, 1988); Edward O. Daniel, "Sam Rayburn: Trials of a Party Man" (PhD diss., North Texas State University, Denton, 1979); Kenneth Dewey Hairgrove, *Sam Rayburn: Congressional Leader, 1940–1952* (Lubbock: Texas Tech University, 1974); D. B. Hardeman, *Rayburn: A Biography* (Austin: Texas Monthly Press, 1987); Booth Mooney, *Roosevelt and Rayburn: A Political Partnership* (Philadelphia: Lippincott, 1971); Alexander Graham Shanks, "Sam Rayburn and the New Deal, 1933–1936" (master's thesis, University of North Carolina, Chapel Hill, 1964); and Alfred Steinberg, *Sam Rayburn: A Biography* (New York: Hawthorn Books, 1975).

43. Sam Rayburn to John McDuffie, July 8, 1932; Rayburn to Amon G. Carter, August 17, 1932, Sam Rayburn Papers, 1822, 1831, 1845, 1903–2007, Series I, Rolls 2, 3, BCAH; Steinberg, *Sam Rayburn*, 100–102.

44. *DMN*, July 28, 1932; Ross S. Sterling to Tom Hunter, July 25, 1932, Sterling Papers, BCAH. Hunter is quoted in Kilman, "Sterling—Texan," 320.

45. *DMN*, August 7, 13, 28, 1932; "We Open the Run-Off," three-page broadside in James Ferguson Scrapbook, 1914–1935, BCAH.

46. *DMN*, August 2, 8, 14, 1932.

47. *DMN*, August 5, 6, 1932.

48. *DMN*, August 6, 9, 19, 27, 1932; Ernest Alexander to G. P. Berry, August 12, 1932, Sterling Papers, BCAH.

49. *DMN*, August 16, 22, 1932.

50. Roy Payne to Ross S. Sterling, July 17, 1932; Wm. W. Snider to Sterling, August 10, 1932, Sterling Papers, BCAH. See also W. I. Cunningham to Sterling, July 20, 1932; Ernest Weaver to Sterling, August 15, 1932; George B. Hays to Sterling, August 27, 1932, in ibid.

51. Gus F. Taylor to Thomas B. Love, August 16, 1932, Love Collection, DHS; *DMN*, August 20, 22, 1932.

52. W. Sterling, *Trails and Trials*, 264–266; Kilman, "Sterling—Texan," 327–328.

53. McKay, *Texas Politics*, 239; Heard and Strong, *Southern Primaries*, 146–148; *DMN*, September 1, 1932; Ross S. Sterling to G. W. Dabney, September 1, 1932, Sterling Papers, BCAH; "Texas Tangled in 'Ma's' Apron-Strings," *Literary Digest* 114 (September 1932): 11.

54. "Texas Tangled," 11; Harold Preece, "'Ma' Ferguson Wins Again," *The Nation* 135 (September 21, 1932): 255–256; Mildred Adams, "Again the Fergusons Rouse the Texans," *New York Times*, October 23, 1932, in James E. Ferguson Scrapbook, 1914–1940, BCAH. See also Owen P. White, "Keeping Texas in the Family," *Collier's* 91 (February 4, 1933): 10–11, 26.

55. *DMN*, September 2, 4, 6, 7, 10, 1932; Edna M. Pollard, *Man from Edom* (Ft. Worth: Branch Smith, 1972), 87; Raymond Brooks to Charles E. Marsh, August 31, September 1, 1932, Sterling Papers, BCAH; James V. Allred to Mr. and Mrs. R. Allred, September 8, 1932, Allred Papers.

56. *Ferguson Forum* 15, September 8, 1932; *DMN*, September 10, 11, 12, 13, 14, 1932; Raymond Brooks, *Political Playback* (Austin: Eugene C. Barker Texas History Center, 1961), 37; Ouida Wallace Ferguson Nalle, *Fergusons of Texas: Or "Two Governors for the Price of One"* (San Antonio: Naylor Co., 1946), 215–217. There was some substance to the rumors of Ranger intervention. "The Lubbock Convention presented a sad spectacle," W. W. Sterling wrote in his memoirs. "Hot oil men and other corrupt groups had put up money to pack it with the rag tag and bobtail of Texas. My boys were ready to get some justice in a practical way, but our attorneys warned that there must be no fights or bloodshed. Captain Frank Hamer used his sarcastic wit. 'There will be no bloodshed, Judge. If we jump that bunch, the only thing that will be shed will be a lot of filth and corruption.' At a caucus in Governor Sterling's room, it was decided to pass up the convention and try to get relief in the courts." W. Sterling, *Trails and Trials*, 270.

57. *DMN*, September 14, 1932. There are six boxes labeled "Voter Irregularities, Sterling vs. Ferguson" in the Sterling Papers, BCAH.

58. *DMN*, September 17, 18, 1932; Ross S. Sterling to Charles I. Francis, September 17, 1932, Sterling Papers, BCAH.

59. *DMN*, September 29, 30, October 3, 4, 6, 7, 8, 9, 1932.

60. *DMN*, September 21, October 14, 1932. On Bullington, see Orville Bullington Biographical File, BCAH.

61. *DMN*, October 12, 18, 19, 1932; S. E. Bingham to Ross S. Sterling, November 2, 1932, Sterling Papers, BCAH; "Crane Reviews Ferguson Rule as Governor," *DMN*, August 27, 1932, clipping in Mrs. Miriam A. Ferguson Biographical File, BCAH; "Nomination Procured by Fraudulent Vote Not Binding, Says Gen. M. M. Crane," one-page broadside in Miriam A. Ferguson File, Campaign Materials, Texas State Archives and Library.

62. Thomas B. Love to William G. McAdoo, September 14, 1932; Love to W. L. Evans, September 14, 1932; W. R. Ely to Henry C. Porter, September 1, 1932, Love Collection, DHS; *Ferguson Forum* 15, September 22, 1932.

63. *DMN*, October 10, 1932; Ross S. Sterling to T. J. Crowe, October 10, 1932, Sterling Papers, BCAH. See also Sterling to Amon G. Carter, October 10, 1932; Sterling to Clarence E. Farmer, same date; Sterling to Walter C. Woodward, October 11, 1932, Sterling Papers. [Editor's note: As stated in my note in chapter 4, Brown did not always specify in his notes which Sterling archival collection held the cited correspondence, and both the Briscoe Center for American History and the Texas State Library and Archives Commission contain correspondence from Sterling's years as governor. I have left the reference in as Brown wrote it: "Sterling Papers."]

64. Ross S. Sterling to J. C. Lyon, October 12, 1932; Sterling to George Hunter Smith,

October 14, 1932; Sterling to Thomas B. Love, October 20, 1932, Sterling Papers, BCAH; *DMN*, October 21, 23, 1932.

65. *DMN*, October 21, 26, 29, 1932.

66. *DMN*, October 14, 19, 23, 30, 1932; *Ferguson Forum* 15, October 13, 1932.

67. James E. Ferguson to Franklin D. Roosevelt, September 22, 1932; Roosevelt to Ferguson, October 6, 1932, Democratic National Committee, Box 735, Roosevelt Presidential Library, Hyde Park, NY; *DMN*, October 11, 1932.

68. "Do Not Be Bluffed or Bulldozed," broadside in James E. Ferguson File, Campaign Materials, Texas State Archives and Library; Thomas B. Love to James C. Farley, September 30, 1932, Love Collection, DHS.

69. *DMN*, November 1, 1931; Dick Vaughan, "Jim Ferguson's Reminiscences—12," Houston *Press*, October 17, 1932.

70. *DMN*, November 1, 1932; Heard and Strong, *Southern Primaries*, 146–148; McKay, *Texas Politics*, 245–246; Geo. Eakin to Thomas B. Love, November 3, 1932, Love Collection, DHS; Ross S. Sterling to Horace Russell, November 10, 1932, Sterling Papers, BCAH. Other gubernatorial totals: George C. Edwards (Socialist), 1,866; George W. Armstrong (Jacksonian Democratic), 706; Otho L. Heitt (Liberty), 101; Philip L. Howe (Communist), 72. Marburger, *Texas Elections*, 60.

71. *DMN*, December 4, 1932.

72. Thomas B. Love to Dr. J. A. Old, December 15, 1932; Love to Alvin Moody, same date; Cato Sells to Love, December 8, 1932; Love to Sells, December 23, 1932; Love to Moody, January 12, 1933; Moody to Sells, n.d.; Love to Sells, February 10, 1933; Morris Sheppard to Chas. C. Robey, February 18, 1933; Love to Tom Connally, February 24, 1933, all in Love Collection, DHS; Sells to Wyatt C. Hendrick, December 5, 1932; Hendrick to Ross S. Sterling, December 8, 1932; Sterling to Connally, December 12, 1932; Sterling to Sheppard, same date; Sells to Sterling, December 13, 1932; Love to Sterling, December 19, 1932, all in Sterling Papers, BCAH.

73. Joseph W. Bailey Jr. to O. B. Colquitt, May 19, 1933; Thomas B. Love to Franklin D. Roosevelt, December 11, 1933, Love Collection, DHS. On Colquitt's lobbying activities, see Colquitt to Love, December 30, 31, 1933; Colquitt to Morris Sheppard, December 31, 1933; Colquitt to Love, January 1, 1933 [1934]; Colquitt to Love, February 4, 1934, Colquitt to Love, March 17, 1934, in ibid.

74. T. Whitfield Davidson to Edward M. House, January 24, April 15, 1933; Charles I. Francis to James A. Farley, January 25, 1933; Alvin M. Owsley to House, December 15, 1932, January 21, March 3, 1933, Edward Mandell House Papers (MS 466), Manuscripts and Archives, Yale University Library (hereafter cited as House Papers, Yale); Marion S. Adams, *Alvin M. Owsley: Apostle of Americanism* (Waco, TX: Texian Press, 1971), 124–127; *Austin American*, April 30, 1967; *Houston Post*, November 7, 1969, clippings in Charles I. Francis Biographical File, BCAH; *DMN*, January 27, 1974, clipping in T. Whitfield Davidson Biographical File, BCAH.

75. Gregory to J. A. Donnell, December 6, 1932, Thomas Watt Gregory Papers, Library of Congress; unidentified newspaper clipping, 1933, in Thomas Watt Gregory Biographical File, BCAH.

76. Arthur D. Howden Smith, *Mr. House of Texas* (New York: Funk & Wagnalls, 1940), 367–368; Raymond Moley, *The First New Deal* (New York: Harcourt, Brace, 1966), 41n.

77. Editor's note: Brown discusses the relationship between FDR and Colonel House in greater detail in chapter 6.

78. Edward M. House to Franklin D. Roosevelt, March 21, 1933; House to Frank Andres,

August 25, 1933, House Papers, Yale. Roosevelt explained his failure to consult frequently with House during the "One Hundred Days" by saying: "For one whole month I have been meaning day by day, to telephone you or write you but I have realized that through the papers you know as much or more of what is going on that I myself do. And, too, I have felt sure that you would let me know at once if you had any suggestions or specially important information." Roosevelt to House, April 5, 1933, in ibid. In 1935 the president wrote flatteringly to House: "I do wish you carried out splendid missions which you had carried out in Europe before we got into the war—but there is only one *you* and I know of no other." Roosevelt to House, April 10, 1935, in ibid. [Editor's note: Brown did not specify which Edward M. House archival collection he had visited. There are collections housed at the Briscoe Center for American History and at Yale. I have cited the Yale collection here, as it seems to be the more extensive collection.]

79. Ross S. Sterling to Roy S. Holloman, November 25, 1932, Sterling Papers, BCAH; *DMN*, October 15, 1932; W. Sterling, *Trails and Trials*, 517.

80. Robert L. Holliday to Gregory, September 8, 1932; Gregory to Holliday, October 5, 1932, Thomas Watt Gregory Papers, Library of Congress; Ross S. Sterling to Holliday, September 9, 1932; Holliday to Sterling, September 24, 1932; Sterling to Holliday, September 29, 1932, Sterling Papers, BCAH; *DMN*, January 13, 15, 1933.

81. *DMN*, December 30, 1932.

82. Editor's note: See Brown, *Hood, Bonnet*, 137, 358.

83. *DMN*, January 14, 16, 1933.

84. Ross S. Sterling to H. C. Coffee, November 30, 1932; Sterling Papers, BCAH; Sterling to Thomas B. Love, January 20, 1933, Love Collection, DHS; *DMN*, January 10, 13, 1933; Mills, *Public Career*, 217–218; Fred Gantt, *The Chief Executive in Texas: A Study in Gubernatorial Leadership* (Austin: University of Texas Press, 1964), 240.

85. *DMN*, January 15, 17, 1933; W. Sterling, *Trails and Trials*, 277. [Editor's note: The Eighth Commandment of the Protestant Bible is "Thou shalt not steal."]

Chapter 6: Garnering Votes for Cactus Jack

1. Editor's note: A condensed version of this chapter previously appeared as "Garnering Votes for 'Cactus Jack': John Nance Garner, Franklin D. Roosevelt, and the 1932 Democratic Nomination for President," *Southwestern Quarterly* 104, no. 2 (October 2000): 149–188.

2. Thomas Watt Gregory to Edward M. House, December 11, 1930, Thomas Watt Gregory Papers, Library of Congress (hereafter cited as T. W. Gregory Papers, LC); Seth Shepard McKay and Odie B. Faulk, *Texas after Spindletop, 1901–1965* (Austin, TX: Steck-Vaughn, 1965), 119; William E. Leuchtenburg, *The Perils of Prosperity, 1914–32* (Chicago: University of Chicago Press, 1958), 264.

3. Roy V. Peel and Thomas C. Donnelly, *The 1932 Campaign: An Analysis* (New York: Farrar & Rinehart, 1935), 28–32.

4. Frank Freidel, *Franklin D. Roosevelt*, vol. 3, *The Triumph* (Boston: Little, Brown, 1956), 144–146.

5. Thomas B. Love to Daniel C. Roper, June 19, 1931; William G. McAdoo to Love, September 27, November 19, 1930, Thomas B. Love Collection, Dallas Historical Society (hereafter cited as Love Collection, DHS).

6. Freidel, *Roosevelt: The Triumph*, 169.

7. Roosevelt to Jesse H. Jones, January 7, 1929; Jones to Roosevelt, January 30, 1929; Roosevelt to Dan Moody Jr., June 5, 1929, FDR Private Correspondence, 1929–1932, Box 91, 120, Franklin D. Roosevelt Presidential Library, Hyde Park, NY (hereafter Roosevelt PL).

8. Mrs. Percy V. Pennybacker to Madam Hainari, February 25, 1929; Pennybacker to Count Carlo Sforza, April 4, 1928; Eleanor Roosevelt to Pennybacker, [June 1929] November 25, 1930; Pennybacker to Roosevelt, July 15, 1929, February 11, October 27, 1930, February 25, March 31, 1931, all in Mrs. Percy V. Pennybacker Papers, 1878–1938, Dolph Briscoe Center for American History, University of Texas at Austin (hereafter cited as BCAH).

9. James G. Holloway to Franklin D. Roosevelt, February 7, 1931, Louis Howe Papers Corr. 1929–32, January–March 1931, Box 49, Roosevelt PL; Hugh Nugent Fitzgerald, "Now as to Politics," *Austin American*, February 7, 1931.

10. "Texas Straus Poll," Democratic National Committee, Box 728, Roosevelt PL; Alfred B. Rollins Jr., *Roosevelt and Howe* (New York: Knopf, 1962), 315–316.

11. HNF [Hugh Nugent Fitzgerald], "For Mr. Marsh," four-page memorandum enclosed in Charles Marsh to Franklin D. Roosevelt, August 13, 1931, Democratic National Committee, Box 731, Roosevelt PL; Peel and Donnelly, *1932 Campaign*, 41.

12. Edward M. House to Franklin D. Roosevelt, March 10, 22, 1925, and undated note, March [?], 1925; Roosevelt to House, October 8, 1928; House to Thomas Watt Gregory, October 20, 1928; House to Roosevelt, November 7, 1928, Edward Mandell House Papers (MS 466), Manuscripts and Archives, Yale University Library (hereafter cited as House Papers, Yale); *Dallas Morning News*, January 18, 1932 (hereafter cited as *DMN*); Arthur D. Howden Smith, *Mr. House of Texas* (New York: Funk & Wagnalls, 1940), 366–367. [Editor's note: Recent studies of the life and career of Edward House include Romney Clark Bushnell, "'All the World and the Fullness Thereof': The Business Career of Colonel E. M. House, 1885–1920," (master's report, University of Texas at Austin, 1982); Inga Floto, *Colonel House in Paris: A Study of American Policy at the Paris Peace Conference, 1919* (Princeton, NJ: Princeton University Press, 1980); Godfrey Hodgson, *Woodrow Wilson's Right Hand: The Life of Colonel Edward M. House* (New Haven, CT: Yale University Press, 2006); Charles E. Neu, *Colonel House: A Biography of Woodrow Wilson's Silent Partner* (New York: Oxford University Press, 2015); and Joyce G. Williams, *Colonel House and Sir Edward Grey: A Study in Anglo-American Diplomacy* (Lanham, MD: University Press of America, 1984).]

13. Editor's note: "Alberich" refers to a character from Norse mythology—a dwarf who guarded gold treasure.

14. Lela Stiles, *The Man behind Roosevelt: The Story of Louis McHenry Howe* (Cleveland: World Publishing, 1954), 139–140. This account of the conference between House and Howe is based on Field's recollections. In a letter to Roosevelt, House mentions his meeting the previous day with Howe, "of which he will tell you." House to Roosevelt, December 30, 1930, Franklin D. Roosevelt Papers as Governor of New York, 1929–1932, FDR Private Correspondence, 1929–1932, Box 84, Group 12, Roosevelt PL. [Editor's note: For a recent biography of Howe, see J. M. Fenster, *FDR's Shadow: Louis Howe, the Force that Shaped Franklin and Eleanor Roosevelt* (New York: Palgrave Macmillan, 2009).]

15. House to Roosevelt, December 30, 1930, Franklin D. Roosevelt Papers as Governor of New York, 1929–1932, FDR Private Correspondence, 1929–1932, Box 84, Group 12, Roosevelt PL; House to Robert Woolley, November 5, 1930; House to Daniel C. Roper, May 9, 1931, House Papers, Yale.

16. House to Roosevelt, March 23, 1931, Franklin D. Roosevelt Papers as Governor of New York, 1929–1932, FDR Private Correspondence, 1929–1932, Box 84, Group 12, Roose-

velt PL; "Memorandum for Mr. Howe," June 24, 1931, Louis Howe Papers Corr. 1928–32, April–July 1931, Box 49, Roosevelt PL. Attached to the memorandum was the following note: "Will you talk this over with the Colonel when you see him? FDR." See also Freidel, *Roosevelt: The Triumph*, 201; Rollins, *Roosevelt and Howe*, 314; Earland I. Carlson, "Franklin D. Roosevelt's Fight for the Presidential Nomination, 1928–1932" (PhD diss., University of Illinois, 1955), 113–117.

17. House to Albert Sidney Burleson, May 7, 1931, House Papers, Yale. See also House to Gregory, December 20, 1930, T. W. Gregory Papers, LC.

18. House and McAdoo are quoted in Elliot A. Rosen, *Hoover, Roosevelt, and the Brains Trust: From Depression to New Deal* (New York: Columbia University Press, 1977), 16–17.

19. Frank Andrews to House, March 31, 1931, House Papers, Yale.

20. Gregory to House, March 31, 1931, T. W. Gregory Papers, LC. Senator Tom Connally said of House's role in Texas politics in the early 1930s: "Colonel House came originally and liked to give the impression that he carried a great deal of political weight in my state, though actually he had little Lone Star influence." Tom Connally and Alfred Steinberg, *My Name Is Tom Connally* (New York: Crowell, 1954), 97.

21. House to Robert N. Field, April 13, 1931; House to Roosevelt, April 5, 1931; House to Frank Andrews, April 13, 15, 1931, House Papers, Yale; House to Gregory, April 15, 1931, T. W. Gregory Papers, LC; Robert M. Field to Roosevelt, April 10, 1931, FDR Private Correspondence, 1929–1932, Box 57, Group 12, Roosevelt PL.

22. "New York Lawyer Here for Round Up Boosts Roosevelt," unidentified newspaper clipping enclosed in House to Roosevelt, April 22, 1931, FDR Private Correspondence, 1929–1932, Box 84, Group 12, Roosevelt PL; Frank Andrews to House, April 25, 1931, House Papers, Yale.

23. "Memorandum," Democratic National Committee, Box 728, Roosevelt PL.

24. House to Gregory, May 2, 1931, T. W. Gregory Papers, LC. See also House to Frank Andrews, April 30, May 3, 1931, House Papers, Yale.

25. Gregory to House, May 20, 1931, T. W. Gregory Papers, LC.

26. Carlson, "Roosevelt's Fight," 118–119; *DMN*, June 5, 1931; House to Howe, June 21, 1931, Box 49, Roosevelt PL. Mrs. Percy V. Pennybacker informed Howe that House's declaration for Roosevelt was worth that of any other hundred men. Pennybacker to House, June 12, 1932, Pennybacker Papers, BCAH.

27. House to Robert W. Woolley, June 14, 1931, Robert Wickliffe Woolley Papers, Manuscript Division, Library of Congress (hereafter cited as Woolley Papers, LC); Carlson, "Roosevelt's Fight," 119–120. See also House to Thomas Watt Gregory, June 14, 1931, House Papers, Yale.

28. House to Robert M. Field, July 4, 1931, House Papers, Yale; Frank Andrews to Roosevelt, July 13, 1931; House to Gregory, July 4, 1931, T. W. Gregory Papers, LC.

29. Gregory to House, July 9, 1931; House to Robert M. Field, July 17, 1931; Field to House, July 23, 1931, House Papers, Yale; Gregory to Roosevelt, July 17, 1931; Gregory to Gus F. Taylor, August 18, 1931, T. W. Gregory Papers, LC; Howe to Gregory, August 17, 1931, Louis Howe Papers Corr. 1928–32, Roosevelt PL.

30. Editor's note: Gen. Martin McNulty Crane was elected lieutenant governor of Texas in 1892 and attorney general of Texas in 1894. He was also chief counsel in the impeachment trial of Gov. James Ferguson. He had remained active in Dallas politics, especially as an opponent to the Ku Klux Klan, throughout the 1920s and '30s. See David Minor, "Crane, Martin McNulty," *Handbook of Texas Online*, accessed July 27, 2017, http://www.tshaonline.rg/handbook/online/articles/fcro4.

31. House to Howe, July 28, 1931, House Papers, Yale.

32. Archie C. Price to Roosevelt, July 29, 1931; Roosevelt to Price, August 17, 1931, Democratic National Committee, Box 731, Roosevelt PL.

33. T. Whitfield Davidson to Gregory, July 27, 1931; Gregory to House, July 30, 1931, T. W. Gregory Papers, LC; *DMN*, July 30, 1931.

34. Gregory to Davidson, July 30, 1931, T. W. Gregory Papers, LC.

35. Davidson to Gregory, July 31, 1931, T. W. Gregory Papers, LC.

36. Editor's note: In *Hood, Bonnet*, Brown refers to Pat O'Keefe in passing as a "veteran Democrat of Dallas." See page 371n31. It is not clear why O'Keefe is listed here as a "crank," and no biographic information on O'Keefe is readily available.

37. Gregory to House, July 31, August 3, 1931; Gus F. Taylor to Gregory, August 14, 1931, T. W. Gregory Papers, LC.

38. House to Gregory, August 3, 1931, T. W. Gregory Papers, LC; House to Howe, August 3, 1931, House Papers, Yale. See also Howe to Gregory, August 17, 1931, T. W. Gregory Papers, LC. Enthusiastic FDR supporters all over the South were popping up with clubs, many of them headed by people who were going counter to what Howe's hand-picked key men were trying to do. Howe referred to them as "those damned Southern Clubs." Stiles, *Man behind Roosevelt*, 145–146.

39. Gregory to House, August 18, 1931, T. W. Gregory Papers, LC. See also Gregory to Gus F. Taylor, August 18, 1931; Gregory to Davidson, August 20, 1931; Gregory to Howe, same date, in ibid.; HNF [Hugh Nugent Fitzgerald], "For Mr. Marsh," four-page memorandum enclosed in Charles E. Marsh to Roosevelt, August 13, 1931, Democratic National Committee, Box 731, Roosevelt PL.

40. Archie C. Price to Howe, August 27, 29, 1931; Price to Roosevelt, September 3, 1931, Democratic National Committee, Box 731, Roosevelt PL; Davidson to Gregory, September 4, 1931; Gregory to House, August 31, 1931, T. W. Gregory Papers, LC. See also Gregory to Howe, September 29, 1931, in ibid.

41. House to Gregory, September 4, 1931; Davidson to Gregory, October 1, 1931, T. W. Gregory Papers, LC; House to Davidson, September 9, 1931; Davidson to House, September 11, 1931, House Papers, Yale; House to Robert W. Woolley, September 11, 1931, Woolley Papers, LC; Davidson to Howe, September 21, 1931, Democratic National Committee, Box 729, Roosevelt PL.

42. [Louis M. Howe] to Samuel I. Rosenman, October 6, 1931, Democratic National Committee, Box 728, Roosevelt PL; Memorandum for Louis McH. Howe, Esq., October 27, 1931, Samuel I. Rosenman Papers, Roosevelt PL.

43. Davidson to Howe, October 14, 1931, Democratic National Committee, Box 729, Roosevelt PL; Davidson to Gregory, October 22, 1931, T. W. Gregory Papers, LC. In the meantime, Howe had asked Gregory how much of an impression they had made at the Texas State Fair where the club had a booth. "We sent them a considerable quality of literature and a number of rather expensive buttons to use. I gather from a note sent me by their Secretary [Archie Price] that they are having difficulties in their financing." Howe to Gregory, October 21, 1931, T. W. Gregory Papers, LC. Archie Price's note to Howe, dated October 9, 1931, is in Democratic National Committee, Box 731, Roosevelt PL.

44. Howe to Davidson, November 2, 1931, T. W. Gregory Papers, LC.

45. Davidson to Howe, November 5, 1931, Democratic National Committee, Box 729, Roosevelt PL; Davidson to H. C. Carter, November 11, 1931, T. W. Gregory Papers, LC.

46. Carter to Davidson, November 12, 1931; Davidson to Gregory, November 20, 1931, T. W. Gregory Papers, LC.

47. Gregory to House, November 28, 1931, T. W. Gregory Papers, LC.

48. Gregory to House, November 28, 1931; Gregory to Davidson, November 27, 1931; Gregory to Frank Andrews, December 12, 1931, T. W. Gregory Papers, LC.

49. Andrews to House, December 5, 1931, Democratic National Committee, Box 728, Roosevelt PL.

50. Gregory to Howe, October 31, 1931; Gregory to House, November 9, 1931; Gregory to Martin M. Crane, November 17, 1931; Crane to Gregory, November 23, 1931; Gregory to Crane, November 25, 1931; Crane to Gregory, November 28, 30, December 2, 1931; Gregory to Crane, December 7, 1931; Gregory to Dan Moody, same date; Cullen F. Thomas to Gregory, December 9, 1931; Gregory to House, same date; James V. Allred to Gregory, same date; S. F. Brooks to Gregory, December 10, 1931; Gregory to Crane, December 14, 1931; Crane to Gregory, December 23, 1931; Tom Connally to Gregory, December 24, 1931; Gregory to W. A. Keeling, December 24, 1931; Crane to Gregory, December 30, 1931; Moody and Keeling to Gregory, January 2, 1932; Crane to Gregory, January 5, 1932; W. A. Tarver to Gregory, January 5, 1931 [1932]; Gregory to Crane, same date; Gregory to Keeling, January 7, 1932; Moody to Gregory, January 10, 1932; Tarver to Gregory, January 9, 11, 1932; Crane to Moody, January 13, 1932; Gregory to Crane, February 23, 1932, all in T. W. Gregory Papers, LC; *Houston Post*, May 23, 1932.

51. John Boyle to Charles Pope Caldwell, September 23, 1931, Democratic National Committee, Box 728, Roosevelt PL; T. H. McGregor to Mrs. M. H. Wilkison, October 6, 1931, enclosed in Wilkison to Franklin D. Roosevelt, n.d., House Papers, Yale.

52. Howe to House, November 16, 1931; House to Howe, November 17, 1931, House Papers, Yale.

53. Davidson to James A. Farley, December 16, 1931, Democratic National Committee, Box 729, Roosevelt PL.

54. HNF [Hugh Nugent Fitzgerald], "For Mr. Marsh," four-page memorandum enclosed in Charles E. Marsh to Roosevelt, August 13, 1931, Democratic National Committee, Box 731, Roosevelt PL.

55. Thomas B. Love to P. H. Callahan, October 31, November 25, December 10, 1930; Love to William G. McAdoo, March 15, 1931, Love Collection, DHS. See also Love to Daniel C. Roper, March 15, 1931; Love to McAdoo, March 23, 1931, in ibid.

56. *DMN*, July 3, 1932; Charles F. Horner to Love, November 20, 1931, Love Collection, DHS; Woolley to House, June 18, 1931, House Papers, Yale.

57. McAdoo to Love, October 19, 1931; Love to McAdoo, October 24, 1931; McAdoo to Love, October 29, 1931, Love Collection, DHS.

58. *DMN*, December 15, 1931; Cato Sells to Love, October 27, 1931; Love to Sells, October 28, 1931; McAdoo to Love, November 24, 1931, Love Collection, DHS.

59. McAdoo to Love, December 19, 1931; Love to McAdoo, December 23, 1931, Love Collection, DHS.

60. House and Roosevelt are quoted in Carlson, "Roosevelt's Fight," 243n.

61. For Garner's career to 1932, see George Rothwell Brown, *The Speaker of the House: The Romantic Story of John N. Garner* (New York: Brewer, Warren & Putnam, 1932); Marquis James, *Mr. Garner of Texas* (Indianapolis, IN: Bobbs-Merrill, 1939), 1–115; Bascom N. Timmons, *Garner of Texas: A Personal History* (New York: Harper & Brothers, 1948), 1–130. [Editor's note: No current scholarly biography of Garner has been written, but he was been written about most recently in Brown, "Garnering Votes for 'Cactus Jack,'" 149–188; O. C. Fisher, *Cactus Jack* (Waco: Texian Press, 1982); and Patrick Cox, "John Nance Garner,"

in Kenneth E. Hendrickson Jr. and Michael L. Collins, eds., *Profiles in Power: Twentieth-Century Texans in Washington*, rev. ed. (Arlington Heights, IL: Harlan Davidson, 1993), 42–65. In Greek mythology, the story of Damon and Pythias traditionally represents the ideal of loyalty in friendship.]

62. Paul Y. Anderson, "Presidential Possibilities VIII—Texas John Garner," *The Nation* 134 (April 20, 1932): 466; Robert S. Allen, "Texas Jack," *New Republic* 70 (March 16, 1932): 119–120.

63. Garner is quoted in Arthur M. Schlesinger Jr., *The Age of Roosevelt: The Crisis of the Old Order, 1919–1933* (Boston: Houghton Mifflin, 1957), 228; Garner to Gregory, December 24, 1930, T. W. Gregory Papers, LC.

64. See Ray T. Tucker, "Tiger from Texas: A Portrait of 'Speaker' Jack Garner," *Outlook and Independent* 156 (November 26, 1930): 492–494, 516–517; "'A Regular Pepper Pot' Is Texas Jack Garner," *Literary Digest* 111 (December 12, 1931): 28–29; "Gentlemen at the Keyhole, Head of the House," *Collier's* 89 (January 9, 1932): 19; "'Cactus Jack' Garner's Boom," *Literary Digest* 112 (March 12, 1932): 8; Robert S. Allen, "Texas Jack," *New Republic* 70 (March 16, 1932): 119–121; Paul Y. Anderson, "Presidential Possibilities—IX, *Forum* 87 (May 1932): 312–317; Owen P. White, "Garner on Parade," *Collier's* 89 (May 28, 1932): 12, 32; Charles Albert Billings, "The Utopian of Uvalde," *North American Review* 234 (October 1932): 322; Schlesinger, *Crisis of the Old Order*, 227.

65. Timmons, *Garner of Texas*, 152–153.

66. Howe to Gregory, November 23, 1931, T. W. Gregory Papers, LC; Garner to Roosevelt, November 18, 1931, FDR Private Correspondence, 1929–1932, Box 57, Group 12, Roosevelt PL. Garner's letter was in reply to the following letter from Roosevelt: "My dear Garner: Here is the beginning of what will probably be an eventual flood. Do not bother to acknowledge it. I do not need control of the House, and especially of your Speakership." Roosevelt to Garner, November 14, 1931, in ibid. The two men also exchanged cordial letters when Garner was elected speaker. Roosevelt to Garner, December 5, 1931; Garner to Roosevelt, December 13, 1931, in ibid., Box 146.

67. Daniel Calhoun Roper, *Fifty Years of Public Life* (Durham, NC: Duke University Press, 1941), 262.

68. Davidson to Gregory, November 20, 24, December 5, 1931; Davidson to Marcellus E. Foster, November 20, 1931, T. W. Gregory Papers, LC; *DMN*, November 28, 1931.

69. Andrews to House, December 5, 1931, Democratic National Committee, Box 728, Roosevelt PL.

70. Rosen, *Hoover, Roosevelt*, 32–37; Elliot A. Rosen, "Baker on the Fifth Ballot? The Democratic Alternative: 1932," *Ohio History* 75 (Autumn 1966): 231–232; Schlesinger, *Crisis of the Old Order*, 286–288.

71. *New York Times*, n.d., clipping in Stephen L. Pinkney Biographical File, BCAH; James E. Kilday to Basil O'Connor, January 20, 1933, T. W. Gregory Papers, LC; *Houston Gargoyle*, December 27, 1931; Maury Maverick to Jouett Shouse, January 8, 1932, Maury Maverick Sr. Collection, 1769–1954, 1989, BCAH.

72. George Milburn, "The Statesmanship of Mr. Garner," *Harper's* 165 (November 1932): 678; *Ferguson Forum*, December 10, 1931.

73. Sam Rayburn to Thurman Barrett, January 2, 1932, Rayburn Papers, Series I, Roll 2, BCAH; *DMN*, January 5, 1932.

74. Edmond D. Coblentz, *William Randolph Hearst: A Portrait in His Own Words* (New York: Simon and Schuster, 1952), 126–128.

75. Coblentz, *Hearst*, 130; Brown, "Speaker of the House," 5; Milburn, "Statesmanship of Mr. Garner," 670.

76. *DMN*, January 5, 1932; Timmons, *Garner of Texas*, 153-154.

77. Timmons, *Garner of Texas*, 158; Thomas L. Stokes, *Chip Off My Shoulder* (Princeton, NJ: Princeton University Press, 1940), 326.

78. *DMN*, January 5, 1932.

79. Rayburn to Lewis T. Carpenter, January 12, 1932, Rayburn Papers, Series I, Roll 2, BCAH. See also Rayburn to Roy Miller, January 11, 1932; Rayburn to Oscar Callaway, same date; Rayburn to Davidson, January 26, 1932, in ibid.

80. *Baltimore Sun*, January 20, 1932, clipping in John Nance Garner Scrapbook No. 1A, BCAH; Allen, "Texas Jack," 119, 121.

81. McAdoo to Henry H. McPike, April 18, 1932; McAdoo to George F. Milton, January 19, 1932, W. G. McAdoo Papers, 1786-1941, Manuscript Division, Library of Congress (hereafter cited as McAdoo Papers, LC); George Creel, *Rebel at Large: Recollections of Fifty Crowded Years* (New York: Putnam's Sons, 1947), 269-270; Roper, *Fifty Years of Public Life*, 258; Arthur F. Mullen, *Western Democrat* (New York: Wilfred Funk, 1940).

82. William G. McAdoo to George W. Lynn, January 6, 1932, McAdoo to Thomas B. Love, January 11, 1932, McAdoo Papers, LC.

83. William G. McAdoo to Thomas B. Love, January 5, 1932, Love to McAdoo, January 8, 1932, McAdoo Papers, LC.

84. Thomas B. Love to John N. Garner, January 14, 1932; Love to William G. McAdoo, same date; Garner to Love, January 16, 1932; Love to Morris Sheppard, January 22, 1932; Love to P. H. Callahan, same date, all in Love Collection, DHS. After failing to elicit from Garner a statement as to his attitude on Prohibition, Mrs. Claude de Van Watts, the president of the WCTU in Texas, announced that "the W.C.T.U. will not indorse Mr. Garner's candidacy until it is assured of his position concerning the issue of prohibition." Mrs. Claude de Van Watts to Garner, n.d.; Garner to Mrs. Claude de Van Watts, February 21, 1932, Love Collection, DHS; *DMN*, February 25, 1932.

85. McAdoo to Love, January 28, 1932; Love to McAdoo, January 30, 1932; McAdoo to Love, February 9, 1932, Love Collection, DHS.

86. *DMN*, February 19, 1932; McAdoo to Garner, February 24, 1932, McAdoo Papers, LC; McAdoo to Love, February 20, 1932, Love Collection, DHS. Daniel Roper saw a bright side to McAdoo's announcement, writing Roosevelt: "The statement of Mr. McAdoo is wholesome in that it releases those McAdoo men who, like myself, are already committed to you, but who were under a cloud of suspicion as belonging to a McAdoo movement under cover and consequently unable to work as effectively as they would be otherwise." Roper to Roosevelt, February 19, 1932, Box 148, Group 12, Roosevelt PL.

87. Lippmann and Hayes are quoted in Rosen, *Hoover, Roosevelt*, 33, 218.

88. *Houston Post*, February 16, 1932, clipping in John N. Garner Scrapbook No 1A, BCAH; Timmons, *Garner of Texas*, 156; McAdoo to Love, February 9, 1932, Love Collection, DHS; McAdoo to George F. Milton, February 16, 1932; McAdoo to W. E. Woodward, February 10, 1932; McAdoo to H. L. Baggerly, February 12, 1932, McAdoo to W. E. Gonzales, February 17, 1932, all in McAdoo Papers, LC.

89. Joseph Israels II to Alvin S. Romansky, February 11, 28, 1932, Presidential Nomination Campaign 1932 Correspondence, clippings, etc., Texas, Folder 585, Alfred E. Smith Private Papers, New York State Library, Albany. "Smith is not a stalking horse for Roosevelt or anyone else," Israels assured Romansky. "He is out to stop Roosevelt and he is sincere about

it. He knows he is going to be a very long shot and the nomination for himself, but is willing to go a long way to stop the other man.... Don't let anybody tell you that Smith does not really want it, he does want it but even more than that he wants to stop Roosevelt." Israels to Romanski, April 22, 1932, in ibid.

90. Alvin S. Moody to Love, February 17, 1932, Love Collection, DHS.

91. *New York Times*, January 25, 1932, John N. Garner Scrapbook No. 1A, BCAH; *DMN*, February 17, 1932; Timmons, *Garner of Texas*, 158.

92. Ernest L. Bogart, "Melvin Alvah Traylor," in *Handbook of Texas*, vol. 2, edited by Walter Prescott Webb (Austin: Texas State Historical Association, 1952), 797; *Time*, July 30, 1928, 22–23.

93. Guy M. Bryan to House, April 30, 1931; House to Bryan, May 4, 1931; Robert M. Field to House, September 14, 1931, House Papers, Yale; Lewis T. Carpenter to Rayburn, January 6, 1932, Rayburn Papers, Series I, Roll 2, BCAH; *DMN*, August 23, 1931; *Dallas Times Herald*, February 21, 1932, clipping in John N. Garner Scrapbook No. 2, BCAH; Peel and Donnelly, *1932 Campaign*, 42–43; Freidel, *Roosevelt: The Triumph*, 235; Edward J. Flynn, *You're the Boss* (New York: Viking Press, 1947), 91.

94. *DMN*, February 19, 21, 1932; Peel and Donnelly, *1932 Campaign*, 39–41. Murray's campaign is discussed in Keith L. Bryant Jr., *Alfalfa Bill Murray* (Norman: University of Oklahoma Press, 1968), 214–236.

95. Davidson to Andrews, January 11, 1932; Davidson to House, January 11, 22, 23, 1932, House Papers, Yale; Archie C. Price to Roosevelt, January 13, 1932, Democratic National Committee, Box 731, Roosevelt PL; *DMN*, January 11, February 19, 1932.

96. Gregory to House, January 25, 1932, House Papers, Yale; House to Gregory, February 2, 1932, T. W. Gregory Papers, LC. See also Gregory to Hugh R. Robertson, February 6, 1932; Gregory to Judge George W. Anderson, February 23, 1932; Gregory to Archie Price, April 18, 1932, in ibid. Daniel Roper also suggested to Garner that he be temporary chairman of the convention and make the keynote speech. "My idea was to launch him as a candidate for Vice-President with Roosevelt. Shortly thereafter William Randolph Hearst began to support Garner for the Presidency, and the Garner campaign was on, not for Vice-President but for President." Roper, *Fifty Years of Public Life*, 262–263.

97. *DMN*, February 20, 1932; Davidson to Roosevelt, February 20, 1932, House Papers, Yale. See also Davidson to House, February 17, 20, 1932, in ibid.; R. J. Boyle to Roosevelt, March 12, 1932, Democratic National Committee, Box 728, Roosevelt PL.

98. Davidson to House, February 25, 1932; Davidson to Rayburn, February 26, 1932, House Papers, Yale. See also Davidson to Roosevelt, April 4, 1932, Democratic National Committee, Box 734, Roosevelt PL.

99. *Houston Gargoyle*, February 22, 1932; *San Antonio News*, February 22, 1932, clippings in John N. Garner Scrapbook No. 2, BCAH; Alvin Romansky to Josef Israels, February 24, 1932, Alfred E. Smith Papers, 1886–1945, Museum of the City of New York. [Editor's note: While there are some Alfred E. Smith letters at the Franklin Roosevelt Presidential Library, it seems most likely, based on the date of this letter, that it came from the Museum of the City of New York, which covers Smith's entire life, rather than the 1923–1927 period the Roosevelt PL houses.]

100. *Houston Post*, February 23, 1932, clipping in John N. Garner Scrapbook No. 2, BCAH.

101. *Washington Herald*, February 23, 1932, clipping in John N. Garner Scrapbook No. 2, BCAH.

102. House to Gregory, February 28, 1932; House to Howe, same date; Robert M. Field to House, March 1, 1932; House to Field, March 3, 1932; Field to House, March 5, 1932, House Papers, Yale.

103. House to Gregory, February 17, 1932; House to James A. Farley, same date, T. W. Gregory Papers, LC; Cordell Hull, *The Memoirs of Cordell Hull*, 2 vols. (London: Hodder & Stought, 1948), 1:150; Schlesinger, *Crisis of the Old Order*, 287, 289. A copy of a nearly final draft of Roosevelt's speech in the House collection at Yale has the following entry in the colonel's hand: "My addition to Gov. F. R. Roosevelt's speech delivered at Albany Febry 1932 before the Agricultural Society. I disapproved of the entire speech & in particular what he says and did say about the League of Nations. EMN." However, Elliot Rosen suggests that "House's disclaimer may well have been an afterthought following the internationalists' condemnation of the address. Howe consulted him every step of the way." Rosen, *Hoover, Roosevelt*, 99n.

104. House to Gregory, February 17, 1932, T. W. Gregory Papers, LC; House to Woolley, February 10, 1932, Woolley Papers, LC; House to Roper, February 17, 1932, House Papers, Yale; Rosen, *Hoover, Roosevelt*, 112–113.

105. Stiles, *Man behind Roosevelt*, 147; Raymond Moley, *The First New Deal* (New York: Harcourt, Brace, 1966), 86; Rosen, *Hoover, Roosevelt*, 112–115. Rosen favorably assesses House's political acumen: "Eccentric, his role limited by age, the claim that he was simply used by Howe seems exaggerated, at least until March 1932, when he was replaced by the Brains Trust. His inability to deliver the Texas delegation to Roosevelt has been stressed at the expense of his more positive contributions, a political *savoir faire* unmatched by Howe and Farley, and a wide range of contacts among the old Wilsonians.... When he was ignored by Howe and Farley, it was at Roosevelt's political peril" (15–16).

106. *DMN*, February 24, 25, 1932; Freidel, *Roosevelt: The Triumph*, 277; Peel and Donnelly, *1932 Campaign*, 73. In January and February Huey Long of Louisiana had been unfriendly to Roosevelt and seemed inclined toward Garner. But he finally decided early in May to bring his uninstructed delegation over to Roosevelt, giving the credit for his switch to Republican Senator George W. Norris of Nebraska. Norris had told Long that he would not support Garner and that Roosevelt was the country's only hope. Freidel, *Roosevelt: The Triumph*, 279.

107. Schlesinger, *Crisis of the Old Order*; Jordan A. Schwarz, *The Interregnum of Despair: Hoover, Congress, and the Depression* (Urbana: University of Illinois Press, 1970); Jordan A. Schwarz, "John Nance Garner and the Sales Tax Rebellion of 1932," *Journal of Southern History* 30 (May 1964): 162–180; Stokes, *Chip Off My Shoulder*, 327; *DMN*, March 28, 1932; *Washington Post*, March 25, 1932. Until the sales tax defeat, a correspondent wrote, the speaker had been "the King of the House. But ... Jack fell down and broke his crown, and his boom came tumbling after. Whether he will be able to mend the one and inflate the other remains to be seen." Anderson, "Presidential Possibilities—Texas John Garner," 465.

108. *DMN*, March 4, 1932.

109. *DMN*, March 10, 31, 1932; Love to W. O. Huggins, March 11, 1932; Huggins to Love, March 14, 1932; Love to Huggins, March 15, 1932; Love to Dan Moody, April 17, 1932, Love Collection, DHS.

110. *DMN*, April 10, 17, 22, 24, 1932.

111. Love to McAdoo, March 18, 1932; McAdoo to Love, April 16, 1932, Love Collection, DHS.

112. *DMN*, May 4, 1932; one-page typed draft, Alvin Moody Statement, Love to Moody, April 26, May 6, 1932, Love Collection, DHS.

113. *Dallas Journal*, March 21, 1932, clipping in John N. Garner Scrapbook No. 2, BCAH; *DMN*, March 22, 1932; *San Antonio Express*, March 22, 1932; Hugh Nugent Fitzgerald, "Garner Fighters Split Up the Spoils," *Austin American*, March 23, 1932, clippings in John N. Garner Scrapbook No. 3, BCAH.

114. McAdoo to Nellie G. Donohoe, February 25, 1932, McAdoo Papers, LC; Royce D. Delmatier, Clarence F. McIntosh, and Earl G. Waters, *The Rumble of California Politics, 1848–1970* (New York: John Wiley and Sons, 1970), 238; Russell M. Posner, "California's Role in the Nomination of Franklin D. Roosevelt," *California Historical Society Quarterly* 39 (June 1960): 127–128.

115. Henry H. McPike to McAdoo, February 29, 1932; Nellie G. Donohoe to McAdoo, May 8, 1932, McAdoo Papers, LC; Posner, "California's Role," 128. In a telegram to Isidore Dockweiler, Louis Howe suggested that conditions had become "chaotic" in California with the entry of Garner into the picture. He proposed the delegates be divided equally among Roosevelt, Smith, and Garner. Dockweiler demurred. "Roosevelt delegation will win," he replied. Rosen, *Hoover, Roosevelt*, 233.

116. Posner, "California's Role," 130. Roosevelt was told that Garner's majority over him in Los Angeles County was "largely due to the very large number of former residents of Texas, who are now located in Los Angeles." Roosevelt scrawled on the memo: "L.H. *Please note!* FDR," Louis Howe Papers, Correspondence 1928–1932, April–June 1932, Box 51, Roosevelt PL.

117. McAdoo to Bernard Baruch, March 16, 1932; McAdoo to Senator W. A. Smith, July 20, 1932, McAdoo Papers, LC. Mark Sullivan is quoted in Rosen, *Hoover, Roosevelt*, 233–234. "Please accept my hearty congratulations on the great victory Speaker Garner has won in California," McAdoo wired Hearst. "It could not have been achieved without the splendid support you and your great newspapers gave to the movement." To Garner went the message: "California victory most gratifying." McAdoo to Hearst, May 3, 1932; McAdoo to Garner, same date, McAdoo Papers, LC.

118. *Houston Chronicle*, May 5, 1932, clipping in John N. Garner Scrapbook No. 4, BCAH; *DMN*, May 6, 1932.

119. Wardell and Dockweiler are quoted in Carlson, "Roosevelt's Fight," 287–288. Mrs. Montgomery is quoted in Delmatier, McIntosh, and Waters, *Rumble of California*, 244. "We have just heard that Garner is well in the lead in California," Josef Israels wrote Alvin Romansky. "This is fine from our point of view. We did not expect to carry the State for Smith and would much rather have it instructed for Garner than for Roosevelt." Israels to Romansky, May 4, 1932, Alfred E. Smith Papers, 1886–1945, Museum of the City of New York.

120. Roosevelt to Herbert H. Lehman, May 4, 1932, in *FDR: His Personal Letters*, 4 vols., ed. Elliot Roosevelt (New York: Duell, Sloan and Pearce, 1947–1950), 3:277; Carroll Kirkpatrick, ed., *Roosevelt and Daniels: A Friendship in Politics* (Chapel Hill: University of North Carolina Press), 115. Roosevelt and Farley are quoted in Carlson, "Roosevelt's Fight," 288–289. McAdoo is quoted in Richard Oulahan, *The Man Who . . . The Story of the 1932 Democratic National Convention* (New York: Dial Press, 1971), 49.

121. Emily Smith Warner with Hawthorne Daniel, *The Happy Warrior: A Biography of My Father, Alfred E. Smith* (Garden City: Doubleday, 1956), 252–253; Rosen, *Hoover, Roosevelt*, 234–235.

122. *DMN*, April 23, 30, May 1, 1932; *Houston Chronicle*, April 25, 1932, clipping in John N. Garner Scrapbook No. 4, BCAH; Charles E. Marsh to Roosevelt, March 28, 1932; Davidson to Roosevelt, May 2, 1932, Democratic National Committee, Boxes 731, 734, Roosevelt PL; Robert M. Field to House, March 14, 1932; Davidson to House, May 2, 1932; Davidson to T. S. Henderson, same date, House Papers, Yale.

123. *DMN*, May 8, 1932.

124. *DMN*, May 11, 13, 1932; *Houston Post*, May 11, 1932, clipping in Stephen L. Pinckney Biographical File, BCAH; James E. Kilday to Basil O'Connor, January 30, 1933, T. W. Gregory Papers, LC; Paul D. Page Jr. to Roosevelt, May 14, 1932, Democratic National Committee, Box 732, Roosevelt PL; Romansky to Israels, April 29, 1932, Alfred E. Smith Papers, 1886–1945, Museum of the City of New York; John Middagh, *Frontier Newspaper: The El Paso Times* (El Paso: Texas Western Press, 1958), 268. Throwing caution to the winds, T. Whitfield Davidson wired Roosevelt at Warm Springs that his friends had controlled four-fifths of the Texas counties: "I don't believe any publicity should be given to this fact but everything looks harmonious and pleasant," he boasted. "Texas will not be a part of any coalition to stop Roosevelt." Davidson to Roosevelt, May 12, 1932, House Papers, Yale.

125. *DMN*, May 11, 1932; Love to Galloway Calhoun, July 7, 1932, Love Collection, DHS.

126. *DMN*, May 19, 20, 21, 23, 1932; Rayburn to Will H. Evans, April 15, 1932, Rayburn Papers, Series I, Roll 2, BCAH.

127. *DMN*, May 23, 1932.

128. *DMN*, May 25, 26, 1932; Rayburn to Judge Rice Maxey, June 9, 1932, Rayburn Papers, Series I, Roll 2, BCAH.

129. *Dallas Times Herald*, June 19, 1932, clipping in John N. Garner Scrapbook No. 5, BCAH; Jed C. Adams to Ross S. Sterling, June 15, 1932, Sterling Papers, BCAH.

130. Gregory to House, May 27, 1932, T. W. Gregory Papers, LC; Ernest May to Roosevelt, June 1, 1932; Davidson to Roosevelt, May 25, 1932, Democratic National Committee, Boxes 731, 743, Roosevelt PL.

131. Walter F. Woodul to Frank M. O'Brien, June 6, 1932, McAdoo Papers, LC; Gregory to House, June 2, 1932; House to Gregory, June 9, 1932, T. W. Gregory Papers, LC.

132. Freidel, *Roosevelt: The Triumph*, 280; Rollins, *Roosevelt and Howe*, 335–336; Texas data Confidential (1932), Louis Howe Dem. National Convention, Box 53, Roosevelt PL.

133. Billings, "Utopian of Uvalde," 326; Milburn, "Statesmanship of Mr. Garner," 679; *Washington Star*, June 21, 1932, clipping in John N. Garner Scrapbook No. 5, BCAH; *DMN*, June 22, 1932.

134. *Washington News*, June 22, 1932, clipping in John N. Garner Scrapbook No. 5, BCAH; *DMN*, June 22, 1932. Love privately expressed the opinion that Newton D. Baker was the only Wet who had a chance to win the November election. Love to Marion C. Early, June 23, 1932, Love Collection, DHS.

135. Timmons, *Garner of Texas*, 159–160.

Chapter 7: Roosevelt and Garner

1. Russell M. Posner, "California's Role in the Nomination of Franklin D. Roosevelt," *California Historical Society Quarterly* 39 (June 1960): 131; William G. McAdoo to William Denman, May 6, 1923, W. G. McAdoo Papers, 1786–1941, Manuscript Division, Library of Congress (hereafter cited as McAdoo Papers, LC).

2. Robert Woolley to Edward M. House, July 8, 1932, Edward Mandell House Papers (MS 466), Manuscripts and Archives, Yale University Library (hereafter cited as House Papers, Yale). Long is quoted in Elliot A. Rosen, *Hoover, Roosevelt, and the Brains Trust: From Depression to New Deal* (New York: Columbia University Press, 1977), 254. Senator Tom Connally stated in his autobiography that "McAdoo's followers told me that he was hoping a deadlock would develop at the convention, so that he would come riding in on his

white horse and win the nomination in the end." Tom Connally and Alfred Steinberg, *My Name Is Tom Connally* (New York: Crowell, 1954), 139.

3. Joseph Meyer Proskauer, *A Segment of My Times* (New York: Farrar, Strauss, 1950), 71; Rosen, *Hoover, Roosevelt*, 245–249. Kent is quoted in Rosen. "As had been arranged over the telephone two months before, Father and Mr. McAdoo had a conference, and in it they agreed that they and their followers would stand in opposition to Roosevelt," remembered Smith's daughter Emily. "If, when the balloting began, a deadlock were to develop, they agreed to meet again in the hope of uniting in support of some candidate." Emily Smith Warner with Hawthorne Daniel, *The Happy Warrior: A Biography of My Father, Alfred E. Smith* (Garden City: Doubleday, 1956), 257.

4. Thomas L. Stokes, *Chip Off My Shoulder* (Princeton, NJ: Princeton University Press, 1940), 319.

5. *Dallas Journal*, June 25, 1932, clipping in John N. Garner Scrapbook No. 6, Dolph Briscoe Center for American History, University of Texas at Austin (hereafter cited as BCAH).

6. E. F. Smith, *A Saga of Texas Law* (San Antonio: Naylor Co., 1940), 324–325; Amon G. Carter to Ross S. Sterling, June 9, 1932, Sterling Papers, BCAH; Will Rogers with Donald Day, ed., *Autobiography of Will Rogers* (Boston: Houghton Mifflin, 1949), 284.

7. *Dallas Morning News*, June 28, 1932 (hereafter cited as *DMN*).

8. *DMN*, June 28, 29, 1932.

9. Roy V. Peel and Thomas C. Donnelly, *The 1932 Campaign: An Analysis* (New York: Farrar & Rinehart, 1935), 95–96; *Dallas Journal*, June 25, 1932; *Dallas Times Herald*, June 26, 1932, clippings in John N. Garner Scrapbook No. 6, BCAH.

10. Peel and Donnelly, *1932 Campaign*, 95–96; *Dallas Journal*, June 25, 1932; *Dallas Times Herald*, June 26, 1932, clippings in John N. Garner Scrapbook No. 6, BCAH.

11. *DMN*, June 30, 1932; James E. Kilday to Basil O'Connor, January 30, 1933, Thomas Watt Gregory Papers, Library of Congress (hereafter cited as T. W. Gregory Papers, LC).

12. Peel and Donnelly, *1932 Campaign*, 100.

13. James A. Farley, *Behind the Ballots* (New York: Harcourt, Brace, 1938), 132–135; James A. Farley, *Jim Farley's Story: The Roosevelt Years* (New York: Whittlesey House, 1948), 19–20; Fred Israel, *Nevada's Key Pittman* (Lincoln: University of Nebraska Press, 1963), 97–98; Lionel V. Patenaude, "The Garner Vote Switch to Roosevelt: 1932 Democratic Convention," *Southwestern Historical Quarterly* 79 (October 1975): 192–193; Arthur M. Schlesinger Jr., *The Age of Roosevelt: The Crisis of the Old Order, 1919–1933* (Boston: Houghton Mifflin, 1957), 304–305.

14. Farley, *Behind the Ballots*, 138; Farley, *Jim Farley's Story*, 20; Patenaude, "Garner Vote Switch," 193; See also Alexander Graham Shanks, "Sam Rayburn and the Democratic Convention of 1932," *Texana* 3 (Winter 1965): 321–332.

15. Paul Page and others to John N. Garner, June 30, 1932, Richard Fenner Burges Papers, 1897–1940, BCAH. [Editor's note: Brown did not name the archive in which he read the Burges papers. I have noted the Briscoe Center's collection here, as it would have been easily accessible for him on UT's campus, but there is also a collection of Burges papers at the El Paso Public Library.]

16. Peel and Donnelly, *1932 Campaign*, 101; Bascom N. Timmons, *Garner of Texas: A Personal History* (New York: Harper & Brothers, 1948), 162.

17. Peel and Donnelly, *1932 Campaign*, 101, 103; Farley, *Behind the Ballots*, 139–143.

18. Daniel Calhoun Roper, *Fifty Years of Public Life* (Durham, NC: Duke University Press, 1941), 259–260.

19. Connally and Steinberg, *My Name Is Tom Connally*, 141–143; Arthur F. Mullen, *West-*

ern Democrat (New York: Wilfred Funk, 1940), 275-276. I have reconstructed the conversations on the basis of these two accounts, which agree in all major productions.

20. Farley, *Behind the Ballots*, 144-146; Farley, *Jim Farley's Story*, 22-23; Lela Stiles, *The Man behind Roosevelt: The Story of Louis McHenry Howe* (Cleveland: World Publishing, 1954), 187; Patenaude, "Garner Vote Switch," 193-194; Frank Freidel, *Franklin D. Roosevelt*, vol. 3, *The Triumph* (Boston: Little, Brown, 1956), 307.

21. Roper, *Fifty Years of Public Life*, 260; "Because of the Roper-McAdoo arrangement and McAdoo's later belief that Roosevelt had violated its terms, a conflict developed in late 1932-early 1933 involving also Cordell Hull and Edward M. House. McAdoo objected to Roosevelt's failure to consult him in the Treasury and State appointments ... then specifically to William Woodin's selection for the Treasury post. Woodin, he claimed, was identified with Wall Street interests and hardly qualified as a member of the party's progressive wing. House and Hull countered that the spirit of the agreement had been kept in these appointments despite the failure to consult McAdoo directly." Rosen, *Hoover, Roosevelt*, 417n.

22. Edmond D. Coblentz, *William Randolph Hearst: A Portrait in His Own Words* (New York: Simon and Schuster, 1952), 132-134; David E. Koskoff, *Joseph P. Kennedy: A Life and Times* (Englewood Cliffs, NJ: Prentice-Hall, 1974), 44-45; Michael R. Beschloss, *Kennedy and Roosevelt: The Uneasy Alliance* (New York: Norton, 1980), 69-73; Farley, *Behind the Ballots*, 131-132.

23. Mullen, *Western Democrat*, 277-278.

24. Timmons, *Garner of Texas*, 164; Farley, *Behind the Ballots*, 150; Matthew Josephson and Hannah Josephson, *Al Smith: Hero of the Cities* (Boston: Houghton Mifflin, 1969), 441, 483; Proskauer, *Segment of My Times*, 71-72; Warner and Daniel, *Happy Warrior*, 261. Dodd is quoted in Rosen, *Hoover, Roosevelt*, 263-264.

25. Karl Crowley and others to Sam Rayburn, July 1, 1932, petition, in Franklin D. Roosevelt, Papers as President, President's Personal File, 1933-1945, 67, Presidential Campaigns 1932-44, Box 1; Clyde O. Eastus to Franklin D. Roosevelt, April 27, 1933, Franklin D. Roosevelt, Papers as President, Official File, 1933-45, 400, Box 57, Appointments—Texas 1933-45, Franklin D. Roosevelt Presidential Library, Hyde Park, NY (hereafter cited as Roosevelt PL).

26. Timmons, *Garner of Texas*, 165-166; Farley, *Behind the Ballots*, 147; John N. Garner to Richard F. Burges, July 8, 1932, Burges Papers, BCAH. In 1961 Bascom Timmons wrote that Rayburn's "soundings convinced him that it was nip-and-tuck between Roosevelt and Baker in the Texas delegation. It appeared to Rayburn that the surest way to get a majority of the Texans for Roosevelt was for Garner to go on the ticket as vice president. A conference between Rayburn and James A. Farley ... agreed that Garner could have second place. Roosevelt from Albany gave enthusiastic approval. But it still was doubtful Texas could be won for Roosevelt." Bascom N. Timmons, "Key Convention Role: Rayburn Influence Grows," *Dallas Times Herald*, October 13, 1961, clipping in Sam Rayburn Scrapbook, 1960-1961, BCAH.

27. Thomas M. Storke to William G. McAdoo, May 12, 1934, McAdoo Papers, LC; Thomas M. Storke with Walker A. Tompkins, *California Editor* (Los Angeles: Westernlore Press, 1958), 314-317.

28. Rosen, *Hoover, Roosevelt*, 261-262.

29. Storke, *California Editor*, 317-319.

30. C. Dwight Dorough, *Mr. Sam* (New York: Random House, 1962), 208-209; Connally and Steinberg, *My Name Is Tom Connally*, 143-144; Farley, *Behind the Ballots*, 147-148.

31. Farley, *Behind the Ballots*, 148-149; Patenaude, "Garner Vote Switch," 198; James E.

Kilday to Basil O'Connor, January 30, 1933, T. W. Gregory Papers, LC. In his memoirs Cordell Hull stated that "Representative Sam Rayburn, Carl [*sic*] Crowley, a Texas delegate, former Tennessean, and long-time friend, and I met with a large group of the Texas delegates, many of whom were my old friends and acquaintances.... I found considerable opposition in the delegation to Roosevelt, but we argued forcefully for our candidate. The pro-Roosevelt delegate, under Rayburn's leadership, won out, and Texas moved into the Roosevelt's camp." Cordell Hull, *The Memoirs of Cordell Hull*, 2 vols. (London: Hodder & Stoughton, 1948), 1:154.

32. *Dallas Times Herald*, July 2, 1932, clipping in John N. Garner Scrapbook No. 6, BCAH.

33. T. Whitfield Davidson to Lionel V. Patenaude, October 6, 1952, quoted in Patenaude, "Garner Vote Switch," 198.

34. Dorough, *Mr. Sam*; Connally and Steinberg, *My Name Is Tom Connally*, 144.

35. Clyde O. Eastus later sent Roosevelt a list of the fifty-four delegates who voted to switch to him in the caucus. Eastus to Roosevelt, April 27, 1933, Franklin D. Roosevelt, Papers as President, Official File, 1933–1945, 400, Box 57, Appointments—Texas 1933—45, Roosevelt PL.

36. Farley, *Behind the Ballots*, 149; Timmons, *Garner of Texas*, 166.

37. William G. McAdoo to Sam Rayburn, September 20, 1938; Rayburn to McAdoo, March 3, 1939; McAdoo to Rayburn, April 28, 1939, Rayburn Papers, Series I, Roll 2, BCAH. Rayburn told Dwight Dorough twenty-eight years later that his conversation with McAdoo took place after Texas voted to go to Roosevelt. "Then I had to get word to McAdoo, the head of the California delegation. I found him in the hall and he said, 'Sam, we'll vote for Jack Garner until Hell freezes over, if you say so.' But I told him to release his delegation, and he rushed in to his group and had no trouble with his outfit. He convinced them to go for Roosevelt; then he jumped on his motorcycle and struck off for the Convention hall." Dorough, *Mr. Sam*, 209.

38. Patenaude, "Garner Vote Switch," 197–198, 201.

39. Storke, *California Editor*, 321–325; Posner, "California's Role," 135.

40. Storke, *California Editor*, 327–328; Farley, *Behind the Ballots*, 151; William G. McAdoo to Sam Rayburn, April 28, 1939, Rayburn Papers, Series I, Roll 2, BCAH.

41. Storke, *California Editor*, 328–331; Posner, "California's Role," 136–137; H. L. Mencken, *Making a President: A Footnote to the Saga of Democracy* (New York: Knopf, 1932), 163; Grace Tully, *F.D.R. My Boss* (New York: Charles Scribner's Sons, 1949), 51.

42. Peel and Donnelly, *1932 Campaign*, 102–103; James P. Rooney to William G. McAdoo, July 1, 1932, McAdoo Papers, LC.

43. *Newsweek*, December 30, 1933, 15; Timmons, *Garner of Texas*, 167.

44. Roosevelt to McAdoo, July 1, 1932, John N. Garner to McAdoo, July 3, 1932, McAdoo Papers, LC; Posner, "California's Role," 137.

45. Bernard M. Baruch, *Baruch: The Public Years* (New York: Holt, Rinehart, and Winston, 1960), 240–241; Shouse is quoted in Rosen, *Hoover, Roosevelt*, 248, 277n. "McAdoo at the last minute feared Baker," Felix Frankfurter wrote Louis Brandeis, "so [Governor] Ely said—and moved quickly. It's characteristic of him." Quoted in Rosen, *Hoover, Roosevelt*, 417n.

46. Freidel, *Roosevelt: The Triumph*, 309–310. In 1947 Boss Ed Flynn predicted: "It is likely that for fifty years or more differing stories will be told about what finally led up to the more dramatic moment when McAdoo took the platform to announce the shift in the Cali-

fornia vote. And is natural, every man who had anything to do with it is going to claim credit for the decisive change." Edward J. Flynn, *You're the Boss* (New York: Viking Press, 1947), 103. For an incisive analysis of the various claims, see Earland I. Carlson, "Franklin D. Roosevelt's Fight for the Presidential Nomination, 1928–1932" (PhD diss., University of Illinois, 1955), 449–451.

47. Patenaude, "Garner Vote Switch"; Clyde O. Eastus to Roosevelt, July 5, 1932, Democratic National Committee 735—Texas Before Election; Eastus to Roosevelt, April 27, 1933, Franklin D. Roosevelt, Papers as President, Official File, 1933–1945, Roosevelt PL; J. W. Minton to Roosevelt, July 8, 1932, Democratic National Committee, Box 738, in ibid.

48. Joseph A. Stout Jr. and Peter C. Rollins, eds., *Convention Articles of Will Rogers* (Stillwater: Oklahoma State University Press, 1976), 147. One of fifty-four delegates, Mrs. Drew S. Wommack wrote later that "if we hadn't voted for Roosevelt when we did no telling that would have happened. There was a certain element on the Texas delegation which did all they could to prevent it." Mrs. Drew S. Wommack to Mrs. Percy V. Pennybacker, November 12, 1932, Mrs. Percy V. Pennybacker Papers, 1878–1938, BCAH.

49. Farley, *Behind the Ballots*, 152–153; Farley, *Jim Farley's Story*, 25; Flynn, *You're the Boss*, 104–105; Freidel, *Roosevelt: The Triumph*, 312–313n; *DMN*, July 3, 1932; R. G. Tugwell, *The Brains Trust* (New York: Viking Press, 1968), 253; Josephus Daniels to John N. Garner, [July 2, 1932]; Garner to Daniels, July 3, 1932; Daniels to Garner, July 5, 1932; Garner to Daniels, July 8, 1932, Josephus Daniels Papers, Library of Congress; the *Catholic Mirror* is quoted in Oscar Handlin, *Al Smith and His America* (Boston: Little, Brown, 1958), 166. [Editor's note: By 1930 more than 750,000 Catholics lived in the Texas—just under 13 percent of the total population. Anti-Catholic sentiment was on the rise in Texas during this era due to increased immigration. This helps to explain the *Catholic Mirror*'s assessment. Robert E. Wright, OMI, "Catholic Church," *Handbook of Texas Online*, accessed September 21, 2017, http://www.tshaonline.org/handbook/online/articles/icc01; U.S. Census Bureau, 1930 Census of Population and Housing, vol. 1, 1055.]

50. McAdoo Satement, July 5, 1932, McAdoo Papers, LC; Joseph L. Morrison, *Josephus Daniels: The Small-d Democrat* (Chapel Hill: University of North Carolina Press, 1966), 165; Hull, *Memoirs*, 1:153–154; Charles I. Francis to Franklin D. Roosevelt, July 1, 1932, Democratic National Committee, Box 735, Roosevelt PL.

51. Timmons, *Garner of Texas*, 167–168; Sam Rayburn to Edward M. House, July 17, 1932, House Papers; Richard F. Burges to T. Whitfield Davidson, July 7, 1932, Burges Papers, BCAH. "Along with the majority of our delegation in Chicago, I had no illusions concerning Mr. Garner's nomination, and I am sure that Mr. Garner himself had none," Burges advised Jim Farley. "A strongly assertive minority in our delegation was utilizing Mr. Garner's name as an excuse to achieve that which could not be openly avowed. I am sure, however, that Mr. T. W. Davidson advised you fully concerning that situation." Burges to James A. Farley, August 3, 1932, Burges Papers, BCAH.

52. *Dallas Times Herald*, July 2, 1932, John N. Garner Scrapbook No. 6, BCAH.

53. *Dallas Times Herald*, July 2, 1932, John N. Garner Scrapbook No. 6, BCAH.

54. Paul D. Casdorph, *A History of the Republican Party in Texas, 1865–1965* (Austin, TX: Pemberton Press, 1965), 140–141; Peel and Donnelly, *1932 Campaign*, 82–91.

55. Gregory to Edward M. House, July 9, 1932, T. W. Gregory Papers, LC; Ross S. Sterling to John N. Garner, August 11, 1932, Sterling Papers, BCAH; *DMN*, July 5, 1932; S. W. McKay, *Texas Politics, 1906–1944* (Lubbock: Texas Tech University Press, 1952), 244. See also Gregory to Roosevelt, July 11, 1932, T. W. Gregory Papers, LC; Gregory to John Garland

Pollard, July 15, 1932, Gregory Papers, Microfilm Reel 1, Southwest Collection, Texas Tech University.

56. J. Frank Norris to Walter H. Newton, July 14, 1932, Presidential Papers—Republican National Committee—Texas, Herbert Hoover Presidential Library, West Branch, Iowa; Alvin Moody to Walter Newton, July 30, 1932; Thomas B. Love to William E. Borah, November 8, 1932, Thomas B. Love Collection, Dallas Historical Society (hereafter cited as Love Collection, DHS).

57. Donald R. Richberg, *My Hero: The Indiscreet Memoirs of an Eventful but Unheroic Life* (New York: G. P. Putnam's Sons, 1954), 155. "I felt a little embarrassed to deliver this message from the Vice Presidential candidate to the Presidential candidate but promised to do so," Richberg recalled. "My embarrassment was increased when I finally met Governor Roosevelt in his library in the company of Mrs. Roosevelt and Louis Howe. However, I carried my message to Garcia, which tickled F.D.R. immensely." Richberg quoted Garner in his memoirs "with only slight necessary revisions." In an interview on January 3, 1947, Richberg told Arthur Schlesinger Jr. that Garner used the word "shit" and not the more genteel "stuffing" printed in the Richberg book. The unexpurgated version better explains the embarrassment Richberg felt in having to convey so blunt a message to Roosevelt in the presence of his wife. Schlesinger, *Crisis of the Old Order*, 534n.

58. Peel and Donnelly, *1932 Campaign*, 129.

59. Frank Andrews to Edward M. House, July 4, 1932, Series I, Box 5, Folder 156, House Papers, Yale; John W. Davis to John J. Cornwell, July 11, 1932; W. L. Clayton to Davis, July 23, 1932, Box 34, John William Davis Papers (MS 170), Manuscripts and Archives, Yale University Library; editors of the *Reader's Digest* to John N. Garner, July 8, 1932, Democratic National Committee, Box 736, Roosevelt PL. [Editor's note: Brown did not specify from which archival collection the Davis citations came. I have noted the Yale collection here, as it seems to have the largest single collection of Davis's papers, but collections related to him exist in several libraries. See "Davis, John W.," Biographical Guide to the U.S. Congress, accessed February 20, 2019, http://bioguide.congress.gov/scripts/guidedisplay.pl?index=d000121.]

60. "Garner's Campaign Bomb," *Literary Digest* 114 (August 6, 1932): 8; Peel and Donnelly, *1932 Campaign*, 174; Freidel, *Roosevelt: The Triumph*, 328; Schlesinger, *Crisis of the Old Order*, 431. See also William C. Murphy Jr., "The G.O.P. Versus Garner," *Commonweal* 16 (September 14, 1932): 462–464.

61. A. G. Hopkins to Sam Rayburn, July 29, 1932; Rayburn to Hopkins, August 26, 1932, Rayburn Papers, Series I, Roll 3, BCAH; George Milburn, "The Statesmanship of Mr. Garner," *Harper's* 165 (November 1932): 669.

62. E. R. Garner to Roosevelt, July 26, 1932; John N. Garner to Roosevelt, July 23, 1932, Democratic National Committee, Box 736, Roosevelt PL.

63. Roosevelt to Garner, August 1, 1932, Democratic National Committee, Box 736, Roosevelt PL.

64. Garner to Farley, August 1, 1932; Roosevelt to Mrs. John N. Garner, August 7, 1932, Democratic National Committee, Box 736, Roosevelt PL.

65. Timmons, *Garner of Texas*, 168; Garner to Louis Howe, August 19, 1932; Howe to Garner, August 25, 1932; Garner to James A. Farley, September 2, 1932; Garner to Howe, same date; Farley to Garner, September 14, 1932, all in Democratic National Committee, Texas before the Election, Box 736, Roosevelt PL.

66. Garner to Roosevelt, October 3, 1932, FDR Private Correspondence, 1928–1932, Box 63, Group 12, Roosevelt PL; Stiles, *Man behind Roosevelt*, 212–213; Alfred B. Rollins

Jr., *Roosevelt and Howe* (New York: Knopf, 1962), 352; Charles Michelson, *The Ghost Talks* (New York: G. P. Putnam's Sons, 1944), 128–131. Historian Claude Bowers listened to Garner's speech "and thought the talk one of the most effective and devastating speeches of the campaign." Claude G. Bowers, *My Life: The Memoirs of Claude Bowers* (New York: Simon and Schuster, 1962), 255.

67. Timmons, *Garner of Texas*, 170.

68. *DMN*, September 30, 1932.

69. T. Whitfield Davidson to Jed Adams, July 5, 1932; Davidson to Richard E. Burges, same date, Burges Papers, BCAH. Hull is quoted in Freidel, *Roosevelt: The Triumph*, 320. When Miller was selected to head the Roosevelt-Garner campaign in Texas in 1936, the secretary of a group calling itself the Progressive Democrats of Texas wrote the president that "it was a blow to our liberal stand in Texas to discover that Roy Miller, lobbyist and reactionary, had been appointed to conduct a campaign in behalf of yourself, whom we regard as one of today's outstanding progressive thinkers." The group avowed: "Whatever lip service Lobbyist Miller may give the Democratic Party, his actions in Texas affairs have been such as would shame the most reactionary Republican. 'Sulphurcrat' is the only term adequate to define Miller's political stripe." After talking with Karl Crowley and several other Texans, Jim Farley, to whom the letter was referred, reported that "they said that the best thing to do was not to pay any attention to this request." Herman Wright to Roosevelt, February 22, 1936; James A. Farley to Marvin E. McIntyre, April 23, 1936, President's Official File, 1933–1945, Box 300-69, Democratic National Committee—Texas, 1933–1937, Roosevelt PL.

70. T. Whitfield Davidson to Richard F. Burges, August 3, 1932, Burges Papers, BCAH; Davidson to Sam Rayburn, July 11, 1932; Rayburn to Davidson, July 25, 1932, Rayburn Papers, Series I, Roll 3, BCAH.

71. Roy Miller to Sam Rayburn, August 11, 1932; Rayburn to Miller, August 13, 1932; Rayburn to Miller, August 17, 1932; Miller to Rayburn, August 22, 1932, Rayburn Papers, Series I, Roll 2, BCAH; Rayburn to F. M. Stevens, August 17, 1932, in ibid., Series I, Roll 3; W. E. Leonard to Roosevelt, September 22, 1932, Democratic National Committee—Texas, Box 737, Roosevelt PL; Roy Miller Biographical File, BCAH.

72. Roosevelt to Garner, November 8, 1932, FDR Private Correspondence, 1929–1932, Box 57, Roosevelt PL; T. Whitfield Davidson to Edward M. House, November 10, 1932, House Papers, Yale; *DMN*, September 20, 1932; Timmons, *Garner of Texas*, 168, 171; Peel and Donnelly, *1932 Campaign*, 215; McKay, *Texas Politics*, 244–245; Casdorph, *Republican Party in Texas*, 143. O. B. Colquitt wired Hoover: "You fought a good fight; you kept the faith, and time will fully vindicate you." Colquitt to Hoover, November 9, 1932, O. B. Colquitt Papers, BCAH.

73. Rogers and Day, *Autobiography of Will Rogers*, 300.

Chapter 8: The Politics of Relief and Repeal

1. "Housewife Again Becomes Boss of Lone Star State," unidentified newspaper clipping in James Ferguson Scrapbook, 1914–1935, Dolph Briscoe Center for American History, University of Texas at Austin (hereafter cited as BCAH); *Dallas Morning News*, January 18, 20, 1933 (hereafter cited as *DMN*).

2. Raymond Brooks, *Political Playback* (Austin, TX: Eugene C. Barker Texas History Center, 1961), 20.

3. *Texas Weekly* 9 (January 7, 1933): 1–3; (January 21): 12; (January 28): 10–12; (February 4): 12; (February 11): 12; (February 18): 10–12; (February 25): 12; (March 4): 12; (March 11): 11–12; Reinhard H. Luthin, *American Demagogues: Twentieth Century* (Gloucester, MA: P. Smith, 1959), 178.

4. *Austin American*, May 19, 1933; *Journal of the Senate of Texas Being the Regular Session of the Forty-Third Legislature Begun and Held at the City of Austin, January 10, 1933*, 987 (hereafter cited as *Senate Journal*).

5. *Texas Weekly* 9 (January 14, 1933): 2; *New York Times*, February 19, 1933.

6. *Journal of the House of Representatives of Texas Being the Regular Session of the Forty-Third Legislature Begun and Held at the City of Austin, January 10, 1933*, 987 (hereafter cited as *House Journal*).

7. *Senate Journal*, 43rd Leg., Reg. Sess., 2071; S. W. McKay, *Texas Politics, 1906–1944* (Lubbock: Texas Tech University Press, 1952), 251–254; *Texas Weekly* 9, (March 25, 1933): 2.

8. Brooks, *Political Playback*, 66.

9. Mary D. Farrell and Elizabeth Silverthorne, *First Ladies of Texas: The First One Hundred Years, 1836–1936* (Belton, TX: Stillhouse Hollow Publishers, 1976), 290; Ouida Wallace Ferguson Nalle, *Fergusons of Texas: Or "Two Governors for the Price of One"* (San Antonio: Naylor Co., 1946), 220–221.

10. Editor's note: Charles C. McDonald has made little impression on the scholarly record of Texas history so far. He is mentioned as a "lawyer and friend of Pa Ferguson" in John Boessenecker, *Texas Ranger: The Epic Life of Frank Hamer, the Man Who Killed Bonnie and Clyde* (New York: St. Martin's Press, 2016), 408.

11. Alfred Petsch to Morris Sheppard, May 15, 1933; H. B. Thomas Jr. to Thomas B. Love, May 19, 1933; James A. Farley to Harry L. Hopkins, June 22, 1933, Federal Relief Agency Papers, Confidential Political File, 1933–1938, De-Hu, Group 24, Harry L. Hopkins Papers, Container 37, Franklin Delano Roosevelt Presidential Library, Hyde Park, NY (hereafter cited as Hopkins Papers, Roosevelt PL); *DMN*, May 15, 16, June 29, 1933; *Ferguson Forum* 16, May 18, 1933. On Garner's enormous "pull" with Congress, especially the powerful Texas delegation, see Lionel Patenaude, "Vice-President John Nance Garner: A Study in the Use of Influence during the New Deal," *Texana* 9 (1973): 124–144. See also the Garner-Roosevelt letters in John N. Garner, President's Personal File, No. 1416, Roosevelt PL.

12. "Ferguson Mechanism," unidentified newspaper clipping, March 1934, James Ferguson Scrapbook, 1914–1935, BCAH; *Ferguson Forum* 16, March 29, 1934; *Texas Weekly* 9 (March 31, 1934).

13. Wayne McMillen to Fred Croxton, February 15, 1933, Aubrey Williams, "Report of State of Texas," FERA-WPA Narrative Reports, Texas-Field Reports, 1933–1935, Federal Relief Agency Papers, Group 24, Box 60, Hopkins Papers, Roosevelt PL; *Senate Journal*, 43rd Leg., Supplement, *Proceedings of Investigating Committee*, 532–533, 551.

14. Williams, "Report on State of Texas," Texas-Field Reports, 1933–1935, Box 60, Hopkins Papers, Roosevelt PL; *Senate Journal*, 43rd Leg., Supplement, *Proceedings of Senate Investigating Committee*, 551–552, 612.

15. Miriam A. Ferguson to Franklin D. Roosevelt, May 15, 1933, President's Official File, 1933–45, File 400, Box 57, Appointments—Texas, Roosevelt Papers, Roosevelt PL.

16. *Senate Journal*, 43rd Leg., Supplement, *Proceedings of the Senate Investigating Committee*, 576–585; Lionel V. Patenaude, "The Politics of Relief in Texas during the New Deal," 3–4. The author is indebted to Professor Patenaude for a copy of this unpublished paper.

17. Sid. Smith to Tom Connally, June 1, 1933; I. L. Martin to Connally, July 11, 1933; H. J.

Cureton to Connally, July 25, 1933, Tom Connally Papers, Manuscript Division, Library of Congress. [Editor's note: Brown did not specify which Connally Papers collection he had used. There are also smaller collections at Baylor University and at the Briscoe Center.]

18. Williams, "Report on State of Texas," Texas-Field Reports, 1933–1935, Box 60, Hopkins Papers, Roosevelt PL; James T. Patterson, *The New Deal and the States: Federalism in Transition* (Princeton, NJ: Princeton University Press, 1969), 51.

19. Field Report Texas, July 11, 1933, Field Reports-General, Box 56, Hopkins Papers, Roosevelt PL.

20. Harry L. Hopkins to Aubrey Williams, July 18, 1933; N. B. Bond to Hopkins, July 29, 1933; Williams to Hopkins, August 9, 14, 1933, Williams, "Report on State of Texas," Texas-Field Reports, 1933–1935, Box 60, Hopkins Papers, Roosevelt PL.

21. Luthin, *American Demagogues*, 178; Nalle, *Fergusons of Texas*, 228–229.

22. *State Journal*, 43rd Leg., Supplement, *Proceedings of Investigating Committee*, 564; Patenaude, "Politics of Relief," 5–6; Nalle, *Fergusons of Texas*, 229.

23. Patenaude, "Politics of Relief," 6; Aubrey Williams to Harry L. Hopkins, September 18 [1933], General Correspondence, 1933–1940, Box 100; Williams "Report on State of Texas," Texas-Field Reports, 1933–1935, Box 60, Hopkins Papers, Roosevelt PL.

24. "Statement of Aubrey Williams to Joint Session of House and Senate," enclosed in William to Harry L. Hopkins, September 21, 1933, Texas-Field Reports, 1933–1935, Box 60, Hopkins Papers, Roosevelt PL. See also Williams to Hopkins, September 22, 1933, in ibid. *San Antonio Express*, September 23, 1933.

25. *Senate Journal*, 43rd Leg., Supplement, *Proceedings of Investigating Committee*, 550–551, 587–588, 698–715; Patenaude, "Politics of Relief," 7–8; *Austin American*, September 21, 22, 23, 1933; *DMN*, September 26, 1933; *San Antonio Express*, September 23, 27, 1933. "Westbrook was on the stand three hours yesterday afternoon," Williams wrote Hopkins from the Baker Hotel in Dallas. "You will see from the press—always garbed and coloured—what took place. Please read the San Antonio press clippings—it sets out the opposition very well indeed. They are going to try to wreck the present organization by forcing us into the use of county boards of supervisors—I took no stand on whether we would or would not agree to their use." Aubrey Williams to Harry L. Hopkins, September 22, 1933, Texas-Field Reports, 1933–1935, Box 60, Hopkins Papers, Roosevelt PL.

26. Patenaude, "Politics of Relief," 8–9; *San Antonio Express*, September 23, 30, 1933. Alsbury's testimony is in *Senate Journal*, 43rd Leg., Supplement, *Proceedings of the Senate Investigating Committee*, 717–724, 743–760.

27. Williams, "Report on State of Texas," Texas-Field Reports, 1933–1935, Box 60, Hopkins Papers, Roosevelt PL; Rupert N. Richardson, *Texas: The Lone Star State*, 4th ed. (Englewood Cliffs, NJ: Prentice-Hall, 1981), 325; Lionel Patenaude, "The New Deal and Texas" (PhD diss., University of Texas at Austin, 1953), 381–382. [Editor's note: In 1930, a total of 2,123,242 Texans lived in cities or towns with a population over 5,000 people—about 36.45 percent of the population. According to Brown's figures here, more than 68 percent of people receiving relief lived in cities—suggesting that New Deal relief, in this instance, was disproportionately weighted in favor of urban dwellers. Population data from U.S. Census Bureau, 1930 Census of Population and Housing, vol. 1, 1055, 1092–1094.]

28. Williams, "Report on State of Texas," Texas-Field Reports, 1933–1935, Box 60, Hopkins Papers, Roosevelt PL.

29. Williams, "Report on State of Texas," Texas-Field Reports, 1933–1935, Box 60, Hopkins Papers, Roosevelt PL.

30. Patenaude, "Politics of Relief," 9–10; *Austin American*, February 13, 1936.

31. Tom C. Stephenson to James E. Ferguson, January 25, 1934, Miriam A. Ferguson Papers, Files as Governor of Texas, Correspondence, Box 15, Texas State Archives; one-page memorandum with H. B. Thomas's name written at the top, Thomas B. Love Collection, Dallas Historical Society (hereafter cited as Love Collection, DHS).

32. *Austin American*, April 9, 10, 12, 1934.

33. Lorena A. Hickok to Harry L. Hopkins, April 11, 17, 1934, Texas-Field Reports, 1933, 1935, Box 60, Hopkins Papers, Roosevelt PL. Hickok was an experienced newspaperwoman and a friend of Eleanor Roosevelt. Her assignment was to tour some of the worst-afflicted areas of the country and to report freely and frankly on conditions. On Hickok, see Doris Faber, *The Life of Lorena Hickok, E. R.'s Friend* (New York: William Morrow, 1980). [Editor's note: Current scholarship on Hickok has emphasized the emotional, and even romantic, nature of her relationship to Eleanor Roosevelt as well as her significance to the New Deal project: Michael Golay, *America 1933: The Great Depression, Lorena Hickok, Eleanor Roosevelt, and the Shaping of the New Deal* (New York: Free Press, 2013); Susan Quinn, *Eleanor and Hick: The Love Affair That Shaped a First Lady* (New York: Penguin Press, 2016); and Rodger Streitmatter, ed. *Empty Without You: The Intimate Letters of Eleanor Roosevelt and Lorena Hickok* (New York: Free Press, 1998).]

34. Memorandum, "Mrs. Hopkins' telephone conversation today with Colonel [George D.] Babcock," June 7, 1934, Transcripts of Phone Conversation with State Relief Directors and Other Officials, Tennessee—Wyoming, Miscellaneous, Box 78, Hopkins Papers, Roosevelt PL.

35. *Austin American*, June 28, 1934.

36. M. J. Miller to Aubrey Williams, October 1, 1934, Texas-Field Reports, 1933–1935, Box 60, Hopkins Papers, Roosevelt PL.

37. Val M. Keating to M. J. Miller, October 25, 1934; Miller to Aubrey Williams, October 29, 1934, Texas-Field Reports, 1933–1935, Box 60, Hopkins Papers, Roosevelt PL; Edward J. Webster to Harry L. Hopkins, November 29, 1934, "Edward J. Webster—Mo., Okla., Texas, Ark. (1934)," Box 67, in ibid. Garner told Roosevelt that he should "cut down, as far as possible, the cost of government." He went on to say that

> it has been dry in this country, but the people are cheerful and the country in which I live is in splendid shape and can take care of itself. Texas is the same way and, my deliberate judgment is, it can take care of itself if the local communities put up fifty-fifty, he wouldn't have to spend ten percent in Texas of what he has spent in the last year. The local communities know that a great deal of this relief is unnecessary, but as long as they can get it from the federal government, or even the state government, they will continue to be in a very distressed condition. Pardon me for mentioning this matter because it is not my "butt-in," but it does pertain to this expenditure of federal funds which goes with living within your income and paying something on your debts.

Garner to Roosevelt, October 1, 1934, President's Personal File, 1416, John N. Garner, Roosevelt PL.

38. Editor's note: These "Mexicans, blacks and former reliefers" constitute an important part of the story of the Texas Rehabilitation and Relief Commission. African Americans and Mexican Americans tended to be affected the most by the poverty and suffering caused by the Great Depression but often could not access New Deal relief due to the corruption

of these local boards. See Roger Biles, *The South and the New Deal* (Lexington: University Press of Kentucky, 1994); Bernadette Pruitt, *The Other Great Migration: The Movement of Rural African Americans to Houston, 1900–1941* (College Station: Texas A&M University Press, 2013); Debra Ann Reid, *Reaping a Greater Harvest: African Americans, the Extension Service, and Rural Reform in Jim Crow Texas* (College Station: Texas A&M University Press, 2007); Keith Joseph Volanto, *Texas, Cotton, and the New Deal* (College Station: Texas A&M University Press, 2005).

39. M. J. Miller to Aubrey Williams, October 29, 1934, Texas-Field Reports, 1933–1935, Box 60; Edward J. Webster to Harry L. Hopkins, November 24, 1934, "Edward J. Webster— Mo., Okla., Texas, Ark. (1934)," Box 67, Hopkins Papers, Roosevelt PL; Patenaude, "New Deal and Texas," 382. Johnson is quoted in Patenaude, "Politics of Relief," 11. See also "Relief and Human Nature," *Texas Weekly* 9 (July 21, 1934): 7.

40. Jeanne Bozzell McCarty, *The Struggle for Sobriety: Protestants and Prohibition in Texas, 1919–1935* (El Paso: Texas Western Press, 1980), 38–39.

41. Thomas B. Love to Cato Sells, December 15, 1932, Love Collection, DHS.

42. Norman H. Clark, *Deliver Us from Evil: An Interpretation of American Prohibition* (New York: Norton, 1976), 20; Thomas B. Love to Hatton W. Summers, February 18, 1933, Love Collection, DHS. See also Thomas L. Blanton to Love, February 18, 1933, in ibid.

43. Clark, *Deliver Us from Evil*, 205–206.

44. Patenaude, "New Deal and Texas," 112–113; Thomas B. Love to Morris Sheppard, December 28, 1932, Love Collection, DHS. See also Love to Sheppard, December 22, 1932, January 9, 1933, Sheppard to Love, December 22, 1932, January 9, 1933, in ibid. "Your protest against beer is certainly vigorous and forceful," Senator-elect William G. McAdoo said of Love's telegram to the House Ways and Means Committee. "The difficulty is, my dear fellow, that the country has become so disgusted with the way prohibition has been enforced that it has swung to the other extreme." McAdoo to Love, December 22, 1932, in ibid.

45. McCarty, *Struggle for Sobriety*, 41; *Austin American*, January 14, 1933.

46. Don H. Biggers to Thomas B. Love, April 16, 1933, Love Collection, DHS; *Fort Worth Fundamentalist*, April 14, 21, 28, 1933; *Austin American*, April 28, May 6, 12, 1933.

47. McCarty, *Struggle for Sobriety*, 42–44.

48. *Austin American*, June 27, 28, 29, 1933; Nalle, *Fergusons of Texas*, 226–228.

49. *DMN*, June 29, 1933; *Guadalupe Gazette-Bulletin* (Seguin), July 27, 1933, quoted in McKay, *Texas Politics*, 254–255.

50. Pat M. Neff to J. Frank Norris, July 14, 1933, J. Frank Norris Papers, Southern Baptist Historical Library and Archives, Nashville; Alvin Moody to Thomas B. Love, July 15, 1933; Love to Morris Sheppard, August 26, 1933, Love Collection, DHS.

51. *DMN*, August 23, 1933. Farley asked Sam Rayburn to "personally assist in this election in behalf of repeal delegates. Shall appreciate everything you may do." James A. Farley to Sam Rayburn, August 22, 1933, Rayburn Papers, Series I, Roll 2, BCAH.

52. *Austin American*, August 27, 28, 1933; *DMN*, August 27, 28, 29, 1933; McKay, *Texas Politics*, 254–255; Ralph Wright Steen, *Twentieth-Century Texas* (Austin, TX: Steck, 1942), 237.

53. *Galveston Daily News*, August 29, 1933; *DMN*, August 30, 1933; *Fort Worth Fundamentalist*, September 1, 1933; J. Frank Norris to Thomas B. Love, August 30, 1933, Norris Papers, Reel 14; McCarty, *Struggle for Sobriety*, 47.

54. McCarty, *Struggle for Sobriety*, 48; *Austin American*, November 25, 1933.

55. McCarty, *Struggle for Sobriety*, 48; William R. White to Thomas B. Love, January 5, 12, April 5, 1934; Love to White, February 14, April 9, 1934, Love Collection, DHS.

56. McCarty, *Struggle for Sobriety*, 49–50.

57. McCarty, *Struggle for Sobriety*, 50; Gould, *Progressives and Prohibitionists*, 290–291; Steen, *Twentieth-Century Texas*, 238; Brown, *Hood, Bonnet*, 435–436. [Editor's note: As noted in the introduction, according to the Texas Alcoholic Beverage Commission, as of November 2016 there were 7 totally dry counties remaining in Texas. The other 53 counties are wet, but wet ranges anywhere from allowing the sale of beer only to the sale of beer, wine, and liquor. For more information see Texas Alcoholic Beverage Commission, "Wet and Dry Counties," accessed September 2, 2017, http://www.tabc.state.tx.us/local_option_elections /wet_and_dry_counties.asp. Texas still has blue laws that restrict the sale of beer before a certain time on Sundays and prevent the sale of alcohol on Sunday entirely. See chapter 105 of the Texas Alcoholic Beverage Code, accessed September 2, 2017, http://www.statutes.legis .state.tx.us/?link=AL. The legal drinking age in Texas was raised from eighteen to nineteen in 1981. In 1986 it was raised to twenty-one, where it remains as of 2019.]

58. McKay, *Texas Politics*, 255; Raymond Brooks, "Who Against Allred in Run Off Easter Political Question," *Austin Statesman*, April 1, 1934, clipping in James V. Allred Scrapbook, July 9, 1932 to June 16, 1968, BCAH; *Texas Weekly* 10 (June 23, 1934): 1.

59. *DMN*, December 16, 1933.

60. "Allred Defends Little Merchant from Chain Store Monopoly; Urges Graduated Tax," one-page broadside in James V. Allred File, Campaign Materials, Texas State Library and Archives, Austin; "Address of James V. Allred, Attorney General of Texas, in Behalf of His Candidacy for Governor, Delivered at Llano, Texas, on Friday Night, June 15, 1934," twenty-nine-page typescript in James V. Allred File, 1934–1948, Box 10, Lyndon Baines Johnson Presidential Library, University of Texas at Austin (hereafter cited as Johnson PL). I am indebted to Mike Gillette for a copy of this typescript. See also McKay, *Texas Politics*, 255–257; George Manning, "Public Services of James V. Allred," (master's thesis, Texas Technological College, 1950), 39–39; Robert René Martindale, "James V. Allred: The Centennial Governor of Texas" (master's thesis, University of Texas at Austin, 1957), 31–48.

61. McKay, *Texas Politics*, 257–258.

62. McKay, *Texas Politics*, 259–260; *Ferguson Forum* 16, April 5, 1934. For the platforms of Small, Witt, Hughes, and Russell, see McKay, *Texas Politics*, 260–268.

63. Dave Shanks, "James V. Allred: 'He Lived Full Throttle,'" *Austin Statesman*, September 27, 1959, clipping in James V. Allred Scrapbook, July 9, 1932 to June 16, 1968, BCAH; *DMN*, July 14, 1934; Fred Gantt, *The Chief Executive in Texas: A Study in Gubernatorial Leadership* (Austin: University of Texas Press, 1964), 288.

64. McKay, *Texas Politics*, 269; *Austin American*, July 30, 1934.

65. McKay, *Texas Politics*, 265–266, 273; J. Frank Norris to Thomas B. Love, April 25, 1934; V. A. Collins to Love, July 7, 1934; Alvin Moody to Love, July 18, 1934; Love to I. T. Goodnight, July 23, 1934; Love to Alvin Moody, July 24, 1934; Love to Pink L. Parrish, same date; Love to Collins, July 27, 1934, all in Love Collection, DHS.

66. McKay, *Texas Politics*, 274; *Austin American*, July 29, 30, 31, 1934; V. A. Collins to Thomas B. Love, July 31, 1934, Love Collection, DHS; *Texas Weekly* 10 (August 4, 1934): 3.

67. McKay, *Texas Politics*, 275; *DMN*, August 1, 7, 23, 1934; *Ferguson Forum* 17, August 9, 1934; Thomas B. Love to Rev. C. C. Armstrong, August 9, 1934, Love Collection, DHS.

68. Brooks, *Political Playback*, 10; Shanks, "James V. Allred."

69. *DMN*, August 5, 17, 18, 21, 25, 1934; McKay, *Texas Politics*, 276–277; Brooks, *Political Playback*, 39.

70. "For a Texas Recovery: Tom Hunter for Governor . . . An Address to the Voters,"

fourteen-page broadside in Tom Hunter File, Campaign Materials, Texas State Library and Archives, Austin.

71. *DMN*, August 13, 1934; McKay, *Texas Politics*, 279–280; James A. Clark with Weldon Hart, *The Tactful Texan: A Biography of Governor Will Hobby* (New York: Random House, 1958), 175. See also "A Campaign Side Light," *Ferguson Forum* 17, August 14, 1934.

72. McKay, *Texas Politics*, 280–281; *DMN*, August 28, 1934.

73. *DMN*, July 18, 1943; Joseph W. Bailey Jr. Biographical File, BCAH. On the 1934 senatorial campaign, see Frank Herbert Smyrl, "Tom Connally and the New Deal" (PhD diss., University of Oklahoma, 1968), 134–149.

74. Irvin S. Taubkin, "Directness Gains in Texas Politics," *New York Times*, December 21, 1933, clipping in Connally Papers.

75. "Bexar to Boom Joe Bailey," *San Antonio Light*, June 28, 1933, clipping enclosed in Frank H. Bushick Jr. to Tom Connally, June 29, 1933; I. Freidlander to Connally, January 2, 1934, Connally Papers. Tom Love wrote Connally: "I find generally that Bailey's campaign has made little or no impression." Love to Connally, February 7, 1934, Love Collection, DHS.

76. Irvin S. Taubkin, "Patronage Stirs Texas Senate Fight," *New York Times*, January 18, 1934, clipping in Connally Papers; McKay, *Texas Politics*, 281–285; "Vote for Joseph W. Bailey, Jr., The Farmer's Friend for United States Senator, A State's Rights Democrat," brochure; "Joe Bailey's Reply to Tom Connally," one-page broadside; "Congressman Joe Bailey's Radio Address at Fort Worth, July 23, 1934," one-page broadside; "The *Corrected* Record of the Votes of the Candidates for United States Senator in the Democratic Recovery Program together with some other Votes which were not referred to in the Connally Advertisements," one-page broadside, all in Connally Papers. See also Joseph W. Bailey File, Campaign Materials, Texas State Library and Archives, Austin.

77. McKay, *Texas Politics*, 287; R. W. Wier to Tom Connally, May 22, 1933, Connally Papers.

78. McKay, *Texas Politics*, 285–286; "Connally Is Afraid to Meet Joe Bailey in Joint Discussion of Campaign Issues," one-page broadside in Connally Papers.

79. FDR, "Memorandum for the Secretary of Labor," June 11, 1934; Francis Perkins to Franlin D. Roosevelt, June 14, 1934, President's Personal File, Senator Tom Connally, No. 1549, Roosevelt PL; Smyrl, "Connally and the New Deal," 145.

80. McKay, *Texas Politics*, 288–289; *Austin American*, July 29, 1934.

81. Editor's note: Scholars have begun to explore the longer history of the rise of the conservative right in Texas. Keith Volanto notes the importance of Bailey Jr. and the Jeffersonian Democrats to the origins of the small core of business interests that would form the backbone of Texas conservatism in decades to come. See Keith J. Volanto, "The Far Right in Texas Politics During the Roosevelt Era," in David O'Donald Cullen and Kyle G. Wilkison, eds., *The Texas Right: The Radical Roots of Lone Star Conservatism* (College Station: Texas A&M University Press, 2014), 68–86.

82. "Death Takes Capt. Bailey, Attorney," *DMN*, July 18, 1943, clipping in Joseph W. Bailey Jr. Biographical File, BCAH. On the Jeffersonian Democrats, see Patenaude, "New Deal and Texas," 145–173.

83. *Houston Press*, September 12, 1934; Manning, "Public Services of James V. Allred," 44–45; Thomas B. Love to Tom Connally, June 12, 1934; Connally to Love, June 16, 1934, Love Collection, DHS; *Texas Weekly* 10 (September 15, 1934).

84. Alexander Heard and Donald S. Strong, *Southern Primaries and Elections, 1920–1949* (Tuscaloosa: University of Alabama Press, 1950), 172; Martindale, "James V. Allred," 48; Smyrl, "Connally and the New Deal," 149–150.

85. Nalle, *Fergusons of Texas*, 236–237; "Politics Over for Ferguson, He Announces," unidentified newspaper clipping, 1934, in James Ferguson Scrapbook, 1914–1935, BCAH.

86. Nalle, *Fergusons of Texas*, 234.

Epilogue: "Pass the Biscuits, Pappy!"

1. *Ferguson Forum*, June 13, 1935; James E. Ferguson to Franklin D. Roosevelt, June 12, 1935, Democratic National Committee—Texas A–Z, OF 300–69, Franklin Delano Roosevelt Presidential Library, Hyde Park, NY (hereafter cited as Roosevelt PL). See also Ferguson to Roosevelt, December 20, 1934; Roosevelt to Ferguson, January 2, 1935, James E. Ferguson File, No. 2081, President's Personal File, 1933–45, in ibid.

2. Reinhard H. Luthin, *American Demagogues: Twentieth Century* (Gloucester, MA: P. Smith, 1959), 179; Howard Marshall, "Fergusons Still Interested 'in Politics, But Not Office,'" James Ferguson Scrapbook, 1914–1935, Dolph Briscoe Center for American History, University of Texas at Austin (hereafter cited as BCAH).

3. Seth W. McKay, *Texas Politics, 1906–1944* (Lubbock: Texas Tech University Press, 1952), 290–294; Rupert N. Richardson, *Texas: The Lone Star State*, 4th ed. (Englewood Cliffs, NJ: Prentice-Hall, 1981), 331–332.

4. George Norris Green, *The Establishment in Texas Politics: The Primitive Years, 1938–1957* (Westport: Greenwood Press, 1979), 14 [Editor's note: the comment about Ann Richards was my addition. Brown finished writing this manuscript before Richards became governor of Texas and has not offered any commentary on her, to the best of my knowledge. Richards has generally been considered to be a liberal governor, however, and at the time of writing, is Texas's current "last" liberal governor.]

5. Ouida Wallace Ferguson Nalle, *Fergusons of Texas: Or "Two Governors for the Price of One"* (San Antonio: Naylor Co., 1946), 238–240; McKay, *Texas Politics*, 294–302; Richardson, *Texas*, 332; James E. Ferguson to Tom Connally, May 15, 1936, Tom Connally Papers, Manuscript Division, Library of Congress. [Editor's note: Brown did not specify which Connally Papers collection he had used. There are also smaller collections at Baylor University and at the Briscoe Center.]

6. V. O. Key, *Southern Politics in State and Nation* (New York: Random House, 1949), 265.

7. Seth Shepard McKay, *W. Lee O'Daniel and Texas Politics, 1938–1942* (Lubbock: Texas Tech Press, 1944), 14–23; McKay, *Texas Politics*, 309–310; Frank Goodwyn, *Lone Star Land: Twentieth-Century Texas in Perspective* (New York: Knopf, 1955), 252–253. [Editor's note: To the best of my knowledge, McKay's study remains the most current scholarly biography of O'Daniel. However, for those interested in O'Daniel's life, a book of photographs with a short biography was published in 2004. See Bill Crawford, *Please Pass the Biscuits, Pappy: Pictures of Governor W. Lee "Pappy" O'Daniel* (Austin: University of Texas Press, 2004).]

8. On the gubernatorial campaign of 1938, see McKay, *Texas Politics*, 308–325.

9. Goodwyn, *Lone Star Land*, 257–259.

10. Wayne Gard, "Texas Kingfish," *New Republic* 104 (June 23, 1941): 848–850.

11. McKay, *O'Daniel and Texas Politics*; *New York Times*, July 25, 1938; John Gunther, *Inside U.S.A.* (New York: Harper & Brothers, 1947), 848, 850; McKay, *Texas Politics*, 323–325. [Editor's note: The results of this election suggest that in 1938 the Republican Party in Texas was all but expired.]

12. Green, *Establishment in Texas Politics*, 16–17. [Editor's note: To date, scholars of

Texas history have not overturned Green's argument about the importance of 1938 to the eventual rise of the far right in Texas politics. They have, however, begun to explore this history in a broader and longer historical context. See the following works: David O'Donald Cullen and Kyle G. Wilkison, eds., *The Texas Right: The Radical Roots of Lone Star Conservatism* (College Station: Texas A&M University Press, 2014); Sean P. Cunningham, *Cowboy Conservatism: Texas and the Rise of the Modern Right* (Lexington: University Press of Kentucky, 2010) (Cunningham's book, however, dates the beginning of this process to the 1960s); Ricky F. Dobbs, *Yellow Dogs and Republicans: Allan Shivers and Texas Two-Party Politics* (College Station: Texas A&M University Press, 2005); Paul Pressler, *The Texas Regulars: The Beginning of the Move to the Republican Party in Texas* (Garland, TX: Hannibal Books, 2001); Donald W. Whisenhunt, ed., *The Depression in the Southwest* (Port Washington, NY: Kennikat Press, 1980); and Robert Wuthnow, *Rough Country: How Texas Became America's Most Powerful Bible-Belt State* (Princeton, NJ: Princeton University Press, 2014). Green revisited his study in George N. Green, "Establishing the Texas Far Right, 1940–1960," in Cullen and Wilkison's *Texas Right*, 87–100. Though Green cites some more recent works, his essay draws heavily on his 1979 volume. In addition, as noted in the introduction to this volume, some scholars have argued that the story of the rise of conservatism in Texas is complicated by the rise of a multiracial, liberal political coalition in the middle of the twentieth century. See Max Krochmal, *Blue Texas: The Making of a Multiracial Democratic Coalition in the Civil Rights Era* (Chapel Hill: University of North Carolina Press, 2016).]

13. Lionel Patenaude, "The New Deal and Texas" (PhD diss., University of Texas at Austin, 1953), 132–136.

14. Richardson, *Texas*, 333–334; McKay, *O'Daniel and Texas Politics*, 135–143, 166–196, 199–202, 205–206; McKay, *Texas Politics*, 325–327; Green, *Establishment in Texas Politics*, 26.

15. Bascom N. Timmons, *Garner of Texas: A Personal History* (New York: Harper & Brothers, 1948), 240; Thomas L. Stokes, "Garner Turns Off F.D.R.," *The Nation* 144 (June 26, 1937): 722–723; Robert S. Allen, "Roosevelt's Defeat—The Inside Story," *The Nation* 145 (July 31, 1937): 124; Lionel V. Patenaude, "Garner, Sumners, and Connally: The Defeat of the Roosevelt Court Bill in 1937," *Southwestern Historical Quarterly* 74 (July 1970): 36–51; Lionel V. Patenaude, "Vice President John Nance Garner: A Study in the Use of Influence During the New Deal," *Texana* 9 (1973): 132–139.

16. Richard Henderson, *Maury Maverick: A Political Biography* (Austin: University of Texas Press, 1970), 205; Nalle, *Fergusons of Texas*, 246; McKay, *Texas Politics*, 418–419; *Dallas Morning News*, March 10, 17, 23, April 7, 9, 25, 1940 (hereafter cited as *DMN*).

17. Alfred Steinberg, *Sam Johnson's Boy: A Close-Up of the President from Texas* (New York: MacMillan, 1968), 145–146; McKay, *Texas Politics*, 419; *DMN*, April 28, 1940.

18. *DMN*, May 28, 29, 1940; McKay, *Texas Politics*, 337–339; Green, *Establishment in Texas Politics*, 29–30.

19. *DMN*, March 24, April 4, 1940; Nalle, *Fergusons of Texas*, 244–245.

20. *DMN*, March 24, 1940; Nalle, *Fergusons of Texas*.

21. *DMN*, April 14, 1940; "Announcement and Platform of Miriam A. Ferguson Candidate for Governor Subject to Democratic Primary," one-page broadside in Mrs. Miriam A. Ferguson Biographical File, BCAH; McKay, *O'Daniel and Texas Politics*, 257–260; McKay, *Texas Politics*, 330.

22. Richardson, *Texas*, 334; McKay, *O'Daniel and Texas Politics*, 260–278. See also McKay, *Texas Politics*, 328–331; Gard, "Texas Kingfish," 849.

23. John Geddie, "'Two for the Price of One': Old Timers Recall Texas's Fergusons," *DMN*, May 6, 1966, clipping in Jim and Ma Ferguson Biographical File, BCAH; Luthin, *American Demagogues*, 180; *Austin American*, September 22, 1944, clipping in James Ferguson Biographical File, BCAH; Nalle, *Fergusons of Texas*, 246–254; McKay, *O'Daniel and Texas Politics*, 292–297, 327; McKay, *Texas Politics*, 335–336.

24. Key, *Southern Politics in State and Nation*, 267–268n; McKay, *Texas Politics*, 342–345. Gilmer is quoted in Green, *Establishment in Texas Politics*, 34.

25. *DMN*, April 29, May 11, 1941; McKay, *O'Daniel and Texas Politics*, 408–409; McKay, *Texas Politics*, 345–346; Nalle, *Fergusons of Texas*, 255.

26. Steinberg, *Sam Johnson's Boy*, 179–180; "Jim Ferguson Says," paid political advertisement in *DMN*, June 9, 1941, clipping in James E. Ferguson Biographical File, BCAH; *Austin American*, May 17, 1948, clipping in Jim and Ma Ferguson Biographical File, BCAH; Nalle, *Fergusons of Texas*, 255–256; Green, *Establishment in Texas Politics*, 36–37; McKay, *Texas Politics*, 342–366; Jack Guinn, "Screwball Election in Texas," *American Mercury*, 53 (September, 1941): 275–281. Walter Jenkins is quoted in Merle Miller, *Lyndon: An Oral Biography* (New York: Putnam's Sons, 1980), 87.

27. McKay, *Texas Politics*, 370–390; McKay, *O'Daniel and Texas Politics*, 499–618; Green, *Establishment in Texas Politics*, 39. See also George Norris Green, "W. Lee O'Daniel and Texas Politics: The 1942 Campaign," *McNeese Review* 23 (Summer 1977): 3–10.

28. McKay, *Texas Politics*, 460–463; Key, *Southern Politics in State and Nation*, 268–271, 361–362; *DMN*, May 12, 1969. John Gunther called O'Daniel "a kind of American marcher-on-Rome who never marched. His career is an illuminating example of the way a man can rise from nothingness to the Senate, by weapons that include demagoguery, the credulity of the people, and their fedupness with the ordinary run of politicians." *Inside U.S.A.*, 848.

29. Nalle, *Fergusons of Texas*, 256–262; *DMN*, September 22, 1944; *Austin American*, September 22, 1944.

30. *DMN*, September 23, 1944.

31. *Austin American*, September 22, 1944; *DMN*, September 23, 1944.

32. Nalle, *Fergusons of Texas*.

33. *Austin American*, May 17, 1948, clipping in Jim and Ma Ferguson Biographical File, BCAH; Nalle, *Fergusons of Texas*, 262.

34. Green, *Establishment in Texas Politics*, 14. The Ferguson counties were Bell, Cass, Henderson, Lavaca, Leon, Robertson, Sabine, San Augustine, Shelby, and Titus (264n).

35. Mary D. Farrell and Elizabeth Silverthorne, *First Ladies of Texas: The First One Hundred Years, 1836–1936* (Belton, TX: Stillhouse Hollow Publishers, 1976), 293–294; Ralph W. Steen "Governor Miriam A. Ferguson," *East Texas Historical Journal* 17 (Fall 1979): 17.

36. Joe Bertram Frantz, *Texas, A History* (New York: W. W. Norton, 1984), 198–199; "Sissy Haunted by Ma's Ghost," *Austin American*, May 19, 1972.

37. *Newsweek*, January 27, 1975.

Index

Note: page numbers in *italics* refer to figures.

and, 347; cotton and, 164; the "Four
Horsemen," 297–298; highway bond
amendment and, 130; Longhorn pardon
and, 116; at Ma Ferguson's inauguration
(1933), 296; racetrack gambling rider,
300; Small bill and, 56
McIlheney, Marshal, 18
McKay, Seth, 92, 108, 117–118, 332, 345,
354, 425n7
McKellar, Kenneth, 16, 277, 286
McMillen, A. Wayne, 303–304
McPike, Henry H., 252, 280, 284
McQueary, Carl, 396n1
Meade, W. H., 42
Meek, Edward R., 202
Mellon, Andrew, 229, 291–292
Mencken, H. L., 281
Mexican Americans, xix, xx, 421n38
Michelson, Charles, 293
Miller, Barry: 1930 gubernatorial candi-
dacy, 20, 21, 76–77, 98, 103–104, 120;
1930 gubernatorial race and, 111, 118–
120; Moody and, 64; as president of
senate, 65–66; prison reform and, 41
Miller, J. J., 314–315
Miller, Roy, 85–86, 135, 294, 347, 418n69
Miller, Tom, 347
Mills, Larry, 7
Mills, Ogden L., 291–292
Mills, Warner E., Jr., 152, 160, 168, 175
Minor, Fred, 155, 194
Mitchner, C. A., 108
Moffett, George C., 187
Moley, Raymond, 203, 248, 287
Molyneaux, Peter, 43, 67, 101, 102, 298,
380n87
Montgomery, Grace, 253–254
Montgomery, W. R., 34
Moody, Alvin: 1928 gubernatorial race, 70;
1930 attorney general race and, 106;
1930 gubernatorial race and, 20–23,
25, 87, 95, 97; 1930 lieutenant gover-
nor race and, 31; 1932 elections and,
179, 180; 1932 presidential election
and, 288–289; 1932 presidential pri-
mary and, 241, 246, 251; Anti-Tammany
Democrats and, 2–3; congressional run,

possible, 316–317; considering Lt. Gov.
run, 31; patronage and, 12–14; Prohibition and, 177–178, 321; at Republican–
Anti-Tammany conference, 5; Roosevelt
campaign and, 209; *Southern Advance*
and, 30
Moody, Dan: 1930 attorney general race
and, 106–107, 122; 1930 Democratic
state convention and, 123–124; 1930
gubernatorial race and, 21–22, 76–78,
83–91, 94, 109, 112–113, 118–121; 1932
gubernatorial race and, 173–175, 183–
184, 188–190, 192; 1932 presidential
primary and, 215, 217, 223–225; 1942
Senate race and, 354; appointments, 81,
106, 205; bolters issue and anti-bolter
bills, 6–8, 22–24; business progressive
model and, xv; civil service reform, 36;
Colquitt nomination and, 10; cotton
"buy a bale" campaign, 161; East Texas
oil fields and, 144, 145–146, 158; farewell
address, 68–69; Fergusonism, credit for
defeating, 120–121; Ferguson on, 39,
52–53, 56, 73, 121, 186; governmental
reorganization, 35–36; highways, 46–51;
"Honest Dan," 63; Howe on, 260; legacy
of, 62–69; loyalty pledge suit, 250; Ma
Ferguson and, 296; martial law decla-
rations, 57–62; patronage and, 18, 201;
prison reform, 36–42, 375n14; Prohibition repeal and, 318, 319; public utilities
regulation, 44–46; relief funding and,
313; retirement rumors, 22; Robertson and, 195; second inauguration, 33;
second term (overview), 33–34; tax reform, 42–44; vetoes and special sessions, 52–57
Moody, Mildred, 41, 52, 55, 65, 66–67, 83,
86, 90, 383n29
Moore, J. D., 146, 157, 204
Moore, Joe, 85, 155
Moore, John M., 318
Moran, W. J., 305
Morgan, J. P., 232, 290
Morris, Jesse, 187
Morrow, Wright, 106, 175–176
Moses, George, 11, 371n44